To inspire ambition, to stimulate the imagination, to provide the inquiring mind with accurate information told in an interesting style, and thus lead into broader fields of knowledge such is the purpose of this work

The New
BOOK OF KNOWLEDGE
Volume Four

MADE AND PRINTED IN GREAT BRITAIN BY THE AMALGAMATED PRESS, LTD.

KEY TO COLOUR FRONTISPIECE

GRASSES AND SEDGES

Many people think that there is little difference between the various sorts of grasses. This is wrong, of course, and it is equally a mistake to think that their flowers are not as distinct as are those of the other flowering plants. In the colour plate overleaf, to which this is a key, you see a few of the beautiful grasses and sedges found in various parts of the British Isles. Their names are: 1, Barnyard Grass; 2, Hairy Brome; 3, Couch Grass; 4, Meadow Foxtail; 5, Carnation Grass; 6, Ribbon Grass; 7, Field Woodrush; 8, Canary Grass; 9, Common Quaking Grass; 10. Cocksfoot Grass; 11, Giant Bent Grass: 12, Common Reed

SOME BEAUTIFUL BRITISH GRASSES AND SEDGES

Painted by Frank R. Hinkins

Here are some of the beautiful grasses of all shapes, sizes and colours that you may see when you are wandering in the countryside in summer and early autumn. They are shown in full maturity with their distinctive flowers. At the back of this plate is a key which will enable you to identify them.

The NEW BOOK OF KNOWLEDGE

*A Pictorial Treasury of Reading
& Reference for Young and Old*

Edited by
SIR JOHN HAMMERTON

COMPLETE IN EIGHT VOLUMES
Alphabetically Arranged

OVER SIX THOUSAND ILLUSTRATIONS
OVER 600 IN COLOUR AND GRAVURE

VOLUME FOUR
GRAS—LOM

THE WAVERLEY BOOK COMPANY LTD.
Farringdon Street, London, E.C.4

HERE AND THERE IN THIS VOLUME

When you are just looking for ' something interesting to read,' this list will help. With it as a guide, you may wander through storyland, visit far-away countries, meet famous people of ancient and modern times, review history's most memorable incidents, explore the marvels of Nature and science—in short, find whatever suits your fancy at the moment.

HOW MANY QUESTIONS CAN YOU ANSWER?

Here are a few only of the unnumbered thousands which are answered in each one of our eight volumes. You can use this page as a test of your own knowledge, or you can draw up from it a set of ' posers ' with which to puzzle your friends. But odd scraps of knowledge are of little value compared with the result of organized study, and you should refer to the Study Outlines in the Eighth Volume for a reading guide.

COLOUR AND GRAVURE PLATES AND PAGES
IN THIS VOLUME

WHEN YOU ARE IN NEED OF READY REFERENCE

In using THE NEW BOOK OF KNOWLEDGE *as a work of reference, Volume Eight is indispensable. As regards its contents that particular volume is unique, for it is at once a complete Index to the preceding Seven Volumes and an Encyclopedia in itself. Its purpose is fourfold, as indicated below.*

(1) **Through the Year with the N.B.K.** Its opening section takes the form of a Calendar of the Year, giving for each day all the chief events and matters of interest, with references to the pages of THE NEW BOOK OF KNOWLEDGE in which full particulars concerning the event, personality, or other interest of the day may be found. By the intelligent use of this section (a) the young reader can have the daily delight of reading about topics that have special association with the particular day of the year on which he may be making his reference ; (b) father or mother can suggest what would be the most appropriate reading for the day ; and (c) the school teacher can set the lessons for the day with a genuine topical appeal.

(2) **Study Outlines.** This large and important section of the volume provides a simple method of study which should enable any of our young readers to become expert in using THE NEW BOOK OF KNOWLEDGE as an auxiliary manual of home study ; and thus what is learnt in school may be amplified, brought home more vividly, and more securely fixed in the memory.

(3) **The Fact-Index.** Actually this is in itself a complete Encyclopedia. In addition to providing many thousands of references to contents of Volumes One to Seven, it records many more thousands of facts in biography, geography, history, science, the arts, etc., that are not mentioned in its seven predecessors. Therefore, if you look in vain for any subject in the alphabetical order of Volumes One to Seven, turn to Volume Eight and you will almost certainly find it there.

It is a good plan, when using THE NEW BOOK OF KNOWLEDGE *as a work of reference,* **always** *first to look up any subject in the Fact-Index of Volume Eight.*

(4) **Thousands of Additional Entries.** In the main body of the work all important terms are explained as they arise ; but the scientist in every field of learning uses a "shorthand" of words and terms to convey a more precise meaning and to save repetition. Such words and terms are included in the Fact-Index so as to free the reading pages from a burden of thousands of brief cross-references which a more strict following of the full encyclopedic method would involve. When in doubt, therefore, about the significance of a term, *look it up in the Fact-Index ;* often you will find all the information you want there, but if further explanation is required the Fact-Index will give you page references to that more complete account in the main volumes. Remember that apart from its role as a never-failing source of recreative and entertaining reading, THE NEW BOOK OF KNOWLEDGE is designed to make your school and college learning of treble value by fitting that learning into its place in daily life.

KEY TO PRONUNCIATION

Most of the subject-headings in THE NEW BOOK OF KNOWLEDGE require no special indication of the way in which they should be pronounced. There are also many for whose proper pronunciation it is only necessary to know which syllable is stressed; in these cases the stress is shown *after* the syllable, thus, Armadil′lo. Where further guidance is necessary the following signs are employed.

ah = a as in father
aw = a as in ball
ê = vowel sound in fern, word, girl, curl
ow = vowel sound in now, bout
oi = vowel sound in noise, boy
Unmarked vowels have their **short sound,** as a in hat, e in bet, i in bit, o in not, u in but, oo in book
Marked vowels have their **long sound,** as in hāte, bē, bīte, nōte, tūne, bōōn

Vowels in italics have a slurred or obscure sound as in abet (*a*-bet′), recent (rē′-s*e*nt),conform (k*o*n-form′), nation (nā′-sh*u*n), tailor (tā′-l*o*r)

th = first sound in thing, thank
th = first sound in the, that
zh = s in measure, leisure
g = hard g, as in good, girl
j = soft g, as in gem, ginger
kh = guttural in loch

LIST OF ABBREVIATIONS

The abbreviations most commonly used in this work are noted below ; longer lists of abbreviations often met with in reading or conversation are given under the heading Abbreviations in Volume One and also in the Fact-Index that is contained in Volume Eight.

A.D., *Anno Domini* (in the year of our Lord, of the Christian era)
a.m., *ante meridiem* (before noon)
b., born
B.C., before Christ
C., Centigrade
c., *circa* (about)
Co., county, company
d., died
e.g., *exempli gratia* (for example)
etc., *et cetera* (and so forth)
et seq., *et sequens* (and following)
F., Fahrenheit
h.p., horse-power

i.e., *id est* (that is)
lb., pound, pounds (weight)
m., miles
MS., MSS., manuscript, manuscripts
oz., ounce, ounces
p.m., *post meridiem* (after noon)
Pop., population
Pron., pronunciation
q.v., *quod vide* (which see)
sq. m., square miles
St., Saint
U.S.A., United States of America
viz., *videlicet* (namely)
yd., yard

The GRASSY CARPET of the EARTH

No garden is complete without its patch of lawn, and what would our country-side be without its expanses of green fields? We learn something of the importance of grass in agriculture in this article.

Grass. Because of its important quality of persistence and because the greater part of the cultivated portions of the earth is under grass this family of plants is the most important in the plant kingdom. The greatest portion of our food is provided by cultivated grasses—wheat, oats, rye, barley, rice, maize, millet, and sugar-cane ; from grasslands in the ordinary sense come indirectly our beef and mutton, hides and wool, and much more.

Among the grasses found in the British Isles is this crested dogstail. It provides excellent grazing for cattle.

Grasses are the most widely distributed of all plants. Pygmy grasses, moss-like grasses not over 2 inches high, cling close to the cold ground right up to the borders of the Arctic ice and snow fields; small and middle-sized grasses grow in comparative luxuriance in the north temperate zone, increasing the total of the family to over 4,000 species; and there are huge bamboos and other tropical types.

In many quarters grass is still regarded as a form of vegetation that takes possession of land which is not sown to any other crop. Practically no useful grasses have that weedlike quality, and those which do are of a kind that produce worthless grazing or fodder and very little of that. It is true, however, that some grasses have been developed for their ability to hold shifting sand together or to provide a soil cover under shade.

An important key to good grass is that so long as it is grazed or cut to prevent seed heads forming it continues to strive to produce leaf. Considerable research has been devoted to encouraging this leafiness in the different species.

One of the main objects of this scientific work has been to extend the grazing period from the normal five to six months up to eight or nine months. A fundamental example of very early research was the discovery that legumes such as clover harbour nitrogen-fixing bacteria ; sown in association with grass they provide nitrogen (taken from the air) for the grasses, to the benefit of both. Thus it is very seldom that true grasses are sown alone as a farm crop. Usually grass and clover are sown in the same field with a cereal, though a short while after the cereal has been sown. When the cereal is harvested the grass mixture, often referred to as seeds at this stage, remains. If the land is well fertilized a considerable source of fertility is obtained over a period of from one to six years, ready for ploughing under. Thus the ground receives valuable decayed vegetable matter, while the grass has contributed to food production by way of meat or milk.

About 130 species of grass are to be found in the British Isles but only a few are of value as food producers. Those most commonly used are: Perennial rye grass, Italian rye grass, cocksfoot, timothy, the fescues, meadow foxtail and crested dogstail. There are roughly one million seeds in a pound of timothy. Bent, tor, and couch are among the worthless grasses.

The steppes of Russia, the pampas of South America, and the prairies of North America are noted pasture lands of natural excellence; but for a country as a whole New Zealand or Britain have probably the finest grassland in the world, important factors being a temperate climate and well-distributed rainfall.

The botanical name of the grass family is *Gramineae*. The chief characteristics are the jointed stems, with leaves arranged in two opposite rows, and a single leaf at each joint of the stem. The stems are hollow, except in a few varieties which have stems filled with soft pith. The flowers are enclosed in glumes or chaff-like scales, and are arranged in spikes like the wheat-heads, or in panicles (loose compound flower-clusters) like the

The Times

HAY-LIFTING WITH AN AUTOMATIC LOADER

Wet hay cannot be stacked, because it will either rot or generate heat sufficient to set the stack alight ; therefore, the crop must be gathered as dry as possible—and quickly, in case of rain. Tractor-drawn loaders, as here, are sometimes used ; they deliver the hay automatically from ground to vehicle as the machine moves along.

Central Press

AUSTRALIAN HAY CROP

In most parts of Australia the climate is too hot and dry for English grasses, and the hay is a good deal coarser than that in England. Here Australian hay is being fed into a machine which can produce 180 cylindrical bales an hour.

oat. The classification of grasses is determined according to the arrangement of the flower system.

Since grass everywhere must have a dormant season the farmer's problem is to preserve some of the surplus from the peak of the growing season for winter feed for his livestock. Selected fields are set aside for mowing. After eight to 12 weeks' rest in spring and early summer they should yield from one ton to 30 cwt. of hay per acre. After cutting, the grass is dried by wind and sun, and to hasten this the swathes of grass are turned over by a machine. There are ingenious loaders which, drawn behind a lorry, collect and deliver the hay automatically from ground to the vehicle, which is drawn to the stack. To minimise the labour of carting and stacking, however, the modern trend is to bale the hay or, in other words, to tie it up in cube-like parcels weighing from 60 to 90 lb. each. These are more easily handled than loose hay and require less storage space.

To reduce the weather hazard in haymaking, grass is sometimes stacked and compressed in its fresh green state in either pit or clamp

or silo. The process is known as ensilage. The exclusion of air prevents spontaneous internal combustion, and the growth of useful lactic acid forming bacteria is promoted by spraying the grass with molasses. Lactic acid preserves the grass, and the loss of food nutrients is lower than in haymaking.

Although making big demands on transport and fuel, grass drying by hot air is probably the best form of grass utilization. For this process the grass is cut young when only two or three inches high, and placed on trays through which hot air is blown by fans. Four cuts a year are possible, yielding up to 12 tons per acre of grass or about 4 tons of dried grass. The protein content of the product is about the highest of any British farm crop. Carotene, which has the same value in nutrition as Vitamin A, is another important constituent of dried grass, and is reflected in the rich colour of the milk from cows fed in winter on dried grass. As the efficiency of the drying plants increases, this process could make British farmers independent of imported feeding stuffs for livestock. It may also become possible to use only forced ventilation to cure hay indoors.

Quite different species of grass are used for the famous lawns of England which rely on regular rolling, cutting and watering for the production of a dense sward throughout the year. Greenkeeping on golf courses is perhaps an even more intricate subject. Nevertheless no crop repays careful study and management better than grass.

Grasshopper. If a boy could jump as far, in proportion to his size, as a grasshopper, he could easily spring to the roof of an eight-storeyed building, or jump from pavement to pavement of the widest London street. If he could make as much noise, in proportion to his size, as a grasshopper, the ground would tremble with the sound; and if he could eat as much and as fast as a grasshopper, he would devour more than his own weight of food in a day. It is because of the rapidity with which they breed, and the immensity of their appetite, that the kind of grasshoppers called locusts are a plague to Man.

The grasshopper, whatever its species, has a helmet-shaped head, and strong jaws with which it tears big pieces out of leaves or plant stems. The front wings, which are tough and hard, lie straight

R. Clapperton

BALING HAY IN BERWICKSHIRE

There is a definite attraction (at least to the onlooker) in the old, leisurely way of haymaking in Britain—with the carting of swaying loads and the stacking and the thatching. In the new method there is more noise than romance : a crop is compressed into bales on the spot. The bales, each weighing between 60 and 90 lb., are easily stacked under cover.

along the back, protecting the tender film of the hind wings, which do most of the flying—for if you watch one of these insects hop, you will see that it often opens its wings, and flies to lengthen its leap. But some forms are wingless, and must hop with their legs alone. The young nymphs, too, which otherwise resemble their parents, have the wings undeveloped, and they too are hoppers. The leap, in both young and adults, is performed by the much enlarged hind legs.

Grasshoppers are of two kinds which form two separate families. Both kinds are found in Britain. One kind includes the short-horned grasshoppers (family *Acrididae*) which have the antennae, or feelers, shorter than the body. The long-horned grasshoppers (family *Tettigoniidae*) form the other kind. They have thread-like antennae longer than the body.

The short-horned grasshoppers are abundant in grassy places where their chirping or singing tells of their presence. Also, they attract notice by leaping when a person disturbs them by walking through the grass. Their chirping is caused by rubbing the greatly enlarged hardened rib thighs of the hind legs against along the middle of each fore wing. The thigh of each leg bears a row of minute pegs or points along its inner side and, when the leg is rapidly rubbed against the fore wing of its side, the scraping of the pegs against the rib produces the familiar notes of the grasshopper. These grasshoppers have very remarkable drum-like ears on each side of the hind body where it joins the chest or thorax.

Locusts are special kinds of short-horned grasshoppers and are usually of large size. They are particularly abundant in Africa and much of Asia. On rare occasions odd stragglers have reached England, but fail to survive our climate. Locusts differ from ordinary grasshoppers on account of their habit of migrating in large swarms, often covering great distances.

This name locust is often wrongly given to the cicada, and to other swarm insects, but it properly belongs only to certain grasshoppers of the family *Acrididae*. A swarm of locusts, which devoured the grain and left famine in its wake, was one of the 10 plagues of Egypt, told of in the Bible.

Dire Destruction Wrought by Locusts

It is impossible to give an idea of the millions of locusts which compose these swarms. A cloud appears on the horizon like a black storm; it spreads until the light of the sun dies out; it settles down like a vast blanket, burying everything in sight, blotting out the landscape; for mile upon mile there is nothing but a sea of locusts. Then the dread march of the insect army begins. Before it stretch green fields; the dense army moves forward, and the green fields vanish. Behind the locusts, the ground looks as if it had been swept clean with a vast broom—not a blade of grass is left. A river bars the way. The front ranks cast themselves upon the water, clinging together, pile upon pile,

GRASSHOPPER LAYS HER EGGS

This is a long-horned grasshopper, whose long antennae and ovipositor distinguish her at once from a locust, or the short-horned form. Here she has drilled holes with the ovipositor and is using it to lay her eggs. Those on the left have hatched and the tiny grasshoppers are crawling out of the hole.

until a bridge of living insects is formed, and the rear ranks march steadily forward over them.

There is mystery in these swarms, but it is gradually being unravelled. They do not come every year, nor do they always attack the same region; but in each part of the world certain breeding grounds are known. In them is a permanent population of green, solitary locusts. When numbers increase, young hoppers, seeing others, hop with them in the same direction. Gathering others, the swarm begins, and the hoppers, no longer solitary, change to reddish or brownish-black in colour. Still hopping, still increasing in numbers, they grow up; and then the whole swarm takes to the wing, flying a hundred miles or more until, with strength exhausted, it descends to ruin the crops and vegetation.

We are only just beginning to understand the habits of locusts. The more we know about them the better are we placed for coping with their ravages. Prevention is better than cure and, for this reason, the best way of dealing with locusts would be to attack them in their breeding grounds, before they have started to migrate. These breeding grounds consist, in some species, of areas of scrub jungle; in others they lie in the deltas of the Volga, Niger and other rivers. Such areas are usually inaccessible except by aeroplane, but treatment of the vegetation by means of poison discharged from aeroplanes seems to offer a means of attaining control. As things are at present, however, ground baiting is about the best remedy. This consists of broadcasting poisoned bran among the crops before the locusts or their hoppers have reached them. Since they find the bait very appetising they are poisoned in large numbers.

Grasshoppers usually lay their eggs in holes which the females bore in the ground. When the young hatch, they look like tiny awkward models of their parents, except that their wings do not develop for some time. Their appetite, however, is large, and they start at once to eat and destroy.

The long-horned grasshoppers are less numerous, and none is known as a locust. The great green grasshopper is a loud chirper, mostly found in the southern half of England, and is a good example of the family. These insects chirp by rubbing the two fore wings together: a kind of file on the wing rubs against a sort of " sounding board " or " drum" on the other wing. The ears are placed on the shins of the forelegs. Crickets are closely related to short-horned grasshoppers. All grasshoppers, crickets, cockroaches, along with stick-insects and leaf-insects, belong to the order *Orthoptera*.

Grass Snake.
There is no reason for anyone to fear a grass snake (*Tropidonotus natrix*), because these reptiles are harmless, though they may

John Kearton

HARMLESS GRASS SNAKE
Sometimes called the ringed snake, because of the yellow ' collar ' on the neck, the grass snake, largest of our reptiles, is common in some parts of England.

hiss and pretend to bite if alarmed. They are often encountered in England and are widely distributed over Europe, North Africa, and Asia, being rare in Scotland and unknown in Ireland.

The upper part of a grass snake is greenish-grey to brown, with a yellow ring behind the head, which gives it the alternative name of ringed snake; it is bluish-black underneath. Growing to two or three feet in length, the grass snake feeds chiefly on frogs, toads, mice and eggs and is usually found in damp places. The eggs, which are the size of a dove's egg, are laid in damp mould, manure heaps and similar places.

Gravitation.
Although it is taken for granted as an everyday occurrence, it is really a very remarkable thing that, when we let go of something in our hand, it falls to the ground, and in no other direction. Everything on this earth tends to seek a lower position unless it is supported from underneath: even balloons and corks are not the exceptions they seem to be. This is even more remarkable when we remember that the centrifugal force (*q.v.*) due to the earth's rotation is trying to fling us vertically upward, off the earth. The force of attraction which keeps us on the earth is known as gravitation.

What then is this force of gravitation due to, and how does it work? Is it only a local affair, acting on the surface of our earth, or does it extend to the other planets and stars? Many great thinkers have set themselves these problems, and even today

scientists do not agree completely as to the fundamental nature of gravitation. The early astronomers guessed that there might be some force which was controlling the movements of the heavenly bodies, but they were in general far too busy plotting these movements and fitting them into geometrical patterns to do more than make vague suggestions as to why they were so regular. The great mathematician and astronomer, Ptolemy, who lived in Alexandria in the second century A.D., believed that there was some connexion between the force which kept the earth in its orbit around the sun and the force keeping us on our planet; but it was left to that far greater genius, Isaac Newton, to elucidate the precise nature of the force.

When Newton, in the 17th century, proposed his universal law of gravitation, whereby all matter mutually attracted all other matter, he had a vast accumulation of astronomical data, built up in the centuries before, to test it with. Unfortunately he chose to calculate the moon's orbit at first; and, owing to the rather inaccurate figures for the distance between the earth and the moon, his results did not agree with astronomical observations. This led Newton to set aside his ideas for some time; but when, later on, more accurate figures were obtained, his calculations agreed exactly. Further applications of the theory to the calculation of other planetary movements also agreed with experimental observations, and the theory was thoroughly vindicated. To this day the Newtonian theory has been found to hold for most purposes, and it is only in very special cases that the slight modifications brought about by Einstein's later theory come into effect.

Newton's Law of Gravitation

The universal law of gravitation which Newton established states that *every mass of matter attracts every other mass of matter with a force which varies directly as the product of their masses and inversely as the square of the distance between them.* This means that the force acting between two bodies weighing one ton each is one-quarter that acting between two bodies weighing two tons each; further, if the bodies are separated by twice their original distance, the force will then fall off again by one-quarter. At first it seems strange that there should be a force acting between *every* particle of matter, but we must realize that this force is extremely minute when we are dealing with the relatively small masses of everyday objects on this earth. A piece of rock is attracted to the earth by a large force, because the mass of the earth is so big, whereas the attractive force between two similar pieces of rock is extremely small, and can be neglected for all practical purposes. However, it is interesting to note that experiments carried out in the laboratory to verify Newton's Law actually measure this minute force. The great 18th century experimenter, Henry Cavendish (1731–1810), measured the force between two suspended balls of lead, and he found that his results agreed well with those given by measuring the forces between the planets.

If every particle of the earth is attracting the bodies on its surface, why then should they all be drawn towards its centre? Newton solved this problem with the aid of his newly-invented " calculus " (a branch of mathematics to deal with problems of

WHEN LOCUSTS SWARM OVER THE LAND

Paul Popper; American Colony, Jerusalem

In East Africa locusts do millions of pounds' worth of damage to the crops, and sometimes thousands of cattle die of starvation because the ravenous insects have eaten the grass. The swarms darken the sky and extend for miles (lower). When locusts descend on a field they cover it like a living blanket (upper), and the vegetation is devoured in an incredibly short space of time. These locusts belong to the short-horned group of grasshoppers.

FOUR WAYS OF PUTTING GRAVITY TO WORK

PILE DRIVER
This is simplest, most direct use of the force of gravity. When the weight is released it falls straight down on the pile and drives it into the earth. (*See* also explanatory diagram in page 958).

WATER-WHEEL
By the action of gravity alone, the water would fall straight down. But it is compelled to follow the rim of the wheel—where its weight, in the vanes, turns the wheel. (*See* Hydro-Electric Installations).

GLIDER
Here, as always, the pull of gravity is straight down. But the strong air resistance against the broad under surfaces of wings and body opposes the straight-down movement. So the glider, like a sled on a hill, slides off to the right—the direction in which its sharp nose and wing-edges meet the least resistance.

PENDULUM CLOCK
In the old-fashioned clock gravity works in two ways. The pull on the main weight turns the clock's wheels. The pull on the pendulum makes it swing at a precise rate, according to its length, and thus gravity regulates the speed at which the clock runs. (*See* Clocks and Watches ; Pendulum).

motion), with which he showed that the gravitational effect of a sphere of matter was the same as if it had all its mass concentrated at the centre. The gravitational force acting on any body on the earth's surface must then be proportional to the mass of that body, and this leads to the result that all such bodies, if left to fall freely, will have the same acceleration.

Now the Greek philosopher Aristotle (384–322 B.C.) had stated that heavy bodies fall faster than light ones, and such was his great prestige that this dictum was firmly believed until about a century before Newton's time. A young Italian named Galileo (1564–1642) then decided to test out this statement by an experiment. He climbed the Leaning Tower of Pisa and dropped from it two cannon balls of different weight. They both reached the bottom at the same time, and by this experiment the centuries-old legend was exploded. No doubt the earlier scientists had been led astray by the fact that light objects, such as feathers, drop much slower than objects of more concentrated mass. Here the resistance of the air is playing a big part in the observed result. But if a feather is allowed to drop down a tube from which all the air has been exhausted, then it will be seen to fall at the same rate as any other object inside the vacuum.

The statement that all bodies fall with the same acceleration (if air resistance is neglected) means that they are gaining speed at a constant rate. If a stone is dropped down a deep well it will drop 16 feet in the first second, 48 feet in the second second, and 80 feet in the third; while its speed at the end of each successive second will be 32, 64 and 96 feet per second. It is thus gaining speed at the rate of 32 feet per second every second. Now this increase in the speed of the falling stone means that it is gaining energy all the time. In the article on Energy, it is explained that the kinetic energy, or energy due to the motion of a moving body, is proportional to the square of its speed. Thus a stone which has fallen for two seconds has twice the speed, and so four times the energy, of one which has fallen for only one second. This is why it is so much more dangerous to be struck by a stone or brick which has fallen from the top of a house than by one which has fallen only a small distance. There is a much greater chance of injuring oneself by falling from the top storey of a house than by jumping out of a lower window.

The strength of the earth's pull on each object is the weight of that object, and since Newton's law tells us that the strength diminishes as the distance increases, the weight will vary at different points on the earth's surface, due to the earth not being perfectly round. If a pound of lead, or any other substance, were weighed on a spring balance at one of the poles, and then taken to the equator and weighed again, it would be found to stretch the spring slightly less there. This is because the diameter of the earth is greater at the equator than at the poles. Note that we must use a *spring* balance, since the ordinary pair of scales merely compares two masses. The weight of an object also gets less if it is taken to the top of a mountain; the difference in weight from that at sea-level being about 1-2000th for every two miles of elevation. The diagram below illustrates how the pound of lead varies in weight according to its position relative to the earth. Taken down a mine shaft, the weight will diminish directly as its distance from the centre.

The weight of an object—that is, the force of attraction on it by the earth—is also in proportion to its mass, which is, scientifically, the amount of matter it contains. Now this mass is not only dependent on the size of the object, for we all know that a ball of steel weighs less than a similarly-sized ball of lead. The weight depends on the closeness of packing of the particles making up the substance, and this closeness is defined as its density. If the

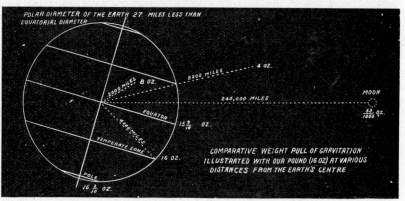

HOW GRAVITATIONAL 'PULL' AFFECTS WEIGHT

This diagram shows how the pull of gravitation varies at different distances from the earth's centre. The unit of comparison is 16 ounces (one pound) weighed in the temperate zone. The general law is that the farther the object is from the centre of the earth, the less it weighs. Because the earth bulges a little round the equator and is flattened at the poles, the pound will lose weight as you move it toward the equator, and gain weight as you move it toward the poles. If the pound were taken to the moon, the earth's pull upon it would be only a fraction of an ounce. At a depth of 2,000 miles in the earth, the pound would weigh only eight ounces. This seems to violate the law about 'the nearer the centre, the greater the pull.' But remember that now the 2,000 miles of earth above our pound weight would be tending to pull it upward.

density is compared with that of water, then the ratio is known as the Specific Gravity (q.v.).

We have seen how Newton showed, with the aid of his calculus, that the force of gravity due to the distributed elements of the earth could be replaced in imagination, by a concentrated mass acting at the centre. In a similar way all bodies, however irregular in shape, have some point within them which can be regarded as the centre of their mass. This point is known as the centre of gravity, and if the body is supported at that point, it will be in equilibrium, and cannot fall. Symmetrically-shaped bodies have their centres of gravity at the geometrical centre, provided they are of the same density throughout. The Leaning Tower of Pisa is an example of an apparently unstable structure which yet stands, because its centre of gravity is in a favourable position, *i.e.* vertically above the base of the tower. If the tower were built higher, however, the centre of gravity would shift upwards and sideways, until eventually it reached a point vertically above the ground not covered by the base, when the tower would fall. All the examples of balance which we practise from day to day, from riding a bicycle to merely standing upright, consist of keeping our centre of gravity above the points of support.

To the scientist, the subject of gravitation is of unique interest, because, although it received very early attention from the great thinkers, and seemed to be so well " explained " by Newton's theory, it was until recently very hard to correlate it with any of the other known properties of matter. How, for instance, does the force of gravity act between the heavenly bodies in the vast expanses of empty space? Is the attractive force anything like that of magnetism, and through what sort of medium does it act? Problems such as these remained unsolved until the coming of Einstein's General Theory of Relativity in 1915. In this he rejects the idea of a " force " altogether, and attributes the phenomena of gravitation to a local modification, where matter occurs, of the curvature of his " four-dimensional " space, in which our normal *three dimensions* (length, height, breadth), and, in addition, the factor of *time* are involved. There is no real physical way of trying to picture what this four-dimensional space is like, but it is a convenient way of expressing mathematical ideas (*see* Relativity). The Einstein theory has been proved only by its application to the explanation of some very specialised occurrences, such as the gravitational bending of a light ray when it passes close to a large mass. In most cases, this new theory approxi-

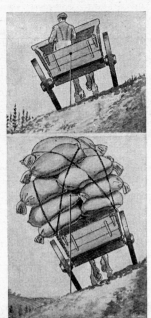

CENTRE OF GRAVITY
A line drawn from the centre of gravity to the ground falls within the wheel base, so the cart (top) can travel safely on the slope. But a slight push will upset it when loaded (lower): now the line falls outside the base.

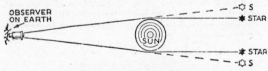

WHEN LIGHT RAYS BEND
During an eclipse, light beams from stars passing near the sun are bent out of their course, so that the stars seem to be farther apart than when the sun is not there. This diagram shows the reason for the apparent shift in position—a shift which Einstein's relativity theory enables us to predict.

mates to that of Newton, and so it does not really supercede it, except in furthering our modern conception of what is, and is not, physical reality.

Gray, THOMAS (1716–71). His most famous poem, the Elegy Written in a Country Churchyard, was published at sixpence in 1751, and a copy of the original edition has since been sold for over £900. Made familiar by many quotations,

it is one of the most beautiful and exquisitely finished poems ever written. The quantity of Gray's poetical work is small, but the quality is such that poems like his Elegy are enshrined in English literature for all time. Also, his letters are among the best in the language, full of sympathy and humour.

Thomas Gray was born in Cornhill, London, on December 26, 1716, and was educated at Eton. After a tour of the Continent he returned to Cambridge in 1742 to resume the classical studies he loved; and at Cambridge he made his home, save for brief intervals, for the rest of his life. He became professor of modern history there in 1768, and there he died on July 30, 1771.

Apart from translations from the classics, Gray's first poem was the Ode to Spring, which was followed by the Ode on a Distant Prospect of Eton College, and the Hymn to Adversity, all of which belong to the year 1742. The Ode on the Death of a Favourite Cat appeared in 1747; the cat in question belonged to his old friend, Horace Walpole. After his father's death Gray's mother had retired to Stoke Poges in Buckinghamshire, and in 1750 came the famous Elegy, which was inspired by the churchyard at Stoke Poges, where his mother and another son were buried. There are monuments to Gray in a field adjoining Stoke Poges churchyard, and in Westminster Abbey.

Great Britain. The " tight little island " of Great Britain is separated from France by a strip of water only 21 miles wide at its narrowest point. But the rough waters of the English Channel, the North Sea, Irish Sea, and St. George's Channel, which surround it, separated the people of Great Britain from their enemies in the days of their weakness; and when they grew strong the sea furnished them with broad highways by which they might carry on commerce with other nations.

This little island—about two-fifths the size of France—which stands at the western approaches of Europe, has been favoured by Nature in many ways. It has a temperate climate, neither very cold in winter nor very hot in summer, and with an abundant rainfall. Its broad, deep rivers —the Thames, Severn, Humber, Mersey and Clyde—admit ships a considerable distance into the interior. On its fertile soil can be grown most crops of the temperate zone. In its mountainous regions of the north and west are to be found valuable deposits of coal and iron.

Before 1603 Great Britain was merely a geographical name. The chief country in the island was England, to which Wales had been added by conquest in 1282; and to the north was the separate kingdom of Scotland. When James VI of Scotland ascended the English throne in 1603 as James I of England, both countries had the same ruler, and he called himself king of Great Britain.

But it has only been since the Act of Union of 1707 that the two countries have been officially united under the name of Great Britain. In 1800 another Act of Union brought Ireland under the same Parliament with Great Britain, and the official name was changed to the United Kingdom of Great Britain and Ireland. Over 100 years later, in January 1922, Southern Ireland was given dominion status as the Irish Free State (later taking the ancient name of Eire), while Northern Ireland remained part of the United Kingdom. In the government of the United Kingdom are included also the other British Isles—the Hebrides, Orkneys, Shetlands, Isle of Wight, Isle of Man and Channel Islands.

The union of Scotland, Ireland, and England is shown by the flag of Great Britain. Before the first Act of Union the flag of England was white, with a large upright red cross; that of Scotland was blue, with a diagonal white cross; and one of the emblems of Ireland was a red diagonal cross. In the modern Union Jack or Union flag, all three of the crosses are united in a single emblem. (*See* also Britain; British Commonwealth of Nations; British Isles; England; Ireland; Scotland; Wales).

Great Lakes.

There is no other system of inland waterways that compares with the large lakes—Superior, Michigan, Huron, Erie, and Ontario—that lie between the United States and Canada. These inland seas cover an area of nearly 100,000 square miles, and the 1,000 or more streams that feed them drain an area of about 288,000 square miles. So vast are they that their storms are like ocean storms, and they have an oceanic effect upon the climate, absorbing heat in summer and giving it out in winter, thus tempering the extremes of climate along their shores.

Varying in depth from 1,180 feet in Lake Superior to 210 feet in Lake Erie, the lakes are open to navigation by large vessels from end to end. You may take a steamer the size of an ocean liner at Buffalo, in the United States, and voyage for 1,000 miles to Duluth or Chicago, nearly half the length of the Mediterranean. On smaller craft you may go farther still, while vessels of 14-feet draught can pass round Niagara Falls by the Welland Canal and down through Lake Ontario and the St. Lawrence River to the Gulf of St. Lawrence and the Atlantic Ocean.

From December or January until April the lakes are in large part ice-bound, and vessels lie idle in the inland harbours of Toronto, Cleveland, Buffalo, and other ports. Terrific storms mark the end of the navigation season. Whitefish Bay, at the east end of Lake Superior, is known as the Graveyard of Ships, from its many wrecks.

The importance of these great waterways to the prosperity of the United States and Canada

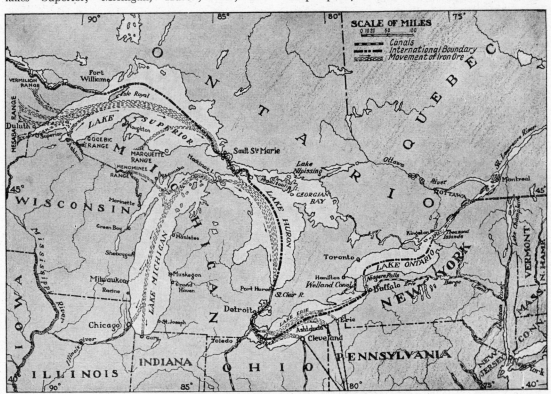

TRAIL OF COMMERCE THROUGH THE GREAT LAKES

Among the busiest bodies of water in the world are the five Great Lakes (above). The heavy broken line shows how the boundary between Canada and the United States divides them. The light lines indicate the routes followed by the iron ore traffic ; this alone maintains a fleet of steamers which are scarcely ever out of sight of each other's smoke, and when you remember that iron ore is only one of the many commodities carried on the Lakes you can appreciate how important they are in North America's life. Note the canals connecting the Lakes with the rivers to the south and east.

Courtesy of the Canadian Government

GRAIN SHIP THAT PLIES ON THE GREAT LAKES

Specially designed ships carry much of the freight on the Great Lakes. This odd-looking vessel was built to transport grain, harvested on the western prairies of Canada, through the Lakes to east coast ports. It is 633 feet in length and has a gross tonnage of 10,000 tons. In the bows are the bridge and the crew's living quarters : the engines are at the stern. Between the two is cargo space capable of holding 550,000 bushels of grain. Similar freighters carry iron ore.

cannot be over-estimated. Without the cheap transportation which the lakes afford, the development of the Canadian prairies would have been far slower. Such Canadian ports as Montreal (on the St. Lawrence), Fort William, Hamilton, Toronto, and Kingston have all thrived in recent years. More vessels enter and leave the port of Chicago than at any other port of the United States excepting only New York. The lake fisheries are the greatest inland fisheries in the world.

There has been a canal with locks on the United States side of Sault Sainte Marie since 1855, to pass round the rushing rapids (*sault*) where the St. Mary's River issues from Lake Superior. Today there are two great series of locks. One of the locks in the United States canal (completed in 1919) is 350 feet longer than the locks of the Panama Canal; and the Canadian locks also are of great size. Great barges and passenger steamers go through the locks at the rate of one every 12 minutes.

The history of the Great Lakes dates back nearly 300 years. The French discovered Lake Ontario in 1611, and four years later the French explorer Champlain discovered Lake Huron. Lake Erie was the last (1669) to be reached by white men owing to the hostility of the Iroquois tribes of Red Indians. The first sailing vessel on the lakes was La Salle's Le Griffon, of 40 or 50 tons, launched on the Niagara River in 1679. The first steamboat appeared on Lake Ontario in 1817. The opening of the Erie Canal in 1825 started emigration westward by canal and lake.

To permit big steamers to carry large cargoes,

commissions of American and Canadian engineers keep constant watch over the water levels. This is necessary because the channel at Niagara and the Drainage Canal at Chicago draw off enormous quantities of water; and if the level of the lakes should be lowered by even a foot below the standard depth, the heavily-laden cargo steamers could not negotiate critical points with safety.

Several important naval engagements were fought on the Great Lakes during the war of 1812 between Britain and the U.S.A. Then in 1817, the Great Lakes were declared neutral by agreement. However, during the Second World War (1939–45), a United States naval station was established at Great Lakes, Illinois, and in 1947 an agreement with Canada permitted the future use of the lakes by the navies of either country.

Grebe. On the water, grebes look like ducks, but they may be distinguished by their pointed bills, short wings, and almost complete absence of tail. On land they are extremely awkward, the legs being placed so far back that when grebes walk they carry their bodies upright, like penguins. The feet are not webbed; the toes are joined only at the base, each having a separate flap of membrane. The grebe's smooth hair-like plumage is waterproof.

The two kinds of grebe seen in Britain are the dabchick or little grebe (*Podiceps ruficollis*), a brownish purple little bird; and the great crested grebe (*P. cristatus*), which is a large bird, with a rosette-like crest on its crown, and long feathers round its neck.

A. Brook

GREAT CRESTED GREBE

Found all the year round on lakes and marshes in England and Ireland, more rarely in Scotland, the great crested grebe builds a floating nest of reeds, leaves and twigs. Before leaving the nest the hen bird covers the eggs with weeds, so that the whole looks like a mass of rubbish.

GREECE and Its PLACE in HISTORY

The past of Greece is of infinitely greater importance to the world than its present, yet by studying its geography at the present day the reasons for its glorious history are made apparent.

Greece. It is often a matter of wonder to the traveller in Greece how so small a country could fill so large a place in history. From Mount Olympus, which marked the northern limit of ancient Greece, you can see over nearly all northern and central Greece; and if you ascend Mount Parnassus (modern Liakoura), which is near the centre of Greece, you can see nearly all the mainland of this wonderful country spread out below you like a map. Travel less than 100 miles south, and from the mountains of Sparta you can see Crete, the southernmost of the 500 islands which make up so important a part of Greece.

But though this little country is only a small patch on the map of the world, it was the cradle of European civilization, and has wielded a greater influence on the course of history than any other single nation. Why? The answer is largely a matter of geography. It was their land and sea, their mountains, bays, and islands, that helped to make the ancient Greeks what they were and determined the course of their history.

Greece is the easternmost of the three peninsulas that Europe thrusts into the Mediterranean towards Africa and Asia Minor, where Man first emerged from barbarism to civilization. Between the mainland of Greece and the coast of Asia Minor the sea is strewn with several hundred islands—the tops of submerged mountains that once formed a continuous land-bridge. These islands are like stepping-stones, leading to the civilizations of Asia.

Look at the map, and you will observe that the sea forms so many gulfs and capes that no part of Greece south of Thessaly is more than 50 miles from the coast. So many are the indentations that the coast-line of the Greek peninsula is longer than that of Spain and Portugal, although that peninsula is five times its size. The greatest of these inlets is the Gulf of Corinth, which all but cleaves Greece in two. The only connexion is the narrow Isthmus of Corinth (which is cut by a canal), so that southern Greece, or Morea, was known to the ancient Greeks as Peloponnesus (Pelops Island).

Thus the sea everywhere invited the Greeks to the adventurous and progressive life of the mariner and trader. Their natural keenness and alertness were increased by this constant intercourse with other peoples and lands; their imagination and thought were stirred.

This call of the sea was supported by the character of the Greek land itself. Four-fifths of its surface is wrinkled by a complex system of mountain ranges. Almost all the arable land is contained in the little isolated valley-patches.

The remainder is divided between the forests from which the Greeks obtained the charcoal that provided their only fuel, and the pasture land, most of it bristling with prickly asphodel and other dry scrub, too juiceless for the taste of any animals but sheep and goats. A few cows and pigs were raised, but sheep and goats supplied most of the meat. The harvests of the sea—chiefly tunny, sardines, and anchovies—largely took the place of meat in the Greek diet. On the scanty areas of tillable land were grown grain, the wine-grape, and the olive, which formed their staple foods. The few rivers are small and rapid.

The story of the coming of the Greeks (Hellenes) into their land takes us back to about 1500 B.C., when wave after wave of barbarian invaders swept over the towns and cities of a great civilization, destroying it and then gradually building up a new one upon its ruins. About the splendid culture which the rude Greek tribesmen found on their coming into the Aegean basin—the Aegean civilization with its gold and bronze and pottery and paintings and its great palaces at Knossos in Crete and at Mycenae and Tiryns on the mainland—you may read elsewhere in our volumes. (*See* Aegean Civilization).

The Greeks who swept down from the north and overwhelmed these cities were simple nomadic herdsmen—a branch of the Indo-European race that had for centuries been drifting to the east and west from their home in the grasslands east and north-east of the Caspian Sea. The first wave of invaders were the fair-haired Achaeans of whom we read in Homer. The Dorians who composed the second wave came, perhaps, three or four centuries later. Other tribes, the Aeolians and the Ionians, settled chiefly on the islands and coasts of Asia Minor.

These Greek invaders must have absorbed much of the culture of the Aegean civilization when they settled down with the people they conquered. But we know little of the earliest stages of the Greek settlement, for these invaders were neither builders nor writers. But we may imagine them moving southward from their pasture lands along the Danube, driving their herds before them, and only stopping in one place just long enough to plant and harvest one crop. These families settled down in the pasture lands of the peninsula,

Extent.—Estimated at about 50,150 square miles, of which the mainland of Greece (roughly corresponding to the ancient Hellas) occupies about 41,328 square miles. Population (1940) about 7,335,675.

Physical Features.—Deeply indented mainland coast, with many small islands, especially Cyclades and Sporades groups in Aegean Sea. Corinth and Saronic gulfs nearly separate northern and central Greece from southern Greece (Peloponnesus, or Morea). Four-fifths of the surface covered by complicated mountain ranges, enclosing many small valleys; chief ranges, Cambunian and Pindus; highest point (in Thessaly), Mount Olympus (9,754 feet). No navigable rivers.

Products.—Wheat, barley, rye, and other cereals; currants, grapes and wine; olives and olive oil, figs, oranges, lemons, etc.; tobacco, silk; sheep and goats; iron ores, lead, zinc, lignite; textile and leather manufactures.

Chief Cities.—Athens (capital) and its port Piraeus (combined population more than 700,000), Thessaloniki (Salonika) (236,000), Patras (61,000).

GREECE : THE HOME OF EUROPEAN CIVILIZATION

The rugged interior of the Greek peninsula is but sparsely populated, the bulk of the inhabitants living close to the sea—in the cities and mountain-ringed plains that lie along the coast or on the islands of the Aegean and Ionian seas.

For nearly 400 years Greece was the centre of ancient culture, and civilization spread thence along the shores of the Mediterranean Sea with the establishment of Greek colonies in Asia Minor, North Africa, Sicily and Southern Italy.

developed a system of farming, and little by little formed communities ruled by kings and elders.

At this point we can begin to picture them, for the background of two epic poems—the Iliad and the Odyssey—is the background of the Age of the Kings. In Homer we read of the Achaeans living very simply, a race devoted to warfare. Their weapons and their songs are the only splendid things they have, except for the gorgeous robes and the beautiful jewelry and metal work they bought from Phoenician traders.

In the Iliad we learn of Greeks from many cities—Sparta, Athens, Thebes, Argos, and the rest—all more or less united to fight their common foe, the city-state of Troy in Asia Minor. In historical times the Greeks were again able to work more or less together when the power of Persia threatened

their very existence. But Greece never became a nation. The only patriotism the Greek ever knew was loyalty to his city. These cities were small, and except Athens, probably no Greek city-state boasted more than 20,000 citizens.

The reason for this disunity we have already touched upon. Ancient Greece or Hellas was divided by its mountain ranges, and even the plains were in many cases subdivided, containing several city-states, each surrounding its acropolis, or citadel. Only in a few instances did the city-state push its holdings beyond very narrow limits. Athens held the whole plain of Attica, and most of the Attic villagers were Athenian citizens. Argos conquered the plain of Argolis. Sparta made a conquest of Laconia and part of the fertile plain of Messenia, the conquered people remaining subjects and not citizens. Thebes attempted to be the ruling city of Boeotia, but never quite succeeded. Similar city-states were found throughout the Greek world, which extended beyond the Aegean basin.

The western shores of Asia Minor were fringed with Greek colonies. In Africa there were, among others, the colony of Cyrene, and the trading post of Naucratis in Egypt. Sicily, too, was colonized by the Greeks, and there and in southern Italy so many colonies were planted that this region came to be known as Magna Graecia, or Great Greece. Pressing farther still, the Greeks founded the city of Massilia, now Marseilles, in Gaul.

The government of many of the city-states—notably Athens—passed through four stages. During the 8th and 7th centuries B.C. the kings disappeared, and monarchy gave way to oligarchy, that is, the rule of the few. Power rested in the hands of the wealthy land-owning nobles—the Eupatrids, or well-born. But the rivalry among the nobles and the discontent of the oppressed masses were too great, and soon a third stage appeared.

This third type of government is known as tyranny. Some Eupatrid seized absolute power—usually by obtaining the favour of the people and promising to right the wrongs inflicted upon them by the other land-holding Eupatrids. He was known as a tyrant, a word which among the Greeks merely implied one who had seized kingly power without the qualification of royal descent.

By the beginning of the 5th century B.C. Athens had gone through these stages and emerged as a democracy—the first in the history of the world. About 621 B.C. the first written laws in Greece were

W. F. Taylor

ROYAL BURIAL CIRCLE AND TOMB AT MYCENAE

On the east coast of Greece, near the port of Nauplia, are the ruins of the ancient city of Mycenae. Within a circle of stones (lower) lie the graves of the Mycenaean kings, in which were found jewelry and gold vessels of elaborate workmanship. The so-called Treasury of Atreus (upper) was really a tomb and, as this reconstruction shows, the interior was decorated with bronze rosettes. The massive vault was shaped like a bee-hive and was built of stone.

COLOURFUL GLORY OF A TEMPLE WHICH ENSHRINED THE WORSHIP OF THE ANCIENT GREEKS

Most of the ancient ruins of Greece are but fragments of once splendid buildings, and it is sometimes difficult to imagine how they looked when they were intact. In this illustration the artist has reconstructed a great Greek temple—the general idea is that of the Temple of Zeus at Olympia. It must be remembered that, though we are apt to think of the Greek buildings as being white, in reality the friezes and pediments (triangular ornamental facing over a portico) were picked out in brilliant colours. The statues that ornamented the temples were likewise coloured. This is not surprising considering that Greek Art was derived from Egypt, where colour was lavishly employed.

ATHENS AT THE HEIGHT OF HER SPLENDOUR, MORE THAN 2,000 YEARS AGO

In the front of this reconstruction of ancient Athens is the Agora or market-place, dominated by the Acropolis on which the statue of Athena Propylaea and the roof of the Parthenon can be seen. At the left is a row of public buildings. The circular pillared structure is the Tholos, in which certain high officials dined at the public expense, with the Senate House behind it. In the centre of the steps leading up to the Agora is the Bema, or rostrum, from which politicians delivered speeches. The hill in the right distance is the Areopagus, where a court of justice sat. Behind the portico supported by figures (right) is part of the Temple of the Mother of the Gods.

compiled from the existing traditional laws. But this code, which was so severe that the adjective draconic, from the name of its compiler Draco, is still used as a synonym for " harsh," did not give the oppressed classes sufficient relief. A revolution was averted by the reforms of Solon (c. 638–c. 558 B.C.), a generation later.

But Solon's reforms only put off the fatal day, and about 560 B.C. Peisistratus, aided by the discontented, made himself tyrant. With two interruptions, Peisistratus ruled for more than 30 years, fostering commerce, agriculture and the arts, and laying the foundation for much of Athens's future greatness. His sons Hippias and Hipparchus attempted to continue their father's power, but Hipparchus was slain in a private quarrel by two youths, Harmodius and Aristogeiton, and Hippias was expelled four years later, the murderers of Hipparchus henceforth being regarded in Greek tradition as patriots and martyrs and as themes for sculptors and poets. By the reforms of Cleisthenes, a statesman who flourished about 509 B.C., the nobles were shorn of much of their power, and the rule of the people was firmly established.

Very different was the course of events in Sparta, which had now established itself as the most powerful military state in Greece. Under the strict laws of Lycurgus, Sparta had maintained its primitive monarchal form of government with little change. Nearly the whole of the Peloponnesus had been brought under its iron heel, and it was now jealously watching the rising power of its rival, Athens.

Suddenly there loomed in the east a menace which threatened to sweep away the whole promising structure of the new European civilization. Persia, the great Asiatic world-empire of the day, had suddenly been awakened to the existence of the free peoples of Greece by the aid which the Athenians had sent to their oppressed kinsmen in Asia Minor. The dramatic story of how the scanty forces of the Greeks drove back the enormous heavily armed Persian hordes is told in the article on Persia.

From this momentous conflict, Athens emerged maimed, but still as the richest and most powerful state in Greece. She owed this position chiefly to the shrewdness of her statesman Themistocles, who had seen that naval strength, not land strength, was henceforth to be the key to power. He persuaded his fellow Athenians to build a strong fleet and to fortify the harbour at Piraeus.

This fleet became the instrument by which the Persians were finally defeated at the battle of Salamis (480 B.C.), and also by which Athens made herself mistress of the Aegean. For, within three years after Salamis, Athens had united the Greek cities of the Asiatic coast and of the Aegean islands into a confederacy (called the Delian League, because the treasury was at first on the island of Delos) for defence against Persia; and in another generation this had become an Athenian empire.

Almost at a stride Athens was transformed from a provincial city to an imperial capital. Wealth flowed into her coffers—tribute from subject and allied states, customs duties on the merchandise

Alinari

REMAINS OF THE PUBLIC STADIUM AT DELPHI

Physical exercise played as great a part as lessons in the Greek system of education, the object being to produce men perfect in mind and body alike. This accounts for the importance in Greek life of athletic contests, called Games, and gymnastics. Above is what remains of the stadium at Delphi, where were held the Pythian Games, second in importance only to the Olympic contests. Athletic meetings were held here not only at the festivals but all the year round.

that poured t h r o u g h Piraeus, and revenues from the Attic silver mines. The population increased fourfold. Learning and art flourished as never before.

This period, which stands out as one of the most remarkable and brilliant in the world's history, reached its culmination in the age of Pericles, 460–430 B.C. But the Athenian state rested on a foundation of slavery. Two-fifths at least, and perhaps more, of the population were slaves (often, if not usually, themselves of Greek blood) whose labour produced a large part of the wealth that gave the citizen the time and money to pursue art and learning and serve the state.

Slavery in Greece was a peculiar institution. When a city was conquered its inhabitants might be often sold as slaves. Kidnapping boys and men in non-Greek lands, and even in other Greek states, was another steady source of supply. If a slave was well educated or could be trained to a craft, he was easily disposed of. Moreover, a slave had a chance of obtaining his freedom, for quite frequently his master would let him work for hire, and this gave him an opportunity to save money. After he had bought his freedom or been set free by a grateful master, he became a metic— resident alien. Many of the slaves who could not be trained, however, had a miserable lot. They were sent in gangs to the silver mines at Laurium, where they worked underground in bad conditions.

Though the citizens of Athens were thus set free from much of the drudgery of life, we must not imagine that they revelled in luxury; the standard of comfort was very low, in comparison with our own. The houses were of sun-dried brick, built two storeys high along narrow, winding streets. Meals consisted of bread, perhaps a broth of beans and pulse, with wine and sometimes fruit. Fish with bread was considered a fine meal. Olives and olive oil were largely used; honey took the place of sugar; cheese was often eaten in place of meat, but butter was practically unknown. The only heat in the house was from a brazier of burning charcoal. There was no plumbing, nor were there any chimneys, the smoke from the stove in the tiny kitchen finding its way out through a hole in the roof. There were no windows on the ground floor, but in the centre of the house was a broad open court, with the men's and women's apartments, and the small cupboard-like bedrooms clustered about it. The upper storey sometimes had a window or aperture looking on the street.

From Journal of Hellenic Studies

A VICTOR'S PRIZE AT THE GAMES

Greek art was greatly affected by the national love of athletics. This vase, though perhaps not of any particular artistic merit, was probably valued highly by its owner, because it was awarded to the winner of a chariot race at the Panathenaic Games. These were held every summer at Athens in honour of Athena, the patron goddess of the city.

The real life of the city was out of doors. The men spent much of their time talking politics and philosophy in the agora, or market-place, exercising or lounging in the athletic fields, performing military duty, sitting in the Assembly or the Council of 500, taking part in the numerous state festivals, or doing jury duty. There were 6,000 jurors on duty all the time in Athens, for all the allied cities were forced to bring their cases to Athens for trial. A daily salary was paid for jury service and service on the Council, and this made up a considerable part of the income of the poorer citizens.

The women stayed at home, attending to the affairs of the house, and spinning and weaving wool for clothing. They were only seen in public at the theatre—where they might attend tragedy but not comedy—and at certain religious festivals.

Such was the life in Athens in the heyday of her glory, before the jealousy of Sparta and other independent Greek states, and the discontent of the subject states of the Athenian Empire flamed up into a war that for ever broke the power of the great city. Already the first of the inevitable clashes between imperial Athens and her rivals, chief of whom was Sparta, had wasted the strength of most of Greece by many years of indecisive struggle. This was the first of the Peloponnesian Wars (460–454 B.C.). In 431 B.C., in spite of the exhaustion of both sides, war again broke out.

The plan of Pericles in the Second Peloponnesian War was not to fight at all, but to let Corinth and Sparta spend their money and energies while Athens conserved both. Therefore, he got all the inhabitants of Attica to come inside the walls of Athens, and let the Peloponnesians enter the plain

PEARL-DIVER OF ANCIENT GREECE

Depicted on the side of this Greek vase is a sailing ship, with a pearl-diver about to plunge into the water. Greek vessels had an eye painted on each side of the prow, and sometimes also on the superstructure, perhaps because the forepart bore some resemblance to an animal's head. This form of decoration is still seen on some boats in the Mediterranean.

commander, Epaminondas, brought Spartan power to an end. The era of Theban leadership was, however, short-lived, for the Theban power was the one-man power of Epaminondas, and when he was killed at the battle of Mantinea in 362 B.C. Thebes really suffered defeat in spite of its victory. The age of the powerful city-states was at an end, and a prostrated Greece invited a conqueror.

Such a conqueror was found in Philip, king of Macedonia, the country lying just to the north of classical Greece. Philip, who came into power in 359 B.C., had spent three years in Thebes as a hostage, and, seeing the weakness of the disunited cities, determined to possess the Greek world.

of Attica year after year and ravage as they would, while Athens, again without losses, harried their lands by sea. But Pericles reckoned without the dangers of overcrowding. Plague broke out in Athens and killed one-fourth of the population, including Pericles himself, and left the other three-fourths without spirit and without a leader. After dragging along for 10 years, this war petered out.

Almost before they knew it, however, the Athenians were plunged by the unscrupulous demagogue Alcibiades, nephew of Pericles, into the Third Peloponnesian War. Wishing for a brilliant military career, Alcibiades persuaded Athens into a great expedition against Syracuse. But this suffered an overwhelming disaster in 413 B.C., being completely destroyed, while the Athenian captives were sold into slavery.

This disaster sealed the fate of Athens. Those of the subject or allied cities about the Aegean that had remained faithful now deserted to Sparta, and the Spartans laid siege to Athens. Then in 405 B.C. the whole remaining Athenian fleet of 180 vessels was captured in the Hellespont at the battle of Aegospotami. Besieged by land and powerless by sea, Athens could neither raise grain nor import it, and in 404 B.C. the Athenian Empire came to an end. The fortifications and long walls connecting Athens with Piraeus were destroyed, and Athens became a vassal ally of triumphant Sparta.

Sparta maintained its supremacy by keeping Spartan garrisons in many Greek cities, and this custom, together with Sparta's hatred of democracy, made its rule unpopular. After various unsuccessful attempts Thebes at length succeeded in shaking off Sparta's heavy rule. At the battle of Leuctra in 371 B.C. the Thebans, under their gifted

Demosthenes saw the danger that threatened, and by a series of fiery speeches against Philip sought to unite the Greeks as they had once been united against Persia. But Philip was too strong for them, and at the battle of Chaeronea (338) established his leadership. Before he could carry his conquests to Asia Minor, however, he was killed and his power fell to his son Alexander, then not quite 20 years old. How Alexander built an empire that embraced almost the entire known world is told in the separate article on Alexander the Great.

Alexander made the whole of the then known world Greek, as he carried out his conquests. Greek culture meant freedom of spirit, and Alexander prevented the inferior culture of the East from being imposed upon the West.

The three centuries that follow the death of Alexander are known as the Hellenistic age, for their products were no longer pure Greek, but Greek plus the characteristics of the conquered nations. It was a time of great wealth and splendour. Art, science and letters flourished and developed. The private citizen no longer lived crudely, but in a comfortable house, and many cities adorned themselves with beautiful public buildings and sculptures.

This age came to its end in another conquest —that by Rome. On the field of Cynoscephalae in Thessaly, the Romans defeated Macedonia in 197 B.C. and gave the Greek cities their freedom as allies. Even so the Greeks caused Rome a great deal of trouble, and were taught their lesson by the burning of Corinth in 146 B.C. and by their reduction to vassalage. Athens alone was allowed to retain a certain amount of freedom, and to its schools resorted many Romans, Cicero among them. Though Rome conquered Greece on the field of

From the painting by Charles M. Sheldon, based on Pausanias

One of the Seven Wonders of the World was the statue of the Greek god Zeus, which adorned the temple of Olympia in Elis. It was the work of Pheidias (born *c.* 500 B.C.), the Athenian sculptor, and like most Greek statues and buildings was brightly coloured. This reconstruction shows how the huge figure of 'Olympian Zeus,' which was wrought in marble, ivory and gold, probably looked

E.N.A

A GREEK TEMPLE GLORIOUS IN DECAY

The Erechtheum, which stands on the Acropolis at Athens, was built in honour
of the Greek hero Erechtheus and contained an image of Pallas Athene, guardian of
the city. It is a building of great beauty, and much of it is still standing, though
it was built well over 2,000 years ago. Here we see its remarkable porch, supported
by six female figures, or caryatides as they are called, instead of ordinary pillars.

L. G. Popoff

GREEK COSTUMES NOW RARELY SEEN

These two girls from northern Greece are wearing their native costumes, in which bold colours are blended with artistic skill. Heavy gold embroidery and delicate needle-work enhance the splendour of their dress, and the girl on the left completes her toilette with a massive belt of embossed silver. The art of executing such elaborate needlework is gradually dying out, and national costumes are now seldom seen.

Fred Boissonas; E.N.A.

The villagers in the upper photograph are wending their way homeward after attending evening service. One of the men is wearing the fustanella, or white kilt of the Greeks, and in front of him are two priests dressed in black. The ancient ruins of the Erectheum (lower, seen also in the second plate), standing on the summit of the Acropolis, tower above modern Athens on the plain below.

FOLK OF MODERN GREECE
Directly above is an elderly Greek woman, spinning wool by hand outside her home. At the top right are two boys in national costume ; lower, some monks are seen in St. Stephen's monastery in Thessaly. The monasteries are built on pinnacles of rock.

Dorien Leigh; George Long

battle, Greece continued to exercise power over Rome in art and letters.

For more than 2,000 years, from the time of Alexander the Great to the third decade of the 19th century, the Greeks passed from one master to another. The last of these conquerors was Turkey, which had established its dominion during the 15th century. In 1821 the Greek nation rose in arms in the Greek War of Independence. Russia was interested because the Greek Catholic Church was also the State Church of Russia, and Russia had for years claimed the right to protect the Greek Christian subjects of the Turks.

Numerous volunteers from Europe joined the Greeks—Lord Byron among them—and fought the troops of the Sultan with varying success. In 1827 the Turkish fleet was destroyed at the battle of Navarino by the combined British, French and Russian fleets, but there the joint action ceased. Next year Russia took matters into her own hands, sent an army into the Balkans, and took Adrianople. In the peace of Adrianople (1829) Turkey signed a treaty whose outcome was the restoration of independence to the Greeks.

In 1832, after serious disorders, the three protecting powers (Britain, France and Russia) raised to the throne of Greece Prince Otto, son of Louis I of Bavaria. Otto ruled after the German manner, with German advisers, and the Greeks in 1862 revolted and deposed him. In the following year Prince George of Denmark became king and reigned until his assassination in 1913. In 1864 Great Britain had ceded to Greece the Ionian Islands, which had been under British protection since

1815. Thessaly, on the north, was secured between 1881 and 1897. The island of Crete was not allowed by the Powers to be a part of Greece until 1913. It was not until 1916 that the Greek railways were connected with those of the rest of Europe.

In the Balkan War of 1912–13, the allied Balkan states defeated Turkey, and Greece gained a broad strip of territory on the north, amounting to some 17,000 square miles and including a great part of ancient Macedonia (*see* Balkan Peninsula). In the First World War (1914–18), Greece proclaimed her neutrality ; but King Constantine, who was married to the sister of the Emperor William II of Germany, was accused by the Allies of secretly aiding Germany and Austria-Hungary.

The prime minister Venizelos, who had piloted his country through the Balkan Wars, revolted after he had twice been dismissed by the king; and in June 1917 King Constantine was forced by the Allies to abdicate in favour of his second son, Alexander, and leave the country. In the peace settlement which followed the close of the war, Venizelos obtained favourable terms for Greece, including the annexation of Thrace as far as the Black Sea (with Adrianople, now called Edirne), together with Smyrna (Izmir), and a large adjacent district in Asia Minor. But in December 1920, following the death of Alexander, Constantine was restored by an overwhelming vote.

The Greek government attempted to enforce their claims to the lands granted them in Asia Minor, but their armies were defeated by the Turks in 1921, and the whole position of Greece was shaken. In August 1922 the Turks attacked the Greek army in Asia Minor, and early in September they occupied Smyrna after the Greek forces had been withdrawn. As a result of a revolutionary movement in Greece, Constantine again abdicated in favour of his son, who succeeded to the throne as George II.

The Greek constitution adopted on October 29, 1864, had placed the legislative power in the hands of a single Assembly elected by manhood suffrage. In 1911 this constitution was altered to provide for a second chamber. Greece was proclaimed a republic in 1924. Business depression resulted in political upheavals and plots to restore the monarchy. Several military dictatorships followed. Then, from 1928 to 1932, Venizelos was in power. After further political upheavals, including an unsuccessful revolt against the royalists which was supported by Venizelos, the monarchy was restored in 1935. Metaxas (who died in 1941), deputy prime minister and minister of war, assumed the premiership, suspended the constitution, and made himself dictator, August 1936.

The Second World War

At the beginning of the Second World War in 1939, Greece remained neutral until on October 28, 1940, she was invaded by Italy from Albania. The Greeks put up a courageous resistance to Mussolini's forces, advanced into Albania, and captured over 20,000 Italians. Britain gave Greece military aid in her fight against the invader, but in April 1941 Germany came to the rescue of her Italian partner, advancing through Yugoslavia. Yugoslav resistance to Hitler's armies collapsed, and after desperate fighting the British and Greek forces were compelled to withdraw, the Greek army in the Epirus capitulating on April 21. The Germans entered Athens on April 26, and the British forces were evacuated to Crete.

King George II with the crown prince and members of the government escaped to Crete. Here, after narrowly avoiding capture by German parachutists, the King was taken aboard a British destroyer, and landed in Egypt. The Greek government set up its headquarters at Cairo and was later reconstituted in London, where it stayed until 1943; it then returned to Cairo until it was possible to go back to a liberated Greece, in 1944.

Under the German occupation sabotage was widespread. The Germans dealt with such outbreaks with their customary severity; in reprisal some 1,500 villages were burnt, the tobacco and currant harvests suffered, and forests were destroyed. Guerilla activities which increasingly harassed the Germans were divided into two politically hostile forces— one loyal to the Government and the other with Communistic tendencies. Threatened in the rear by the advancing Russian armies, the Germans withdrew from Greece in 1944, but the liberation at first brought little relief to the Greek people. Some 480,000 persons had lost their lives through guerilla fighting, famine, executions, and deportation ; and the country was torn by civil war.

As in other war-ravaged lands of Europe, the fight against an invader marshalled men of all tenets in resistance to the oppressor. But when the immediate danger was over, differences in views between monarchists and Communists and other more moderate men who desired a republican form of government became acute. Civil war broke out in December 1944. A lightning visit of Mr. Winston Churchill and Mr. Anthony Eden to Athens on Christmas Day, and the acceptance by Archbishop Damaskinos of the post of Regent, composed the strife.

In London, King George II announced his intention not to return to Greece until invited by the Greek people. The general election of 1946 resulted in victory for the Populist (royalist) party, and the King thereupon returned to Athens. He died on April 1, 1947, and his brother Paul reigned over a country still politically divided, impoverished by the long enemy occupation, and surrounded by hostile neighbours.

In December 1947 a guerilla force calling itself the Greek Democratic Army set up a " Free Greek Government," under its commander, Markos Vafeiadis, as Premier. Markos was a Communist, and his movement received support in arms and supplies from Bulgaria and Yugoslavia. Greek Communist refugees had fled to Yugoslavia after the troubles at the end of 1944, and bands of desperate men had since sallied forth to harass the Greek frontier regions. With American aid in money, arms and military organization, the Greek government at Athens held the forces of Markos in check, but the revolt caused very grave disturbance to Greece's recovery from her wartime troubles.

As a result of the Paris Conference, June 27, 1946, the Dodecanese, a group of islands and islets in the South-Eastern corner of the Aegean, were handed over to Greece on March 31, 1947. (They had been under Italian occupation since 1912.)

A Visit to Present-Day Greece

Of ancient Thebes, Corinth and Sparta little is standing now. Modern Thebes is surrounded by mountains, with the famous Helicon and Parnassus on the west. To the north-west lies Lake Copais, formerly a shallow and unhealthy sheet of water and marsh, but now drained, redeeming 60,000 acres of fertile land.

The most interesting excavations in Greece are in the Peloponnesus at Olympia. As you journey along the Gulf of Corinth you will see luxuriant vineyards and fields set apart for drying currants. Tall dark cypresses and mountain torrents add to the beauty of the landscape.

Olympia, like Pompeii, is a buried city which modern enterprise has brought to light. In the three centuries following the last celebration of the Olympic Games, in the 4th century A.D., the chief temples were overthrown by earthquakes, the treasuries were covered by a landslide, and the whole site buried under two or three layers of sand

E.N.A.

ANCIENT PATRAS, WESTERN PORT OF GREECE

Still a busy and thriving port, in normal times engaged mainly in the export of currants and other fruit, wine, oil, and woollen goods, Patras traces its recorded history back to the 3rd century B.C. Situated on the Gulf of Patras, about 13 miles south-west of Lepanto, it was an early centre of Christianity, one of its churches being traditionally associated with the martyrdom of St. Andrew. Rebuilt after its destruction by the Turks in 1821, it has few relics of the past.

by the two rivers at whose junction it lies. In the museum there is the original Hermes of Praxiteles, one of the greatest pieces of ancient sculpture.

Other important finds have been made at Delphi, once the site of the famous oracle. This beautiful spot is situated on the northern shore of the Corinthian Gulf, whose cold springs and cool air currents from the chasms of Mount Parnassus early excited the awe of the Greeks.

A visit to the little island of Aegina, about 15 miles south-west of Athens, would also be well worth while. This has a prosperous agricultural and fishing community, famous for its pottery, and for the sponge fishing carried on by divers. But it is most interesting for the remains of its splendid temple of Zeus.

The little island of Delos, one of the Cyclades, is uninhabited today except by a few shepherds and the custodian of the excavations, but is rich in archaeological interest—temples, a theatre, and a house with a mosaic floor, and the fragments of a very old colossal statue of Apollo which stood in the sacred precinct near the Apollo temple in the days of the Delian League. If you climb to the top of Mount Kynthos you can see other islands of the group round about, including Naxos, the largest and most fertile, and Paros, still famous for its marble.

Side by side with the antiquities of Greece you will often find Byzantine churches, medieval monasteries of the Greek Catholic Church, and ruins of castles, erected in the days following the Crusade of 1204, when barons from western Europe ruled parts of the land. There are scores of monasteries in Greece, among them those of Mount Athos, which are world-famous.

In addition to the Greek-speaking element of the population, which represents the parent Greek stock much changed by Slavic and other foreign mixtures, Greece today is inhabited by two other wholly distinct racial groups. All over the Attic plain, in Corinthia, Argolis, and various other parts, are found the Albanians, who are chiefly farmers. They are a vigorous and manly race, who make excellent soldiers and sailors and have furnished many famous leaders. The Vlachs, who are found chiefly in the mountains of Thessaly and central Greece, are for the most part nomad herdsmen or carriers; descended from the Latinized population of Roman times, they still speak a language which indicates its Latin origin.

Greek economy was ruined as a result of the occupation of the country by the Italians, Germans, and Bulgarians during 1941–44. One-fifth of the mainland was still forest land. The methods of agriculture are still for the most part of the primitive kind. In many places the old wooden plough is still employed. The use of fertilizers and rotation of crops are rare outside the wheat-growing areas of Thrace and the reclaimed bed of Lake Copais, so Greece imports much of its food, especially cereals.

The absence of good native coal has handicapped manufacturing, though textiles, leather goods, soap, paper, glass, and some other articles are produced, in addition to olive oil and wine. Currants, i.e. the small dried grapes shipped from Corinth (the word currant is a corruption of Corinth), are still among the most valuable exports. At the beginning of the Second World War Greece had a flourishing merchant marine which consisted of some 600 ships. These went into the Allied wartime shipping pool and many were sunk.

Greece, like other European countries freed from enemy occupation by the victory of the Western Allies in 1945, received much help through U.N.R.R.A. (q.v.). In addition, British experts gave advice in the organization of the government departments, and American ones later continued the task after British forces were withdrawn.

The GLORIOUS ART of OLD GREECE

Thousands of years have not dimmed the ' glory that was Greece,' and the major part of that glory lies in her superb plastic art, the perfection of which no later race of men has ever since achieved.

Greek Art. Excavations in Crete have revealed that this island was the centre of a highly cultured people—the Minoans—as early as 1500 B.C. Much of their civilization was borrowed from the Egyptians, and eventually spread to the Greek mainland.

Discoveries at Mycenae and Tiryns, in southern Greece, have shown that these cities produced a highly formalised art, which doubtless influenced primitive Greek pottery and early sculpture; though no relation has yet been traced between the well-wrought figures and reliefs of Mycenae and Knossos and the beginnings of Hellenic sculpture in the 7th century B.C.

Decorated with a representation of a boxing match, this vase was a prize at the Games dedicated to Athena.

The Greeks used colour in both their sculpture and their architecture, though time has almost entirely washed away the bright hues of their work. The work of the great Greek painters also has disappeared; it lives only in what ancient writers tell us about it. Polygnotus in the 5th century B.C. was renowned as a draughtsman; while in the 4th century Parrhasius, Xeuzis, and Apelles were famous as colourists.

The earliest Greek art is represented almost entirely by pottery, at first adorned with geometric patterns and crudely drawn figures, but later borrowing from Oriental models a wealth of plant and animal forms. The most familiar designs show figures of men and gods, painted in black against the natural red of the clay, or, as later became more common, with the figures left red against a black background. From these vases we are able to form some idea of what Greek painting was like, and they give us further examples of that wonderful feeling for form and line and movement which made Greek art supreme.

When we see how primitive and stiff are the Greek statues of the 7th century B.C., and compare them with the masterpieces of two centuries later, we cannot but marvel at the rapid development of Greek art. Through the Phoenicians the early Greeks came into contact with the art of Babylonia, Assyria and Egypt. They borrowed many of their decorative forms from these peoples, but transformed them by their own artistic genius.

The Persian invasion (490–479 B.C.) aroused the virile young Greek race to great achievements. Having driven out the Asiatic invader, the Greeks suddenly grew, in the 5th century B.C., to full stature. What the Persians had destroyed the Greeks set to work to rebuild. Their poets sang the glories of the new epoch, and Greek genius, as shown in the great creations at Athens, came to full strength and beauty. It was then, under Pericles, the great statesman and patron of art, that the Athenian Acropolis was restored and adorned with the matchless Parthenon, the Erechtheum, and other beautiful buildings. (*See* Acropolis ; Athens.)

There were beautiful temples in other cities of Greece, too, notably that of Zeus at Olympia, which we know from descriptions by the ancient writers and from a few fragments that have been discovered in recent times. A striking feature of Greek architecture is the skill with which the fullest advantage is taken of natural surroundings.

The 5th century B.C. was made illustrious in sculpture also by the work of three great masters, all known to us in some degree by surviving works. Myron is famous for the boldness with which he fixed moments of violent action in marble, as in his famous Discobolus, or Disk-Thrower, which we know through a copy at Rome (see page 1532). The Doryphorus, or Spear Bearer, of Polyclitus, who worked in bronze, was called by the ancients the Rule, or guide in composition,

Vatican Museum, Rome: photo Alinari

GREEK VASE PAINTING

The quaint paintings with which the ancient Greeks decorated their pottery are interesting not only for their artistic value but also for the stories they tell. In this one, for instance, dating from about 460 B.C., we see the legendary king Oedipus answering the riddle of the Sphinx and thus saving his country from destruction.

THINGS *of* BEAUTY WE OWE *to* GREECE

Alinari

'Lysicrates, son of Lysitheides of Cicynna, was choragus (i.e. instructor of the chorus) when the boys of the tribe of Acamantis conquered . . .': so reads the inscription round the architrave (stone course immediately above the columns) of this lovely little monument, which was dedicated to Dionysus, the god of wine. Erected in Athens in 335–34 B.C. by Lysicrates to celebrate his team's victory in the theatrical contests held during the feast of that god, it was built of white marble and is a graceful and pleasing example of the Corinthian style.

2 D 4

E. P. Co.; Professor Rossmahith

The temple of the 'Wingless Victory' (Athene Niké) in the lower photograph is one of the greatest glories of the Acropolis at Athens, and a superb miniature work in the Ionic style. Notice the capitals (tops of the columns) and compare them with those of the Corinthian monument (page 1529) and of the Doric temple (top), which is at Bassae, near Phigalia, in Arcadia. Designed by the Athenian architect Ictinus, who in the 5th century B.C. was associated with Callicrates in the building of the Parthenon at Athens, this temple was dedicated to Apollo.

FIGURES FROM THE ATHENIAN ACROPOLIS

 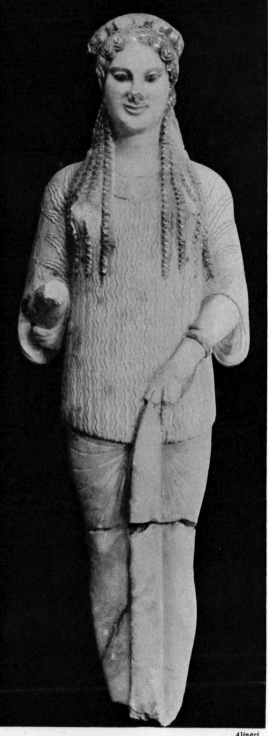

Here can be seen what the Athenian ladies wore during the 6th century B.C., for it is from that time that these two sculptured figures date. The one on the left, slightly the earlier of the two, was done in soft stone, which accounts for the rather clumsily rounded contours. The far finer work of the right-hand figure is due to the use of marble, which can be carved with greater sharpness. The prevailing colour of Greek men's dress was white, but women used gaily-coloured materials. Sandals or shoes were worn out of doors, women's shoes often being highly decorated.

THE ATHLETE IN ACTION AS MIRON SAW HIM

Anderson

Finest of the various copies of Miron's Discobulus, this magnificent sculpture (now in the Vatican Museum at Rome) is an example of Greek art at its best. It is a perfect representation of an athlete in a pose assumed naturally as he prepares to throw the discus, an action peculiarly suited to the display of free muscular movement. Miron, who was born about 480 B.C., was one of the most celebrated of Greek sculptors and portrayed the human figure accurately in the most difficult and momentary attitudes. He also directed his genius towards animals.

PRAXITELES'S HERMES, A MASTERPIECE IN MARBLE

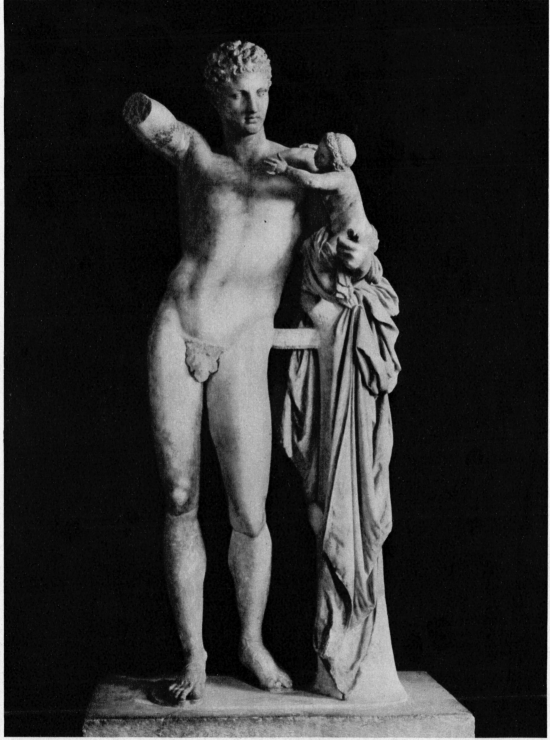

Alinari

In this glorious statue, which is an original work of the famous Greek sculptor Praxiteles, we can admire the artist's supreme skill in delineating beauty of form. It represents the god Hermes bearing the infant Dionysus on his left arm. It is believed that, originally, he was probably dangling a bunch of grapes in his right hand. This sculpture, which was done in marble, was discovered at Olympia, and is now in the museum there. In the 4th century B.C. a greater play of emotions was introduced into their work by Greek sculptors, typified by Praxiteles.

DIGNITY AND FEELING IN A GREEK BRONZE

Alinari

Greek bronzes are far less common than statues in stone or marble, and this figure is one of the finest of existing examples of that art. Found at Delphi, where it is housed in the museum, it depicts a charioteer, reins in hand, standing erect as he guides his horses. The simplicity of the work in no way detracts from its greatness and does in fact emphasize the intensity of expression which is one of its chief qualities. Chariot races were held at religious festivals, teams of two or four horses being used.

W. F. Mansell

Dating from the second century of the Christian era, near the end of the greatest period of Greek art, the Aphrodite of Melos (above) shows how the Greek sculptors best treated the subject of a female nude. Aiming at something more than a mere representation of feminine beauty, they produced an idealized type of figure which gives the impression of a goddess in marble rather than of a mere human being. Found on the Greek island of Melos or Milo in 1820, this statue, which is better known as the Venus de Milo, is now one of the treasures of the Louvre, Paris.

PAINTED WARE
OF GREEK POTTERS

These two vessels give some idea of the heights to which the potter's art rose in ancient Greece, and especially in Attica, where this art was practised with the greatest success. That on the left is especially interesting, for it is of a type, having coloured figures on a band of white ground, which was principally reserved for vessels to be placed in tombs. It shows a Greek woman seated on a diphros—a sort of stool—and is probably an oil-jar (lekythos). The other vase (above), of the better-known red-figure ware, shows a truly typical Greek subject—a warrior for whom the figure of Victory is pouring out wine; one of her wings and the wine-vessel are visible on the right. Both these vases are in the British Museum, London.

because it was believed to follow the proportions of the human body with greater perfection than any other work.

But the greatest name in Greek sculpture is that of Pheidias, who expressed in his magnificent works the noblest and loftiest ideals of Greek religion. It was under his direction that the sculptures decorating the Parthenon were planned and executed, and some of them may have been his own work.

We can form some idea of his genius from the remains of the sculptures of the pediments and frieze of the Parthenon now preserved in the British Museum and known as the Elgin Marbles, from Lord Elgin, who brought them from Athens in 1801–12 (see Elgin Marbles). These sculptures, in their composition, in their exquisite modelling, and in the noble ideas which they embody, are the greatest surviving works of Greek art.

Another famous work that is believed to belong to the school of Pheidias is the Aphrodite of Melos, or Venus de Milo, a marble statue now in the Louvre, Paris (see page 1535). It was discovered in the 19th century in the island of Milo, or Melos, one of the Cyclades. Although some think it belongs to a later date, its perfect proportions, dignity and serenity typify the qualities associated with Pheidias.

British Museum

GREEK POTTER AND WHEEL

Much of our knowledge of the manners, customs and crafts of ancient Greece is derived from the ornamentations of their pottery. The figure (left) of a Greek potter modelling on his wheel was found on the island of Cyprus. The terra-cotta potter's wheel (right) was discovered in Crete and has a central depression in which its pivot was inserted.

Pheidias was followed by Praxiteles (flourished 360–340 B.C.), Scopas and Lysippus. Of Praxiteles, who has been called the sculptor of the beautiful, we have an original work, the statue of Hermes with the child Dionysus. Most of the sculptors, it must be remembered, are known to us only through copies of their work by Roman artists. The figure of Hermes, at once strong and active and graceful, finely proportioned, having a surface of exquisite texture, the well-poised head and the face expressive of nobility and sweetness, is beautiful beyond description. The child, who is held in the left hand, is reaching out to grasp something, perhaps a bunch of grapes—held in the missing hand of Hermes. The so-called Satyr, or Faun, of Praxiteles, is probably the work of another sculptor of the same school. Praxiteles' conceptions are less lofty and dignified than those of Pheidias, but they are full of grace and charm. (See illus. page 1533).

Scopas carried farther the tendency to portray dramatic moods. Lysippus harked back to the athletic type of Polyclitus, but made his figures lighter and more slender, combining manly beauty

British Museum; Mansell

PART OF THE PARTHENON'S SCULPTURED FRIEZE

The famous frieze of the Parthenon at Athens ran around the top of the cella (chamber containing the image of Athena), inside the collonnade and high up under the roof. The Greek sculptors were such masters of their art that they realized that the modelling of the frieze as seen from the ground should allow for the angle of vision. They overcame this difficulty by increasing the depth of the relief (prominence of the figures) from below upwards, as seen in this group. The bas-relief, with those shown in pages 1143 and 1144, is in the British Museum, London.

2 E   4

and strength. He was at the height of his fame in the time of Alexander the Great (356–323 B.C.), who, it is said, desired that Lysippus only should portray him. How far this age had advanced can be seen in the celebrated sculpture known as the Winged Victory of Samothrace, now preserved in the Louvre, Paris (see illus., page 1276).

Greek art later lost much of its simplicity and ideal perfection of form, its serenity and restraint; but it gained in intensity of feeling, in expressing physical suffering and anguish. It had also become more realistic, portraying not only ideal types of men and gods, but portraits of individuals, and not only Greeks, but barbarians as well. This is especially true of the Hellenistic age—the three centuries following the death of Alexander. One of the most

apparent after the Roman invasion, when the sculpture became more emotional. Many beautiful examples of Greek sculpture were taken to Rome, and both Greeks and Romans continued to work in stone in that city.

From that time on, however, Greek art gradually decayed, until classical art appeared to be lost entirely. It was not until the revival of ancient culture in the Italian Renaissance that original and creative art arose once more in Europe.

The influence of Greek art has been visible, off and on, for the last 2,000 years, not merely in the Mediterranean countries, but also in England. For the style named Palladian after the great Italian architect, Palladio, and brought back to England by Inigo Jones (1573–1652), was derived

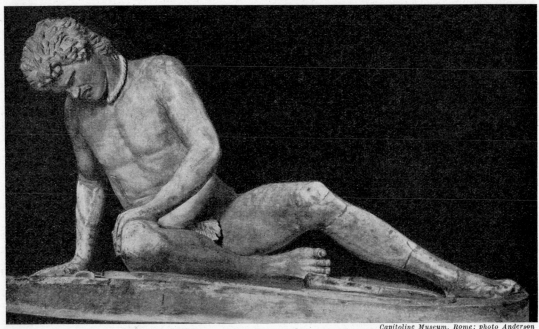

Capitoline Museum, Rome; photo Anderson

THE DYING GAUL : A CELEBRATED GREEK STATUE

Attalus I (241-197 B.C.), King of Pergamum, in Asia Minor, carried out a successful campaign against the Gauls, and to celebrate and commemorate his victories erected statues of defeated Gauls on the Acropolis at
Athens and at the city of Pergamum. The above statue by an unknown sculptor, a copy of the bronze original at Pergamum, belongs to the Hellenistic age of Greek art, which began soon after the death of Alexander the Great, 323 B.C.

famous works of this period is the Dying Gaul, sometimes called the Dying Gladiator. In the Laocoön group, which depicts the Trojan father and his sons crushed to death by deadly serpents, we find the extremity of physical torture and exaggerated pathos as represented in sculpture. To the Hellenistic period belongs also the famous Apollo Belvedere (see page 187), so called from having been placed in the Belvedere gallery of the Vatican.

The first and most glorious period of Greek art, as we have seen, began in the 5th century B.C., following the Greeks' success in repelling the Persian invasion. The heart of the movement was in Athens, a large part of which had been destroyed, and which was rebuilt. The character of the art was its simplicity, its chaste outline, its restraint, and the ideals it expressed. The second great period was in the 3rd century B.C., though even then it was altering in character. This became still more

from Greek origins. The use of columns, whether plain or fluted, which became characteristic not only of that architecture, but also of the later work done during the following century and comprising those buildings which we now know as Georgian, is derived almost directly from the Greek.

Sir Christopher Wren (1632–1723), again, in his west front of St. Paul's, uses Greek columns with outstanding success, and it is no exaggeration to say that most of the best productions of the finest age of English architecture were directly influenced by the work of ancient Greece. One striking example of a later date is the colonnaded façade of the British Museum, completed in 1852. Not only in England is this debt owed to Greece; in France and Germany, too, one sees ancient Greece providing the model for many a fine building, while in sculpture there has never been any lack of support for work in the classical Greek manner.

The Classic TONGUE of Ancient GREECE

One of the loveliest languages of the world, and one in which the world's finest literature and noblest thoughts have been composed, is Greek. From Greek literature all that is best in modern letters is derived.

Greek Language and Literature. If by some happy miracle the Greek philosopher Plato and the orator Demosthenes could return to earth, and sit down in some café of modern Athens, they would probably be surprised to find how easily they could read the morning paper. Of course, it would take them a minute or so to focus their eyes on the print, which is so much smaller than anything done with the reed-pen of their day, and they would find the shape of some of the letters changed.

They would discover many new words, and, perhaps, they would accuse the journalist of careless grammar. But, all the same, the written literary Greek of today is intelligible to anyone who knows the Greek of 2,500 years ago. (The Greek schoolboy can read the literary masterpieces of 2,500 years ago far more easily than we can read Chaucer.) It is another matter with the spoken tongue, however. Many words in modern Greek, concerning the intimate things of daily life, were borrowed during medieval and modern times from the Italians, Turks, or other neighbours, and the pronunciation is so changed as to make modern spoken Greek almost unintelligible to one who knows only the classical tongue.

There is much of the Greek language in the present-day speech of Great Britain and the rest of the world. When we want to make a new word for a new thing we are likely to borrow from the Greek. For example, " photograph," " telegraph," " telephone," " gramophone," " periscope," and scores of other words that have found their way into our dictionaries as names of modern inventions, are formed directly from old Greek words.

Nor are we indebted to Greek only for "new" words like these. Many others, some of them centuries old, are woven into the very warp and weft of our language. So, if you know even a little Greek, you can work out the meaning and pronunciation of a word that at first glance appears difficult.

Ancient Greek was graceful and harmonious, full of light and shade and colour, subtlety and music; it could pile words together into compounds as German does—only the words were more musical to begin with. Moreover, in this language was written one of the most wonderful literatures of all time. Of this we can get only half an idea through even the most careful translations. Poetry is always difficult to translate, but Greek poetry loses more, perhaps, than any other, since English often takes two or three times as many words to say the same thing. A prose translation of Homer is clumsy, and a translation in English verse is incomplete. Neither gives any true idea of the simplicity

THE POET PINDAR
Writing his first choral ode at 20, Pindar (*c.* 522–443 B.C.) rapidly came to be regarded as the national lyric poet of ancient Greece.

and resonance and movement, the inevitability which never becomes monotony. Greek lyrics are even harder to translate, though there have been published free renderings of great beauty which give the English reader some notion of the originals.

Greek prose also loses much by translation, for Greek is much subtler an instrument of expression than English. The Greek particles, for instance, little words only a letter or two long and amounting only to a slight gesture of the hand or the flicker of expression on a person's face, must be translated in English by some such awkward words as "moreover." A translation makes things tedious where the Greek expresses them compactly. This is because Greek is a rather highly inflected language—one in which alterations of the endings of words express grammatical changes. A single word of, perhaps, no more than two syllables in Greek may become a whole sentence with us.

The history of the Greek language may be roughly divided into the following periods: Attic (500–300 B.C.); Hellenistic (300 B.C.–A.D. 600) ; Byzantine (600–1453); and modern (1453 to the present day).

The oldest Greek literary works that we have are the Iliad and the Odyssey of Homer, still the most splendid examples of epic or narrative poetry. These were not the first poems of the Greeks. They come from an age that was already rich in folk poetry—hymns to the gods, and marriage hymns, and lays recounting the deeds of ancient heroes. In that age, however, the Greeks had no writing, and of all the songs that the wandering bards carried from city to city and recited from memory, few but the Homeric poems survived to be written down. The only exceptions are a few of the so-called Homeric hymns—the invocations to Apollo or some other god, with which it was customary for the singer to prelude his recitation of the Homeric stories. From a slightly later period we have the poems attributed to Hesiod. He lived at the hamlet of Ascra, near Mount Helicon, in Boeotia, probably in the 8th century B.C., and drew many faithful pictures of the country life he knew so well.

With the 8th and 7th centuries we come to the beginnings of the historical period. The old ways of life were giving way to new. Commerce, discovery, colonization and political change widened the horizon of the Greeks and quickened their feeling and imagination. To express the thoughts and feelings aroused by this fuller national life, new literary forms were invented—all still in verse, however, for prose had not yet begun to be used as a literary medium. The greatest national lyric poet was Pindar (*c.* 522–443 B.C.), whose magnificent odes yield the scholar a pleasure which alone is enough to recom-

W. F. Taylor

GREEK THEATRE SPLENDID IN RUIN

At Epidaurus are the ruins of a vast Greek theatre, dating from the 4th century B.C., which the Greek writer Pausanias (c. A.D. 150) said was the most beautiful in the whole country. It held 16,000 and almost every seat remains as it was originally, though of the stage only the foundations have survived. In front of the auditorium are marble seats reserved for the favoured few.

pense him for the labour of learning the Greek language. Sappho, who wrote about a century before Pindar, is generally esteemed the greatest of all women poets, though little of her work survives.

As the Greeks invented the epic and lyric forms of verse, and brought them to perfection, so too they invented the drama (considered as a literary form), and produced the masterpieces which are still reckoned as the world's crowning achievements. In the crowded glorious age which followed the repulse of Persia (490–479 B.C.), the awakened national consciousness of Athens found expression in a series of superb tragedies which have never been equalled except, perhaps, by a few of Shakespeare's. The story of how the simple choral songs and dialogues performed at the festivals of the god Dionysus flowered into the majestic tragedies of Aeschylus (525–456 B.C.), Sophocles (495–405 B.C.) and Euripides (480–406 B.C.), and how each made improvements in the dramatic form, is told elsewhere in these pages, in the article on Drama.

From Greek comedy only the plays of one man have survived—those of Aristophanes (c. 445–385 B.C.). His comedies are gay, poking fun at the things of his own day.

As always in literary history, Greek prose was late in developing. In the 6th century some of the early philosophers formulated their ideas in brief prose maxims, but the first truly literary use of prose is in the History written by Herodotus (c. 484–424 B.C.), about the middle of the 5th century. The theme is the struggle between East and West, ending in the Persian wars. His great successor, Thucydides (c. 464–404 B.C.), told the story of the Peloponnesian War. Thucydides' critical use of sources, his inclusion of documents, his laborious research into the cause and origin of important events, make him the most "modern" of the Greek historians, far removed from Herodotus or from Xenophon (430–354 B.C.).

The 5th century also saw the rise of the art of oratory, with its companion art of rhetoric, which taught the technique of making successful speeches. With the establishment of democracy in Athens and other Greek cities, the ability to make convincing speeches, and especially in the law courts, soon became of the greatest practical value.

Litigants were usually compelled to plead their own cases, instead of hiring others to plead for them ; so rhetoric became part of the ordinary education of the youth, and a new profession arose—that of the writer of speeches for men to speak in their own behalf. A large proportion of the speeches of the Attic orators that have come down to us were meant to be used in this way. The 4th century B.C. was the golden age of oratory.

The same lively curiosity and interest in the spectacle of the universe which led the Greeks to invent epic and lyric verse, drama and history, also made them the first philosophers. Their craving to find a reasoned answer to the riddles of life resulted in the creation of another department of prose literature, represented chiefly by the great names of Plato and Aristotle.

Beginning with the 6th century, one thinker after another advanced his theory of the material causes of the basis of the universe, of knowledge, and of conduct. Many of the fragments of their teachings, which have been preserved in the form of terse, epigrammatic statements in prose or verse, seem crude and childish, but serve to remind us how long and toilsome is the road that leads to wisdom.

The first to lay a really scientific basis for philosophical inquiry was Socrates (born c. 470 B.C.), whose tireless questioning into the roots of conduct and searching criticism of all traditional doctrines so outraged the orthodox and narrow-minded that he was put to death. He wrote nothing himself, but his great pupil Plato (427–347 B.C.) carried on and developed his teaching in a matchless series of dialogues, packed with fresh and stimulating ideas which have inspired every philosophical thinker since his day.

Third of the immortal trio of Athenian thinkers was Plato's pupil, Aristotle (384–322 B.C.), often called the father of science. Aristotle sought to map out nearly the whole field of human knowledge into the various sciences. In the history of literature, his work cannot rank with the superbly artistic Platonic dialogues, but in the history of thought he is acknowledged as " the master of those who know." Theophrastus, who succeeded Aristotle as head of the school called the Lyceum, is chiefly remembered for a series of lively character sketches which have found imitators in every age.

With these names the story of classical Greek literature ends, but the Hellenistic age (period of three centuries after the death of Alexander) in Alexandria offers us a second rich store of literature. The name that stands out in poetry is that of Theocritus (3rd century B.C.), who wrote exquisite pastoral poetry picturing the rural life of his native Sicily. Imitators, from Virgil to those of our own day, have tried to recapture the charm of the pastoral form as Theocritus first used it.

Poets of the Hellenistic Age

Other poets of this age are the lyric poet Callimachus (d. c. 240 B.C.); Bion and Moschus (c. 280–250 B.C.), writers of pastoral verse; and Apollonius Rhodius (c. 222–188 B.C.), who wrote the Argonautica, an epic in four books on the quest of the Golden Fleece. Greek prose, too, continued to flourish far into Roman times, and from these later days we have our first forerunners of the novel, as well as important works of geography and history.

The most noteworthy of these later writers are the historians Polybius (c. 204–122 B.C.), Diodorus Siculus, Josephus (A.D. 37–c. 100), and Appian (c. A.D. 98–161); the geographers Strabo (c. 63 B.C.–A.D. 19) and Pausanias (c. A.D. 174); the biographer Plutarch (c. A.D. 48–122), who has given us more general information about antiquity than any other single writer; the critic Longinus (c. A.D. 213–273), the supposed author of one of the best of all works of literary criticism, the treatise On the Sublime; the humorist Lucian (c. A.D. 120–180), whose Dialogues of the Gods are almost as outrageously laughable as a comedy of Aristophanes; and the two Stoic philosophers Epictetus and Marcus Aurelius (A.D. 121–180), one a slave and the other an emperor.

In different regions the Greek language was spoken and written with variations sufficient to cause three chief dialects to be recognized. The Ionic dialect, the language of Homer and Hesiod, was spoken in most of the Aegean islands and on the west coast of Asia Minor. With a few modifications, the Ionic is identical with the Attic, the chief literary dialect. The Doric, the language of Pindar and Theocritus, was spoken at Corinth and throughout most of the Peloponnesus. The Aeolic, in which Sappho wrote, was the speech of Boeotia, Thessaly, and Aeolis (northern Asia Minor). The language of the New Testament (Judaeo-Greek or Hellenistic Greek) differs only slightly from classical Greek.

In modern Greece there is a sharp cleavage between the dialect of the people, called Romaic, and the literary language, which represents an attempt to return as far as possible to the standards of classical Greek. The style of most of the current literature and journalism of Greece represents a compromise between these two ideals, but the most powerful poetry and fiction are written in the popular dialect.

Greenland.
An immense continental island, which lies to the north-east of Canada and almost wholly within the Arctic Circle, Greenland is nearly covered in an impenetrable sheet of ice thousands of feet deep. Its narrow rocky shores are fringed with ancient worn-down mountains (some more than 10,000 feet high) and deeply cut by fiords and valleys. A chain of mountains in the vicinity of Scoresby Sound was discovered in 1933. Greenland, the only colonial possession of Denmark, is the second largest island in the world, with an area now estimated at 826,000 square miles. Only 31,000 square miles of this total are ice-free. Its length is about 1,600 miles and its breadth from 700 to 800 miles.

The east coast is almost uninhabited, but the west coast is warm enough to permit the growth of a narrow belt of green tundra, and some 15,000 Eskimos live there. In the uncertain climate of fogs and snows and icy winds (bitterly cold in the sunless north, but in the south-west often mild enough to breed mosquitoes), these people live an outdoor life hunting the seal, whale, walrus, polar bear and fox, and fishing for salmon, cod and halibut. Nearly all trade is with Denmark, the principal exports being whale and seal oil, cured fish, eiderdown, and skins. Cryolite is also mined and exported. This is a mineral used in smelting aluminium and in

Danish Legation

GREENLAND'S RUGGED SCENERY
Most of the interior of Greenland is buried under an ice-cap, but in the south-west the climate is warmer and in the summer the inhabitants can fish in the ice-free streams. Here a fisherman is spearing his quarry.

making soap, soda, and a fine quality of glass. Coal, copper, gold and iron have been discovered.

Greenland was named by the Norwegian, Eric the Red, who about the end of the 10th century reached its south-western coast and founded a colony. Communication with Norway ceased in 1410, and Greenland became lost to the world until the close of the 16th century, when it was rediscovered by English explorers. In 1702 Danish settlers founded Godthaab on the west coast.

In April 1941 during the Second World War (1939–45) the United States took the country under its protection to forestall possible German invasion.

HOW GREENLAND WAS EXPLORED

Routes taken by some of the exploratory expeditions to Greenland are shown in this map. The Norseman Eric the Red landed on the south-west coast in the 10th century and apparently gave the country the inviting name of Greenland to attract settlers from Iceland. Greenland is Denmark's only colonial possession and is the second largest island in the world, ranking next to Australia. It has a length of about 1,600 miles.

Permission was obtained from the Danish government to establish air, wireless and meteorological bases. The population is 18,430.

Gregory. POPES.

Sixteen Popes have borne the name of Gregory, and short accounts of the most important are given here.

GREGORY I, called the Great (540–604), was a Roman of old family and great wealth, who became a monk in the monastery of St. Andrew at Rome, which he himself endowed. His interest in the Roman island of Britain was aroused by seeing some beautiful English boys sold as slaves in the market-place at Rome. Their blue eyes and golden hair attracted his attention, and he inquired : " Whence come these fair youths? " On being told that they were Angles from the province of Deira, ruled over by Aella, he replied: " Truly, they should be called angels, and not Angles, for they have the faces of angels." After he became Pope in 590, he sent St. Augustine as missionary to England to convert the people to Christianity. Gregory defended Rome against repeated attacks of the Lombards, and exercised much of the power in the West which had fallen from the hands of the weak Eastern emperors. As a teacher and a theologian he is notable. In the realms of liturgy and church music his name is still commemorated in what is called the Gregorian Sacramentary, and in the Gregorian plain-chant. He died on March 10, 604.

GREGORY VII (c. 1025–85) was the mighty Hildebrand. He was chosen Pope in 1073, and his pontificate is memorable for the beginning of the great investiture conflict with the Holy Roman Emperor Henry IV, in which he sought to stop the practice of lay persons—those not in Holy Orders—making ecclesiastical appointments.

A Catholic historian sums up Hildebrand's ideas of a league of nations in these words: " Seeing the world sunk in wickedness and threatened with impending ruin, and believing that the Pope alone could save it, he conceived the vast design of a universal theocracy, which should embrace every kingdom of Christendom, and of whose policy the Ten Commandments should be the fundamental principle. Over this commonwealth of nations the Pope was to preside. The spiritual power was to stand related to the temporal as the sun to the moon, imparting light and strength, without, however, destroying it or depriving princes of their sovereignty."

His struggle with Henry IV lasted many years. Finally Gregory, forced to leave Rome, took refuge first in the Benedictine monastery at Monte Cassino, and then at Salerno, where he died on May 25, 1085. He was canonized in 1606.

GREGORY IX (Pope 1227–41) is chiefly memorable for his conflict with the Emperor Frederick II. GREGORY XI (Pope 1370–78) was a Frenchman who instituted many reforms and transferred the Papacy back to Rome from Avignon, where it had been for some 70 years. GREGORY XII (Pope 1406–15) upheld the rights of the Roman pontiffs against the Avignon " Anti-Pope," Benedict XIII. GREGORY XIII (Pope 1572–85) made the great reform in the calendar (q.v.) in 1582. GREGORY XVI (Pope 1831–46) encouraged learning and founded the Egyptian and Etruscan museums in the Vatican.

Grenfell, SIR WILFRED THOMASON (1865–1940). Labrador fisher-folk will always remember how this doctor-missionary, during 40 years, brought comfort and health to their desolate land.

SIR WILFRED GRENFELL

As a doctor-missionary Sir Wilfred Grenfell spent more than 40 years among the fisher-folk of Labrador, a desolate region on the east coast of Canada, establishing churches, hospitals and schools. Here he is seen leaving his home to visit patients. Knighted in 1927, he died in October 1940.

Grenfell was born near Chester on February 28, 1865, and upon his graduation from Oxford University he entered the London Hospital to study medicine and surgery. Having decided to devote his life to missionary work, he believed that practical help in improving health and living conditions should go hand in hand with religious teaching. Among his patients were many seamen, and in 1889 he joined the Royal National Mission for Deep Sea Fishermen, fitting up an old sailing vessel as a mission ship to cruise in the North Sea among the fishing fleets. Within a few years he built a sailors' hospital, a co-operative store, a mill, an orphanage and a school. He attracted so much attention by his brilliant success in this unique work that Lord Strathcona (1820–1914), the pioneer of railways in Canada, gave him a steamer.

From Lord Strathcona Dr. Grenfell heard of the deplorable condition of the English, Scottish and French-Canadian fisher-folk of Labrador. During the short summer, ministers and doctors from Newfoundland visited the fishing villages, but for nine dark months of every year the people were frozen in, with no means of communication with the outside world except by dog-sledge.

In 1892, when he was 27 years old, Dr. Grenfell went to Labrador, and made that forbidding region the field of his missionary labours. He fought epidemics of smallpox, made the villages sanitary, instructed the women in nursing, and took the seriously ill and injured to his hospitals in Battle and Indian Harbours. He opened a road along the coast, introduced reindeer herds for their milk and for rapid travel, and started a travelling library. Knighted in 1927, he died on October 10, 1940.

Grenville, SIR RICHARD (1541?–91). In British history there are few more dramatic events than the last fight of the Revenge, which had been Sir Francis Drake's flagship at the defeat of the Spanish Armada ; in 1591 it was the flagship of Sir Richard Grenville, Lord Thomas Howard's second-in-command in the Azores, a group of islands in the Atlantic Ocean. The incident is immortalized by Tennyson's poem, The Revenge.

King Philip of Spain, fearing the rising naval power of England, had forbidden his treasure-ships to return from Central and South America. At last he could delay them no longer, because he required the money. He, therefore, equipped a strong fleet which was to meet the Spanish treasure fleet in mid-ocean and convoy it home. Howard had only 16 ships, while Don Alonso de Bazan, the Spanish commander, had a fleet of 53 vessels.

While Howard was in Flores Bay, Azores, a pinnace brought a warning that Don Alonso was approaching, and Howard put to sea.

When Grenville was ready to leave the bay, the Spaniards were between him and Howard. Despite the entreaties of some of his officers, he steadfastly rejected their counsel to seek safety in flight. Grenville played a hero's part. The first Spanish galleon to meet him was the San Felipe, which got to windward and took the breeze out of his sails so that his vessel lay motionless upon the water.

The fight began at three o'clock in the afternoon and was continued throughout the night. " Fifteen naval armadas," writes Raleigh, " were brilliantly repulsed by this one English ship, which received

After Sir O. W. Brierly

GRENVILLE'S LAST FIGHT ON THE REVENGE

A stirring struggle against hopeless odds is the subject of this painting. It shows the last moment of the battle, when Sir Richard's ship was dismasted, but, though surrounded by the Spanish fleet, kept her ensign flying at the stern. It was not until only 20 men of the original crew of 150 were left to serve the guns, and Sir Richard himself had been mortally wounded, that the Revenge surrendered. Grenville died aboard the Spanish admiral's ship a few hours later.

in the course of the action eight hundred shot of great artillery, besides many assaults and entries." Grenville was wounded twice, but refused to go below. At length, his ship leaking like a sieve, her masts gone, the upper deck torn away, and 40 dead, Grenville ordered the master-gunner to be prepared to blow up the battered hulk with the remaining barrel of gunpowder. Then he addressed those of the crew who were still unwounded, saying that " as they had, like valiant, resolute men, repulsed so many enemies, they should not now shorten the honour of their nation by prolonging their own lives by a few hours or a few days." The master-gunner readily agreed, and so did several of the others ; but the captain and the master besought Sir Richard to have care of them.

The master of the Revenge was then rowed to Don Alonso's flagship, and the admiral agreed that the officers should be released on payment of a ransom. As Grenville was borne away from the Revenge he fainted, but shortly afterwards recovered consciousness, only to die later on board the Spanish flagship.

Grey of Fallodon,

EDWARD, 1ST VISCOUNT (1862–1933). Numbered amongst the statesmen who strove to avert the First World War (1914–18), this British leader by his honesty, his quiet dignity, and because he exemplified much of what was best in the national character, won the respect and complete confidence of the nation.

Russell

VISCOUNT GREY
British Foreign Secretary at the outbreak of the First World War (1914–18), Sir Edward Grey was created a Viscount in 1916.

He was born on April 25, 1862, and was educated at Winchester College and Balliol College, Oxford. He succeeded to the family baronetcy in 1882 and first entered the House of Commons in 1885. At the outset he displayed little political activity and no bent for foreign affairs, so that it was a surprise when he was chosen Under-Secretary for Foreign Affairs in 1892. Gradually the Liberals came to regard Grey as one of their leaders, and in 1905 he was made Foreign Secretary, remaining in that office for 11 years.

He was handicapped by a certain narrowness of outlook—his knowledge of foreign languages was elementary—and, more seriously, by his dislike of making decisions. It fell to him to conduct the last negotiations with Germany, and those with France, in July and August 1914, and to explain the British position to Parliament and the nation. He strove hard for peace, but when he had to announce failure he had no difficulty in committing Britain to the struggle with the full assent of the people. He resigned in December 1916.

Already a Knight of the Garter, he was created a viscount on July 6, 1916, after refusing an earldom. He died on September 7, 1933. His little volume Fly-fishing (1899), a standard work on this subject, was followed in 1927 by Charm of Birds.

Grey, LADY JANE (1537–54).
Sad is the story and tragic the fate of this young girl, the " nine days'

queen" of England, who was sacrificed to the self-seeking ambition of shameless intriguers. Daughter of Henry Grey, Duke of Suffolk, great-granddaughter of Henry VII (1457–1509), and cousin of Edward VI (1537–53), she was remarkable for her beauty and accomplishments. She acquired great proficiency in Greek, Latin, Italian, French and Hebrew, and her learning aroused the admiration of the great scholars of the day. In pursuance of a plan to alter the royal succession from the Tudor to the Dudley family, the unscrupulous Duke of Northumberland caused her to be married to his son, Guilford Dudley. Edward VI was persuaded to settle the crown in her favour, and after his death, on July 6, 1553, Lady Jane was proclaimed Queen on the

LADY JANE GREY REFUSES THE CROWN
When Edward VI died on July 6, 1553, Lady Jane Grey was at Sion House, Brentford, Middlesex, the residence of her husband's father, the Duke of Northumberland. When she was informed that she was Edward's successor she at first refused to accept the crown, but her reluctance was at length overcome. This painting by Charles Leslie, R.A. (1794–1859), shows the messengers making the announcement of her accession, and her husband, Lord Guilford Dudley, and his mother trying to persuade her to become Queen of England.

10th. By the 19th the scheme had collapsed, for Mary Tudor (sister of Edward VI) was proclaimed Queen in London. Northumberland was arrested, and Lady Jane Grey was imprisoned in the Tower of London. She was never to be free again, and remained locked in the gloomy Tower for many months. Then an uprising against Queen Mary, in which Lady Jane's father took part, led the Queen to sign Lady Jane's death-warrant. She was beheaded at the Tower on February 12, 1554.

LIFELINE for BRITAIN'S LIGHT and POWER

Slung from the latticed steel towers which dot the countryside are the aluminium cables which carry electricity at 132,000 volts pressure from the giant power stations. Here is the story of the Electric Grid.

Grid, ELECTRICITY. The supply of electric power began on a very small scale, and it was usual to have the generating plant on the actual premises which utilised it. Thus, in London, amongst the earliest recorded installations were those at the Gaiety Theatre, Billingsgate Market, and The Times office in 1878. In Britain the first occasion upon which electric power was offered to the public was in Godalming, in 1881—with cables laid in the gutters. Brighton followed early in 1882. Most of these were what would nowadays be considered tiny plants—with a capacity of a dozen or so arc lamps, and from these beginnings has grown up the public supply industry as we know it today, with an annual output of more than forty thousand million units (kilowatt-hours).

In the beginning, not only the power stations were small, but also the areas that they served ; at one time it was considered uneconomical to supply electricity outside a radius of about a mile from the power station ! This, of course, was due to the low pressure (about 100 volts) used. As you can read in our story of Electricity, the amount of power present in a circuit, in watts, is equal to the voltage multiplied by the current in amperes, so that 10 amps. at 100 volts is the same power (1,000 watts, or 1 kilowatt) as 1 amp. at 1,000 volts. Now, the power lost in a conductor (as heat), due to its resistance, depends on the current only. But it varies *as the square of the current*, so that our 1 amp. at 1,000 volts would waste only one-hundredth of the power that 10 amps. would do at 100 volts. Or, putting it another way, for the same losses, using 1,000 volts, we can use a conductor one hundred times the resistance (i.e., one hundred times as long), and our power station can feed a much bigger area.

A thousand volts, however, is much too dangerous and inconvenient as a supply to our houses. By the

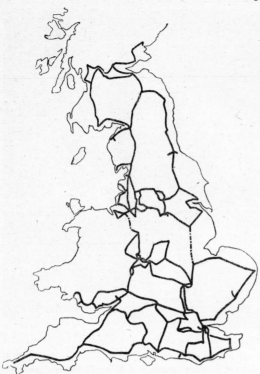

GRID TRANSMISSION LINES
England and the south of Scotland are well served by the
Grid system, as can be seen from this map. There are more
than 5,000 miles of transmission lines, which interconnect
with the main power stations, thereby preventing a complete breakdown in any one area.

use of alternating current we can employ transformers as a simple method of changing from one
voltage to another; we can " step-up " our voltage
(far higher than 1,000 volts) for transmission over
long distances, and then " step-down " again to a
convenient voltage at the user's end.

The advantage of easy transmission of electricity
over distances is that we no longer have to locate
the power station in the centre of the area which
it is supplying. Nowadays, it would be quite
impossible to find room for a power station in the
middle of a crowded city—quite apart from the
fact that we have to supply it with something like
two thousand tons of coal a day, and anything
up to twelve million gallons of water per hour.
If the generating plant should happen to be worked
by water power (*see* Hydro-Electric Installations)
it must be near the source of the water.

In 1887 the London Electric Supply Corporation,
advised by Dr. Sebastian Ziani de Ferranti, projected what was then a gigantic station to be
located at Deptford, on the Thames, where land
was cheap and where coal could be brought in by
water. This station was to send its power to
London's West End at 10,000 volts. Owing to one
trouble and another it was 1891 before the scheme
was effectively operating. Power systems tended
to remain small (with a few notable exceptions)
and self-contained. In 1926 a body known as the
Central Electricity Board (now merged with the
British Electricity Authority) was set up to carry

out a programme of interconnexion of all public
supply authorities, to enable them to be supplied
with electricity on a wholesale basis, from a small
number of large power stations. Within the next
ten years the Electricity " Grid " came into full
operation. The name is an apt one, for the cables,
on their lofty supports, criss-cross the country
rather like the bars of a gridiron.

The Grid, then, is a vast network of transmission
lines (more than 5,000 miles) which covers the whole
of Britain, except for parts of Wales and the North
of Scotland. It interconnects the main power
stations, and acts as a kind of " wholesale " distributor. It does not " retail " electricity—your
house is not connected to the grid, nor is your local
sub-station—and it is not a distribution network in
the ordinary sense. It is a network of power
systems, enabling the whole of the generating plant
in the country to be operated—and planned—as
one enormous power system. Now, what advantages are there in this ?

First and foremost there is continuity of supply.
If you lived in an area served by a single power
station, without Grid interconnexion, and there
was a serious disaster—a fire or an explosion—
which wiped out the entire station, you might be
without electricity for weeks or months while
repairs were made. In an emergency, power is today supplied by other stations through the Grid.
Second, there is load sharing. A district where
the load has outgrown the power station would
be in sad trouble if it were not able to obtain extra
power from the Grid. Again, power stations.

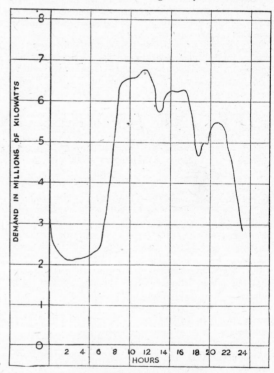

CONSUMPTION OF CURRENT
The amount of electric current used during a period of 24
hours varies enormously from time to time. The line on
this chart shows how peak or maximum loads occur at
certain times, imposing a great strain on the plant.

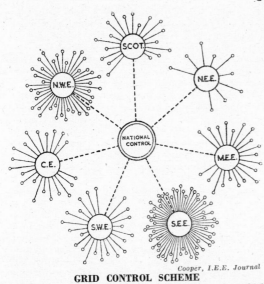

Cooper, I.E.E. Journal

GRID CONTROL SCHEME

Under the National Control centre are seven areas, which operate a network of power stations (represented by small circles). The power stations in each area work together under the area control to give the most economical results.

machines turning round, even if they are generating practically no electricity.

By using the Grid to transfer power backwards and forwards where it is wanted, the main load can be carried by the most efficient plant (known as " base load " plant). The smaller and less efficient stations can be shut down except at times of peak load, and only sufficient plant kept running to supply (with a reasonable safety margin) the amount of load expected. There is also a considerable economy due to what is known as " diversity of demand." Peak loads occur at different times in different parts of the country. By transferring power from one area to another as required, the Grid helps to spread the load.

Another advantage of the Grid is the ability to maintain a steady controlled frequency all over the country, thus enabling us to use mains-driven synchronous clocks. (*See* Electric Clocks).

More than 5,000 miles of transmission lines go to make up the Grid, of which nearly 4,000 miles operate at a working pressure of 132,000 volts. The conductors are of aluminium strand, suspended by large porcelain insulators from the steel lattice towers which are a familiar sight in most parts of the country. The highest towers are those where the lines cross the River Thames at Dagenham; here, in order to obtain the necessary clearance, the towers are 487 feet high.

The system is that known as three-phase (*see* Electricity), and either three or six conductors (for

as we have seen, must be built where land is cheap and water and coal available, but no one commercial concern could afford to build a new power station on a fine site, and let it stay there " twiddling its thumbs," waiting for factories and houses to grow up around it to take its supply. As it is, the station can feed into the Grid straight away— its load is there waiting for it.

Third—and possibly most important of all—the Grid system makes for economy. Power stations vary considerably in their efficiency—i.e., the amount of electricity they can produce by burning a certain amount of coal. One station may produce a kilowatt-hour (unit) for 1·2 lb. of coal ; another might take 1·3. A difference of one-tenth of a pound does not sound much, but on a large station it may mean two or three hundred tons of coal per day extra.

Also, the load on a power system varies during the day, and a typical curve of variation during the 24 hours is shown in page 1546. This is a Grid curve for the whole country, and shows how " peak " loads occur at different times of the day. During the night the load is comparatively small. In a system of separate areas, with no Grid interconnexion, every power station must keep on running—no matter how small the load. You would not like it if you woke suddenly during the night and found that nothing happened when you pressed the light switch— because the power station had shut down! The station must keep on running no matter how light the load, and power stations are not very efficient at light loads, because it still takes a lot of coal just to make steam enough to keep the

NERVE CENTRE OF THE GRID SYSTEM

The National Control Engineer is responsible for the entire Grid, and he conducts his operations from the National Control room (above), which is in direct communication with all the areas. Every night an estimate is made of the amount of power required in the next 24 hours.

single or double circuits) are slung from each tower. The additional conductor which you may have noticed strung along the tops of the towers, without any insulators, is an earth wire to guard, as far as possible, from damage by near-by lightning strokes. Lines end and meet at Grid substations, which are located at power stations and other important centres. They are either purely " switching " stations, so that the various lines may be connected together or disconnected as necessary for operating requirements, or to cut out any damaged or faulty line; or they may be " transformer " stations, where the voltage is changed to 66,000 or 33,000 volts for interconnexion with power stations. In the London area, there is a " cable grid " or network of underground cables, operating at 66,000 volts.

It was originally planned to operate the Grid in seven self-contained areas, and it is only from 1939 onwards that it has been operated as a complete network, covering the whole country. Those responsible for the operation of the Grid do not run the individual power stations. They do not perform any actual switching operations themselves, nor do they start up or shut down generating sets—any more than the conductor of a large orchestra plays a musical instrument. The Area Control Engineer, or System Operating Engineer of the Grid, is concerned that his " orchestra "— the network of power stations under his control— shall operate together, each at the amount of load planned for it, so as to give the most economical and safest results.

The National Control Engineer conducts all seven " orchestras "—Grid areas—at once. He is responsible for the overall running of the entire Grid, and he conducts his operations from the National Control Room, which is in direct touch with all the Area Control Rooms by telephone and teleprinter. The Area Control Rooms, likewise, are in close touch with the power stations and Grid switching stations in their areas; the chain of connexions is as shown on page 1547.

Normally, the entire day's operations are planned the night before, when the probable total load required over the whole country is estimated (with remarkable accuracy) from various factors, chief of which is the weather forecast. When we tell you that the appearance of a black cloud over the Central London area can cause a load increase of half a million kilowatts in a few minutes, owing to people switching on their lights, you will realize that the weather plays a very important part in load forecasting. Having estimated the total load, arrangements are made to meet it in the most economical manner by using the most efficient plant as much as possible. The exact amount generated by each area, and the loads which will be transferred from one area to another at different times, are all planned. In addition the operating engineers must be prepared to meet any emergency —such as a sudden change in the weather, a breakdown, or the heavy " power swing " which occurs as factories in the North shut down for dinner.

G.P.A.

TOWERING PYLONS CARRY THE ELECTRIC CABLES

From the generating stations the cables that carry electric current to homes, shops, offices and factories where it is consumed are borne over the countryside on these steel lattice towers. Those at Dagenham, Essex, are the tallest, having a height of 487 feet. The cables carry current at enormous pressures, mainly at 132,000 volts, and on the top of each pylon is an earth wire to guard against damage by lightning. In built-up areas the cables are laid underground.

The Grid gives remarkable service in sharing out the load—but it cannot produce power from nowhere! In Britain the use of electricity has increased faster than new power stations can be built; at times (such as cold winter mornings when so many persons switch on electric fires, on top of the factory load) the system cannot produce the power required. Then the giant machines, overloaded, begin to slow down, and the frequency drops. (That is when our synchronous clocks begin to go wrong.) The frequency must not be allowed to fall by more than a certain amount or everything would come to a standstill, so what is termed " load shedding " must take place and, according to a pre-arranged plan, various loads are switched off to relieve the situation.

This, then, is the Grid, and next time you see the lattice towers with their cables they will mean a great deal more to you. Standardization of voltage, of frequency, of the kind of apparatus used, all make for more economical working. Now the rural village has plentiful electric current for lamps and for the household machines which make work easier in the home. Cookers, cleaners, refrigerators and radio sets can be installed in village as well as town. In a thousand ways the Electricity Grid is adding to our comfort and convenience. It is, of course, giving parallel benefits to the factories and industrial plants throughout our land, and enabling village industries to have cheap and plentiful motive power.

Grieg, EDVARD HAGERUP (1843–1907). The rhythms and strange harmonies of Scandinavian folk-music were the inspiration that brought Grieg (pron. grēg) to a position among the great composers of the 19th century. He was born in Bergen, Norway, on June 15, 1843, but was sent to Leipzig, Germany, for his musical education ; his early compositions give evidence of this German influence. On his return to his native land his imagination was captured by the entrancing Norwegian folksongs, and he determined to develop the full beauty of these simple tunes by making them the basis of compositions for piano and orchestra. Thus he did for Norway what Chopin, in even greater degree, did for Poland, and Liszt for Hungary.

When Grieg was 31 years old the Norwegian government granted him a life pension. Thus relieved from the necessity of teaching music, he devoted himself entirely to composition, with occasional concert tours. As a conductor he was magnetic, and everywhere he was acclaimed as a most individual and enchanting pianist. He played only his own compositions—beautiful lyrics, tonepoems for the piano. Of his orchestral works the frequently heard Peer Gynt suites are most popular. His songs have a distinctive haunting quality. He died on September 4, 1907.

Grimm, JAKOB LUDWIG KARL (1785–1863) and WILHELM KARL (1786–1859). One of the most delightful books for children is Grimms' Fairy Tales, compiled by two German brothers famed for their researches into philology and folk-lore. Jakob, the elder, was born on January 4, 1785; Wilhelm was

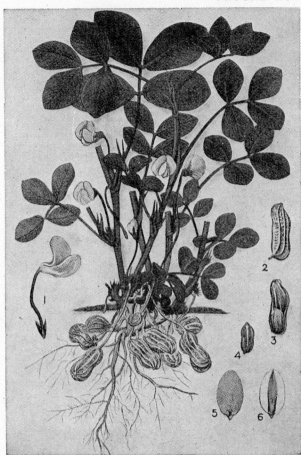

GROUND-NUT PLANT AND FRUIT
The fruit of the ground-nut (monkey-nut) is a pod. Here is a plant in bloom, showing also the flower stalk (1) from which the pod develops ; a whole pod (2) ; a pod opened (3) to reveal the seeds ; a seed (4) ; a seed with the skin removed (5) ; and a seed split (6).

born on February 24, 1786. Their first collection of fairy stories was published in 1812. These tales, translated into many languages, have immortalised the brothers Grimm. Jakob's most important works were his German Grammar (1819) and History of the German Language (1848). In his monumental German Mythology (1835) he covered the whole range of his vast subject. Grimm's Law—the regular sound-shifting or interchange of consonants between (1) Sanskrit, Greek, and Latin, (2) Low German, and (3) High German—was named after Jakob. The brothers began a German dictionary and edited many old German classics. Wilhelm's chief independent work was German Heroic Saga (1829). Otherwise his life was the counterpart of Jakob's. Wilhelm died on December 16, 1859, and Jakob on September 20, 1863.

Ground-nut. In the United States this strange plant is called the peanut, other names being earth-nut and monkey-nut. It is a member of the pea family, and its fruit is a pod rather than a nut. The plant (*Arachis hypogaea*) originated in Brazil, but is grown today in many other lands, notably in North America, Africa and China. In semi-arid regions it is particularly valuable, since it can live

GROUND-NUT HARVEST IN EAST AFRICA
Vast areas in Kenya and Tanganyika are devoted to the cultivation of ground-nuts. To harvest the crop mechanical diggers (top) pass down the rows, lifting the plants from the soil (lower left). The nuts are left to dry and are then mechanically stacked in rows. They are bagged (bottom right) by a combine harvester, the leaves being discarded. World shortage of fats after the Second World War increased the importance of this crop.

British Official

contain large amounts of protein, carbohydrates and fat, so that the ground meal is a valuable ingredient in soups and other dishes.

After the end of the Second World War (1939-45), when the former war zones suffered a loss of agricultural produce, the cultivation of the ground-nut as a source of edible oil was taken up by several countries. Britain opened up in East Africa a wide area of bush formerly infested by the tsetse fly; the ground was cleared by bull-dozers and other modern machinery and was sown with ground-nuts. Harvesting was done by mechanical diggers which passed down the rows, lifting the plants and shaking off the soil. Next, after the nuts had dried, mechanical rakes stacked them in long rows, and a combine-harvester traversed the rows to bag the nuts and reject the leaves. The African ground-nut scheme may revolutionize the life of the people dwelling in the region, besides supplying food to Britain.

Grouse. The distinction of being the only purely British bird is borne by the red grouse (*Lagopus scoticus*), for it is found native nowhere but in these islands. It is well protected all over the

through drought and make speedy growth when rain comes. In parts of North America it yields 30 to 60 bushels of nuts in pod per acre, together with a ton or more of fodder.

A strange thing about this plant is that it sows its own seeds, before they are ripe, and they complete their development in the ground. After the flowers have been fertilized and have fallen, the flower stalks bend down and push themselves into the earth, where the " nuts " in their pods continue to grow larger and to ripen. The leaf and flower resemble those of the common pea. Ground-nuts, roasted to bring out the true nutty flavour, are sold in the streets of the U.S.A. and have become popular in Britain. Peanut butter, made from the oil extracted from the nuts, is used for cooking and as a spread. The most important use of this plant, however, is as a source of edible oil from which margarine and cooking fats can be prepared. The nuts

A. Brook

RED GROUSE ' FREEZING '
When danger threatens and they wish to avoid being seen, many birds ' freeze '—that is, remain absolutely still, trusting to their resemblance to their surroundings for safety. The red grouse, which lives on moors, is found native nowhere but in the British Isles.

PTARMIGAN IN WINTER

In Great Britain the ptarmigan, which is a species of grouse, is restricted to the highest parts of the Scottish Highlands and to some of the western islands. In winter it changes its normally brown plumage for white, but at any season of the year it closely resembles its surroundings.

W. S. Berridge

grouse moors of Wales, northern England and Scotland, and every year in normal times just before August 12, the opening day of the grouse shooting season, there is an exodus of sportsmen from London and the south, so important is this event. In shooting grouse, the birds are usually driven by a line of beaters towards a row of butts, semi-circular walls of turf, behind which are the shooters.

Beside the red grouse, which is actually a rich red-brown, with a scarlet wattle over the eye, we have the fine black grouse, or blackcock. This handsome blue-black and white bird has a sombre mate, aptly described by her name, grey hen. The blackcock goes farther south than the grouse, being found in Somerset and in South Wales, but many attempts to acclimatize the other bird in the apparently suitable Exmoor and Dartmoor country have failed. Farther north still, and especially on the higher mountains, is found a smaller bird, the ptarmigan, a species of grouse whose plumage turns white in winter. Close relatives of the grouse family are the capercailzie, the pheasants, and the partridges. All these birds are members of the same order as our familiar domestic fowls.

Of the North American species the best known is the ruffed grouse (*Bonasa umbellus*). It is about 18 inches long and has tufts of black feathers on each side of its neck.

Guadeloupe. In the French West Indies, about 75 miles north of Martinique, lie the twin islands of Guadeloupe, which, with five near-by islets, constitute the largest French colony in this region (area, 688 square miles). A strait divides the two main islands, one of which, Basse-Terre, is crowned by lofty mountains, while the surface of the other, Grande-Terre, nowhere exceeds 500 feet. The products are chiefly sugar, coffee, cocoa, bananas and rum. Terrible damage is often done here by earthquakes which sweep the Caribbean Sea. The capital is Basse-Terre (13,600 inhabitants), but Point-à-Pitre (43,500 inhabitants) is the largest town and the chief port.

Guadeloupe was discovered by Columbus in 1493. Except for short intervals, when it was held in turn by England and Sweden, it has been French since 1635. In 1947 Guadeloupe became a Department of France. Its population is about 304,000, chiefly Negroes and mulattoes.

Guatemala (Pron. gwah-tem-ah'-la). The most populous and the most important State of Central America, Guatemala lies immediately to the south of Mexico and to the north of the Republics of El Salvador and Honduras. With an area of 45,450 square miles, the country includes a remarkable variety of scenery and climates.

Most of the people live in the highlands at heights of 3,000 to 8,000 feet. This is a region of eternal spring, with a mild sunny climate, where coffee, the most important crop, is grown. Not all of Guatemala is mountainous. On the Pacific side, along the 200 miles of coast, is a plain about 50

Percy F. Martin

GUATEMALA : RUINS OF OLD ANTIGUA

Once one of the richest cities in Central and South America, Antigua was the capital of the Spanish colony of Guatemala until it was destroyed by earthquake in 1773. Though the capital was removed to Guatemala city, 25 miles away, many of the inhabitants refused to leave and their descendants still live there.

miles wide; and there is another small area of low-land on the Caribbean coast. Thousands of square miles of scrub and jungle have been cleared on these coastal plains for banana plantations.

The plain of Peten, which forms a wedge between Mexico and British Honduras, is partly grassy low-land and partly jungle. From its forest are obtained supplies of chicle (a gum), from which chewing gum is made, and valuable timber, including mahogany and pine. Although Guatemala has a large variety of minerals, the difficulty of transportation has discouraged the development of mining. Gold is found, and there is a limited production of chromium, manganese, lead and mica. There is little manufacturing, the principal products being cotton goods, flour, sugar, soap, pottery, leather goods, bricks and furniture. There are over 700 miles of railway, and some 5,000 miles of motor-roads. Air services are well developed.

The capital is Guatemala (population 186,000), which has been destroyed three times by earth-quakes and rebuilt, so that few old buildings remain. The only other towns of any size are Antigua, Quezaltenango, and Coban, centre of the coffee trade.

All children between seven and 14 years of age must attend school, but only about one in five of the people can read and write. Secondary schools exist only in the largest towns; the National University is in Guatemala city.

During the first thousand years of the Christian era, the ancient Mayan civilization flourished here, followed by the Aztec culture; and there are many architectural remains of these races. The country was conquered by the Spaniards between 1522 and 1524, and was ruled by Spain for nearly 300 years, gaining its independence in 1821. The Republic of Guatemala was established in 1839, after the country had formed part of the Confederation of Central America for 18 years. In 1946 and 1948 Guatemala put forward territorial claims to British Honduras, but these were strongly repudiated by Great Britain, and Guatemala did not press the matter further. The population of the republic is 3,451,000.

Guiana. (Pron. gē-ah'-na). Geographers give the name of Guiana to that little-known part of South America between the River Orinoco, the River Amazon and its tributary the Rio Negro, and the Atlantic Ocean. In common usage, however, Guiana means especially the three colonies of British Guiana, Dutch Guiana, and French Guiana.

The coast is everywhere low, being nowhere much above sea-level. For 20 miles inland the land was once a mangrove swamp, but it was drained by the early settlers, and thus made into fertile plantations. Along the coast and on the banks of the numerous rivers live the scanty population. Farther inland the country rises into a rocky, hilly plateau (3,000 to 4,000 feet above sea-level), covered with almost impenetrable forests, except where grassy plains or savannas occur. The ranges of low mountains and hills which traverse this plateau are rich in gold, aluminium ore, and other minerals.

In the perpetual summer of the hot, moist climate vegetation flourishes. The district is noted for the height and variety of its trees, many of them furnishing valuable woods. Orchids sometimes grow in large masses with flower-stems 12 feet high, and gigantic vines festoon the trees. In the lagoons and rivers grow many kinds of water-lilies; the largest, the famous *Victoria regia*, with leaves five or six feet across, was brought from British Guiana and distributed over the civilized world. Alligators and fish of innumerable species abound in the rivers, and the forests are filled with brightly-plumaged birds, such as the scarlet ibis and pink flamingo ; with reptiles, and with such other animals as the tapirs, sloths, ant-eaters, jaguars, and monkeys. The insects are remarkable for number and brilliance of colour.

The Guiana coast was first sighted on the third voyage of Columbus in 1498. During the 16th century many Spanish and Portuguese adventurers made un-successful visits to its rivers in search of the fabled El Dorado or Golden City. By the middle of the 17th century several British, Dutch, and French settlements had been founded. The colony of Surinam, now known as Dutch Guiana, was given up in 1667 by the British to the Dutch in return for New York.

British Guiana has an area of about 89,500 square miles and is the only British possession in South America. Sugar, rice, coconuts, coffee, rubber and bauxite (aluminium ore) are the chief exports. Gold is mined. There are only about 100 miles of railway, and trans-portation is carried on chiefly by water. The capital, Georgetown, which has a population of some 72,000, is below high-water mark, and is protected from the sea by a stone wall a mile long, and the older houses are built on piles. The United States have a naval and air base on the Demerara river. More than two-

SOUTH AMERICA'S THREE GUIANAS
Three colonies—British, Dutch and French—comprise the greater part of the territory which is known to geographers as Guiana. As can be seen from this map many rivers flow from the high forest-covered plateau to the narrow coastal plain, where are the chief towns.

Guilds. During the Middle Ages the men of each trade in every important town of Europe were organized into associations known as craft guilds (often spelled gilds) for the purpose of regulating their occupations and controlling the entry of new members.

The weavers seem to have been the first to organize, but later the goldsmiths, saddlers, fishmongers, bakers, dyers, glovemakers, and men of many other occupations,

thirds of the inhabitants are Negroes, or coolies brought from the sub-continent of India as labourers; there are also about 8,800 native Indians. The population of the Colony is 367,000.

Dutch Guiana, sometimes called by its old name Surinam, is about 50,000 square miles in area. Cacao, coffee, sugar, rice, maize, bananas, and gold are the chief products. A third of the population live in Paramaribo, the capital, which has a population of 60,700. Hindu coolies, Chinese, Javanese and Negroes form the bulk of the population. The most interesting people are the "bush negroes," descendants of runaway slaves, who at one time terrorised outlying settlements. The population of the Colony of Dutch Guiana is 191,000.

Dorien Leigh; A. V. L. Guise

BRITISH AND DUTCH GUIANA SCENES
Seaport and capital of British Guiana, Georgetown (upper) is near the mouth of the Demerara river; among its chief exports are sugar, rum, timber and aluminium ore. The principal river of Dutch Guiana is the Surinam (lower). The Dutch received their colony from the British in 1667 in exchange for New Amsterdam, now New York.

French Guiana is the smallest of the three territories, with an area of about 32,000 square miles. It has always had a bad name from the terrible disasters which attended early attempts at settlement. In 1763 a colony of 12,000 came here from Alsace and Lorraine, and was reduced, after two years of hunger and disease, to a band of less than 1,000. During the French Revolution it was made a convict settlement, and was so used until 1946. There is little industry except agriculture, the chief exports being rice, cocoa, bananas and timber. The capital of French Guiana is Cayenne (population about 11,700). French Guiana, which became a Department of France in 1947, has a population of approximately 31,000.

some with only a handful of workers, formed separate guilds. Usually they were authorized by the local governments, but sometimes they obtained a charter from the king. The Guilds or Livery Companies of the City of London remain today as an interesting reminder of these medieval days. The rules of the guild usually provided that no one who was not a member should practise the trade within the town.

The guilds also kept up standards of quality, especially by barring entry to a trade unless the man had "served his time" as an apprentice. The young craftsman was bound by his parents or guardians to an employer for a number of years—usually seven—during which time he was fed and clothed and lodged. When his apprenticeship was finished he became a journeyman—that is, a qualified craftsman, free to work for another master.

In addition to the craft guilds, there were older and more powerful organizations called merchant

OLD GUILD HOUSES AT ANTWERP

The craft guild of the Middle Ages was not unlike the modern trade union in some respects ; but there were also more powerful guilds of merchants who traded with foreign countries. The headquarters of the merchant guilds were usually in large towns, and shown above are the guild halls or houses, dating from the 16th and 17th centuries, in the Grand' Place at Antwerp, Belgium.

rodent, related to the hares and rabbits. It was domesticated in Europe in the 16th century.

These cavies are about six inches long, and there are several varieties, some of which have short and others long, curiously ruffled hair. The colours are varied, usually black and white, tan and white, or a mixture of all three. Guinea-pigs are gentle and make amusing pets. They live on vegetable food. (*See* illustration in opposite page).

In recent years the guinea-pig has become almost indispensable in the biological and pharmacological laboratories of the world for the standardization of medicines and serums.

Gulf Stream. The largest and most important of all the ocean currents, the Gulf Stream has been called the heating apparatus of north-western Europe, because the warm water which it carries from the tropics tempers the climate of northern Europe. This great ocean "river," several degrees warmer than the surrounding ocean, is 50 miles wide at its narrowest point, and its depth is about 2,000 feet. It flows at a speed of two to six miles an hour.

The stream receives its name from the Gulf of Mexico, where it originates. The North-East Trade Winds cause a great drift of water across the Atlantic Ocean north of the Equator. Part of this current skirts the West Indies, but the greater portion enters the Caribbean Sea, thence passing to the Gulf of Mexico. Here the influx of water causes a current to issue from the gulf between Florida and Cuba. This current unites with the West Indian branch to form the Gulf Stream. It rounds the Florida shore, and then runs close along the coast of North America. Off Cape Hatteras, in northern Florida, it curves to the east, under the influence of the increasingly westerly winds. Fan-like, it spreads as it flows, growing gradually wider, shallower, and cooler, until it merges in the general drift of warm water flowing north-eastwards from the North Atlantic Ocean to Europe. As this Gulf Stream drift approaches the eastern Atlantic it splits into two parts, one going south along the coast of Africa, and another turning north and dividing into three smaller currents which warm the seas washing the British Isles, Scandinavia, and parts of Iceland. That is one reason why London and Paris, although no farther south than parts of Labrador and Canada,

guilds, composed of men who made a business of buying and selling, and engaged in what we should call wholesale trading to distant places. On the Continent the merchant guilds had a great influence in the city government, and the guild hall of the merchants is today one of the striking buildings in many European cities.

Nowadays, though the older meaning and function of the guild have been revived by associations of artists or craftsmen, the term generally has a wider use—for an association of persons having some common object, *e.g.* a society for mutual aid.

Guinea-fowl. (Pron. gin'i-). Guinea-fowl have thick, greyish plumage, with small white spots, and are the only representatives of the pheasant family found in Africa, where they are common from the Guinea coast southward to the Cape of Good Hope. They run swiftly, but seldom fly.

The guinea-fowl has been domesticated since early days, and was highly appreciated by the Greeks and Romans.

The continual calling of these birds at the slightest alarm is one of their outstanding characteristics, and they are often unpleasantly noisy if kept near the house.

Guinea-pig. In spite of its name, this little animal is not a pig, and not a native of Guinea, but of Guiana, Bolivia, Brazil, and other parts of South America. Belonging to the cavy family, it is a

SPECKLED GUINEA-FOWL

A member of the pheasant family, the guinea-fowl is a native of Africa but is found domesticated in many countries. The plumage is grey with white dots, and the flesh is dark.

GUINEA-PIGS : SMALL RODENTS KEPT AS PETS

Members of the cavy family and related to the hares and rabbits, these animals are neither natives of Guinea in Africa nor pigs. Guinea-pigs came to Europe from South America in the 16th century, and the name Guinea may be a corruption of Guiana. They may be descended from the black cavy of Peru, which had been domesticated by the Indians. (*See* facing page.)

C. Reid

from the Gulf of Mexico is about 84° F., and by the time it has reached mid-Atlantic it has decreased only by about 14°.

Gulls AND TERNS. Most familiar of all the creatures of the seaside are the gulls, and in many parts of the coast of Britain their cousins, the terns, or sea-swallows, are found. They are all excellent fliers, the gull's wings being very long and

enjoy a fairly mild climate, and why Norway and Iceland are habitable despite their high latitudes.

Although scientists today consider the Gulf Stream a less important factor in the climate of Europe than they once did, there seems little room for doubt that it is an active agent in warming the south-westerly ocean winds which give the western coast of Europe so much milder a climate than the corresponding latitudes on the east coast of America. The Gulf Stream serves another important purpose in keeping the harbours of north-western Europe free from ice. It also enables trawlers to establish fisheries as far north as Barents Sea.

The waters of the Gulf Stream are a deep blue, strongly contrasting with the lighter blue of seas it passes through, and they carry along great quantities of seaweed, detached from the coral islands round Florida, and the island of Cuba. The temperature of the Gulf Stream in summer as it issues

powerful, enabling it to make steady headway against the strongest gales. It has webbed feet.

Gulls are great travellers, though the record for long-distance travelling does not belong to the gull, but to the Arctic tern. This bird regularly makes a round trip of about 22,000 miles between its winter and summer homes, for it nests in the Arctic, and as soon as the young are grown the whole family flies to the Antarctic continent.

Gulls and terns are the most widely distributed group of birds, for there are about 50 species of each scattered throughout the world. Together they comprise the family of *Laridae*. Gulls range in size from that of a pigeon to that of a goose; terns are smaller, with more slender bodies and comparatively much longer wings and tail. All these birds are sociable and nest in colonies. But such havoc has been wrought in some of their breeding colonies, for the sake of their edible eggs, and so many of the

Courtesy of United States Coast Guard

A PERIL WHICH THE GULF STREAM KEEPS FROM BRITISH WATERS

According to their latitude the British Isles should have winter temperatures as low as those of certain parts of Canada and Russia ; but we are saved from such conditions by the Gulf Stream, which flows from the Gulf of Mexico across the Atlantic Ocean to our western and northern shores. The iceberg seen here is slowly melting in the warm waters of the Gulf Stream. Were it not for this current, ice might well be a danger to shipping in the English Channel.

A. Brook

BLACK-HEADED GULLS AT THEIR NESTS
Perhaps the most familiar seabird is the black-headed gull. It is often seen inland, especially during severe weather and in the breeding season, and flocks are a common sight in London during the winter. These gulls usually nest in marshy coastal regions as above, congregating sometimes in considerable numbers.

black-backed gull, and the so-called common gull.

It is easy to distinguish terns from gulls, if you look closely at them. They are more graceful in flight, as their nickname sea-swallows indicates. Gulls usually have square tails, while most terns' tails are forked. In terns the beak is more slender and often seems longer, and their feeding habits also differ from those of gulls, for gulls often alight on the water to feed, while terns hover and plunge into the sea for their food. Another distinction is that gulls usually fly with their bills on a line with the body, while terns carry theirs pointed downward.

The common tern is found in all parts of the Northern Hemisphere, as well as in South America and Africa. It often hovers over schools of fish, and fishermen find it of great service in locating a shoal. Other British species are the Sandwich, noticeably larger in size than the other species, the roseate, easily distinguished by its pinkish underparts, and the little tern; occasionally, the Arctic and black tern are seen on our coasts. Terns, which nest usually on sandy shores rather than

adult birds have been slain for their plumage, that gulls have disappeared from many districts.

The increasing use of oil fuel at sea is an important contributory factor to the destruction of sea birds like the gull and tern. Ships discharge oil waste, which floats on the surface of the water and this clogs the wings and feathers of birds that alight there.

The prevailing colour of most adult gulls and terns is white below and pearl-grey above, but the black-headed, and greater and lesser black-backed gulls, have the plumage implied by their names, while many others have black tips to the wing and tail feathers. Terns, too, usually have a black-capped head, and one species is more black than white. A few are dull grey all over, while young birds are brownish for a year or more. The feet and bill are usually bright yellow or red.

All gulls and terns are fond of fish, and will eat dead ones as well as any edible refuse found floating on the water; thus harbour and shore gulls are valuable scavengers. Inland gulls are valuable friends to the farmer, because they eat field-mice and the insect pests which do such harm to crops and trees. Among the commonest of the birds are the black-headed gull, which haunts marshy coastal districts; the herring gull, a large and handsome bird; the lesser black-backed gull, the great

on the sea cliffs, defend their nests very vigorously, flying at intruders and attacking them.

Gums. By-products of the plant kingdom, gums are the juice or sap exuded from certain trees or shrubs. There are about 150 varieties known to commerce, most of which are used in varnishes, confectionery, drugs, and industrial preparations.

In popular usage the word gum is applied to true resins and to gum-resins or mixtures of gum and resin, as well as to gums proper. True gums, however, dissolve more or less in water, whereas true resins do not dissolve in water.

Good quality " gum " supplied by stationers is a solution of gum arabic, one of the most useful of the gums, and is used as the adhesive for postage stamps, etc. Gum arabic is brought into the market in the form of roundish " tears," which vary in colour from garnet red to light straw, and are always more or less transparent. The lightest-coloured varieties are the best. It is employed in the manufacture of confectionery, such as marsh-mallows and Turkish delight, and has many uses in pharmacy, being added to mixtures and cough syrups, and in making pastilles, and emulsions. It is also employed to give lustre to crêpe and silk, and to stiffen other fabrics. It comes from varieties of

Spread throughout the world, gulls and terns form the family *Laridae*. Terns are smaller and more slender than gulls, but the prevailing colour of both is white below and pearl-grey above, though certain species have distinctive markings, as can be seen here. A black-headed gull (1) returns to her nest on the shores of an estuary, and another (2) guards a fledgling. The great black-backed gull (3) is the largest of the family. A yellow beak, red legs and yellow rings round the eyes make the herring gull (4) easy to distinguish. The Arctic tern (5) nests in the Arctic regions; as soon as the young are full-grown the families fly to the Antarctic continent. The roseate tern (6) makes its nest among rocks. The dainty least tern (not shown) is pale blue above and white beneath; it was once so sought after for its feathers that it came near to extinction and is still rare.

acacia which are grown in Turkey, in certain parts of Australia and in northern Africa.

Gum tragacanth, which comes from a shrub that grows in Asia Minor, will take up as much as 50 times its weight of water, and by doing so makes a thick sticky solution, having many valuable uses. It is employed as a thickener in calico-printing; in medicine as a means of binding insoluble powders ; and in the mounting of all kinds of beetles and other insects in museums or private collections.

Kauri gum is the resin of the kauri pine of New Zealand. Most of it is obtained in fossil form. It is used in making fine varnishes. The copal gums, which are also used in varnishes, are fossil resins from East Africa, Madagascar, and many places in the East.

Gunpowder.

It is not known when gunpowder was invented. In fact, it cannot be said to have been invented by any one man, for it was a gradual development from various " fire " substances, long known in many countries before they were adapted to explosive or military use. The Chinese early had a knowledge of some such incendiary substance; and the Greek fire, first used by the defenders of Constantinople against the Saracens in 673, is believed to have been somewhat similar to modern gunpowder. The English Franciscan friar, Roger Bacon (died about 1294), and the German monk, Berthold Schwartz (early 14th century), share the honour of having been the first to give a scientific account of the composition of gunpowder.

The gunpowder of early days was much the same as the common black powder of today. It consisted of a mixture of saltpetre (potassium nitrate or nitre), charcoal, and sulphur. This mixture is a purely mechanical one, there being no chemical association of the ingredients. The proportions of these chemicals have varied greatly from time to time, a fair modern standard being 75 per cent saltpetre, 15 per cent charcoal, and 10 per cent sulphur. These ingredients are ground to a fine dust, thoroughly mixed into a moist paste, pressed into cakes, and dried. The cakes are then broken by rollers into grains of varying sizes, which are glazed by friction against each other in revolving barrels. Each operation in a gunpowder works is carried on in a separate shed, usually surrounded by water and high embankments, so that the danger of widespread damage being caused by explosions is minimized.

Except for fireworks, blasting and certain special military purposes, the old-style gunpowders have been almost entirely replaced by the smokeless powders and the high explosives. Smokeless powders were first perfected about 1884. (*See* Explosives).

Gustavus Adolphus, KING OF SWEDEN (1594–1632).

The greatest military genius of his age, Gustavus Adolphus was the first of modern commanders to supply his army from a fixed base instead of leaving it to live off the country by foraging and pillage. He was born at Stockholm, on December 9, 1594, the son of Charles IX of Sweden, and was trained from childhood for his kingly duties. In addition to proving himself an able scholar and brilliant linguist he showed great skill in the practical arts of statecraft. In 1611, on his father's death, he ascended the throne, enthusiastically supported by the people.

Gustavus soon showed his political wisdom by terminating the senseless wars with Denmark and with Russia by treaties in Sweden's favour. By 1640, after a successful struggle with Poland, he had extended his kingdom round the whole eastern shore of the Baltic. He had also reorganized the government, finances, and legal system, and under his rule industry and commerce both prospered.

Gustavus Adolphus entered the Thirty Years' War (1618–48) not only because he was an enthusiastic Protestant and therefore wished to help the German Protestants against the Emperor Ferdinand, ruler of the Holy Roman Empire, but also because he dreamed of extending his kingdom even to German shores, so that the Baltic might indeed become " a Swedish lake."

The Imperialist generals, Tilly and Wallenstein, were sweeping all before them; and the Baltic ports, and thus Sweden herself, were threatened. Gustavus realized that, despite the risks, he had to carry the war into the enemy's camp. He began by landing his army in Pomerania, Germany, in June 1630, and in a few weeks had captured the port of Stettin and swept the Imperial troops out of the province. As a consequence, Magdeburg, the strongest fortress of north Germany, became his ally.

GUSTAVUS ADOLPHUS
One of the most brilliant generals of all time, Gustavus Adolphus (1594–1632) was also the best king Sweden ever had. This portrait is from the painting by Van Dyck (1599–1641).

It was at once besieged by the Imperialists. Gustavus improved his position by an alliance with France and set off to relieve the hard-pressed city. But Magdeburg fell on May 20, 1631, and the horrible story of its sack and pillage not only shocked all Europe but also spurred Gustavus to greater efforts.

Reinforced by the Saxon army, he threw himself on Tilly and utterly routed him at Breitenfeld near Leipzig, on September 7, 1631, afterwards sweeping on towards the Rhine, and capturing Frankfort and Mainz. Settled in the latter town, he strove hard to bring about a coalition of the Protestant German states, but the advance of Tilly from the Danube in 1632 compelled him to advance into Bavaria. His campaign was a triumph, and the mortally wounded Tilly was pursued to Ingoldstadt, where he died.

In this emergency the emperor recalled the dismissed Imperialist general Wallenstein who, with a reorganized army, advanced to cut off Gustavus from his base in Saxony. At Nuremberg the two armies faced each other for two months, beset by sickness. At the end of August 1632, Gustavus gave up his intention of reaching Saxony and withdrew to the south, but later he caught Wallenstein and on November 6, 1632, brought him to bay at Lützen. Again the Swedish troops gained the victory, but at the cost of the life of their king.

Gutta-percha.
(Pron. gut'-a-pêr'-cha). In the Malay Peninsula and the neighbouring islands grow forests of gutta-percha trees (*Palaquium oblongifolia*), members of the order *Sapotaceae*. Their spongy wood is useless, but between the wood and the bark is found a milky juice, or latex, which, when it is boiled, produces a reddish-grey substance like india-rubber.

This is the gutta-percha which today has many important uses. It is a non-conductor of electricity, is unchanged by water, and can be very easily worked when it is made warm, while it retains its shape and becomes leathery and very tough, but pliant, when it cools.

Like rubber, gutta-percha is waterproof and can be treated with sulphur or vulcanized; but it is not elastic, and, unlike rubber, when softened in warm water, it can be drawn into fine

E.N.A.

GUTTA-PERCHA TREE
Down the grooves cut in the bark of the tree by this Malay will run the latex or milky juice which, when boiled, produces the rubber-like substance we call gutta-percha.

sheets or moulded into any form, retaining impressions to the finest detail when it becomes cool and hard. It is used for making certain kinds of surgical instruments, in the moulding of plates for artificial teeth, and many other purposes. Nowadays, however, there is a tendency to use synthetic plastics instead of gutta-percha.

Gutta-percha has been known in western countries only since the middle of the 18th century, but in China it has been used much longer. Some times the trees are tapped, but as the juice flows very slowly, it is more usual to cut down the trees to collect the latex, a large tree yielding only 2 or 3 lb. This wasteful practice has denuded some of the forests, and plantations of gutta-percha forests have been started to replace the loss.

Gwalior.
The premier Mahratta state in Central India, Gwalior forms part of the republic of India, and has an area of some 26,000 square miles. Gwalior, the ancient capital, is the most historic town in the state; Lashkar, the modern capital, is really an extension of Gwalior city, their combined population being 80,000.

The state is fertile, watered by the rivers Chambal, Narbada, and Sind, and its agriculture is aided by big irrigation works. Millet and wheat are grown.

There are extensive forests, and deposits of mica, iron, limestone and sandstone. The chief industry is the manufacture of cotton goods. The population of the State is a little over 4,000,000.

Gypsum.
Occurring in Nature as a soft white rock, usually associated with rock salt, gypsum is composed of calcium sulphate in combination with water. Transparent varieties are known as "selenite," and very fine grades of the material, of white colour and special lustre, make the familiar alabaster. When gypsum is heated, part of the water evaporates and the mineral becomes a white powder known as plaster of Paris, the name being due to the fact that gypsum was early used near Paris for the making of plaster or cement. If moistened, this powder hardens as it dries, and plaster of Paris is therefore widely used for making sculptors' casts and surgical splints. Plaster of Paris is also used sometimes as a fertilizer on the land, where it facilitates the decay of certain forms of alkali.

For making plaster of Paris the gypsum is ground in mills and burned in large kettles, which are usually about six feet deep and eight feet round. Heat is applied from below, and revolving arms stir the gypsum.

Quantities of gypsum are used in the preparation of cements, as a basis of paints, and for making imitation marble; as a flux in melting nickel ores; and for improving water for brewing beer.

Gypsum occurs in Cheshire, Derbyshire and Nottinghamshire, and is also found in many places in the United States.

Gyroscope.
Any wheel or disk-shaped body when rotating quickly tends to stay in its plane of rotation. That is, for example, the reason why your cycle ceases to wobble when you have pedalled a few times and have got up speed. The cycle wheels rotate in a vertical plane, on a horizontal axis. Again, let us take a spinning top: it stays upright until the speed gets low, and then it begins to lean over and to wobble. The spinning top rotates in a horizontal plane, on a vertical axis. Most people have seen a toy gyroscope, and have accepted its behaviour without understanding the reason why it acts so strangely.

The simple gyroscope consists of a wheel or a disk with a heavy rim, fixed to a spindle and mounted in a ring-shaped frame so that it can turn freely. This is the form we know in the familiar toy, seen at the left in the illustration below. The compound gyroscope has its ring-shaped frame mounted by pivots in another (outer) ring or frame, so that the axes of the two rings are at right angles. This type is shown in the centre diagram; the outer ring is fixed to a stem which fits in a stand. With the simple gyroscope we can try the interesting experiments shown in the picture.

But the gyroscope will do these wonderful things only so long as its disk, or rotor, is spinning rapidly. Then it has rigidity in space, and if we start it spinning with its axis (or spindle) pointing in any given direction, it will tend to keep in that plane of rotation. For example, you may rest the gyro end in a loop of string, as illustrated, or may rest it on the edge of a tumbler; it will not fall off,

the gyroscope, as it overhangs the support, corresponds to your finger applying pressure to the outer end of the spindle.

Let us examine this picture carefully. The weight of the apparatus is giving a downward push to the outer end of the spindle. As a result of this attempted tilting, the frame—and of course the whole apparatus—moves round in the circular path shown by the arrows, at right angles to the direction in which the tilting push is being given by gravity. This effect is called *precession*, and in the case shown by the right-hand diagram such precession is continuous, because the tilting force (gravity) is being constantly applied. The centre diagram on this page shows the same phenomenon, but here a finger is being used to apply a tilting pressure. Note that if we reverse the process, and

SOME OF THE QUEER ANTICS OF THE GYROSCOPE EXPLAINED

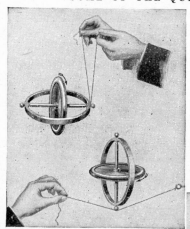

This shows the gyroscope's tendency to 'stay put' where it first starts spinning. A toy gyro-top (left) is horizontal although only one end is supported by the string. A second top is 'walking a tight-rope.' Below we see the result of disturbing the 'rigidity in space' of a small laboratory gyroscope. Instead of tipping when pressed down lightly (F), it turns around its vertical axis in the direction P. This effort of the wheel to get around so that its edge will be moving (arrow R) in the same direction as the finger pressure is 'precession.' Right, 'continuous precession'; a gyro-top whose free end is subjected to the pull of gravity turns round its supporting stand.

PATH OF ROTATION

or move out of the horizontal, so long as the rotor spins quickly. Or you may make it walk a tight-rope by using a sloping piece of twine as its support, as shown in the lower part of the left-hand diagram. If, when the gyro is standing out horizontally, you try to push it out of this position, you will find that it resists you with a force equal to many times its weight.

If you apply sufficient force to overcome this resistance, and you actually tilt the gyroscope— and you may safely tilt it to almost any angle short of really toppling it over—a surprising thing happens. The wheel goes on spinning merrily in

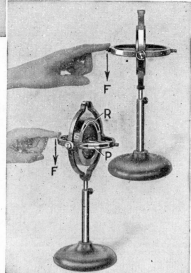

its new plane of rotation, but the whole apparatus turns in a circle about the spinning point, thus compounding two simultaneous rotations. (One of these rotations is that of the disk in its frame; the other is that of the frame on its own support.) The right-hand picture on this page shows such an experiment, the frame of this laboratory model being provided with a hooked extension by which the frame is supported in a stand, but is free to turn, or to tilt up or down. Here the weight of

try to move the axis around horizontally, it will tilt instead. Both these properties are used in gyroscopic instruments.

Now for the reason which makes the gyro-compass possible. If the gyroscope is started with its axis pointing in a North and South direction, it will stay in this direction, because its axis of rotation is now in the same plane as the axis of the earth itself. If we start the gyroscope with its plane of rotation a different one from that of the earth, the earth's revolution will gradually tend to bring the gyroscope axis into a position coinciding with the earth's axis. So here we have a non-magnetic North-seeking pointer which can replace the magnetic compass—so long as we set it first in a North-South axis and maintain its rapid rotation.

Léon Foucault (1819–68), a French scientist, tried an interesting experiment with a pendulum which illustrates this property of the gyroscope. He suspended a heavy pendulum bob by a long and fine wire, and started it swinging. He marked out on the floor the track of the pendulum bob. He found that the pendulum kept on swinging in a fixed direction, but that after a time the track marked on the floor did not coincide with the path followed by the pendulum; instead this track deviated to the right (in the Northern hemisphere). In fact, the pendulum kept swinging in a fixed direction relative to space; but owing to the rotation of the earth, the track *appeared* to shift relative to the earth. Foucault's experiment, made in 1851, demonstrated the rotation of the earth. It also stimulated him to invent the gyroscope soon after. In the Science Museum, London, is a big Foucault pendulum, demonstrated daily.

In the gyro-compass a rotor (corresponding to the disk of the simple gyroscope) is driven by an electric motor at about 6,000 to 9,000 revolutions per minute. Some form of weight is used to exert a tilting pressure at one end of the gyro axis. In earlier models a small lead weight was used, but today some liquid is employed, flowing in a sort of U-tube from one side to the other if and when the axis should tilt in relation to the axis of the earth's rotation. The moving liquid transfers weight from one side of the rotor system to the other, and applies a correcting force which, should the gyro axis deviate from the North-South line, causes the system to precess towards this line.

In our story of the Compass we explain the handicap which modern ships, built of steel and having much electrical machinery in them, impose on the magnetic compass. The compass has to be shielded from the influence of electrical machinery, and to be corrected for the presence of steelwork in its neighbourhood. There is an even bigger difficulty in fighting-ships: the officer who controls the ship must be protected from enemy missiles by armour plating; there must be several control positions, each with its reliable compass, in case one after another should be damaged or destroyed in battle. This is where the gyroscopic instrument is so valuable; it can be made to transmit direction-indications to a large number of "repeaters," installed in suitable positions in the ship. The gyro-

FOUCAULT'S EXPERIMENT
As a pendulum swung to and fro over a table covered with sand the point on the bob of the pendulum traced a line. Owing to the Earth's rotation, this track after a time appeared to deviate to the right.

compass—master instrument—can be located in a non-vulnerable place, well protected. The repeaters are free from the drawbacks attendant on magnetic compasses.

Briefly, the gyro-compass works as follows : The rotor—in some types weighing four or five pounds, and in others weighing ten times as much—is driven by electricity. Its framework, sometimes called the "phantom," is driven independently in step with the rotor system. When the ship alters her course she moves the phantom with her, but the rotor system goes on pointing Northwards. Thus the phantom and the rotor system are no longer in step and aligned with one another. This lack of alignment is used to make the phantom send a signal to its driving motor, which now moves the phantom backwards until it is again in step with the rotor system. In thus moving, the phantom traverses, perhaps, several degrees of the compass circle, or only some fractions of a degree. As it moves back into step the phantom sends out electrical impulses to the repeaters, so many for each degree that it traverses.

The impulses transmitted by the phantom cause the indicating cards of the repeaters to move round and to show the new course which the ship is following. It is still necessary to carry magnetic compasses for reference and in case of emergency. The gyro-compass rotor must be continually driven by electricity, and if there is a break-down

DEMONSTRATING THE EARTH'S ROTATION
To demonstrate the rotation of the Earth by the same method as that used by the French scientist, Jean Foucault, in 1851, this girl is burning the cotton thread in order to release the pendulum and set it swinging in an even and regular manner. The pendulum will continue swinging in the same plane while the Earth turns around.

of the ship's generating plant, and the rotor should stop, several hours are necessary to get the gyro-compass back again into the true North direction. The same delay may occur when the rotor's action is disturbed by some outside cause.

Aircraft compasses are almost always of the magnetic type, though gyroscopes may be used in the transmission system which operates repeaters. The gyro-compass needs a steady location, and is easily upset by shocks, or by violent changes in the speed of the carrying vessel. This is why it has not displaced the magnetic compass in aircraft. But several other aircraft instruments utilise the peculiar properties of the spinning rotor—for example, the artificial horizon, the turn-and-bank indicator, and the automatic pilot which keeps the aeroplane on a pre-set course and frees the pilot from manual operation of the controls on long flights. In the flying-bomb (q.v.) several gyroscopes are used for the same sort of purposes.

HOW A GYROSCOPE IS TURNED INTO A COMPASS

To understand the picture at the right imagine yourself suspended in space and looking at the earth from south of the Equator. A giant gyroscope aboard a ship is being carried around by the earth's rotation. The gyro-axis W-E points west and east. As the gyroscope is carried around, note that its 'rigidity in space' holds the wheel parallel to its original position, so that the W end of the axis, still pointing west, dips more and more toward the earth. Below, the original conditions are the same, except that a U-tube with enlarged ends, containing mercury, is fastened to the axis supports of the wheel's frame. As soon as the west end of the axis starts to dip towards the earth the mercury, under the levelling force of gravity, flows to that side of the tube. This results in greater downward pressure on the west than on the east end of the axis, and what was the west end of the axis turns toward the north. The turning

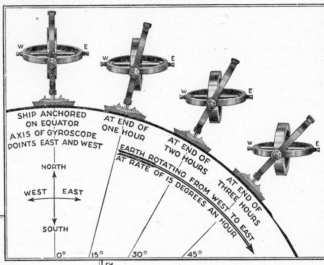

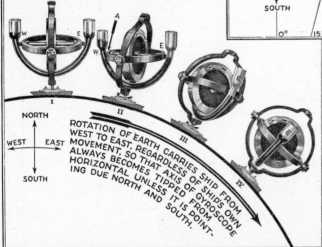

continues until the mercury is balanced in the U-tube, a condition that can only exist when the axis of the gyro and the axis of the earth are in the same plane—or in other words, when the axis of the gyro points in exactly a north-and-south direction. This is the principle of the gyro-compass.

Foucault, as we have mentioned, worked out the theory of the gyro-scope, following on his discovery that a free pendulum kept in its original plane of swing in space, irrespective of the rotation of the earth. He saw that a gyroscope could be used as a North-South indicator, in the manner which we have described. Between the years 1900 and 1906 a German, Dr. Anschütz, produced a gyro-compass for the Kaiser's navy. In 1911 Elmer A. Sperry, an American, produced his gyro-compass, which soon became one of the standard types. The invention was followed up in other countries, and today there are a number of different patterns in use. Sperry also used a very big gyroscope to prevent rolling in ships. Louis Brennan, an Irishman, notable for his invention of a torpedo, invented a mono-railway, in which the train ran suspended on a single rail and was kept stable by a gyroscope.

Gyroscopes form part of many different types of apparatus and machines today besides those mentioned, including gun-stabilizers and tanks.

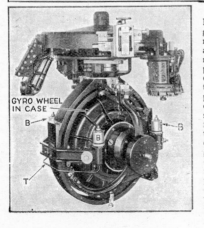

In this Sperry compass, the gyro is part of an electric motor and is kept spinning about 6,000 to 9,000 times a minute inside the case. A pair of mercury containers B on each side correspond to the ends of the U-tube in the previous picture. The tube T connecting each pair is so small that the mercury will not flow rapidly back and forth as the ship rocks, but will respond only to prolonged tipping of the gyro-axis. The gyro then precesses, and the motion is communicated by its vertical supporting ring through electrical contacts to an auxiliary motor which keeps the compass card aligned with the gyro.

H

Habeas Corpus. (Pron. hā'-bi-as kor'-pus.) Throughout the British Commonwealth, when a person is imprisoned, or held anywhere against his will, a court of law may upon reasonable demand issue an order compelling the gaoler or other custodian to produce the person in court and show for what reason he is held captive. If no lawful reason is found, the prisoner is released. This court order is called a writ of habeas corpus, often known as " the great writ of liberty."

Habeas corpus is a Latin phrase meaning " you must have the body." The principle is of ancient English origin, for in Magna Carta King John (1167-1216) was forced to promise that " no free man shall be taken or imprisoned except by the lawful judgement of his peers and by the law of the land." Under this principle no one could be arrested and held in confinement on mere suspicion, without being formally accused of a crime.

This remained one of the mainstays of English liberty until Charles I (1600-1649) set up the claim that a royal command was a sufficient answer to a writ of habeas corpus. This misguided policy, with similar arbitrary acts, cost the king his throne and his life. The result was that under Charles II it was deemed necessary to pass, in 1679, an Act of Habeas Corpus, which has since become famous. This extended the principle to mean that any person who was imprisoned for any crime except treason or felony might demand and obtain his freedom under bail until called upon to stand his trial. Bail is the pledge or bond of some responsible person to pay a fixed sum of money if the accused person fails to appear for trial.

In times of national emergency the Habeas Corpus Act may be suspended by a special Act of Parliament which gives power to the Crown alone to imprison suspected persons for a limited period without stating the reason. Habeas corpus is also suspended automatically if martial law is proclaimed.

In the United States of America, too, the individual is protected against imprisonment upon suspicion without a formal charge being brought against him. The Constitution of the U.S.A. declares that " the privilege of the writ of habeas corpus shall not be suspended unless, when in cases of rebellion or invasion, the public safety may demand it."

Haddock. An important and popular food fish, belonging to the cod family, is the haddock. Its scientific name is *Gadus aeglefinus*, and it is distinguished from the cod by the dark lateral line that runs along the sides of the body, and the black spot behind each pectoral fin. In other respects it is a typical member of the cod family, feeding on shell-fish and crust-aceans, and ranging in large shoals through the North Atlantic and into the North Sea. In size the haddock is usually less than two feet long, though sometimes as much as three.

While large quantities of fresh haddocks are regularly consumed, particularly in the fried fish trade, the most popular forms of this fish are the whole smoked haddock, renowned the world over, and the smaller, smoked fillets; the best variety of the smoked haddock comes from Finnon or Findon in Kincardineshire, where they are dried and smoked in a special way. A large export trade in these is conducted from the chief Scottish and English fishing ports. Haddock, which are usually found over a muddy or sandy bottom, are caught by trawling, or on lines baited usually with mussel.

Hague, THE. (Pron. hāg.) The seat of the Netherlands government and capital of the province of South Holland is known as The Hague, a town situated two miles from the North Sea in a broad pleasant plain. It is prosperous and attractive, and famed for its cleanliness, but it is not a commercial city. As well as the Dutch Parliament, the Government offices and the Supreme Court are at The Hague. The royal palace, an 18th-century building which was enlarged during 1816-17, is the residence of the Court of Holland; and The Hague was for long the diplomatic capital of Europe, where many momentous international conferences were held.

Since 1899 The Hague has been the seat of the International Court of Arbitration, or Hague Tribunal, for which a splendid palace, The Palace of Peace (opened in 1913), was built. From 1920 also the town has been the seat of the Permanent Court of International Justice which deals with disputes referred to it under international law; and since 1946 the Court of the United Nations has been established there.

The original Dutch name of the city was 's Gravenhage (the Count's Grove), which has been

HADDOCK, RELATION OF THE COD
One of the most important of our food fishes, the haddock is distinguished from the cod by its forked tail and pointed dorsal (back) fin, and by the dark lateral line on its body. It is caught on the same fishing grounds and by the same methods as the cod. In size the haddock is usually less than two feet long.

Dorien Leigh

THE HAGUE, SEAT OF THE NETHERLANDS GOVERNMENT

Just as Washington is the political capital of the United States and New York the commercial capital, so The Hague is the political and Amsterdam the commercial capital of the Netherlands. This photograph shows the sheet of ornamental water near the centre of the city known as the Vyver. Behind the buildings at the edge of the lake is the Binnenhof, a square in which are situated the Parliament buildings. The Hague, which is about 14 miles north-west of the port of Rotterdam, is the meeting-place of the International Court of Justice and the Court of the United Nations.

shortened to den Haag. The name comes from the fact that long ago the counts of Holland had a hunting-lodge there. The city was once in a dense wood, most of which was cut down by the Germans during the Second World War (1939–45). Only a little patch is left between The Hague and Scheveningen, a popular seaside resort.

Broad, tree-lined streets, intersected by many picturesque canals and with fine old buildings, make the city one of the handsomest capitals of Europe. Its greatest pride is in its celebrated picture-gallery, the Mauritshuis. Here are masterpieces by the Dutch artists Rembrandt, Rubens, Van Dyck, Vermeer, and others. There is also a fine gallery of modern paintings, the greater number of which were collected by the eminent Dutch painter, Hendrik Willem Mesdag.

During the Second World War (1939–45) the city received some air-raid damage, and was in German hands from May 15, 1940 until May 8, 1945. It was here that an exceptionally courageous low-level attack was made by R.A.F. Mosquitoes on May 3, 1944, on a building which housed documents of the Gestapo ; the building was entirely ruined. The population of the city is 476,300.

Haig, EARL (1861–1928). During the First World War (1914–18) the British commander-in-chief in France and Belgium from December 1915 until the Armistice on November 11, 1918, was Sir Douglas Haig, who in 1919 was created Earl Haig. He was born on June 19, 1861, and was educated at Clifton and at Brasenose College, Oxford, whence he went to the Royal Military College, Sandhurst, joining the 7th Hussars in 1885.

Haig saw his first active service under Lord Kitchener in the Nile Expedition (1898), where he distinguished himself and was raised to the rank of major. He served also in the Boer War (1899–1902). He succeeded Lord French as commander-in-chief in France in December 1915 and was promoted Field-Marshal in January 1917. He led by far the largest British forces that had ever taken the field up to that time. At the close of the War he received a large number of honours, among them the Order of Merit. Haig founded the British Legion in 1921, and gave his name to the Poppy Fund. He died in London on January 29, 1928, and was buried in the family burial place at Dryburgh Abbey, Berwickshire.

Hail. Pellets of ice which fall from thunder clouds or large cumulus clouds are known as hail. They are of various shapes and sizes, complex in structure and transparent. Hailstones as big as grape fruit and weighing over 2 lb. have been observed. They result from the growth of ice crystals at the expense of water drops lower in the same cloud. These crystals, condensed directly out of the rising air in the higher regions, grow to pellets sufficiently heavy to overcome the resistance of rising air currents. They fall through the cloud, strike super-cooled water drops supported by the ascending air, and freezing occurs, the water uniting with the ice. When the air can no longer support it, the hailstone falls to the ground as a mass of ice. Hail does great damage to crops, fruit trees and glass.

Hair. The possession of hair is a characteristic feature of the great group *Mammalia*, and was one of the factors which enabled mammals to develop so far beyond their ancestors, the reptiles. This is because the outer covering enabled them to live in cold as well as hot climates, at high as well as low altitudes. Animals which live in cold regions—for instance, the reindeer and the polar bear—show a tendency to grow much heavier coats than those which live in a temperate climate. In some mammals, like the pig, the hair develops into stiff bristles; in others, like the porcupine and hedgehog, the bristles form protective spines.

In human beings no hair is found on the palms of the hands and the soles of the feet. The hair of the head is protective; the presence of hair elsewhere is probably only a relic of the heavy, hairy coat worn by our remote, prehistoric ancestors. Most of the lower animals have shedding periods when the hair begins to come out and to be replaced with new.

Hair originates in the epidermis (*see* Skin) and consists of modified horn cells. Each hair grows at its root from a tubular follicle or sheath, formed in the papillae of the skin. It is provided with a blood-vessel which feeds it and carries away waste material, with glands which provide oil to keep it moist and soft, and with nerves which control the contractions and expansions of the blood-vessel. It has also a muscle (the hair erector or *erector papillae*) which by contracting makes the hair bristle or stand on end, like the hair on the tail of an angry or frightened cat, or the hair of the coat of an angry dog.

Each hair is a strong, flexible, elastic thread, composed of many horny cells. Some hairs are straight, others wavy, and still others "frizzy" or woolly. Microscopic examination of a cross-section of a straight hair shows that it is round, while a curly hair is elliptical in a cross-section. Scientists have used these and other differences in the texture of human hair as a basis for classifying mankind into the straight-haired, the wavy-haired, the woolly-haired, and finally the frizzy-haired races. The first includes Chinese and other yellow peoples and the North American Indians, the second the white peoples, the third the Negroes, and the fourth the aboriginal Australians and Nubians.

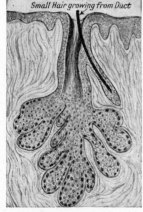

HAIR: ITS LUBRICATION
A gland opening into the sheath from which the hair emerges, emits a greasy secretion, thus preventing dryness.

Haiti, REPUBLIC OF. (Pron. hā′-ti). One of the Greater Antilles and second in size only to Cuba, the island of Haiti lies in the centre of the chain of the West Indies, close to the eastern end of Cuba. Only the western portion is occupied by the Republic of Haiti, but this area of 10,200 square miles contains about three times as many people as the Dominican Republic in the east of the island.

Forest-clad mountains occupy about 80 per cent of the country; the largest rivers are the Artibonite (navigable for 100 miles), the Grand Anse, and the

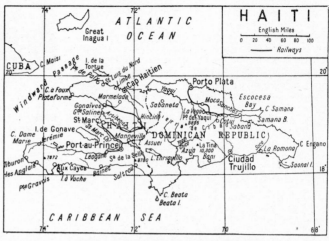

HAITI, ISLAND OF THE WEST INDIES
Also known as Hispaniola, the island of Haiti is divided between the Dominican Republic and the Negro republic of Haiti, as shown here. In 1697 the western, or Haitian, part of the island was taken from the Spaniards by the French, and Haiti's official language is still French.

Trois Rivières. Little has been done to exploit the mineral resources; among the minerals known to exist are gold, silver, copper, tin, nickel, antimony, gypsum, limestone and porphyry. Rainfall is abundant, and the valleys are exceptionally fertile, producing coffee, cotton, cacao, sisal, tobacco, bananas, rice, pineapples and sugar-cane.

Port-au-Prince is the capital and chief port. There are only 158 miles of railway and 975 miles of motor road in the republic. Elementary education is free

E. Peterffy
IN PORT-AU-PRINCE, HAITI'S CAPITAL
On an arm of the Gulf of Gonaives, Port-au-Prince is the capital and chief port of the republic of Haiti. Coffee, sugar, hemp and fruit are the main exports. With its population of 115,000 the city is by far the largest in the republic.

and compulsory. The inhabitants are Negroes, and the official language is French, though many of the people speak a dialect called Creole French.

Haiti was a French Colony from 1677 until 1801 when the Negro slaves revolted against the French, driving them from the island. A kingdom was established which lasted until 1820, after which a republic was proclaimed. Years of misgovernment and revolts reduced the country to a miserable condition, and in 1915 the United States formally undertook to restore law and order. Yellow fever and smallpox were stamped out; sanitation was improved, hospitals erected, prisons cleansed, and banditry suppressed. The American forces and advisers to the Haitian Government were withdrawn in 1934. The estimated population of the Republic is 3,000,000.

Halibut. *Hippoglossus vulgaris*, as the halibut is called by naturalists, is perhaps the most important of the flat fish. Its flesh is pleasant and is valuable as food, and the oil of its liver is an even richer source of vitamin A than is cod-liver oil. When the halibut liver oil is prepared for use as a vitamin source, Vitamin D is added to it in a

W. S. Berridge
HALIBUT, A LARGE FLAT FISH
Differing slightly in shape from its relatives, the sole and the turbot, in having a thicker and more elongated body, the halibut is found in the northern waters of the Pacific and Atlantic oceans. Specimens more than seven feet long have been caught, but the male rarely exceeds four feet.

certain proportion. Halibut are sought by deep-sea anglers for sheer sport, one great centre for this kind of deep-sea fishing being Valencia Island off the coast of Kerry in Eire. Apart from this it is caught by trawling, since it is found up to 600 feet deep at some distance from the shore. Mostly from four to five feet long, the halibut has been known to grow to over seven feet.

Halifax, NOVA SCOTIA. Possessing one of the finest harbours in the world, Canada's chief winter port stands on a hill overlooking Chebutco Bay, 747 miles east of Montreal. Halifax is the terminus of two trans-continental railways, and the headquarters of the Atlantic section of the Royal Canadian Navy.

Exports are fish and lumber, and its many industries include shipbuilding, sugar and oil refining, and the manufacture of furniture, soap, paint, tobacco, cotton and woollen goods, and agricultural implements.

The city was founded in 1749, and named after the Earl of Halifax (1716–71); it was made the capital of the province of Nova Scotia in 1750. The population is 70,400.

Hallowe'en. The night of the 31st of October, which precedes All Saints' Day, is known as All-Hallow-Even (holy eve) or Hallowe'en. Superstitious folk used to believe that almost anything could happen on that day; for they thought that witches then rode abroad on broomsticks, elves played pranks upon sober folk, and that the future might be foretold by jumping over a lighted candle, or by many other magic rites.

Many of these superstitions have come down to us from our pagan ancestors of 2,000 years

Canadian Official News Bureau
HALIFAX IN NOVA SCOTIA, CANADA
One of the chief ports of Canada, and the capital of Nova Scotia, Halifax is a fine city with a magnificent harbour, which you see here together with some of the great docks which lie along the city's water-front. The large open space and regular buildings in the centre are the remains of an ancient fortress, now used as barracks.

ago or more, for our Hallowe'en occurs about the time of the ancient Druidic autumn festival. This was also the season of the ancient Roman festival in honour of Pomona, goddess of fruit and gardens; and so, after the Roman conquest of Gaul and Britain, some of the Roman beliefs and ceremonies were added. Later, after the spread of Christianity, November 1 was a day for the honouring of all the saints, and the eve of that day was called Hallowe'en. Many of the old pagan customs were retained, and even today some people still crack nuts, and bob for apples, throw apple peelings over their shoulder and look in a mirror with a lighted candle in order to see the face of their future spouse, and so forth. Hallowe'en observance as a time of merry-making is more popular in Scotland, where dances are frequently held on that night.

Halogens. The four elements fluorine, chlorine, bromine, and iodine are classed together under the general name of "halogens" (Greek *hals*, meaning salt; Latin *generare*, produce) because, in some chemical properties, they are related to one another. Their atoms have electronic structures which bring them into related positions in the Periodic Table (*see* Chemistry).

Fluorine is often found in nature combined with calcium as the mineral fluorspar (calcium fluoride, CaF_2). Fluorspar is used as a flux in steel-making and other metallurgical processes, for the preparation of hydrofluoric acid (HF), and for the manufacture of some kinds of glass, including opal glass. Another fluoride, the mineral cryolite (Na_3AlF_6), is used, mixed with fluorspar and bauxite (aluminium hydroxide), during the commercial production of aluminium metal by electrolysis, a very important process in these days, when enormous quantities of aluminium are needed for light alloys to make anything from a saucepan to an aeroplane.

Fluorine compounds have other uses, *e.g.* fluorides are used in insecticides ; and volatile organic fluorine compounds have been used as cold-producing liquids in refrigerators.

The element fluorine is a yellowish, extremely reactive gas. It combines violently, and often with incandescence, with many elements ; and attacks all metals, even the noble metal platinum. Hydrofluoric acid (HF), manufactured by heating fluorspar with sulphuric acid, comes on to the market in the form of a concentrated aqueous solution, which can be safely stored and manipulated in vessels made of paraffin wax, platinum, or some plastics. The acid attacks glass, and is used for etching marks and designs on glass vessels: the design is cut in a protective layer of wax, and the acid is then applied and allowed to eat into those parts of the glass not protected by wax.

Hydrofluoric acid and the fluorides are very poisonous, but, strangely enough, it is now thought that small quantities of fluoride are desirable for the proper development and growth of the bones and teeth of animals and man. It seems likely that, for the development of healthy bones and teeth, drinking water should contain about one part of fluoride in one million parts of the water. Too much fluoride causes "fluorosis" disease, with mottled discoloration of the teeth.

Chlorine, a greenish-yellow reactive corrosive gas, used as a poison gas during the 1914–18 war, occurs in nature combined with metals, the most important compound being sodium chloride (common salt, NaCl), which is found in literally enormous quantities in the waters of our oceans,

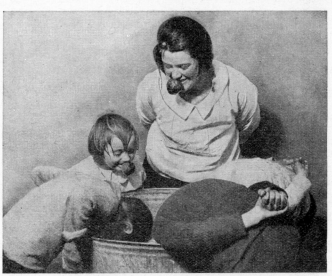

APPLE-BOBBING ON HALLOWE'EN
Amongst old customs connected with Hallowe'en is that of picking up with the teeth apples floating in a tub of water. Some of the beliefs and observances associated with the celebrations arose long before the Christian era, in the autumn festivals of pagan peoples.

in the concentrated water of the Dead Sea, and as rock salt in Cheshire and many other places.

Chlorine gas is made in large quantities by electrolysing aqueous solutions of common salt, and has many uses, including the preparation of bleaching solutions (used in bleaching cotton fabrics and for bleaching wood-pulp to be used for paper-making), the manufacture of organic compounds like carbon tetrachloride (used in some fire extinguishers), the preparation of dyestuffs, and the sterilization of drinking water.

The third halogen, bromine, discovered by Balard in 1826, in evaporated sea water, is chemically rather like chlorine, but is a reddish-brown liquid at ordinary temperatures and gives off a pungent, corrosive, and poisonous vapour. It combines with metals to form bromides, the main sources of supply of bromine now being the bromides present in ordinary sea water and in the waters of the Dead Sea. Ordinary sea water contains only about 0.007 per cent of bromides, yet the Americans have a plant which extracts about 15,000 lb. of bromine per day from sea water. Bromine has many uses ; it is present in the silver bromide of your photographic roll film, it is used in medicine, and it is present as ethylene dibromide in anti-knock petrol for motor vehicles. The fourth halogen, iodine, is a solid (*see* Iodine).

Hals, FRANS. (1580?–1666). One of the greatest of portrait painters was the Dutch artist Frans Hals (pron. hahlz). He is said to have been born in Antwerp about 1580 or 1581, and went as a young man to live at Haarlem in the Netherlands. In 1616 he began to paint the first of the great series of shooting-guild groups and of public officials that show his genius so well. In the Town Hall at Haarlem, 84 men and women look down from the walls in eight great canvases. The last of the series was painted in 1661, when Hals was over 80. There in that collection may be traced the artist's development. A picture painted in 1633 reveals him at his most vigorous period, when his use of brilliant colour and quick grasp of fleeting expression were at their height. In these later groups the colouring has been toned down to sombre grey tints.

Many other examples of Hals's work are scattered throughout the world in public and private galleries. Best known of all his works is The Laughing Cavalier, now in the Wallace Collection in London. This portrait reveals an amazing gift of capturing an expression. Many others, from small portraits to big family groups, are to be seen in great art galleries. Although he did many fine paintings of the upper classes, it is perhaps for his rollicking tavern scenes and groups of musicians that Frans Hals is now best known.

Underwood

IN HAMBURG'S OLD QUARTER
During the Second World War (1939–45) great damage was inflicted on the German port of Hamburg by the Allied air forces. This pre-war view shows one of the narrow waterways intersecting the old quarter, with the spire (483 feet high) of St. Nicholas Church in the distance.

His work was almost ignored for two centuries after his death, and so lightly was he esteemed that some of his paintings were sold for a few pounds. Yet of late years as much as £26,775 has been paid for a single work by him. Critics put him next to Rembrandt (1606–69), at the head of the Dutch school, and some call him the greatest painter for truth of character.

Hamburg, Germany. Germany's largest seaport, Hamburg lies many miles inland, being situated on the north bank of the river Elbe, 75 miles from its mouth. The city bestrides a little stream called Alster, and this forms two connected lakes (the Inner and Outer Alster) in the heart of Hamburg. The older part of the town, to the east, was intersected by a great number of narrow canals, lined with warehouses and squat dwellings that seemed to rise right out of the water.

Owing to wartime destruction our story here is of Hamburg mainly as it was before 1939. Viewed from the left bank of the Elbe, Hamburg and the adjoining towns of Altona and Harburg-Wilhelmsburg looked like a single city. With a continuous river frontage of 10 miles, crowded with shipping in normal times, and with its densely packed houses in the background surmounted by lofty church spires, the city gave an impression of massive grandeur. On the borders of the Inner Alster, the smaller of the two lakes, were grouped fashionable avenues and the more important business streets, lined with magnificent buildings.

In the Hopfenmarkt, one of the largest public squares, stood the church of St. Nicholas (Nikolaikirche). Rebuilt as a memorial of the fire of 1842, it was the third highest religious building in the world, its spire soaring 483 feet above the street level. The new Rathaus was the most important of the secular buildings. Hagenbeck's zoological gardens, which formerly contained the largest and most complete collection of wild animals in captivity, was also noted for life-size models of prehistoric monsters. The sites of the old ramparts and fortifications were converted into gardens.

Hamburg had its origin in a fortress and bishopric founded here by Charlemagne in 808–811. Its importance as a centre of commerce began in the 12th century when the Emperor Frederick I granted it free navigation of the Elbe, with the right of levying toll on foreign shipping. In 1241 it joined in the formation of the Hanseatic League (an association of the commercial cities of North Germany). This gave a tremendous impetus to its rapidly increasing wealth and commercial importance. In 1510 Maximilian I reorganized Hamburg as a free imperial city. Under Napoleon the French occupied the city from 1806 to 1814.

Hamburg's modern greatness came in the middle of the 19th century with the development of great steamer lines to all parts of the world. Lying on the most south-easterly inlet of the North Sea, with a harbour ice-free all the year and with waterways to carry goods cheaply to the interior, it soon became the chief seaport of continental Europe. Its industries included shipbuilding, machine works, sugar refining, chemical manufactories, corn and oil mills and the clothing trade.

After 1933 Hamburg was ruled by a Governor who was a personal representative of the German

THE 'LAUGHING CAVALIER' PAINTED BY FRANS HALS

W. F. Mansell

Although the title of this portrait (which is in the Wallace Collection, London) is mystifying, because the sitter is not laughing, there is no doubt about the craftsmanship and artistry that have gone to make it. No man has yet equalled Hals in ability to catch the fleeting expressions that pass across the human face, especially those of laughter and merriment. His detail work was also perfect, as can be seen in the lace and embroidery. Hals is now recognized as one of the greatest portrait painters of all time, but little was thought of his work while he was alive.

leader Adolf Hitler; but the place regained its status as a free city in 1947. The area of the free city is about 160 square miles and includes the outlying port of Cuxhaven at the mouth of the Elbe, with a vast system of docks.

During the Second World War (1939–45), Hamburg was frequently attacked by Allied aircraft, and enormous damage was done. The dockyards and port facilities were almost destroyed, and two-thirds of the industrial and residential quarters were wiped out. Most of the museums escaped with repairable damage, and the greater part of the city's art treasures was saved.

Hamburg surrendered to the British 2nd Army on May 3, 1945, and was the headquarters of the British zone of occupation in Germany until the amalgamation of the administration of the British and United States zones in 1947. The estimated population is 1,380,000.

Hamlet. By almost universal consent this is regarded as Shakespeare's greatest tragedy. The opening of the play reveals Hamlet, the young Prince of Denmark, plunged in bitter grief by the sudden death of his royal father, who, according to report, had been poisoned. The fact that the queen, his mother, has almost immediately married the dead king's ill-favoured brother adds to the Prince's sorrow. To him appears from the tomb the spirit of his father, revealing that he had been put to death; and calls upon Hamlet to revenge this "foul and most unnatural murder."

Hamlet's brilliant, sensitive mind is thrown into feverish activity by the horror of this deed, yet he would make sure of his uncle's guilt. He feigns insanity, the better to watch the guilty pair, and in a court play gets the actors to insert a scene like that of his father's murder, so that he may observe its effect upon the usurping king. The latter's confusion confirms the ghost's revelation; but Hamlet, distracted between his grief and his inability to form a plan of revenge, contemplates his own suicide. " To be or not to be "—to live or die—he muses bitterly, " that is the question "—

Whether 'tis nobler in the mind to suffer
The slings and arrows of outrageous fortune;
Or to take arms against a sea of troubles,
And, by opposing, end them? To die: to sleep;
No more; and, by a sleep, to say we end
The heartache, and the thousand natural shocks
That flesh is heir to, 'tis a consummation
Devoutly to be wished. To die, to sleep;
To sleep; perchance to dream: ay, there's the rub.
For in that sleep of death what dreams may come
When we have shuffled off this mortal coil,
Must give us pause. There's the respect
That makes calamity of so long life;
For who would bear the whips and scorns of time,
The oppressor's wrong, the proud man's contumely,
The pangs of despised love, the law's delay,
The insolence of office, and the spurns
That patient merit of the unworthy takes,
When he himself might his quietus make
With a bare bodkin? Who would fardels bear,
To grunt and sweat under a weary life,
But that the dread of something after death,
The undiscovered country from whose bourn
No traveller returns, puzzles the will,
And makes us rather bear those ills we have
Than fly to others we know not of?
Thus conscience does make cowards of us all. . . .

While Hamlet thus postpones revenge, the king resolves on Hamlet's instant death. But before he can effect it, Hamlet has, by accident, slain old Polonius, the king's counsellor, whereupon the daughter of Polonius, Ophelia, a gentle girl with whom Hamlet is much in love, goes insane and drowns herself.

Laertes, the son of Polonius, swears revenge, and is thereupon used by the king to carry out his own wicked designs. A duelling match is planned with Hamlet, in which Laertes shall use an untipped foil, poisoned at the point, while the king will furnish a cup of poisoned drink to quench Hamlet's thirst.

DRAMATIC MOMENT IN THE PLAY SCENE FROM 'HAMLET'

Here is the tense scene which occurs in Shakespeare's Hamlet, when the King of Denmark sees, reproduced in a play, the murder of his brother which he himself has committed. Lying at Ophelia's feet is Hamlet, watching the king; the old man standing opposite him is Polonius, Ophelia's father; behind her chair is her brother Laertes, who kills Hamlet in a duel. This scene is reproduced from an engraving, after a painting by Daniel Maclise (1806–70).

In this tragic duel and end of the play, Hamlet is, indeed, slain as planned, but in the scuffle Laertes himself is pierced with his own envenomed sword. The queen, by mistake, drinks the poisoned cup and dies, and Hamlet, in the instant of his death, stabs the wicked king. About the only comic relief to the play is the dialogue of the grave-diggers who dig Ophelia's grave.

It has been the ambition of most serious actors to play Hamlet, and success in the part has usually set the hall-mark upon a player's ability. David Garrick played Hamlet from 1742 to 1776, when he bade farewell to the stage, and is said to have been during that time the foremost interpreter of the part, as well as the greatest Shakespearean actor of his day. Mrs. Siddons was the first woman to play the name part of Hamlet, though she only did so a few times (in the provinces), and never in London; her Ophelia, however, was considered excellent, and was played in 1785 to John Kemble's superb Hamlet. Edmund Kean played Hamlet in the 19th century. Sarah Bernhardt (1845–1923) played the part, and, among other great actors, Sir Henry Irving (1838–1905), Sir Johnston Forbes-Robertson (1853–1937), Sir John Martin Harvey (1867–1944), John Barrymore (1882–1942), John Gielgud (born 1904) and Donald Wolfit (born 1902). Laurence Olivier (born 1907) portrayed a bolder, harsher Hamlet in the film, made in 1947 and first shown in 1948.

Hampden, JOHN (1594–1643). One of the most gallant and determined of the band of Puritan statesmen who opposed the autocratic government of Charles I, Hampden was a man of wealth and position, a cousin to Oliver Cromwell, and one of that leader's ablest supporters.

Probably born in London, he was educated at Thame Grammar School, Oxfordshire, and at Magdalen College, Oxford. Entering Parliament in 1621, Hampden was imprisoned for refusing to pay a share of a forced loan raised by Charles I, and in 1635, on the king's attempt to raise ship money from inland places, he refused again and was prosecuted. A majority of the judges voted against him, but Parliament reversed their judgement. His courageous stand on a matter of principle made him a popular figure and he became one of the leaders of the Parliamentary party.

In the early days of the memorable Long Parliament (1640–60) Hampden was right-hand man to the redoubtable John Pym, then leader of the Puritan cause, and was one of the five members whose attempted seizure by King Charles on January 4, 1642, led rapidly to armed conflict. When hostilities began, Hampden joined the Parliamentary army, contributed liberally to its support, raised a regiment of infantry, and in the

struggle displayed great bravery and generalship. He was mortally wounded at Chalgrove Field on June 18, 1643, and died on June 24.

Hampshire. In geniality of climate and in variety and charm of scenery few English counties can claim to surpass Hampshire. It is bounded on the west by Dorset and Wiltshire, on the north by Berkshire, and on the east by Surrey and Sussex. The chief rivers are the Itchen, Test, Avon, Hamble and Lymington. The Isle of Wight is officially included in the county, which has an area of nearly

J. Dixon-Scott

ABBEY RUINS AT BEAULIEU, HAMPSHIRE
On the fringe of the New Forest is the village of Beaulieu, where stand the ruins of a Cistercian Abbey (above) founded by King John in 1204. The New Forest, which covers a large part of Hampshire, is an ancient royal hunting ground, where a breed of wild ponies and a few deer still roam.

1,650 square miles. It is mainly an agricultural county ; large numbers of sheep and pigs are reared and wheat, barley and oats are grown. Inland, it is sparsely populated, but this is compensated for by the large towns on the coast, which include Portsmouth, its suburb, Southsea, Southampton and the seaside town of Bournemouth, whose equable climate makes it popular as a winter as well as a summer resort. At Eastleigh, five miles north of Southampton, the Southern Region of British Railways has important engineering works. The county town is Winchester (*q.v.*).

The chief glory of the county is the New Forest, lying between Southampton and the River Avon, and having an area of 144 square miles. A few deer still roam about this old hunting ground of the Norman kings. A stone, known as the Rufus Stone, in one of the glades, is supposed to mark the spot where William Rufus (1056–1100) was killed by an arrow, said to have been shot by Sir Walter Tyrell. The first cricket club in England was formed at Hambledon. In the county are the ruins of the Abbeys of Netley and Beaulieu (pron. bū'-li), and two very beautiful churches, Romsey Abbey and Christchurch Priory.

The novelist, Jane Austen (1775–1817), was born at Steventon Rectory, and passed most of her life in the county; and Hampshire is the scene of Gilbert White's (1720–1793) Natural History of Selborne. The population of the county is 1,102,000. (*See* Portsmouth; Southampton; Wight, Isle of.)

Hand. Placed at the end of the arm, with the ball-and-socket joint at the shoulder, the hinge joint at the elbow, and a peculiar joint at the wrist, the hand is a wonderful piece of mechanism, and with a wide range of movement.

The eight bones of the wrist are called carpal bones, the five of the palm are the metacarpals, and the 14 in the fingers are the phalanges. All these bones are bound together by tough flexible ligaments. (You should compare the description and illustrations of the hand with those of the foot given in pages 1342 and 1343.)

The muscles that move the hand are mostly upon the forearm, and have long tendons connecting them with the different bones. You can feel and see some of these tendons in your wrist when you bend your fingers. There are more than 30 pairs of muscles producing hand motions. The thumb is arranged so as to work against the fingers in very useful grasping movements.

Sensibility is highly developed in the hand. There are many little elevations or papillae on the skin of the palm, and fine nerve fibres extend from these to the brain, thus making the skin very sensitive to touch, heat and cold.

Because it possesses both strength and lightness of touch, the hand is adapted to all sorts of uses. It is the instrument with which the brain accomplishes its greatest direct achievements—including those " handicrafts " which made British mechanics and engineers the peers of any in the world.

Handel, GEORGE FREDERICK (1685–1759). Although born a German, Handel won his first great fame in Italy with his Italian operas. He later became an English citizen, and today is chiefly remembered for his English oratorios.

Handel was born at Halle, Saxony, on February 23, 1685, and at a very early age revealed the possession of great musical gifts. He received no encouragement from his father to develop them, but eventually became a pupil of the cathedral organist at Halle.

At the age of 11 Handel was master of the organ, clavichord, violin, and other instruments, and was

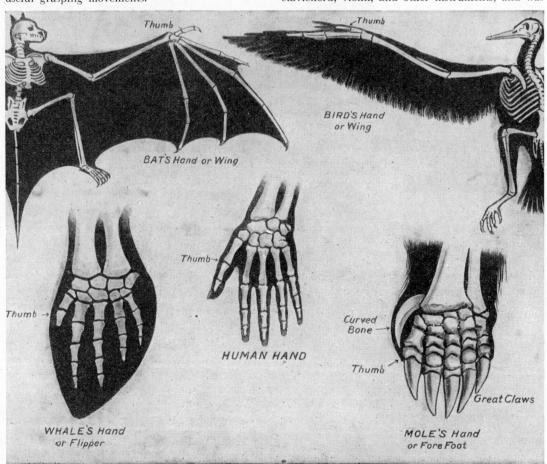

'HANDS' FOR FLYING, SWIMMING, DIGGING AND GRASPING

Although the human hand is the most perfect instrument of all, other creatures also have hands adapted to various purposes. The fingers of the bat, as seen here, have grown very long to support the wings, the thumb remaining free to be used as a hook. The bird's hand or wing has lost almost all its fingers, stiff feathers taking their place. In the whale the hand has developed into a flipper, but all the fingers are plainly represented. The mole not only has the usual five digits but an extra bone to make the palm broader for digging, and the finger nails have become sharp claws.

proficient in musical composition. When he was 20 years
of age he produced his first
opera, which was favourably
received. He went to Italy to
study the Italian style of opera,
and there his brilliant perform-
ances on the harpsichord won
him the highest recognition.

Handel came to London in
1710, where his triumph was
repeated. England offered so
much in the way of oppor-
tunity and appreciation that,
in 1726, he became a nat-
uralized Englishman. Seven
years later he began his career
as an English composer, using
from that time only English
texts for his oratorios. To
these his greatest fame is due,
perhaps the best-known being
his Messiah. Other musicians
were composing operas, but
English oratorio, as composed
by Handel, was quite new.
The English people loved his
music, and the royal family
were always his staunch supporters. The bitterest trial of
his life came in his later years,
when he became totally blind.
Yet he still played, and con-
ducted his oratorios. Handel will never cease
to be revered as one of the greatest of composers.
He died on April 14, 1759.

Hangchow, CHINA. When Marco Polo,
the greatest of medieval travellers, visited Hangchow, towards the end of the 13th century, he
declared it was the finest and noblest city in the
world. It still ranks as one of the richest cities
in China, though it has lost much of its ancient
magnificence. Its shops are noted for their excellence, and its silk, paper fans, tapestries, ivory
carvings, and lacquered ware are famous.

Hangchow is about 118 miles south-west of
Shanghai, lying near the head of the estuary of
the Tsien-tang River, 50 miles from the ocean.
Although a bore—a tidal wave varying in height
from a few feet to 20 feet—comes up twice daily,
the river is constantly crowded with small craft,
which carry vast quantities of merchandise to and
from the southern provinces. An immense amount
of traffic is also carried by the Grand Canal.

The old city, now partly modernized, lies on the
shore of the Si-hu or West Lake. The shores of
this lake and its many islands are crowded with
monasteries and Buddhist shrines. Japanese
forces seized the city in 1937, holding it until the
defeat of Japan by the Allied nations in August
1945. The population of Hangchow is 507,000.

Hankow, CHINA. Though it is 600 miles
up the Yangtze River from Shanghai, ocean-going
steamers can reach this river port of Hupeh province.
Hankow stands at the junction of the Han and
Yangtze rivers. Across the Han is the city of
Hanyang, and on the south bank of the Yangtze
is Wuchang. This triple city of Hankow, Hanyang

Naples Museum; photo Alinari
HANNIBAL OF CARTHAGE
Master of strategy and tactics, Hannibal (c. 247-
184 B.C.) exploited the principle of surprise,
defeating the Romans repeatedly until Scipio
Africanus learnt to beat him at his own game.
But his final failure has left undimmed
Hannibal's fame as a military genius.

and Wuchang is called Wu-
Han and is the industrial and
commercial heart of central
China. To its mills, factories
and docks come hides, wheat,
tobacco, cotton, silk, rice,
beans, iron, coal and antimony.

Of the three cities Hankow is
the most important, handling
the export trade. Wuchang
is chiefly a receiving centre
for trade with the interior;
while Hanyang is almost entirely industrial.

During the war between
China and Japan (1937–45),
Hankow became the pro-
visional capital of China in
1937, after invading Japanese
forces had captured Nanking.
Japanese troops entered the
city in October 1938, but the
Government had retired to
Chungking. Though bombed
by Allied aircraft, Hankow
remained in Japanese hands
until August 1945. The combined population of the three
cities is 778,000.

Hannibal (about
247–183 B.C.). " I swear that
so soon as age will permit, I
will follow the Romans both at sea and on land.
I will use fire and steel to arrest the destiny of Rome."
This was the oath sworn by Hannibal when a
nine-year-old boy, as he and his father, the famous
Carthaginian general Hamilcar Barca, were setting
out to fight the Romans in Spain.

Hamilcar hoped to gain conquests that would
compensate Carthage for the possessions that Rome
had wrested from her in the disastrous war recently
ended—the First Punic War (264-241 B.C.). He
was taking Hannibal that he might learn the ways
of war and, also, to prepare to renew the struggle
with Rome for the supremacy of the Mediterranean.

So well did Hannibal learn his lesson that, after
his father's death, he succeeded to the command
of the army in Spain, and three years later (218
B.C.) was prepared to renew the contest to which
he had been dedicated. While the Roman Senate
was planning invasion, Hannibal was already starting on the most daring march hitherto known.

Along the eastern coast of Spain, over the
Pyrenees, and across the swift waters of the Rhône
he led his force of 50,000 foot soldiers, 9,000 horse-
men, and scores of elephants. It was already
autumn and the cold was intense when this army,
accustomed to the sunny lands of Africa and Spain,
began to cross the Alps. Blinded and almost overwhelmed by snowstorms, over steep and narrow
paths they struggled. In places the natives rolled
heavy stones down the mountain sides upon them;
many men slipped down precipices and were killed;
others perished of cold and hunger, so that the army
was reduced to less than half its original number
when it descended upon the plains of Northern Italy.

By skilful use of cavalry, in which the Romans
were weak, Hannibal won two great victories, at the

HANNIBAL'S ARMY CROSSING THE RHÔNE

When the Carthaginian army on its way to invade Italy crossed the river Rhône in southern France, special rafts had to be built for the elephants. In battle these beasts were said to have been protected by armour and were used somewhat as tanks are today. Hannibal led his forces over the Alps and defeated the Romans at the Trebia river and Lake Trasimene (217 B.C.).

Hannibal now showed that he could be a statesman as well as a soldier. Elected chief magistrate, he reformed and strengthened the government of Carthage and contrived to pay, without hardship to the people, the heavy tribute exacted by Rome. The Romans, alarmed by this prosperity and by the charges of his enemies that he was plotting to renew the war against Rome, demanded Hannibal's surrender. To avoid falling into their hands, he fled to Asia Minor, to the court of Antiochus III, at Ephesus. In the war which followed he took no important part, but when peace was concluded the surrender

River Trebia and at Lake Trasimene. Alarmed at these disasters, which had shattered one army and nearly destroyed another, the Romans appointed a dictator—an official invested with extraordinary power. Their choice fell upon a wise statesman named Quintus Fabius Maximus. Instead of risking an engagement at once, Fabius adopted a policy of following the Carthaginian army, delaying it and harassing it in every possible way. From this he was nicknamed *Cunctator*, or delayer, and even today the expression "a Fabian policy" is used to denote one of caution and deliberation.

At last, in the summer of 216 B.C., a Roman army of between 70,000 and 100,000 met Hannibal's force at Cannae, near the south-eastern coast of Italy. Though far outnumbered, Hannibal managed by clever strategy to surround the forces of his enemy, and to annihilate them. Ex-consuls, senators, nobles, thousands of the best Roman citizens were among the 60,000 slain. Of the gold rings which they wore as an indication of their rank, Hannibal is reported to have sent a bushel to Carthage.

But the victory bore little fruit, for Hannibal was one man fighting against a united nation. He failed to receive support either from his own countrymen or from the tribes whom he subdued during the 15 years that he remained in Italy. His brother Hasdrubal, coming to his aid with reinforcements from Spain, was met by a Roman force, completely defeated, and slain.

Still Hannibal struggled on, until in 204 B.C. a Roman army under Scipio Africanus attacked Carthage, and he was forced to return home. At Zama, in his own country, the lion-hearted commander, who for 15 years had ravaged Italy, suffered a crushing and final defeat in 202 B.C. The battle for supremacy was ended and Rome, mistress of the Mediterranean, dictated peace terms in 201.

of Hannibal was one of the conditions. Foreseeing this, he had fled to Bithynia on the shores of the Black Sea, and when, several years later, the Romans hunted him out, he took poison, which, we are told, he always carried with him in a ring. (*See* Carthage.)

Hanover, GERMANY. At one time the kings of Great Britain were also German princes, ruling the electorate (later the kingdom) of Hanover, in North-Western Germany. This state of things lasted from the accession of George I, the first of the Hanoverian (or Brunswick) dynasty, in 1714, until the death of his great-great-grandson, William IV in 1837—a period of over 120 years. In 1814 the elector George William Frederick (our George III) had become the first king of Hanover. Owing to a law forbidding female succession in Hanover, that land passed to the Duke of Cumberland, younger brother of William IV, when Queen Victoria ascended the British throne in 1837.

In the war between Prussia and Austria, in 1866, Hanover was allied with Austria, and after the defeat of Austria was annexed by Prussia. After the Second World War (1939–45) it was part of the British zone of occupation and in 1946 was merged into the newly-formed state of Lower Saxony. The area of Hanover was 14,970 square miles, and its population about 3,367,000.

The city of Hanover (spelt in German Hannover), the capital of the former province, about 60 miles south-east of Bremen, contained an irregularly built old town, with handsome new quarters to the north and east. Numerous manufactures—hardware, chemicals, machinery, linen, tobacco, contributed to the city's rapid growth in the past half-century. Hanover was devastated by Allied bombing during the Second World War. The population of the city in 1939 was 443,000.

Hanseatic League. In the spring of 1368 a fleet of tall-masted ships met in the Sound, off the coast of Denmark. They came from the towns of Northern Germany belonging to the Hansa or Hanseatic League, which was at war with the King of Denmark.

For two years they harassed the Danish coasts and waters, sacked the Danish cities, and plundered their treasures. At the end of that time the King of Denmark was glad to make peace, although the terms exacted were humiliating. The towns comprising the League demanded a share in the Danish revenues for 15 years, the possession of Danish strongholds, and the final voice in the election of the Danish kings.

The Hanseatic League was the first systematic union of its kind known in the history of European nations, and the high political influence which it rapidly attained was due to its development of sounder principles of trade than hitherto. The foregoing episode in the history of this confederation of North German towns gives an idea of the power it then possessed. It had been growing up gradually. More than 100 years earlier, some towns had formed alliances or *hansas* to protect their traders from the plundering barons along the highways and the pirates upon the seas. These alliances proved so useful that gradually more towns joined the strongest league, of which Lübeck was the centre, and this union became known as the Hanseatic League.

When the League was at the height of its power in the 14th century it probably comprised nearly 100 towns, extending right across Europe, from Dinant, in Belgium, to Cracow, in Poland.

Merchants of the League were exempt from the taxes and tolls levied upon others. And in some places they had a monopoly of a certain trade. The League grew to be so powerful, that it not only protected its merchants, but maintained its fleet, and engaged in war to safeguard its interests.

But quarrels between the towns gradually weakened the influence of the League, and by 1630 most of them had deserted the alliance, although the free cities of Hamburg, Lübeck, and Bremen continued to be known as Hanse towns, and retained their local self-government, until the latter part of the 19th century.

Hapsburg. On the top of the Wülpelsberg (1,682 feet high), in Northern Switzerland, near the junction of the little River Reuss with the Aar, stands the ruined Hawk's Castle (*Habichtsburg*) which was the original seat of the famous Hapsburg (or Habsburg) family. The castle was erected in 1020, and its owners ruled Austria from 1278 to the end of the First World War (1914–18). With the single exception of Charles VII (1742–45), all the rulers of the Holy Roman Empire, from 1438 until the abolition of the empire in 1806, were members of the Hapsburg House. The Emperor Charles V (1519–56) was by descent on his father's side a Hapsburg (*see* Charles V, Holy Roman Emperor). After the division of his dominions there were two Hapsburg Houses, one ruling Spain until the extinction of the line in 1700, and the other Austria. A full lower lip and a long pointed chin— the famous Hapsburg chin—became family features after a marriage with a Bohemian princess in the 15th century. (*See* Austria-Hungary).

BUILDINGS OF THE HANSEATIC LEAGUE IN OLD BERGEN

Reconstruction by R. Christiansen, from Schäfer, Die Deutsche Hansa

The Norwegian port of Bergen with its shipping and fishing industries attracted the German merchants of the Hansa as an ideal place for their purposes ; and from the middle of the 14th to the middle of the 16th century the Hanseatic League was established there, controlling most of the trade. Above is a reconstruction of the so-called German bridge on the north side of the harbour. It consisted of a row of gabled wooden houses and warehouses facing the busy quay.

Harbours. Ships need "harbours of refuge," where they may shelter from storms; such sheltering places may often also serve as commercial harbours, where goods can be landed and taken in conveniently. A harbour is designed to provide safe accommodation, and to allow easy access to and from the open sea in any weather. A natural harbour is an inlet or an arm of the sea which is protected from storm danger by the shape of the land. An example is Milford Haven, on the coast of Pembrokeshire. The mouths of some rivers (for example, the Thames, Mersey and Humber) form other natural harbours, though here Man has to supplement the protection.

Artificial harbours are made by building breakwaters to afford protection. Ancient Tyre and Sidon were early examples of such harbours. Dover Harbour, with its fine basins enclosed or shielded by massive banks of masonry, is a modern instance.

The commercial prosperity of a nation depends a great deal on the nature of its coast-line. For commerce, with the progress in civilization which follows on its heels, most readily springs up where there are well-sheltered harbours, in which ships may safely load and unload their cargoes.

Despite its vast potential wealth, Africa, with the exception of the narrow strip along the Mediterranean, remained undeveloped until the 19th century, largely because it has so few natural harbours. The civilization we enjoy today was born in the Mediterranean lands, where safe harbours tempted men to traverse the sea, and interchange products and ideas.

Rivalry between nations for harbours has brought many wars, for the state without a coast-line is at the mercy of any state whose territory it must cross to reach the ocean. The inland country strives for a strip of land along the sea, a single port, or even the establishment of a " free port " where its goods may be shipped without customs duties. The treaties that followed the First World War (1914–18) brought Poland a " corridor to the sea " through German territory, and access to a port in the free city of Danzig. The treaties at the same time deprived Austria of its sea-coast along the Adriatic. This land, with the ports of Trieste and Fiume, went to Italy.

Australian National Travel Association

SYDNEY HARBOUR: FAMED THROUGHOUT THE WORLD

Capital of New South Wales and one of the chief seaports of Australia, Sydney owes its origin and subsequent prosperity to the fine natural harbour on whose shores it is built. From the Pacific coast the harbour extends some 13 miles inland and has an area of about 22 square miles, with a coast-line of 188 miles, so indented that the wharves are close to the heart of the city. In this view the famous Sydney bridge is seen in the foreground.

Germany's determination to repossess herself of the Polish Corridor, and to incorporate Danzig again in the Reich, led to the war with Poland in 1939—and thus to the Second World War. At the end of that struggle, Trieste was made an internationally controlled region—an arrangement which satisfied none of the neighbouring States.

The discovery of America turned the eyes of Europe westward, and the excellent harbours on Europe's west coast brought wealth and power to the countries owning them. Nearly all the early centres of settlement in North and South America were at some bay or river mouth, which afforded shelter to the vessels coming to the new land.

The rapid growth of the United States and its commercial and industrial importance are due, in part, to its long strip of coast on the two great oceans dotted with fine harbours.

Immense sums have been spent on improving natural harbours or constructing artificial ones. Tremendous breakwaters and jetties have been built far out into the sea to afford a safe refuge within. Other jetties have been built to narrow the channel and increase the scouring effect of the current, thus deepening the water in the fairway. Constant dredging is necessary in many harbours to remove the sand and silt deposited by tides and rivers. London, Liverpool, Bristol, Le Havre, and many other ports with tidal harbours have immense " wet docks," with miles of basins, to which ships are admitted by gates that retain the waters at low tide.

The profits of commerce repay the immense expense of constructing artificial harbours. Dover has one of the largest artificial harbours. More than two miles of concrete breakwaters enclose a square mile of water, which has a minimum depth of 40 feet.

In many cases, river channels have been dredged deeper, or canals have been dug to turn inland towns into harbours large enough to receive ocean-going vessels. An example is Manchester, which is connected with the ocean by the River Mersey and the Manchester Ship Canal, 35 miles long, allowing steamers to unload cargoes from foreign ports in its docks. The River Clyde, home of shipbuilding, is the outstanding example whereby a tortuous, shallow river, miles from the sea, has been made navigable for the largest ships afloat. Another notable instance is the port of Hamburg, 75 miles from the sea. Continuous dredging deepened the channel of the Elbe from 15 feet to about 40 feet.

All great harbours are equipped with dry docks and other facilities for repairing ships and cleaning their hulls. (*See* Dock; Dredger).

While commercial harbours almost always are made where Nature has at least provided a starting point, the demands of wartime may call for the creation of a harbour on an open beach. A striking example of this last was the building of what came to be known (for wartime secrecy) as the " Mulberry " (*q.v.*) harbours constructed for the use of Anglo-American armies when they invaded France from the Normandy beaches in 1944. Immense units made of reinforced concrete in Britain were towed out to the French coast and there assembled—a magnificent engineering enterprise.

Hardy, THOMAS (1840–1928). One of the few authors whose works have been accepted as classics in their lifetime, this great tragic novelist was born near Dorchester in Dorsetshire on June 2, 1840, and passed most of his long life in that region of woodland and heathy moor which he called by the old name Wessex (kingdom of the West Saxons), and which forms the setting of most of his writings.

He was educated at local schools and by private tutors, and for a time studied at King's College,

Photochrom

THOMAS HARDY'S BIRTHPLACE
At Upper Bockhampton in Dorset is this thatched house in which Thomas Hardy was born. His novels immortalize the people of ' Wessex,' especially those of Dorset. Hardy was awarded the Order of Merit in 1910. See portrait in page 1215.

London. At the age of 16 he began the study of architecture, and later went to London as assistant to an architect. He had already begun to write, and for a time was uncertain whether to make architecture or letters his profession, but after the publication of his first really successful novel, Far From the Madding Crowd, in 1874, he decided to retire to Dorset and devote himself to writing.

Hardy was interested in the simple primitive folk of the countryside, with their strong, elemental instincts and passions. Still more was he concerned with Nature in all its moods and changes, not merely as the great background against which he showed Man moving onward to his destiny, but also as a power which enters into the very life of Man, sometimes sympathetic, more often cruel. In The Return of the Native, for example, it is Egdon Heath, in its sombre power, that dominates the life of his characters. In his poetry, however, he is less troubled, yet always conscious of the inexorable Fate over all men and women.

The intense, almost overwhelmingly sombre Jude the Obscure (1895) brought such an outcry from critics and public alike, that thereafter Hardy refused to write further novels, and devoted himself to poetry. Thus his work falls into three periods: first, as a novelist (till 1896); then came The Dynasts, a dramatic, blank verse chronicle of England during the Napoleonic Wars; finally his work as a lyric poet. He died on January 11, 1928.

Hardy's chief other novels are: Under the Greenwood Tree (1872); The Trumpet Major

(1880) ; and Tess of the D'Urbervilles (1891), one of the greatest novels in the language. His poetry includes Wessex Poems (1898) and Poems Past and Present (1901).

Hare. Noted for their great speed, hares are members of the large family, *Leporidae*, of rodents. Their upper lips are cleft and that is why a deformity of the upper lip in human beings is called hare-lip. Their colouring is mostly grey or brown, and they are remarkable for their long ears and hind legs, and their short curved tails. The common hare is distinguished from the rabbit by its larger size and longer legs and ears. It also differs greatly in its habits, especially in not living in burrows.

Hares usually live in the open, crouching in a furrow or in a hollow in the grass, only taking shelter in thickets in wet weather. They sit so very closely that often they will not stir until almost trodden upon. They feed mainly on grain, vegetables, and bark of young trees.

The common hare inhabits all parts of Europe except Ireland, Scandinavia and Northern Russia. It is 20 to 22 inches in length and weighs six to eight pounds. The Alpine hare is found in Scandinavia and Northern Russia and resembles the Arctic hare of North America. A related species, *Lepus hibernicus*, is found in Ireland.

Hargreaves, JAMES (1730?–78). The obscurity of this inventor contrasts sharply with the world-wide importance of his invention, the spinning jenny. He was born probably at Stand-hill in Lancashire. Then, as now, Lancashire was the centre of England's manufacture of cotton goods, but the industry was still confined merely to workmen's homes, and the cards, spinning wheels and looms were operated by hand. Hargreaves became a skilled carpenter and spinner, and made an ingenious carding machine for a neighbour.

The story goes that an accident gave Hargreaves the idea for his spinning jenny. In his crowded cottage, which was both home and workshop, he had been experimenting with spinning two threads at once, with the wheel upright and the two spindles held horizontally. But the threads were in too close contact, and constantly became tangled. Then one of his children upset the wheel so that the spindles were vertical and the threads flew apart as wide as the wheel's diameter. Hargreaves seized the idea and set the spindles vertically in a frame. This invention, made some time between 1764 and 1767, enabled him to spin eight threads at once. He called it a spinning jenny, in honour of either his wife or his daughter.

The amount of cotton yarn Hargreaves began to turn out alarmed his rivals, who feared that his machine would leave nothing for them to do; so they broke into his home and destroyed his jenny. He moved to Nottingham, where he set up a fairly profitable yarn mill, and in 1770 he patented the spinning jenny. As he had previously sold several of his machines, the patent was declared void according to the law. This left others free to seize upon his invention without paying him royalties. Consequently, it came into wide use. The production of cotton yarn increased vastly. Even during his lifetime jennies were built to spin as many as 20 threads at once.

Other inventors were also at work in solving the same problem, and before Hargreaves's death, in 1778, mechanical spinning was fully developed by Richard Arkwright and Samuel Crompton. The stories of these two inventors, told in separate articles, are sequels to this sketch of James Hargreaves, as is also that of Edmund Cartwright, the man who invented the power loom.

Chicago Mus. of Science and Industry
HARGREAVES'S SPINNING JENNY
The first machine to spin 20 threads at the same time was invented by James Hargreaves (1730?–78). The loosely twisted yarn was wound on bobbins (1), from which they passed through a movable clasp (2) which the operator pushed to and fro with his left hand. From the clasp they extended to the spindles (3), and when they were attached to these the operator turned the large wheel with his right hand. A belt from the wheel turned a cylinder (4), and smaller belts carried the power to the bottoms of the spindles. As these revolved, the yarn slipped off their tops and was spun into thread. When the threads had received the proper twist, the operator pulled a wire which caused a bar (5) to drop down over the threads so that they were wound on the spindles instead of slipping over the tops.

Harold, KINGS OF ENGLAND.   Only two kings of England have borne the name of Harold; both reigned before the Norman Conquest (1066).

Harold I (died 1040) was the son of the Danish monarch Canute (c. 994–1035), who ruled Denmark and Norway as well as England.   When

HARPS OLD AND NEW
Of extremely ancient origin, the harp as we know it today (right) resembles in many respects the instrument played by an Egyptian girl (above) in a tomb painting of 2000 B.C.

Canute died in 1035 Harold claimed the English crown in opposition to his half-brother Hardicanute.   Both claimants had powerful supporters, but finally, in 1037, Harold became king.   His reign was uneventful except for minor invasions of England by the Welsh and Scots.

The reign of Harold II (c. 1022–66), the last king of the Anglo-Saxon period, lasted less than nine months.   For several years before the death of Edward the Confessor, in 1066, Harold had been the chief man in the kingdom, and when Edward died without direct heirs, Harold was chosen by the nobles to succeed him.

William, Duke of Normandy, laid claim to the English throne on the strength of a promise made by Edward that the crown should descend to him, and because of an oath sworn by Harold to aid in obtaining it.   When William invaded England to make good his claim, Harold was in the north, where he had been called to repel an attack by the Danes, whom he defeated at Stamford Bridge. Hastening south, Harold met the Norman invaders, only to fall in the Battle of Hastings or Senlac on October 14, 1066.   (*See* illus., page 1196).

Harp.   From primitive times men knew that a stretched bowstring gave out a pleasant, twanging sound when it was plucked; it is easy to understand how some musically-inclined genius conceived the idea of adding other strings of different lengths, thus producing a primitive harp on which simple melodies and chords could be produced.   Greek legend gives an account of how the cithara or lyre, a harplike instrument, was invented by the precocious god Hermes (Mercury), who put strings across a tortoise's shell not long after his birth, and made sweet music.   The great antiquity of the harp is also indicated by Egyptian paintings thousands of years old, which picture the harp in various stages of development, from a form obviously derived from the hunter's bow to elaborately carved, triangular instruments much like the harp of today.   Some of these early Egyptian harps, dating from about 1500 years before Christ, are to be seen in the British Museum, London.   Much like these were the harps used by the ancient Hebrews, in their religious ceremonies, and by the early Irish.

In the modern harp the strings are stretched between the sounding board, which rests against the player, and a gracefully curved bracket connecting the top of the sounding board with an upright pillar.   Through this pillar pass rods, worked by pedals at the base of the harp, by means of which the pitch of the strings is changed, so that the harp can be used in various keys, the fingering remaining the same.

If a pedal is pressed half-way down, the note is raised a semitone; if pressed fully down, it is raised a tone.   At one side of the grooves in which the pedals work, in the pedestal of the harp, are two notches into which they can be hitched when required.   So three different tones can be produced on every one of the strings, of which there are usually 46; this gives the harp a very wide range.

These ingenious double-action pedals—of which there are seven—were invented by Sebastien Erard (1752–1831), a French manufacturer of musical instruments, who was also noted for his improvements of the piano.   By perfecting the harp in this and other respects, Erard greatly amplified its possibilities for orchestral use.   The harp is one of the most difficult instruments to play.

Harte, FRANCIS BRET (1839–1902).   When he caught the spirit of the lawless, primitive life of the early California mining camps and put it into his vivid short stories, Bret Harte started the American story of local colour and atmosphere, which sprang into instant popularity. Harte was born on August 25, 1839, and at the age of 15 went to California, where he spent three years as a gold-miner and schoolteacher.   While he was at work in a San Francisco newspaper office, he wrote the first of his sketches, and was at once promoted to the editorial staff.   He became

BRET HARTE
Famous for his stories of life in the western United States, Bret Harte died in England in 1902.

editor of the Overland Monthly in 1868, and contributed to it The Luck of Roaring Camp (1868) and The Outcasts of Poker Flats (1869), the most famous of his stories of rough western life. Harte had a talent, too, for humorous verse, and the world laughed at his Heathen Chinee (1870), the Chinaman with the " smile that was childlike and bland," who turned the tables on two white men who tried to cheat him at cards.

Bret Harte's fame had spread so far, meanwhile, that the Atlantic Monthly asked him to write for it alone. He went east in 1870, lectured awhile on California life, then was sent as consul to Crefeld in Germany, and later to Glasgow, Scotland. His last years, after 1885, were spent in England, where he died on May 5, 1902. He was the author of many other short stories and one long novel. He wrote some serious poems, too, of which certain ones deserve a wider reading than they receive.

Harvest.

With the coming of August, the thoughts of all who live in the country turn to the harvesting of the corn. Some kind of crop is being harvested in almost every month of the year, but it is as August merges into September that the farmer and his assistants have their busiest season. The word corn is a general term, and is applied to practically all kinds of grain. It may mean wheat, oats, or barley, and is generally used to denote the kind of grain (or cereal as it is called) most widely grown in the district. (In America it is used for maize.)

Among the chief cereals, barley is allowed to remain standing until the grains are fully ripe and the ears bend down, while oats and wheat are cut before fully mature, as otherwise the grain is liable to fall out and be lost. The sickle for reaping, and hand labour for making up the sheaves, have been superseded by the reaping machine and self-binder—or by the combine-harvester. Wagons may be loaded by means of a mechanical loader, and stack-building is done by employment of an elevator. When stacks are built in the open the principles of construction and thatching are similar to those generally used for hay. It is usual to raise the stack from the ground on supports

which prevent or hinder attacks by rats and mice.

Ceremonies and celebrations associated with the gathering of the harvest are of immemorial antiquity. They originated in worship of the Nature deities associated with the growth of crops. Among the Romans, the Cerealia were feasts in honour of Ceres, and many widely disseminated customs are linked with the Greek legends of Demeter (goddess of agriculture) and her daughter Persephone, who spent half the year in the underworld.

One custom which, with but slight variations. can be traced among widely separated peoples, is the forming of a crude figure—sometimes merely a handful of corn decorated—which is borne in procession as a personification of the crop, and made the central figure of the festivities. This custom still survives in parts of England, Ireland, and Scotland, where a harvest doll or kern, i.e., corn baby, is fashioned from some of the last corn into the semblance of a human figure, dressed up, and carried with the last wagon-load of the harvest.

In Scotland, the last sheaf, called the Maiden or the Old Woman, according to whether it is cut before or after Hallowe'en (October 31) may be kept till Christmas morning, when it is distributed to the cattle to give them health throughout the next year, or is hung up until replaced by its next year's successor. Similar customs are recorded in various other European countries, and are believed to be relics of the far distant times when human beings were sacrificed to make the crops grow.

Another custom is the harvest supper, given by the owner of the crop to all who help to garner it. The Jews feasted at the gathering of the harvest and made a thank-offering of the first fruits, and among the pagan peoples the heads of families feasted on terms of equality with their servants. In England, the supper was the crowning celebration of the harvest home, and from the fact that a goose was the principal dish on these occasions the custom of eating a goose on Michaelmas Day (September 29) originated. In Scotland, too, the " kern supper," upon the completion of the harvest, became an important social event.

HARVEST GRAIN FOR THE BIRDS
Observances connected with the gathering of the harvest are very old. Here the rector of Ackworth, Yorkshire, is hanging up wheat for the birds. More than 1,000 years ago, Norsemen offered grain to the mythical ravens who acted as messengers to the god Odin.

In these feasts, as in many more primitive customs, it is easy to see a reflection of the farmer's joy that his labours have been rewarded.

Harvey, WILLIAM (1578–1657). Most people know the heart is a pump which sends blood constantly circulating through the arteries and veins. Yet though for centuries it had been realized that blood courses throughout the body there were various strange theories as to its journeying. It was not until the year 1616 that William Harvey announced in his lectures his discovery of the organized circulation of the blood, by way of arteries, arterioles, venules, and veins, through the regular pulsations of the heart. He pointed out that the small size of the heart made it impossible that it could be anything but the same blood that goes and returns. His discovery opened up a new field of research into nutrition and the chemistry of the blood, proving as it did that the blood is the vehicle by which all food reaches the tissues.

Harvey was born at Folkestone on April 1, 1578, and was educated at Canterbury and Caius College, Cambridge. He afterwards studied at Padua, Italy, but returned to London in 1602. He became a fellow of the College of Physicians in 1607, and was appointed physician to St. Bartholomew's Hospital in 1609. During the years of the Civil War (1642–48) he occupied himself with his scientific studies and wrote important works on the subjects of generation and respiration.

He was distrusted by many fellow physicians after his discovery, but he lived to see it fully recognized. Harvey died on June 3, 1657, and there is a statue of him on the Leas, at Folkestone, Kent. (*See* Blood ; Heart.)

Harz Mountains, (Pron. harts), GERMANY. Quaint old towns, ruined castles, and fantastic rock masses, rich with the romance of many centuries, abound in the deep, wooded valleys of the beautiful Harz Mountains. This range lies in west-central Germany, between the rivers Elbe and Weser, extending 57 miles to the north-west, and averaging about 20 miles in width.

The upper slopes are bare of trees, but grazing is plentiful. The lower slopes support forests of pine and fir, and all the valleys are thickly wooded.

The highest elevation is the Brocken, a dome-shaped mass of granite, 3,745 feet high—the highest peak in Central Germany. Many legends have sprung up about the Brocken, which was a stronghold of Teutonic paganism long after the rest of Germany had been converted to Christianity. The peak is also famed for the Spectre of the Brocken. This is the hugely magnified shadow, seen on the clouds, of anyone standing on the summit between the clouds and the sun.

The richest stores of minerals in all Germany lie in these mountains, making mining the chief industry. Veins of lead with a mixture of silver abound, and gold, copper, iron, and sulphur are also found in the region.

Hastings, BATTLE OF (1066). The engagement commonly called the Battle of Hastings was actually fought at Senlac, about six miles away. Duke William of Normandy, who claimed the throne of England against King Harold, succeeded in landing his army without active opposition at Pevensey Bay, on the Sussex coast. At dawn on

Royal College of Physicians

HARVEY, PIONEER PHYSICIAN
In the list of great doctors William Harvey occupies a high place, because he discovered that our blood is circulated by pulsations of the heart. Here we see him as painted by his Dutch contemporary, Cornelius Janssen (c. 1593–1664).

October 14, 1066, he roused his troops and set out on an eight-mile march to attack the English, who had occupied the crest of a steep hill.

The English were about as numerous as the Normans, and were packed closely together on foot, protected by their great shields. They repulsed attack after attack of the mounted Normans, using long-handled battle-axes with terrible effect.

Towards evening Harold was struck by an arrow and fell mortally wounded. His two brothers had already been slain, and the picked troops who guarded his standard were killed. The rest then fled, leaving the Normans victorious. In after days Battle Abbey was erected to mark the battlefield.

Hastings, which gave its name to the battle, is a thriving Sussex town and seaside resort, with a population of about 65,000.

Hastings, WARREN (1732–1818). Clive may have laid the foundations of the British power in India, but it was his successor, Warren Hastings, who built on those foundations in such a way as to create the Indian Empire.

Hastings was born at Churchill, Oxfordshire, on December 6, 1732, and was early left an orphan under the care of an uncle who sent him to Westminster School, London. In 1750 a clerkship in the East India Company was obtained for him, and he arrived in India at the age of 18.

When Suraj-ud-Dowlah, the ruler of Bengal, attacked the British in Calcutta, Hastings was at a cotton factory near the town, and for a time was held prisoner. Clive marched against the Indian prince, and Hastings joined his force as a volunteer, to help in the recovery of Calcutta. Clive recognized his abilities, and made him agent of the East India Company at the court of a native prince.

After 14 years in India, Hastings returned to England in 1764. In 1772—following Clive's retirement and the most terrible famine in India's history—Hastings was appointed Governor of the province of Bengal, and later was made Governor-General in India for the Company.

His administration, which lasted until 1785, marks a great epoch in the extension of British rule. In the beginning, the East India Company was merely a trading corporation, having nothing to do with governing the land outside its own trading posts. Now it took over, in addition, the chief work of government in wide stretches of the land— collecting the taxes and maintaining armies, and leaving to the native rulers only shadowy power. Elsewhere, also, the Company undertook to furnish the princes with military protection, in return for large money payments.

Hastings had to watch the interests of the Company, and to wage wars for the protection of their territories. Meanwhile the French were plotting in the south with powerful Indian princes.

National Portrait Gallery

WARREN HASTINGS

First Governor-General of British India, Warren Hastings (1732-1818) ranks, with Clive, as one of India's greatest administrators. This portrait is by Sir Thomas Lawrence (1769-1831).

Hastings found difficulty in finding money for these various wars, for many of the princes had failed to pay the sums due for their protection.

Hastings accordingly forced the Rajah of Benares to pay the amount he owed, and also collected arrears from a weak prince in Oudh—using high-handed methods. These two debts collected, Hastings was able to send an army to Madras, where Hyder Ali with a huge army was laying waste the land. After defeating two British generals, Hyder Ali was routed by General Coote, and his French allies were driven from the sea by a British fleet.

Hastings retired in 1785, after completing Clive's great work, but the methods he used to raise money in India had created for him a host of enemies. Chief of these was Sir Philip Francis, a member of the Council of Bengal, whom he had wounded in a duel at Calcutta. Hastings was now accused of extorting money from the native rulers, and of oppressive and tyrannical rule. At home the orator Burke and the playwright Sheridan took the lead in demanding his formal accusation and his trial by Parliament. For seven years the trial dragged on; it ended in Hastings' acquittal but the expense made him a poor man. He died on August 22, 1818.

A GLANCE *at the* WORLD'S HEADGEAR

*E*xcept *on formal occasions, many people today go hatless in countries where climate and weather permit. But there is plenty of interest and variety still in the making and wearing of the world's hats and caps.*

Hats and Caps. We must distinguish between head coverings, of which the original function was protection, and head-dresses, worn for display or distinction. As we might expect, the first class developed into the second very often, and the simple hat or cap became the elaborate or gaily ornamented headgear of the soldier, the sailor or other official persons. Rank came to be indicated by a distinctive headgear as well as by other dress styles. On the other hand, in lands where head protection from the weather was not required, the elaborate, grotesque or highly decorated head-dress came to mark out the chief and the priest or the medicine-man from the rest of the community.

The kaleidoscopic changes in head coverings throughout the centuries are best shown by pictures, and the colour plate facing page 1584 illustrates a series ranging from the Phrygian cap and the skull-cap of the ancient Egyptians to the Highland bonnet and the tweed cap of today.

Until the train and the motor car brought about more frequent intercourse between people of different lands, and opened up towns and villages formerly isolated by natural boundaries or barriers, distinctive national dress was common. In Britain easier communications have obliterated most of these national distinctions in headgear, but we still have the steeple-crowned hat of Welsh women, worn on ceremonial occasions, and the Scots bonnets still commonly worn. On the Continent of Europe different regions or even villages had their quaint and pretty hats and caps, and many are worn today.

Protective or merely convenient hats and caps are worn by workers in certain trades or crafts. Examples are the flapped leathern hats worn by dustmen and sewermen; the leather hat worn by miners; the broad-rimmed and padded hat worn by fish porters for ease of carrying the boxes of fish on the head.

From the protective hat to the helmet is a short step. Military helmets and those worn by the other fighting services and Civil Defence personnel belong to "armour," but there are others, such as the padded crash-helmet worn by racing motorists, which are not very different from hats. One reason why some building trade workers wear hard felt hats is that these afford some protection from falling objects on the building site. But the city man's

PROCESSES IN THE MAKING OF MEN'S HATS

1. To start, the furs are cleaned and strengthened with nitrate of mercury, applied with a coarse brush. This is called "carroting"

2. After seasoning in storage they are dampened, brushed, and passed through cutting machines, which remove the hide. The cut fur is then sorted and stored

3. Before making into hats the fur is "blown" or passed through rotating machines, which pick it apart

4. An air current then sucks it onto the damp surface of a forming cone, which soon is covered with a thin layer of "felt." This is the hat body

5. After careful treatment and toughening, the body is shrunk

6. In the "pulling out" department the body begins to resemble the familiar shape

7. Exact shape and size are obtained by "blocking"

8. The felt is now given a smooth finish in the "pouncing" machines—

9. —and steamed, sponged, and ironed

10. The hat is then placed in a wooden form and the brim, cut to the right width, is "flanged" or curled-under a huge bag of heated sand

11. In the trimming department the hat is completed, and after one more "flanging" it is ready to pack and ship.

Fur alone is used only in the manufacture of the finer grades of men's felt hats, as shown above. Cheaper hats are made from a mixture of wool and fur, or wool alone. Women's hats are produced in factories, wholesale workrooms, and—the more expensive ones—in small shops which sell direct to the customer. The factories and shops buy hat 'bodies,' usually of felt or straw, which have been cut on a form, and then shape, block and trim them.

bowler hat is nothing more than a durable protection from the weather. The straw boater, once commonly worn in summer months, was rivalled by the soft straw hat but held its place, though the widespread custom of wearing no hat at all in good weather stole its popularity. The straw boater, with its wide flat brim, is worn still by meat-market salesmen, butchers and fishmongers to some extent.

Examples of hats and caps worn today as marks of rank or office are the cardinal's hat, the bishop's mitre, and the clergyman's biretta. Ministers of religion once generally wore a round, wide-brimmed felt hat as a mark of their office, but more and more of them adopt an ordinary soft felt hat of normal shape. Then there are the various flat caps worn at colleges, to one of which the nickname of mortar-board has become attached.

The many processes through which a felt hat passes before it is ready for the wearer are shown in our full-page picture (page 1583). In England the felt hat industry has its centre around Manchester; straw hats are made in large numbers at Luton. Hats for women are made from all kinds of material beside felt and straw; the shape, style and material vary from season to season.

How a Felt Hat is Made

If ever you get the chance, visit one of our great felt-hat factories, and see how a soft felt hat or a bowler is made. For the finer grades, fur alone is used; but cheaper hats are made from a mixture of wool and fur, or wool alone. The first step is to clean and brush the fur while it is still on the skin. Then a machine shears off the fur, which passes on an endless belt to blowing machines. In these, the soft fluff is torn apart by steel teeth, and freed from hairs or foreign material.

Now begins the transformation into a hat. The exact amount of fur needed to make one hat is passed to a boxed-in machine, which contains a minutely perforated copper cone, about three feet high. As this cone revolves, myriads of the mist-like fur particles are drawn by suction to its damp outer side, forming a thin covering of felt. A wet cloth is thrown over this matted fur, another cone is pressed over it, and the whole is placed in a tank of hot water, until it " felts" or mats together.

The delicate cone of felted cloth is then shrunk to the proper size, dyed, and given a bath of shellac, or some similar resin, to stiffen it—weak shellac for soft hats, and a denser solution for stiff hats. The cone is now plunged in boiling water and flattened at the crown, so that it begins to take on the appearance of a hat. It is stretched, blocked (pressed to shape on a mould or block), and pulled with the aid of hot water, steam, and machinery, until it has taken the desired form.

Stiff hats are put in a hydraulic press to increase their rigidity, and the brim is curled by being pressed on a flange. The rough surface is smoothed by rubbing with abrasive, the trimming is put on, and, last of all, the leather band is attached inside—and the hat is ready for the wearer.

Straw boaters and similar hats are made from carefully prepared imported straw. The braids, except in some of the finer grades, are sewn and pressed into shape by machinery, after being sized with waterproof gum. Panama hats are made from a very fine light " straw " (toquilla) obtained from

the leaves of a shrub that grows in South America, chiefly in Ecuador, though it is also found in Colombia and the forests of the upper Amazon.

In the manufacture of silk (" top ") hats, now chiefly used for ceremonial occasions, several layers of cotton material are cemented together with shellac. This " body " is pressed into shape on a block, and the rim is cemented to it. Then it is coated with shellac, covered with silk plush, trimmed and finished.

Did you ever notice the tiny bow that decorates the lining or inner band of most hats, both men's and women's ? Not so very long ago hats were made in only a few sizes, and a draw-string was inserted in the lining, which was tightened or loosened to fit the head. The little bow is a relic of that old practice, now obsolete.

During the 14th and 15th centuries women's hats, caps, and hoods were of the most extravagant shapes and sizes. Some were horned, others were great cones like a dunce's cap, from one foot to three feet in height. Sometimes a veil would be draped over these towering structures, falling the length of the dress.

Hats have often had an important place in distinguishing sects and parties. The Puritan wore his severe, high-crowned hat over his cropped head as a rebuke to the cavalier of the time, with his hair in curls, and a great sweeping plume on his low-crowned hat. The Quaker affected a broad-brimmed, grey hat. During the greater part of the 18th century two rival political parties in Sweden, known as Hats and Caps, were in constant struggle, the " Hats " representing the nobles, and the " Caps " the common people.

In the House of Commons, members may wear their hats while seated, but take them off when they rise to speak. But in one special case—after a debate has been closed and a vote ordered, but before it is actually taken—a member who wishes to raise a point of order must speak seated, and with his hat on.

Havana. Largest city of the West Indies, and the capital of Cuba, Havana is situated on the north coast of the island and is a busy commercial centre. It is connected by railway and motor roads with all the chief towns, and there are air services to the North American cities. The Bay of Havana affords one of the safest harbours.

Havana consists of the Old and New towns. The old quarter, lying within the limits of the ancient walls, built between 1671 and 1740, and almost completely dismantled between 1863 and 1880, is very cramped. The new town is on more spacious lines, and generally presents a clean and well-planned appearance, with fine promenades, squares and streets, some of them lined with trees. The remains of Christopher Columbus lay for a century in the Cathedral, which was completed in 1724, until they were moved to Spain for internment at Seville in 1898.

The main industry is the manufacture of cigars and tobacco. Sugar is also produced in large quantities, other manufactures being carriages, wagons and machinery.

Founded by the Spaniards on the south coast in 1515, Havana was removed to its present site in 1519. It was captured by the English in 1762, and restored to Spain in 1763. On February 15,

HATS & CAPS OF MANY LANDS AND AGES

Specially drawn by J. F. Campbell

A key naming the fifty-six types of headgear seen in this page is given on the back of this plate.

HEADGEAR THROUGH THE AGES

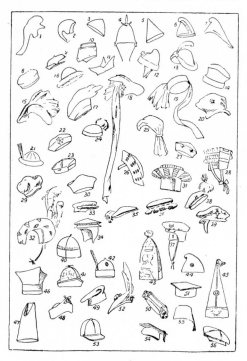

1, Phrygian. 2, Ancient Egyptian skull-cap. 3, Ancient Greek felt cap. 4, Cap of priest in Ancient Rome. 5 and 6, Anglo-Saxon. 7, 8, and 9, Anglo-Norman. 10, Spanish, 13th century. 11, English *c.* 1300. 12, Cap of Doge of Venice *c.* 1300. 13, English, 14th century. 14, Italian, *c.* 1400. 15 and 16, English, *c.* 1400. 17 and 18, French, *c.* 1400. 19, Roundlet, 15th century. 20, Jewelled bag cap, 15th century. 21, 22, and 23, Middle 15th century. 24, English, late 15th century. 25, Burgundian, 1456. 26, 27, and 28, Late 15th century. 29, Cardinal's, *c.* 1500. 30, Bishop's, *c.* 1500. 31, French, 16th century. 32, Milanese, 16th century. 33, 34, and 35, English flat caps, 16th century. 36, Middle 16th century. 37, German, *c.* 1550. 38, Cap of Knight of Garter, 16th century. 39, English, 16th century. 40 and 41, Indoor caps, 17th and 18th century. 42, Running footman's cap, early 18th century. 43, Grenadier cap, middle 18th century. 44, French Cap of Liberty, late 18th century. 45, Jacobin cap, worn doubled over. 46, Laplander's. 47, Persian. 48, Russian. 49 and 50, Spanish 51, Polish. 52, Highland Chief's. 53, Huntsman's. 54, College cap. 55, Fez. 56, Tweed cap, 20th century.

To face page 1585

1898, the United States warship Maine was blown up in the harbour, the incident leading to the Spanish-American War of 1898. When the independent Republic of Cuba was proclaimed in December 1898, Havana became the capital of the new State. The population of the city is 783,000.

Havre, (Pron. ah'-vr), FRANCE. Called Le Havre (the harbour) by the French and situated at the mouth of the River Seine is Havre, one of the chief seaports of France. Almost entirely modern, the town has few features of interest, being purely a commercial centre. There are important engineering works, shipbuilding yards, oil refineries, chemical and dye works, and a State tobacco factory. Havre is the main centre for French trade with North America, the docks being extensive and well constructed.

During the First World War (1914–18) Havre was a base of the British Expeditionary Force, and between October 1914 and November 1918 was the seat of the exiled Belgian Government. In the

IN HAVANA, LARGEST CITY OF THE WEST INDIES

Capital of Cuba, and possessed of a magnificent harbour, Havana consists of two towns, the old and the new. The modern quarter has well-designed buildings, generally constructed of white coral limestone, bordering tree-lined streets. Here is the important residential and business thoroughfare Paseo de Marti, or Prado, in which stands the Capitol, or Houses of Parliament.

Second World War (1939–45) it was again a British military base and was occupied by German forces on June 14, 1940. It became a German port for the intended invasion of England and as such was frequently bombed by the R.A.F.

After the Allied landings on the coast of Normandy in June 1944 the isolated German garrison in Havre offered stubborn resistance, and the town suffered an intensive bombardment from the sea and air. By the time that the Germans surrendered on September 12, 1944, the port had been devastated. The population is 107,000.

Hawaiian Islands. (Pron. hah-wī'-yan). In the middle of the Pacific Ocean, 2,000 miles from North America and Asia, are the Hawaiian Islands. They are really the tops of 15 or more enormous volcanoes which have been built up from the bottom of the ocean. Hawaii, the largest and most southerly island, consists of five volcanic mountains, which have encroached upon one another by their eruptions. There are now no active volcanoes, except on Hawaii; but all the islands are mountainous, in many places rising from the sea in sheer cliffs hundreds of feet in height.

Cooled in summer and warmed in winter by the ocean winds, this group of islands is seldom too hot and never cold; the temperature being about 10 degrees lower than in other lands of the same latitude. Owing to the north-east trade winds

Dorien Leigh

HAWAIIAN ISLANDERS SURF-RIDING

At Honolulu, on the Hawaiian island of Oahu, one of the favourite sports is surf-riding. Here riders on their surf-boards are being carried shorewards on the crest of a wave. Honolulu is a busy port, sending abroad sugar and tinned fruit; six miles to the west is the United States naval base of Pearl Harbour.

FRUIT AND FUN IN THE HAWAIIAN ISLANDS

E.N.A.; *Dorien Leigh*

Pineapples are the most important of the fruits grown in the Hawaiian Islands, and in the warm climate they ripen quickly in the open. Straight rows of the spiny plants cover mile upon mile of fertile, red, volcanic soil in the rolling uplands (top). The girls dancing at Honolulu (lower) are wearing skirts made of strips of the inner bark of the paper mulberry tree and garlands of flowers. The Hawaiians are a tall handsome race, with brown skin and black hair. They are fond of riding, bathing and other outdoor sports, and they have a passionate love of music and dancing.

the islands are well watered on their northern side, the rainfall amounting in some places to 250 inches a year. The southern slopes, however, are almost arid, and crops are grown under irrigation. The decomposed lava rock makes a rich, deep, red earth most favourable to agriculture.

The area of the group, which is a Territory of the United States, is 6,420 square miles. On Hawaii, which is twice as large as all the other islands together, are the volcanoes of Mauna Kea and Mauna Loa. Mauna Loa, the largest active volcano in the world, has erupted frequently in modern times. Hilo, the chief town of the island and the second port of the archipelago, lies on the north-east coast. Cattle and sheep ranches in the interior raise most of the Territory's meat. Sugar-cane and pineapple plantations cover the plains.

Oahu ranks only third in size; but it is considered the main island because it is the site of Honolulu, the chief port and capital of the Territory. Six miles west of Honolulu lies Pearl Harbour, the United States naval base, with its barracks, workshops and huge dry docks. On Oahu, as on the other large islands, the arable lowland up to about 2,000 feet is occupied by sugar-cane plantations, and above that level pineapples are grown.

Kauai is called the Garden Island because of its prosperous plantations of sugar-cane, rice and pineapples. It was here that Captain James Cook first trod Hawaiian soil in 1778; and it was here that he was killed by natives in 1779.

Cook called the group the Sandwich islands after the Earl of Sandwich, who was the head of the British Admiralty at that time, but they are now known by their native name of Hawaii. They were then ruled by chiefs who were constantly at war with one another, but in 1795 they were all united under the famous King Kamehameha I whose descendants reigned for almost 100 years. In 1893 the Queen Liliuokalani was deposed, and annexation to the United States was applied for. A treaty of annexation was concluded in 1898.

On December 7, 1941, Japanese aircraft and submarines attacked Pearl Harbour. They sank or severely damaged 13 warships and set fire to hangars, warehouses and dock installations, the onslaught bringing the United States into the Second World War (1939–45). The estimated population of the Territory is 502,000.

Hawk. Except vultures, eagles and owls, most birds of prey, including goshawks, sparrow-hawks, buzzards and harriers, are called hawks.

The sparrow-hawk, which is one of two common British birds of prey, is still largely treated as a foe and mercilessly killed. Yet this bird feeds largely

John H. Vickers

YOUNG SPARROW-HAWK

When first hatched, hawks, like most other fledglings, are just balls of fluffy down, though none the less fierce for that. This youngster is growing out of the downy stage ; the first wing feathers have appeared, and the strong beak and talons typical of the bird of prey are well developed.

on vermin. It does, however, eat large numbers of small birds, and sometimes seizes chickens to feed its young, but the damage it does is probably little in comparison with its services to the farmer. It is a short-winged hawk, bluish-grey above, with a pale breast barred with grey or black. The nest, built in a tree, is made of sticks and roots, and there are from three to six eggs, pale bluish-white, with red-brown spots and blotches. The young are at first covered with white down and are very fierce little birds. In former times the sparrow-hawk was much employed in the sport of falconry (*q.v.*).

Even more common than the sparrow-hawk, especially in more open country, is the kestrel. This is the bird you may see apparently motionless in mid-air, its wings spread out, its head slightly dropped, its tail flickering up and down to help it keep stationary. Actually, the tips of the wings are also just moving, but this is barely noticeable. This habit has earned for the kestrel its apt name of wind-hover. It feeds on mice and insects, as well as small birds, and it is perhaps even more useful than the sparrow-hawk in destroying vermin. The kestrel uses the old nest of some other bird, such as a crow, or builds in a hollow tree or hole in a cliff or in masonry. Its eggs are covered all over with red-brown blotches. In colour it is a

Fred Jefferson

MALE HAWK ON THE NEST

Cock birds of many species assist in the incubation of the eggs, taking their turn with their mates. Here is a male kestrel (member of the hawk family) sitting on the reddish-brown eggs in the nest of sticks. This bird can be recognized by its regular spots and by the bar across the tip of its tail.

much browner bird than the sparrow-hawk, from which its long wings and tail further distinguish it.

The harriers, of which three species—the marsh, hen, and Montagu's harrier—all breed in Britain, are very rare, and were it not for protection would certainly become extinct, as indeed they almost were some years ago. They feed largely on partridge and poultry chicks, and are therefore very unpopular with gamekeepers and poultry-farmers. East Anglia is the home of these birds, though the hen harrier usually breeds in the Shetlands. All the harriers nest on the ground.

Other hawks in Britain, besides the buzzard (*q.v.*), are the merlin and the hobby, both small and fierce. The merlin is the typical hawk of the northern moorlands, the hobby of the woodlands in the south and southern midlands. But whereas the merlin is quite common, the hobby suffers from the foolishness of egg collectors, who rob many nests and make this interesting bird very rare. The merlin nests on the ground among deep heather; the hobby nests in trees.

F. Jefferson

MERLIN GROWING UP

Common on the northern moorlands of Great Britain, the merlin is the smallest of the British hawks. This young bird has nearly lost its down and will soon have adult plumage.

Hawkins, SIR JOHN (1532–95). Among the bold and ruthless seamen of Elizabethan England, none gained a greater reputation for reckless daring than Sir John Hawkins, who played a prominent part in the prolonged naval warfare with Spain during the reign of Queen Elizabeth.

S. V. Waters

HAWTHORN BLOSSOM

Commonly called the may tree, the hawthorn grows wild in Asia, Africa and Europe. The sweet-scented flowers may be white or pink or red, single or double. The blossom is succeeded by small red berries ('haws').

The son of a sea captain, Hawkins, like Sir Francis Drake, was a Devon man, having been born at Plymouth. He made several trading voyages to the Canary Islands, and in 1562 had three vessels under his command.

The naval commanders of those days were not very scrupulous in the pursuit of their ambitions, but some of the enterprises of Hawkins were very questionable even by the standards of those times. He had, for example, the unenviable reputation of being the first Englishman to engage in the slave traffic.

He made voyages to the coast of West Africa, where he bartered his goods for cargoes of Negroes. These unhappy people he took out to the Spanish settlements in Central and South America, and sold them into slavery in exchange for such commodities as sugar, ginger, and pearls.

A later expedition in 1567 proved unfortunate, however. The fleet of Hawkins was surprised by a Spanish admiral in the Bay of St. Juan de Vloa, off the coast of Mexico, and, after a desperate encounter, all the English ships with the exception of two were captured or sunk, with their treasure.

One of the two vessels afterwards foundered at sea, the only one to return safely to England being a small vessel commanded by Francis Drake. Hawkins managed to escape in that vessel, and afterwards rose to high rank in the Navy, becoming treasurer in 1573.

When England was threatened in 1588 by the Spanish Armada (*see* Armada, Spanish) Hawkins was vice-admiral of the fleet sent to meet the Spaniards. In association with Sir Francis Drake (died 1596), Hawkins showed great courage and ability in connexion with the operations and engagements which resulted in the complete defeat of the Armada. He was knighted for his services.

In 1595 Hawkins and Drake set forth on a joint expedition against the Spaniards. But they quarrelled, and this, together with the failure of their schemes, hastened Hawkins's death. He died of fever off Puerto Rico, in the West Indies, on November 12, 1595. (*See* Drake, Sir Francis).

Hawthorn. Milton mentions the hawthorn in his descriptions of happy pastoral scenes :

> And every shepherd tells his tale
> Under the hawthorn in the dale.

Many of our other poets have commemorated the charm of this lovely shrubby tree, which is often known as may.

The hawthorn (*Crataegus oxyacantha*), a member of the rose tribe, grows wild throughout Europe, in northern Africa and western Asia. It is often more bush than tree, and is frequently less than 25 feet high. It forms a dense growth of handsome foliage and in the early spring there is a profusion of fragrant bloom, sometimes tinged with pink, but mostly white.

The fruit, known as "haws," and usually red, with hard seeds, is as fine a sight in autumn as the flowers are in spring, but birds soon strip the trees when frosty weather comes. Besides the wild hawthorn, many fine members of the genus *Crataegus* are cultivated in gardens. One very interesting type is the Glastonbury thorn, named after Glastonbury Abbey in Somerset. This variety flowers at Christmas-time, and according to the old legend the original tree sprang from the staff of St. Joseph of Arimathea, being planted there by the saint himself.

Hawthorne, NATHANIEL (1804–64). A true artist who took time and pains to make his language the fitting expression of his thought, this American novelist also had a penetrating insight into human hearts. Nathaniel Hawthorne was a native of Salem, Massachusetts. He was a lonely boy, for his father, a sea captain, died when he was four, and his mother shut herself away from the world.

After he left Bowdoin College, in the state of Maine, in 1825, he lived almost like a hermit until he was 33. But he was very busy all this time, thinking and writing, though he published little. For a time Hawthorne lived at Brook Farm, where a group of literary men and women were trying an experiment in community life, and so he got the idea for his Blithedale Romance.

He married Miss Sophia Peabody in 1842, and for a time they lived in Concord, Massachusetts, in the Old Manse.

Then, because he was unable to earn enough by writing to support his family, he took a position in the Customs Department. Under the influence of the old Puritan atmosphere that had so strongly touched his imagination, his thoughts began to take definite shape in the story that made him famous, The Scarlet Letter (1850). After it was published, his future was secure. The House of the Seven Gables and A Wonder Book for Boys and Girls appeared in 1851, and Tanglewood Tales in the next year.

Later, when consul at Liverpool, Hawthorne travelled in Europe, visiting France and Italy. Broken by ill-health and saddened by the American Civil War (1861–65), he did not live many years after his return to the U.S.A. in 1860, dying at Plymouth, New Hampshire, on May 19, 1864.

None of Hawthorne's novels could be called bright and cheerful, though they have touches of quiet humour. They are overhung with a sense of mystery and unseen influences. His stories for children were treated with the same care and thought as his novels for older folk.

Haydn, FRANZ JOSEPH (1732–1809). No musician was better liked than Haydn (pron. hī′-dn), and the nickname Papa Haydn, by which he was known, expresses the great affection in which he

HAYDN CONDUCTING A DRAWING-ROOM CONCERT

The father of instrumental music, as he was called, the Austrian composer Franz Haydn occupies a position of the highest importance in musical history if only for the skilful construction and mastery of technique displayed in his later symphonies. The impulse which he gave to music of both concert-hall and drawing-room is still felt. In this reproduction of the painting by A. Rosier he is seen (right) directing some musicians in his own home.

was held. He was like a father to his associates, as he was also to all young and struggling men of talent.

Haydn was born at Rohrau, near Vienna, Austria, on March 31, 1732. His father was fond of music, and the evenings of Haydn's early childhood were spent listening to the father playing the harp while Haydn's mother sang the folksongs of Hungary, the themes of which later found their way into some of the finest compositions of the master. As a child Haydn showed marked ability along musical lines, and at the age of eight was made a chorister in the chapel of St. Stephen, in Vienna. At the age of 17 his voice broke. Because of some boyish prank, he was expelled, and found himself destitute.

Ten long hard years followed. Hungry, cold, ragged, but always devoted to the art of music, Haydn struggled against poverty, and at last fortune smiled. He was made director of the orchestra of a Hungarian nobleman, Prince Esterhazy, at that time the finest in Austria, and for 30 years he held this position. During this time his fame as a composer spread to Leipzig (Germany), Paris, and London.

The friendship which sprang up at this period between Haydn and the great Mozart was one of great value to both the composers. It was from Mozart that Haydn derived much of the mastery of orchestral effect that marked his later symphonies. When 58 years of age Haydn came to England. He was received with enthusiasm, and Oxford University conferred on him the degree of Doctor of Music. During his stay of 18 months he produced his opera Orfeo, nine symphonies, and many other compositions, among them the accompaniments of more than 100 Scottish songs.

In 1798 Haydn's great oratorio The Creation was produced. Among the compositions of his declining years was the Austrian national anthem. He died in Vienna on May 31, 1809. Haydn's compositions include 150 symphonies, 77 quartets (which are the most distinctive of his works), three oratorios, 54 sonatas, 16 masses, and a large number of smaller pieces of church music.

Hazel. The hazel provides rods for hoops and baskets and crates, and is noted for its nuts. The nuts of some cultivated varieties grown in England, such as the filbert, are collected for the market, but the majority of the members of this group are mere shrubs or bushes, and the nuts have little market value. Hazel-nuts lie in leafy cups in clusters of two, three, or four, and from their reddish-brown shade we get the colour term hazel. The oil pressed from hazel-nuts is used by perfumers and painters, and for medicinal purposes.

In certain European lands, including England, a forked hazel twig is used as a divining rod for pointing to the place where precious minerals or other objects lie hidden, or where water may be found. The person using the twig holds it in his hands, and on approaching hidden water or metal the rod twists. The explanation is uncertain.

The hazels belong to the birch family (*Betulaceae*). The scientific name of the common hazel is *Corylus avellana*.

Health, MINISTRY OF. All matters concerning the health of the people of England and Wales are looked after by the Ministry of Health. It was established by Act of Parliament in 1919, and took over the work previously performed by the Local Government Board in the organization of the National Health Insurance (function transferred to the Ministry of National Insurance in 1945); certain duties connected with the welfare of children from the Board of Education; others formerly discharged by the Privy Council; together with most of the powers of the Home Secretary under the Lunacy and Mental Deficiency Acts. The department is presided over by the Minister of Health.

Its establishment just after the close of the First World War (1914–18) was a sign of a change in the public and official attitude towards health and disease. It was a recognition of the fact that good health is a national asset, and that it is one of the duties of the State to see that its citizens are enabled to live healthy lives. By the National Health Service Act of 1946, The Ministry of Health became responsible for free medical treatment for the population, in the home, doctor's surgery, hospital, or Health Centre. Maintenance of certain hospitals also became the responsibility of the Ministry. The public health services now cover the whole country, and there are many hundreds of doctors in the Health Service whose job it is not only to cure people who are ill but to see that, as far as is possible, they do not become ill.

This change from curative to preventive medical action on the part of the State is one of the brightest features in modern social legislation. And so we see the constant multiplication of ante-natal (before-

E. J. Bedford

HAZEL NUTS AND LEAVES

Whether wild or cultivated, hazel bushes are very fruitful, and the nuts (above) are popular alike with humans and with squirrels. They are plentiful in the British Isles. Each nut is held in a leafy cup, or shuck, until it is ripe, when it falls to the ground. The filbert is a cultivated variety.

SCHOOLROOM OPEN TO THE SUN'S HEALTH-GIVING RAYS

Ideas as to the value to health of fresh air have changed during the past 40 or 50 years. It was once thought that in cold and wet weather fresh air was dangerous to health, and nurseries and schoolrooms were kept at a high temperature with the windows closed. Nowadays children are kept as much in the fresh air and sunlight as possible. This photograph shows a modern classroom with outer walls of glass. The front wall is a folding glass screen, drawn back in fine weather, so that the children are practically in the open air, while in bad weather the screen forms another wall.

birth) clinics, infant welfare centres, open-air schools, orthopaedic institutions (for the treatment of deformities), and other similar organizations designed solely to promote health and to convert citizens into members of the community physically and mentally equipped to play their part for the good of the commonwealth. Inspired by the Ministry, slums are being demolished in our great cities, and are being replaced by houses that are healthy and comfortable to live in. In conjunction with other Government departments the Health Ministry rigorously controls the standard of purity or freshness of all foodstuffs offered for sale.

Heart. Situated rather to the left of the thorax, bounded on either side by the lungs, and lying on the diaphragm (the great domed muscle which divides the thorax from the abdomen), the whole encased by the bony cage of the ribs, is the heart—most vital among all the organs of the body. This amazing mass of organized muscle, this all-important pump, works day and night from birth until death. The tired animal sleeps and rests, but through all the hours of unconsciousness the heart keeps at its uniquely important task of driving the blood round and round through the blood vessels of the body, so that the cells may be fed and their waste matter removed.

It is not really possible to consider the heart except as a pump in a closed system of fluid-carrying conduits. These conduits include arteries, capillaries and veins. First we have the arteries, conveying the arterial blood, red because oxygen-laden. They become smaller and smaller, breaking down eventually after the fashion of a tree's branches

into twiglets called the capillaries, so named because they are of hair-like fineness in the bore. At this point takes place the real business of gaseous exchange, which is of the very essence of life. The blood cells give off through the extremely thin walls of the capillaries their load of oxygen, for transformation into substance or energy, and take on a load of carbonic acid gas, the waste matter of living. Because of this carbonic acid gas the blood is now purplish in colour as it runs on into the veins, which finally empty it into the heart. From the heart the blood is pumped to the lungs, there to reverse this gaseous exchange. The immeasurably fine walls of the blood vessels and the equally thin walls of the air-spaces of the lungs lie alongside one another; carbonic acid gas passes across to the lung-air, and oxygen from the lung-air passes to the blood. The blood-stream pours into the heart and is driven round again—the same circuit, the same task. So it goes on while life lasts. The process takes some two minutes to complete. This circulation of the

BLOOD VESSELS
The conduits along which the heart pumps the blood through the body consist of arteries, capillaries and veins. The circuit is shown diagramatically.

blood has been recognized only in relatively recent times. (*See* Blood; Harvey, William).

The heart has four cavities, two on either side of a central "cross." The upper chambers are called the right and left auricles (the early anatomists felt they looked like little ears), and the lower chambers are named the right and left ventricles (the anatomists thought they resembled little bellies).

The auricles have relatively thin walls, for they are *receiving* chambers; the ventricles have thick and powerful walls, for their function is to *pump the blood* onwards. A series of valves prevents the blood-stream leaking backwards under this pressure. The right auricle and the right ventricle (*see* diagrams) are connected by the tricuspid valve (which has three flaps when dissected out); the left auricle and left ventricle are connected by the mitral valve (which when dissected out has two peaks reminiscent of a bishop's mitre). The aortic valve lies where the left ventricle forces the blood into the aorta (the main artery of the body); and the pulmonary valve guards the junction of the right ventricle with the pulmonary vessels (through which

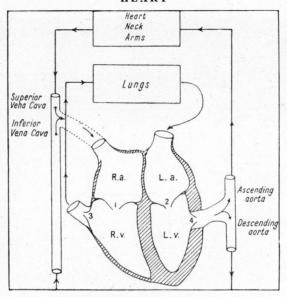

THE HEART'S VITAL ROLE
The circulation of the blood is shown in this diagram. R.a. and L.a. indicate the right and left auricles of the heart; R.v. and L.v. the right and left ventricles. The heart valves are : 1. Tricuspid ; 2. Mitral ; 3. Pulmonary ; 4. Aortic.

the blood is driven to the lungs). Let us trace the path of the blood from that point where it returns, oxygen-laden, from the lungs and is poured into the left auricle. This contracts, and the blood passes through the mitral valve into the left ventricle; as the left ventricle contracts, this valve closes under back-pressure while the blood rushes out into the aorta through the aortic valve which, in its turn, closes and prevents the return of the stream. Thence the blood finds its way to every tissue of the body—via artery, capillary, vein—until two great veins, the upper and lower vena cava, collect it and pour it into the right auricle. This contracts and the blood is thus emptied into the right ventricle; the right ventricle contracts, closing the tricuspid valve behind the stream which now passes through the pulmonary valve on its way to the lungs for purification, the pulmonary valve shutting down on its heels. The purified blood is borne back by other great vessels to the left auricle.

The real work of the heart is done during the contraction of the ventricles. While the auricles are filling, it rests and feeds from the small arteries

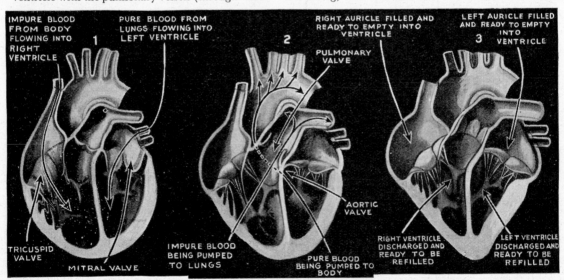

HOW THE HEART KEEPS THE BLOOD STREAM FLOWING
The heart is a pumping machine, its action consisting of a contraction from top to bottom on both sides at the same time. In (1) both auricles are filled with blood, the right with impure blood from the body and the left with pure blood from the lungs, and the beginning of the contraction is forcing the blood through the valves into the ventricles. In (2) the contraction has passed to the ventricles. The back pressure has closed the valves to the auricles and is forcing the blood from the right ventricle to the lungs and from the left ventricle to the body. In (3) the contraction has ended. The ventricles have been discharged, the auricles have been filled, and the process is about to be repeated. (*See* also top diagram).

(the coronary arteries), which ramify in its sub-stance. In Man the heart beats some 72 times per minute—some 100,000 times per day. The rate of the heart-beat is under the control of two great nerve branches; the sympathetic nerve, which increases its pace, and the vagus which slows it. But the heart carries in its own walls the mechanism which keeps it beating. Anxiety or fear, because of the sympathetic nerve control, makes it beat more quickly, thus getting all the tissues on the top line for fight or flight, whatever the nature of the animal: the deer will run away from danger; the lion will turn to rend its foe. The heart-beat is also increased in fever. Its rate can be measured by the pulsations of the arteries, of which the walls are elastic. The well-known pulse in medicine is measured most simply where the artery of the wrist can be compressed against the wrist-bone. "Blood-pressure" implies the measurement by an instrument of the tension in the arteries when the heart is contracting, and again when it is relaxing.

The physician can hear the sounds of the heart through the stethoscope, an instrument designed to carry sounds from an organ to the ear of the examiner, who can thus form a very fair idea of the condition of the heart and of its valves. The use of an electrocardiograph is another method of checking up on the behaviour of the heart. An electric current is passed through the heart, and the reactions traced on a graph. Gramophone records of heart sounds are now made, and the sounds magnified for the training of medical students.

The heart muscle can suffer from over-strain, as in the well-known condition called "athlete's heart." The valves may become diseased by bacterial attack; rheumatism is the most virulent of such enemies, its germs having a special affinity for the substance of the heart's valves. Prolonged and absolute rest is the only preventive of permanent damage. The valves may show no damage at the moment, but in the course of years, when the responsibilities of life are probably heaviest, the formation of fibrous tissue causes them to contract; then the valves do not let enough blood pass, or else they fail to dam it back so that the victim, not getting adequate gaseous exchange, is always a bad colour, breathless and fatigued. Valvular disease of the heart was once a term more dreaded than now, when the capacity of a heart is measured not by its alterations in structure but by what it can achieve.

The MYSTERY of HEAT EXPLAINED

Since a primitive man first made heat by rubbing two sticks together, people have wondered what it really was; many have even thought it was a separate substance. How Science has unravelled this problem is told here.

Heat. What is heat? In olden times, fire, which produced heat, was worshipped as a deity, for many were the wonderful and terrible things that it could do. Later, fire was thought to be one of the four elements making up all matter, the other three being earth, air, and water. But gradually, however, as experimental enquiries were carried out as to its nature, the idea grew up that heat was some kind of weightless fluid, called "caloric," which in some way flowed from a hot body to a cold one. It was weightless, because experimenters found that, by heating up a body, the body did not increase in weight; it did increase in size, however. The caloric theory held sway for many years. Thus, caloric was said to flow from the hot coals to the water in a kettle when the latter was put on the fire. Then, round about the year 1800, fresh evidence showed that heat could not be a material substance. This evidence was provided by two men, Benjamin Thompson, better known as Count Rumford (1753–1814), and Sir Humphrey Davy (1778–1829).

In the course of boring brass cannons, Rumford noticed that his boring tool, and the brass block used in the process, got very hot. He made careful measurements of the heat produced, and he communicated the results of his experiments to the Royal Society of London in 1798. With a blunt borer, and with felt covering the outside of the brass block, so that no heat could get in from outside, he found that a much greater quantity of heat was produced than before, yet the amount of brass chips removed by the tool was smaller. This led him to speculate on where the heat came from, and he was forced to the conclusion that the caloric theory must be false. In his account he wrote: "It is hardly necessary to add that anything which an insulated body can furnish without limitation cannot possibly be a material substance. It must be motion." He meant the motion of the particles of the body.

The next year Sir Humphrey Davy furthered Rumford's experiments by contriving to rub two pieces of ice together in a vacuum, when the air around it was below freezing-point. (It was a very cold day on which the experiment was carried out.) Davy managed to melt the ice by friction, and this was conclusive that no such substance as caloric could exist, since all the bodies near the ice were below its freezing-point, and could not have given up heat to melt the ice. To the question: "Where can the so-called caloric come from?" the only answer was: "There is no such substance as caloric. Heat is simply motion given to particles or molecules."

Although these experiments were so conclusive, it took a long time for the caloric theory to be rejected completely. Not until 1840 was the full realisation made of the equivalence of heat and mechanical work. In this year a Manchester man, James Prescott Joule (*q.v.*), carried out careful measurements on the amount of work needed to produce one unit of heat. He did this by churning up water with paddle wheels, measuring both the mechanical work done by the paddles and the rise in temperature of the water. The "mechanical equivalent of heat" was thus first measured, and we now know from Joule's work that it takes 778 foot-pounds of work to produce one British Thermal Unit of heat.

We must be careful not to confuse "quantity of heat" with "temperature," as the early scientists often did. Temperature is a measure of the degree of heat of a substance, and tells us in what state of agitation are its constituent molecules. Quantity of heat, on the other hand, is a measure of the energy which flows when a body rises or falls in temperature (or changes its physical state)—that is, when it gains or loses heat.

Heat is, then, the motion of the molecules making up a substance. In the case of a gas, the molecules are free to move about in space, only occasionally bumping into one another. We can calculate at what average speed the molecules of a gas are moving, by knowing its temperature. For the gas oxygen, at ordinary atmospheric temperature and pressure, this speed is about 1,000 miles per hour. As the gas is heated up, the speed of the molecules increases. The molecules of a liquid are likewise moving about, but in this case they are not quite so free to move, but are bound together to a certain extent. In solids the molecules merely oscillate about a mean position, but they are still vibrating with a speed corresponding to the temperature of the solid. When we hit a piece of iron with a hammer, it gets hot, because the energy of the blow goes towards speeding up the vibration of the iron molecules. Two pieces of wood rubbed together similarly get hot, by the change of mechanical energy into molecular energy, or, in other words, into heat.

Can we ever cool down a substance until the molecules all stop moving? Theoretical reasoning goes to show that this would happen at a temperature of −459° F. (or −273° C.). This temperature is known as the " absolute zero," the temperature at which a body loses all its heat. Although it is found impossible to cool a substance right down as far as this, scientists have managed to get to within a fraction of a degree of it by liquefying gases in a strong magnetic field (see Freezing and Refrigeration). Substances have very interesting properties at these low temperatures, when their molecules are moving about so slowly. All gases become liquids or solids, and the molecules in a metal near the absolute zero are so close together that its electrical resistance becomes very small, and if a current is once induced in the metal, it will go on flowing for many hours. This phenomenon is known as " super-conductance." Of course, at these low tempera-

Heat is created and transmitted by the motion of molecules.

Molecules of the bar carry the heat to the hand by 'conduction.'

Heated air rises, carrying heat by convection currents.

Heat travels in all directions by ' radiation ' through the air.

Impact between objects speeds up their molecules and so causes them to become heated.

The rapid motion of molecules undergoing chemical changes is the cause of heat in fire.

A heavy electric current passing through resisting wires creates heat.

The British Thermal Unit is the amount of heat needed to raise one pound of water one degree Fahrenheit in temperature.

FACTS ABOUT HEAT

tures no life can possibly exist, for heat is needed to maintain life.

If, on the other hand, we *add* motion to the molecules of a body, we make it hotter. There are a great number of ways of heating a substance, from the direct transference of mechanical energy into heat, as in Joule's paddle-wheel, to the passing of a current of electricity through it, if it be a metal. In the article on Energy, it was explained that heat is only one form of energy, and can be produced by the conversion of any of the other forms, as long as the Law of Conservation of Energy is obeyed. Thus we use chemical energy when we burn something, electrical energy in an electric fire, and radiation energy if we put something in the sun to warm. The hottest temperature that can be readily obtained on this earth is produced in an electric arc, when the gas molecules in it are given sufficient energy to raise them above 7,000° F. Enormous temperatures, of many millions of degrees, were, however, momentarily produced in the explosions of atomic bombs. The sun is also at an extremely high temperature, the surface being at about 10,000° F., while the inside is far hotter.

Two very practical questions concerning heat must occur to us. They are: " How can we get heat when we want it? " and " How can we transfer heat from place to place? " Our great source of energy, the sun, is continually sending out heat by radiation. The amount of heat we receive from the sun cannot be controlled by us, and we can only make the best use we can of it. Only in the sunniest parts of the world, as, for example at Pasadena, in California, is it economically worth while to collect the sun's heat directly, and use it to produce steam to drive an engine. Usually, it is used indirectly—as water-power. The sun evaporates water from the oceans, which later on condenses as rain on the slopes of high mountains. The accumulated rain runs down the mountain side, and we collect it to drive the water-turbines of our electricity generators.

Different parts of the world get very different amounts of the sun's heat, and these different quantities of heat cause our seasons. In winter, in northern and far southern regions, the sun's heat is not enough to keep our houses warm, and so we must get our heat artificially. The power needed to drive the various engines and machines of our industrial civilization must also, to a large extent, come from artificial sources. The chief source of artificial heat is the burning of wood, coal, oil and gas, but it must be borne in mind that much of this heat is "stored sunshine" from past ages (*see* Fuel; Energy). Chemical energy is transformed into heat energy when the oxygen of the atmosphere combines with the carbon and other elements making up the fuel. There are many other chemical reactions which produce heat, but the burning of coal and oil are the only ones where large quantities of heat can be cheaply obtained.

As mentioned above, heat can be generated in a variety of ways. One of the most convenient for producing a local supply is caused by passing an electric current through a wire. The electric current causes the molecules of metal in the wire to vibrate at a higher rate, and so the wire gets hot. Electrical heating is used very widely nowadays, but it must be remembered that the electrical energy one uses was obtained originally by burning coal in the furnaces of the power station, or in some other way which can be eventually traced back to the sun for its origin. The only independent source of energy is the atomic pile, the newly invented source of controlled atomic energy. In this, heat is developed directly by the annihilation of very small quantities of matter, actually uranium atoms. This heat, we hope, will in the future be made to drive our generators for us, and so relieve the miner of his task of digging the many millions of tons of coal that we at present need.

Without these external sources of heat, such as the sun, and the burning of fuel, everything on this earth would take up the same temperature, just as a number of hot and cold bodies, left in a room together, will even up in temperature. Now it is a well-known fact that a steam-engine cannot work without a supply of heat at a high temperature. Thus, if all things on the earth were at the same temperature, no mechanical energy could be obtained from heat energy. It is here that we are at a disadvantage, and this "one-way" nature of the transformation of mechanical energy into heat energy forms one of the basic laws of heat. All the heat lost in friction, for instance, is no longer available for doing useful work again.

Heat travels in three ways: by conduction, by convection, and by radiation (*see* the series of diagrams in the opposite page). If one end of an iron bar is placed in a fire, the rapidly moving molecules of the hot coals and hot gases strike against the iron molecules, and so the iron molecules that touch the fire are given violent motion. These first molecules pass the motion along to the other molecules farther back in the iron; and soon the heat travels, or is conducted, to the hand that holds the iron. That is, in *conduction*, the heat motion passes along just as motion passes along a row of balls which bump against one another.

The best conductors of heat are the metals. Wood is a poor conductor. This is the reason

SUNSHINE RECORDER
The sun's rays are focused by the glass sphere upon a strip of paper placed in the curved framework. The heat chars the paper, giving a record of the duration of sunshine.

why you can hold a burning match, even while the wood burns only an eighth of an inch away. A metal wire would have to be several inches long for you to hold it in your hand when one end was red hot. We wrap steam pipes with felt and asbestos because these substances are poor heat conductors.

If, now, the hot iron bar is taken out of the fire, the air about it is heated, and, being less dense than the surrounding colder air, it rises In this case, the heat travels upwards by *convection*—that is, by being conveyed by the currents of heated air. Similarly, in the hot-water system of a house, the hot water rises to the top by way of one pipe, and cold water returns, by another, to the heating boiler, without any pumps being employed to move it. Once again, heat has been conveyed by convection, and this method is distinguished by the fact that the heat is here conveyed by the moving matter itself. It is evident that heat convection can only take place in a liquid or gas, where the molecules are free to move.

But heat can reach your hand when it is at some distance beneath the iron bar. Here it cannot be carried by a convection current of hot air, for hot air rises. Nor is it reaching your hand to any appreciable extent by conduction from molecule to molecule, for air is a very bad conductor. It flies to us directly across space, just as heat comes to us from the sun, having travelled through miles of empty space. This method of transfer is called *radiation*. And what is this radiation? Evidently it is not the same as the heat which is the vibrating motions of the molecules of matter, for there is no matter in the long stretches between the earth and the sun.

A hot body, by the motion of its molecules, sets up waves in the surrounding ether, similar to light waves, but invisible (*see* Ether; Light). These waves are electromagnetic in character, and travel with the same velocity as light (186,000 miles per second); but they have a slightly longer wavelength than the visible radiations, and so are known as infra-red rays (*i.e.* those rays beyond the red, in the light spectrum). These infra-red rays are not really heat at all, but are only capable of producing it in a body when they fall on it—that is, they are capable of making its molecules vibrate faster. All the radiation is not absorbed, but some is reflected away again, and different substances absorb different fractions of the radiation falling upon it. Thus a black cloth will absorb more radiation than a white one, becoming hotter in the process. This is the reason why people find light clothes cooler than dark clothes in summer.

The sun, being a very hot body, gives off radiation to a very great extent, some being of the visible type, but by far the greater part being the non-visible infra-red radiation. The amount of heat we get from it is enormous in comparison with any other source. Every square foot of the sun gives off as much heat as would be produced by burning 1,500 tons of coal on this area every hour. The infra-red heat radiation can be reflected and refracted, as well as absorbed. Thus a lens will focus both the visible (light) and invisible (heat) radiations, and if the sun's rays are focused on to a piece of paper in this way, it can be set alight. By using special photographic plates which are sensitive to infra-red radiation, photographs of hot bodies can be taken in the dark; or, for instance, two hot flat-irons can be used to "illuminate" other objects in a dark room, and photographs of them again taken by infra-red photography. Even special "heat-ray" searchlights and telescopes have been developed, for seeing things in the dark. The telescope used in this case focuses an image of the object that is

looked at on to a special screen. where it is transformed into a visible image, appearing on a sort of television screen.

The degree of heat, or the temperature, of a substance, is a measure of the rate at which its molecules are moving, as we have seen. Temperature is measured on a thermometer, and the most useful instrument of this type is the mercury thermometer. In this, mercury is contained in a glass bulb, and, when heated, it can expand up a narrow glass stem, sealed off at the other end, and which is graduated in degrees. On the Fahrenheit scale, the freezing point (of water) is 32° F., and its boiling point 212° F. The Centigrade scale, which is used for most scientific purposes, has 0° C. and 100° C. for these two standard points. Temperature can be measured on a variety of other types of thermometer, all of which depend on some change in the physical properties, such as volume, pressure, or electrical properties, of a substance when it is heated. Two bodies can have the same temperature, yet contain different quantities of heat—first, on account of the mass of the body; and second, because of the kind of matter it contains. This is made clear when their temperatures are changed by the same amount. Obviously, a bucket of water needs more heat added to it than a cupful of water, to raise its temperature one degree, which illustrates the first point. It will be found that it takes about 30 times as much heat to raise one pound of water by one degree as is needed to raise a pound of mercury by the same amount. This property of a substance is known as

its specific heat. Quantity, as opposed to degree, of heat is measured in terms either of calories or of British Thermal Units. A calorie is the amount of heat, or thermal energy, needed to raise the temperature of one gramme of water by one degree Centigrade. This is the unit used in most scientific work. A British Thermal Unit (B.Th.U.) is the quantity of heat needed to raise the temperature of one pound of water one degree Fahrenheit. The B.Th.U. is the unit used in most cases by engineers. Thus we read in an engineering paper that a certain kind of coal "gives 13,000 B.Th.U. per pound of coal." This means that the amount of heat which is produced by burning a pound of this coal is enough to raise 13,000 pounds of water one degree Fahrenheit. Similarly, measuring the food value of a substance in calories really gives a value of its heating ability when it is broken up chemically in our bodies. Some of the heat, of course, appears in the work done by our muscles.

We have seen the various ways in which heat can be produced from other kinds of energy. The reverse process, however, is far more important—how to get mechanical work or electrical energy from heat. The great engineers of the past, with James Watt at their head, showed how this could be done, and the later additional inventions of the internal combustion engine, and now the gas turbine, have extended their great work. However, we must not forget the forerunners of these men, who showed us what

Kodak Research Laboratories

PHOTOGRAPHY BY HEAT RAYS
By using photographic plates sensitive to infra-red radiation photographs can be taken of an object illuminated only by invisible heat rays from two electric irons (lower). The arrangement of the bust and irons, taken by ordinary light, is shown in the upper photograph.

heat was, and by their study of thermo-dynamics, as the science of heat is called, laid the foundations of our great modern industrial civilization.

Heather AND HEATH. The song and story of Scotland are filled with praises of heather, that small shrub which covers the rugged Highlands with purple. Heather (*Calluna vulgaris*) is found throughout northern and western Europe. It is a small evergreen shrub, of the order *Ericaceae*, sometimes rising only a few inches above the ground, but often growing to a height of three feet or even more.

On its purplish brown stems are close-leaved green shoots and feathery spikes of tiny flowers, usually rose-lilac in colour, but ranging from deep purple to pure white. White heather is somewhat rare in the wild state; in Scottish legend this beautiful plant is regarded as a bringer of good luck. Heather tops afford winter forage for Highland sheep and cattle, as well as for birds such as grouse. The flower is a favourite of the bee, and heather honey has a delicious flavour. The larger stems are made into brooms, the smaller into brushes.

Owing to the scarcity of wood, the Highlanders in former times built their sheilings, or cabins, of heather stems cemented with mud, and used it as a thatch; while heather laid on the ground with the small twigs uppermost formed a warm, comfortable bed.

Often wrongly called heather are the various species of heath, members of the genus *Erica* and closely related to true heather. A number of these are common in Britain, the most familiar being the cross-leaved heath, or " bell-heather " (*E. tetralix*), and the fine-leaved heath (*E. cinerea*). The former has pale, almost pink flowers, the latter's blooms being of a rich purplish

A. W. Dennis

TRUE HEATHER AND HEATH
Sometimes called ling, heather (left) is found in Britain and throughout northern and western Europe. The tiny flowers are usually rose-lilac in colour. Various species of heath are common in Britain, the most familiar being the cross-leaved heath or bell-heather (right).

hue. Other species, which are very local, are the Cornish heath (*E. vagans*), which in that county often covers large tracts of land; the ciliated heath, *E. ciliaris*, found in Dorset and Ireland; and the Irish heath, *E. mediterranea*. Of these, *E. ciliaris* is the finest, bearing long spikes of crimson-purple flowers.

MAKING an ARTIFICIAL CLIMATE

Though our bodies have automatic heat regulators, and can more or less adapt themselves to climatic changes, we still have to guard them against extreme variations of heat or cold. How Man does this is described here.

Heating and Ventilation. If you have stood in front of a watchman's brazier, with its red-hot glowing coals or coke, you have experienced some of the advantages and drawbacks of the " open-fire " method of creating warmth. The flaming fuel radiated heat to your body through the space separating you from the brazier ; the shimmering warm air from the top and sides of the brazier warmed you by convection; if you were so unwise as to touch your finger to the metal fire-basket, you received warmth by conduction— perhaps too much warmth, locally applied!

If you have read the article on Heat, these terms will be familiar to you; if not, you should read this earlier story before going any farther. To return to the brazier, if the weather was cool, you at once noticed that you were warmed only in front, at the part of the body turned towards the fire. You may have thought: " Why did not the watchman put his brazier inside his hut or shelter? " The answer is, that if he had done so he might have been suffocated by the fumes given off by the burning fuel. Burning coal, coke or wood gives off carbon monoxide, which is a lethal gas (we are ignoring the smoke, which in a coke fire is negligible). So he would have secured more even warming, but at the risk of danger to health or life.

The open fire has many of the drawbacks of the brazier, but its flue and chimney carry off the fumes and smoke from the room harmlessly. Moreover,

the draught provided by the flue and chimney conduces to steady and regular burning of the fuel. The open fire warms us mainly in front, but if the apartment is ventilated reasonably, without too much inflow of fresh air from outside, the air inside soon becomes nicely warm and we feel the comforting heat all round us. Long before fires were placed at one side of a room, with a chimney contrived in the wall, the hearth used to be sited more towards the middle of the apartment, and a mere hole in the roof let out the smoke; much of the fumes escaped into the chamber, to cause coughing and sneezing and irritation to the eyes.

In colder countries than Britain it was a pressing problem to make the best use of the fuel—often mainly wood, and difficult to procure. Benjamin Franklin (*q.v.*) made one of his many contributions to science by inventing a closed stove made of iron, which could safely stand in a room; smoke and fumes were taken away by an iron stove pipe passing upwards through the roof, or going across the top of the room to make its exit through a wall, high up. Now all the family could sit or work around the stove in comfort. The iron casing of the stove, and the smoke-pipe, became heated and gave out warmth by convection; some warmth was also emitted by radiation. You must have experienced the difference between the feeling in a room warmed by a closed stove, and that in a cosy sitting-room where there was an open fire. The open fire gives radiant heat in a greater degree, but comparatively few can enjoy it; the stove is useful because it warms bigger rooms more efficiently.

The open fire is a luxury, one might say, for only a small percentage of the heat energy of the burning fuel reaches the room. But fire grates have been much improved of late years. You will notice that the fireclay back is shaped so as to compel the smoke to pass outwards over the top of the fire, where much of it is consumed. Smoke consists mainly of unburned particles of carbon from the fuel. The same shaping of the fireback forces the burning gases to come outwards before passing up the chimney. The fireclay becomes heated, and radiates warmth. Gas-fires are built on much the same plan, imitating the coal fire. The elements or radiants, as the glowing members are named, are made white hot by a row of Bunsen burners below; they send out their warmth into the room, helped by the fireclay backing. In all but small and portable gas-fires there is a flue with a chimney, to take away the products of combustion.

The electric fire gives out warmth because the passage of an electric current through wire elements made of special metal, having a high resistance, heats up the wire until it becomes red hot. There is no need for a flue here, and many electric fires are portable, able to be plugged in wherever the room is suitably wired for them.

Closed stoves range from the simple type familiar in our schoolrooms—with a cylindrical casing—to the more ornamental ones used in sitting-rooms or nurseries, these last being often provided with doors having mica-panelled windows through which one can see the glowing fuel. Because they are closed, and the draught (inflow of air) can be regulated, such stoves are termed slow-combustion stoves. By opening a damper we can admit more air (which means supplying more oxygen), and burn up the fuel more quickly. More fuel burnt in a given time means more heat produced in that time. The two ways of obtaining more warmth from a given appliance are, then, to burn more fuel, and to ensure that the heat output is used in the most efficient manner, and that little is wasted.

Now we must consider ventilation. For comfort we need ample supplies of fresh air, constantly and regularly renewed as the air in a room becomes stale and vitiated by the carbon dioxide we emit from our lungs, and by gases from any fuel-burning appliance we use for warming the room. Doors and windows fit loosely enough to allow plenty of fresh air to reach a room normally. If the room has a flue and chimney, there is a natural draught— even when no fire is burning—to cause an air circulation. Air in a room becomes warmed by heat given off by our bodies, and is almost always

HEAT TRANSMISSION

Warm air rises from the stove, carrying heat by convection. Heat is transferred from the tip of the poker to the handle by conduction. Direct rays from the fire warm objects they strike, heat being transmitted by radiation.

warmer than air outside. So the warmer air, being less dense and therefore lighter, is forced upwards by the weight of the cooler and denser air entering from outside. Thus a circulation is brought about which ejects used air and brings in fresh air. On warm days we open windows and speed up this circulation. By opening two windows on opposite sides of the room we obtain cross-ventilation and a still more rapid air-change.

It is not sufficient for comfort that fresh air shall be exchanged for stale air ; there must be air movement, so that continually new portions of the air in the room are brought in contact with our bodies, to remove the warmth and humidity brought about by perspiration, and by transpiration from the lungs. Unless this is achieved, the room feels stuffy ; upon opening a window (or on starting an electric fan in the room) we at once feel relief. The air we inhale contains the following quantities of oxygen, nitrogen, carbon dioxide and vapour, on an average, expressed in parts per 10,000 cubic feet of air. The second column shows the composition of the air we breathe out or exhale.

Air inhaled		Air exhaled
Oxygen	2,026 parts	1,620 parts
Nitrogen	7,800 „	7,500 „
Carbon dioxide	4 „	400 „
Vapour (about)	150 „	500 „

You can see from this little Table that a large amount of oxygen is abstracted from the air in breathing, and that a hundred times as much carbon dioxide is present in out-breathed air as compared with that in fresh air breathed in. It will at once be realized that it is useless to try to

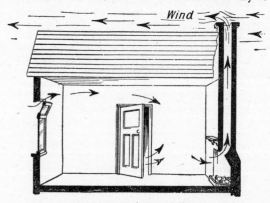

HEAT AS A VENTILATOR

A room heated by a gas or coal fire is ventilated by a natural process. Fresh air comes in through the window or door, and stale air is drawn down from the upper part of the room and sucked up the chimney by the draught from the fire.

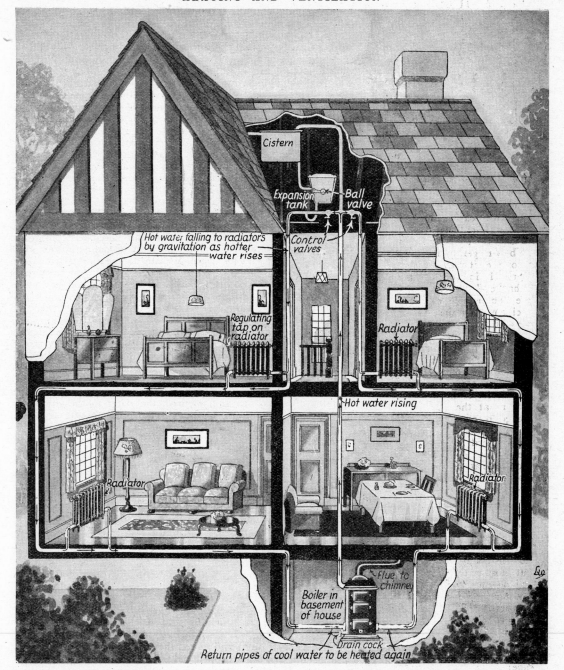

Cistern

Expansion tank — Ball valve

Hot water falling to radiators by gravitation as hotter water rises

Control valves

Regulating tap on radiator

Radiator

Hot water rising

Radiator

Radiator

Flue to chimney

Boiler in basement of house

Drain cock

Return pipes of cool water to be heated again

CENTRAL HEATING SYSTEM IN A MODERN HOUSE

The usual method of warming a house by central heating is shown here. In the basement is a boiler to heat the water which, as it becomes hot, rises through pipes to the top of the house. There it begins to lose some of its heat, and as the hotter water from the boiler takes its place it descends by gravitation, passing through various radiators.

keep a room warm by shutting out air, for we must have enough new air entering to provide comfortable and healthy conditions. The body naturally loses surplus heat, and must be allowed to do so gradually by contact between the skin and the cooler air surrounding it..

The body has a natural and automatic heat-regulating mechanism, which keeps its temperature down to normal. But if we throw too much strain on this mechanism, and expect it to deal with too great extremes of temperature, we shall be far from comfortable. The proper warming and ventilation of rooms, therefore, comes down to this: it must allow the body to *lose* excess heat in a comfortable manner. Heat cannot pass from a colder object to a warmer one; therefore the air in a room should be cool enough to allow the passage of bodily heat which is produced in excess of the body's needs.

The burning up of food in our bodies generates heat ; muscular exercise, even the least exertion, generates more heat. There is a comical story of a pioneer who often kept himself warm in the winter with logs, but did not burn them. When he felt cold he walked half a mile to his log-pile, loaded fuel on to a sled, and drew it to his hut. There he sawed the wood into logs, and split them with an axe. By this time he was warm enough, and had no need to burn them on a fire !

Types of Central Heating

Many houses, and most big ones, besides public buildings, are centrally heated. Warm air, steam, or hot water are circulated throughout the rooms, in conduits or in pipes. The air, steam or water yield up their heat to the colder air in the rooms. Warm and filtered air is circulated in ducts from a jacket around a furnace or other warm appliance and is blown gently into cinemas, theatres and halls; some of it may be re-circulated along with new, warm air, in order that the requisite number of " air changes " per hour may be obtained to provide comfortable conditions in the building. If the cinema contains few people, as at the beginning of the day's programme, more warmth is needed. As more people enter, and their bodies give up warmth, the air entering can safely be cooler than that supplied earlier.

An adult person wearing ordinary indoor clothing, when at rest, gives off about 220 British Thermal Units of heat per hour (supposing the temperature at the time is 60° Fahrenheit). If you engage in sedentary work, you dissipate about 340 B.Th.U. per hour; while if you perform moderately hard work your surplus heat output will be about 440 Th.U.—double the amount when you were at rest.

Steam heating is used in big buildings, with many rooms. The steam is generated in a boiler (q.v.) and is circulated in pipes around the walls or others buried in the concrete of the floor, or in the plaster of the walls or ceilings. Or steam may be piped to those iron or steel appliances we call " radiators " in order to get a bigger transfer of heat to the room. The radiators, by the way, give out most of their warmth by convection and conduction—not by radiation.

Hot-water systems are most common for warming small houses. The water is led to a boiler by one pipe (the return pipe) entering low down in the boiler; it becomes warmed and is pressed up by the greater weight of cooler water coming in below; the warmed water flows up a second pipe (the flow pipe) which leads off from near the top of the boiler. So we get a flow of warmed water which is actually moved by gravity through the pipes to radiators in the rooms. From the radiators it goes by piping around the circuit and again reaches the boiler by the return pipe, to be made hotter again. There are various arrangements of piping, and sometimes the hot-water supply for baths and basins or sinks is combined with the heating system.

In all these systems, we are really warming our rooms by coal or coke, which made the air, steam or water hot before it was circulated to the rooms.

But there is a strange system of heating buildings in which Nature warms the water for us ! The city electrical engineer of Norwich and his staff, in 1945, began to use what you or we should call " cold " water from the River Wensum for warming the office and workshop of the city's electrical department. They had put together a " heat-pump " installation, using a second-hand compressor and other material which happened to be available. (It was wartime, of course.) The river runs near the buildings.

River water, at an average temperature of 40° F., was pumped to an evaporator. This evaporator formed part of what one might call a " reversed refrigerator " (see Freezing). The pressure inside was lowered until the " refrigerant "—sulphur dioxide in this case—was made to boil by the heat taken out of the river water. Then the sulphur dioxide (now in the form of vapour) was taken to a condenser, after the vapour had been compressed to a pressure which raised its temperature to one useful for warming water for heating the building. (Sulphur dioxide, if compressed to a pressure of 22 pounds per square inch, will boil at 30° F., two degrees below normal freezing point.)

In the condenser the sulphur dioxide turned into a liquid again, and now yielded up its heat to water circulating in pipes which ran through the building to warm it. Then the sulphur dioxide was carried back to the evaporator, to begin its cycle again. The river water, after passing through the refrigerator, was discharged again into the Wensum. It had lost 2° to 4° F. only, yet by the reversed refrigeration method, the water in the circulating pipes which warmed the building was as hot as 120° F. At one time, during the first season in which the installation was used, the temperature of the river water fell until it was only half a degree F. above freezing point !

In case you find it hard to understand how we can " reverse a refrigerator," and get hot water from fairly cold water, you may bear in mind that a common type of refrigerator—the absorption type—uses a small gas flame to supply the energy which freezes ice or keeps our food cool and fresh.

Hebe. (Pron. hē′-bē). In Greek mythology the goddess Hebe typified eternal youth and joyousness. She was a beautiful maiden, with sparkling eyes and rounded form, ever smiling; and Milton in his famous poem L'Allegro speaks of—

> Nods, and becks, and wreathèd smiles,
> Such as hang on Hebe's cheek.

She was the daughter of Zeus (Jupiter) and Hera (Juno) and served the gods as cupbearer, until one day she tripped and fell. Then the youth Ganymede took her place, and Hebe became the wife of Heracles (Hercules) after he had been made a god.

Hebrew Language AND LITERATURE. To most persons of European descent, the chief representative of the Semitic tongues is Hebrew, the language in which the Old Testament was written (except for a few passages in the Aramaic dialect), and in which its Scriptures are still read in the Jewish synagogues. It is the best-known member of a group of Asiatic and African languages known as Semitic.

The Semitic languages are divided into two great branches, the northern and the southern. To the former belong Hebrew, Phoenician, Aramaic, and Assyrian, while Arabic and Ethiopic are of the second group. Hebrew and Phoenician are so closely related that they are considered as dialects of one tongue.

The Hebrew language is very ancient, and was spoken in Palestine as early as 2,000 years before Christ. The words are short, for the most part, and the grammar and sentence construction are simple. Much is expressed in a few words, and the language is full of strength and grandeur, with a deep sonorous quality that makes it well suited to poetry and the expression of religious feeling.

In common with other Semitic tongues, the parts of speech are derived from roots or word-stems having three letters. Originally the Hebrew alphabet was made up entirely of consonants, and the vowel sounds were omitted. Early in the Christian era, vowel signs were inserted underneath the consonants. Hebrew, printed with the vowel-sounds indicated, is known as pointed, and without them as unpointed. It reads from right to left, and from what we call the back of the book to the front.

With the exception of parts of the books of Daniel, Ezra, and one verse of Jeremiah, which are in Aramaic, the Old Testament is written in Hebrew. This and a few inscriptions are all that remain to us of ancient Hebrew literature. In their daily speech, the Jews came to use the Aramaic language of their Syrian neighbours, but Hebrew was preserved as a religious and literary language.

In the first four or six centuries of the Christian era, there grew up a great body of writings known as the Talmud (meaning teaching or learning), consisting of two parts. The first of these, the Mishna or oral law, was written in Hebrew ; and the second, the Gemara, or commentary on the law, in Aramaic. The Mishna is a systematic collection of religious-legal decisions, developing the laws of the Old Testament. The Gemara is a great unordered mass containing arguments and opinions on the law, and much miscellaneous material. In its pages are poems, prayers, anecdotes, and maxims, together with science and mathematics; tears and laughter are mingled, while side by side with the investigations of the learned are the wisdom and superstition of the unlearned. The Talmud formed a bond between the scattered Jews, and kept alive their learning during the Dark Ages, making it possible for them to play a large part in the restoration of learning and the cultivation of science at the time of the Renaissance.

In the Middle Ages arose a body of literature which included the Cabala, a mystical interpretation of the Scriptures based on the belief that every letter and number had a hidden meaning.

From early days the Jews have adopted the language of the country in which they happened to

American Colony, Jerusalem

JEWISH SCRIPTURES READ IN HEBREW
In synagogues the Scriptures are still read in Hebrew from a scroll. This Jew, who is holding the form of scroll used at a service, is dressed for prayer ; on his forehead is a phylactery—a small black box containing a miniature scroll to remind him to keep the law—and on his head and shoulders is a fringed scarf, worn in accordance with the scriptural command, ' Thou shalt make the fringes in the four corners of thy vesture.'

dwell. Even in the 1st century A.D., Josephus, the great Jewish historian, had written for the most part in Greek, probably because he could thus reach the greatest number of readers. His immortal History of the Jewish Wars was written first in his native Aramaic and then in Greek; but only the more easily read Greek version has survived.

The Jews in Germany adopted German as their language, but they wrote it in Hebrew characters; and when persecution drove great numbers of them to the countries of eastern Europe, they carried this language with them. Mixed with some Hebrew and Slavic words, and written in Hebrew letters, this German dialect developed into the language known as Yiddish (from the German *jüdisch*, Jewish), spoken today by Jews in many parts of the world. (*See* Jews).

Hebrides, SCOTLAND. Lying off the northwest coast of Scotland is a large group of widely scattered islands known as the Hebrides (pron. heb′-ri-dēz). They are usually divided into the Inner and Outer Hebrides, which are separated from each other by the Minch and Little Minch. The Inner Hebrides, which are the nearer to the mainland, include Skye, Rum, Coll, Tyree, Mull, Colonsay, Eigg, Jura, Islay, Staffa and Iona. The Outer Hebrides form a continuous chain of islands extending for about 120 miles. The largest is Lewis-with-Harris, others being North and South Uist, Benbecula and Barra. Altogether there are over 500 islands, but only about 100 are inhabited, and many are simply islets of bare rock.

Rainfall is heavy, but on the whole the climate is mild and pleasant. In most parts the soil is scanty and agriculture is difficult, but fair quantities of oats, barley and potatoes are grown. Sheep-rearing and fishing are the staple industries. Stornoway, on Lewis, is an important centre of the herring fisheries; whisky is distilled on Skye,

F. Hardie

GATHERING KELP IN SKYE
In the Hebrides the tenant-farmers use kelp, or seaweed, to fertilize the poor and scanty soil. This woman is carrying a load of it, from the beach to a field, in the basket slung from her shoulders.

Mull and Islay; tweeds are made on Harris, and slate is quarried on Luing, Easdale and Seil. The total area of the group is about 2,800 square miles. Gaelic is spoken in most parts.

St. Columba landed on Iona and founded a monastery there in A.D. 593, the island becoming the centre of Celtic Christianity. The Hebrides became a part of the kingdom of Norway about 890, and the Scottish kings did not regain them until 1263. They remained semi-independent under the rule of native chieftains until 1745, when the chiefs

R. K. Holmes; J. J. Farquhar

CATHEDRAL AND COTTAGE OF THE HEBRIDES
On the island of Iona, one of the inner Hebrides, are the ruins of a cathedral (lower), founded in 593 when St. Columba landed there from Ireland, and almost destroyed during the reign of Henry VIII (1509–47). It was partially restored in 1899 and 1907. On the left is a typical cottage home in Skye, which is famed for its beautiful mountain scenery.

were deprived of much of their authority as punishment for the support they had given to the unsuccessful rebellion to restore the Stuarts to the English throne. Following the failure of the potato crop in 1846, which brought many of the people to the verge of starvation, numbers of the Hebrideans emigrated to Australia and Canada. In 1918 the first Lord Leverhulme purchased Lewis and part of Harris to develop the fishing and weaving industries. The population of the islands is 79,000.

Hector. In Greek legend the hero of the Trojans, " glorious Hector " was the son of King Priam of Troy and Hecuba and the husband of Andromache. In his Iliad, the Greek poet Homer tells of Hector's valour during the siege of Troy by the Greeks, and of his death at the hand of Achilles.

To avenge the slaying of his friend Patroclus by Hector, Achilles tied Hector's body to a war chariot and dragged it round the walls of Troy, as is told in the accompanying story. On the personal intervention of the aged Priam, Achilles gave back the body to the Trojans for burial. Hector is represented not only as a brave warrior, but as a devoted son, husband, and father. One of the most touching passages in the Iliad describes his final parting from his wife Andromache and his infant son.

THE STORY OF THE DEATH OF HECTOR

HIGH on the great tower of Troy stood the white-armed Andromache (pron. an-drom'-a-kē), wife to Hector, bravest of the Trojan warriors. By her side stood a nurse bearing his infant son Astyanax (as-tī'-a-naks). All day long the dreaded Greeks had been pressing her countrymen hard, and she looked out over the plain before the city, weeping and wailing like one frenzied, for she feared the coming disaster.

Suddenly she caught sight of her dearly loved husband, who had come to the city to bid the elders and the women pray to the gods for help. Andromache ran swiftly to meet him, and with her went the nurse and the child. She clasped her hand in Hector's and begged him with tears not to return to the battle.

" Come now, have pity and abide here upon the tower, lest thou make thy child an orphan and thy wife a widow."

But Hector of the shining helmet could not be turned from the path of duty. " My soul forbiddeth me to shrink away from battle like a coward," he answered, and he stretched out his arms to his boy. But the child shrank crying to the nurse, frightened at the gleaming bronze and the horse-hair crest that nodded fiercely from his father's helmet. Laughingly, the great warrior swept the helmet from his head, and, taking his son in his arms, kissed him and prayed to the gods that he might grow to be a great man.

With the return of Hector, the sun-god Apollo befriended the Trojans. So it was that, with the aid of this swift-arrowed deity, Hector killed Patroclus, the most loved of the friends of Achilles, who was the greatest warrior in Greece. Because of this Achilles swore vengeance and went out to do battle with Hector.

Once more, when Achilles entered the fight, the tide turned for the Greeks, and they swept the fleeing Trojans back to the gates of Troy. The massive portals closed, and all the Trojans were safe inside save Hector, who stood without the wall awaiting the coming of Achilles.

Now Hector was the bravest man in Troy, but when he saw Achilles, god-like and terrible in shining armour which Hephaestus (Vulcan) had made for him, his heart was filled with a great fear, and he fled. Three times round the city they ran, and neither lost nor gained. As they came near, for the fourth time, to the hot and cold springs where the maids of Troy were wont to wash their garments, the goddess Athena (Minerva), who loved the Greeks, whispered to Achilles to stop and take breath. She promised to bring about his meeting with Hector. Then the goddess went to Hector, and, taking the shape of Deïphobus (dē-if'-o-bus), Hector's brother, said to him, " Wait, and we shall meet Achilles together. Thus shall you slay him."

Hector took heart and closed with Achilles. The Greek threw his spear, but Hector bent low and it flew past him. The goddess Athena returned the spear to Achilles, but Hector did not see this and, throwing his own spear, struck the shield of the Greek. It bounded back from the god-made armour. Turning to seize a second spear from Deïphobus, Hector found him gone, and knew a goddess had tricked him. So, certain that he must die, he drew his sword and rushed towards Achilles, but the famed warrior bore down upon him like an eagle on its prey.

With one thrust, Hector lay dead at the feet of Achilles. To take full vengeance for the death of Patroclus, Achilles fastened the body of Hector to his war chariot, and dragged it round the walls of Troy. Andromache fell fainting into the arms of her maidens, as she looked upon the dishonour done to the body of her husband.

Great was the weeping in Troy that the body of Hector had come into the possession of the enemy, for Achilles's heart was wroth, and he would not give it up for any ransom.

Then to Achilles came his goddess-mother Thetis. " I am the messenger of Zeus (Jupiter) to thee, my son. The gods are displeased at thee because thou holdest Hector and hast not given him back. Come, restore him, and take ransom for the dead."

And Zeus sent a messenger to King Priam, saying : " Be of good cheer, O Priam. Zeus, though he be afar off, hath great care and pity for thee. He biddeth thee ransom noble Hector, and carry gifts to Achilles that may gladden his heart."

Hermes (Mercury), the wing-sandalled messenger of Zeus, guided Hector's aged father to the camp of the enemy. At his entreaty and in return for gold and rugs, mantles and cloaks and cauldrons, Achilles gave up the body.

There was a nine-day truce between the Greeks and the defenders of Troy, while the Trojans wept and mourned over Hector. With many tears they burned the body of their dead hero on a lofty pyre, and then gathered his ashes in a golden urn and buried them under a great mound of stones. " Thus held they funeral for Hector, tamer of horses."— *Retold from Homer's Iliad, Books vi, xxii, xxiv.*

Hedgehog. In the ordinary course of events you are not very likely to come across this little animal, for it is seldom seen in the daytime, which it spends asleep in hedges and thickets, coming out at night to feed.

Hedgehogs are about 10 inches long and have a short tail, a snout somewhat like a pig, and very short legs. They can roll themselves up into a ball, with the head and limbs tucked in so that nothing but an array of spines is presented to an enemy.

The hedgehog, whose scientific name is *Erinaceus europaeus*, is our largest and most important member

A. Brook

HEDGEHOG LOOKING FOR FOOD
After sleeping all day the hedgehog comes out from its hiding place at night to search for such food as insects and snails ; it is also fond of eggs. It is found in many parts of Europe, and it sleeps through most of the winter. When threatened it rolls itself into a ball, presenting an array of inch-long spines to its enemy.

of the order *Insectivora*, to which also belong the shrews and the mole. It eats eggs and snails as well as insects, and is common in Britain. It hibernates during the winter months, sleeping rolled up in a ball beneath a mass of dead leaves or moss. In other lands, too, there are other species, some of them without any spines. (*See* Hibernation).

Heidelberg (Pron. hī'-dl-bärg), GERMANY. Nestling between a wooded height and the beautiful river Neckar, which here leaves its gorge to enter the plain of the Rhine, this quaint university town is one of the most attractive and interesting places in Germany.

The old city consists principally of a long narrow street following the course of the river for about two miles. It grew up at the foot of the castle begun in the 12th century, which crowns the wooded heights in the background. Added to in different periods, the castle became one of the largest and grandest in Germany; but it was almost destroyed during the devastating wars of Louis XIV of France in 1693, and, though later rebuilt, it was struck by lightning and again ruined in 1764.

Its reddish ivy-clad ruins are still beautiful, and in an old cellar beneath the castle is still preserved

the great Heidelberg tun, an enormous wine cask capable of holding about 48,700 gallons.

Heidelberg University was founded in 1386, and in the 17th century was a stronghold of Protestantism. Normally Heidelberg manufactures cigars, leather, fountain pens, surgical instruments, and furniture. Formerly the capital of the Rhine Palatinate, Heidelberg became part of Baden in 1803. Population, about 84,000.

Heine, HEINRICH (1797–1856). "I am a Jew—a Christian. I am tragedy—I am comedy." This is what the most gifted poet in Germany of his century said about himself. Heine (pron hī-'ne) was born of Jewish parents in Düsseldorf, in western Germany, on December 13, 1797; later he joined the Lutheran Church in order to practise law, which he had studied at the universities of Bonn and Göttingen.

Heine's heart was in literature, not in law. During a visit to a wealthy uncle, his life-long benefactor, he fell in love vainly with a very beautiful cousin. His spurned love found expression in exquisite poems which were published in 1822, and created a sensation. Although Heine wrote much about philosophy, literature, and politics, his fame rests on his poems. Many of these lyric gems have achieved the popularity of folksongs, and with good cause, for they have the true folksong qualities. They are simple and full of warmth, and have the freshness and melody of the skylark's note. Some of them, such as The Lorelei and the Two Grenadiers, are universally famous. His songs have been set to music by many famous composers. One of his delightful poems, My Child, We Once Were Children, pictures two children playing at mothers and fathers, and entertaining company, amongst the many distinguished guests present being the neighbour's cat; and the sweet, pensive mood of the poem is broken by the satiric stanza:

> Politely we asked how her health was
>   In the course of a friendly chat.
> (We've said the same things since then
>   To many a grave old cat.)

It is in his prose writings that Heine's most bitter flashes of wit appear. The Pictures of Travel, the most popular of all of Heine's prose writings, is full of sparkling wit.

The nervous headaches of his university days at length were followed by a disease of the spine, which resulted in paralysis. He died February 17, 1856.

Helicopter. When men turned their minds to building flying-machines most of the inventors tried to imitate the flapping movements of a bird's wings; this attempt was doomed to failure for reasons explained under Aeroplane. A few experimenters had the idea of raising a machine directly into the air by the "pull" exerted by a bladed screw rotating horizontally on a vertical shaft.

Some of these pioneers—Leonardo da Vinci (1452–1519) was one—made daring experiments on paper, sketching out designs for machines sometimes fantastic but sometimes also approaching very close to engineering projects of the 19th and 20th centuries. In medieval times engineering skill would not permit the building and testing of machines which might conceivably have proved successful; the current knowledge of metals (and the supply of those metals) lagged far behind the theoretical ponderings of contemporary scientists.

The idea of a helicopter (the name comes from the Greek word *helix*, spiral; and *pteron*, wing) filled the minds of many 19th century flying-machine experimenters. Two Frenchmen, Ponton d'Amécourt and Alphonse Penaud, built model flying-machines on this principle without success. Penaud later gave up the attempt and turned to aeroplanes; he died in 1880 when only 30 years of age. Sir Hiram Maxim also began his flying-machine research by trying to design a helicopter.

Meanwhile, the success which attended the making of gliders and, later, of aeroplanes diverted inventors away from the helicopter type of machine. But in 1908 Louis Charles Breguet achieved a flight of about 25 yards with a helicopter designed by himself. He, again, was a pioneer who later deserted helicopters for conventional aeroplanes. In 1921 Etienne Oemichen tested a helicopter of which the airscrews lifted a weight of nearly 600 lb., the engine being one of 25 horse-power. No provision was made for balancing or forward movement.

In 1925 Juan de la Cierva's autogiro (*q.v.*), or windmill-plane, made successful flights in England.

had spurred on inventors. Success would have been impossible but for the phenomenal increase in power and efficiency of the internal combustion engine.

The Vought-Sikorsky helicopter of 1940 had a single lifting screw with three blades, 28 feet in diameter. There were also three auxiliary airscrews, much smaller, one mounted on the tail and the other two placed on outriggers from the tail end of the main fuselage. These last two were for controlling the lengthwise stability of the machine—that is, in inclining it up and down. Since the pitch of the screws could be varied by the pilot, he could, by giving a different pitch on one side from that of the opposite screw, use them in the manner of ailerons to give side-to-side control. The screw at the tail-end, also with variable pitch, functioned as a rudder.

In making an ascent, the blades of the main rotor were given a fairly large pitch, so that they " bit " the air strongly. Forward movement was obtained by using the two small side-positioned auxiliary screws to incline the nose of the machine downwards slightly. When making a descent without engine power, the main rotor blades automatically took up a smaller pitch, and the aircraft then glided down somewhat in the same manner that an autogiro does. The engine was a 90-horse-power Franklin motor, and the aircraft weighed 1,290 lb.

On test, Sikorsky's helicopter hovered over an area of about an acre for more than an hour. Fitted with cigar-shaped floats, it took off from, and landed on, the Housatonic River. The helicopter which the U.S. Army adopted in 1943 weighed 2,400 lb. and was driven by a Warner engine. A speed of 82 miles an hour and a climb to 5,000 feet were achieved.

Development of the American pioneer machine was rapid, and in Europe also aircraft designers worked out their own versions of a direct-lift aircraft. In 1948 the British G.P.O. held trials of

This was not a helicopter, since the rotor, on a vertical shaft, turned freely and did not lift the aircraft. But experience gained with the autogiro aided the development of the helicopter. In the U.S.A. Igor Sikorsky built an aircraft with a horizontal lifting airscrew which enabled it to rise directly into the air. In 1941 he made a flight of 1½ hours; and in 1943 the United States adopted his helicopter for use in the armed forces. Wartime demands for a flying-machine which could rise or land in a small space, could travel slower than a conventional aeroplane—which *had* to travel fast in order to stay airborne—and, above all, could hover,

P.A.-Reuter; Charles E. Brown

HELICOPTER DEVELOPMENT

Novel features are incorporated in the two helicopters shown here. In the lower aircraft, the Cierva W9, the normal propeller at the tail is replaced by a vent through which gases from the engine are ejected. Ideas giving greater safety, speed and comfort are embodied in the machine at upper left. This is the Fairey Gyrodyne, which made its trial flight in 1948.

helicopters for delivering mails—between Peter-borough, Norwich and Great Yarmouth. American Westland-Sikorski helicopters were used for these trials, since no British machine had then been developed enough for practical work. But Britain was not idle. The Fairey Gyrodyne, combining features of the autogiro and the helicopter, had averaged a speed of about 120 miles per hour and had a top limit of 18,000 feet for altitude. Its rotor was 52 feet in diameter and it weighed about 1½ tons. The engine was an Alvis Leonides which gave 500 horse-power for take-off.

The " Air Horse," built by the Cierva Company, had three lifting rotors, each over 50 feet in diameter, and was the first British freight-carrying rotor air-craft—able to take three tons of cargo, or 24 passengers. The engine was a Rolls-Royce Merlin, of 1,640 horse-power. Another British type was the Bristol 171, designed as a four-seater air-taxi or to take passengers to the bigger air liners ; other projected uses were as a rescue aircraft and for artillery spotting.

By 1948, then, the direct-lift aircraft had come into its own ; like the autogiro, its speed was much slower than that of the aero-plane, but, as we have explained earlier, this was an advantage. The realization of Leonardo da Vinci's dream had taken four and a half centuries !

Heligoland. Form-erly described as the Gibraltar of the North Sea, the island of Heligoland lies 44 miles north-west of the mouths of the Elbe and Weser rivers. Its red sandstone cliffs, 200 feet high, rise sheer from the ocean on all sides except the south-east, where there is a flat bank of sand. It has an area of ⅓ square mile and a circumference of three miles. Until the Second World War (1939–45) it was peopled by Frisian fisherfolk.

Great Britain took Heligo-land from Denmark in 1807, and in 1890 she gave the island to Germany in exchange for the recognition of certain rights

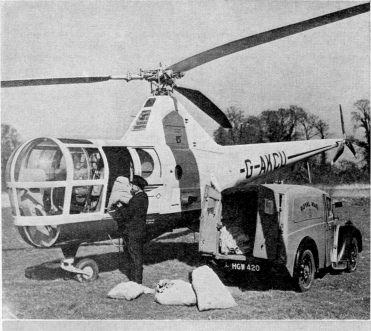

Keystone; Graphic Photo Union

HELICOPTERS AS A POSTAL-VAN AND AS AN AIR LINER

In September 1948 a Cierva ' Air Horse ' was produced and was then the biggest aircraft of its type in the world. It had three rotors (lower), each of three blades, and accommoda-tion for 24 passengers or space for three tons of cargo. The engine was a Rolls-Royce Merlin of 1,640 horse-power. Helicopters are in use to deliver and collect mail in districts where road and rail communication is poor. Top, experiments with such a service were carried out at Yeovil, Somerset

in the island of Zanzibar, off the east coast of Africa. The Germans turned Heligoland into a powerful fortress and naval base to protect the ports of Emden, Wilhelmshaven, Cuxhaven, and Hamburg and the Kiel Canal. The fortifications were dismantled at the end of the First World War (1914–18), and the island was used as a bird observatory; but after the German leader, Adolf Hitler, assumed power in 1933 the island was refortified.

Many attacks were made in this area by Allied aircraft on German warships during the Second World War, and in 1944 the civilian population was evacuated to the German mainland. The island was very heavily bombed in April 1945 and on May 14 the German garrison surrendered to British troops. The town of Heligoland had been completely destroyed, but much of the fortifications had suffered only slight damage. In April 1947 tunnels, gun emplacements and strongpoints were blown up; two minor explosions preceded the final one to scare away the thousands of birds resting on the island during their migration.

Topical

HELIGOLAND BEFORE THE SECOND WORLD WAR
Formerly so heavily fortified by the Germans that it was known as The Gibraltar of the North Sea, the island of Heligoland lies about 28 miles from the German mainland, north-west from the mouth of the Elbe. This photograph shows it as it was before the fortifications and buildings were destroyed by the Allies during and after the Second World War (1939–45). The island was later used as a practice bombing target by the R.A.F.

Helium. By the use of the spectroscope scientists had actually discovered helium on the blazing surface of the sun before they knew of the existence of the gas here on earth. Hence its name, from the Greek *helios*, which means " sun." Strangely enough, this namesake of the hottest body known to Man has since been used to produce the most intense cold ever observed. Helium under great pressure, cooled with liquid air and liquid hydrogen, itself becomes liquid at −269° C., and when this liquid helium is evaporated an even more intense cold (−272° C.) is produced, freezing the liquid. (*See* Heat; Freezing).

Helium is the lightest of inert gases—that is, those that refuse to combine chemically with other substances. Because it will not burn it has been used to inflate the gas-bags of airships instead of hydrogen, which is highly inflammable. In the First World War (1914–18) the United States attempted to produce helium in quantities for this purpose. Up to 1915 the world's total output of this gas was probably less than 100 cubic feet, and its market value was about £340 a cubic foot. Scientists, however, had discovered that helium occurs in some of the natural-gas fields of Canada

and the United States, and plants were erected for its extraction. The process consists in refrigerating the natural gas under very high pressure, and then allowing it to expand. As it expands it becomes so cold that all of its constituents become liquid except helium, which is easily separated. Helium can thus be produced much more cheaply.

Helium exists in very small quantities in the atmosphere, in volcanic gases, and in gases from mineral springs. In addition, it is generated by radium, that amazing element which is constantly breaking down and producing other substances; helium is given off by other radioactive substances, such as thorium, and some scientists believe that all the earth's helium has been derived from this source. (*See* Chemistry; Atom).

Helsinki. Beautifully situated on the Gulf of Finland, the capital of Finland possesses a fine harbour and is also the country's principal port. Considerable export trade is carried on with Russia, Sweden and England in timber, paper, and cellulose. The chief industries are sugar-refining, brewing and distilling, engineering and carpet making. Among notable buildings are the Diet House where the Finnish Parliament meets, the President's palace, the Lutheran church of St. Nicholas and the Uspenski Cathedral of the Greek Church. The university, founded at Abo (Turku) in 1640, was moved to the capital in 1827.

Founded by the Swedes in 1550 on a site about five miles to the north-east of the present one, to which it was moved in 1642, Helsinki was captured

Finnish Legation

IN HELSINKI, CAPITAL OF THE FINNISH REPUBLIC

On the Gulf of Finland, 250 miles by railway west of Leningrad (in the Soviet Union), Helsinki has three harbours, the one seen here being the South Harbour. In the centre is the Lutheran Church of St. Nicholas. As Finland's chief port, in normal times, it carries on a considerable export trade with Britain, Russia and Sweden in paper, cellulose and butter. Founded in 1550 on a site five miles to the north-east of its present one, the city was moved in 1642.

by the Russians from the Swedes in 1808. When the Finnish Republic was established in 1919 Helsinki became the capital of the new State. In the Russo-Finnish War of 1939–40, the city was bombed by Russian aircraft. Finland joined Germany in her attack on Russia on June 22, 1941, and Helsinki was bombed repeatedly by the Russians until the armistice of September 1944. The population is 355,000.

Hemlock. One of the most poisonous plants of the British countryside, hemlock is a tall, not ungraceful plant, with the typical deeply-cut leaves and flat clusters (umbels) of white flowers of the order *Umbelliferae*, the parsley family. Its distinguishing feature is that the hollow, shining stems are liberally spotted and blotched with red or purplish markings; no other similar plant is marked in this way. Hemlock is a very deadly poison, and all parts of the plant are poisonous.

The hemlock tree is a conifer of the genus *Tsuga*, found in Canada and the United States. It has a slender, pyramidal shape, with the typical tall, straight trunk of the forest conifer, small flattened needles, and much smaller cones than have most trees of this type. Of this hemlock there are several species, one of which is called the hemlock spruce, from its resemblance to the better-known spruce. The bark is used extensively in tanning.

Hemp. Since very early times the fibre of the hemp plant, a native of Asia, has been employed in making coarse cloth and rope, and its cultivation is an important industry in China, the sub-continent of India, various parts of Europe, and the United States. Some hemp is grown in England. In India and China hemp is cultivated not only for its fibre, but for its flowers and leaves, from which is prepared an intoxicating drug, called hashish, charas or bhang.

Hemp fibre, which comes from the inner bark of the stem, is valuable because of its length, toughness,

E. J. Bedford

DEADLY HEMLOCK IN BLOOM

A member of the parsley family, hemlock reaches a height of from two to six feet. All parts of it are poisonous. It has red or purplish markings on the shiny, hollow stems.

pliability, and resistance to water. American dew-retted (softened) fibre is grey and coarse, but Italian fibre, which is retted by soaking in soft water, is soft, lustrous, and white. The retting process resembles that used for flax (*q.v.*).

Hemp is chiefly used for making rope, twine, shoe and harness thread, and the coarse cloth known as sacking. At one time it was used extensively in the manufacture of sail cloth and sheeting, and some of the finer quality is still made into cloth in China and Japan. Hemp seeds produce an oil which is used in the manufacture of soap and varnishes and are a bait for certain fish.

The term hemp is also used to designate many kinds of fibre in no way related to the hemp plant—among them Manila hemp, sisal hemp, and the Sunn hemp of India. Manila hemp is a product of the Philippines, and is obtained from a species of banana plant, *Musa textilis*.

All cultivated true hemp is produced from *Cannabis sativa*, a member of the mulberry family, *Moraceae*, varying under cultivation from three to 16 feet in height and having angular rough stems.

Henry. HOLY ROMAN EMPERORS. There were seven emperors of this name in the history of medieval Germany and Italy. Perhaps the most important was Henry IV, who reigned from 1056 to 1106. He succeeded his father, Henry III, when he was less than six years old, and grew up wilful and headstrong. A few years after he took power into his own hands he refused to give up at the command of Pope Gregory VII the right to invest German bishops with their lands. These clergy were not only high officers of the Church but great feudal princes exercising power in the State as well. In 1077 revolts in Germany forced Henry IV to cross the Alps into Italy in the dead of winter, and to humble himself before the Pope, Gregory VII (*q.v.*), at Canossa. But the reconciliation did not endure.

HENRY VII (reigned 1309–13) was the last emperor who sought to maintain the traditions of the medieval Empire. He died in Italy, frustrated in his attempts to restore any effective union of Italy and Germany. His son was John, the blind King of Bohemia, who fell at the battle of Crécy, 1346, fighting with the French against the English.

Eight HENRYS *of* ENGLISH HISTORY

In following the careers of the eight kings named Henry who have sat on the throne of England, much is learnt of our history during the four centuries between Norman and Tudor times.

Henry. KINGS OF ENGLAND. Eight Henrys have sat on the English throne since this name was first introduced into the royal line in the person of Henry I, youngest son of William the Conqueror; and all except two of these royal Harrys (Henry III and Henry VI) were among the ablest of the long line of sovereigns of our island kingdom.

HENRY I, who reigned 1100–35, was called Beauclerc because, unlike most princes of that age, he was a good scholar (*beau clerc* in Norman-French). He is credited with saying that " an unlettered king is only a crowned ass." During the 35 years of his reign England enjoyed peace and prosperity.

At his accession Henry I issued a famous Charter of Liberties, which became the basis of Magna Carta, the foundation of the liberties of the Anglo-Saxon world. He also favoured the Church in order to win its support against his elder brother Robert, who claimed the English throne as well as the Duchy of Normandy, left him by their father.

England was pleased by Henry's marriage with Matilda, a descendant of the Anglo-Saxon kings, and the support of the common people was assured by his successful measures to curb the power of the Norman nobles, and by the justice he administered through the King's Court.

One misfortune darkened Henry's later years. His only son was drowned when, in 1120, the White Ship sank in the English Channel. This accident left his daughter Matilda and his nephew, Stephen, contestants for the throne at his death. (*See* Stephen, King of England).

HENRY II (reigned 1154–89) was the son of Henry I's daughter Matilda (or Maud). His father was Geoffrey, count of Anjou, called Plantagenet from his habit of wearing a sprig of the broom plant (*planta genista*) in his cap; so with Henry II, in 1154, the first Plantagenet king ascended the English throne. Two years before he became king, as a lad of 18, Henry had led an army from France to assert his mother's claim, and the wearied Stephen had agreed to a treaty by which Henry was recognized as his successor.

Henry II was the most powerful prince in Christendom. In addition to England and Normandy, which he held by his mother's right, he inherited from his father, as French fiefs, the important provinces of Anjou, Maine, and Touraine, and by his marriage with Eleanor of Aquitaine he acquired Poitou, Guienne, and Gascony, so that he held most of the British Isles and about one-half of France. Wars with the French king followed.

Henry re-established law and order after the anarchy of Stephen's reign. He improved the military service by permitting the barons to pay scutage or shield money in place of serving in the army; with this he hired soldiers who would fight whenever and wherever he wished—an important means of keeping in order the powerful nobles of the land. His greatest work, however, was the reform of the law courts. The Curia Regis or King's Court was brought into every part of England by the sending of judges on circuit through the land to administer what was called the king's justice, so that gradually one system of law took the place of the many previous local customs.

He also established the grand jury, by which accusations could be brought by a body of representatives of the community against evil-doers who were so powerful that no single individual dared accuse them. To him, also, we owe the growth of the petty or trial jury, especially in cases relating to land; this substituted the weighing of evidence, and testimony by sworn men, for the old superstitious trial by battle, or by ordeal. (*See* Jury). Henry even attempted to bring

HENRY II AND HENRY III IN STONE AND BRONZE

Daveau, Rouen; Royal Commission on Historical Monuments in London

Some of the Norman and Plantagenet kings were buried in England and some in France. The tomb of Henry III (lower) is in Edward the Confessor's Chapel, London. It rests on a pedestal and is surmounted by a gilded bronze effigy of the king, who is wearing his coronation robes and a simple crown. The right hand, now empty, probably once held a sceptre. Henry II's tomb (upper) is in the abbey at Fontevrault, a town of Western France situated on the Vienne river. At his side is the figure of Isabella, wife of his youngest son John, who succeeded his brother Richard I. During the last years of Henry II's reign his sons, even John, his favourite, rebelled against him.

churchmen who committed crimes under the king's courts, but the scandal caused by the murder of Archbishop Thomas Becket forced him to give up this reform. (See Becket).

Henry's last years were embittered by the rebellion of his sons, aided by Philip Augustus, king of France, and by their mother. The king, old, sick, and discouraged, had to consent to the terms demanded of him. When he saw the name of John, his favourite son, among those of his enemies, he exclaimed, " Now let all things go as they will; I care no more for myself, nor for the world." He died in France on July 6, 1189.

HENRY III (reigned 1216–72), son of King John (1199–1216), was a religious man, and a good husband and father, but he was a weak and incompetent ruler. Until he became of age, nobles trained under his grandfather, Henry II, directed affairs, and good order and prosperity prevailed. When Henry III took the administration into his own hands, he squandered the revenues of the kingdom on greedy relatives and favourites. The nobles seized upon his misgovernment as an excuse for rebellion in the Barons' Wars (1264–65), under the leadership of the great Simon de Montfort. After Simon was defeated and slain in the battle of Evesham (1265), the people looked to the king's son, Edward, for good government, and during the last seven years of Henry's reign the country was quiet and flourishing.

HENRY IV (reigned 1399–1413), founder of the royal House of Lancaster, was unjustly exiled in 1398 by his cousin Richard II. The following year he landed in England with only 60 supporters, but these soon became 60,000, for all classes of people were tired of the mingled tyranny and weakness of Richard II, grandson and successor of Edward III, and he was deposed and imprisoned. Henry IV, claiming descent from Henry III, was then seated on the throne by Parliament.

Throughout his reign of 14 years his position was insecure and trying. The claim later asserted by the House of York was felt to be a better hereditary title to the throne than that of Lancaster. Scotland was restless, newly conquered Wales broke into open revolt, and the powerful family of Percy took up arms against the king.

So Henry was obliged to keep on good terms with the Church, and to permit the newly established Parliament to exercise powers in the government of the country which became a notable precedent in later struggles between Crown and Parliament.

HENRY V (reigned 1413–22) succeeded his father Henry IV in 1413 and acquired the reputation of being " the most virtuous and prudent of all the princes reigning in his time." He followed his father's advice to " busy giddy minds with foreign quarrels " by putting forth again the claim to the French throne, formerly raised by Edward III, thereby renewing the Hundred Years' War (1338–1453). By his brilliant victory at Agincourt (1415) he conquered all the northern half of France, and by a treaty five years later he married Princess Catherine of France; it was also agreed that he should become King of France after the death of Catherine's father, the insane Charles VI. In the midst of his victories, Henry V died of camp fever at Vincennes on August 31, 1422, leaving as heir to his rights in both kingdoms his infant son Henry, then only nine months old.

HENRY VI (reigned 1422–71) was one of the most unfortunate kings who ever sat on a throne. While he was still a baby his uncle, the Duke of Bedford, ruled for him, and for a time maintained and even extended the English conquests on the Continent. Then the French were aroused by Joan of Arc, who raised the siege of Orleans and brought the young French king, Charles VII (1403–61), to Reims to be crowned. (See Joan of Arc).

National Portrait Gallery

HENRY VI OF ENGLAND

Devout and learned for his time, Henry VI had an unhappy reign. Whilst he was king, England lost all her French possessions, save Calais, and the Wars of the Roses began. To him England owes Eton College, Buckinghamshire, and King's College, Cambridge.

Matters did not mend for the English when Henry VI grew to manhood. He was truthful, upright and just, but he had the strength neither of mind nor body to rule a kingdom, and for long periods he was insane like his French grandfather. War and business were never to his liking; he would rather have lived the life of a monk. So, bit by bit, the English lost the lands which they held in France, until only Calais was left to them when the Hundred Years' War ended, in 1453.

Meantime, the misgovernment of Henry's ministers at home led to a rebellion under Jack Cade, in 1450, in which London was taken before the insurgents were overpowered and their leaders executed. Five years later began the merciless Wars of the Roses. In these Queen Margaret, Henry's French wife, was the real head of the Lancastrian party. But in the course of the contest he lost his throne to the Yorkists, his young son Prince Edward was slain, and the king himself was finally imprisoned in the Tower of London, where he was eventually murdered. (*See* Roses, Wars of the).

HENRY VII (reigned 1485–1509), who claimed descent from the Lancastrian House, gained the throne by overthrowing the last of the Yorkists. When the battered crown of the usurper Richard III was picked up on Bosworth Field, on August 22, 1485, and placed on the head of Henry Tudor, the seventh Henry, the Wars of the Roses ended, and with them the Middle Ages in England. He was the first modern king of our land. He united the Houses of Lancaster and York by marrying Elizabeth of York, niece of Richard III. War had no place in the policy of this Tudor king, who was called the Solomon of England, and was regarded by his subjects as the craftiest prince of his time.

Abroad, he secured his aims by treaties and by the marriage alliances of his children. At home he increased his power by forbidding the great nobles to maintain lawless bands of followers, and by compelling them to obey the laws by means of his famous Court of Star Chamber. He thus laid the basis of that powerful Tudor monarchy, as it came to his son, Henry VIII, and the great Elizabeth.

Henry VII is also to be remembered because in his time the Renaissance (*see* Renaissance) was established in England. William Caxton had introduced printing into England shortly before this; and it was John Cabot, sailing in 1497 to Newfoundland by permission of Henry VII, who laid the foundation for England's claim to Newfoundland and the mainland of North America. Henry died on April 21, 1509.

HENRY VIII (reigned 1509–47), whose elder brother Arthur died in 1502, was a clever, gay and handsome youth, well skilled in all manner of athletic games, though in later life he became coarse, fat and ungainly. For nearly 40 years he ruled England with a strong hand, and brought about one of the most far-reaching changes ever effected in the institutions of any kingdom. For policy he was betrothed to his brother's girl-widow, Catherine of Aragon.

During the first 20 years of his reign he left the government of the country largely in the hands of his great counsellor, Cardinal Wolsey. On one occasion Henry took part in France in the gorgeous display of the Field of the Cloth of Gold, where

National Portrait Gallery

HENRY VII, WISE BUT MEAN

First Tudor king of England, Henry VII compelled the nobles to obey his laws and laid the foundations of the power wielded by his successors of the Tudor line. This painting by an unknown artist shows him four years before his death in 1509.

he and the young French king, Francis I, met to wrestle, dance, watch tournaments, and talk of international relations and policies.

The decline of Wolsey's power began when Henry professed doubts as to the power of the Pope to grant him the dispensation which the laws of the Church had required in order that he might marry his brother's widow. For Henry had grown tired of Catherine and had fallen in love with a young court lady, named Anne Boleyn.

When the Pope would not annul his marriage, Henry in furious anger turned against Wolsey, and had him arrested for treason. He then obtained a divorce through Thomas Cranmer, whom he appointed Archbishop of Canterbury, and it was soon announced that he had married Anne Boleyn. The Pope was thus defied. All ties that bound the English Church to Rome were broken. Appeals to the Pope's Court were forbidden; all payments to Rome were stopped; and the Pope's authority in England was abolished.

By an Act of Parliament, Henry himself was declared Supreme Head of the Church of England, and to deny this title was made an act of treason. Some changes were also made in the Church services; the Bible was translated into English and copies were placed in the churches. The monasteries throughout England were dissolved, and their vast lands and goods turned over to the king, who in turn granted those estates to noblemen who would support his policies. Soon, in the northern part of the kingdom, the people rose in rebellion on behalf of the monks, but the uprising was put down with extreme cruelty.

Although Henry reformed the government of the Church, he refused to allow any changes to be made in its doctrines. Before his divorce he had opposed the teachings of Luther in a book which had gained for him from the Pope the title Defender of the Faith—a title British kings still bear. And after the separation from Rome he persecuted with equal severity the Catholics who adhered to Rome, and the Protestants who rejected its doctrines.

Anne Boleyn, his second wife, he had executed, and Jane Seymour, his third wife, died in a little more than a year. Anne of Cleves he divorced, Catherine Howard was executed, but Catherine Parr, his sixth wife, survived him. Henry died on January 28, 1547.

Henry. KINGS OF FRANCE. The name of Henry has been borne by four kings of France, and of these the last was the greatest. HENRY I (ruled 1031–60) was defeated by William, later the Conqueror of England, when he attempted to assert his authority over the Duchy of Normandy.

Under HENRY II (ruled 1547–59) began the religious persecution of the Huguenots (French Protestants), which was the cause of the religious wars that started after his death. He died on June 30, 1559, of a wound received in a tournament. HENRY III (king 1574–89) was the last of the three weak sons of Henry II and Catherine de' Medici.

HENRY IV, King of France and Navarre, who reigned from 1589 to 1610, was the last and greatest of the Henrys. He was king, not only of France, but also of the small independent kingdom of Navarre, on the northern slope of the Pyrenees. In 1569, when he was 16 years old, his mother, Jeanne d'Albret, the Huguenot Queen of Navarre, placed him in the care of Admiral Coligny, the brave Huguenot leader, (see Coligny, Gaspard de). From that time until his accession as king of France, Henry of Navarre was the recognized leader of the Huguenot party; but for a short time after his marriage to the king's sister, Margaret of Valois, and the subsequent massacre of St. Bartholomew's Day (August 24, 1572), he seemed to renounce the Protestant faith.

At the death of Henry III, in 1589, Henry of Navarre was the heir to the throne of France. But his right of succession was disputed by the powerful Catholic League, aided by the King of Spain, and he was not crowned until he had enforced his claim by arms and had become a member of the Catholic Church in 1593.

Henry IV set about restoring the prosperity of the land. The improvement in the condition of the people, in which he was aided by his great minister the Duke of Sully, and his own agreeable personality, combined to render him the most popular king France had ever had. On May 14, 1610, he was struck down by the dagger of a religious zealot, leaving the throne to his son, Louis.

Although he conformed to the Catholic Church, Henry IV did not forget the claims of his former religious associates. The Edict of Nantes, which he issued in 1598, gave the Huguenots equal political rights with Catholics; freedom of private worship in their own homes, and public worship in certain places (not including the king's court or within five leagues of Paris); and La Rochelle and a few other strong places as cities of refuge. This edict remained in force for nearly 100 years.

Henry THE NAVIGATOR (1394–1460). A famous figure in the history of exploration was the fifth son of John I, King of Portugal, and of Philippa, daughter of the English John of Gaunt. He became known as Henry the Navigator in honour of the discoveries he inspired. He early distinguished himself at the conquest of Ceuta in 1415. Soon afterwards he moved to Sagres, a town

From Major: Prince Henry
THE NAVIGATOR
Son of John I, King of Portugal, Prince Henry was nicknamed the Navigator—after the voyages of discovery he sponsored.

close to Cape St. Vincent, in south-west Portugal, where he resided for a great part of his life.

While warring against the Moors of Africa, he became greatly interested in this continent, and longed for a better knowledge of the western ocean and the discovery of unknown regions. He founded an observatory and also a school where young men could learn navigation. Then he began sending out expeditions. One by one the rich islands of the Azores, Madeira, the Canaries, and Cape Verde were discovered, and the African coast was explored as far as Sierra Leone. "Explore, trade, convert!" said Prince Henry to his men. All this they did, and unfortunately also began trading in African slaves.

Prince Henry died on November 13, 1460, before the full results of his work were realized.

Henty, GEORGE ALFRED (1832 - 1902). How many of the writers of thrilling books for boys have actually experienced any of the adventures described in their pages? In one case, at least, the author was able to use many of his own experiences, because G. A. Henty, who in the last quarter of the 19th century was without a doubt the chief writer in this field, had a most varied and exciting career.

Henty, who was born near Cambridge on December 8, 1832, served as a volunteer in the British Army during the Crimean War (1854–56), and almost immediately became a journalist as well, for he reported the operations at Sevastopol for a London newspaper. In 1866 he became correspondent for The Standard and saw much fighting.

By the time he was 45, in fact, Henty had accumulated enough experiences to enable him to settle down and turn out, at the rate of three or four every year, those books for which he was to become famous. With Clive in India; The Lion of the North: a Tale of Gustavus Adolphus; Redskin and Cowboy; In the Reign of Terror—these are enough to give some idea of the range he covered.

Even in his leisure he showed his adventurous spirit, for he was a pioneer in the sport of ocean-racing, sailing in his own yacht. It was on this yacht that he died on November 16, 1902, in Weymouth harbour, Dorset.

Hephaestus. (Pron. hē-fēs'-tus). In Greek mythology, the lame god Hephaestus (Roman Vulcan), the son of Zeus and Hera, was the god of fire and the forge. He was lame from birth, according to some stories; but others assert that he was crippled by being hurled down to earth by Zeus, falling on the island of Lemnos in the Aegean Sea, where he built a palace, with a workshop and anvil. He also had a beautiful palace in Olympus, Greece, or, according to others, under Mount Etna, on the island of Sicily. Here with the help of the Cyclopes, the one-eyed giants, he made the thunderbolts of Zeus, the armour of Achilles, and the weapons of Hercules. He was also aided by handmaidens whom he had made of gold and endowed with life. All the palaces of Olympus were built by him. He was the patron deity of the metal-workers.

Hera. By the side of the supreme god Zeus on Mount Olympus, Greece, as the Greeks believed, reigned his stately wife Hera (called by the Romans Juno), queen of the gods. Their life was not always one of harmony, however, for Hera was quick to anger and Zeus frequently gave cause for jealousy. Hera was the goddess of womanhood, of marriage, and of maternity. The peacock, the cuckoo, and the pomegranate were sacred to her. She was usually represented as a beautiful, majestic woman of mature age, with large wide-open eyes and grave expression inspiring reverence. The Greek poet Homer speaks of her as the "white-armed goddess" and the "ox-eyed queen." The most famous statue of Hera was the one by Polyclitus in the temple of Argos, Greece. This was a colossal image, in ivory and gold, representing the goddess seated on her throne, wearing a crown and bearing in one hand a pomegranate and in the other a sceptre with a cuckoo placed at its summit.

Heraldry. In the Middle Ages, when knights wore armour that completely covered their heads and bodies, there grew up the custom of emblazoning devices on shields, banners and surcoats so that the wearers could be distinguished on the field of battle.

By slow degrees an elaborate science of heraldry developed. Strict rules were laid down regulating

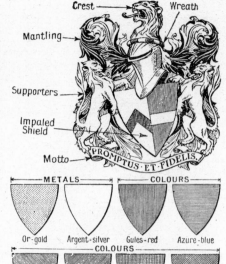

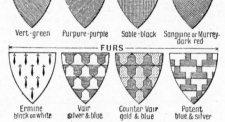

HERALDIC DEVICES

The method of impaling or joining a man's arms (chevron) with those of his wife (bar or fess) on a shield is shown in the imaginary coat of arms at the top. Lower, are the tinctures or devices by which metals, colours, and furs are indicated.

the assumption and design of armorial bearings, and colleges of heralds were founded to enforce observance of the rules. Most of the terms used in heraldry are French, because that language was most widely used while the science was growing up.

Several coats of arms are often arranged, or marshalled, on the same shield, or escutcheon, to show descent, marriage, alliance, or territorial possessions. To enable this to be done, the shield is divided into halves by a single line extending across it vertically, diagonally, or horizontally; or it is divided into quarters by a cross-shaped arrangement of lines, and these quarters may be further subdivided. The metals and colours used in heraldic devices are called *or* (gold), *argent* (silver), *gules* (red), *azure* (blue), *sable* (black), *vert* (green), *purpure* (purple), *sanguine* (dark red).

The "charges" or devices are of infinite variety. Some are wide bands, variously named according to the direction in which they cross the shield. Thus the "pale" extends from top to bottom, the "fess" is a horizontal band in the middle, and the "bend" crosses diagonally from the upper left-hand corner (*dexter chief*) to the lower right-hand corner (*sinister base*) of the shield.

Among common charges are simple geometrical designs, and representations of animals, flowers, or trees. The animal most used is the lion, which may be

HERALDS AT THE PROCLAMATION OF KING GEORGE VI

Much heraldic pageantry marks the accession of a monarch to the throne. Here is seen the proclamation of King George VI at St. James's Palace, London, on December 12, 1936. Between the mace-bearers, reading from left to right, are Clarenceux King of Arms; the Earl Marshal; Garter King of Arms, who read the proclamation; and Norroy King of Arms. At Trafalgar Square the proclamation was read by Lancaster Herald, at Temple Bar by Norroy King of Arms, and at the Royal Exchange by Clarenceux King of Arms. The tabards or official cloaks worn by the Kings of Arms and Heralds are emblazoned with the royal arms. The Earl Marshal is the head of the College of Arms.

placed in several positions: *rampant* (erect on the hind legs), *passant* (walking), *couchant* (lying with the head raised), *dormant* (asleep), and others.

Grants of coats of arms to those entitled to bear them are made by the College of Arms or Heralds College. It is composed of three Kings of Arms (Garter, Clarenceux and Norroy), six heralds (Windsor, Chester, Lancaster, York, Richmond and Somerset), four pursuivants (Rouge Croix, Bluemantle, Rouge Dragon and Portcullis), and two extra heralds. They are appointed by the Earl Marshal, and their duties, in addition to the granting of arms, are to proclaim the accession of the Sovereign, to make proclamations on other important occasions, to attend the Sovereign in the House of Lords, to attend the installation of Knights of the Garter and to marshal processions.

The head of the College of Arms is the Earl Marshal, who nominates the members. The college was established and endowed by Richard III in 1483, and occupies a building in Queen Victoria Street, London, built about 1669 by Sir Christopher Wren.

Hercules. (Pron. hêr′-kū-lēz). By far the most celebrated of the Greek mythical heroes was the mighty Hercules (or Heracles, as the Greeks called him), the son of the supreme god Zeus and the mortal Alcmene. The goddess Hera (Juno) was hostile to Hercules from his birth, and sent two serpents to destroy him in his cradle, but the infant strangled them with his hands.

Obtaining in marriage Megara, daughter of the king of Thebes in Greece, as reward for having slain Erginus, king of Orchomenus, the oppressor of the Thebans, he had by her several children. But in a fit of madness, sent by his old enemy Hera, he slew the children. Then, the myth goes on, he purified himself of this deed by a journey to the Delphic oracle, which instructed him to serve Eurystheus, the king of Tiryns, for 12 years. Eurystheus compelled him to perform the twelve labours; this term, or the phrase " Herculean task," is still used to describe any task of extreme difficulty.

The first labour was the slaying of the Nemean lion, a monstrous beast that terrified the country of Nemea. Hercules, at the command of Eurystheus, strangled the animal with his own hands.

Next he slew the Hydra, a terrible nine-headed water serpent. As soon as he crushed one of the monster's heads with his club, two more grew in its place, but finally, with the help of his companion Iolaus, who seared each neck with a blazing branch, Hercules succeeded in killing the Hydra. He then dipped his arrows in its poison.

His third task was to capture and bring alive to Eurystheus the Arcadian stag, an animal with golden horns and brazen hoofs, so fleet of foot that it scarcely touched the ground. The capture of the wild Erymanthian boar was the fourth labour. Hercules returned from the chase with the huge beast on his shoulders. A greater task was the fifth, the cleansing of the Augean stables. Augeas, king of Elis, had a herd of 3,000 oxen, whose stalls had not been cleansed for 30 years. By turning the rivers Alpheus and Peneus through the stables, Hercules finished the work in a single day.

As the sixth and seventh labours, he killed with his poisoned arrows the monster Stymphalian birds, which fed on human flesh, and captured the Cretan bull. This bull had been sent by Poseidon (Neptune) for Minos, king of Crete, to sacrifice. But Minos was so pleased with the beauty of the animal that he kept it for his own; whereupon Poseidon drove the bull mad and it caused great damage. Next came the capture of the mares of Diomedes the Thracian king, which ate human flesh. Hercules killed Diomedes and threw his body to the horses, before bringing them to Eurystheus.

Hercules was then dispatched to obtain the beautiful girdle of Hippolyte, queen of the Amazons. The hero defeated the warrior-women, killed the queen, and escaped with the girdle. The tenth labour was the capture of the oxen of Geryon, a monster with three bodies, who dwelt on the fabulous island of Erythia, beyond the strait of Gibraltar. On his journey the hero erected the rocks on each side of the strait, known as the Pillars of Hercules.

The eleventh exploit was to obtain the golden apples of the Hesperides, which Gaea, or Mother Earth, had presented to the goddess Hera as a wedding gift. Hercules succeeded through the help of the Titan Atlas, father of the Hesperides, the four sister-nymphs who guarded the apples with the assistance of a sleepless dragon. Atlas, whose task it was to support the weight of the heavens on his shoulders, went to get the apples, while Hercules relieved him of his burden. While engaged in this labour, the hero encountered some other strange adventures, for on the way he met the tiny race of men called Pygmies, and slew the giant Antaeus, son of Poseidon and Gaea, who compelled all strangers coming into his country to wrestle with him, on condition that if he conquered they would suffer death. He also set free Prometheus, who had been chained to a rock in the Caucasus for stealing fire from the gods and giving it to mortals.

Last Labour of Hercules

The last labour was the bringing up of Cerberus from the lower world. Braving the dread regions of Hades, he captured this three-headed dog, who guarded the entrance, and brought him before Eurystheus, who was so terrified that Hercules had to take back the monster.

Having finished his appointed tasks, Hercules was now freed from bondage. But these were not the only feats he performed. He gave way to violence at times, and once, in a fit of rage, slew his friend Iphitus; but, for the most part, his strength was used to relieve those who suffered pain or oppression. For example, he brought back from the grave the noble Alcestis, who had given her life for her husband.

As the life of Hercules was a hard one, so also was the manner of his death. With his wife Deïanira he came to the bank of a river across which travellers were carried by the centaur Nessus. Hercules waded across the stream, while Nessus carried Deïanira. But when the centaur attempted to run away with Deïanira, Hercules shot him with one of his poisoned arrows, The dying Nessus called to Deïanira to take some of his blood and keep it as a charm to preserve her husband's love.

Before long, Deïanira, fearing that Hercules was in love with another woman, sent him a robe which she had steeped in the blood of Nessus. No sooner had he put on the robe, when poison spread through

HERCULES FIGHTS THE MANY-HEADED HYDRA

One of the most famous characters in the mythology of ancient Greece is Hercules, son of the supreme god Zeus and a man of enormous strength. In a fit of madness he slew his own children, and to atone for his crime he was forced to serve King Eurystheus, ruler of the Greek city of Tiryns, who set him the tasks which are known as the twelve labours of Hercules. The second task was to slay the Hydra, a nine-headed monster which dwelt in a swamp. As soon as Hercules struck off one head, two others grew in its place. Eventually Hercules conquered the brute with the help of his companion Iolaus, who, to stop the heads growing, seared the wounds with a torch and buried the last one, supposed to be immortal. This illustration is from a 17th-century engraving by Bernard Picart.

his body like fire, and caused him such agony that, fleeing to Mount Oeta, he built a funeral pyre on which he threw himself to die. But as the flames consumed his body, Zeus caught up the immortal part and bore it to Mount Olympus, where, purged of mortal sin and sorrow, Hercules dwelt among the gods in eternal happiness.

Hercules has been a favourite character in literature, and his heroic strength has inspired many beautiful works of art. The finest representation of the hero in sculpture is the Farnese Hercules in the Naples Museum, Italy. Festivals were celebrated in honour of Hercules, at which his exploits were sung in long poems called Heracleia.

Heredity (Latin *hereditas*, heirship). That like begets like is a self-evident truth. The acorn becomes an oak and not a gooseberry bush. The lion's cub is not a deer. But beyond this very obvious fact observation shows that, apart from these great subdivisions of species, some laws are at work controlling colouring, height, shortness, cleverness, stupidity, and all those attributes that go to make the personality of the animal equally with its structure.

How is this miracle accomplished? For miracle it is that from two specks of matter, less in size than the full-stop ending this sentence, so much of import should spring.

Many great names in modern science are associated with this problem and its solution. Lamarck (1744–1829) believed in the transmission of acquired characteristics. Thus, according to him, the giraffe got its long neck by stretching up to reach the foliage of tall trees, and this neck was transmitted to young giraffes. Wingless birds arose because their owners did not fly.

August Weismann (1834–1919) in the 19th century got near the correct solution in the quest when he felt that in the nuclei of the germ cells lay hidden the secret. Sir Francis Galton (1822–1911), another scientist, calculated that each individual takes half of its equipment from its parents, a quarter from its grandparents, and so backwards in decreasing fractions.

Darwin proposed the theory of natural selection: the fittest survive, the less adequate running into disaster and extinction. So new forms evolve, and so new species arise.

In order that variations may be transmitted, there must be a mechanism. Weismann was right: it lies in the germ cells. Each individual in the higher scale of life is the product of two microscopic cells, one male and one female. Indeed they may be called half cells, for prior to their fusion the nucleus of each loses half its chromosomes—rod-shaped bodies tightly packed into particles; in these are housed all the physical, spiritual, and mental characteristics of the new organism. Each nucleus now carries 24 chromosomes which, joining together, make 48 chromosomes, and the new cell increases rapidly by splitting up into an ever-increasing number of new cells. Characteristics do not modify one another. It is not like mixing coffee and milk in a cup. It is rather like throwing handfuls of coloured beads into a bowl. The mating of two people, one with a hot and one with a mild temper, does not result in an offspring with a medium temper. He will either be hot or mild tempered. The young animal throws clear cut to one or the other.

The mating of dark or fair does not result in mouse-colour. The young animal will breed true to one or other colouring. Characteristics which come down in the first generation are known as *dominant*; those that occur later, as *recessive*. The mating of two recessives will result in a dominant. These chances of inheritance follow recognized mathematical laws of chance and average.

In animals, speed in racehorses, milk production in cows, egg-laying in hens are traits which can be accentuated by intelligent breeding. Eugenics is the name given to this type of work. In human beings it is more difficult to breed scientifically because of the complexities of personality, of intellect, of social setting, and of individual likes and dislikes.

Diathesis is the term which describes predisposition to a disease, such as tuberculosis, rheumatism, and diabetes. Such diseases themselves are not transmitted, but weak resistance to them. Epilepsy and mental disorder come down definitely in a stock, not necessarily showing themselves in the immediate new generation but turning up distressingly at last. Some conditions come down in one sex to appear in the other. Such is haemophilia, the failure of blood to clot. Transmitted by the female it shows itself only in the male. Marriage between cousins is undesirable because any flaw in the stock is thus reinforced. (*See also* Genetics; Mendel).

Herefordshire. One of the least-spoilt counties of England, Herefordshire lies on the eastern borders of South Wales, with Shropshire on the north, Worcester on the east, Gloucester and Monmouth on the south, and Brecknock and Radnor on the west. With an area of 842 square

B. C. Clayton

HEREFORD CATHEDRAL
Begun about 1079, Hereford Cathedral has been much restored since its completion in the 12th century. It possesses a unique map of the world made about 1313. In the Middle Ages Hereford was a centre of the wool trade.

miles, it is fairly level in the centre, but on its borders are hills, the Malverns in the east and the Black Mountains in the south. The chief river is the Wye, which flows across the county.

The principal industry is agriculture. Orchards abound; and Hereford cattle and cider are well known. This border county contains the remains of many old castles, the chief ones being Hereford, Clifford, Weobley, Wilton, Goodrich and Wigmore.

The county town, Hereford, stands on the river Wye and has as its chief industries the making of cider, tanning, brewing, fruit canning and preserving, and tile making. The Cathedral was begun in 1079, on the site of an earlier one, and was completed about 1150. The west front was reconstructed in 1900–05. There is a remarkable map of the world designed about 1313, and a collection of chained books and manuscripts. The population of the county is 112,000.

Hereward THE WAKE. Here is a name that symbolises the virtues of patriotism, gallantry, selflessness, and bravery. The "last of the English," as the author Charles Kingsley (1819–75) has styled Hereward the Wake, is one of the heroic figures of English history. He was by no means the last of the English in a literal sense; the Angles and the Saxons, or the English, as they had come to be called, continued to represent the bulk of the population of England even after they had passed under the rule of William the Conqueror. Hereward was the last of the English in the sense that

Courtesy of Geo. Harrap & Co., Ltd.

HEREWARD KILLS A GIANT

According to Charles Kingsley's (1819–75) book, Hereward the Wake, Hereward went to Cornwall where he quarrelled with a giant named Ironhook. With the giant's own sword, which had been given him by the Princess of Cornwall, the English hero slew Ironhook.

he was the last outstanding defender of the soil of England against the Norman invaders.

The particulars of Hereward's parentage and birth cannot be stated with certainty. It seems certain, however, that he was of noble birth, and belonged to the land-owning class, otherwise he would never have risen to the eminence he did, or been in command of the last remnant of the English defenders in the Isle of Ely, or have had under him great English noblemen like Earls Edwin and Morcar.

He appears to have been banished from England in the reign of Edward the Confessor (1042–1066), because of his hatred of the Frenchmen whom that king had about his court, and to whom he had given high positions in his realm. Hereward accepted his outlawry not unwillingly, believing that he would gain for himself fame and honour by his courage and skill in arms. The passion of his boyhood had been to listen to the stories of great warriors and the battle-songs of the Saxons.

His mother had hoped to make a monk of him, but he hated the cloister, and loved the open air; loathed study, and longed for the life of the camp. He had a companion, too—Leofric by name—who equally loathed the idea of a monkish life, and one day this lad, while in company with Hereward and the latter's brother Alfgar, took a harp in his hands, and sang thus to Hereward:

Before thine eyes the future dim
  Seems to unroll its shadows grey,
And only thee, my lord, I see—
  Athwart the foeman's blood-stained way;
  A path of glory 'fore thee spread,
  Some mighty deed marks each new day.

The youthful harpist Leofric thus became Hereward's first faithful follower. He served him for many years, and afterwards became his biographer, and it is to his account that we are indebted for much that we know of Hereward.

Hereward returned to England on hearing that his mother's estates had been given to a Norman, and one of his first exploits was to attack the wealthy monastery of Peterborough, ostensibly to prevent its riches falling into the hands of the newly appointed Norman abbot, Turold.

Hereward's Alliance with the Danes

The last invasion of England by the Danes took place in 1069. Hereward and the warlike remnant of the English flocked to their standard, hoping, with their help, to drive out the Normans. In the course of this raid, Peterborough was burnt and sacked, and the indignant and ruined monks excommunicated Hereward, while the Danes embarked with their plunder, leaving the English to the armies of William the Conqueror.

Undismayed by the formidable forces which King William brought against him, Hereward entrenched himself in Ely, where the monks, who had forgiven Hereward, armed themselves in his service, and where the surrounding fens protected them against being taken by assault. He made a heroic defence, but at last William built a causeway, crossed to the island, and Hereward and a few of his followers fled through the marshes. What happened to Hereward afterwards is not known, but according to one account, for which there is some evidence, he made peace with the Conqueror, who gave him honours and lands. An idealized version of Hereward's life is given in Charles Kingsley's novel, Hereward the Wake.

Hermes. An adept in robbery and possessed of great cunning was the Greek god Hermes, also called Mercurius (Mercury) by the Romans. He was

Florence National Museum; photo Anderson

HERMES, MESSENGER OF THE GODS
In this bronze statue by Giovanni Bolgna (c. 1530–1608) the Greek god Hermes, whom the Romans called Mercury, is shown as a youth wearing the traditional winged and brimmed hat, wings on his feet, and carrying a staff entwined with serpents and bearing another pair of wings.

the son of Zeus and Maia, daughter of Atlas, the giant who held up the heavens on his shoulders. He began his career by escaping from his cradle when a few hours old, and going out in search of adventures. Finding a tortoise, he took the shell and stretched cords across it, thus inventing the lyre. That evening he stole the oxen of Apollo, god of the sun, hid them in a cave, and killed two of them. When Apollo discovered the theft, Hermes so charmed him by playing on the lyre that he allowed the little thief to go unpunished. Hermes gave his lyre to Apollo, and received in return Apollo's own golden shepherd's staff, which bestowed wealth and prosperity on its owner, turning everything it touched into gold.

Hermes was made the herald and messenger of the gods, and in this capacity one of his many duties was to conduct the shades of the dead to the lower world. Among men he became the patron of merchants, the god of eloquence, of good fortune, of prudence and cunning, of fraud and theft. He was also regarded as the god of the roads, and the pro-

tector of travellers. Pillars with his image at the top were erected as sign-posts.

Hermes was represented most commonly as a slender youth, wearing a broad-brimmed hat adorned with two small wings, and carrying his magic wand in his hand. On his sandals were wings that bore him over land and sea with the swiftness of the wind.

Hero AND LEANDER. One of the supreme accounts of ill-fated love is the Greek legend of Hero, priestess of Aphrodite, and Leander, the stalwart youth who nightly swam the Hellespont (Dardanelles) to meet her. According to the story as told by various Greek and Roman poets (notably Musaeus in the 5th or 6th century A.D.), Hero used to place a lamp at the top of her lonely tower at Sestos each night to guide her lover through the waves from Abydos, in Asia Minor, on the other side of the strait.

Venturing to make the passage one stormy night, he was drowned, and his body was washed up at the tower. Seeing the lifeless form of her lover, Hero plunged into the water that she might join him in death. Christopher Marlowe (1564–93) wrote a fine poem on Hero and Leander, and Byron (1788–1824), who himself accomplished the difficult

Painting by Lord Leighton; Manchester City Art Gallery

HERO'S LAST WATCH
According to the Greek legend every night Hero used to watch her lover Leander swimming to her across the Hellespont, now known as the Dardanelles. One night she watched in vain, for he had been drowned. Learning this, Hero drowned herself in the waters that had engulfed him.

feat of swimming the Hellespont, refers to the tale in these well-known lines:

> The winds are high on Hellas' wave,
> As on that night of stormy water
> When Love, who sent, forgot to save
> The young, the beautiful, the brave,
> The lonely hope of Sestos' daughter.

Herod. Several rulers in Palestine were named Herod; Herod the Great, king of Judaea from 37 B.C. to 4 B.C., being the most noted.

HEROD ANTIPAS AND JOHN THE BAPTIST
Alinari
Decorating one of the walls of the cloister of the Scalzo, Florence, is this painting by Andrea del Sarto (1486–1531) of John the Baptist being bound before Herod. Like his contemporaries, del Sarto clothed his figures in the dress of his own period.

It is generally accepted that Jesus of Nazareth was born towards the end of his reign. Herod Antipas, son of Herod the Great and ruler of Galilee from 4 B.C. to 39 A.D., is the Herod most frequently mentioned in the New Testament; to him Jesus was sent by Pilate, the Roman governor of Judaea.

Herodias, the granddaughter of Herod the Great and wife of Herod Antipas, prompted Salome, her daughter by her first husband, to ask Antipas, whom she charmed by her dancing, for the head of John the Baptist on a charger (a large flat plate), thus bringing about the prophet's execution. John had angered Herodias by denouncing Herod Antipas for divorcing his first wife in order to marry her.

Herodotus. (484–*c.* 425 B.C.). Commonly known as the father of History, Herodotus was born at Halicarnassus, in Asia Minor; and as it was then under Persian rule, he was technically a Persian. He early devoted himself to a literary life, and travelled extensively, visiting the northern shores of the Black Sea (Euxine), as well as Persia, Egypt, Italy and Sicily.

He investigated both the customs and religion of the peoples and the history of the countries through which he passed. He made use of the material which he gathered in his great work—the first specifically historical work ever written. The special purpose of Herodotus's work, which consists of nine books, is to give an account of the conflict between the Greeks and the Persians; but he often turned aside from his main purpose to describe interesting things he had seen or heard. His work is thus a rich source of information for the early history of all the lands about the eastern Mediterranean.

Herring. One of the most important of all food fishes is the herring; its family, the *Clupeidae*, is indeed the most valuable of all fish families from an economic point of view. For besides the herring itself (*Clupea harengus*) it includes the sprat, sardine or pilchard, anchovy and various species of shad, the last of which are more important as food fishes on the North American than the European side of the Atlantic.

Not unnaturally, we know more about the life history of the herring than about that of many food fishes, for its presence or absence is a matter of vast importance to the herring fleets. It is known, for example, that the herring migrate to definite localities in such waters as the North Sea, when spawning time comes; that they spawn in spring and autumn; that they are not mature and do not spawn until the age of five years; and that they are of the class known as demer-

THE HERRING : IMPORTANT FOOD FISH
A. H. Jacob
Owing to its nourishing qualities and its great abundance, the herring is an important food fish ; and oil is extracted from herrings for use in food preparation. This fish is found, in vast shoals, near land in the North Atlantic and in the North Sea.

sal fish, that is, they spawn at the bottom of the sea, or among sea-weed. Another thing about the herring is that not only does it, after spawning, frequently run up into salt-water lochs for a while, but it can also survive in those which are practically pure fresh-water.

The herrings which have the habit of frequenting lochs are

H. H. Goodchild; W. S. Berridge
SPRAT AND PILCHARD
Two of the smaller members of the herring family are the sprat (left) and the pilchard (above). Pilchard fishing is carried on off the Cornish coast during the late autumn. Young sprats are known as whitebait.

considered to belong to a race quite distinct from those found in the deeper waters, and these two races are known as coastal and sea herring respectively. The best commercial variety of coastal herring is the Loch Fyne. Moreover, while the loch-frequenting herrings spawn in the spring, those of the open sea do so in the autumn. Since 1935 the British herring-fishing industry has been organized, developed and regulated by the Herring Industry Board. In 1948 the Board opened a processing factory at Wick, in Caithness, to extract oil from herrings for use in food preparation. This was one measure to deal with the glut often experienced by fishermen, when more herrings are landed than the market at the time can absorb (*see* page 1307).

Herrings are caught in curtain-like nets by drifters—that is, boats which put out their nets and then drift across or through the fishing grounds. The net is of the type illustrated in page 1299, in which the fish become trapped by their expanded gill-covers. Headquarters of the English industry are at Grimsby, Yarmouth, and Lowestoft on the East Coast ; while the Scottish herring fishery is largely carried on from Wick and Aberdeen, the boats operating off the Shetlands in spring, and off the Orkneys as well as the East Scottish coast later in the year. There are great fisheries for spring herring off the coasts of Norway, and in the Baltic.

An important industry is the pilchard fishery, carried on largely off Cornwall. The pilchard (*C. pilchardus*), formerly regarded as rather a delicacy is now familiar to all in its canned form. Small pilchards are the " sardines," which are caught off the west coast of France. Sprats (*C. sprattus*), found especially in estuaries and firths of the Scottish coast, are also the subject of an extensive fishery. Young sprats are known as whitebait.

Yet another food fish which is closely related to the herring is the anchovy (*Engraulis encrasicholus*), a migratory species inhabiting the southern North Sea, the English Channel, and the Mediterranean. It is only eaten salted, or in the form of a flavouring.

Hertfordshire. (Pron. har-fordshĭr). A beautiful pastoral English county, 632 square miles in extent, Hertfordshire stretches northwards

for 30 miles from the northern suburbs of London to the borders of Bedfordshire.

It is a pleasant and undulating district, with many woodlands, and wide stretches of arable land, peculiarly suitable for wheat growing. An extension of the Chiltern Hills, in the form of grassy downs, stretches across it.

There are no large rivers, but quite a number of small streams. The most important of these are the Lea, Ash, Beane, Hiz, Ivel, Maran, Stort, and

H. & V. Joel
A HERTFORDSHIRE MANSION
For more than 300 years the seat of the Cecil family, Hatfield House, near Hatfield, is one of the most notable examples of Jacobean architecture in Britain. Completed in 1611, it contains part of the old palace of the bishops of Ely.

Ver. The artificial New River, which supplies much water to London, runs nearly parallel with the Lea. Agriculture, market gardening and the growing of fruit for the London market are the main industries.

Herts (pron. harts), as it is abbreviated, is rich in historical sites. In Roman times the capital of southern Britain was Verulamium, near St. Albans (*q.v.*), itself one of the oldest towns in Britain. There are many famous houses in the county, including Hatfield, Knebworth, and Panshanger. The principal towns are Watford, now an important industrial and agricultural centre, St. Albans, Hertford (the county town, population 11,300), Hitchin, Welwyn Garden City, and Letchworth, also a garden city. Part of Whipsnade, the country branch of the London Zoo, lies within Hertfordshire. Other modern developments in the county are the film studios centred on Elstree, the aircraft works at Hatfield, the B.B.C. wireless transmitter at Brookman's Park, and an agricultural experimental station near Harpenden.

Hertfordshire is rich in literary associations, and is particularly connected with the name of Charles Lamb (1775–1834), whose early memories of the county are recorded in his essays. The philosopher Francis Bacon (1561–1626) lived at Gorhambury, near St. Albans; the poet Cowper (1731–1800) was born at Berkhamsted and introduced into Ware his poem, John Gilpin. Bulwer-Lytton (1803–1873), the novelist, inherited Knebworth from his mother, and it still remains the seat of his family. The population of Herts is about 535,000.

Hertz, HEINRICH RUDOLF (1857–1894). The discovery of the "Hertzian waves" of wireless telegraphy will always be associated with this German physicist.

To Hertz the 20th century owes much of all it has enjoyed and benefited from, following the discovery that light consists of electro-magnetic vibrations ; or, to put it in another way, that electro-magnetic effects are propagated through space in the same manner and at the same speed as those of light —at 186,000 miles per second.

Hertz was born at Hamburg on February 22, 1857. Leaving school, he went to study at Munich University, and there, under the influence of the great Helmholtz, physiologist and physicist, the young student devoted himself to physical science. Soon he became Helmholtz's chief assistant, and in the short space of three years his original theories and papers had won for him a high place among the scientists of the world.

The British scientist, James Clerk-Maxwell (*q.v.*), had several years before given mathematical expression to the relationship between electric and magnetic forces. His formulae proved that ordinary light waves were comparatively short electro-magnetic waves. But it took 20 years to prove practically what Clerk-Maxwell deduced from calculation, and Hertz was the genius to demonstrate it. He proved to the world of science the existence and nature of those waves to which the name Hertzian Waves was given, and so paved the way for wireless communication. This brilliant scientist was only 30 years of age when he discovered and proved experimentally the correspondence between light waves and other electro-magnetic waves.

Hertz connected the secondary circuit of an induction coil (*q.v.*) to two metal rods ; on the end of each rod was a sphere of polished metal, the two spheres being separated by a small gap. He found that an electric charge was built up on the spheres, as it is on the plates of a condenser (*see* Electricity), until that charge grew powerful enough to break down the air insulation and jump the gap, with the passage of an electric spark. This set up electro-magnetic oscillations. Hertz found also that, with a loop of wire having two balls at the open end (separated by a gap as in his " oscillator"), he could receive electro-magnetic energy which produced similar sparks in the loop— even when the loop (which he called a " resonator") was as far away from the oscillator as 13 yards.

Hertz made many further discoveries regarding the propagation of electro-magnetic waves through space: the measurement of the length and speed of such waves; how they are reflected and refracted in the same manner as light waves. At this period, 1887–1889, he just missed discovering the X-rays which another German physicist W. K. Röntgen announced to the world in 1895.

Hertz was able to measure the wavelength of the oscillations by means of a similar resonator. He found out that the passage of a spark across the gap "ionized" the air and made it a conductor ; also that ultra-violet light rays (*e.g.* from a carbon arc light) ionized a similar spark-gap. We know today that the ultra-violet radiations cause the metal to emit electrons which thus form a conducting path.

After a long illness, this brilliant scientist died at the age of 36 at Bonn, Germany, on January 1, 1894.

Hibernation. The pet garden tortoise, or the hedgehog, which you used to see in the summer months, disappears underground during the winter; you may dig them up in the leaves of the ditch, or find them hidden beneath the tool shed. In these creatures you are witnessing the strange problem of hibernation (from the Latin word *hibernare*, to pass the winter).

In northern countries the great majority of adult insects, worms, etc., and of the marine life fixed

HEINRICH HERTZ
Beginning the study of electro-magnetic waves in 1885, this German scientist achieved practical results on which wireless communication is based.

between high- and low-tide range, die in winter, leaving immature stages to revive their race in the succeeding spring. Fishes of brooks and shallow streams, and of the shallows near shore, retire to deeper water, and some bury themselves in the mud. Many birds fly southward and almost all of them retire to countries where there is more easily obtainable food. This leaves quite a large number of animals of various classes which, so far as passing the winter is concerned, may be divided roughly into two classes—those able to obtain food during the snowy season, and those whose food supply is cut off by the winter.

For these latter, the only alternative to death is hibernation—" sleep," or a torpid state, in a sheltered place; and it is resorted to by all kinds of northern land creatures. Earthworms burrow below the reach of frost. All manner of insects in their pupal stage lie inert within cocoons, while others remain dormant as eggs or larvae. Frogs and other amphibians bury themselves deeply in the mud of the pond, or in loose soil and rotting stumps. Snakes coil up in crevices of rocks or holes in the ground. And some four-footed animals occupy deep burrows or warm nests, where many pass the winter.

In most cases of hibernation, the animal is one that is unable to get its accustomed food in winter, and has not learned—like the squirrel and the dormouse—to gather and have under cover a store of imperishable supplies such as nuts, seeds, dried fungi and the like. Other hibernators prepare unconsciously for the ordeal by eating amply in the abundance of autumn, when Nature's bounty is greatest, and storing up, in the fat which then covers their bodies, fuel destined gradually to be absorbed as nourishment during hibernation.

What is the nature of this dormancy ? We term it, loosely, winter sleep, but this does not explain it, and it differs a good deal from sleep. The body temperature falls lower; heart-beat and respiration are slowed down, along with other bodily functions. Some normal functions of active life cease altogether for the time being. It is a " resting state."

There is a parallel state called aestivation (sometimes spelled estivation) or " summer sleep "; some mud-fishes, when the rivers dry up in the hot season, pass a period until the coming of the rains in a sort of mud "coccoon," coiled up waiting for better times! Certain land snails go to ground, or retire into crevices, during dry seasons; they seal up the opening of their shell with a film of matter which they secrete, and stay dormant until wet weather comes.

Hibernating animals differ much in the soundness of their sleep. Some, such as the squirrel, are light sleepers, and often on mild days will wake up, come out, and move about indolently until the return of cold sends them back to bed. Bears are among the most irregular. In very cold and snowy countries the females " lie up " early, and may be snowed under for weeks. They lie quietly, subsisting on their accumulated fat. It is thus that the female polar bear passes the cold months, but the males are abroad during all the long, dark, polar night, even in the farthest north. In the case

of other northern species, the males also hibernate, each by itself, but are liable to come out at times in search of food.

Another irregularity is shown in the marmot, which retires underground very early while plenty of green herbage remains for its nibbling. This may be due to a habit inherited from former conditions, when winter came earlier and ended earlier, for the marmot often comes out in spring long before he should. An even more striking example is shown by certain bats, which retire in July, when insects are still plentiful.

Hieroglyphics. The picture characters which the Egyptians used in writing are commonly called hieroglyphs or hieroglyphics (from the Greek *hieros*, sacred; and *gluphein*, carve). In the early Roman period the knowledge of hieroglyphic writing was lost, and all attempts to decipher it failed until

HIEROGLYPHICS OF ANCIENT EGYPT
The earliest form of Egyptian hieroglyphics is shown, all the characters being pictures and generally easily recognizable. In a later form only the salient features of the pictures were used, and eventually they became merely conventional representations of the original hieroglyphics.

the early years of the 19th century, when some of the characters of the Egyptian alphabet were deciphered. The difficulty was solved at length by the discovery of the Rosetta Stone, now in the British Museum, and of a stone obelisk from Philae. It was customary for kings to publish their edicts in two or more languages, and each of these monuments bears both a Greek and Egyptian version of an inscription. By studying and comparing them it became possible to translate Egyptian hieroglyphics. (*See* Egypt ; Young, Thomas).

High - Frequency Currents. In the story of Electricity we read about alternating currents, and learn that the ordinary " frequency " of supply from the mains is 50 cycles (i.e. 50 complete reversals) per second. In the present pages we consider some of the remarkable effects which we encounter when dealing with currents having frequencies measured in kilocycles (thousands a second) and megacycles (millions a second).

Up to about 10 kcs. (10,000 cycles a second) alternators of special design (known as high-frequency alternators) can be used. Above these frequencies, generation is by means of a thermionic valve (*see* Electronic Devices ; Radio) which, by suitable arrangement of inductance and capacity in its circuits, is caused to oscillate, and to generate high-frequency currents.

High frequencies are used by the telecommunications engineer for radio and " wired-wireless " or carrier telephony . The chief use which the power engineer has for them is in high-frequency heating —induction heating, and dielectric heating.

Induction heating depends on Faraday's principle of electro-magnetic induction. A stationary conductor in an alternating magnetic field behaves just like a moving conductor in a stationary field, and has an E.M.F. (electromotive force) induced in it in the same manner. Depending on the size and resistance of the conductor, what are known as eddy currents will be set up in the latter—i.e., currents which circulate inside the conductor itself and give rise to internal heating. The E.M.F. induced in a conductor is proportional to the *rate at which the field changes*—that is, the speed of rotation, if we are considering a dynamo (moving conductor in a stationary field) ; or the frequency, if we are considering a stationary conductor in an alternating field. If, then, we raise the frequency high enough, we can induce a considerable quantity of heat in a conductor simply by placing it inside the field produced by a magnet coil fed from the high-frequency supply. One of our illustrations shows a graphite crucible (which, although non-metallic, is a conductor) being heated by the "work coil" surrounding it; this coil is being energised at several megacycles per seond. The remarkable point is that while the crucible is white-hot, the coil remains comparatively cool, since the only heat in it is caused by its own resistance to the h.f. (high-frequency) current, and a certain amount radiated back to it from the hot crucible. The coils are, in fact, water-cooled to guard against this un-useful heating.

Another queer trick of electricity, known as "skin effect," enters into this type of heating. Any alternating current flowing along a conductor will tend to forsake the centre, and to crowd into the outer layers of the conductor. The higher is the frequency and the higher the current, the more does this happen. Even at low frequencies and high currents, it is often found that a tube is just as good a conductor as a solid rod of the same diameter. At high frequencies such as we are considering, most of the heating is produced in a thin outer skin, and the heat spreads from the outside inwards. It is possible, by carefully choosing the amount of power, the frequency, and the " coupling " between the coil and the work, either to heat all the work, or only a small part of the outside of it. Fig. 2 shows an example of such partial heating, where the teeth of a chain sprocket are being heated, leaving the centre cool. This principle of partial heating is becoming widely used in the heat-treatment (for hardening) of steel parts; such operations on small parts which, at one time, required careful individual heating of each part can now be done automatically at the rate of hundreds an hour.

It is explained in the story of Electricity, when describing capacity and condensers, how the dielectric of a condenser is subject to a considerable strain at each reversal of charge. This sets up a certain amount of heating (depending upon the " loss factor " of the material) which, although almost unnoticeable at ordinary power frequencies, may be quite considerable at high frequencies. This immediately suggests another new method of obtaining heat, which is in constant practical use.

The General Electric Co., Ltd.; Rediffusion Ltd.

HIGH-FREQUENCY CURRENT AS A SOURCE OF HEAT

Heat can be induced in a conductor by placing it inside the electro-magnetic field produced by a coil fed from a high-frequency supply. A graphite crucible (1) is brought to white heat by currents induced in it by the high-frequency currents flowing in the coil. A cycle sprocket wheel (2) is being heated by high-frequency current, the most intense heat being developed on the surface of the teeth. 'Welding' a plastic mackintosh material (3) by dielectric heating.

HIGHWAYMAN DUVAL AND A ROADSIDE DANCE

Of the well-known highwaymen, Claude Duval (1643–70) was famous for his daring robberies and the gallant way in which he treated ladies who were involved in them. According to a story, he once waylaid a coach in which a man and his wife were travelling with £400 in cash. Duval requested permission to dance with the lady by the roadside. The dance having been performed before the lady's husband, Duval asked and received £100 for the entertainment, then allowed the couple to go on their way. The scene is here depicted by W. P. Frith, R.A. (1819–1909).

Most non-conductors of electricity are very poor conductors of heat. If, for example, we wish to dry quickly a large piece of wood, and we put it between steam-heated plates, it takes hours for the heat to penetrate to the centre. But if we place the piece of wood between two condenser plates, connected to a high-frequency supply, we are making it act as the dielectric of that condenser, and can induce heat in it. Furthermore, the heat is induced fairly evenly throughout the wood, and it is possible, by applying sufficient power, to heat a piece throughout in minutes—or even seconds.

This principle is applied to many operations which could not be carried out any other way, since heat cannot be conducted through some materials in any considerable quantity without making the outside so hot that it is damaged. Plastic sheet can be welded, for example, by dielectric heating. If you look at a transparent mackintosh, you will probably find no sewing in the seams: they are all high-frequency welded.

Food can be cooked by dielectric heating, but it is not a great success as yet for various reasons. Different materials have different loss factors, and it is possible to burn the fat off a piece of meat, and leave the lean part almost raw. Also, since the food cooks from the inside, there is no browning and, although a cake can be baked in less than a minute, it is not particularly nice to look at. But high-frequency heating can be used for re-heating food which has already been cooked by normal methods. Thus in America there are automatic machines which, upon the insertion of a coin, deliver a cellophane-wrapped sandwich, piping hot from its high-frequency "heat treatment"!

Highwaymen. In the late 17th century and in the 18th no traveller along the public roads of England could be sure of reaching his destination safely; for this was the age of the highwaymen. And this state of things lingered on until the early 19th century.

These desperadoes waited in ambush and held up coaches at the point of the pistol, then proceeding to relieve the passengers of all the valuables they had about them. If the orders of these " gentlemen of the road " were disobeyed, then woe betide the unfortunate traveller.

Many are the stories and legends which have grown up around the highwaymen. Most people have heard of Dick Turpin and his ride to York on Black Bess. Turpin was certainly a historical character; he lived from 1705 until 1739, and made quite a business of cattle-lifting, smuggling, and thieving, as well as being a notorious highwayman. The story of Turpin's ride, however, is mythical, despite Harrison Ainsworth's description in Rookwood, and is probably based on the amazing feat of one " Swift Nick " Nevison, who in 1676 is said to have robbed a sailor near Rochester, in Kent, at 4 a.m. and to have established an alibi by reaching York at 7.45 p.m. on the same day. Nevison, like Turpin, came to an untimely end on the York gallows.

The most romantic figure among the highwaymen was undoubtedly Claude Duval (1643–70), a native of Normandy. The epitaph on Duval's grave in Covent Garden church in London indicates his place in popular estimation:

Here lies Du Vall: Reader, if male thou art
Look to thy purse: if female to thy heart.

Himalaya Mountains.

(Pron. hi-mah'-la-ya *or* him-*a*-lā-ya). Compared with other ranges such as the Andes the Himalayan is not extensive, for its length is only about 1,500 miles, and its average breadth about 200 miles. In elevation, however, it is unique. From the southern of its two parallel ranges between 40 and 50 peaks rise more than 23,000 feet in the air, overtopping most other mountains on the earth. Mount Everest, the highest of the Himalayas, is 29,141 (officially 29,002) feet, or nearly 5½ miles high (*see* facing page). The average height of the passes is 18,000 feet.

Lying on the northern frontier of the sub-continent of India, the Himalayas extend from the borders of Afghanistan to Upper Burma on the east, and separate the plateau of Tibet from the plains of the Ganges. They are in the sub-tropic latitude, so the snow-line is at about 16,000 feet. The lofty southern range forms a wall which intercepts the rain-laden clouds brought by the monsoon winds and at some points 600 inches of rain fall in the course of a year, while the inner range and the Tibetan table-land are dry, cold, and half-desert.

Up to 5,000 feet on the southern slope the tea plant is cultivated, as in the famous gardens of Darjeeling, and other places. Grains and fruits are grown up to 12,000 feet, and in the summer months cattle and sheep are pastured on slopes up to a height of 18,000 feet.

Tigers and leopards, bears, deer, goats, yaks and rhinoceroses are all found at various heights. The passes are blocked with snow from November to May. From melting snow and glaciers, innumerable streams and cascades drop down through wild gorges to feed the Ganges, Indus, Jumna, Sutlej and Brahmaputra, which all rise in the Himalayas.

The Hindus from ancient times have held the Himalayas in reverence as the home of the gods. Pious pilgrims still ascend to the source of the sacred Ganges to spend a time in penitence and prayer. To people coming from the steaming heat of the valleys, the greatest marvel of all is the snow-mantled, jagged ridge-pole of this " roof of the world." The name Himalaya is from two Sanskrit (ancient language of India and Ceylon) words which mean dwelling-place of the snow. (*See also* Everest; and map of Asia facing page 264).

Hinduism.

Of the 388 million people in the sub-continent of India, more than 250 millions are Hindus, and the name Hinduism is given to their complicated religious beliefs and the social customs that arise from them.

When the Aryan conquerors first appeared in northern India, about 1500 B.C., there gradually arose a series of sacred writings in the Sanskrit language called the *Vedas;* these expressed a lofty and mystical belief in one divine Being which included all knowledge and all Nature within itself. This earliest form of Hinduism has been greatly modified.

According to these Vedas this early Aryan society was divided into four social castes or classes— the Brahmans, or priestly caste; the Kshatriyas, or soldier caste; the Vaisyas, or farmer class; and the Sudras, or labourers. Early in their history, the Brahmans gained political as well as religious supremacy over the Kshatriyas, and established the religion called Brahmanism, set forth in writings called Brahmanas, which are little studied. Gradually, the worship of one supreme Being gave way to a religion of personal gods of which Brahma, the Father of all; Vishnu, the Preserver; and Siva, the Destroyer, were the most important.

As the native tribes of India were conquered one by one by the Aryans, the Brahmans found it wise to allow the new converts to retain many of their old beliefs, and primitive religious customs. This has left a permanent mark upon the Hindu religion, especially in Southern India, where primitive customs like animal sacrifice, and superstitious

A. R. Slater

HINDU OF THE HIGHEST CASTE

Of the many castes into which the followers of the Hindu religion are divided, the Brahman or priestly caste is the highest. This young Brahman, who is studying a religious work, is wearing the sacred thread of his caste over his left shoulder. On his forehead is painted the trident of the god Siva, one of the chief Hindu deities.

THE CHALLENGE OF UNCONQUERED EVEREST

Courtesy of the Mount Everest Committee

Extending for some 1,500 miles along the northern boundary of the sub-continent of India, the Himalayas (*see* article in facing page) contain many peaks more than 23,000 feet in height. In the centre background of this photograph is the 26,000-feet North Peak; the snow-tipped peak farther to the right is Everest, 29,141 feet above sea-level, whose summit has not yet been reached by any mountaineer, though a British aeroplane flew over it in 1933. Because of their inaccessibility, the native peoples have from ancient times reverenced the Himalayas as the home of the gods. Among the hundreds of rivers rising here are the Ganges, the Indus and the Brahmaputra.

beliefs in demons and local deities still prevail. Opposition to this adulteration of the old religion was in part responsible for the foundation in the 6th century B.C. of the creeds of Buddhism and Jainism, but the Brahmans retained the adherence of the majority of Hindus.

Today Brahmanism has ceased to exist as a distinct faith, being swamped beneath the mass of popular beliefs and rituals, and incorporated in Hinduism. Scores of sects have grown up, some emphasizing the worship of Vishnu, others of Siva, and still others of newer gods.

Most of the sects base their practices upon popular religious treatises of about A.D. 700, called

puranas. At the same time the old four-fold caste system has split into thousands of branches and sub-castes.

Most true followers of Hinduism continue to look upon the Brahman caste as their leaders, and to observe broadly similar rules regarding food, marriage, and burial. One of the most interesting of the Hindu beliefs is that in the transmigration of souls, or metempsychosis. According to this doctrine the soul of a person passes at death into some other creature, either human or animal. If the person has led a good life, the soul goes upward in the scale of existence —a low-caste, for instance, will be reborn

as a high caste; but if the person has led an evil life, the soul may pass into the body of an animal. As a result of this doctrine, the Hindus believe that during his life a man cannot leave the caste into which he is born, and he must take his wife from the same caste, and his childen after him are members of the same caste.

Hippopotamus. With its body like an undersized elephant, its little pig's eyes, its broad-muzzled head, showing formidable tusks when it yawns, the hippopotamus is perhaps the ugliest mammal in existence. Its great clumsy body, and short stocky legs, would scarcely lead one to think of it as an expert swimmer and diver. But it is more at home in the water than on land.

The name hippopotamus means river horse (from two Greek words: *hippos*, horse; and *potamos*, river), but this African animal is really related to the pigs. The hippopotamus (*Hippopotamus amphibius*) is the largest existing land mammal next to the elephant. The finest specimens of the common hippopotamus measure 12 to 14 feet in length, and about 5 feet or more in height, and may weigh more than 4 tons. The body is covered with a hide which is over an inch thick

W. F. Taylor; F. W. Bond

HIPPOPOTAMI IN CENTRAL AFRICA
Nestling against its mother's huge muzzle is this baby hippopotamus. The nostrils, protruding eyes and ears of this animal are set in the upper surface of the flat face so that they alone project above the water when the beast swims, leaving the great head concealed. The upper photograph, taken in Central Africa, shows hippopotami wallowing in a marsh.

'WIDER, PLEASE'—THE WORLD'S LARGEST YAWN

Autotype

Even a hippopotamus feels bored at times, and this one decided to yawn just when the photographer was about to press the button. So we have a fine view of the inside of the animal's huge mouth, armed with great yellow, tusk-like teeth. Notice the stiff bristles on the upper lip. His eye is set on a raised brow so that he can still see when nearly every other part is submerged.

To face page 1628

Fox; left, E.N.A.

HIPPOS IN THE HERD

HERE are two photographs of that huge and extraordinary beast, the hippopotamus. Above, a big herd of them are stampeding in a wild, surging mass, terrified as much by the noise as by the sight of the passing aeroplane from which this photograph was taken. Even here you can see their bulky, cumbrous build and huge, rounded snouts. These features are seen better still in the lower photograph, a close-up of some of these beasts having their after-dinner nap in the shallows of the Zambezi river. How like they are to huge, half-submerged rocks or balks of timber! Were it not for their bright, twinkling eyes one would hardly recognize them as animals at all. Indeed, it is hardly surprising that in ancient times this beast was regarded as a semi-fabulous monster, the ' behemoth ' of the Bible.

To face page 1629

on its back and sides, and is hairless except at the tip of the tail. It can close its large nostrils and short ears when under water.

During the day hippopotamuses (or hippopotami) remain in the water, often in herds of 20 to 40. At times they disappear beneath the water for four or five minutes at a time. When these creatures are excited or in pain their bodies become covered with drops of a reddish fluid, which gives rise to the saying that the hippopotamus " sweats blood"; but blood forms no part of this reddish sweat. At night they leave the water to feed on shrubs and grasses.

They often journey eight or nine miles in search of good pasture, and sometimes make inroads on cultivated fields. For this reason they have been exterminated in most settled districts. The natives hunt hippopotami for their flesh as well as for their teeth, which are superior to ivory in hardness.

Though formerly plentiful in Egypt, the hippopotamus is now found only in equatorial Africa. It is thought that the common hippopotamus was found formerly in the Jordan valley also, and that it is the behemoth mentioned in the Bible. It is not difficult to keep in captivity.

Fossil remains of the common hippopotamus have been found even in the north of England, thus showing that there must have been a widespread distribution of the species at one time.

In addition to the common hippopotamus there is a pigmy species (*H. liberiensis*), about two and a half feet high and six feet long, which weighs, when full grown, only about 400 lb. This species is found chiefly in Liberia and neighbouring regions of the West African coast.

Hirohito, EMPEROR OF JAPAN (b. 1901). Descendant of a line of rulers going back, so the Japanese claim, to Jimmu Tennu, 660 B.C., and regarded as divine because of this line's descent from the Sun God, Hirohito had an upbringing far different from that of Western princes. But he proved to be one of the most enlightened rulers of Japan.

The son of the Emperor Yoshihito, he was born on April 29, 1901, entering the Peers' School in 1909. At the age of 10 Hirohito was made a lieutenant in the Japanese Army and Navy and attended military exercises. In 1921 he visited Europe, being the first Japanese Crown Prince to do so. On December 25, 1926, he ascended the Imperial throne, his reign being given the name of Showa, or light and peace. He did much to further the acceptance of Western ideas and industrial practices by his people, but took little active part in affairs of State.

Although Hirohito, being regarded as divine, was held to be above politics, he did approve (or at least acquiesce in) the various acts of aggression carried out by Japan, from the seizure of Manchuria in 1932 to the attack on the United States naval base at Pearl Harbour, in the Hawaiian Islands, on December 7, 1941. During the greater part of the Second World War (1939–45) he remained in

semi-seclusion, but towards its close he issued an Imperial proclamation admitting that the war situation was very serious.

Following the surrender of Japan to the Allied nations in August 1945, Hirohito was allowed to retain his throne. He declared that in future Japan would have a parliamentary form of government on Western lines, and in December 1945 he stated that the belief in the divinity of the Japanese Emperor was false.

Hiroshima. Situated at the head of a bay on the south coast of the Japanese island of Honshu, Hiroshima occupies a plain bounded by hills on the north-west and north-east. Commercially important, it carried on a brisk trade in lacquered ware, bronze goods and artistic products of all kinds. There were also engineering plants.

During the Second World War (1939–45) the city suffered little damage from air raids until August 6, 1945, when a bomber of the United States Army Air Force released over it the first atomic bomb used in warfare. The bomb exploded about 1,000 feet above the centre of Hiroshima, blast spreading destruction in all directions. Fires burnt for days, completely gutting the old quarter and the industrial area surrounding it. Of the city's population of 343,000 more than 78,000 were killed and nearly 59,000 injured, many of those injured dying later. By 1947 temporary buildings had been erected, and commercial life was beginning again.

Topical

HIROHITO : EMPEROR OF JAPAN
Succeeding his father on the throne in 1926, Hirohito was allowed to retain it after the defeat of Japan by the Allies in the Second World War (1939–45). Stripped of much of his power by the Allies, he is here seen with the Empress in the garden of the royal palace in Tokyo.

TRAVELLING BACKWARDS *through* TIME

*T**he** History we learn by rote may appear dull because it involves memorising many dates ; but in later life this knowledge enables us to understand the story of the present—for to some extent at least ' History repeats itself '!*

History. All the major events of the past have affected the course of history in later centuries —sometimes directly but often indirectly. Man, though he has changed immeasurably in habits and culture, and in the development of his mind and intelligence, tends to do the same kind of things today as he did 10 or 20 centuries ago. Thus the history of past ages is a pointer and a clue, broadly, to what the future picture of our story may contain. Here is one enormously important aspect of historical study. Then, if we read it intelligently, history is absorbingly interesting. In the historical articles throughout our volumes we try to open your eyes and your mind to the salient facts in Man's story.

How does the historian set about his task? Of course, he is familiar with research carried out by other scholars, but he does much original investigation. He makes sure that his statements are based on sound documents or sources which go back to the time of the facts themselves. Those sources are of all kinds—ruined monuments, old tombs and other material remains ; state documents and records, legal papers, letters, diaries, newspapers, and written or printed narratives of eye-witnesses; he must even take into account myths and fables. Sometimes the discovery of the key to new sources adds whole new realms to our historical knowledge.

The historian needs to be continually on his guard so as not to be misled by his sources. A document may be entirely forged ; its author may be deliberately lying ; he may be so prejudiced by national, religious, party, or personal bias as to be grossly unfair to the other side; and, if honest, he may be misinformed as to the facts and mistaken in his inferences. A writer may have coloured the facts in order to curry favour with a ruler; or he may have been afraid to tell unpleasant facts. Scores of pitfalls must be avoided by the research worker in this fascinating field.

Four Periods of Recorded History

To the long period before written records begin, when Man was taking his first steps in the arts of civilization, we give the name Prehistoric Age. Ancient history covers well over half the span of our recorded knowledge. It stretches from the beginnings of Assyrian and Egyptian inscriptions, through " the glory that was Greece, the grandeur that was Rome," to the coming into the Roman Empire of the Germanic barbarians, who overthrew classical civilization (about 3000 B.C. to about A.D. 375).

The Middle Ages extend from A.D. 375 to about 1500. This period starts with an epoch of confusion and transition which lasts to about A.D. 800. Then comes the height of the Middle Ages, from the Emperor Charlemagne to the Italian poet Dante (800 to 1300), when feudalism, monasticism, scholasticism, the Crusades, and Gothic architecture flourished. The period closes

with a second epoch of transition (1300 to 1500), which is called the Renaissance (*see* Renaissance). After 1500 comes the Modern Period, characterized by the organization of national states, the spread of discovery and European settlement of new lands, the progress of science and the rise of democracy.

Written records appear to go back only about 5,000 years. Some geologists however, believe that the Earth is at least 1,000,000,000 years old, and that Man has perhaps inhabited it for 50,000 years. The whole of recorded history from the earliest Assyrian and Egyptian inscriptions to the present day, would scarcely cover the last of 10,000 pages dealing with that stupendous period.

Fascinating Story of Man's Social Life

If history as a study often appears dull and dry, a mere catalogue of names and dates of rulers and battles and treaties, it is the fault of the books and not of history itself. Nothing can be more fascinating than the story of how men and women have spent their lives in the past and in far distant lands—their houses, food and clothing, how they cultivated their fields and manufactured goods, and traded with their neighbours, the games their children played, their beliefs about God and the world of Nature, their laws and manner of government, the songs their poets sang, and the beautiful things their artists made. All of this is history.

Even wars and political struggles are interesting, when we once know what they were about, and how they were carried on, and become well enough acquainted with the heroes and leaders to feel that they were real men and women.

Since the times of the Greek historians Herodotus (*c.* 484–424 B.C., the Father of History, and Thucydides (*c.* 464–404 B.C.), the writing of history has been recognized as a distinct form of literature. Among the Roman authors Livy (59 B.C.–A.D. 17) and Tacitus (*c.* A.D. 55–*c.* A.D. 119) were pre-eminent as historians. One of the greatest of all writers of history was Edward Gibbon (1737–94), who in his Decline and Fall of the Roman Empire dealt eloquently and ably with a great subject. Among other English historians who have written great works are Macaulay (1800–59), Carlyle (1795–1881), Froude (1818–94), Henry Hallam (1777–1859), W. E. M. Lecky (1838–1903) and John Richard Green (1837–83). Two outstanding historical works are A History of England by G. M. Trevelyan (b. 1876), and A History of Europe by H. A. L. Fisher (1865–1940).

You may be wondering how the chroniclers of the stirring events of our own times gather their material. We will take the period of the Second World War as an example. Sir John Hammerton's History of the Second Great War was begun in September 1939 ; week by week articles by observers in the theatres of war were prepared; trained compilers scrutinised the reports sent out by headquarters of the warring nations, and built from them a narrative as detailed as the requirements of military security permitted. All important official publications of the various governments were read, and salient facts recorded. So the recording and chronicling process went on throughout the years of war—with the chroniclers often under aerial bombardment and the printing works, too, undergoing perils of fire and explosives.

Later came the stories told by newspaper correspondents in war-ravaged lands, and the reports brought by returning diplomats. Later still, real historical accounts of some of the greatest events of the war came to be written—though usually in a form which demanded much pruning and condensing before they could be incorporated into a necessarily sober history of the war. Despatches from naval, military, or air force commanders were not made public until years after the events with which they dealt, so that much that had been written earlier needed to be clarified or modified in the light of the precise new information when this became available to the historian. For a really definitive account of the war events, historians must await the issue by governments of official histories, which take years to compile and publish. So you see that the chronicler must take a long view, and must stand a good way back from the period of which he compiles a history.

As to current history, week by week, this is recorded by such bodies as the Royal Institute of International Affairs, which issues fortnightly its Chronology, and publishes monthly a magazine, The World Today, in which are articles by writers having special knowledge. In the U.S.A. there is the Council on Foreign Relations, which publishes quarterly the review, Foreign Affairs.

Hitler, ADOLF, GERMAN FUEHRER (1889–1945). There is no stranger story in history than that of this unknown and obscure Austrian who, between 1920 and 1933, gathered together a new political party in Germany and eventually obtained so much support for his theories of government that President Hindenburg called upon him to take the post of Chancellor of the Reich. When the aged president died in 1934 Hitler combined in his own person thereafter the offices of Chancellor and President. Later he adopted the title of "Fuehrer" (leader), probably copying Benito Mussolini who, in Italy, had taken a similar title (Duce).

The rise of Hitler to absolute and untrammelled power can be understood only if we bear in mind the state of Germany after her defeat in the First World War (1914–18). Humiliated by the utter collapse of her armies, perplexed by the abdication and flight of her Emperor, stunned by the enormous sums she was called upon to pay in reparations, she had to face economic chaos also, with poverty and unemployment followed later by a complete collapse of her monetary system. Communism and other political "isms" which promised better times grew apace; riots, party faction fights and brawls made an end of law and order in the cities. Big landowners and business magnates lent a ready ear to

political leaders who told them that they could put an end to Bolshevism and "red" Socialism.

Army generals had their own plans for resurrecting Germany's armed forces. The big chemical and dyestuff combines, and the mighty armament works, were ready to back a leader whom they thought might recreate conditions in which their factories and engineering works could flourish again in a new and powerful Germany. Thus they favoured the National Socialist Party (q.v.), once it seemed likely to win power. Hitler was the origin and personification of this Party.

Hitler was born in Braunau-am-Inn, Austria, on April 20, 1889, the son of Alois Hitler, an Austrian customs official, and Klara Poelz Hitler, a Bohemian. The details of Hitler's early life are scanty. He spent his childhood in Lambach, Austria. At 18 he was left an orphan. In Vienna, where he had gone at the age of 14, he did various jobs and suffered poverty ; his hardships are said to have awakened his mind to social and political problems. Austria was a country of many races, and Hitler, feeling himself a thorough German, looked longingly across the border at the powerful, energetic German nation. Hitler already carried in his mind the seeds of his later political doctrines when he left Vienna for Munich in 1912. In Munich he worked as carpenter, architect's draughtsman and water-colour painter. There the outbreak of the First World War found him in 1914.

He enlisted as a private on August 3, 1914. He served on the Somme, and was made lance-corporal. He was twice wounded, gassed, and temporarily blinded. When he returned to a much-changed Munich, he joined the German Workers' Party, and his gifts as an orator soon made him a leader. In 1920 he organized the Storm Troops to prevent any interference with his meetings by the Communists. The name of the

New York Times Photos

HITLER COMES TO POWER
In 1933 Hitler became Chancellor of Germany, and here he is seen, at the left of the front row, next to President Hindenburg whom he succeeded in 1934. Hitler was the Leader or Fuehrer of Germany from 1934 until his death by suicide in Berlin on April 30, 1945.

Party was changed to National Socialist German Workers' Party (*Nationalsozialistische Deutsche Arbeiterpartei*), abbreviated to "Nazi" (pron. naht'-si). The Nazis gained ground so fast that, on November 8, 1923, aided by General Ludendorff and his Nationalist followers, they attempted to seize control of the Government by an armed rising. The revolt was easily put down by the authorities ; Hitler was arrested and sentenced to five years in the fortress of Landsberg-am-Lech. There he wrote Mein Kampf (My Struggle), setting out his theories and plans for a new form of State. He was released from prison after he had served only eight months of his sentence.

The years from 1924 to 1928 were fairly prosperous for Germany, and revolutions seldom flourish on prosperity. In 1928 the Nazi Party had gained 800,000 votes and won 12 seats in the Reichstag. But in 1930 there came a great economic crisis which affected most countries. This was the Nazis' opportunity. Hitler himself, having smarted at German defeat in the war and gone hungry in poverty, was in the closest touch with German thought and feeling, and his oratorical powers enabled him to play skilfully on the emotions of the masses. He salved national pride by blaming war defeat on Jews and Marxists, and promised a return to order.

In 1930 the number of Nazis in the Reichstag had grown to 107, supported by nearly six and a half million voters. Two years later they polled over thirteen million votes, winning 230 seats. Then came a check, but on January 30, 1933, Hitler was called to be Chancellor by the old president. When Hindenburg died in 1934, Hitler unified the offices of Chancellor and President and became the nation's Fuehrer.

Immediately he began to convert the republic into a totalitarian state, in which all the power was vested in his own hands, directed through trusted members of his party. The governments of the states of the Reich lost most of their powers, and Germany was unified for purposes of administration and control. In 1934, after a revolt of Nazi chiefs, many prominent men in the Party were shot in a " blood purge."

Then, step by step, Hitler broke the shackles imposed on Germany by the Treaty of Versailles. At first in secret, and then openly, he directed the country's rearmament ; in 1936 Germany's occupation of the demilitarized zone of the Rhineland opened a series of events that culminated in the open defiance of the treaty Powers by a Germany now rapidly growing strong enough to contemplate seizing the territory of her neighbours. For the annexation of Austria, the spoliation and subsequent seizure of Czechoslovakia, and the attack upon Poland which in September 1939 ushered in the Second World War, Adolf Hitler must bear the

ADOLF HITLER

B.N.A.

Though he developed plans for the regeneration of Germany, Hitler brought about her destruction by the ruthless pursuit of his own desire for her territorial expansion.

personal responsibility ; the evidence disclosed in the trials of war criminals at Nuremberg in 1945–46 showed that the master-plan for all these doings was his own.

When opposed by his army, navy and air force chiefs, who pointed out the danger of armed intervention by Britain, France, and Russia, Hitler overbore the service advisers and determined to take the risk. Disunity among the other Powers and a knowledge of their unpreparedness played into his hands, and he had free play in his predatory schemes. He had many times declared his peaceful intentions towards his neighbours, but in these utterances, as in the many treaties which Germany signed and later broke, Hitler disclosed his utter disregard of truth and good faith. To secure his rear in the invasion of Poland he had signed a pact with Russia in 1939; he broke it in 1941 by invading Russia in turn.

The collapse of France in June 1940 seemed to have proved all Hitler's claims, and henceforth his generals lost their fears and scruples, though there were some who were against the Russian adventure a year later—with good reason, since the Russian campaign proved the downfall of all Nazi hopes. An atrocious feature of all the campaigns was the murder of Jews, which went on until millions had been slaughtered in death camps, or shot by special formations of the armed forces when territory was overrun. This foul crime began with the killing of the Jews in Poland, and continued with the mass deportation of Jews to slavery or death from Holland, Belgium and France. Later the same process was carried on in central and eastern Europe—with special ruthlessness in Russia. Here again we trace Hitler's personal influence; as no doubt one might in the arrangements made, when defeat stared the Nazis in the face, for the mass starvation of hundreds of thousands of political offenders and others who had been incarcerated in prison camps throughout Germany.

This strange man, who had gifts of genius, and developed creative plans for the regeneration of Germany, seems to have shown in his private life some of the ordinary virtues. But his actions as German leader showed him to be a war-lord, ruthless and unscrupulous to a degree unparalleled outside the history of the Middle Ages; and with a taint of ferocious hatred and loathsome cruelty which it would be difficult to match even then.

When at length it became clear that Germany was faced with a defeat more catastrophic even than that of 1918, with invading armies closing in from east and west, and the Russian forces fighting a way through Berlin itself, Hitler killed himself. With his intimates and Party leaders he had retired to a concrete stronghold in the grounds of the Berlin chancellery. Shortly before his death he married Eva Braun, who died with him on April 30, 1945.

Hittites. When the tribes of Israel entered Canaan after their long journey from Egypt, they found many people living there, and among them were the Hittites, who reached great power in the near East before fading away into obscurity. Apart from several mentions of them in the Bible they were unknown to modern scholars until their monuments and inscriptions were dug up by archaeologists.

The Hittites are first heard of about the year 2500 B.C., when they still occupied their original home country in Asia Minor. From there they spread southwards and eastwards. In 1925 B.C. they sacked Babylon, and brought to an end the first Babylonian dynasty. Subbiluliuma, the Great King of the Hittites, came to the throne about 1400 B.C., and by his efforts added greatly to the strength of the Hittite empire. During his reign the Hittites invaded the far-flung boundaries of the great Egyptian empire, and we find a later Hittite forming an alliance with the Egyptian pharaoh. But attacks from the Assyrians, and from the so-called sea-peoples—the Thracians, Phrygians, and Armenians—first weakened and finally overcame the Hittite empire, and Carchemish, the capital, was captured by the Assyrian king, Sargon II, in 717 B.C. This may be said to mark the end of the Hittites, for their kingdom was gone, and their civilization became a fading memory.

It is one of the great benefits of archaeology that it shows us not only the warlike but also the domestic life of ancient peoples. From their inscriptions, which have only in part been deciphered, we know that the Hittites were well organized and administered politically, and had a code of laws much milder and humane than the Assyrians and Israelites. They mostly followed agricultural occupations, and were expert in raising cattle and keeping bees. They also bred and domesticated the horse. Their religion was very involved, and they worshipped many gods. Some elements of their culture, such as the use of a silver coinage, seem to have been borrowed from the Babylonians.

Hobart. Capital of Tasmania and the second oldest city in Australia, Hobart stretches along the hills on the shores of the Derwent estuary on the south side of the island. It has a fine harbour deep and well-sheltered, and is a port of call for European mail liners and for Australian inter-state steamships. Industries include tanneries, foundries, saw-mills, breweries, flour mills and fruit-preserving; the main exports are apples, wool, zinc, jam, timber, and cocoa.

Hobart, which was founded in 1803, has a climate comparable to that of southern England and has a population of 71,000.

Hockey. It seems likely that the word hockey has some connexion with the hooked stick with which the game is played, probably being derived from the English hook, or the Old French *hoquet*, a crook. Exactly how the game came to be introduced into Britain is unknown. According to one authority, it originated in France in the 14th century, but it is more than likely that modern hockey is but a variation of a game that the ancient Greeks played. It is certain, at least, that the game grew and developed in England. There is a similar game in Ireland known as hurling, in Scotland as shinty, and in Wales as bandy.

In some form or other hockey is played in most parts of Europe, several Asiatic countries, and North and South America. Originally, it was undoubtedly very rough, and it was discouraged in many quarters for this reason. In 1875 the Men's Hockey Association was formed, and eight years later rules were drawn up by the Wimbledon Club.

There are 11 players on each side : namely, a goal-keeper, two backs, three half-backs, and five forwards, the object being to score by hitting the ball into the opponents' goal. Each player has a curved stick, made of ash, the handle of which is usually about 2 feet in length, and the blade 1 foot long. The end must be rounded—not pointed, or cut square. The head of the stick is smooth—sharp edges are not allowed—and the surface of the face of the stick is flat. The weight of the stick, including that of any protective binding, must not exceed 28 ounces. Occasionally the game of hockey is played with a solid rubber ball, but more often a ball covered in white leather is used. It is common

HITTITE GOD IN STONE
Carchemish, situated in what is now known as Syria, was the capital of the Hittite Empire and reached the height of its glory in the 13th century B.C. Excavations there have revealed statues of royal personages and gods ; above is the statue of a Hittite deity. The Hittites' home was in Asia Minor, whence they spread South and East.

centre-forward of each team strikes the ground on his side of the ball, and his opponent's stick above the ball, three times alternately, after which either is free to strike the ball, which is then in play. This procedure is called the bully. When the ball is hit over either side-line, it is rolled in by a player of the opposing team from the point on the line at which it left the field of play, no other player standing within seven yards.

Where a foul occurs in the striking circle, the referee awards a penalty bully or a penalty corner, either of which offers a reasonable prospect of a goal. In taking a penalty corner the ball is hit from the goal-line at any spot at least 10 yards from the nearest goal-post, all the defending players meanwhile being behind their goal-line, and the remainder of the attacking side outside the circle. A goal may be scored only from within the striking circle, described below.

The measurements of the hockey field are as follows : length, 100 yards; breadth, 55 to 60 yards. The longer boundary lines are called side-lines and the shorter, goal-lines. A line is drawn 7 or 5 yards inside and parallel to the side-lines. In front of each goal a line 4 yards long is drawn parallel to the goal-line. The ends of this are carried round a curve, forming a quarter circle, until they reach the goal-line at a point 15 yards from each of the goal posts. This semi-circle is called the striking circle. Goals are 4 yards wide, and 7 feet high. Ice Hockey (q.v.) is a popular form of the game.

HOCKEY INCIDENTS

Typical features of this popular winter game are (1) the 'bully,' (2) a tussle for the ball, (3) play near goal, (4) goalkeeper clearing, (5) mid-field play. Below right, the field of play.

for the players, especially the backs, to wear shin-guards. The goalkeeper usually wears, in addition, pads and other protection.

Anyone with a good knowledge of the laws of football will find little difficulty in following the laws that govern hockey. A player cannot be off-side if he is in his own half of the field, if the striker or roller-in is nearer the opponents' goal-line, or if there are three opponents between him and the goal-line.

In the act of striking the ball, a player must not raise his stick above his shoulders. The penalty for this offence is a free hit. It is not permitted to play left-handed ; to undercut the ball ; intentionally use any part of the body, except the hand, to stop the ball ; to hook, hold or strike an opponent or his stick; to obstruct an opponent; or to interfere with the game unless with stick in hand. To start the game, the

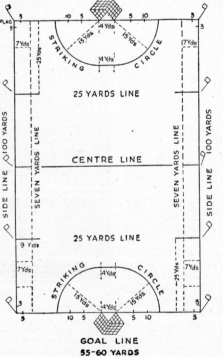

GOAL LINE
55-60 YARDS

Hogarth, WILLIAM (1697-1764). Few men have had a keener eye for the expressions of the human face than the English painter and engraver, William Hogarth. No artist has reproduced those expressions with more biting irony.

Hogarth has been called a master of caricature, and he did contribute greatly to the development of technique in this field. But a caricaturist, in the modern sense of the word, usually ridicules individuals by exaggerating their conspicuous features. Hogarth made fun of humanity as a whole, satirizing its weaknesses and vices.

In his own day, many critics called Hogarth vulgar, and thought his art inferior. Now he is generally placed high among English artists for his technique, his originality, his superb rendering of costume and setting, and, above all, for the vital humour and trueness to life of his characters. Most of his works are stories on canvas or copper, though he also did some excellent portraits.

Born in London on November 10, 1697, Hogarth early showed a remarkable gift for mimicry and drawing. He was apprenticed to a silver-plate engraver, and at the age of 22 established his own business. Soon he began to paint portraits and groups, and eventually found his true sphere in ridiculing human folly. His practice was to make a series of paintings, and from them engravings, which were sold by subscription. He was a bitter opponent of hypocrisy, corruption, and extravagance, and crusaded against drunkenness and cruelty to animals. He died on October 26, 1764.

Among Hogarth's famous works are the series The Rake's Progress (1735 ; Soane Museum, London), Marriage à la Mode (1745; Tate Gallery), and The Election (1755–58; Soane Museum).

HOGARTH RIDICULES HUMAN FOLLY

Hogarth satirized many aspects of life in the 18th century and exposed the follies of the fashionable life of his time. In his series of paintings called Marriage à la Mode he depicted the misery of a loveless marriage. This is one of his most successful works.

Holbein, HANS (1497–1543). The son of a painter and a designer for wood engraving, and perhaps the first man in England to paint what are now known as portrait miniatures, Hans Holbein (pron. hŏl-bīn), a young German artist, left his father's studio in the Bavarian city of Augsburg in 1514 to seek his fortune in Basle, Switzerland. His intention was to furnish illustrations for the wonderful new printed books that were there being published.

There he met the Dutch scholar Erasmus, who had come to Basle to oversee the publication of the first printed edition of the New Testament in the original Greek, and other works which he had edited. He and the young artist at once struck up a friendship, and Holbein drew pictures for a very clever satire, called The Praise of Folly (*Encomium Moriae*), which Erasmus had written.

Holbein illustrated many other books, among them the German religious reformer Martin Luther's translation of the Bible into German. He displayed great skill, further, in painting portraits and miniatures and religious subjects; he designed stained-glass windows; he even drew designs for women's costumes.

After a time Holbein, with a letter from his friend Erasmus to Sir Thomas More, the English statesman and author, again set out to try his fortune in a strange land. In London the young painter met with a favourable reception and on a later visit he painted the famous series of notabilities at the court of Henry VIII, which are still at Windsor Castle.

Although much of his life was spent in Switzerland and England, Holbein is regarded as a German artist. Comparing him with the other master artists of that nation, it is said: " Dürer was the greater genius, a greater thinker, a greater engraver, but Holbein was the greatest painter Germany produced."

His paintings and drawings are found in most of the larger galleries of Europe, and one of his finest works—a portrait of Christina, Duchess of Milan, painted in 1538—is in the National Gallery, London. (*See* illus. p. 1455; *also* National Gallery).

Holidays AND FESTIVALS. Since ancient times and amongst nearly all peoples certain days each year have been observed as religious anniversaries, public festivals, or as periods of rest. The Greeks had their Olympic games and many other festivals. The Romans celebrated Lupercalia in the spring, and Saturnalia in mid-winter, marked by games, fantastic amusements, and the giving of presents. The earliest of all festivals seem to be connected with the dead, to whom offerings were made. Later, the sun and moon or the seasons were recognized by festivals; sowing and harvest were occasions for special rejoicing.

All early festivals were in some measure religious. Thus the word holiday was originally holy day. Political holidays, celebrating historical events, are of later growth.

In England and Wales the Bank holidays are Easter Monday, Whit Monday, the first Monday in August, and the first week-day after Christmas Day (Boxing Day, when Christmas boxes or gifts of money used to be given to local tradesmen). Banks are closed then, and on Good Friday and Christmas Day. In Scotland the Bank holidays are New Year's Day (or the first week-day after, if it falls on a Sunday), the first Monday in May and the first Monday in August. Scottish banks are closed also on Good Friday and Christmas Day. Bank holidays may also be proclaimed on days of public rejoicing.

The institution of Bank holidays was due to John Lubbock, M.P., afterwards Lord Avebury, who in 1871 secured the passing of the Bank Holidays Act.

In Lancashire and other parts of the North of England, in towns largely engaged in one industry, all the works close during the same week. This mass-holidaying is called a wake.

Holland. This name is used loosely in Britain for the country properly called The Netherlands (*q.v.*). It belongs really to two of the Netherlands provinces—North Holland and South Holland, with areas respectively of 1,142 and 1,130 square miles. During the Second World War

(1939–45) the name Holland Line was given to a defence line from the Ijssel Lake to the mouth of the Maas, enclosing the zone known as Fortress Holland.

Holly. Usually associated with the Christmas season, the holly is a native of Great Britain, though foreign species were introduced from North

America as far back as 1726. The leaves are usually spiny and dark green, though there are smooth and variegated sorts; the red or yellow berries are borne in autumn and winter.

The holly flowers are small, and white in colour, and they appear quite early in the year. Often, the berries are ripe at the same time as most other fruits, namely in a u t u m n; sometimes they may still be on the tree when spring comes round again.

HOLLY BERRIES
Associated with Christmas decorations, the holly is a hardy evergreen tree, usually having spiny leaves and red berries.

The holly (*Ilex aquifolium*) if left to itself will grow into a large tree, but often they are clipped for hedges. English hollies are, as a rule, the largest, the tree growing especially well in oak and beech woods. The wood is hard, close-grained—for the tree grows slowly—and white in colour. It is not much used now, but formerly was a popular wood in English native furniture, being often dyed green or black to imitate ebony. Straight young shoots of holly make, perhaps, the finest and strongest of all walking sticks.

The reason why holly is used for Christmas is rather a strange one, and not Christian at all! For holly was among the decorations used in ancient Rome at the Saturnalia, when all Romans exchanged greetings with their friends. This festival was celebrated at about the same time as Christmas, so the early Christians living in Rome exchanged the same emblems of good cheer as their pagan neighbours, the custom later spreading throughout the Christian world.

The holly has, too, a butterfly of its own, the little holly blue, pale grey-blue with black tips to its forewings; you may see it in early spring or late in summer, flitting around the trees on whose flower buds the caterpillar feeds; it also eats the flower-buds of ivy.

Hollyhock. Clothed with dark green leaves and thickly studded with large bright-hued blossoms, the tall stems of this old-fashioned plant make a beautiful background to herbaceous borders. Reaching a height of six or eight feet, its spikes stand in soldierly array, seeming to guard the more modest blossoms that cling closely to Mother Earth.

The hollyhock (*Althaea rosea*) has been developed from a species of wild mallow, native to the Mediterranean countries, and originally it had single, rose-coloured blossoms, but through centuries of cultivation numerous varieties of both double and single flowers have been produced, in several shades of pink and purple, as well as in yellow and white.

Holmes, OLIVER WENDELL (1809–94). Of American authors who have won a large reading public on this side of the Atlantic, one of the most famous is Oliver Wendell Holmes. His best-known work is The Autocrat of the Breakfast Table, a volume of essays, witty and wise, humorous and kindly. He followed that success with two other books of the same kind, The Professor at the Breakfast Table and The Poet at the Breakfast Table. He also wrote two novels, and poetry.

He was born at Cambridge, Massachusetts, on August 29, 1809, and his success as a writer was the more remarkable because writing was not his chief business. He was a busy physician and a professor of Harvard University, who, besides attending to a big practice, made original scientific investigations and wrote medical works.

His fame as a writer began while he was still a student at Harvard University, with his poem Old Ironsides, which was instrumental in saving the old frigate, Constitution, from destruction. The volume that contained the funny My Aunt, and the humorous-pathetic Last Leaf, also appeared while he was at Harvard.

Holy Roman Empire. On Christmas Day of the year 800, Pope Leo III, in the church of St. Peter's in Rome, placed a crown on the head of the Frankish King, Charlemagne, as he knelt in prayer. It was then that the organization

HARDY HOLLYHOCKS
One of the favourite old English garden flowers is the tall hollyhock, developed from a species of wild mallow. Originally it had single rose-coloured blooms, but through centuries of cultivation numerous varieties, with double or single flowers of various colours, have been produced.

known as the Holy Roman Empire first came into existence. (*See* Charlemagne.)

A few years later, through the break-up of the Frankish kingdom after Charlemagne's death (814), the Empire for a time disappeared. It was revived by the Saxon Otto I, king of Germany, in 962. From that time until its final abolition in 1806, the Empire maintained some sort of existence; but in its last three centuries it had become, as Voltaire said, "neither holy, nor Roman, nor an empire."

In theory the Holy Roman Empire was the counterpart, in civil government, of the universal Catholic Church in religion. Just as God had placed the Pope over His Church, so, it was reasoned, He had placed the emperor over all kings and princes. In practice, the Empire after 962 included only Italy and Germany, though Switzerland, the Netherlands and parts of France were also loosely connected with it.

In theory again, the Empire was elective. The Golden Bull of 1356, issued by the Emperor Charles IV, placed the hereditary right to elect in an Electoral College composed of the Archbishops of Mainz, Cologne, and Treves (Trier), the King of Bohemia, the Count Palatine of the Rhine (Pfalzgraf), the Duke of Saxony, and the Margrave of Brandenburg (Bavaria and Hanover were added later). In practice the Empire was virtually hereditary in some one princely house, though election sometimes took place.

After the Carolingian and Saxon lines, the imperial crown was worn by the members of the following houses: the Franconian or Salian house (1024–1137), the Hohenstaufen (1138–1254), [Great Interregnum, 1254–73], various houses (1273–1347), the Luxemburg-Bohemian line (1347–1437), the Hapsburgs (1438–1806, except for one reign, 1740–45).

From the foundation of the Holy Roman Empire by Charlemagne in the year 800, until the 16th century the story of the Empire is mainly concerned with Germany, and with the Popes, and Italy. Its history in the 16th century became almost entirely merged in the history of Germany. This German phase lasted into the middle of the 17th century, when the Empire became Austrian; it finally disappeared in the early years of the 19th century, when Francis II of Austria dropped the ancient title, calling himself Emperor of Austria.

Home Guard. Originally called the Local Defence Volunteers, the Home Guard was formed on May 14, 1940, during the Second World War, in response to an appeal for volunteers from men of all ages between 17 and 60 who were capable of handling a rifle. The primary object of the force was to oppose possible landings on British soil of German parachute troops. In 10 days 400,000 volunteers had joined, and within three weeks the figure had risen to one million.

In the early days members armed themselves with shotguns and any other personal weapons on which they could lay their hands, but eventually the battalions were equipped with rifles, automatic weapons, heavy machine-guns, mortars, grenades and light mobile artillery. The basis of training was the defence of their own locality.

In 1942 any man who was of suitable age and not performing work of national importance which might suffer in consequence was compelled to enrol in the Home Guard. Service was unpaid, but out-of-pocket expenses could be recovered, and Army uniform was provided.

Though the Home Guard never had to resist an enemy invasion of our shores, its members saw actual service with the heavy and rocket batteries of Anti-Aircraft units and helped to capture crews of German aircraft forced down over Britain. The existence of this large part-time national Army enabled the military authorities to liberate regular forces engaged in defence duties for training at home and for service overseas.

The official date of the disbandment of the Home Guard was December 31, 1945.

Home Office. One of the most important Government Offices, and one that closely affects our daily life, is the Home Office. It is presided over by the Home Secretary, who is the senior of the eight Secretaries of State. As such he is in close relation with the Sovereign, who issues through him all communications to his subjects and takes his advice as to pardoning those convicted of crime. He is also required to be present at the birth of royal children.

The Home Secretary signs the death warrant of those condemned to be hanged. Until the reign of Queen Victoria the warrants were signed by the Sovereign, but the Queen found this duty so distasteful to her that it was transferred to the Home Secretary.

Many of the former functions of the Home Office have been taken over by other Government departments, but it is still responsible for the Metropolitan Police and has a limited control over other police forces; all prisons are under its jurisdiction. The inspection of factories and mines is carried out by Home Office officials, who also administer the laws relating to aliens, the licensing of hotels and public-houses, burial laws, fire brigades, and many other matters. The Home Office is in Whitehall, London.

Homer. There is no greater name in poetry than that which stands for the reputed author of the famous epics of Greece, the Iliad and the Odyssey. According to the ancient historian Herodotus, Homer was an Asiatic Greek who lived about 850 B.C. But seven cities—Smyrna, Chios, Colophon, Salamis, Rhodes, Argos and Athens—claim the honour of having been his birthplace, thus giving rise to the saying:

Seven cities contend for Homer dead
Through which the living Homer begged his bread.

Tradition describes him as a blind old man, who wandered about reciting his poems.

Many scholars, however, hold that the poems were not composed by a single person, and were not written until centuries after they took the form in which we know them. It is almost certain that they were long handed down from memory, as there is little evidence that writing was practised in Greece at so early a period.

One theory of their authorship is that they are the work or compilation of a company of poets or minstrels, who composed, collected and handed down in this form the legends of the Trojan War.

But the question of the authorship of the Iliad and the Odyssey is of little importance beside the poems themselves, which are the greatest epics that have ever been produced in any age or country.

The Iliad—from Ilium, one of the names of Troy—describes the events of a few days in the last of the 10 years of the war between the Trojans and the Greeks. Paris, a Trojan prince, had gone on a visit to Menelaus, the King of Sparta, and while there had fallen in love with Helen, wife of Menelaus, and reputed the most beautiful woman in the world. Paris persuaded Helen to run away from her husband and go to Troy with him, and, when Helen refused to return, Menelaus called upon the other princes of Greece to avenge his injury, and thus began the war. Achilles was the great warrior on the Greek side, and Ulysses, also a Greek, was famous for his wisdom.

The Greek war with Troy forms the basis of the poems. The Iliad tells the story of " the wrath of Achilles," while the Odyssey relates the many adventures of Odysseus (Ulysses) on his voyage home. Even though the poems contain only a shadow of historical fact, scholars owe a great debt to them for the information they furnish concerning early life in the lands about the Aegean sea. Excavations on the site of Troy and elsewhere have abundantly confirmed the information obtained from the poems. (*See* Aegean Civilization; Schliemann, Heinrich).

One does not need to be a scholar to appreciate the wonderful stories in Homer ; only a student of the Greek language, however, can fully appreciate the simple and lofty beauty of the style of the original. (*See* Achilles; Circe; Cyclopes; Hector; Odysseus; Trojan War).

Honduras, BRITISH. Formerly called Belize, this British Colony in Central America has the Caribbean Sea on the east, Guatemala on the west and south, and Mexico on the north and north-west. Its area is about 8,867 square miles. The coastal regions are low-lying and swampy; the mountains in the west and south are covered with forests, yielding mahogany, cedar, pitch-pine and logwood.

The principal crops are coffee, bananas, maize, rice, citrus fruits and sugar-cane. The capital is Belize, which was devastated by a hurricane in 1932, and from which there is an air service to the United States.

The Colony was probably founded by wood-cutters from Jamaica in the 17th century, and in 1786 the British Government appointed a super-intendent to administer the district. In 1862 British Honduras was declared a Colony, sub-ordinate to Jamaica, but it became independent in 1884. In March 1948 the Republic of Guatemala put forward a claim to British Honduras. Great Britain refused to admit Guatemala's right to the territory, but offered to put the case before the International Court of Justice of the United Nations, to which Guatemala would not agree, allowing the matter to drop. The population is about 64,000.

Honduras, REPUBLIC OF. Third largest of the Central American republics, Honduras is bounded on the north by the Caribbean Sea, on the south by the republics of Nicaragua and El Salvador, and on the west by Guatemala. It has an area of 46,322 square miles.

Most of the surface is mountainous, with heights ranging up to 10,000 feet. The low coastal areas are hot and damp, especially in the wet season, which is from May to November. In the warm valleys coffee and tobacco are grown for export, and bananas are the main crop in the lowlands near the Caribbean coast. Maize, beans, rice, potatoes and fruit are also raised. The mineral wealth of the country includes gold, silver, antimony, copper, iron, and coal. There are but few industries, among the manufactured products being clothing, straw hats, soap and leather goods. There is much valuable timber, including mahogany, beech, cedar, pine and white poplar.

Railways cover about 900 miles, but there are only some 700 miles of motor roads. Difficulties of transport have been largely overcome by a network of air services, linking nearly every town, and even many villages. Tegucigalpa, the capital, has a population of about 47,000, and is the only Central American capital without a railway.

Columbus landed in Honduras in 1502, the Spaniards completing the conquest of the country in 1522. With the

BELIZE : CAPITAL OF BRITISH HONDURAS
E.N.A.
At the mouth of the Belize river, the town of that name is surrounded by swamps which render the climate unhealthy. It has a poor harbour, accessible only to small vessels through a channel between coral reefs. Timber, bananas, and tortoiseshell are chief exports. Belize has a population of 17,000.

rest of Central America, Honduras achieved independence from Spain in 1821, being a member of the Central American Federation until 1838, when the independent Republic of Honduras was established. The population is 1,200,000.

Honeysuckle. With its sweet-scented yellowish-white or pinkish trumpet-shaped flowers, honeysuckle (*Lonicera periclymenum*) or woodbine is a familiar plant in gardens or growing wild in hedgerows. The fruit, which is a small, red, single-seeded berry, is poisonous. There are many species of honeysuckle, growing wild or under cultivation, scattered through the Northern Hemisphere. One well-known variety, the evergreen or trumpet honeysuckle, that bears scarlet or yellow blossoms in the spring, is a North American plant. Especially beautiful is the Japanese honeysuckle which has white or purplish blossoms and opens its buds only in the evening. The snowberry, which has little pink flowers and big, waxy white berries, belongs to the same order, *Caprifoliaceae*.

Hong Kong. When Britain in 1841 took the mountainous little island of Hong Kong, it was a barren place frequented chiefly by pirates. Since that time the colony has become a great commercial centre and an outpost of British defence in the Far East. Besides the island, which is 11 miles long and from two to five miles wide, the colony includes the Kowloon peninsula on the mainland of China, the total area being 391 square miles. Lying at the mouth of the Chukiang or Pearl river, the island has a superb harbour on the north-west coast, and here has grown up the port and city of Victoria, the capital.

E. J. Bedford

FRAGRANT HONEYSUCKLE
Known in parts of Britain as the woodbine, the wild honeysuckle has fragrant, tubular flowers of yellowish-white. Cultivated varieties include shades of rose and crimson, and the Japanese honeysuckle has white or purplish blooms.

The town stretches for four miles along a narrow strip of land between the hills and the sea, and in normal times is the distributing centre for one-fourth to one-third of China's foreign trade. Local

E.N.A.

HONG KONG'S CAPITAL CITY OF VICTORIA
On the north-west coast of the island of Hong Kong is a magnificent natural harbour, on the shores of which is the port of Victoria. The British Colony of Hong Kong includes the Kowloon peninsula, which is on the mainland of China. The climate is sub-tropical, cool and dry in winter, hot and humid in summer. The most important industries are cotton-spinning, sugar-refining, rope and cement making, shipbuilding, fishing and stone-quarrying.

industries include such varied activities as ship-building, rope and cement making, sugar manufacture, tin refining, and deep sea fishing.

Hong Kong was created a British Crown Colony in 1843, and in 1946 plans were announced for granting a large measure of self-government to the people. During the Second World War (1939–45) the colony was captured by Japanese forces on December 25, 1941. Allied air raids damaged Victoria before the Japanese occupation was terminated on August 30, 1945, many public buildings, including the university, being destroyed. The population of the colony is about 1,100,000, the majority being Chinese.

Hood, THOMAS (1799–1845). "There was a dash of ink in my blood," was the explanation given by this punster and poet for his youthful adoption of a literary career. His father was a Scotsman, who devoted his spare time to fiction and other writing, and Thomas Hood began to follow in his father's footsteps at an early age. He was born in London on May 23, 1799, and is one of the most delightful punsters in English literature. The fountain of fun was always bubbling up in his writings, which were for the most part in verse. Many of his comic verses, like Miss Kilmansegg and her Precious Leg, and Ode on a Distant Prospect of Clapham Academy, can still be read with delight; but Thomas Hood is chiefly remembered today for his Song of the Shirt, published in Punch in 1843, which exposed the hardships endured by women who made garments for the wholesale clothing trade. He died on May 3, 1845.

Hooke, ROBERT (1635–1703). Philosopher and scientist-craftsman, Hooke was a contemporary of Sir Isaac Newton, with whom he often disputed. It has been said that but for Hooke's moroseness and hot temper he might even have rivalled Newton in his services to science. Towards the end of Hooke's life he is said to have remained night and day at his table engrossed with his inventions, not undressing or going to bed. He became secretive and would not tell the results of his researches to the Royal Society, of which he was one of the original members; in 1667 he became secretary of the Society, and curator of experiments.

What, then, did Hooke contribute to science and invention ? A remarkable example of a man who could scheme out new appliances, and make them with his clever hands, Hooke rendered invaluable services to clockmaking. He used Huyghens's pendulum in a practical manner, connecting it to the wheelwork of clocks so as to regulate the timekeeping. He invented the anchor escapement which, with the pendulum, made the clock substantially what it is today—a simple and

accurate measurer of the hours. He is said to have introduced the flat spiral spring for the balance of portable clocks and watches; it is certain that he made original researches into the elasticity of metals, as part of his experiments with springs. To him we owe " Hooke's law "—which first stated that elastic deformations, such as twists or bends or stretches, are directly proportional to the forces which produce them. A practical use of this property of a stretched metal filament is in the spring balance; a two-pound weight pulls out the spring twice as far as does a one-pound weight.

Working with the Irish chemist Robert Boyle, Hooke produced an air-pump with which Boyle could continue his famous experiments on gases. Hooke made researches into the nature of light and sound. He improved the microscope of those days, and published his Micrographia (1665), dealing with the result of his investigations of, among other things, animal and vegetable tissues. As a surveyor to the City of London after the Great Fire (1666), Hooke made a model for rebuilding the city.

Hooke was born at Freshwater, Isle of Wight, on July 18, 1635. He became professor of geometry at Gresham College, London, in 1665. Two years later he took up the post of secretary to the Royal Society. He died on March 3, 1703.

Hooker, SIR JOSEPH (1817–1911). If the Zoo is a paradise for animal-lovers and students of zoology, the choicest site of study for botanists in London must be Kew Gardens, Surrey. But few realize that they owe the continued existence of the Gardens almost entirely to the great Sir Joseph Hooker, who was Director of Kew from 1865 to 1885. For it was he who, backed by public opinion, saved Kew from becoming a mere recreation ground. But Hooker was more than the saviour of Kew; he was the most distinguished botanist of his day, and he was almost as travelled as an explorer. Scarcely any part of the world was unvisited by Hooker, who is, however, best known for his classic Student's Flora of the British Isles.

The son of Sir William Hooker, director of Kew Gardens from 1841 to 1865, he was born at Halesworth, Suffolk, on June 30, 1817, and educated at Glasgow University. In 1839 he accompanied an expedition to the Antarctic, publishing on his return an account of the flora of the south temperate and sub-Arctic regions. In 1848 he led a botanical expedition to Northern India, and in 1855 was appointed Assistant Director at Kew Gardens, where in 1862 the first part of his Genera Plantarum was prepared. Three years later he succeeded his father as Director at Kew, holding this post for 20 years.

The value of Hooker's work did not go un-

R. A. Malby

HOOKER AND HIS RHODODENDRON
One of the plants brought to the botanical gardens at Kew, Surrey, by the botanist Sir Joseph Hooker was the Sikkim rhododendron (right). Succeeding his father as Director of Kew Gardens in 1865, he was knighted in 1877. He died in 1911.

recognized. In 1873 he became president of the Royal Society ; in 1877 he was knighted; and in 1907 he was presented by King Edward VII with the Order of Merit. He died on December 10, 1911.

Hops AND HOP-PICKING. When the green, cone-like blossom-clusters of the hop-vine take on a yellow tinge and rustle like paper flowers, the hop grower sends his pickers into the field, for the value of his harvest depends on gathering this flower-fruit at precisely the right moment. The aromatic, resinous substance called lupulin, which is contained in the fruit, gives hops their medicinal value and their importance in brewing malt liquors. A pillow stuffed with hops was an old remedy for sleeplessness. Because of the bitter principle in the fruits, hops are made into medicines to aid appetite and digestion.

The common hop (*Humulus lupulus*) is a perennial climber, which each year produces several twisting stems that reach a length of 15 to 20 feet; it belongs to the nettle family, and has lobed, heart-shaped leaves. Each plant is either male or female, the respective flowers being very dissimilar. The small green male blooms are clustered in branching sprays, while the females form spikes in which the flowers are hidden by overhanging scales, so that they resemble catkins. The vines grow upwards, clinging in the wild state to other hedge plants. When grown commercially in the hop-fields they are trained to upright poles or wire (*see* illus. page 1642). Hop-vines always twist in a right-handed spiral.

E. A. Botting

HOPS IN THE SUNSHINE

As summer advances the female hop flowers develop into cone-like scaly heads (above), which are the hops of commerce. At the base of each scale there are glands which exude a bitter, yellowish, resinous substance—and this gives hops their importance in the brewing of beer. Both the leaves and the stems have small hooks, which enable them to cling to any available support. *See also page 1642.*

The best hops come from fields where only female plants are grown. This prevents seed production, which would lessen the value of the fruit. Plants grown from seed are not true to type ; therefore, hops must be propagated by root cuttings or sets.

The principal use of hops is in flavouring beer and other malt beverages. Bohemian hops are noted for their excellence, and Germany, France, and Belgium also cultivate them. In the United States, the principal hop-fields are in New York State, and on the Pacific coast.

To pick the hops labour is brought from London and other large towns to the hop-fields in Kent, Surrey, Hampshire, Herefordshire, and Worcestershire. Men, women and children work in the hop-fields. The conditions under which the pickers lived were very primitive, their only shelter being often barns and outhouses. But much has been done in recent years to improve this. Special trains transport them at the beginning and end of the season.

Horace. (QUINTUS HORATIUS FLACCUS) (65–8 B.C.). There is nothing new under the sun, and the youth of Horace, the great Roman poet, born more than 2,000 years ago, has many points of resemblance to the life of an ambitious scholarly boy in our own time. He was born on a farm in Southern Italy, within the Roman Empire, on December 8, 65 B.C. His father was determined to give him the best education possible. After six years' schooling in Rome Horace was sent to Athens at the age of 18 to complete his studies. Not only did this wise father see that no social or intellectual advantage was withheld from his promising son; he also, by precept and example, sought to develop in his boy a noble character. That Horace was not ungrateful for all his father did for him is shown by the tributes he pays to his father's memory in his writings.

Horace settled in Rome, and there soon won fame for his verses. He also gained the friendship and patronage of the wealthy Maecenas, the generous patron of authors, upon whom in return he bestowed immortality, for the name Maecenas is widely used to this day to describe a rich man who helps literature and learning by his wealth. Horace's poetry is famous for two reasons. In the first place he displayed unsurpassed dexterity in handling Latin verse. Secondly, his writings reveal a shrewd philosophy of life, a calm judgement of men and motives, and a smooth and polished wit in exposing folly and wickedness.

It is the greatest tribute that can be paid to his genius to say that today, 2,000 years after his birth, acquaintance with his odes, his satires, and his epistles is an essential part of a classical education.

There are many English translations of Horace. None has been wholly successful; but perhaps the best were the versions of Professor John Conington (1825–69) and of Sir Theodore Martin (1816–1909).

Horn. There are two kinds of horn, one the continued growth of bone, the other a hardening of the epidermis or outer layer of skin. True horn is a modification of the tissue of the outer layer of

AUGUST IN THE HOP GARDENS OF KENT

The Times; Sport & General; Topical

Towards the end of August hops are usually ready for picking, and here are scenes from the Kentish hop gardens taken at the height of the season. The hop is a climbing plant and in the gardens twines itself about lengths of cord or wire suspended from horizontal wires supported on poles. The vines, or bines as they are called, are grown in regular rows (lower). The yield of dried hops per acre **averages** about 10 cwt. In the top left photograph, in front of a row of oast-houses—buildings in which hops are dried—a load of hops is being carted away to a brewery. The stilt man (top right) walks up and down the rows picking hops from the tallest shoots, which may be as much as 20 feet off the ground. The hop was introduced into England from Flanders in 1524, and is chiefly cultivated in Kent, Hampshire and Herefordshire. Its main use is to flavour beer. See article and illustration in page 1641.

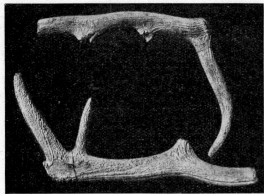

HORNS USED FOR DIGGING
Found in Grimes' Graves—flint mines near Weeting in Norfolk—these red deer antlers were used by prehistoric men for excavating flints. Many thousands of years ago red deer were widely distributed over Britain, but they disappeared long before the beginning of recorded history.

the skin, and is seen in the nails and hair of human beings, the hair, claws, and hoofs of animals, and beaks and feathers of birds. The scales of snakes are of a horny nature; tortoiseshell and the hard spots on animals' bodies are different varieties of horn.

In the horns of cattle, sheep and antelopes the central part is bone, the outer portion only being the true horn tissue. Except for those of the prong-horn antelopes, such horns are never shed. The antlers of deer are really a bone outgrowth and during the growing period such horns are covered with a sensitive skin, known as velvet—which later peels off, leaving the hard, solid antlers. These are usually shed once a year. The horns of the rhinoceros are composed wholly of horny matter, which is in the form of longitudinal fibres so that the horns appear to consist of a compressed mass of coarse bristles. Horns may be solid or hollow; in the latter case they are usually found on the female as well as on the male.

Primitive men used horn for weapons, drinking cups, and handles; then later for powder horns and musical horns. Since true horn can be softened and split into thin sheets which are tough, pliable, and easily moulded, many articles both useful and ornamental are made from it. By a dexterous mixing of dyes, common horn can be made to look like expensive tortoiseshell. Formerly thin horn plates were used in window-panes and lanterns, and horn is still used in making combs, buttons, and handles for umbrellas, canes, knives and forks.

With the invention of celluloid, the earliest, perhaps, of the synthetic substances we call today Plastics (q.v.), natural horn went into disuse for many articles. Better artificial compositions without the inflammable nature of celluloid were made from casein and other compounds. These, since they could be coloured in pleasing patterns, and turned out in uniform grades, took the place of horn—always a material of uncertain behaviour.

Hornbill. A great beak, surmounted by a bony crest and, in some species, prominent eyelashes distinguish these queer ungainly birds (*Bucerotidae*) of Africa, India and Malaya. Their plumage is mainly black and white and, except in the case of the helmet hornbill, the bony excrescence is honeycombed with air spaces, making it very light. The hornbill's food consists chiefly of fruit and insects, but the larger species (about four feet long) kill and eat snakes. These birds spend most of their time on the ground, being slow and rather awkward fliers.

The hornbill breeds in holes in trees, and during the incubation period the male plasters up the entrance to the hole with mud, leaving only a small opening through which he passes food to his mate.

Hornets. In general behaviour and mode of life hornets resemble wasps, and they belong to the same family (*Vespidae*) and genus, the hornet's scientific name being *Vespa crabro*. In England hornets are found in the southern and midland counties and can be readily recognized by their large size, and by the reddish bands and markings which take the place of the wasp's black stripes. The male is about an inch long, a queen even larger.

Hornets do a certain amount of good in killing other harmful insects. They build their nest almost invariably in hollow trees or on the beams of outhouses. Their sting is very painful, and like bees and wasps they become pugnacious if their nest is disturbed. This aggressiveness has given rise to the saying "a veritable hornets' nest," in connexion with an uncomfortable or dangerous situation. (*See* illustration below).

Horns AND TRUMPETS. The early forms of the musical instrument from which the modern horn is descended were made of the horns of animals. The next step was to fashion them out of a long metal tube, and in time the tubes were improved by the addition of valves, worked by keys that shortened or lengthened the air spaces in the tube, thus making it possible to produce any note of

HORNET SEEN FULL-FACE
Largest members of the wasp family in Britain, hornets are not very common, being restricted to the midland and southern counties of England. Above is a highly magnified full-face view of a hornet clutching a twig. On either side of, and immediately behind, the antennae are the large compound eyes. Hornets do some damage to fruit, but make up for it by killing harmful insects.

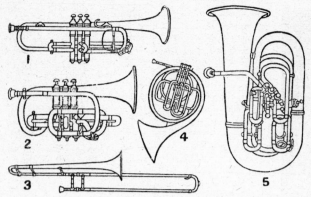

FRENCH HORN AND TRUMPETS

The trumpet (1), the cornet (2) and trombone (3) are all spoken of as trumpets. The French horn (4) is derived from the hunter's horn. In military bands the euphonium (5) is the chief bass solo instrument.

Handel wrote. An inquisitive player discovered, about 1770, that the pitch could be altered by inserting his hand into the bell of the instrument, producing "stopped" notes; so composers, with whom the horn was a favoured instrument, could then use more freedom in scoring parts. Crooks (extra coils of tube) of different length were introduced, by adding which to the horn the pitch could be lowered.

At length piston valves were introduced, admitting wind to several U-shaped turns of the tube which could thus be connected to the main tube at will. You can see these turns and the valves in our illustration of a three-valved French horn on the left.

In the modern orchestra only the French horn is technically called a horn. The trumpet, cornet, and trombone are spoken of as trumpets. The powerful tubas are the tenor and bass instruments of the brass group. The saxhorns, which are chiefly used in military bands, are keyed instruments with long winding tapering tubes, made in several sizes. They get their name from a Belgian, Adolphe Sax (1814–94), who invented them. The euphonium is a bass instrument of the saxhorn type.

the scale. By varying the shape and width of the tube, of the mouthpiece, and of the bell (the flare at the end), various types have been developed.

The long tube was coiled upon itself for convenience of handling. Different notes were produced by varying the lip pressure at the mouthpiece. Even with the simple (valveless) hunting horn, quite elaborate fanfares could be played. Then came the horn as an instrument for the orchestra (about 1700). The scales were incomplete, by the nature of the instrument, so that horns in several keys had to be used to play music such as Bach or

Each of these instruments has its own interesting history and its own distinctive quality. The French horn is derived from the hunter's horn. Straightened out, it would be from seven to 10 feet long. The tube was bent in a circle large enough for the hunter to slip over his head or shoulder, and in this way he carried it.

The trumpet's brilliant and penetrating tone is due to its long, narrow tube, eight feet in length; it is only three-eighths of an inch in diameter until within 15 inches of the bell. The trumpet is very difficult to play, and therefore the cornet often takes its place.

The cornet is the smallest of the brass instruments generally employed. For all its small size, it is the most important member of many brass bands, and fills a useful place in the orchestra.

The sliding trombone is the curious instrument that the performer plays by extending and drawing back his arm as he works the slide and thus lengthens and shortens the tube.

Although the tuba is the deepest voiced of all the brass instruments, it produces rich tones. Its long cone-shaped tube is bent and rebent before it finally ends in a great flare. Like the cornet, horn and trumpet, it is played by valves.

ALPENHORN USED BY SWISS PEASANTS

In the Alps a long, curved, wooden instrument (above) is used occasionally by peasants and cowherds to communicate with one another from a distance. Some of these horns are very long, but their size and shape differ with the locality. Formerly they were used to convey signals in war time. Similar instruments are played by the lamas of Tibet.

The FAITHFUL SERVANT of MANKIND

Man's helper through the ages, the horse is being supplanted by the motor vehicle. Seldom today does he carry the cavalryman into battle. But he still pulls the plough and draws the farm cart.

Horse. The affection, docility and intelligence of the horse have made it the best-loved friend of Man. From the earliest times of human history we know that Man used the horse, first for food and later as a beast of burden and draught animal. The horse and other members of the same family, the ass and the zebra, are especially interesting because scientists have been able to trace their history more completely than that of any other animal group. So many fossil skeletons of horses have been discovered, in all parts of the world, that we know the history of its development for a vast period of time. We know that the remotest ancestral horse was a small animal about the size of a hare, with five toes on each forefoot and four on each hindfoot.

Fossil remains of early horses, named *Eohippus* or dawn horse (Greek *eo* meaning dawn; *hippus*, horse) have been found with four complete toes on the forefeet and three on the hind. As we follow down the series of fossil skeletons, we can see how these little animals took to running on the tips of their toes to escape their enemies, and how gradually they came to throw more and more weight on the centre toes. With each generation, therefore, these toes became stronger, and the unused toes became weaker and finally disappeared. (*See* Evolution; Foot).

That is why the horse now has only one toe on each foot. The hoof which encases it is just a greatly enlarged and thickened toe-nail. Traces of two of the lost toes may be found in the splint-bones which grow on either side of the cannon-bone of the foot. The upper joint of the toe has also become much larger and stronger. It is known as the fetlock. The joints that are usually called the knees of the horse correspond to the ankles and wrists of a human being. The true knees and elbows are concealed within the body of the horse, but their action may be seen clearly when it is in motion.

The horse has a symmetrical form, strong limbs, a long head with large eyes,

small pointed ears which it can move, and wide-open dilating nostrils. The neck is long, the body rounded and fleshy; the hair is soft and short, and lies close to the body, growing into long coarse strands in the mane and tail. The mane falls down one or both sides of the neck and over the eyes. The tails of the ass and the zebra are tufted at the ends, but in the horse the long hairs grow from the base and sides as well as from the tip.

The horse eats grass and grain, but does not chew the cud. It has from 36 to 40 teeth—three incisors, or cutting teeth, and six grinders on either side of both jaws. The grinders (molars) are peculiar in that they grow from the gums as fast as they wear off at the crown. In addition to these the males have four small canines, or dog-teeth. Between the canines and the grinders there is a space where the bit is placed, an arrangement by which Man has been able to subdue this vigorous animal.

The foal, or baby horse, is born with its eyes open and its body fully covered with hair. It is able to stand and walk a few minutes after birth. Within two weeks the " nippers," or central teeth, appear; when the colt is about six months old it has a full set of milk-teeth, which it begins to shed during its

Topical

MARE AND HER TWO LONG-LEGGED FOALS

Very young horses are called foals, then colts when about six months old. Unlike the young of many of the larger animals a foal is active almost from birth, being able to walk almost immediately. The legs are out of all proportion to its body—because, in order to be able to escape from its enemies in the wild state, it must be capable of running some distance at a good speed while still very young. The first teeth begin to appear when a foal is two weeks old.

third year. The dog-teeth, or canines, make their appearance, but only in the males, during the fourth year, and at the age of five years the set of permanent teeth is complete.

The growth and changes in appearance of the teeth are so regular up to the tenth year that the age of a horse may be judged by them. During its second year the colt's hair loses the curliness which distinguishes its first season, and becomes more lustrous. The hair, except the mane and tail, is shed annually in the spring. In the autumn it grows longer for the winter.

From the piles of horse-bones found in the haunts of the early cave men, we know that the wild horse was first pursued for food. As a tamed servant of mankind the horse was unknown to Egypt of the

Pyramid Age (3000–2500 B.C.), and to the Babylonians before 2100 B.C. The first to tame the horse were Aryan (Indo-European) peoples who inhabited the vast grasslands that stretched north of the Caspian Sea and the Black Sea.

All the early monuments and records indicate that for many centuries the horse was used chiefly to draw chariots in war. As beasts of burden, the ox and the ass were used long before the horse.

Several animals similar to the ass are still found wild in Central Asia, such as the kiang and onager, but the only wild horse is Przevalsky's horse, which occurs still in herds in Mongolia. This is a small shaggy, pony-like animal, its tail being more like that of an ass than a horse. When white men first went to America the horse was entirely unknown to the natives and increased their awe of the newcomers. The wild horses later met with in South America and the mustangs, or Indian ponies, which, until quite recently, ranged wild over a great part of western North America, are descendants of tamed horses that escaped from the Spaniards in the 16th century. Likewise the wild horses of Australia are descended from stock imported by the early settlers.

Most of the ordinary horses of north-western Europe are descended from the ancient dun-coloured Norse horse. The ancestors of our modern draught-horses were first bred as war horses, because a very large and powerful animal was needed to carry the weight of a mail-clad knight. Breeds from France, Belgium, and Germany were long ago imported into Great Britain, where some of the most famous

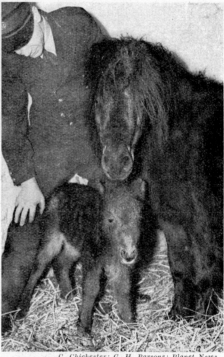

C. Chichester; G. H. Parsons; Planet News

SOME EQUINE CONTRASTS
Three widely differing breeds of domesticated horses are shown. The Arab (top) is noted for its speed, intelligence and endurance. Of agricultural horses, the Shire (centre, left) is the biggest and heaviest, and though of immense strength is remarkably docile. The Shetland pony (lower) is the smallest of the horses; the foal seen here is only 14 inches high. Shetland ponies are very strong for their size and exceedingly hardy.

modern types originated, such as the Cleveland Bay, the Shire, the Suffolk Punch, and the Clydesdale. The Cleveland Bay has long been bred in Yorkshire as a carriage horse and is red or reddish in colour. The Shire, which has been bred for centuries, is of immense weight—from 1,800 to 2,200 lb.—with a plentiful covering of long hair extending from the hoofs to the knees. The magnificent Clydesdale, a Scottish breed named from the valley of the Clyde, is not quite so large as the Shire, and is noted for its activity, strength, and endurance. The Suffolk Punch of East Anglia, generally of reddish-brown colour, is a splendid draught horse, docile yet full of courage.

The Shetland pony is a diminutive creature, a product of the cold, barren Shetland Islands off the northern coast of Scotland. Its small size is doubtless due to generations of battling against adverse physical conditions in its native haunts. It possesses great strength for its size, will fatten on almost any kind of food, and is patient and gentle. It possesses a long, shaggy mane, and a bushy tail.

The Arab steed is the ideal horse for speed and endurance. It is also noted for its graceful proportions, and its intelligence and docility. The original home of the Arabian horse was not the country after which it was named. The Arabs were without horses until after the Christian era. The Egyptians, however, as early as 1500 B.C., possessed horses which appear to have resembled the modern Arabian horses, while those that appeared in Babylonia, Palestine, and Greece about that time were coarse, thick-set animals. Classical literature, moreover, proves that about 1000 B.C. North African steeds were highly esteemed and eagerly sought after by the nations of the Mediterranean area. The Barb horse from Morocco is perhaps as famous as the Arab itself, and the Irish hunters almost equally noted in recent times were originally derived from Spanish horses of Barb descent.

The thoroughbred racehorse was developed in the 18th century from old English stock improved with Arab or Barb blood. These animals were bred for speed, and a good racehorse will attain a speed of 35 m.p.h. (See also Horse Racing; Riding).

Horse Chestnut. The beautiful tree which adorns many of the public parks, and which in springtime, especially about Whitsuntide, bears pyramidal white or pink flower spikes is the horse

E. J. Hosking

HORSE CHESTNUT IN FULL BLOOM
Native to Asia and Eastern Europe, the horse chestnut was introduced into Britain about 1550. It is quite different from the sweet chestnut (see p. 782) of which it is no relation. Its fruit, popularly known as conkers, is not edible by Man. The timber, white and soft, has little commercial value but is used for decorative inlays.

chestnut. It belongs to the *Sapindaceae* family, and the scientific name of the common horse chestnut tree is *Aesculus hippocastanum*. It is not a native of Great Britain, though it grows well there; it originated in Asia and Eastern Europe.

The name is said to come from the scar, resembling a horseshoe, which appears on the main woody stem after the shedding of the leaf-stalk.

The large sticky buds containing the leaves and flower-spikes appear in late winter and early spring; if picked and placed in water in a warm room they will gradually open out and form an attractive indoor decoration. The seeds, contained in a spiny ball-like casing, are the conkers with which every boy delights to play. The seeds look rather like the sweet chestnut, though they are not eaten by Man; they do, however, form a useful food for pigs, goats and sheep, and, when boiled, for poultry.

The trees, planted mainly for their ornamental value, grow quickly into fine shapely ones which afford ample shade in summer, and live for quite 200 years or more. Planted carefully, they form beautiful avenues, examples of which can be seen in Bushy Park, near Hampton Court, in Middlesex. The wood of this tree is too soft for timber.

Horse Racing.

One sport in England which has attracted the public for centuries is horse racing. It is essentially a spectators' sport, as few can afford to breed, train, and race thoroughbred horses. In England the word racing is usually understood to denote horse racing.

The first authentic account of a horse race concerns one between Richard II, when Prince of Wales, and a certain earl of Arundel in 1377. Henry VIII was interested in the sport, likewise his daughter, Queen Elizabeth. By the time of James I (1566–1625) there was a celebrated course at Croydon, Surrey ; and at the end of Charles I's reign races were being run in Hyde Park, and continued during the time of Charles II (1660–85). In 1607 winners at York had been rewarded with a prize of a small golden bell, which in Charles II's time was altered to a silver bowl valued at 100 guineas. Under the Puritanical Oliver Cromwell, racing was banned, though he did not forbid the breeding of horses. After the Restoration Charles II established Newmarket races in 1667.

During Anne's reign (1702–14) racing was started at Epsom, and annual meetings have been held there since 1730. The annual meeting at Ascot, Berkshire, was begun in 1820. The first race for the St. Leger stakes was run in 1776 at Doncaster by Col. St. Leger, and thereafter the race was named after him. The Duke of Richmond started in his park at Goodwood, Sussex, the races of that name in 1802. King Edward VII, when Prince of Wales, developed a keen interest in the Turf, winning the Derby and St. Leger with his famous Persimmon in 1896 and the Ascot Gold Cup in 1897 ; and in 1900 with Diamond Jubilee he won the Derby, St. Leger and Two Thousand Guineas. He also won the Derby and Two Thousand Guineas with Minoru in 1909. George V and George VI both carried on the royal tradition of successful racing and breeding.

Amateurs frequently ride in steeplechases or over hurdles, but it is usually only professional jockeys who ride on the flat. The Jockey Club, founded 1750, controls all flat racing; while the National Hunt Committee is responsible for all steeplechases and hurdle races.

Many training stables are at Newmarket, Cambridgeshire, and others are on the Sussex and Berkshire Downs and in Yorkshire. In Eire there is a considerable amount of horse-breeding, and not far from Dublin is the famous Curragh racecourse, said to be the finest in the British Isles.

Hospitals.

In the early days of Christian civilization in our own land, as well as throughout Europe generally, caring for the sick was rightly regarded as a religious duty. The erection of hospitals was therefore an honoured enterprise of the Church. At first only the most helpless sufferers, such as lepers, were provided for; and the hospitals were always a branch of some monastery or priory maintained by religious revenues, and staffed by devout members of some religious order.

St. Bartholomew's Hospital in London, said to be the oldest general hospital in Britain, is a good surviving example of a hospital dating from medieval times, with a history going back 800 years. It was founded as an annexe of the Priory of St. Bartholomew in the same parish, and the priory church still stands on the opposite side of the road.

No doubt caring for the souls of the poor patients, rather than for their bodies, was the primary aim of those early hospitals. Ignorant as people then were of surgery and medicine, and indeed of sanitation, it must have been hopeless to attempt to cure the ills of most of the poor sufferers whose condition was so desperate as to secure their admission to some one or other of the very few and primitive hospitals existing at that time.

Today, however, all this is changed, and hospitals are " temples of healing." Money cannot put into the most luxurious home the advanced medical and surgical facilities which even the poorest can get in a hospital. There the sick can have the expert care of the best physicians and surgeons, trained nurses in attendance night and day, all the discoveries and appliances of modern science, and skill to find out what the matter is and put it right; a trained dietician to see that they have the proper food; and almoners to ensure that convalescence is not interfered with by undue money worry, or to arrange for the transfer of patients to the convalescent homes now run in connexion with every large hospital.

The principles of modern hospital organization had their rise, through the genius of Florence Nightingale (q.v.), out of the ghastly sufferings of the Crimean War, as did the profession of nursing, without which the modern hospital could not exist. A few years later the chemist Pasteur discovered the relation of germs to putrefaction; and the great surgeon, Lister, applying Pasteur's discoveries to surgery, revolutionized operating room practice by the use of antiseptics. Almost every year since then has seen some advance, great or small, in medical science and hospital practice. Most hospitals have, in addition to free wards, provision for paying patients in private wards.

In the medical schools of many great hospitals the doctors and surgeons of the future receive their training. Until 1948 many British hospitals were kept up largely by voluntary payments made by public and patients. Now State medicine has taken over the cost of administration of the British hospitals, and public sympathy is shown in funds to provide extra amenities for the patients.

In addition to general hospitals, there are a number of hospitals devoted to special classes of disease, such as children's diseases, eye troubles, nervous and mental diseases, tuberculosis or cancer.

Hudson, HENRY (died 1611).

This English explorer ventured on four voyages in the early years of James I's reign. Nothing is known of Henry Hudson's life before 1607, when he set out on his first expedition. All his voyages were made for the purpose of discovering north-east or north-west passages to China, to reach the rich trade of the Orient. His first and second voyages were for the Muscovy Company, an English trading company. During the first, he explored the coasts of Greenland and Spitzbergen (archipelago 360 miles north of Norway), where he realized the possibility of establishing a whale fishery. During the second, he reached Novaya Zemlya (islands in the Arctic Ocean), trying in vain to force a passage through the ice-locked Kara Strait, separating the islands from the north coast of European Russia.

The third voyage was undertaken for the Dutch East India Company. In 1609, he sailed with a crew of only 20 men and explored the river which bears his name (and on which New York now stands) with the vain hope that it might lead to the Pacific Ocean. The last voyage was for an English company formed especially for the purpose. He set sail in April 1610, passed through the strait which was named after him, and explored and charted Hudson Bay. Winter overtook him, and he and the members of his crew endured terrible hardships.

His men became increasingly discontented and broke out in open mutiny in June 1611. Hudson was overpowered and, together with his young son, the ship's carpenter, and several sick men, was cast adrift in a small boat. The boat was never heard of again. The ringleaders of the mutineers were killed by the natives. Others won their way back to England with Hudson's records.

Hudson's voyages were of great value in extending geographical knowledge, and they were instrumental in developing the rich fisheries of Spitzbergen and the fur trade of the Hudson Bay region.

Hudson, WILLIAM HENRY (1841–1922). A British writer and naturalist who became better known after his death, Hudson was born on August 4, 1841, near Buenos Aires, Argentina, of British parents, and until he had reached the age of 33 remained in South America.

Hudson's special interest in South America, as, later, in England, was the study of bird-life in its natural surroundings. His books at first reached only a small circle, and it was not until after his death on August 18, 1922, that he really became famous. From 1874 onwards he lived in England, mainly in London, in poor circumstances; but by 1901 the value of his work was being recognized, and in that year he received a pension from the British Government. His name was first made familiar in 1925 by the establishment in Hyde Park, London, of a bird sanctuary dedicated to him and containing the famous mural sculpture by Jacob Epstein, representing Rima, the heroine of Hudson's Green Mansions. His books are as full of scientifically correct detail as they are of unforgettable pen-pictures of Nature, both human and animal.

In Hudson's many books about birds, every fact of interest and many previously unknown details about birds are chronicled in charming style. His works on the countryside in general give vivid pictures of its natural beauties, and evince deep insight into the home life of country districts and rural customs and traditions. Such books include Nature in Downland, Hampshire Days, which contains a delightful account of the wild life of the New Forest, Afoot in England, and A Shepherd's Life. Green Mansions is a romance, set amid the tropical beauty of the upper Orinoco in South America; and Far Away and Long Ago, Idle Days in Patagonia, and History of My Early Life describe his early years as a student of Nature.

Hudson Bay. In north-eastern Canada is the third largest inland sea in the world, which is named after Henry Hudson (q.v.), who explored it in 1610. This is Hudson Bay—a mighty gulf with an area of over 500,000 square miles. It is entered from the Atlantic Ocean by way of Hudson Strait, and from the Arctic Ocean by Fury and Hecla Strait and Fox Channel.

Although never entirely frozen over, it is so obstructed by drift ice that navigation is safe only during June, July and August. The Nelson, Churchill, Hayes and Severn are the most important of the numerous rivers flowing into the bay.

In the short summer season steamers find their way there to load up with thousands of pounds worth of furs. Then, too, the Indians and Eskimos living in scattered bands near the shore venture out after seals, porpoises, and walrus, and fish for cod, salmon, and many other edible fishes.

Except for a few trading stations and scattered settlements, the shores—low except for certain high bluffs on the east and north-east—are the haunts chiefly of caribou and musk ox, of ducks and loons (diving birds) and ptarmigan. The only good harbour is Fort Churchill, and the Hudson Bay railway from Le Pas, Manitoba, to the port has reduced the journey from Winnipeg and Edmonton to Liverpool by 500 and 1,000 miles respectively. Large quantities of wheat from Manitoba's grain-growing areas are shipped from Churchill to England.

The Cabots (q.v.) entered Hudson Strait in 1498, and several Elizabethan mariners did likewise.

The Hudson river has no connexion beyond its name with Hudson Bay. It rises in the Adirondack mountains in the United States, and flows through New York State to the Atlantic. New York and Jersey City stand on its banks.

Topical

HUDSON'S MEMORIAL IN A LONDON PARK
In the bird sanctuary dedicated to the famous naturalist, William Henry Hudson, in Hyde Park, London, is this sculpture by Jacob Epstein, representing Rima, the heroine of Hudson's novel, Green Mansions. Born in Argentina in 1841, Hudson made a study of bird-life in its natural surroundings, both in England and South America, and wrote many delightful accounts of wild life in Britain.

Hudson's Bay Company.

The early history of north-western Canada is the history of the Hudson's Bay Company and its rivals. Their trading-posts were the first settlements in the western plains, around which many a thriving city has grown. The Hudson's Bay Company dates from 1670, when Prince Rupert (1619–82), a cousin of Charles II, received reports of the rich harvest of furs that the French were gathering in the Hudson Bay area. With 17 associates the prince obtained from King Charles II of England a charter giving them the sole rights of trade over all the unoccupied lands whose rivers flow into Hudson Bay.

It was thought that the region so described was not more than a few hundred miles in breadth, and years of exploration were necessary before it was discovered that Rupert's Land, as it was at first called, included nearly all of the present provinces of Manitoba and Saskatchewan, a large part of Alberta, and even certain territory now a part of the United States.

The Hudson's Bay Company had something more than mere trading privileges, for it owned the land and governed the people also. This arrangement was intolerable to the settlers, and in 1869 the company was forced to surrender most of its privileges, though it was paid £300,000 and allowed to keep its trading posts and large tracts of land.

Hugo, VICTOR MARIE (1802–85).

If the sole object of poetry is to achieve beauty of metre and phrase, then as a poet, but not as a dramatist or orator, this French master of Romance merits the great reputation he gained. Born at Besançon in eastern France on February 26, 1802, the son of an officer of the French Army, Victor Hugo spent his childhood in Paris with his mother, and in military camps in foreign countries, his father being a general. His mind and emotions were stimulated by public life, travel, and the atmosphere of glory which invested Napoleon Bonaparte's conquering armies, and the precocious boy wrote a tragic drama at 14. At 17 he took the French Academy prize for a poem, and at 22 was recognized as a master of the lyric and ballad.

By 1831 he had written Notre Dame de Paris, the book which made him popular with English readers. He headed a literary revolt from the classics, and founded the French romantic school of writers. Most of his followers are forgotten, but Hugo had such original ideas, command of language, and splendour of sentiment, that he is assured of literary immortality.

VICTOR MARIE HUGO
Poet, novelist and dramatist, Victor Hugo was born in 1802. He won a prize for poetry when 17. At the age of 60 he wrote Les Misérables (The Unfortunates), which is ranked amongst the world's greatest novels.

Hugo was tremendously in earnest as a patriot and social reformer, and a number of his poems, plays, and works of prose fiction are criticism of the laws and social customs of his time. As a political opponent to Napoleon III (1808–73), whom he nicknamed "Napoleon the Little," Hugo made himself so dangerous by his eloquence that he was banished from France, fleeing to Brussels in 1851.

Making his home in the Channel Islands, he wrote notable historical papers, rhapsodic memories inspired by personal sorrows, and novels. He was 60 years old when he wrote Les Misérables (The Unfortunates), an epic work of fiction, which is justly ranked with the greatest novels of all countries. This was in 1862. Three years later came Les Travailleurs de la Mer (Toilers of the Sea). Hernani (1830) is thought to be his best drama, and Les Châtiments (1833) is a collection of his finest lyrical poems. After the fall of the empire of Napoleon III in 1870, Hugo returned to Paris, where he became a popular idol.

His songs were set to music, his banned play Le Roi s'amuse (The King's Diversion) was revived, and he was the chief figure of the French Academy. When he died on May 22, 1885, at the age of 83, the Panthéon—a church in Paris dedicated as the tomb of illustrious men—was opened for the first time for 75 years for his burial.

Huguenots.

(Pron. hū′-ge-nŏz). This name, given in the 16th century to the French Protestants who adopted the Calvinistic form of Christianity, is thought to be derived from the German word *eidgenossen*, meaning "confederates bound by an oath." They were to be found chiefly among the humbler classes in the industrial towns, though Paris remained strictly Roman Catholic. In their struggles for religious freedom, the Huguenots were driven to become a political party.

By the middle of the 16th century their numbers and influence had aroused the fears of the Catholic party, and there was a series of wars between the Catholics and Huguenots from 1560 to 1598. The first war began with an attack by the Duke of Guise and his followers on Huguenots assembled for worship in a barn. The peace which concluded the third war was broken by the massacre of Huguenots on St. Bartholomew's day, August 24, 1572. (*See* Coligny, Gaspard de).

The Huguenot wars ended in 1598, when their leader, Henry IV (1589–1610)—who though formerly a Huguenot had conformed to the Catholic

Church—issued the Edict of Nantes, which gave the Protestants certain political rights, and religious freedom. (*See* Henry IV, King of France).

When Louis XIV revoked the Edict of Nantes in 1685, all legal protection was withdrawn from the Huguenots. Although they were forbidden to leave France, more than 250,000 of them, many of them France's best industrial workers, managed to escape, and carried French arts and manufactures to England, Brandenburg (Germany), the Netherlands, and North America.

Hull. The full name of this city and seaport of the East Riding of Yorkshire is Kingston-upon-Hull, a name given to it in place of Wyke-upon-Hull in 1296 by Edward I, when he bought the town and created the port. It stands where the River Hull flows into the broad Humber estuary. Hull owes its importance to its fine position 20 miles from the North Sea, and within easy reach of the industrial areas of the North and Midlands. The docks cover over 200 acres, King George V dock being the largest on the East coast outside London, and normally handle a large trade with Germany and Scandinavia, as well as coastal traffic. Hull is, moreover, the premier fishing port in the United Kingdom. Local industries—apart from seed crushing and oil extraction—include shipbuilding, flour milling, cement making, aircraft manufacture, and manufactures of chemicals, paper, and paint. In the Second World War (1939–45) the city suffered 82 attacks by German aircraft in which 83,000 of its 92,660 houses were destroyed or damaged. The centre of the town had to be completely rebuilt. The estimated population is 287,300.

Mansell

BEGGING MERCY FOR THE HUGUENOTS
The massacre of the Huguenots (French Protestants) on St. Bartholomew's Day, August 24, 1572, horrified many Catholics who knew of the plan and did their best to prevent it succeeding. Here one of those who were to take part in the massacre is being called by a monk to come out and slay, while a nun on her knees is begging him not to obey the summons. This painting by Sir John Millais (1829–96) is entitled Mercy : St. Bartholomew's Day, 1572. It is in the Tate Gallery, London.

Humming-bird. Belonging exclusively to the North and South American continents these exquisite little birds comprising the *Trochilidae* family derive their name from the sound produced by the rapid vibration of their wings as they hover beside a flower. There are about 750 species and sub-species, ranging from Alaska to Patagonia, the Andean regions of Ecuador and Colombia having the greatest variety. All have long slender bills—sometimes longer than head and body together—tiny bodies, brilliant plumage, and strong wings.

The humming-bird feeds on the nectar of flowers and minute insects which it finds within flowers too small to support even its light weight. To enable the bird to feed it has developed very strong wings which sustain it above a blossom, vibrating so rapidly that the human eye cannot follow their movements. The beak is long and slender, and the long tongue is in the form of a double tube which can be extended to an extraordinary length, to seize insects in flowers or under the bark of trees.

Like the bee, the humming-bird is very useful in the cross-fertilization of plants, for specks of pollen cling to its body and are carried from flower to flower as the little bird searches for its food ; and indeed there are some tropical blossoms specially adapted to cross-fertilization by these tiny creatures.

The nest of a humming-bird is a tiny cup-shaped affair, and it is made of plant-down, the outside

Mass. Institute of Technology

HUMMING-BIRDS ON THE WING

While it hovers in the air to feed, the wings of a humming-bird vibrate at an average rate of 55 strokes a second, making the humming sound which has given the birds their name. Here a special high-speed camera has caught three of the birds feeding, the wings showing clearly instead of as a filmy haze.

covered with moss and strands of spider's web. The eggs are pure white, never more than two in number.

Among the humming-birds are the smallest known birds, only about two inches in length, but some members of the family are eight and a half inches long. The ruby-throat humming-bird of North America is about three and a quarter inches long, and the upper feathers of the male are the glistening green of an emerald, with changeable amethyst lights over the wings and tail; the under feathers shade from pearl grey into the darker upper feathers, and the throat is like a glowing ruby, with all its variations of colour. The females are more soberly clad.

The racket-tailed humming-bird, found only in the upper Amazon valley, South America, is one of the smallest and most remarkable members of the family. It has a curious tail, the second pair of feathers being wire-like, and crossing each other after forming a loop. The ends are formed into a racket-like expansion of a purple colour.

In the Andes lives the great humming-bird, the largest of all, which is about eight and a half inches long and has a wing span of $15\frac{1}{2}$ inches. Its plumage is dull, and its flight is one of its characteristic features, for when hovering over flowers it continually opens and shuts its tail feathers like a fan.

The double-crested humming-bird has amber-like feathers over each eye, a wonderful red crest, and long green-spotted tufts of red feathers extending from either shoulder. Its tail is wedge-shaped. This bird, four inches long, lives in Brazil.

Hundred Years' War (1338–1453).

Instead of winning the French throne for England, this protracted struggle cost her all her continental possessions except Calais, and developed in the French a sense of unity which they had never had before.

The causes of the conflict, which started in 1338, were to be found in the constant clashes between the two nations arising out of the

English kings being the rulers of Guienne in south-west France; in the aid given by the French to the Scots in their wars against the English; and finally in the interference of Philip of France and his vassal, the Count of Flanders, with the profitable wool trade of England with the Flemish cities.

In addition there was the claim that Edward III himself was rightfully king of France, because his mother was a sister of the late king, while Philip VI was only a cousin.

The conflict was really a series of wars, truces, and peaces, lasting through the reigns of five English kings, from Edward III to Henry V, and of five French kings, from Philip VI to Charles VII. At the time of the battle of Crécy, 1346, the English had already won command of the English Channel by a spectacular naval victory at Sluys (1340); and after Crécy, the town of Calais on the Strait of Dover surrendered to them on September 28, 1347.

For nearly 10 years after that the fighting almost ceased, partly owing to the plague, called the Black Death, which swept over Europe, killing more than a quarter of the population. Not until 1355 was the struggle between the countries renewed. At Poitiers (1356) the Black Prince with a small army of Englishmen was confronted by an overwhelming French force. The Black Prince arranged his troops on a little plateau protected at the flanks by a hedge and by rough and marshy ground. The brave but inefficient French King John threw away his advantage of superior numbers by ordering his knights, weighted down with their armour, to dismount and advance on foot against the hail of

British Museum

CAVALRY ACTION AT POITIERS

Second of the English victories over the French in the Hundred Years' War (1338–1453) was the battle of Poitiers, fought on September 19, 1356. Victory was largely gained by the English bowmen, whose arrows pierced the armour of the French. This illustration, from a contemporary manuscript, shows an encounter between English and French knights.

Painting by J. D. Penrose; photo, Mansell

QUEEN PHILIPPA INTERCEDES FOR THE BURGHERS OF CALAIS

When Calais after a year's siege surrendered in 1347 to the English army under King Edward III, six of the leading citizens, with halters round their necks, presented the keys of the town to the king, offering their own lives in exchange for those of the starving inhabitants. Edward, who was enraged by the stubborn resistance he had encountered, would have killed the envoys had not his wife, Queen Philippa, successfully pleaded for their lives, as shown here.

English arrows. One after another the three divisions of the French army were thrown into confusion. King John and his youngest son, refusing to flee, were taken captive by the English and sent to England, where the king remained a prisoner until 1360.

The horrors of a peasants' revolt and civil strife were now added to the miseries of France. A treaty with England was concluded in 1360; but in 1369 the new king of France, Charles V, found an excuse for renewing the war. He regained a good deal of his land, and only Calais in the north and Bordeaux in the south remained to the English at the time of Charles's death in 1380.

There was little fighting during the next 30 years, each country being occupied with its own internal troubles. Soon after the accession of Henry V in 1413, the hero king of England, the war began again. At Agincourt (q.v.), near Crécy, a small English force was again confronted in 1415 by a large French army.

As in the two former great battles, the French forces consisted chiefly of dismounted knights weighted down with heavy armour. And again they were packed close together, in a narrow newly-ploughed field, in which they sank almost to their knees. Shakespeare makes Henry V say, the night before the battle, that he "wished not for a single man more" to share the glory of the impending fight. A third great English victory ensued.

By the Treaty of Troyes (1420) the defeated and disunited French agreed that Henry V should marry Princess Katherine, the daughter of Charles VI of France; that during the life of this insane king, Henry should act as regent; and after Charles's death Henry should reign as king of France as well as England.

Henry V did not live to wear the French crown, for he died seven weeks before Charles (1422). The death of these two monarchs left the inheritance to both thrones to Henry VI, the nine-months-old son of Henry V and Queen Katherine. Under the direction of the Duke of Bedford the English armies continued their conquest of France, but their claims were disputed by the disinherited dauphin of France, later Charles VII, who refused to accept the Treaty of Troyes. At the end of seven years it seemed that Orleans, his last important stronghold, would surely fall to the English.

Just at this darkest moment in the fortunes of France, a new force appeared in the person of Saint Joan of Arc, the Maid of Orleans (see article on Joan of Arc). Inspired by her patriotism the French forced the English to raise the siege of Orleans. Victory followed victory in rapid succession, until in 1429 the dauphin was crowned at Reims as King Charles VII. Even after Joan's capture in 1430 her spirit inspired the French, and they fought to such effect that when the war ended in 1453, only Calais remained in English hands.

PRAIRIE LAND *of the* DANUBE PLAIN

A country of wide pastures and magnificent scenery is Hungary, where gaily-costumed peasant farmers grow, on the small holdings they received at the breaking up of the big estates, much of the grain that feeds Central Europe.

Hungary. (Pron. hung'-ga-ri). Within half an hour of its capital city, Budapest, lies the heart of the Republic of Hungary—the great *Alföld* (lowland plain), one of the richest agricultural lands of Europe, as level as a threshing-floor and of amazing fertility. Through its fruitful expanse flow the broad, winding Danube and its sluggish tributary the Theiss, fringed with marshes.

It is a peaceful land of broad meadows, strips of clover, huge windmills; of vineyards, long stretches of bright red peppers, and purple fields of lucerne; of huge rectangles planted with tobacco, cabbage, potatoes or sugar-beet. The landscape is everywhere dotted with splashes of red and blue—the full skirts and kerchiefs of the peasant tillers of the plain. Stubble-fields, gorgeous with poppies and sunflowers, contrast vividly with patches of fallow land or pasture, where boys tend flocks of geese.

Splendid roads, shaded by long rows of Lombardy poplars, lead off in every direction—past one village after another of whitewashed walls; red-tiled or straw-thatched roofs, church spires, and often the graceful stone minaret of a mosque, to remind one of 150 years of Turkish rule (1526–1683). The long narrow peasant houses look out on the street over gardens enclosed by walls of white washedbrick.

In his home, the Magyar (pron. mod'-yŏr), as the true Hungarian calls himself, has reached a high state of peasant culture. When he can afford a floor of wood, he has it, even in the kitchen; when he must put up with an earthen floor, it is compact, hard and wonderfully clean. In his kitchen, as clean and orderly as his front room, his wife cooks in a pot which hangs over an open fireplace, or on an earthen or tile stove with a tiled chimney. His passion for china and earthenware, dishes and bowls, and the pitchers and mugs which line the walls of his house, is only exceeded by his love of flowers.

The Magyar's furniture must be decorated, his chairs and benches painted, his great chests carved. The walls are tinted, as are the great beams and boards of the ceiling. He even decorates his veranda, and always the gable ends of the house, with tasteful designs. His pig-pens, mangers, stables and barns are substantial, and often decorated in colours. The yard about the house is clean, either gravelled or covered with compact turf. His unfenced fields are not disfigured by weeds.

Vast estates belonging to the Church and nobility formerly occupied a large part of the Alföld; many of the peasants owned no land at all. After the First World War of 1914–18 most of the

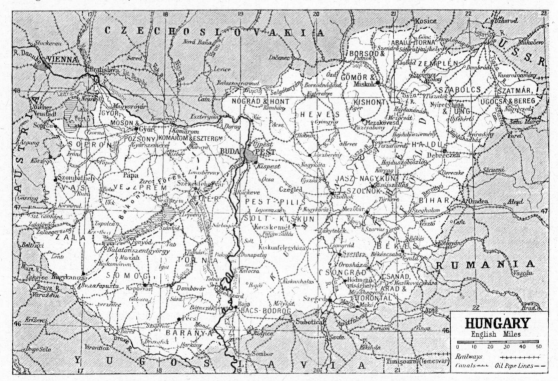

HUNGARY, THE GRANARY OF CENTRAL EUROPE
Between the First and the Second World Wars Hungary was a kingdom with a vacant throne, a regent exercising the functions of a monarch. In 1946 a Republic was established, and changes took place in the social structure of the country.

estates were broken up into small holdings which were distributed among the peasants.

Between the Alföld and the vineyard-clad Carpathian foothills lies the *puzta*, or steppes of Hungary. Treeless, save for small clumps of locust trees near the widely-scattered peasant homes, it is the grazing-ground of thousands of long-horned Hungarian cattle and flocks of sheep, tended by men in sheepskin greatcoats and cowhide sandals.

Here, too, are seen many camps of the Tzigany (pron. tsĕ′-gah-ni) or gipsies. About their queer brown tents, naked dark-skinned children roll in the grass; and the men, with gaudy spangled waistcoats, flapping trousers and broad-brimmed hats, stroll lazily about, while the gaily bedecked women tend the pot that hangs above the fire.

The Magyar, a little shorter in stature than the average Englishman, is strong and healthy. His appreciation of the beautiful—so evident in his architecture, his innate orderliness and cleanliness, his passion for flowers— is second only to his love of his land and his absolute independence of spirit. He is a natural

musician, and the influence of the Tzigany is heard in the works of the great Franz Liszt (*q.v.*), Bela Bartók, Kodály, and Dohnányi. He is generous to a fault and extravagant, but hard working. All Hungarian children must attend a " general school " between the ages of 6 and 14.

The Magyar tongue is closely related to that of the Finns and Lapps, and bears little relation to the other languages of Europe except Turkish. Although the Roman alphabet is used, no word on a Magyar printed page gives us any hint as to its meaning, since the language has practically no Latin or

Hungarian Legation; Ewing Galloway

HUNGARIAN PEASANTS IN TRADITIONAL COSTUMES

Despite political changes, Hungary is a land where the peasants still cling to their old customs and costumes. On special occasions they wear the brightly coloured and elaborately embroidered clothes peculiar to their country (upper), not merely to attract tourists, as do the peasants in some parts of Europe, but to satisfy their own love of colour. The shepherds (lower) are tending their sheep on the banks of the river Tisza in south-eastern Hungary. The Magyars, as the people of Hungary are called, descend from a race that came out of Central Asia 1,000 years ago.

Teutonic roots. This makes the very extensive literature written in the Hungarian language a sealed book to most Europeans.

Budapest, the seat of government, with a population of over a million, is beautifully situated on both sides of the Danube. It was much damaged during the Second World War (*see* Budapest). Other important cities are Szeged, Debreczen, and Miskolc. More than 6,000 miles of railways, most of them operated by the government, connect the leading cities with one another and with the outside world. The Danube in normal times is a great avenue of commerce. Hungary exports chiefly agricultural products—wheat (its main crop) and other grains, flour, livestock and meat, poultry and eggs, and sugar. The chief manufactures are iron and steel, machinery, cloth, flour, sugar, and alcohol. Its cotton mills have multiplied about five times during the past 30 years. Its deposits of bauxite, the aluminium ore, are among the largest in the world. Hungary's main imports are machinery, metals, coal, textiles, paper, and timber.

The Magyars, a Finno-Ugrian race, first came as raiders from Asia up the valley of the Danube as early as the 9th century. After their defeat by the Germans at Lechfeld (in Bavaria) in 955, they settled down as permanent residents—an "island of Asia" in the heart of the Slavonic east of Europe—in the broad valley of the Theiss. In the year 1000 their leader, later known as St. Stephen, accepted Christianity and took the title of king. In the 15th century John, or Janos, Hunyady, the great national hero of Hungary, defended the land against the Turks, until his death from plague a few days after his relief of Belgrade from Turkish siege (1456).

On the fatal field of Mohács (August 29, 1526) the young king Louis II was killed by the Turks and two-thirds of the kingdom passed under Turkish dominion. Over the small remnant of non-Turkish Hungary, the Hapsburg Ferdinand of Austria (brother of the Emperor Charles V) was chosen to rule. Not until 1718, after much sanguinary fighting, did his successors complete the redemption of Hungary from Turkish rule.

Restiveness under the sway of the Austrian Hapsburgs led Hungary in the course of the ill-fated Revolution of 1848 to establish a short-lived republic, with Louis Kossuth as president. This was put down, but Austria was obliged (1867) to grant Hungary equal partnership in what was

thenceforth known as the Dual Monarchy of Austria-Hungary, which lasted until 1918.

The new Hungary (native name *Magyaria*), was less than one-third the area of the old Hapsburg kingdom. It extended from the River Drava on the south to the Danube on the north, and from the neighbourhood of Bratislava on the west to the mountains enclosing Transylvania. The Treaty of Trianon (Versailles) after the First World War (1914–18) gave the Slovak strip along the Carpathians to Czechoslovakia, gave Transylvania to Rumania, and handed the Slavonia-Slovene-Croatian territory on the south and south-west to Yugoslavia. All this deprived Hungary of some 10,000,000 of her population, about one-third of them pure Magyars. In October 1938, a strip of Czech territory (4,630 square miles) was awarded to Hungary, with its 1,029,000 inhabitants, including the towns of Kosice and Uzhorod. In November 1939, Hungary took possession of the former Czech province of Carpatho-Ukraine (Ruthenia). Both these awards were annulled after the Second World War (1939–45), and Hungary was left with an area of 35,875 square miles.

After the First World War, Hungary was a republic from November 1918 until March 1919, when a Soviet government, headed by the adventurer Bela Kun, took command for a few months. Opposition governments were set up, however, and with Rumania's help Bela Kun was driven out of the country, the Soviet government overthrown, and a national government established, with the old monarchical constitution in force. Hungary was forbidden to restore a Hapsburg to the throne without the consent of the Allied Powers, and Admiral Horthy, who had been war minister and C.-in-C. of the Hungarian army, was appointed regent, and took over the duties of the king. The national parliament consisted of two Houses. Women's suffrage was introduced in 1929.

Hungary, like her neighbours in central Europe, became involved in the Second World War and in the disturbing political changes which preceded that conflict. Her rulers sought to profit by the troubles of those neighbours, siding with Mussolini and with Hitler in schemes of aggression and receiving in return slices of territory. Hungary declared war on Russia in June 1941 (when Germany began her invasion of that land); in the following December Hungary declared war upon Britain and

MATIAS·GEWESEN·KINIG·IN
VNGERN·VND·PEHAM·DALM

From Franknoi's Matthias Corvinus

HUNGARY'S KING MATTHIAS

Son of John Hunyady, the Hungarian national hero, Matthias Corvinus was elected King of Hungary in 1458. He drove the Turks out of the country and conquered the whole of southern Austria, making Vienna his capital.

HOW THEY CELEBRATED HARVEST-HOME IN HUNGARY

The harvest festival was celebrated in Hungary at the end of August with elaborate ceremonial. A delegation of farmers and peasants dressed in their festival clothes presented a crown of wheat to the lord of the manor. Sometimes it was drawn in a decorated ox-wagon by six oxen. This photograph shows the crown borne by picturesquely-garbed men of the Mezökövesd district. After the Second World War (1939–45) the big estates were divided among the peasants.

BRIDE AND BRIDEGROOM OF HUNGARY

The bridal couple are a won'rous sight in Hungary when they are dressed in colourful wedding garments such as have been worn there for centuries. Upon the girl's head is a 'creation' of tinsel and flowers, and flowers also are fastened in the man's hat. Under his cloak he has on a white garment with very full sleeves.

To face page 1657

the U.S.A., in time with Japan's assault on the Pacific possessions of the Western Powers.

Menaced on all sides in 1939, the Hungarian leaders had had little choice but to side with Germany and Italy; but their territorial greed and intense nationalism brought upon the country great disaster when the tide turned and Germany and Italy suffered catastrophic defeat in early 1945. By April 1945 the Russians had swept the Germans from the country, and a Government of Liberation was established. The Regent, Admiral Horthy, fell into American hands in May 1945, and he was imprisoned for a time at Nuremberg, being released in January 1946.

In February 1946 a Republic was proclaimed. Communist influence was growing, and in 1947 the Prime Minister, Mr. Ferencz Nagy (pronounced Nahdj), who favoured a conservative policy, was forced to flee the country after the discovery of a pretended " plot against the people." But despite this and similar incidents (as when the new Republic's first president, Zoltan Tildy, was compelled to resign after the implication of his son in a similar plot), Hungary retained the forms of democracy. The population is 9,320,000.

Huns. The name of this race, of Asiatic origin, which invaded Europe in the 4th century is a synonym for a people of savage instincts, waging warfare with merciless cruelty. Europe had several times been scourged by the raids of people of Mongol, Turanian or Tartar stock from central Asia, who in vast migratory hordes swept across the land killing and robbing, subduing local populations or wiping them out. The Huns were one such horde (troop of Asiatic nomads). Various contemporary or later accounts of these invaders depict them in horrific terms, and tell of the stern and cruel discipline and training which their menfolk received from earliest childhood.

In A.D. 374, coming from their homes in Central Asia, the Huns invaded Europe for the first time and occupied the region north and west of the Black Sea. There they lived for more than 70 years, before they began their second and greater invasion. In 451, under Attila, whom Christians called the Scourge of God, they swept into Germany and crossed the Rhine into what is now France.

Defeated there at the battle of Châlons (451), the Huns descended into Italy, devastating the country. They would probably have taken Rome, as Alaric had done 40 years before, had it not been for the bravery of Pope Leo I, who in an interview so overawed Attila that he spared the city and withdrew from Italy. With the death of Attila in 453 the empire of the Huns, which included all the peoples from the Volga to the River Rhine, quickly fell to pieces, and the race probably became absorbed among the latter hordes pressing into Europe.

The Magyars, who several centuries later settled in what is now Hungary, were related to the Huns.

The WORLD-WIDE SPORT of the CHASE

In all quarters of the globe, and from the earliest times, Man has indulged in this most thrilling of all sports—at first for food and later for pleasure alone. Here are described most varieties of hunting.

Hunting. One of the first occupations of Man must have been hunting of some sort, and since the first, brutish, stone-age hunters stalked and slew their game, Man has hunted, in all parts of the world, animals of every type. Moreover, it cannot have been so very long before hunting for sport came into being. In the monuments and writings of all the earliest peoples, hunting is a subject of frequent mention, and more than one of the greatest early races were hunters—the Assyrians, for example.

Except where there is still an abundance of wild life and comparatively little other food, hunting has long ceased to be of importance to Man's economy, and it flourishes now chiefly as a sport.

Whatever our views on the desirability of carrying on a blood-sport such as fox-hunting, there can be no doubt of the picturesqueness of the scenes which it occasions. The colour of the huntsmen's coats— pink, as it is called, although it is more scarlet, really—the black-and-tan and white of the hounds, and the splendid horses, combine to make the meet of a foxhunt one of the brightest and most characteristic of all sights in our English countryside.

It is only since about 1756 that fox-hunting has been popular as an organized sport. The hunting season starts with cub hunting—that is, hunting of the young foxes with the new, more or less untried hounds—in September, and it is not until November that the real hunting begins. The hunt starts with the meet, held perhaps at the home of some important member. At other times, the meet is held at some spot in the country which is to be hunted that particular day—for each pack of hounds has its country divided into different sections, and one of these is generally hunted on one particular day in the week.

Meets for cub-hunting are held early in the morning, and are largely confined to the coverts, as woodlands are called in hunting terminology. The ordinary hunt, too, starts at a covert, for it is there that a fox will most likely be found. The huntsman will let the hounds run about in the covert until they pick up the scent of a fox, when they set off in full cry after it. The huntsman and the master alone may ride close behind the hounds, the rest of the " field " following them. When the hounds are running straight across country on a scent so strong that they can follow easily without a check of any sort, they often run silently, but when they first pick up such a scent they all give tongue together. And no one, however he may disapprove of hunting, can be quite unmoved by the " music " of the pack in " full cry." As the fox is viewed or seen, the cry of " Tally-ho ! " is given, another welcome sound, which as often as not is unheard until the fox is almost beaten and the hounds are right on its tail. At the end of the hunt, the mask (head), brush (tail) and pads (feet) of the fox are given to favoured members of the field, usually

THE HOUNDS ARRIVE
Instead of walking from the kennels to the meet, as they
used to do, hounds are often taken in a motor-drawn
trailer. Foxhounds are generally believed to be descended
from the old type of bloodhound and the pointer.

to hunt the fox now—are similar in colour to foxhounds, but smaller and shorter in the leg. The
hare is hunted on foot, giving fine sport and exercise.

Otter-hounds are of various types, bred mostly
from fox- or stag-hounds, but the finest—the rarer,
true otter-hounds—are big, rough-coated, heavily-
built dogs that have been bred especially for this
sport, and are as much at home in the water as on
land. Then we must mention the drag-hunt,
where the hounds follow an artificial scent, purely to
give the " field " the sport of riding after them.

Hunting, as practised by the English, has been
introduced by them into many other parts of the
world. But in general, each country has its own
form of hunting. On the Continent, the wild boar
gives great sport, and in the sub-continent of India,
boar-hunting, under the name of pig-sticking, is an
art of its own, mounted men endeavouring to kill
the boar with a short spear. In some countries
big-game hunting is almost an industry. It is
especially carried on in Central and South Africa,
and North America.

Huntingdonshire. With an area
of 366 square miles, this inland county of England
is one of the smallest. Bedfordshire lies to the
south, Cambridgeshire on the east, Lincolnshire on
the north, and Northamptonshire on the west.
Huntingdonshire is within the low-lying district of
the Fens, and has much rich agricultural land.
The main industries are brewing, brick and paper-
making and flour milling. The chief river is the Ouse,
on which the county town, Huntingdon (population,
about 5,290) stands. In All Saints' church, Huntingdon, Oliver Cromwell (1599–1658) was baptized.
On the opposite bank of the Ouse is the old town of
Godmanchester. St. Neots, another busy market
town on the Ouse, is situated on the southern

those who are " in at the death," and after their
removal the fox's body is thrown to the hounds.

The modern foxhound, of course, is very highly
bred. They are for the most part sleek, smooth-
coated, black-and-tan and white creatures, but in a
few packs, such as the Seavington, in Somerset, the
true old English, shaggy, long-haired foxhound is
still used. In the north of
England, and in Wales, foxes
are hunted on foot in the
mountains.

Besides the fox, the red
deer, hare and otter are all
still actively hunted in Britain.
The modern staghound is a
very similar animal to a foxhound in most ways, only
rather larger and often with
more white about it. In a
staghound pack, the hounds
are divided into two sections,
one of which, known as the
" tufters," selects and rounds
up the chosen stag, driving it
towards the others, which
then give chase; and as often
as not this hunt ends with the
escape of the quarry. When
the stag is cornered, it may be
put to death with a humane
killer; while in the case of
most stag-hunts, where the
stag is an animal liberated for
the hunt, the last thing the
master wants to do is to kill it.

Beagles, as the hounds used
for hunting hares are called—
since harriers, originally used
for hares, have been bred up

Sport & General

OTTER-HUNTING AS A SUMMER SPORT
Still popular in the west of Britain from Cornwall to Scotland, otter-hunting is the one
form of hunting engaged in during the summer months. Otter-hounds are of various
types, some, such as those seen here, being bred from foxhounds or staghounds.
The true otter-hound resembles the harrier, but has a rough, thick, greasy coat.
The poles carried by the huntsmen are for maintaining a foothold when wading in
streams, and for exploring holes in which an otter may be hiding.

PACKS OF FOXHOUNDS MOVING OFF TO A HUNT

Fox

Late in September cubbing commences, when young foxes are hunted by inexperienced hounds and the younger members of the hunt form the 'field.' Meets for cub-hunting (lower) are held early in the morning and are largely confined to coverts or woods. One of the premier packs of foxhounds, the Quorn (upper) hunts over rolling grassland around Melton Mowbray in Leicestershire. The Quorn country, which derives its name from the village of Quorndon, near Loughborough, has been hunted over since the 17th century. *See* article in pages 1657 and 1658.

boundary of the county. The church of St. Mary in this town is one of the finest in Huntingdonshire. St. Ives is distinguished by having been the home of Cromwell when he was a farmer, and in the town there is a fine statue of him with the inscription: " Oliver Cromwell, a Citizen of St. Ives." Stilton, on the Great North Road, has given its name to a famous brand of cheese. The population of the county is 56,200.

Hurling. A winter game played in Eire, it closely resembles hockey, but the stick or hurley is shorter than a hockey stick and the striking surface is very much broader. The goal posts are like those used in Rugby football. Hurling is a very old game; it goes back, in fact, into the legendary times of the old Gaelic heroes, and in any case was played before the Romans arrived in Britain. In those days it was a royal game, in which the king himself might well take part.

As played now, " hurley," its popular name, takes place on a field some 150 yards long and over 80 yards in width. There are 15 players on each side, though formerly the usual number was 17. There are a goalkeeper, three backs, three half-backs, two " mid-field " men, and usually two lines of forwards. The ball is a largish one, of cork and yarn, covered with leather, and the aim is to drive it between the goals, as in hockey. But if it goes over the cross-bar, between the posts, a point is scored. A goal counts three points.

Another game of the same name survives in Cornwall. In this type of " hurley " a small silver-coated ball is used, which must be borne by a member of one side (their number is unlimited) back to his own goal—usually some landmark or conspicuous object, the members of the other side trying to prevent him. The bearer of the ball must carry it for all to see and run with it until caught, when he must throw it towards his own goal. But apart from this there are few rules.

Huss, JOHN (about 1369–1415). " I am prepared to die in the truth of the Gospel which I taught and wrote." Like so many other religious reformers, John Huss, the Bohemian priest, defied the authority of the Church and was ready to defend his principles to the uttermost. In his case the uttermost was demanded, and for his views he was burned at the stake as a heretic.

Huss was born of humble parents in the little Bohemian village of Husinec. He was christened Jan, or John, and from his birthplace was called John of Husinec, or, in shortened form, John Huss. Having decided to become a priest, he entered the University of Prague, with which his name was henceforth to be indissolubly connected, and after his graduation became a lecturer there on philosophy. He also took a prominent part in the nationalist Bohemian protest against the undue influence of Germans in the University, which in 1409 led the German masters and scholars to found the rival University of Leipzig.

As a preacher Huss won the hearts of the people by his powerful sermons in the Czech (Bohemian) tongue, as well as by the purity and nobility of his life. His attacks on evil living among the clergy made him many enemies.

Huss had early come under the influence of the religious and philosophical writings of John Wycliffe (c. 1325–84) and adopted many of his teachings. When Huss opposed the Papal Bull ordering that Wycliffe's books should be burned, he was charged with heresy and forbidden to preach. The climax came when Huss attacked the granting of Papal indulgences in Bohemia, and the Pope's Bull was burned by his followers. Huss was now excommunicated, and for two years went into retirement to devote himself to writing.

When the Council of Constance met in 1414 to consider the question of reforms in the Church, Huss attended it under a safe-conduct from the emperor, Sigismund, to justify his views. On his arrival at Constance, in Germany, Huss was thrown into prison, despite the safe-conduct. When he steadfastly refused to recant his teachings,

Fox

HURLING IS A NATIONAL WINTER GAME IN EIRE
A very old game, hurling or hurley is played in Eire during the winter months. It was once held in such high esteem that even kings took part in it. Play was also very rough, serious injuries being common. Each side consists of 15 players who may hit or carry the ball with the stick, but must not handle it. The sticks or hurleys resemble those used in hockey, but are shorter and have a broader striking surface. The goal-posts are like those seen on a Rugby field, with the cross-bar eight feet from the ground.

Painting by C. F. Lessing; photo, Bruckman

JOHN HUSS BEFORE THE COUNCIL OF CONSTANCE

The Bohemian religious reformer, John Huss, won the hearts of the people by the purity and nobility of his life. But his attacks on evil living among the clergy earned him many enemies, who accused him of heresy. When the Council of Constance met in 1414 to consider reforms in the Church, Huss attended under safe conduct from the Holy Roman Emperor Sigismund. But he was arrested, tried as a heretic (above), and burnt at the stake on July 6, 1415.

unless shown that they were in conflict with the Scriptures, he was condemned to death.

Huss met his death (July 6, 1415) with heroic constancy, as also did his disciple Jerome of Prague, a year later. "Thinking to extinguish heresy," says an English historian, "the Council of Constance had made it the national faith of Bohemia, and had made the martyr Huss the national hero and the national saint."

The immediate result was the terrible Hussite War, a struggle on the part of the Bohemians for national, religious and social revolution, in which they resisted the combined force of Europe in numerous "crusades," and for nearly a score of years prevented Sigismund from securing his inheritance of the Bohemian crown.

John Huss is now regarded as a national hero, and a fine statue of him is a prominent feature of Prague.

Huxley, THOMAS HENRY (1825–95). This intellectual giant was the chief supporter of Charles Darwin when Darwin in 1859 published his book called On the Origin of Species by Means of Natural Selection. No work had caused more controversy or aroused more hostility than this pronouncement

of the then novel theory of organic evolution. It enraged religious leaders, and distracted scientists and philosophers. On the one hand, it was roundly denounced as rank heresy and the production of an atheist; on the other, it was praised to the skies as a work of genius which explained the universe and all in it. (For an explanation of Darwin's theory, *see* Evolution).

Son of a schoolmaster, Thomas Henry Huxley was born on May 4, 1825, at Ealing, London. Self-educated for the most part, he won a scholarship to Charing Cross Hospital at 16, and three years later published his first scientific paper. In 1846 he became a naval surgeon on the survey ship Rattlesnake, spending the next three years in the Torres Strait off the north coast of Queensland, Australia. His researches and papers proved so brilliant that he was elected a Fellow of the Royal Society in 1851, and awarded the Medal of that society in 1852. Thereafter Huxley lectured to students, continued his biological researches and published scientific papers until 1859, the year when Darwin's Origin of Species was published.

He now became the leading champion of the new evolutionary doctrines, so much so

THOMAS HENRY HUXLEY
A pioneer of modern scientific thought, Huxley supported Darwin's evolutionary doctrines. This portrait by the Hon. John Collier (1850–1934) is in the National Portrait Gallery, London.

that he was styled " Darwin's Bulldog." By this time Huxley was recognized as one of the greatest figures in scientific and educational life. Between 1862 and 1884 he served on 10 important Royal Commissions, and from 1870–72 he was a member of the London School Board.

Huxley was president of the Royal Society (1881–85) and president of the British Association. He refused all titles and official honours except that of a privy councillorship in 1892, and three years later he retired from public life. He had left an indelible mark not only upon science, but upon education and social reforms. Huxley died at Eastbourne, Sussex, on June 29, 1895.

Among Huxley's best-known writings are : Man's Place in Nature (1863); Lay Sermons, Essays and Reviews (1872); The Crayfish: an Introduction to the Study of Zoology (1880); Scientific Memoirs (1898–1902); Science and Hebrew Tradition (1894).

Huxley's great intellectual gifts were inherited by some of his descendants. His eldest son, LEONARD HUXLEY (1860–1933), after being a master of Charterhouse school, in Surrey, became editor of the Cornhill Magazine, and wrote some polished verse and an admirable life of his father.

Leonard was the father of two famous sons, Julian and Aldous Huxley. The former of these, JULIAN SORELL HUXLEY (born 1887), after a brilliant career at Oxford University established himself as one of the foremost scientists. He became senior demonstrator in zoology at the University in 1919. He was honorary lecturer in zoology at King's College, London, 1927–35, and Fullerian professor of physiology at the Royal Institution, 1926–29. He was secretary of the London Zoological

Society from 1934 to 1942, and was made a Fellow of the Royal Society in 1938. In March 1946 he was chosen first Director-General of the United Nations' Educational, Scientific and Cultural Organization (Unesco). Besides many contributions to scientific literature, Julian Huxley has written many popular books on scientific subjects. ALDOUS LEONARD HUXLEY (born 1894), third son of Leonard Huxley, gained fame as an exponent of the modern school of English fiction. One of the best-known of his books is Brave New World, in which he forecasts possible future developments in civilization.

Hwang-ho. Winding down through mountains and over the fertile plains of northern China flows the great and terrible Hwang-ho (Yellow River). In its keeping are the lives and the fortunes of millions of people, and like a capricious giant it deals out death or wealth by turns. For thousands of years, since the earliest dawn · of Chinese history, the people have struggled with it, trying to curb the floods, which have earned the river the nickname of " China's Sorrow."

The Hwang-ho rises in the mountains of Tibet, and through the first two-thirds of its course the river, which is 2,600 miles long, flows through mountains, finally entering the Yellow Sea in the Gulf of Chih-li. The Hwang-ho is too shallow in winter and too swift in summer to be navigable. The soil of the region drained by the river is a yellow earth which dissolves easily and is washed down in enormous quantities by the river, staining its waters the deep yellow from which it, and the Yellow Sea, get their names. But as the river leaves the mountains and starts across the flat plains it begins to deposit this sediment. By degrees the bed rises and the people build embankments to prevent the river from overflowing.

As the bed continues to rise so the embankments must be heightened, too, until the stream is flowing many feet above the level of the surrounding country. As time goes on, the situation becomes more and more dangerous; finally a breach occurs and the whole river pours over the country, carrying destruction and ruin with it. If the breach cannot be repaired the river leaves its old channel entirely, and finds a new exit to the sea. Many times it has thus changed its course, entering the ocean through different mouths as much as 500 miles apart.

In 1851 the river made such a change, flowing to the north instead of to the south of the rocky peninsula of Shantung. It took 15 years to repair the damage. The southern valley from being a well-watered fertile plain was left practically without water. The northern valley could not be cultivated for a time, because the river deposited three feet of sand and mud over the fields, but became later very fertile, because of the new water supply. In 1887 another flood occured which swept away whole villages, killing more than a million people and flooding 50,000 square miles of territory.

During the war with Japan (1937–45) the Chinese cut the banks near Changchow in Honan to hold up the advancing Japanese. Hundreds of square miles were flooded and eventually the river found a new channel to the sea. It was not until 1947, with the help of U.N.R.R.A. (United Nations' Relief and Rehabilitation Administration), that engineers were successful in setting it back on its old course.

E.N.A.

BESIDE THE HWANG-HO
This photograph shows a section of the bridge which crosses the great Hwang-ho river at Lanchowfu, where the river is 700 feet wide. On the right is a portion of the city wall, and beneath it is the market.

Hyacinth. The ancient Greeks told this story of the origin of the beautiful and fragrant hyacinth. One day, said they, the god Apollo was playing a game of quoits with a young mortal, Hyacinthus, whom he dearly loved, when Zephryus, the god of the west wind, passed by.

Being jealous of Apollo, the west wind blew the latter's quoit aside, and caused it to strike Hyacinthus, inflicting a mortal wound. In a few moments Hyacinthus died in Apollo's arms. The grieving Apollo then caused these beautiful clustered blossoms to spring from the fallen drops of his blood.

At all events, the cultivated hyacinth, *Hyacinthus orientalis*, was originally found in Greece and Asia Minor. Brought to western Europe in the 16th century, the hyacinth was extensively cultivated by Dutch horticulturists. They succeeded so well that the original blue and purple blossoms were varied to numerous shades of pink, rose, yellow, scarlet, and pure white, while many varieties are also double-flowered. The bluebell (*q.v.*) is also often called a wild hyacinth, but it belongs to a different genus and has drooping flowers and stems less stiff than those of the true hyacinth.

Hyderabad. In the centre of the Deccan plateau in the sub-continent of India, between the states of Bombay and Madras, lies Hyderabad, largest and most important of the former independent states, with an area of 82,300 square miles. Once under British rule, it is now part of the Indian republic.

Hyderabad is a plateau about 1,200 feet above sea-level. It is rich agriculturally and has great mineral wealth, especially coal. Agriculture is aided by irrigation projects, which include a dam two miles long across the Manjra river. Railways and manufactures are well developed. The products include millet, rice, wheat, cotton, tobacco, sugar-cane, tussore silk, lac (resin), gums, and oils.

S. L. Bastin

HYACINTHS GROWN INDOORS
Introduced into Britain from the continent of Europe in the 16th century, hyacinths were extensively cultivated by Dutch bulb-growers, who developed both single and double varieties in many shades of colour. These plants may be flowered indoors in bowls filled with fibre.

But of greater interest to visitors are the relics of India's historic past which abound in this region. Chief among these are the marvellous temples at Ellora and at Ajanta in the north-western corner of the Nizam's dominions The majority of these temples consist of caves carved out of the rock and decorated at the cost of enormous labour.

At Ajanta, in a lonely ravine, a great horse-shoe-shaped cliff is excavated into a score of monasteries and temples of remarkable beauty. The inner walls of the rock-hewn chambers are painted with frescoes of ancient workmanship, and the colours, even after a lapse of many centuries, are still clearly visible. A part of one of these frescoes is reproduced in this page, and another in page 1712.

The Kailas temple at Ellora, built in the 8th century, is looked upon as one of the wonders of the world, for not only was its interior hewn out into great chambers and altars and bas-reliefs, but the outside of the rock-bound hill which forms its roof was fashioned into graceful and intricate design.

Hyderabad was a province of the Mogul Empire until the decline of that power in the 18th century, when the Nizam, its ruler, became independent. In the Indian Mutiny of 1857 Hyderabad remained loyal to the British and was her faithful ally during the two World Wars. In 1947 Britain's Indian Empire came to an end with the creation of the Dominions of India and of Pakistan. Nearly all the independent native states adhered to one or other of the Dominions, but the Nizam of Hyderabad, the Mahomedan ruler of a largely Hindu population, announced the independence

HYDERABAD : FRESCOES AT AJANTA
In the north-west corner of the State of Hyderabad, at Ajanta, there is a collection of Buddhist monasteries and shrines, which flourished from about 200 B.C. to A.D. 600. The walls are decorated with frescoes representing semi-divine beings, who were believed to live among the peaks of the Himalayas.

F. Deaville Walker

HYDERABAD'S ANCIENT TEMPLE OF KAILASA

Called the Kailasa after the celestial palace of the great Hindu god Siva, this rock-hewn temple at Ellora in the State of Hyderabad dates from the eighth century of the Christian era. Here is only a small portion, surrounded by cliffs, over 100 feet high, which were created by the excavators. The elephant is about life-size and, like so many of the sculptures there, has been mutilated by Mahomedans. The cliffs around the court are deeply undercut with a colonnade along which pilgrims used to march ; but the Kailasa has been deserted for centuries.

of his country. The Government of the Dominion (later republic) of India, whose territory surrounds Hyderabad, tried, unsuccessfully, to induce the Nizam to join the Dominion. In 1948 the Government established a blockade, stopping all trade with Hyderabad, and troops of the Indian Dominion invaded and occupied the State. In 1949 the Nizam agreed to join.

The city of Hyderabad, capital of the State, is the fourth largest city in the sub-continent (population about 740,000). The population of the state of Hyderabad is about 16,330,000.

By the Indus delta, in the Sind region of Pakistan, is another city called Hyderabad, but it is of less importance than the one described above. It has a fortress, however, and an arsenal, and produces good lacquered ware, silks and embroideries.

Hydra. Gather in a bottle some of the floating green weeds or submerged plants or stones from a stagnant pond and empty them into a glass bowl filled with clean pond water. You may then find attached to the plants the tiny freshwater creatures known as hydras. They are named after the Hydra, the many-headed monster of Greek mythology. To the small creatures on which they prey these pond hydras are monsters too.

Hydras are usually about half an inch long, and one end is sticky to anchor it to objects in the ponds and streams where it lives. At the other end is its mouth, capable of opening wide and surrounded by six or eight threadlike tentacles. Stinging cells in the tentacles poison and paralyze tiny crustaceans, worms and other small creatures which touch them. Then the tentacles sweep the prey into the hydra's mouth (*see* illustrations opposite).

The body structure is simple, consisting of two layers of cells—an outer layer for protection and an inner one to perform digestive operations.

The hydra was one of Nature's first experiments in building animals out of different kinds of cells (*see* Cell). But, once discovered, its plan was used for all the great branch of animals to which the hydra belongs—thousands of kinds of polyps, sea anemones and jelly-fishes.

Young hydras develop from buds growing on the sides of older ones, and also from eggs. When a hydra is injured, lost parts are quickly restored. If it is cut into pieces, each piece will soon form a complete hydra. This ability to survive mutilation made naturalists think at first that hydra was a plant.

The few species of hydra, mostly world-wide but seldom abundant, are almost the only fresh-water representatives of their great branch of the animal kingdom (the *Coelenterata*). Two of the more common species of hydra are the brownish *Hydra fusca*, and the green *Hydra viridis*.

Hydrangea. One of the showiest flowering bushes is the hydrangea, with its huge globular masses of small blooms. In the wild species the flowers are peculiar in that those on the outside of each cluster are not " complete." They are sterile, having no parts for bearing pollen or producing ovules ; but they attract pollen-carrying insects, and these deposit pollen in the fertile blossoms to be found within the cluster.

In the cultivated hydrangea, all the flowers are sterile, thus reproduction is only possible by taking cuttings from the growing plant.

The hydrangeas, which belong to the saxifrage family, form a numerous group of about 35 species and are natives of North and South America, Japan, China and the Himalayas. One species, *Hydrangea arborescens*, was introduced into England from North America in 1736 ; the common hydrangea (*Hydrangea hortensis*) came from China some 50 years earlier.

The flowers are naturally pink and white, but by treating the soil with a solution of saltpetre and oxide of iron blue blossoms are produced. In Britain some species thrive in the open air in sheltered positions.

Hydraulics AND HYDRAULIC APPLIANCES. No doubt, when about to pump up your cycle tyres, you have at some time or other tested the pump by placing a finger over the outlet, while pushing down the piston : you found that you *could* press down the plunger to some extent, although the air outlet was blocked. This is because air is compressible. But if you tried the same experiment with a syringe filled with water or some other liquid, you found that this liquid was *not* compressible : if the outlet was completely blocked, and the pump washers were sealing properly, the piston could not be pushed down.

This fact, of practical non-compressibility, is one of the salient ones about hydraulics. Brakes in motor vehicles utilise it, for there is a cylinder with

R. A. Malby

HYDRANGEA MASSES

As shrubs in the open, or as pot plants for house decoration, hydrangeas make a most attractive display. Colours vary, but in all species the flower-heads remain showy for a remarkably long time. The hydrangea most commonly seen outdoors in Britain came from China.

a piston attached to the brake blocks, and a kind of pump connected to a lever which the driver moves when he wants to check the vehicle. The movement of the lever operates a piston in the pump ; oil—the usual fluid used in such braking systems—is forced along pipes to the brake cylinders,

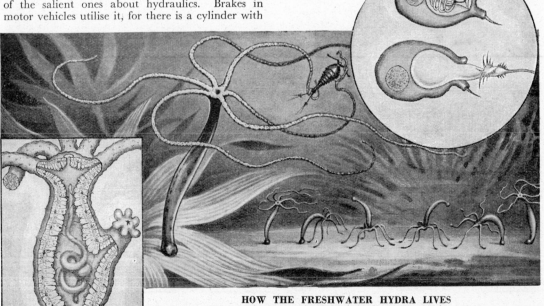

HOW THE FRESHWATER HYDRA LIVES

The greatly enlarged hydra immediately above is attached to a leaf under water and has just caught a minute creature with its tentacles. To the right of this, hydras are shown in movement to new anchorages. The cut-open view at the lower left is of a hydra that has swallowed a tiny worm ; at the upper right is one of the stinging cells. (*See* facing page).

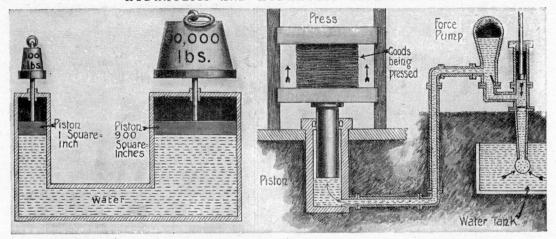

HOW A HYDRAULIC PRESS EXERTS ENORMOUS PRESSURE

The reason why a hydraulic press develops such great power is shown in these diagrams. The small piston (left) has a surface equal to one square inch ; therefore, it pushes on the water with a pressure of 100 lb. to the square inch. When this pressure is transferred through the water to the larger piston, with a surface area of 900 square inches, the total pressure exerted on that piston is 90,000 lb. How this principle is used in an actual press is shown on the right.

and there forces out the pistons which apply the brakes. Now look at the diagrams explaining the action of a hydraulic press (*see* above). The left-hand one shows a piston whose ram or plunger has an area of 1 square inch and is pressed down by a weight of 100 lb. The bottom of the cylinder communicates with the bottom of a much bigger one, in which works a piston with an area of 900 square inches. The diagram shows that a weight of 90,000 lb. on top of the bigger piston can be balanced by the 100-lb. weight on the smaller.

The pressure per square inch is the same on the lower surface of both pistons (100 lb. ÷ 1 inch on the first ; 90,000 ÷ 900 inches on the second); it is 100 lb. per square inch of piston area. The right-hand diagram shows how this principle is applied in the hydraulic press for baling goods. Water from a reservoir is sucked up by a pump and

forced through the pipe to the base of the piston—usually termed a ram—beneath the platform of the press; this platform moves up and down on guides, and forces the contents of the press against an immovable top plate. You will notice that on the pipe-line there is a funnel-shaped air chamber; this, because it contains a compressible gas (air), smooths out the pulsations of the liquid caused by the pump strokes, and permits a more steady action. The principle is explained in our story of Pumps.

A pile of material is placed on the platform of the press, the ram then being in its lowest position. Now the man operating the press gives a number of strokes to the pump handle. We assume the area of the pump piston is 1 square inch, and that the man applies a pressure of 100 lb. So he generates a pressure of 100 lb. per square inch in the pipe-line, and this pressure is transferred to the base of the ram, which has an area 30 times as great as that of the pump piston—i.e. 30 square inches. Thus the operator, working the handle of a quite small pump, can apply a pressure of many tons upon the material in the baling press—all because water is for all practical purposes incompressible, and because any pressure applied to it in a closed vessel is transmitted equally in all directions. This principle was discovered by Blaise Pascal (*q.v.*), that brilliant French scientist to whom the world owes many such discoveries.

But although a small force applied to the pump piston produces a very much greater force on the larger area of the ram, there is no gain in " work "—the product of *force × distance moved*. In order to raise the ram by 1 inch, the pump piston must, by successive short strokes (short in order to make the action easy enough for the man to apply), depress the surface of the water in the pump and pipe-line by 30 inches. What the hydraulic press does, then, is to enable the force exercised to be applied easily and in a useful manner. There is a certain loss of power by friction and by leakage at valves, for however well the latter are made, the enormous pressure always causes some leakage.

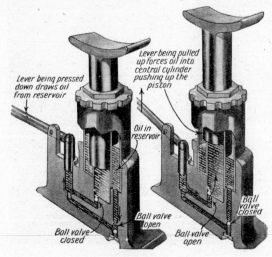

AN HYDRAULIC JACK

Oil is the liquid used in this hydraulic jack. It is pumped into the central cylinder, thereby raising the piston on which the load rests. Oil is often employed in hydraulic tools, because it does not freeze or cause the metal to rust.

A common application of hydraulic power is in the lifting jack (*see* diagrams in page 1666), which acts in the same way as the baling press. Hydraulic lifts for goods or passengers were more common years ago, before electric power had been developed to the high degree we know today. Here again there is a ram, and gearing or other mechanical linkage to apply the force. Lifts in commercial garages are often hydraulic ones. Lead pipe is made in hydraulic machines by which the metal is forced through dies which shape the outside wall and form the central bore, turning out a continuous length of pipe. Aluminium and other softish metals are forced through dies to produce rods, tubes and moulded lengths such as are used for shop-fitting purposes. This process is known as extrusion, which means, literally, thrusting out. It saves an enormous amount of time which would be occupied in machining such forms of metalwork out of the solid, and is also instrumental in saving a great amount of material.

Quite another side of hydraulics is the use in transmitting power. If a series of pulsations is imparted to a column of liquid in a closed system of pipes, etc., at one end, the pulsations can be transmitted to the opposite end, for control or the

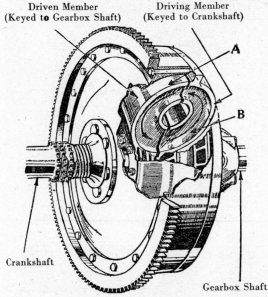

Driven Member   Driving Member
(Keyed to Gearbox Shaft)   (Keyed to Crankshaft)

A

B

Crankshaft

Gearbox Shaft

FLUID FLYWHEEL OF A MOTOR CAR
Power from the engine is transmitted to the gearbox through oil in the flywheel casing. A is the driven member on the gearbox shaft ; B is the driving member on the crankshaft. Curved arrows indicate the flow of oil.

working of machinery. The so-called " fluid fly-wheel " is a means of transmitting motion smoothly from an internal combustion engine to the shaft or wheel-work it has to drive. It is in effect a " clutch " (*see* Motor Vehicles), but instead of mechanical connexion between the driving member and the driven one, the connexion is by a quantity of oil contained in a casing around these parts. The *driving* shaft turns a sort of paddle, which gives a rotary motion to the oil; this motion is imparted to another vaned member fixed on the *driven* shaft (*see* diagram above).

The engineer's vice for gripping work for filing and shaping is usually of the type in which the jaws are opened or closed by turning a screw. In the hydraulic vice the jaws are moved by a ram, and the operator gives one or two strokes to a pump lever to force oil into the ram cylinder. The jaws are instantly released by turning a valve. Engines of the reciprocating (piston) type also are driven by high-pressure water, but piston engines are little used except for special purposes today. Turbines and water wheels are the principal forms of water-engine ; both are described under the heading Turbine.

In a form of pump called the hydraulic ram the flow of water from an elevated source is used to drive some of the same water to a greater height. (*See* Pump).

Hydraulics (from the Greek *hydor*, water and *aulos*, pipe) is the science which deals with the flow of water or other liquids in motion. The designing of dams, aqueducts, canals and pipe-lines is an important application of this science. (*See* Hydro-electric Installations ; Water).

Hydrochloric Acid. One of the most important acids in scientific work and in industry is this colourless compound of hydrogen and chlorine (HCl). It is manufactured by treating common salt (NaCl) with sulphuric acid (H_2SO_4), yielding sodium sulphate as a by-product; also by burning chlorine gas inside containers filled with hydrogen. The pure product is a gas (hydrogen chloride), which develops acid properties only when dissolved in water. A cubic foot of water will absorb 455 cubic feet of the gas.

Gastric juice contains normally about 0·2 to 0·4 per cent of hydrochloric acid. It helps to dissolve the minerals in our food and acts in part as an antiseptic. Medicinally, it is given in treating indigestion arising from a deficiency of the acid in the gastric juice. Hydrochloric acid unites with most metals and metallic oxides to form salts known as chlorides (*see* Chlorine). It was used as a source of chlorine for the bleaching industries, but nowadays chlorine is usually produced by electrolysing common salt. (*See* Halogens).

Formerly, when soda factories produced sodium sulphate by the Leblanc process of treating ordinary salt with sulphuric acid, the hydrochloric acid gas was allowed to escape into the atmosphere. As it killed neighbouring vegetation and was generally objectionable, very high chimneys were built to disperse it. But this method only spread destruction further afield, and led to the practice of dissolving the gas in water and allowing the hydrochloric acid so formed to run into the nearest river. Unfortunately, it was found that this killed all the fish, and complaints against soda factories became greater than ever.

Then came steam printing and a need of more paper, which created a demand for bleached wood pulp as a suitable raw material for paper. This led to experiments with the waste hydrochloric acid of the soda works, for it was well known that the chlorine element of the acid was a powerful bleaching agent. A simple inexpensive method of making chlorine gas from the acid was soon discovered, so that, instead of being allowed to run to waste, this by-product became of great value.

HYDRO-ELECTRIC STATION IN NEW ZEALAND

English Electric Co., Ltd.

On North Island, New Zealand, is this hydro-electric installation at Piripaua. There are two vertical reaction water turbines, each of 26,000 horse-power and running at 333 revolutions per minute. The head of water—the vertical distance between the level of the water in the dam and that of the turbines—is 360 feet. As explained in the text, this scheme would be classed as a medium head one. The turbines are in the building at right centre.

PRODIGIOUS POWER *from* FALLING WATER

Nothing would seem more simple than to harness a stream or waterfall to generate power, and indeed it was the earliest method. But, as our story shows, the modern hydro-electric plant is a complex engineering installation.

Hydro-Electric Installations.

Power has been obtained from falling water for centuries, and the water-wheel mill for grinding corn used to be a familiar sight in the English countryside. For many hundreds of years the principle of the water-wheel remained unchanged —wooden compartments or " buckets " around the edge of the wheel being filled with water and emptied at a lower level, the weight of water turning the wheel (*see* Hydraulics ; Turbine). The largest wheel of this type ever built is at

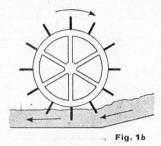

OVERSHOT AND UNDERSHOT WATER-WHEELS
In the overshot wheel (Fig. 1a) it is the weight of water falling from above which provides power to drive machines. In the undershot wheel (Fig. 1b) the force of a fast-running stream below drives the wheel.

Laxey, Isle of Man ; it is 72½ feet in diameter, and generates between 130 and 150 h.p. Two types of water-wheel are shown in Fig. 1, *a* and *b*.

The idea of using water-power to drive dynamos and produce electric power has always seemed attractive, because it looks as if one gets the electricity "for nothing." This is very far from being the case, since the engineering works for a water-power scheme are so large and expensive that the power usually costs as much as if coal were burned in a steam power station—and sometimes costs even more. If you can find a high waterfall, tap water from the top of it, and take it down a short pipe to a water turbine, you can get a certain amount of power quite cheaply—but such things are not easily found. If you want a lot of power all the year round, and have to build huge dams to hold back a river, the costs can very easily make the enterprise not worth while.

Also, you must be certain that you will have enough water all the year round—it is no use finding, after you have built your station, that a dry summer will stop it running. That is why so many places which seem—to the average person —to be ideal for a hydro-electric project are not worth developing : there is not enough water always to make it worth while spending hundreds of thousands of pounds. There are other objections, too, to be taken into consideration. A position which is ideal for a scheme may be too far away from anywhere requiring electricity. Although electricity at high voltages can be transmitted over long distances (*see* Grid) the losses may be so high as to make it uneconomical.

A certain amount of power can be obtained either from a comparatively small amount of water at a high " head " or from a large quantity at a low head. High heads are obtained by tapping a waterfall or a mountain lake, and putting the power station at the foot, anything from 800 to several thousand feet below. Medium (150–700 feet) and low heads are frequently obtained, where the country is suitable, by building a dam across a river, thus holding back the water and causing the river to overflow its normal channel and form an artificial lake. One of the largest schemes of this type is at Boulder Dam on the Colorado river in the United States. A sectional drawing of it appears facing page 960. The head is 475 feet, and

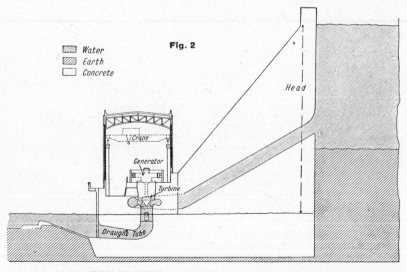

INSTALLATION WORKING ON A LOW HEAD
The ' head ' of water is the height of the upper level above the lower. In this scheme (shown simplified) the power station is situated just below the dam which impounds the water. The penstock, a huge pipe taking water to the turbine, is shown.

the station develops 115,000 h.p. A good example of the low head type is Wheeler Dam, also in the United States, which develops 45,000 h.p. at a head of 48 feet. A large scheme in the British Isles is that in Galloway, Scotland, which develops 150,000 h.p. in five power stations located between Loch Doon and the sea, at heads varying from nearly 400 to 65 feet. The turbine house of one of these power stations, at Tongland, is illustrated in Fig. 7 in the opposite page. There are also extensive hydro-electric works in the North of Scotland, and some smaller ones in North Wales.

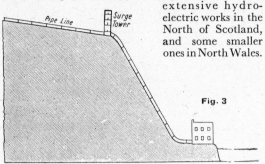

Fig. 3

HIGH-HEAD INSTALLATION
The power station is some distance from the water source, which is high above. The surge tower will allow the stream of water to expand its energy harmlessly if the station suddenly ceases working.

A simplified drawing of a low or medium head scheme, with the power station just below the dam, is shown in Fig. 2. The water impounded by the dam flows through a large flume or pipe line, cut through the dam, and enters the turbine casing by way of a regulating valve. After working the turbine it flows out through the draft tube or exhaust pipe to the " tail race " at the lower river level, where it continues its journey to the sea—or to another dam lower down. When a river flows in a bed which falls steeply, it is often possible to arrange several power stations at different points on its route.

Fig. 3 shows a high-head installation where the power station is some distance from the source of water, and a long pipe line or " penstock " is used. Wherever possible, " surge towers " are placed as near as possible to the station. These are to guard against damage from the hammer-blow action of the water in case it is necessary to turn off the supply suddenly. Water flowing at a good speed takes a great deal of stopping, and the surge tower provides a sort of safety-valve—the water can pile up in the tower instead of expending all its energy in a hammer-blow on the pipes and valves. It is rather like providing an empty siding for a train to run into, instead of letting it run into buffers. Energy cannot merely be " blocked "; it must be used up harmlessly in some way or other.

Water turbines can be divided into two main classes: impulse turbines which get their power by a series of impulses from a high-pressure jet of water; and the type known as reaction turbines in which the water flows through the wheel or runner, and the turning force

is obtained by the push of the water on shaped vanes. The best-known impulse turbine is the Pelton wheel which, at first glance, resembles an old-fashioned water-wheel. The buckets surrounding the wheel are specially shaped, and a high-speed jet of water is directed into them, causing the wheel to revolve (Fig. 4). The jet has a specially-shaped steel needle-valve in the centre, which is used for regulating the flow of water.

Reaction wheels are of two main types, the Francis, which has a wheel or runner with a number of curved vanes (Fig. 5) and is usually employed for medium head working; and the propeller type, which works like a ship's propeller and is used for low head work, sometimes reaching quite large sizes (Fig. 6).

The kind of alternator (*see* Dynamo) used varies with the type of turbine. A Pelton wheel is much more conveniently mounted with its shaft horizontal, and the wheel revolving in the vertical plane; and the alternator does not differ greatly from one driven by a steam turbine, except that it is designed to run at a much lower speed.

With reaction turbines, either Francis or propeller type, it is easier and more efficient to mount the runner horizontally, when the water can be admitted from a circular casing all round the wheel, and allowed to run away directly below the centre (Fig. 8). With this arrangement the shaft is, of course, vertical, and the alternator is mounted directly above. This type is frequently known as the " umbrella " type, from the way in which the arms of the large rotor, or magnet wheel, droop from the shaft like the ribs of an umbrella. The exciter is perched above the alternator. Except for the actual alternator, the remainder of the electrical gear does not differ from that fitted in steam stations. (*See* Power Stations).

Water turbines, if the load is suddenly removed, will tend to speed up and " run away." This

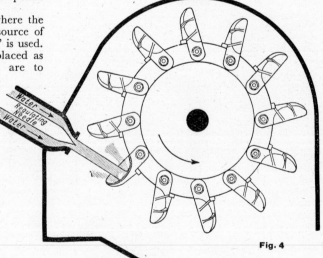

Fig. 4

PRINCIPLE OF THE PELTON WHEEL
The best-known 'impulse turbine' (*see* text) is the Pelton wheel. A high-speed jet of water, controlled by a needle-valve, is directed through a nozzle on to scoop-like buckets, causing the wheel to revolve. The thick black line is the casing. (*See* also facing page).

English Electric Co., Ltd.

The group of water-turbine runners (5) includes Pelton wheels, Francis wheels, and several of the propeller type. At 6 is a large runner of the propeller type. The various types are explained in the opposite page. At 7, inside the turbine house of the Tongland power-station of the Galloway water-power scheme in Scotland. This view, from the elevated platform, shows three generating units each producing 11,000 kilowatts of electrical energy.

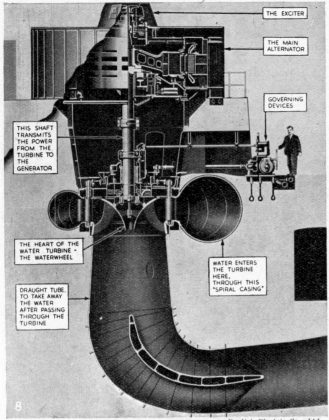

THE EXCITER

THE MAIN ALTERNATOR

GOVERNING DEVICES

THIS SHAFT TRANSMITS THE POWER FROM THE TURBINE TO THE GENERATOR

THE HEART OF THE WATER TURBINE - THE WATERWHEEL

WATER ENTERS THE TURBINE HERE, THROUGH THIS "SPIRAL CASING"

DRAUGHT TUBE, TO TAKE AWAY THE WATER AFTER PASSING THROUGH THE TURBINE

English Electric Co., Ltd.

HOW A WATER-TURBINE WORKS

The wheel or runner is the 'heart' of a turbine. The governing devices are explained in the text. The flow of water against the wheel turns it, rotating the alternator above. For the exciter see page 1062.

might have serious results—the wheel might burst under the centrifugal forces (*q.v.*) and wreck the station. Governor gear is provided to prevent this. The actual governor is often similar to that used on a steam engine—the centrifugal forces acting on revolving weights tending to raise a lever when the speed increases. The valve of a turbine fed by a pipe anything up to 20–30 feet diameter is a heavy one, and the actual moving of the valve is done by an electric or hydraulic mechanism under the control of the governor. Pelton wheels may be governed in three ways: one is to close the jet-opening by pushing forward the needle and, at the same time, to open a by-pass valve, allowing the water to go straight to the tail race without passing through the turbine—otherwise the shock of a sudden stop might burst the pipes. A second method is to use a movable jet, and for the governor to deflect it so that the water misses the buckets. The third method is to cause little vanes inside the jet to spring out and break up the solid stream of water into a kind of spray, thus diminishing its force.

When the by-passing of any type of turbine is used, or if, for any reason, water has to be discharged without having given up its energy, it will emerge as a solid stream like that from a gigantic fire hose. This would cause considerable damage, perhaps even washing away the station foundations. It is necessary, therefore, to use a diffuser, which consists of a cone-shaped nozzle.

English Electric Co., Ltd.

DIFFUSER DISCHARGE OPERATING IN NEW SOUTH WALES

As explained in this page, when water has to be discharged without first giving up its energy to the turbines the stream must be broken by a cone-shaped nozzle (with another cone inside it). This diffuser changes the solid stream into a fine swirling spray, as seen above at the Burrinjack Dam, New South Wales, and allows it to discharge harmlessly, without causing damage to the foundations of the power-station, which otherwise might possibly be washed away.

Keystone

EXPLODING HYDROGEN DESTROYS A GIANT AIRSHIP

This remarkable photograph shows the terrible force with which hydrogen explodes when mixed with air. The giant airship Hindenburg blew up just as she was being moored to the steel tower at Lakehurst, New Jersey, U.S.A., on May 8, 1937. Had the ' ballonets ' inside her hull been filled with the inert gas helium the tragedy could never have occurred, for helium cannot explode. But helium is very expensive, and only about one-half as buoyant as hydrogen.

This breaks up the stream into a fine swirling spray (like a rose on a watering-can), and discharges it harmlessly, without damage (Fig. 9).

Hydrogen AND HYDROGENATION. Hydrogen is a gas, the lightest of all known gases, in fact the lightest of the elements, having an atomic weight of 1·008, and being the first element in the Periodic Table. Ordinary hydrogen contains a very small proportion of "heavy" hydrogen. (*See* Deuterium).

Hydrogen is colourless, tasteless, and odourless ; it burns in air or oxygen to form water, and suitable mixtures of hydrogen with air or oxygen will explode with great violence if ignited. A mixture of hydrogen and oxygen is used in the oxy-hydrogen blowpipe, which gives such a hot flame that it can be used for melting and working materials like quartz and platinum.

Our atmosphere contains only about one part of hydrogen gas in 20,000 parts of air, but the outer parts of the sun are believed to be largely a mass of blazing hydrogen flames over 300,000 miles in height. The world contains an enormous quantity of hydrogen in one form or another, for one ninth part by weight of all water (H_2O) is hydrogen, and a great deal of water is found in our oceans, seas, lakes, and rivers, as well as in the soil, underground, and in the atmosphere. In addition, the rocks of the earth's crust contain combined hydrogen; and free hydrogen is sometimes found in natural gas (*see* Gas). But this is not all, for hydrogen is present, in combination with carbon and other elements, in the chemical compounds (proteins, fats, and carbohydrates) from which our bodies and the bodies of animals and plants are built up (*see* Chemistry); and body fluids, such as milk and blood, are largely water solutions of similar compounds. Petroleum, coal gas, and tar are many mixtures of hydrocarbons, which, as the name suggests, are compounds of carbon and hydrogen.

In the laboratory, hydrogen gas is usually made by dissolving a metal, such as zinc, in dilute hydrochloric or dilute sulphuric acid, thus:

$$Zn \quad + \quad H_2SO_4 \quad = \quad ZnSO_4 \quad + \quad H_2$$

The metal dissolves with brisk effervescence, caused by the escaping hydrogen. The gas can also be prepared by other methods (e.g. by electrolysis) but hydrogen is now usually obtained industrially from water gas, prepared by passing steam over hot coke:

$$H_2O + C = CO + H_2$$
steam   coke   carbon   hydrogen
                monoxide

(water gas)

The carbon monoxide in the water gas is now made to react with more steam in the presence of a catalyst (usually iron oxide with a little chromium oxide),

$$CO + H_2O = CO_2 + H_2$$

and we now have a mixture of carbon dioxide and hydrogen, from which the carbon dioxide may be dissolved out with water under pressure, leaving us with hydrogen gas, which is not appreciably dissolved by the water. Hydrogen is also obtained as a by-product during the production of caustic soda by electrolysis. (*See* Hydrochloric Acid).

Gaseous hydrogen, being very light and buoyant, is used to fill barrage balloons. Airships, like the German Zeppelins and our R101, were filled with hydrogen, but the dangers from fire and explosion were so great that this type of aircraft is now rarely used. The Americans use some airships filled with helium, a non-inflammable rare gas obtained from natural gas. (*See* Helium).

Hydrogen is used for preparing pure hydrochloric acid from chlorine, and for other purposes; but its most important industrial uses nowadays are for the production of synthetic ammonia, and for "hydrogenation."

Very large quantities of ammonia (NH_3) are needed every year to supply us with nitrogen compounds, such as sulphate of ammonia, for fertilizers. Much of this ammonia was, and still is, obtained as a by-product during the manufacture of coal gas for heating and cooking; but large quantities of ammonia are now made by passing a highly compressed mixture of hydrogen and nitrogen over a hot catalyst. A German chemist, Haber, developed this process. The nitrogen is obtained from our atmosphere.

If it were not for hydrogenation, we would probably not be able to have so much margarine, for margarine contains "hardened" oils, prepared by hydrogenation of edible oils. Some oils to be used for making soap are also hardened.

Certain animal and vegetable oils, such as whale oil and ground nut oil, are liquid at ordinary temperatures, and cannot therefore always be used directly for foods like margarine or for making soap. They are liquid because they contain "unsaturated" oils (*see* Chemistry). These liquid unsaturated oils can be converted into solid saturated fats by treatment

with hydrogen gas in the presence of a catalyst (usually finely divided nickel). Thus we obtain solid fats to help us to keep up the supply of margarine and soap.

Other materials can be hydrogenated to produce very useful substances. By heating coal under pressure with hydrogen and a catalyst (such as a mixture of iron, aluminium, and titanium oxides), we can produce lubricating oils and motor spirit. This is known as the Bergius process, or as "Berginisation," so named after the German chemist who invented it. Creosote, tar, and other substances can also be hydrogenated to convert them into more useful materials; and, during the production of petroleum products by "cracking" (decomposing by heat) heavy oils and tars, a better yield of saturated compounds, for motor spirit and other uses, may be obtained if the cracking is performed in an atmosphere of compressed hydrogen. Hydrogenation may be used in a more exact way for making some organic compounds.

Chemists in the U.S.A. are producing petrol by hydrogenating carbon monoxide, suitable gases being manufactured cheaply from natural gas.

We can understand from these brief details how very important hydrogenation processes now are. Shortage of fats, during the Second World War (1939–45), caused the Germans to produce margarine by a complicated series of chemical processes starting from water gas. It was not very nice margarine, but it made a welcome addition to the diet of hungry people. (*See* Catalyst; Coal; Fats and Oils; Petroleum.)

Hydrometer. A floating body sinks deeper in a light liquid than in a heavy one. This principle is applied in the hydrometer (from Greek words *hydor*, meaning water; and *metron*, measure), an instrument for determining the specific gravity, or relative density, of liquids. It is usually a glass tube weighted at one end to keep it upright, and marked with a scale. This scale may directly indicate specific gravity or it may consist of arbitrary degrees, as in the Baumé scales. Common uses of hydrometers are to measure the specific gravity of beers and spirits and so determine the proportion of alcohol in them; to test the solutions in storage batteries and motor-car radiators, and to determine the richness of milk.

The density of a substance is its weight divided by the volume which that substance occupies. The specific gravity is the weight of a substance divided by the weight of an equal volume of cold water. In his legendary test of a golden crown Archimedes (*q.v.*) used the king's crown, in fact, as a sort of hydrometer, the vessel being his bath-tub. Density

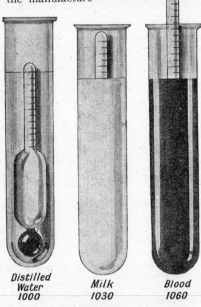

Distilled
Water
1000

Milk
1030

Blood
1060

HYDROMETER IN USE

The varying specific gravity (given under the diagrams) of the three common fluids shown above is demonstrated by testing them with a measuring instrument known as a hydrometer.

and specific gravity are sometimes confused, but you can easily remember that density gives a *direct* statement of the weight, or amount of matter, of the substance for a given volume: for example, in our story of aluminium we state that a cubic foot of this metal weighs about 170 lb. Elsewhere in the same article the specific gravity is given as 2·7, so that to find the weight of a given volume of the substance we must multiply that of an equal volume of water by 2·7. That is what is meant by relative density—i.e., density as compared with that of another substance.

Hyena. (Pron. hī-ē′-na). About the size of a large dog, this unpleasant and ungainly animal is noted for its cowardice and uncanny shrieks, like the laughter of a maniac, which it utters when excited. The various species live in caves and holes in southern Asia, and in Africa, sleeping by day and coming out at night to feed on carrion.

The hyena performs a valuable service to the health of the communities which it infests by devouring dead animals and thus acting as a scavenger. So cowardly that it rarely attempts to defend itself,

it hardly ever attacks an animal that is standing still; but it often so terrifies horses and cattle that they run till they fall from exhaustion. Then the hyena tears its victim to pieces. It was formerly much dreaded in South Africa, where it often entered native dwellings at night and carried off children even when they were sleeping by the the side of their mothers.

These carnivorous animals are related in structure to the cats and the civets. They are ungainly creatures with large heads, and their forelegs are longer than the hindlegs, which gives them an awkward, shambling gait. They are distinguished from all other large carnivora, except the African hunting-dog, by having only four toes on each foot. Their powerful teeth and jaws are capable of crushing even the leg bone of an ox. There are three varieties of the hyena: the striped (*Hyaena striata*), the spotted (*H. crocuta*), and the brown (*H. brunnea*). Probably no other animal has such a bad reputation, and it is therefore surprising that even the hyena, when in captivity, has the capacity of regarding his master with affection.

The SCIENCE of HEALTHY LIVING

The ancients thought that Health could be secured by some magic gift or process. But we know that a healthy body can be ensured by the practice of a few simple rules, aided by what we call ' preventive medicine.'

Hygiene. Modern medicine has a very important subdivision — preventive medicine — which seeks to prevent ill-health before there is need to cure ill-health. It treats of Hygiene (named after Hygeia, Greek goddess of Health), the art of healthy living.

Exercise has an important and interesting department all to itself. Structures rust out in dull disuse sooner than they wear out; muscle and sinew, nerve and organ, all demand strenuous use to achieve their perfection of fashioning and of functioning. Swimming, rowing, skating, dancing, cycling and a sharp heel-and-toe walking are types of admirable exercise for the physically sound. Cricket, football, tennis and team games in general train mind and body to quick decision and quick co-ordination, not only in the interest of the player but of a group. In health, exercise should be short and sharp, rather than prolonged and slow, to achieve its object—that of causing the blood to run quickly and so carry off from the cells of the body and the brain the clogging products of fatigue.

Sleep is all-important. "Eight hours for work, eight hours for play, eight hours for sleep" is a good rough rule. But this is a very personal question. Some very healthy and normal people can do with four hours' sleep; others need twelve. The nature of sleep and of its recreating power is not yet understood. Children, of course, need more sleep and more play than do adults. Play for a child, as for all young animals, is a form of work, an instinctive preparation for future living.

Food, the energy-fuel of the living cell, is of paramount importance. A mixed diet which comprises all the foodstuffs is best for human beings, since all foods are necessary to their complete health. But it may be wiser to ease digestion by eating only certain types of food together rather than all types

at once (e.g. proteins and green vegetables together; starches and sugars together). Meals should be eaten at regularly spaced times so that the digestive organs fall into a regular rhythm of activity and of rest.

Adequate chewing is necessary in order to mince up the food sufficiently fine for treatment by a digestive tract which, unlike that of the birds, has no gizzard; and furthermore to bring the starchy elements into intimate contact with the saliva, which contains an enzyme capable of transforming the unabsorbable starch into the accessible sugar.

The mechanism of biting needs care. The baby teeth must be carefully brushed and any cavities filled by the dentist so as to hold the jaw firm and wide for the second teeth. Teeth should be brushed after every meal; but the most important toilet of the teeth is at bedtime. Decay is caused by fragments of food lodging between the teeth, obviously least disturbed during the night-hours, and forming an ideal breeding ground for the germs that cause decay. A visit to the dentist twice a year is now not an occasion for fear, but part of a wise scheme of living.

Water, fruit drinks, tea—indeed any fluid— should be taken freely *between* meals. Drinking with meals dilutes the digestive juices and often causes trouble. The body consists of some 90 per cent of water, it should be remembered, and it therefore needs a high fluid intake.

Dead skin, dried sweat, dust and so forth clog the pores, and need removing by a bath and by scrubbing with soap. The real way, however, to achieve deep cleanliness of the skin is by sweating exercise. A ploughman's skin is more clean, in the medical sense, than that of the "fashionable beauty." Hair should be washed every 14 days or so. This again is a personal question. Sometimes it should

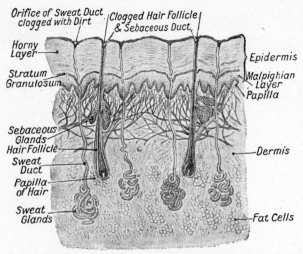

Orifice of Sweat Duct clogged with Dirt
Clogged Hair Follicle & Sebaceous Duct
Horny Layer
Stratum Granulosum
Epidermis
Malpighian Layer
Papilla
Sebaceous Glands
Hair Follicle
Sweat Duct
Papilla of Hair
Sweat Glands
Dermis
Fat Cells

HYGIENE : EFFECTS OF SKIN POLLUTION

The surface of the skin is studded with a multitude of small openings through which the sweat and the sebaceous glands pour out their secretions. Insufficient washing has the result shown in the above diagram—the orifices of the gland ducts become blocked with dirt and with dried skin secretions.

be washed more often, sometimes less often. Brushing with a clean stiff brush after frictioning the scalp with spirit may be the more advisable, for water often relaxes the oil glands of the scalp, causing the hair to be too greasy.

Breathing should be deep and full, expanding the lungs. Deep breathing before an open window, on waking, is a healthful beginning to the day, enriching the blood-stream with oxygen. Many Eastern philosophies enjoin this first activity. Windows should be kept widely open. It is the narrow opening which causes a draught. The danger of "night air" is an out-worn fallacy. It is the play of air on the skin that is the surest preventive of disease, the surest step towards health. Cool air on the skin surface, like a cool daily sponge-down, challenges the adrenals, the small glands above the kidneys, and they secrete adrenalin, which braces the body against disease invasion.

Breathing should be through the nose and not the mouth, so that the air may be warmed and filtered through the nasal passages. If there is difficulty in breathing through the nose, medical aid must be sought—for adenoids may be present, or a malformation of the nose. Adenoids are an excessive growth of lymphoid tissue in the space between the back of the nose and the throat. They are a source of infection; and by spoiling the air and blood supply to adjacent parts, they cause stupidity and a poor bone development of the face—the distressful "rabbit jaw." Enlarged tonsils often accompany adenoids, but they are, generally speaking, less disastrous in their effects.

Clothes should be loose, light in weight, adequate in conserving warmth or in protecting from heat. Women are always the better for a firm corset, because the greater width between their pelvic bones allows the blood to gather in the abdomen, and the heart has difficulty in driving the stream out and round. This is a real consideration quite apart from personal vanity. A well-fitting brassière slings the weight of the breasts on to the shoulders; this is also good "mechanics" for a once four-footed mammal now walking upright. Shoes play a special part in health and happiness. Ill-fitting or ill-chosen shoes throw the weight awry, and nerve strain results. The shoe should be long enough for the wearer to wriggle the toes. The shoe heel should lie in the gravity-line

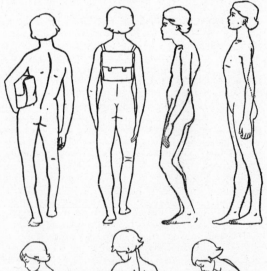

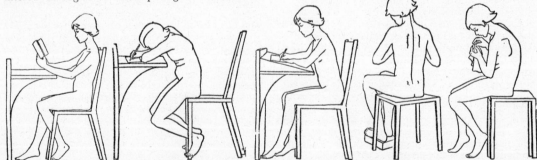

IMPORTANCE OF POSTURE IN HYGIENIC LIVING

Young people in particular are apt to adopt faulty attitudes, both when sitting and standing. The first drawing on the left shows a good position to adopt when reading, the whole length of thighs, spine and arms being supported. The second and fifth drawings are of bad sitting positions, the thighs being unsupported, the spine curved, and the lungs cramped. The third and fourth drawings show good postures for writing and for sewing. Top right, examples of bad carriage, from which spinal curvature and other ills can result ; the corresponding good postures are shown.

of the wearer—directly under one's heel, and should have a broad tread. The height should be that which is comfortable to the wearer, and this depends on the length of the *tendo Achilles*—the long tendon at the back of the leg. All things being equal, if this tendon is short, a high heel is comfortable; if it is long, a low heel is better. The shoe should be bound to the arch of the foot, so that the heel stays in the shoe-heel, otherwise the foot slips forward, barking the toes against the shoe roof and causing corns. The prevention of "bad feet" is of special significance in preventive medicine.

The importance of an upright posture while sitting or standing; the care of eyes and ears; the use of vaccines and serums against disease; the war against flies and disease-carrying insects; the cleanliness of food and its conserving—all these belong to hygiene, this fascinating subdivision of Medicine. From it the great public Health Services have sprung. One important phase of their work is represented by the laws which make compulsory the notification to the authorities of every case of certain diseases. Being early informed of the appearance of such cases, they can take prompt measures for the isolation and removal to hospital of sufferers. The seaports, too, are now narrowly watched by their special health officers, and suspicious cases of illness on vessels arriving in harbour are at once dealt with.

In the domain of industrial hygiene great strides have also been made. Formerly, the dust and foul air of factories were responsible for a great number of serious diseases, but the measures taken have been highly successful, and comparatively few instances of diseases of this nature are now recorded.

Preventive medicine is the medicine of the future. It is positive *not* negative in its implications, enjoining as it does, by checking the occurrence of ill-health, the ideal of health and of happiness.

Hygrometer. One of the important factors which the Meteorological Office must take into account in making its forecasts is the humidity—the amount of moisture in the atmosphere. To measure this, instruments are used, called hygrometers. One of the simplest is the toy known as the "weather house," at the door of which a man appears if the weather is about to be wet, and a woman if it is to be fine. It is operated by cat-gut threads, which grow shorter as the humidity increases and lengthen as it decreases, thus moving the figures. Hair also contracts when moist, and is used in the hair hygrometer, moving a needle on a scale as it changes in length.

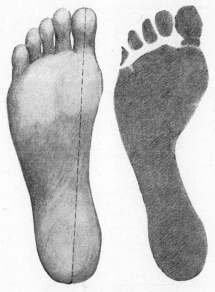

HYGIENE OF THE FEET
One essential for healthy feet is correct weight distribution. Meyer's line—an imaginary axis —shows how the normal well-arched foot rests on the ball of the great toe, the outside edge of the foot, and the heel.

The wet and dry bulb hygrometer, also called the psychrometer, is the most generally used. In the sling psychrometer two thermometers are fastened side by side on a stand, exactly alike except that the bulb of one is covered with wet muslin. The thermometers are then whirled or fanned, and the evaporation of the moisture in the muslin causes a fall in temperature in the wet-bulb thermometer—rapid if the day is dry, and slight if it is damp. The dry thermometer records the actual temperature of the air, and by comparing the two readings the humidity can be determined from a set of prepared tables.

Another type is the dew-point or condensing hygrometer. This makes use of ether, which evaporates very quickly and soon cools one of the thermometers down to the point at which the moisture in the air begins to condense as dew. From the dew-point, and the temperature of the air as given by the other thermometer, the relative humidity can be determined. In chemical hygrometers the moisture in a given volume of air is absorbed by calcium chloride or sulphuric acid, and the increase in weight gives the amount of moisture.

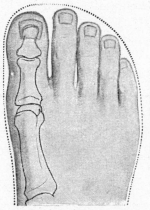 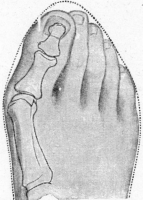

DANGER OF ILL-FITTING SHOES
The sole of a shoe should have a straight inner line (left). If it tapers (right), the natural action of the foot is damaged, and the toes, particularly the great toe, may be so crushed that they overlap, thereby causing painful and crippling distortions.

Another type of instrument used to measure humidity or rather to gauge the cooling effect of air upon a human body, is called the Kata thermometer. It was invented by the English physiologist Sir Leonard Hill (born 1866), and is really a thermometer with a larger bulb than usual. It is raised to blood heat (98° F.) by immersing it in warm water. Next a record is made of the time taken by the air around it to lower its temperature

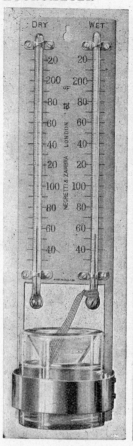

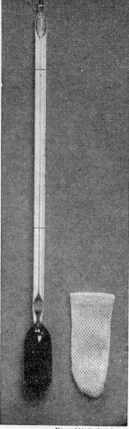

Negretti & Zambra

TYPES OF HYGROMETER
Left, wet and dry bulb hygrometer which measures the
amount of moisture in the air. Right, the Kata thermometer which is used to test the cooling power of air in
buildings ; the cap is placed on the bulb for wet readings.

by a certain number of degrees. After this, a
" finger-stall " of silk net is placed over the bulb
and a " wet-bulb " reading taken. From these
readings and from the time record, the cooling
effect of the air can be estimated.

Hygrometers are used in many public schools and
office buildings to measure the humidity, so that
moisture can be supplied when the air becomes too
dry (*see* Heating and Ventilation). They are also
used in industries in which humidity is a factor,
such as in the manufacture of textiles and tobacco.

From measuring the humidity in an apartment
the next step is to make the recording instrument
automatically vary the humidity within certain
limits set beforehand. The appliance which does
this is called a hygrostat. One type opens or closes
a valve in the air line when a certain degree of
moisture in the air being supplied to the room or
building is attained.

We spoke, above, of certain substances absorbing
moisture. A substance which does this is said to be
hygroscopic: glycerine is a good example.

Hymns. The singing of songs that express
adoration, praise or religious fervour has always
occupied a prominent place in Christian worship.
But hymns are older than Christianity. The Greeks

had their hymns, and the word hymn is derived from
the Greek *hymnos*, a poem. It is said that Clement of
Alexandria (150–220) composed one of the first
Christian hymns. Strictly speaking, a hymn is a
solemn song addressed to God. A versification of
the Psalms of David is called a psalm, and that of
other parts of Scripture, a paraphrase.

The popularity of hymns arises from the fact
that they furnish a religious congregation with the
opportunity of taking an active part in the service,
instead of being merely listeners to a preacher.

As early as 633 the use of hymns was sanctioned
in churches, and since that time religious poets and
versifiers have been pouring out a stream of hymns,
some of which have gained world-wide popularity.
In modern church hymnals there are translations
from Latin and Greek hymns of the early Christian
Church. Other hymns, again, in common use are
from the German, as for example Now thank we all
our God. Martin Luther (1483–1546) did much
to promote the use of hymns in the German
Protestant Church. Amongst the great English
hymn writers are Charles and John Wesley, Isaac
Watts (1674–1748) and William Cowper (1731–
1800). John Henry Newman should be included,
too, if only because of his poem, Lead, Kindly
Light, written in 1833. English hymns have been
translated into many languages, and are sung
from one end of the world to the other. Perhaps the
most popular hymns in the language are Onward,
Christian Soldiers, Abide with Me, Rock of Ages,
Nearer, my God, to Thee, and Jesu, Lover of my
Soul; while one of the first hymns children learn to
sing is There's a Friend for Little Children.

The story of the origin of some of our most
popular hymns is in many instances very interesting. Who would ever have thought that the
Rev. S. Baring Gould's (1834–1924) Onward,
Christian Soldiers, composed as it was for a Yorkshire Sunday School procession, would emerge
from obscurity and become one of the most popular
hymns in the whole world?

The beautiful hymn Abide with Me was written
by the Rev. Henry Francis Lyte, a clergyman at
Brixham, Devonshire, in 1847, two months before
his death, and no doubt it was the consciousness of
his failing health that inspired the beautiful words—

Swift to its close ebbs out life's little day.

This faithful minister had preached his last
sermon in his beloved church, had said farewell
to his flock of hardy fishermen who loved him
like a father, and had returned home to muse on
the past and the future. And as he sat and con-
templated the nearness of his end, the inspiration
of Abide with Me came to him in a moment.
He wrote the words down and gave them into the
care of his wife, and when the news of his death
came to Brixham a few weeks later his parishioners
sang the hymn for the first time in the parish
church.

It is said that the first verse of Our Blest Redeemer, ere He breath'd, came to the composer,
Harriet Auber, when she was musing by her
window in a house at Hoddesdon, Hertfordshire.
As she had no pen or paper handy, she scratched
the words on the window-pane with the diamond
in her ring. There the words remained for years
after the hymn had become widely known.

I

Ibex. (Pron. ī'-beks). Some four species are included in this small group of wild goats, all being distinguished by fine curved horns. Ibex live in mountains above the line of perpetual snow, only descending from the heights at night to graze. They feed in small herds, but the older males usually live alone and at higher altitudes than the females and young animals.

The splendid horns of the male, 30 to 60 inches long, rise from the crest of the skull in a long, backward sweeping curve, and are marked in the front with bold cross ridges; the horns of the female are much smaller. The forelegs are shorter than the hind, making it easier for the animal to go up a slope than down.

The Alpine ibex (*Capra ibex*) is almost extinct in the wild state, but a few herds are preserved by the Italian Government. The Asiatic ibex (*Capra siberica*), which inhabits the mountains of central Asia, is brown to white in colour and about 40 inches high at the shoulder. The Arabian species (*Capra sinaitica*) is yellowish brown, with dark markings, and is found in Palestine and Egypt, as well as in Arabia. The Abyssinian ibex is darker than the Arabian and has black horns, with a curious projection on the forehead.

Ibsen, HENRIK (1828–1906). Although the plays of Henrik Ibsen are limited almost completely to Norwegian themes, they have a universal appeal and have had a tremendous influence on later dramatists. Ibsen was a stern and lonely man who saw more evil than good in life. His pessimism no doubt sprang in part from the hardships and disappointments which he experienced in his youth.

He was born at Skien, in southern Norway, on March 20, 1828, and was apprenticed to a chemist at the age of 15, suffering seven years of drudgery. When he was 19 he began to write poetry, his first play, Catalina, being published in 1850. He entered the University of Christiania (now Oslo) in the same year, but did not have enough money to complete his studies. Thereafter for some years he was successively a journalist, manager of a theatre at Bergen, and the author of lyrics and unsuccessful plays.

Ibsen was long in discovering his true bent, and he waited still longer for recognition. His play The Warriors in Helgeland (1858), which marked an epoch in Norwegian literature, and Love's Comedy, the first of the social satires for which he is particularly famous, were coldly received. In 1864 Ibsen went to live in Rome, where he wrote the dramatic poem Brand, which aroused his native country to belated acknowledgment of his genius. The Norwegian Parliament granted him a pension in 1866, and asked him to come home, but until 1891 he chose to live abroad.

Success won, he devoted himself to writing satiric comedies of modern social life. Misfortune had developed in him a biting irony; and his plays were so audacious, pessimistic and scornful of social hypocrisy that they could not be ignored.

His recognition was greater abroad than in his native land. Some thought of him as a preacher, but Ibsen insisted his plays had no moral purpose. He was simply a commentator, prescribing no remedies for social evils; and in time it was recognized that his chief claim to distinction was as a playwright. He scorned the " happy ending," and restored to the sentimentalized drama something of Greek simplicity. His plots are masterly. Ibsen's plays have been translated into all

HENRIK IBSEN
Norwegian dramatist and poet, Ibsen's Peer Gynt (1867) established him as a writer of genius.

IBEX ENGAGED IN A DILEMMA
Fine curved horns are a distinguishing mark of the ibexes, members of a small group of wild goats. The Alpine ibex of Europe is nearly extinct, except for a few herds preserved by the Italian Government. These animals live in mountains above the snow-line, descending at night to lower levels to graze.

European languages, and performed in many lands. He died at Christiania (Oslo), May 23, 1906.

To English readers and playgoers Ibsen's best known works are Brand (1866); Peer Gynt (1867); The Pillars of Society (1877); A Doll's House (1879); Ghosts (1881); The Wild Duck (1884); Hedda Gabler (1890); and The Master Builder (1892).

Icarus. The ancient Greek legend of this young man is certainly one of the earliest of all those stories of which the moral is the tragic end that awaits excessive ambition. For Icarus was the son of the famous Greek, Daedalus, and with his father, he was flying away from the great king Minos, who had imprisoned them in Crete. Their wings, the invention of Daedalus, were of feathers, fastened to their shoulders with wax. Daedalus flew safely along, but his son, ambitious to go higher, went so high that he came too near

C. J. Gregory

WHERE THE ICE AGE LEFT ITS MARK
When, during the Ice Age, great sheets of ice swept over the existing rock-surfaces they literally smoothed them down, rounding off sharp parts and grinding projections flat. Small, rounded rock-surfaces like those seen in this photograph are relics of that time, and from their resemblance to the backs of a flock of sheep, are called, from the French for rocks and sheep, *roches moutonnées.*

the sun. The wax which secured his wings was melted and the youth dropped to his death in that part of the Aegean Sea which has ever since borne his name, the Icarian Sea. (*See* Daedalus).

Ice. When water is sufficiently cooled six-sided needle-like crystals begin to form, and these increase and interlace until the whole mass becomes solid ice. In water which freezes naturally this change to a solid state begins at the surface and spreads gradually downwards. When the freezing process is complete the crystals are so closely packed that they cannot be discerned as separate bodies.

Fresh water normally freezes at 32° Fahrenheit or 0° Centigrade at atmospheric pressure, salt water at a lower temperature. But if oil is poured over water in a vessel, and the vessel is kept absolutely still, the water may be cooled to 10° Fahrenheit without freezing. If the vessel is slightly shaken or

jarred, however, the water solidifies at once. Most substances contract as they freeze, but this is not true of water. Water expands upon freezing by one-eleventh of its own bulk, its point of greatest density being 4° C., above and below which temperature expansion takes place. (*See* Freezing and Refrigeration).

Ice Age. The early part of the geological period known as the Pleistocene is called the Great Ice Age. Half a million years ago, when the mammoth and the mastodon still roamed the trackless forests, vast ice sheets formed over the northern part of Europe and America. The ice was so thick that only the highest mountain peaks were visible above it. The ice sheets formed because there was not enough heat during the warmer months of the year to melt the previous winter's snow and ice.

In North America the ice reached great thickness, especially in Labrador, near the western shore of Hudson Bay and in the mountains of British Columbia. In Europe the ice was at least 6,000 feet deep over Norway. Scotland, Ireland and all but the southern part of England were covered by a thick layer of ice which extended right across the North Sea to the Scandinavian ice-cap. (Most of Greenland is still an ice-cap.) Much of Germany and Russia was also buried beneath ice.

The interglacial period, or Great Ice Age, consisted of several glacial epochs, each separated by "interglacial" epochs of milder climate, during which the ice sheets were reduced or perhaps disappeared altogether. Together the glacial epochs and those of milder climate which separated them may have covered half a million years—a short span as geologists measure time. The melting of the ice produced quantities of water, which gathered into lakes wherever basins were present.

The melting of the last ice sheet left a thick deposit of debris, called drift, on the area which it had covered. The drift consisted of rocky and earthy debris which the ice had scraped and broken off from the land over which it passed. The irregular distribution of the drift, as well as erosions made by the ice, left many depressions without outlets, and in these ponds and lakes formed.

Indeed, the ice sheets made great changes in the physical features of the regions they covered. In addition to the lakes formed, they left the surface strewn with boulders of various kinds of rock, many of great size. Some of them had been transported hundreds of miles from the places where the ice broke them from the bed-rock. Some of the lakes occupy basins made by the damming of river valleys by drift which the ice left. By means of these boulders, and of the smoothing off and scratching of the rocks over which the ice sheets passed,

Daedalus, legendary Greek sculptor and inventor, was employed by King Minos of Crete to build a labyrinth in which to imprison the monstrous Minotaur. Later, Daedalus incurred the king's displeasure and was himself shut up there with his son Icarus. They both escaped with the aid of wings invented by Daedalus. But Icarus flew too near the sun, and the wax with which the wings were secured melted and he fell into the Aegean Sea. In this painting by Herbert J. Draper sea-nymphs are mourning the death of Icarus. See article in facing page.

American Museum of Natural History

ICE AGE LANDSCAPE IN NORTHERN FRANCE

During the Ice Age it was, as one would expect, intensely cold, and those animals which survived did so because they had thick coats. Above is a scene in the flat country of Northern France during one of the periods in which snow and ice covered the greater part of the Temperate Zone. The beasts in the foreground are woolly rhinoceroses; in the distance are antelopes and elephant-like mammoths. Some animals became extinct, while others moved southward.

the extent of the sheets and the direction in which they moved can be worked out quite accurately.

The many waterfalls within the area covered by the ice are in most cases due to changes of drainage caused by the great glaciers; for many valleys were filled by deposits made by the ice, and when it melted the surface waters sought new courses. In the glaciated area there have been found many peat-beds, evidently formed from marshes which developed in shallow basins after the ice sheet melted.

The ice, which encroached gradually on regions previously warm, must have submitted all living things to new and disturbing conditions. In consequence, some animals became extinct at this time, others moving southward. Man existed in Europe during the early interglacial epochs, and also in central North America. (*See* the articles on Geology and Glacier).

Icebergs. Masses of ice which have broken away from a glacier or ice sheet and slid into the sea are known as icebergs. They vary in size from small flat pieces to great masses a mile or more in diameter. Although some icebergs stand as much as 200 feet above the water, only a small portion of the whole berg is actually visible. Calculations show that only about a ninth of an iceberg is above the surface of the ocean.

These wanderers of the sea overwhelm the onlooker with their beauty. Over their dazzling surface tints of delicate green mingle with blazing sapphire veins, contrasting with the deep dove-coloured caverns carved by the waves, and at dawn and sunset gleams of purple, azure and rose colour the scene. As they drift along, now and then sloughing off great fragments with a tremendous crash, many of them assume fantastic shapes—like castles, triumphal arches or domed mosques. Once afloat, most icebergs are soon melted by the warmer ocean water and the sun. Some bergs, however, are so huge that they travel 2,000 miles before disappearing.

Most bergs in the North Atlantic come from Greenland's great ice-cap. Here in early spring a procession of floating ice islands

Courtesy of United States Coast Guard

TRAVELLING ICEBERG SLOWLY MELTING

Breaking off from the Arctic ice-sheet at the edges of Greenland's glaciers, icebergs float many miles southward into warm water. There the waves and the heat of the sun carve the ice into fantastic shapes, forming pinnacles and arches. Some icebergs are so large that they may travel 2,000 miles or more before disappearing from sight.

begins to travel southward; and about April, May or June they reach the northern Atlantic steamer routes, where they constitute a grave menace to shipping. Here they come under the influence of the Gulf Stream flowing north-eastwards; their course southwards is stayed and they quickly melt.

When night has fallen the icebergs glow with a peculiar white sheen called ice blink, due to the reflection of scattered rays of light from the sky on the white surface of the ice.

It has often been observed that the presence of birds far from land, or the absence of waves, means that floating ice is near, as does the sudden echo from a siren or a horn.

Ice Hockey. Though its actual origin is unknown, this game was played in the English Fen district as far back as 1813, and was introduced into Canada some 40 years later. Said to be the fastest game in the world, ice hockey has become Canada's national winter sport and, since the beginning of the 20th century, has gained much popularity in England and on the Continent.

Ice hockey is played by two teams of six; substitutes may replace players during the match. Owing to the great speed at which the game is played and the risk of injury, players may wear protective equipment. Ice hockey skates resemble those used in racing, but have shorter blades. The sticks of wood or other approved material must not be more than 53 inches in length from the heel to the end of the shaft, or more than 14¾ inches from the heel to the end of the blade. The blade must not be more than three inches high, except for the goal-keeper's stick, which is not allowed to exceed three and a half inches, except at the heel, where it may

THE GREAT WHITE PERIL OF THE OCEAN LANES

About nine-tenths of an iceberg are below the surface of the water; and the underwater part may extend far beyond that which is visible, constituting an unseen and serious peril to shipping. The liner shown here, though avoiding the obvious danger, is menaced by the 'shelf' of ice under the sea. Since 1912, when the British liner Titanic struck an iceberg on her maiden voyage and sank in two hours with great loss of life, under an international agreement special vessels have patrolled the danger zone, sending out wireless reports of the presence and movements of icebergs.

Sport & General

ICE HOCKEY : THE WORLD'S FASTEST GAME

Canada's national winter game of ice hockey has gained considerable popularity in
Britain and on the European continent since the beginning of the 20th century. The
sticks are longer than those used in ordinary hockey, and a disk of vulcanised rubber is
used instead of a ball. On the right is a rink marked out for a game.

measure four and a half inches. A puck, a round
flat disk of vulcanised rubber, one inch thick and
three inches in diameter, is used instead of a ball.

A game is divided into three periods of 20
minutes play, with 10 minutes rest between periods.
Playing positions are: goalkeeper, left and right
defence, right wing, centre, and left wing. Primarily
the stick must be used for playing the puck, but
kicking is permitted. A kicked goal, however, is
disallowed. The puck may be stopped by the hand,
but it must not be held except by the goalkeeper.
A player is sent off the ice without replacement for
two minutes as a minor penalty, and for five minutes
for a major infringement. For certain offences the
offender is sent off the ice, but may be replaced.

Iceland. In the North Atlantic, just
outside the Arctic Circle, is the oldest existing
democracy—the Republic of Iceland. In the
year 930, Icelanders established a Parliament; within the next century they took a
step which other nations did not take until
centuries later: they instituted a scheme of
mutual insurance against loss of property.
They had trial by jury long before England,
and in no country is the general level of
education higher or is there a more widespread love of good literature.

Iceland is about 150 miles east of Greenland and some 500 miles from the north coast
of Scotland. It has an area of 39,700 square
miles. Because of its northern situation the
island has little more than two hours of
daylight on the shortest day in winter, and
about the same number of hours of darkness
on the longest day in summer. Of its whole
area barely one-quarter is habitable, mainly
the lowlands in the south and south-west and
the valleys running up from the numerous
bays and fiords that indent the coast. The
interior is a plateau from 2,400 to 2,700

feet above sea-level, strewn with glaciers, lava
fields, volcanoes, hot springs, rivers, lakes and
waterfalls. The active volcano Mount Hekla (5,108
feet) is situated in the south of the island. Its last
serious eruptions were in 1912 and 1946.

In spite of its name Iceland has a remarkably
mild climate for a country so far north, due in
large measure to the moderating influence of the
Gulf Stream. The rainfall is much heavier in
the south than in the north; in the winter gales
blow almost continuously. There are few trees of
any size; rich grass provides excellent pasture for
sheep and horses.

The only minerals of value are calcareous spar
(kind of crystal) and sulphur. Some of the richest
fishing grounds in the North Atlantic lie off the
coasts of Iceland, and fish and fish-products are
the principal sources of the island's wealth. The

THE SOVEREIGN STATE OF ICELAND

rearing of cattle, sheep and horses is an important industry. There are no railways in the country, but inland communication is maintained by means of motor-buses and aeroplanes, steamers handling the coastal traffic.

The capital of the Republic is Reykjavik, a well-built town with a population of 46,578. Here, as in a number of other places, many of the houses are heated with water from hot springs. The second largest town is Akureyri, and Isafjördur is the centre for the herring fisheries.

The people of Iceland are intensely proud of their literature, especially of their ancient sagas or stories. These sagas are tales of ancient heroes and combine fact with legend. They were collected and written down by Snorri Sturlason (1179–1241) and by later writers, and so little has the Icelandic language, which resembles Norwegian, changed in the course of centuries that the people of today can read these old tales with but little difficulty.

The first Norse settlers came to Iceland in 874. Between 930 and 1262 the island was an independent republic, but in 1263 it became part of the kingdom of Norway. In 1381 Iceland, together with Norway, came under the rule of Danish kings, but when Norway was separated from Denmark in 1814, Iceland remained a Danish possession. From 1918 to 1944 the country was a sovereign State united with Denmark only through the fact that the king of Denmark was also king of Iceland. In May 1944 the people decided to sever all ties with the Danish Crown, and a Republic was officially proclaimed.

During the Second World War (1939–45) a small force of British troops landed in Iceland in

H. Felton

ICELAND'S NATURAL HOT-WATER SYSTEM
At Reykjavik, the capital of Iceland, and elsewhere, hot springs supply water for doing the washing. This natural system is also used to heat buildings and glasshouses in which vegetables and flowers are grown all the year round. Iceland is a highly volcanic region, but serious eruptions are rare.

May 1940 to forestall any movement that the Germans might be preparing to make against it. Coast defence batteries were installed and aerodromes constructed. In 1942 United States forces assumed responsibility for the defence of the island, remaining there until the end of the war. The population of Iceland is 130,000.

Ichneumon Flies. Despite their name these four-winged insects are not "flies," but are members of the order Hymenoptera, to which belong ants, bees and wasps. Ichneumon flies vary greatly in size, but all have thread-like antennae, long slender abdomens and long legs which trail behind them in the air. The females have a needle-like ovipositor (egg depositor) which is sometimes as long as the rest of the insect.

By means of their ovipositors the females lay their eggs in the larvae of many kinds of harmful insects. After the eggs hatch the ichneumon larvae feed on their hosts and kill them, thereby checking the increase of noxious insects.

Idaho. Because of its wild and lovely scenery, the Red Indians gave the name of Idaho (gem of the mountains) to the region now included in this north-western State of the United States. Idaho lies west of the Rocky Mountains and is bounded on the north by British Columbia, on the east by the states of Montana and Wyoming, and on the west

J. J. Ward

ICHNEUMON FLY AND ITS LONG OVIPOSITOR
Relatives of the bees and wasps, ichneumon flies vary greatly in size, but all have long slender abdomens ; from that of the female (above) extends a thin egg-laying organ, called an ovipositor, by means of which the insect pierces the skin of the larvae of certain other insects and deposits eggs therein. When the eggs hatch, the ichneumon larvae feed on their hosts.

by Oregon and Washington. It has an area of 83,557 square miles, much of it being mountainous. Forests cover more than a third of the state.

The Snake or Shoshone river drains most of Idaho, but its waterfalls render navigation impossible. Huge dams, reservoirs and more than 10,000 miles of irrigation canals along the course of the river have transformed what was once a desert into rich farmland.

The state has deposits of lead, silver, zinc, copper, gold, antimony, mercury, tungsten, cobalt and manganese. Its potatoes are famous and it yields more apples than any other state save Washington. Other products are wheat, alfalfa, oats, barley, sugar beet, fruit, meat, wool and dairy produce. Cattle and sheep are raised ; and among the industrial establishments are beet sugar factories, flour and saw mills, and fruit canneries. Boise, with a population of 26,130, is the capital.

Idaho was explored in 1805–06, the first settlements being established in 1855. The territory became a State in 1890. The population is 524,873.

Iguana. (Pron. ig-wah′-na). Despite their formidable appearance the members of this family of queer-looking lizards are harmless, if left alone, though they will bite savagely if cornered. They vary widely in size and are found only in the tropical regions of America, except for two species native to the island of Madagascar and one found in the Fiji Islands. Curious teeth, saw-edged at the tips, distinguish the family, as do the large

dewlap or pouch under head and neck, and the scaly crest extending down the back. Most are green, though some change colour at will. They usually live in trees, or in holes in the ground.

The common iguana (*Iguana tuberculata*) of Central and Southern America sometimes attains a length of six feet. Greenish in colour, with brown bands and bars, it feeds mainly on fruit and leaves. The great sea iguana of the Galapagos Islands, in the Pacific Ocean, is four or five feet long and a strong swimmer. It feeds mainly on seaweed. Its shorter-tailed relative, the Galapagos land iguana, which is orange and red in colour, eats berries and cacti. The rhinoceros iguana, which is confined to the islands of San Domingo and Puerto Rico in the West Indies, had three blunt horns on its snout. Another curious member of the iguana family is the helmeted or hooded basilisk of Central America, which derives its name from the fleshy crown or crest upon its head.

Iliffe, EDWARD MAUGER ILIFFE, 1ST BARON (born 1877). The life-story of Lord Iliffe would embody a romance of modern journalism which began with the enterprise, foresight and sagacity of his father, William Isaac Iliffe, more than half-a-century ago. In the limited space that is available here we can only hint at the astonishing advance from the most modest beginnings in 1881, when W. I. Iliffe ventured into the unfamiliar world of technical journalism with a periodical which he called The Cyclist, and which afterwards became The Cycle Trade Review, and still later The Motor Cycle and Cycle Trader.

Coventry, the home of the cycle trade, was naturally the home of its first representative journal. The Bicycling News was another successful journal founded by Iliffe, and it had the distinction of employing on its staff a brilliant young man named Alfred Harmsworth, who later became Lord Northcliffe.

The element of fortune entered with the coming of the motor-car, for though Iliffe had foreseen the tremendous expansion of cycling, he could not have foreseen the invention of the internal combustion engine some years later.

But he was alert and readily did for the motor-car what he had so successfully done for the bicycle. The Autocar has held the chief position in motoring journalism for many years. A bare description of the other journals that have grown up around The Autocar would fill a page of our book, covering as they do agriculture, electricity, photography, nursing, yachting, and other activities. Edward Iliffe and his brother, W. Coker Iliffe, carried the business after their father's death to heights of success undreamed of by its founder.

Edward Iliffe's organizing abilities were nationally recognized when he was appointed controller of machine tools in the Ministry of Munitions during the First World War (1914–18). From 1923 to 1929 he was M.P. for Tamworth. He was raised to the peerage as Baron Iliffe of Yattendon in 1933. (*See* Camrose, Viscount.)

Ewing Galloway

A GIANT MARINE IGUANA
Although one of the largest members of its family—it may be as much as five feet in length—this sea iguana of the Galapagos Islands, off the coast of Ecuador, is harmless enough. The scaly crest all along the back is one of the distinguishing marks of these particular lizards.

Illinois. (Pron. il-i-noi'). From a happy hunting ground of Red Indians to one of the busiest regions of North America is the story of this north-central state of the United States. Illinois lies to the south-west of Lake Michigan, which forms part of its eastern boundary, and has an area of 56,400 square miles. The largest rivers are the Mississippi, which forms the western boundary; its tributary the Illinois; and the Wabash and the Ohio on the eastern and southern boundaries respectively. With its gradually sloping hills and wide shallow valleys, Illinois is one of the flattest states in the country.

The rich black soil is extremely fertile, making agriculture the leading industry. The principal crops are wheat, oats, barley, rye, potatoes, hay, fruit and nuts. Meat packing rivals agriculture. The stockyards and packing establishments of Chicago—the largest city in the state—are, indeed, the biggest in the world. Steel-milling and the manufacture of watches, furniture, musical instruments, soap, glass, machinery, and men's clothing are other leading industries. The capital of the state is Springfield (population, 71,000). First settled in 1750, Illinois was an organized territory by 1809, and 1818 it was admitted to the Union as a State. The population is 7,900,000.

Impressionism. In 1863 the dissatisfaction of a large number of French artists with their treatment by the authorities controlling the Salon—the French equivalent of our Royal Academy—led to what amounted to an open revolt. The dissatisfied painters set up on their own, striving to make themselves as independent

Han;staengl

VAN GOGH'S SUNFLOWERS
Many of Vincent Van Gogh's best-known works, including this study of sunflowers, were painted while he was in an asylum at Arles, France. As an artist Van Gogh (1853–90) belongs strictly to no group, though he is generally considered to be one of the leading Post-Impressionists.

as could be from the tyranny of the academic painters of Paris. Then the emperor, Napoleon III, opened the *Salon des Refusés,* for the exhibition of works by those whose pictures had been rejected by the Salon proper. (*See* France, Art).

Thus arose a new movement in art, which came to be called Impressionism. This name was borrowed from the title of Monet's painting, Sunrise, an Impression, which was exhibited in 1874. The Impressionists were not an organized body but included painters of all types, whose principal common bond was revolt against conventions of lighting and composition. Using only seven or eight colours, they sought to reproduce in pictures the fleeting moods

PARISIAN SCENE IN THE IMPRESSIONIST MANNER
One of the first masters of Impressionism was the French artist Édouard Manet (1832–83), who painted this work entitled Bar aux Folies Bergère, now in the National Gallery, London. Reflected in the mirror behind the central figure of the barmaid is the auditorium. The Impressionists revolted against conventions of lighting and composition, seeking to reproduce in their work the effect of a fleeting impression.

National Geographic Magazine

EXTRAORDINARY INCA MASTERPIECES OF MASONRY WITHOUT MORTAR

Among the wonders of the New World are these two ruins in Peru, South America. positions, fitting closely together without mortar of any kind to bind them, so cunningly were they shaped. In the lower picture the town of Machu Picchu is seen perched high above the surrounding country and also constructed of huge stones. In the tremendous walls of the hill-top fortress of Sacsahuaman (upper) some of the stones are 20 feet high and weigh many tons. Yet they were transported for more

of Nature—the exact effect in one single moment, rather than the more permanent, static, conventional effects favoured by the academic painters. The Impressionist painter, in fact, showed things as they looked when he saw them, not as they might really be. Thus, where before there had been, perhaps, a convention that all trees are green and must therefore be painted green, while shadows are grey or black, and must therefore be painted grey or black, the Impressionist departed from this convention. As we all know, on a hot summer day the trees may seem golden with reflected sun, the shadows brilliant blue with shimmering heat; and this is precisely the way in which the Impressionist painted them.

Put in another way, the Impressionists were not concerned with the colour of an object so much as with the play of light on it. Therefore, they used no colours but those which occur in the spectrum. For example, they would build up a compound colour (e.g., green) by painting with its components (yellow and blue).

At the same time the Impressionists were carrying on another battle, that against the standards of beauty imposed on the art world by the same academic " tyrants " already referred to. They saw that there might be beauty in anything, from a mud-flat to a mountain, and that it was in Nature that beauty really lay. So the Impressionists turned their attention to all manner of subjects, and to all they brought the sense of light and airy colour, of transparency and life.

The criticism was levelled against them that they painted only the moment, not the lasting form; but in rescuing painting from the depths to which it was sinking, they created the most beneficial movement in art for centuries.

Chief among the Impressionists were Claude Monet (1840–1926), Édouard Manet (1832–83), Hilaire Degas (1834–1917), Pierre Renoir (1841–1919) and Camille Pissarro (1830–1903). The Englishman Alfred Sisley (1840–99), who lived and painted entirely in France, and the American James Whistler (1834–1903), were also notable exponents of Impressionism. Among later painters influenced by this movement Walter Sickert (1860–1942) and Henry Tonks (1862–1937) and Wilson Steer (1860–1942) are pre-eminent in Britain.

The Impressionist theory of division of tone was re-stated in 1886 by Seurat (1859–91) and Signac. Pure, separated tints, balanced according to a scientific method, were used to depict some visual impression.

Impressionism was followed by Post-Impressionism. The Impressionists, in their search for light and transitory effect, tended to lose sight of the form and solidity of their subject. The Post-Impressionists worried less about what the object

looked like to the eye at any given moment than about the actual content or meaning of the object. But in so doing, they did not mind if they distorted it or even made it unrecognizable. A good picture, to them, was one which conveyed the *spirit* of a scene, whether it reproduced the scene or not.

Post-Impressionism, therefore, was the first step beyond a representational art. Indeed, its exponents despised mere representation. At the same time they produced the effect which they set out to produce. When their paintings were first shown in England, at a special exhibition held in 1911, the three great Post-Impressionists, Paul Cézanne (1839–1906), Vincent Van Gogh (1853–90), and Paul Gauguin (1848–1903), were regarded almost as madmen. Yet later they came to be appreciated as the leaders of a great movement—who took art for the first time successfully beyond mere representation.

From them, too, can be traced many of the numerous phases of abstract art, such as Vorticism, Cubism, Futurism and Expressionism, of which the last two were the especial product of Italy and Germany respectively. And even the Surrealist artists of a later day owe a good deal, indirectly, to the Post-Impressionists.

The word Impressionism is also applied to music and literature which show the same basic movement as painting. The music of Claude Debussy (1862–1918) and Frederick Delius (1862–1934), for example, is considered as typically Impressionist; while the writings of Gustave Flaubert (1821–80) and Emile Zola (1840–1902) represent something of the same spirit in literature.

Incas. Scattered over the central highlands of the Andes of South America are the remains of massive stone temples, palaces, fortresses, terraces and dwellings. These are the only traces so far

Giraudon

IMPRESSIONIST PORTRAITS BY GAUGUIN
Dissatisfied with life under modern civilized conditions, Gauguin (1848–1903) migrated to Tahiti and later to the Marquesas Islands in the South Seas, where he produced his finest work. This picture of two Tahitian women on a beach, brilliant in colour and beautiful in pattern, is in the Luxembourg Museum in Paris.

with post-houses at intervals over the wildest mountain ranges and across desert for hundreds of miles.

The fall of this thriving and industrious race when confronted by Pizarro and his handful of Spaniards forms one of the tragedies of history. The Inca ruler, Huayna Ccapac, had just died, and the legitimate heir was his young son. But a pretender, Atahualpa, laid claim to the throne, raided Peru and captured the heir. The whole country became paralysed by doubt as to who was the divine ruler. Pizarro by a sudden and treacherous move thereupon captured Atahualpa, and so obtained control of the whole of the over-organized Peruvian empire. The spirit of the Incas was broken, and after a few disastrous rebellions they declined into the submissive apathy which marks the Peruvian Indians of today. Slaughter and oppression, continued through centuries, thinned their numbers until the pure-blooded descendants of the Inca tribes are now fewer than 3,000,000, though the ancient population is said to have been between eight and 10 millions.

British Museum

PRE-INCA POTTERY
Though very similar to Inca pottery, these two pieces date from an even earlier time. That on the left, worked in red clay, shows the craftsmanship of these ancient Peruvian potters. The handle-less vessel on the right, with its spout at the back, represents an important dignitary.

discovered of the ancient civilization of the Incas, a race of Peruvian Indians that ruled over territory extending from what is now Chile, north into Ecuador, from the 13th to the 16th century.

Above the city of Cuzco in Peru, their ancient capital, tower stupendous ramparts made of individual stones of prodigious size. No mortar was used, yet after centuries these stones fit so perfectly that it is impossible to insert the blade of a knife between them. Some are 20 feet high and weigh many tons. Ruins like these are found in many parts of the Andes, together with remains of stone causeways and carefully terraced fields where maize and potatoes were grown, all telling of a highly gifted race. The Incas were ignorant of writing; but they kept records and accounts by means of knotted cords (called *quippus*), the knots being of various kinds and colours.

The Incas were skilful weavers, and seem to have been proficient in every style of hand weaving we know today. They also knew how to smelt metals and cast in moulds; and in the making of pottery they were artists. Evidently, also, they had made some progress in music, for among the remains of their civilization are found flutes made of bone and of cane, clay trumpets and trumpets of shells, bells of different tones, some made of bronze, some of pure copper. They built paved roads, with suspension bridges, and

Mervyn Palmer

INCA HOUSE IN CUZCO, PERU
In the walls of many of the houses in Cuzco, capital of the ancient empire of the Incas, are incorporated the remains of old Inca dwellings. The stones in the lower half of the above building, called the House of the Seven Pumas from carvings over the door, were laid by Inca masons ; the upper storeys are Spanish additions.

WONDERLANDS *of a vast* SUB-CONTINENT

One-sixth of the human race live in Britain's former Indian Empire, now divided into two parts known as the Indian Union (or Republic of India) and the Dominion of Pakistan, both remaining in the British Commonwealth. This chapter is concerned with the sub-continent of India as a whole.

India. The great Asian sub-continent of India was never truly one land. This vast peninsula, thrusting 1,900 miles southward from the Himalaya Mountains into the Indian Ocean, and inhabited by 389,000,000 people—one-sixth of the whole of mankind—has been since the dawn of its history the home of many different races, different in their languages, their customs, their religious beliefs. Now divided politically into two countries, the Indian Union of the Hindus and the Pakistan of the Moslems, it is inhabited still by a bewildering variety of contrasting races. They speak more than 200 distinct languages and dialects; they profess many shades of religious belief; they are split into different social castes; and within the framework of the two countries they belong to hundreds of provinces and petty states. Though their civilization looks back 5,000 years, four-fifths of them cannot read or write. Some of the hereditary princes are among the wealthiest men in the world, possessors of fabulous treasures of gold and jewels; yet the great mass of Indian peasants are miserably poor.

You can read in the article on the History of India how this great land, "the brightest jewel in the Crown of England," was granted self-government in 1947, and how it then was split up into two Dominions. Pakistan consists of two entirely separate regions, one in the north-west, the other in the north-east. The rest of the country is still called India—or, to avoid confusion with the sub-continent, and as its constitution describes it as a Union of States, it is called the Indian Union.

A broad view of the sub-continent shows four separate and well-defined physical regions. The mountain and hill districts of the Himalayan ranges, and the slopes of the Afghanistan and Baluchistan highlands form the northern and north-western borders. Then come the great river plains of the Indus, the Ganges and the lower Brahmaputra forming a broad belt from the head of the Arabian Sea to that of the Bay of Bengal.

Next is the tableland known as the Deccan, which includes the southern half of India; it is bounded by a range of hills, the Eastern Ghats, sloping down to the Coromandel Coast, and by the Western Ghats descending to the Malabar Coast.

Extent.—N. to S. 1900 miles ; E. to W. 2,000 miles. Area 1,800,000 square miles. Population about 389 million.

Physical Features.—Himalaya Mountains, the highest in the world (20,000 to 29,000 feet) ; Vindhya Range and Eastern and Western Ghats, enclosing the Deccan plateau ; deserts in Sind and Rajputana. Principal rivers ; Indus, Ganges and Brahmaputra.

Products.—Millet, rice, wheat, barley, oil-seeds, cotton, jute, sugar, indigo, coconuts, tobacco, tea and opium ; cotton and silk manufactures, metal work ; coal, gold, precious stones, and petroleum.

Chief Cities.—Calcutta (pop. 2,109,000), Bombay (1,499,000), Madras (777,500), Hyderabad (740,000), Delhi, capital of Indian Union (522,000), Karachi, cap. of Pakistan (359,500).

History.—Aryan invasion, about 1500 B.C. ; rise of Buddhism 6th century B.C. ; Alexander the Great's conquest of the N.W., 327 B.C. ; Mahomedan conquest, A.D. 1001 ; Mogul Empire established 1526 ; English East India Company obtained trading posts at Madras (1639), Bombay (1668) and Calcutta (1696) ; battle of Plassey established British supremacy over French, 1757 ; Indian Mutiny, 1857 ; British Crown took over government from East India Company, 1858 ; divided into two dominions (India and Pakistan) 1947 ; Dominion of India became a republic within the British Commonwealth, called the Indian Union, in 1950.

The northernmost portion of India, and one of the most important of the native states is Kashmir (or Cashmere) which extends over the first Himalayan ranges, and includes the famous Vale of Kashmir. Beyond the Indus, between Kashmir and Afghanistan, stretches the North-west Frontier Province—a wild rocky region, which forms a barrier against the raids of the untamed Afghan tribes. Here is the approach to the Khyber Pass, a defile 33 miles in length, through which a railway runs to the Afghan frontier.

Equally wild and unsettled is Baluchistan, immediately to the south, which borders on Persia as well as on Afghanistan; it has now been incorporated into Pakistan. Nepal and Bhutan, on the borders of Tibet, are independent mountain kingdoms; from Nepal come the gallant Gurkha troops who have fought so splendidly for Britain in two world wars; and within its borders is situated the highest mountain in the world, Mount Everest.

These mountain states and border districts form a picturesque background for the far more important river plains. Here is a tract of level cultivation about 2,000 miles long, and from 200 to 400 miles broad. The soil is composed of river sand and silt, washed down through ages from the northern slopes.

The Indus in the west and the Brahmaputra in the east have their sources in Tibet behind the snowy peaks of the Himalayas. These rivers form the western and eastern boundaries, respectively, of that portion of northern India which is properly known as Hindustan. This country, in turn saturated by warm rain, chilled by light frosts, and scorched by desert winds, is the cradle of ancient Indian civilization. The Ganges valley is one of the most crowded regions in the world, many extensive districts supporting more than 600 persons to the square mile, all of whom get their living directly from the soil. In contrast, Baluchistan is very sparsely populated indeed, with six persons to the square mile.

In this rich plains region are the Punjab, or Land of the Five Rivers, now partitioned between India and Pakistan, and containing the important cities of Lahore, Amritsar, Simla, and Delhi.

Here, too, are Rajputana, a collection of about a score of small native states, with the cities Jaipur,

Jodhpur, and Bikanir; the United Provinces of Agra and Oudh, with the famous cities of Allahabad, Cawnpore, Lucknow, Benares, Agra, Bareilly, and Meerut; and the Bengal district with Calcutta, the largest city of India, and Patna as the principal places. All are in the republic of India.

Eastern Bengal and the Sylhet district of Assam, which lie beyond the Ganges, form the Eastern part of the Dominion of Pakistan, though the rest of Assam belongs to India.

The third physical division of India, the peninsula known as the Deccan, offers a marked contrast to the northern plains. The hill country begins not far south of Delhi, capital of the Indian republic, and spreads fan-wise south-east and south-west; while farther south a series of ranges crosses the peninsula from west to east. The Western Ghats

W. Stokes

CLOUDS THAT FORETELL INDIA'S MONSOON

Climate, rainfall and agriculture in the sub-continent of India are affected by seasonal winds called monsoons. The great or south-west monsoons blows from the Indian Ocean between June and October, bringing moisture to the parched earth. If the monsoon fails, crops are ruined over wide areas and hundreds of thousands of people are faced with starvation. The lesser or south-east monsoon of November and December brings moisture from the Bay of Bengal to eastern districts.

follow the coast, closely rising in an unbroken wall to an altitude of 8,000 feet behind the old Portuguese port of Calicut. Close to the coast as they are, the Western Ghats form the true backbone of India, for from their rugged sides the whole country slopes generally eastward; the rivers which rise in the narrow gorges on their eastern side flow for the most part right across the peninsula and empty into the Bay of Bengal. The Eastern Ghats, on the other hand, are of no very great altitude, averaging less than 1,000 feet. They are broken through in a great number of places by rivers, both large and small, which cut deep gashes on their way to the sea.

The central Deccan consists principally of rough hills, some covered with dense forests, others with tall jungle grass, and still others bare. At intervals are broad, well-cultivated plateaux, and the banks of the numerous streams are dotted with tiny irrigated farms and cleared pasture lands.

The political divisions of southern India are more confused than are those of the north. Bombay State includes more than 350 small native states all of which are now under the control of the government of the republic of India. Its chief city is Bombay. East of Bombay State lie the states of Central India and the Central Provinces. The cities of Gwalior in the north and Nagpur in the south are the most important. Farther south and occupying the very heart of the Deccan is Hyderabad (*q.v.*), which was the largest and most populous of the independent states. Hyderabad State did not join the dominion of India until it had been occupied for some months by troops of the dominion.

Madras, the largest state of the Indian Union, begins south of Bengal, includes the whole east coast to Cape Comorin, and extends to the west coast, almost completely surrounding the large state of Mysore. In the south-west corner of the peninsula are the states of Cochin and Travancore. The city of Madras is the third largest in all India, and extends for some distance along the Coromandel coast; among the other important places may be mentioned Madura, Trichinopoly, Tanjore, Calicut, Negapatam, Cuddalore, and Tuticorin.

The Andaman and Nicobar Islands in the Bay of Bengal are under Indian Union administration. The former group, consisting of the Little and the Great Andamans, divided by the Duncan Passage, with a total area of 2,508 square miles, has been used as a penal colony. The Nicobar group consists of nineteen islands, twelve inhabited. The total area is 635 square miles.

The French, who were once supreme in India, retained in early 1950 Pondicherry on the Madras coast; Karikal and Yanaon on the Coromandel coast; Mahe on the Malabar coast. Chandernagore, formerly French, broke away and joined the Indian Union in 1949. The remaining French possessions, total area about 200 square miles, are administered by a governor residing at Pondicherry. The Portuguese retain some territory on the Malabar coast; Gôa (1,469 square miles), the seaport of Damão, which is situated about 100 miles north of Bombay; and the island of Diu, on the other side of the Gulf of Cambay.

Picture to yourself a typical Indian scene during the months of April and May. The burning and pitiless sun looks down upon a land sapped of its strength. The baked earth seems dead, the dried grass rustles with the scorching breath of the wind; the very blue of the sky seems to turn brassy in the intolerable white light of noon.

Presently a dust-storm advances. Behind this rise great black clouds, rolling forward like a tidal wave. The storm bursts overhead with a roar

CUSTOMS AND COSTUMES OF INDIA

Topical

At Puri in Orissa there is a temple dedicated to the Hindu god Juggernaut, Lord of the World, and once a year the image of the deity is dragged in a colossal car by devotees from the temple for about a mile and back again. The vehicle is 50 feet in height, and owing to the weight of the car and the nature of the road the journey takes several days.

Bourne & Shepherd

LORD HIGH EXECUTIONER OF OLD IND

Tradition dies hard in the sub-continent of India, especially in the former semi-independent native States. This weird figure wears the traditional uniform of the office of State executioner of Rewa. But Rewa is now included in the republic of India. and the one-time executioner merely attends ceremonial functions.

TRIBESMEN OF THE NORTH-WEST FRONTIER

All along the north-west frontier of Pakistan dwell turbulent tribes who have harried their neighbours for centuries. These two seasoned warriors are fine specimens of hardy manhood and well-versed in mountain warfare. The collective name for these frontier people is Pathans, but they are divided into many tribes.

A 'COOLER' BENEATH THE TORRID INDIAN SUN

Edward E. Long

When the scorching midday sun beats down on the plains, the cattle wander to the nearest water to wallow in the shallows. Here, beside them, mahouts (elephant drivers) have brought their charges down to the stream for a welcome bath and drink. Tame elephants are the only ones that will be seen in the plains ; the wild herds are now almost entirely confined to the hills, where they are rounded up in great drives every 10 or 12 years in order to be trained for the service of Man.

E.N.A.

n the Hindu religious play Ram Lilla, which is seen being performed at Cawnpore, a city in the republic of India, this grotesque
igure represents Ravana, the demon king of Ceylon. It is made of bamboo and paper and is filled with fireworks. Ravana is
ventually slain by firing a blazing arrow into his inflammable interior, so that his brief life ends in a great display of fireworks.

INDIAN IVORY-CARVER AT WORK

The craftsmen in the Indian bazaars have inherited through the ages delicacy of execution and beauty of design in their artistic products. This photograph shows a worker in ivory putting the finishing touches to a model of a ceremonial elephant. Great patience is needed to achieve the accuracy of detail which such carvings show.

Central News

DANCING GIRLS OF A HINDU TEMPLE

Attired in brightly-coloured dresses, these nautch girls are performing a ceremonial dance in a temple. Nautch girls are dedicated to the service of the gods and are chosen for their good looks, though the fifth daughter of a family is generally considered the most eligible. The dance consists of posturing with arms and body.

Underwood

WHERE A GREAT RAJAH LIES ENTOMBED

In the city of Alwar, capital of the former State of that name (now in the republic of India), is the white marble mausoleum (background, above) of Bakhtawar Singh, a ruler who aided the British against the Mahrattas in 1803. In front of it is an artificial pool around which are a number of graceful pavilions. In the precincts live hundreds of blue pigeons.

and the water strikes the ground in sheets. The great monsoon has come, the annual south-west wind which brings life-giving rains to northern India. Within a week, the bleak country has become again a mass of green.

The monsoons are the salvation of the millions in India who live on the fruits of the soil. There are two of these winds, the great or south-west monsoon, which blows from June to October; and the lesser or south-east monsoon, which blows during November and December. The mountainous wall of the Western Ghats causes the more southerly currents to release most of their moisture on the west coast. The winds which enter over the Sind coast do not strike a cooling mountain range until they have crossed the Sind desert and most of Rajputana, so that they carry a great part of their moisture far into the Punjab, or sweep eastward along the Himalayan barrier, shedding their rain upon the United Provinces and Bengal. In eastern Bengal these winds meet the monsoon coming up the Bay of Bengal, and the two together sweep onward until they strike the Assam hills, where they drop their double charge of moisture. This explains why Assam has the largest rainfall of any country in the world, the average in the Cherra Punji district being 424 inches a year.

The south-west monsoon blows itself out in October, and in November the south-east monsoon sets in. This carries rain to the east and south-east and to the central plateau of the Deccan, which, as we have seen, are deprived of their due share of the earlier moisture by the barrier of the Western Ghats. A good monsoon season means plenty of food for India; a bad monsoon season means famine, misery, and death for hundreds of thousands of helpless victims.

In general, southern India enjoys a more equable climate than the river plains or mountain regions. The latter are subject to extremes of heat and cold, dryness and moisture. In Sind and the Thar desert are places where day after day in the summer the thermometer reaches 110° in the shade, and it is not uncommon to see a drop or a rise in temperature of 70° within a space of 24 hours.

The Himalayan climate is favourable to a tremendous variety of plant life. Below the snow line are to be found vast fields of rhododendrons, then thick forests of evergreens, and on the damp lower slopes to the east a rank and tangled undergrowth of coarse grass, bushes, cane-brakes, bamboo and great trees whose branches are thick with orchids.

The plains region is notable for the babul, a species of acacia, the mango, the banyan, banana trees and the betel-palm. The northern Deccan forests consist chiefly of scrub trees, but in the south teak, sandal-wood and satinwood flourish.

Wild animals abound all over India, for the Hindu religion forbids the people to kill most living creatures. The tiger is found in all the wilder forest regions. Lions, once plentiful in Hindustan, are now confined to the Kathiawar peninsula between the Gulf of Cutch and the Gulf of Cambay. Bears are numerous in the mountains and leopards infest many of the more remote tracts. Elephants still exist in the forests of the south-west.

The *gaur* or Indian buffalo, and the wild pig offer exciting sport to the hunter. The wolf, the jackal, the wild dog, and the striped hyena are plentiful. All these are extremely destructive to game. Monkeys are numerous near settlements and do great damage to crops. The larger rivers are filled

E.N.A.

INDIA'S HALF-TAMED WATER BUFFALOES
Similar in many ways to the Cape buffalo of South America (*see* page 71) the Indian species has for many years been semi-domesticated, although wild herds still exist. During the hottest part of the day these animals like to stand in water or wallow in the mud. Though usually quite docile with the native inhabitants they are liable to attack Europeans.

with crocodiles; snakes abound in all districts, the cobra and the tiny dust-coloured krait being the most dangerous, causing thousands of deaths annually. Insects are incredibly numerous, only a few, such as the bee, the silkworm and the lac-insect, being useful.

The population of India may be roughly placed in five groups: (1) The descendants of the earliest known inhabitants of India, sometimes called Dravidians, who are represented by the savage Bhils and Gonds of central and western India, and by the Tamils of the south. (2) The pure-blood descendants of the successive tides of Aryan invaders who conquered the Dravidian inhabitants and who are best represented by the Rajputs. (3) The great mass of Hindus formed by a mixture of the two preceding types. (4) The descendants of the Mahomedan invaders from Persia in the 7th century, now composing the people of Pakistan. (5) The Mongol

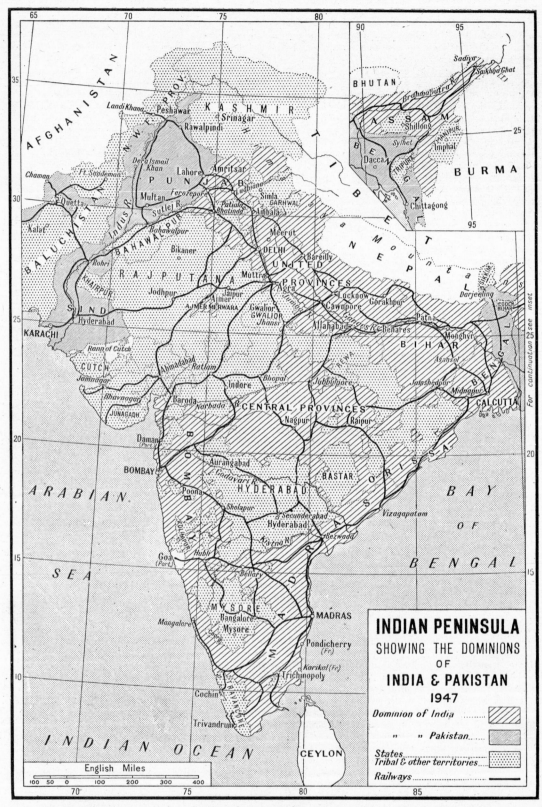

INDIAN PENINSULA
SHOWING THE DOMINIONS
OF
INDIA & PAKISTAN
1947

Dominion of India ....

" " Pakistan ....

States ....
Tribal & other territories ....
Railways ....

The independent States are here shown as they were before their accession to either India or Pakistan.

However, it is not so much linguistic or racial differences which divide the people of India as differences of religion. The chief religions are Hindu, Mahomedan, Buddhist, Sikh, Jain, Christian and Parsee. Next to the crude beliefs of the primitive hill peoples, who see gods in rocks and trees, Hinduism is the oldest religion and includes in its numerous sects more than 270 million persons, about 70 per cent of the total population. Hinduism has many forms, all of which are marked by a belief in many gods and in universal reincarnation. The Sikhs form a religious community whose history dates back to the 16th century. Their faith is a curious mixture of Mahomedanism and Hinduism, great stress being laid on the ethical side, and for a time they constituted a powerful and formidable military brotherhood. At the last census, in 1941, the Sikhs numbered 5,700,000.

The Jains tend to combine the Buddhist and Hindu religions. There are about 1,500,000 Jains, and among them are many of the richest and most influential of Indian merchants. Their temples which include the famous ones on Mount Abu, are the finest in all India. The Buddhists, once exceedingly powerful in the land, have virtually disappeared from India.

By far the largest and most influential group after the Hindus are the Moslems or Mahomedans. There has always been hostility between Moslem and Hindu in India, and this reached such a pitch when after the Second World War (1939–45) the form of India's self-government was being decided that a joint government was impossible, and no

E. Watts

INDIAN BATH
Among the Hindus personal cleanliness is considered of the greatest importance, and the mother sees that her children have a daily bath. There are no bathrooms in the villages, so washing takes place in the open.

or Tibetan types, found chiefly in the extreme north-east and in the Himalayan border regions.

The people of Dravidian stock are short and dark, with curly or wavy hair and broad noses. In contrast, the Rajputs are tall, slender and handsome. Many Indians have settled overseas. There are three-quarters of a million in Ceylon and almost as many in Malaya; 270,000 in Mauritius, and over 100,000 in Trinidad, British Guiana, Fiji, and East Africa.

The many languages of India can be generally divided into those derived from the ancient Sanskrit and those from the early Dravidian tongues, with a mixture of Malayan and Chinese elements. In the north the common dialect is Hindustani or Urdu, a blend of Persian with the Hindi language. In the south Telugu and Tamil, both Dravidian tongues, are spoken.

D. Leigh

SACRED COW ON A CITY PAVEMENT
Considered holy by the Hindus, cows are allowed to come and go as they wish, even in the cities, where they help themselves freely to fruit and vegetables from the greengrocers' stalls. They lie on the pavements (above) and even on the tram lines, no one daring to move them. Hindus neither eat beef nor drink milk and will not kill a cow, no matter how diseased or feeble the animal may be.

PAGEANTRY AND PRIMITIVE LIFE SIDE BY SIDE

At Srinagar, capital of the State of Kashmir, the river Jhelum is spanned by several primitive wooden bridges, one of which is seen in the lower photograph. In the foreground is a fishing-boat of the type used by the riverside folk for hundreds of years. Kashmir is noted for its beautiful scenery, and normally is used as a summer resort by people who can escape from the plains of the sub-continent of India. Though most of the Kashmiris are Mahomedans, the ruler is a Hindu. In the top photograph the Maharajah of Gwalior is passing through the merchants' quarter of Lashkar, the capital of the State, riding on an elephant and attended by his retinue. Gwalior, which became a part of the Dominion of India in August 1947 when British India was divided into the Dominions of India and Pakistan, has an area of 26,000 square miles and a population of four millions.

FIGURES OF THE ROADSIDE IN PICTURESQUE INDIA

W. Stokes; Dorien Leigh

Life on the great highways in the sub-continent of India was vividly described in Rudyard Kipling's book entitled Kim, and it is still much the same. In the lower photograph a member of a band of wandering entertainers carries around with him four weaver birds which he has taught to do simple tricks. Top left, a peasant at a roadside well in Rajputana is filling his waterskins and loading them on his donkey. Top right, a workman in the Lakoi bazaar, Simla, shapes rolling-pins out of blocks of wood, steadying with his feet the tool he holds in his left hand.

DEVOUT MAHOMEDANS AT DELHI'S GREAT MOSQUE

Fox

In Old Delhi is the Jama Masjid, or Great Mosque, which is one of the finest buildings of its kind in the sub-continent. Built in the middle of the 17th century, the domes are of white marble, and in front of the edifice is a courtyard 450 feet square, which is crowded with worshippers during Mahomedan festivals (above), when thousands cannot be accommodated in the mosque itself. There are about 90 million Mahomedans in All-India, most of them living in the Dominion of Pakistan. Other important religious sects are the Sikhs, Jains, Christians, Parsees and Hindus.

GIGANTIC BULL REPRESENTING THE GOD SIVA
Carved from stone, this enormous bull is not far from the city of Mysore in the south of the republic of India. Devotees worship the beast because it is a representative of the god Siva, the supreme deity of the Sivaite sect of Hinduism. There are some 270 million Hindus in the sub-continent, worshipping many different gods but all accepting the caste system.

alternative was found to the creation of a separate Mahomedan state, now called Pakistan.

The Parsees are descendants of Persian Zoroastrians—fire and sun worshippers, who fled to India to escape the Mahomedan massacres of the 7th century. They form now a rich merchant class of great power in the Bombay area, though they number only just over 114,000.

The Christians of India total over six millions, the Roman Catholics being far the most numerous.

The followers of Hinduism are grouped into numerous castes which are half social, half religious. The caste system had its foundation in the old Aryan law, which divided the people into four classes—the priests or Brahmans, the warriors or Kshatriyas, the farmers or Vaisyas, and the labourers or Sudras. These four castes have been subdivided again and again until it is almost impossible to tell the number of separate castes. Estimates vary between 2,000 and 3,000 distinct groups. The members of each handicraft tend to form separate castes which amount to trade guilds or unions.

The restrictions which surround members of a caste are innumerable. Generally speaking, a person may not marry outside his caste, nor may he touch or associate with a member of a lower caste. Caste offences are judged by a tribunal.

Lower yet than the Sudras are the Harijans or scheduled castes—a mass of nearly 50 million people, one-eighth of all the population of India. These so-called "untouchables" were formerly not allowed to use public roads, bridges and temples. They were forced to live outside villages and were permitted to follow only such despised occupations as street-sweeping and leather-working.

At the dawn of history India was already famous for its wealth, its gold and silver and precious stones, its fine silks, its spices and drugs and rare woods. Treasures from India reached the ancient courts of Assyria and Egypt. Today India's wealth is not reckoned in gold or precious stones, but in the products of the fields and factories and steelworks. Agriculture is the most important industry, two-thirds of the population living by farming, forestry, and stock-raising.

The millet grains form the chief crop, for these hardy, drought-resisting, and prolific cereals are the staple food of the lower classes. Next in importance are rice (particularly in the south), wheat, and pulses (lentils, chick-peas, and others).

Oil-seeds and oil-producing plants, such as linseed, rape, mustard, sesamum, ground-nuts, and castor-oil plants are extensively grown; the Indians use vast quantities of oil for cooking, for burning in their primitive lamps, and for anointing themselves, and large quantities are exported.

Cotton is one of India's most valuable products. Other crops of importance are barley, jute, sugar-cane, indigo, tea, and tobacco.

It is estimated that there are more cattle in India than in any other part of the world, but they are a hump-backed species of inferior quality, and since the religion of Hindus forbids eating meat, the animals are chiefly used for draught purposes. Half-tamed buffaloes are also employed in many regions for farm work, as are camels in the north-west, particularly in the Indus valley.

The principal minerals found in the sub-continent are coal, iron, manganese, mica, nickel, aluminium ore, tungsten, chromite and salt. Tex-tiles are the chief products; but with the rapid development of the iron and steel industry, the manufacture of all kinds of machinery has increased. Other leading industries are sugar refineries and oil mills, tanneries, paper mills and tobacco factories.

There are about 40,000 miles of railway in opera-tion, consisting of broad-gauge lines connecting the large towns, and of a network of narrow-gauge tracks. There are regular air services with Europe and various parts of the Far East.

INDIAN CONTRIBUTIONS *to* CULTURE

There is a distinctive character about the artistic and literary products of the sub-continent of India which is easy to recognize. The word India here is to be taken as meaning the entire country.

India: ARTS AND LETTERS. As one might expect of a land whose peoples have for so many centuries been highly civilized, the art and archi-tecture of India contain many memorials of the most impressive size and the highest artistic merit. Some of the earliest are small figures of gods and goddesses which date from 3000 B.C.; the 3rd century B.C. gives us many fine religious monu-ments; and from then until recent times an almost unbroken succession can be noted.

A feature of the early architecture of Buddhist and Jainist times is the *tope*, or *stupa*. This was originally a simple funeral mound, which came to be developed, with walls and all manner of carved erections, gateways and avenues, into almost a museum of contemporary art and, especially, sculpture. The *tope* at Sanchi in the state of Bhopal is one of the finest of such works. One of the most important events in Indian history was the invasion of that great country by the Macedonian king Alexander the Great in 326 B.C., and this has left a permanent mark in the Graeco-Buddhist sculpture of which many remains have been dis-covered. The greatest school of art is the Gandhara, which flourished in north-west India. Much of its finest work dates from the 1st century B.C. and the 1st A.D., from which period, too, date some of the amazing rock-cut shrines and monasteries. A number of these are lined with pillars and intricate sculptures hewn from the solid walls. After them came the Gupta period (320–600) with monuments alike of Buddhist and Hindu art in brick and stone. Some of these are weird to western eyes, and have a beauty relying on forms completely foreign to those devised in any other part of the world. At this time, too, the famous Ajanta cave-temples in Hyderabad were excavated, as remarkable for the paintings which adorn their walls as for their sculpture. Throughout all its long development, Indian architecture, and the sculpture and painting which went with it, grew more compli-cated.

From the 10th to the 13th centuries, Mahomedan armies were invading India, and in the northern part especially they have left their mark. Among the peoples whom they drove from their original homes were the Raj-puts. To the Rajputs we owe the lovely miniature paintings which are India's chief contribution to illustrative art. The finest were done in the 17th and 18th centuries; and in those times, too, much very fine wood-carving and metal-work was carried out. Moreover, their

British Museum; photo, Mansell

GREEK INFLUENCE IN INDIAN SCULPTURE
Showing Buddha being attacked and tempted by the prince of demons, Mara, this relief is a typical example of the Graeco-Buddhist sculpture of the Gandhara school, which flourished in north-west India after the invasion by Alexander the Great in 326 B.C. Greek influence is noticeable in the clothing, especially, and in the posing of the figures, and the whole work is simpler in character than a purely Oriental sculpture.

INDIAN ART IN STONE AND STUCCO

F. Deaville Walker

The most famous and perfect of all ancient Buddhist monuments is the great ' tope,' or temple mound, at Sanchi in the former State of Bhopal, republic of India, dating from the 2nd century B.C.   Above is one of the four superb stone gateways, ornamented with marvellous carvings illustrating the story of the Buddha's life.

ROCK TEMPLES CARVED BY LONG-DEAD HANDS

At Karli in the Western Ghats is a great Buddhist temple (lower), entirely hewn from the solid rock and still with its original teak roof. Much of the work dates from the beginning of the Christian era or even earlier. The Hindu temple (upper). with a very intricate exterior. is in Orissa, a province of the Indian republic, and belongs to the 9th century

A MODERN MARVEL OF INDIAN ARCHITECTURE

One of the loveliest and most impressive buildings in the whole sub-continent, this 'Hall of the Winds' at Jaipur in Rajputana is faced with pink and white stucco. It was built during the 18th century, and thus is a comparatively recent example of Indian architecture, showing well how the native manner continued to thrive in later times.

K. de B Codrington: Indian State Railways; British Museum

The cave-temples at Ajanta in Hyderabad are as remarkable for their paintings as for their sculpture. Examples are seen in the two lower photographs : left, a lady at her toilet ; right, a hunting scene, showing the Mogul Emperor Akbar (1542–1605). At Konarak, Orissa, is the finest of all Indian animal sculptures—a huge 11th-century War Horse (upper).

truly Indian style still exists, for all over the great country there are to be found traditional workers in metal and stone, who, when European influence is not at work, still build and decorate their temples in the same manner as has been used for hundreds of years. This Rajput tradition has survived especially in southern India, while in Bengal efforts have been made to preserve an Indian pictorial art which shall be entirely free from western influences.

To the Mahomedans, however, India does owe one of its greatest periods, both in architecture and in painting, and that is the period of the Mogul emperors. It was one of them, Shah Jehan, who had erected in the 17th century India's most glorious building of all, considered by many people to be the loveliest in the world—the magnificent Taj Mahal (q.v.) at Agra.

There has always been a vast production in India of the art of the people, the instinctive art of the village potter, the weaver and maker of coloured textiles. In many of them there is a great beauty as that in the more highly organized work. Moreover, Indian art extends far outside its own country, all over the East Indies and through the adjoining lands. In Ceylon, Siam, Indo-China and Burma, the architecture especially is much the same as that found in the sub-continent.

The earliest Hindu literature consists of the Vedic hymns, of which the Rig-

International News Photos

ROYAL ASTRONOMER'S OBSERVATORY, DELHI
Outside Delhi is this observatory dating from about A.D. 1725. It was built by the famous royal astronomer Maharajah Jai Singh, ruler of Jaipur. The photograph was taken from the top of an enormous sundial. The two circular buildings, with pillars in their centres, were used for measuring the ascension and declination of the stars. These huge instruments indicate an astronomical knowledge of high degree.

Musée Guimet; photo Giraudon

SIVA DANCING : AN INDIAN BRONZE
The great god Siva, in one or other of his numerous forms, is the most popular of all subjects for Indian artists, and here he is seen dancing on the body of the demon Tripoura-Soura. The movement and liveliness of this lovely bronze figure make realistic the four-armed form of the Hindu god.

Veda, written about 1500 B.C., is the oldest collection. This consists of 1,017 short poems, giving a definite picture of a high civilization existing about the time the Aryan invaders had reached the banks of the Indus and were fighting the dark people of the south. To the Vedic poems were attached prose works called Brahmanas, explaining the duties of the priests; then were added the Sutras, telling of laws and ceremonies; and later the Upanishads, treating of God and the soul; the Aranyakas, giving directions for leading a holy life; and finally the Puranas, or sacred traditions.

During the period from the 1st to the 8th century of the Christian era were composed a number of Sanskrit epics, and dramas filled with adventure and romance. The old Hindu fables of animals, which were translated into the Persian as early as the 6th century and so found their way into Europe, are said to be the basis of many of the familiar nursery stories that have charmed the children of England and other lands.

Under the influence of modern education, many Hindu writers are developing a new and interesting national literature. Most distinguished among these was Sir Rabindranath Tagore (1861–1941), who attempted to embody in his poems, tales, parables and dramas the advanced ideas of European civilization, while keeping the best traditions of ancient Hindu idealism. In 1913 this eminent Hindu writer was awarded the Nobel prize for literature, and in 1915 he was knighted, but later renounced this honour for political reasons. Among his well-known works are The Crescent Moon: Child Poems; The Gardener; Gora, a novel; and The Religion of Man.

Indian music is strange to Western ears in that it contains no harmony. It is made up of melody and rhythm only. There is no accompaniment to the melody as in Western music. No two different tones are sounded at the same time. It is seldom that several instruments are used together, and when they are they play in unison. Songs, which are of the greatest importance in Indian life, are sung in unison also. Among instruments, drums and flutes are favoured. There are also many varieties of stringed instruments, some of ancient origin.

Centuries ago Hindu astronomers and mathematicians were highly honoured, and contributed an important share to the development of knowledge. They exchanged ideas with the Greeks at the time of Alexander's conquest, and in the 9th century important Hindu scientific works were translated by the Arabs and so reached Europe, but with the advent of the Mahomedans science declined, and it has remained for the universities of Calcutta, Madras, Bombay, Allahabad, the Punjab, Patna, Nagpur, Andhra, Agra, Rangoon, Lucknow, Dacca, Annamalai and Delhi, and their large number of affiliated colleges to bring back the traditional love of learning to the Indian youth. There is a Hindu University at Benares, the first private and sectarian university to be established by law in India, and a Mahomedan University at Aligarh. (See also the separate articles on the sub-continent's chief states and cities).

INDIA'S LONG and TROUBLOUS HISTORY

The history of all-India is largely a chronicle of invasions, from those of the Aryans of antiquity to those of more recent times. British guidance led the peoples of the sub-continent at length to self-government.

India, HISTORY OF. The early history of India is merely tradition. The Hindu poem called the Rig-Veda, written about 1500 B.C., tells of the old struggle between the Aryan invaders and the " black people " who were in possession of the soil. By the 6th century B.C. 16 Aryan states had been established south of the Himalayas, and Brahmanism was flourishing, In 327 B.C. the armies of Alexander the Great reached the Hydaspes (Jhelum) river, and the Greek settlements he left behind made a profound impression upon the art and literature of the country. The next 1300 years were marked by a succession of bitter struggles for power between the Indian princes, and by a succession of invasions.

The first attacks of the Mahomedans were repelled, but in the 11th century the Turkish leader Mahmud established the Ghazni dynasty in the land. The great Mongol invasion of Genghis Khan followed in 1219, and in 1397 Tamerlane's Tartar hordes poured into India. In 1526 Babar, who was a descendant of Genghis Khan as well as of Tamerlanc, seized the throne at Delhi, establishing the great Mogul empire, which remained intact until the close of the 18th century.

The south of India was never completely conquered, but the empire of the north, under such rulers as Akbar and Shah Jehan, was perhaps the most brilliant in the history of the Orient. During the reign of Aurungzebe (1618–1707), the last of the great Mogul emperors, the Mahratta nation, from west and central India, became very powerful and gradually undermined Mogul rule.

Advent of the East India Company

Meanwhile, the struggle between Europeans for supremacy in Indian affairs had begun. With Vasco da Gama's discovery of the ocean route around the Cape of Good Hope in 1498 there began a race for the rich Indian trade between Portugal, the Netherlands and France. In 1600 the English East India Company joined in the rivalry, and soon had trading posts at Madras, Bombay and Calcutta (then called Fort William). The history of India from that time forward dealt largely with the long commercial struggles of these European rivals. The French enlisted native troops, and interfered so successfully in native quarrels that by 1751 the regions of the Carnatic and the Deccan were under French influence.

At the moment when British influence was threatened with extinction in India, the genius of Robert Clive (1725–74) turned the tables. His storming and successful holding of Arcot in 1751, and then his victory at Plassey in 1757, overthrew the French power and laid the foundations of the rule of the East India Company (see Clive, Robert). Later, trading rights gradually grew into political domination. It was one of the strangest conquests in history, this by which a private trading company conquered an empire by the use chiefly of native soldiers (sepoys) raised in that land itself.

Expansion under Warren Hastings

Warren Hastings (1732–1818), who became Governor-General for the East India Company in 1774, built soundly upon the foundation Clive had laid. He subdued the Mahratta princes and crushed the famous Haider Ali, sultan of Mysore (see Hastings, Warren). In the next 30 years the rule of the Company was extended over a great part of India. Between 1848 and 1856 the Sikhs were defeated and the Punjab was annexed.

But certain high-handed methods employed by the Company stirred up a wave of unrest. In 1857 a rumour was circulated among the native troops enlisted under the British flag that the cartridge papers, which the soldiers must tear with their teeth, were greased with the fat of cows and pigs— the former held sacred by the Hindus, and the latter abhorred by the Mahomedans. This rumour set fire to the tinder of discontent, the great Indian Mutiny of 1857 being the result. The insurrection spread rapidly in the north. Nana Sahib, a Mahratta prince, besieged a British force in Cawnpore and, after promising safe conduct, treacherously massacred his prisoners, including women and children. Another British force was besieged in Lucknow, but after the commander, Sir Henry Lawrence, and many others had been killed, the survivors were rescued. Not until Delhi was captured in September 1857 was the mutiny crushed.

This tragic outbreak put an end to the political rule of the Company, and in 1858 its rights of government were transferred to the crown. From then on greater respect was shown to the religious and other susceptibilities of the people, and about two-fifths of India was left to its native princes. In 1877, under the viceroyalty of Lord Lytton, Queen Victoria was proclaimed Empress of India.

Benefits of British Rule

British rule brought not only the great gift of peace but factories, railways, hospitals, police, Western justice, modernized cities, irrigation systems, schools and universities, and brisk trade. At the beginning of the 20th century the movement for independence from British rule came into prominence. The conflict between the two races was greatly intensified after the First World War (1914–18). During the war, India loyally sent money and men to the aid of Britain. These men returned with a new sense of the importance of India to the Empire, and demanded a larger share in the government. The Act of 1919 promised it to them. India signed the peace treaty and was made an independent member of the League of Nations. But the Indians were not satisfied, and the demand for home rule was intensified.

In a rebellion against British domination and Western civilization, the strange ascetic, Mohandas Gandhi (1869–1948) initiated the Swaraj, or Home Rule, movement (see Gandhi). He urged peaceful methods of opposition by non-co-operation, and passive resistance to the British, and tried to end the cruel caste system, and the hatred between Maho-

medans and Hindus, so that India might present a united front against everything British. But another faction of Swaraj urged violence, and, by propaganda and terrorism in Bengal and in the Central Provinces, almost succeeded in destroying all respect for law and order. Only strong disciplinary measures, imposed by the government, restored the situation.

At the same time Communism was gaining ground, and the country was more and more torn by the religious feuds between Hindus and Moslems. Conditions became so bad that in accordance with the act of 1919 the government of 1927 appointed a commission to inquire into the advisability of altering the constitution, and to investigate all phases of the government of British India. But there were no Indian representatives on this commission, and Indian Nationalists were enraged. Opposition by the Indian National Congress increased, and the campaign of what Gandhi called "non-violent civil disobedience" continued with greater intensity than ever.

Gandhi's Demand for Dominion Status

In March 1930 Gandhi demanded immediate Dominion status for India, and when it was not granted he inaugurated his Salt Rebellion, attacking the government monopoly of salt production as typifying unjust oppression. As before, he stressed his policy of non-violence, but without avail. Rioting broke out afresh and Gandhi and his associates in the campaign were imprisoned.

The report of the Royal commission of 1927, made public in June 1930, outlined a new constitutional organization for British India on the basis of a federation of self-governing provinces. With the exception of Burma, which was to develop separately towards self-government, all the prov-

ENGLAND'S FIRST AMBASSADOR TO INDIA

The foundations of British supremacy in India were laid by Sir Thomas Roe, who was sent in 1614 on an embassy to the Court of the Mogul Emperor, Jehangir (1569-1627) by the East India Company. After a six months' voyage round the Cape of Good Hope, Roe arrived in September 1614, and remained at the Court of the Emperor for a year, during which time he concluded a commercial treaty and arranged for a continuation of the existing concessions to English merchants. This picture by Sir William Rothenstein (1872-1945) shows Sir Thomas Roe before the Great Mogul.

inces were included in this proposed system. A so-called " round-table conference " of British and Indian leaders to consider the details of such a scheme met in London in November 1930. But the Nationalists of India refused to participate and there was disagreement between Moslem and Hindu delegates. As a result the conference was not successful; but an outline for a new constitution was drafted.

After a series of conversations, Gandhi agreed that the India National Congress would discontinue the passive resistance campaign and take part in a second conference in 1931. Gandhi himself went to the conference, but negotiations again failed because of the irreconcilable positions taken up by Hindus, Moslems, and other religious groups, who could not be persuaded to agree on a common plan. The Prime Minister of the day, Mr. Ramsay Mac-Donald, insisted that no constitution could be framed until after a Hindu-Moslem agreement was reached. The failure of the conference was the signal for a renewed outbreak of civil disorder in India. Early in 1932 Gandhi and many other leaders were imprisoned and the Indian government took vigorous steps to repress demonstrations.

Under these inauspicious circumstances a third round-table conference was held, as a result of which a constitution was made ready for sub-mission to Parliament in 1933. This constitution was accepted by the British Parliament in 1935 and came into force on April 1, 1937.

The constitution of 1935 provided for the feder-ation of 11 self-governing Governor's Provinces and five Chief Commissioner's Provinces in British India and the numerous native Indian states. Burma was not included in the federation but had a separate government (*see* Burma). Under the Constitution the Governor-General, known as the Viceroy, appointed by the British Government, exercised the chief executive authority on behalf

of the King-Emperor with special responsibilities. He was assisted by an advisory Council of Ministers, responsible to the Federal Legislature. The Legis-lature consisted of two chambers. The members were chosen chiefly by the provincial legislatures and by the rulers of the native states, a small number being appointed directly by the Governor-General. Each province had a local governor and a legis-lature elected by the population, though only a few were entitled to vote. The native states were ruled by native princes, but were subject in certain respects to Britain.

Moslem Demand for Partition

With the coming of the Second World War (1939–45) Indian demands for complete self-government increased in vehemence; and a new element became evident when in 1940 the Moslem League under its leader Mahomed Ali Jinnah demanded the partition of India to create an independent Mahomedan state. This introduced a stumbling-block that made agreement among the Indian leaders impossible. A British Cabinet mission which visited India in 1942, under Sir Stafford Cripps's leadership, with the object of getting Indian leaders to agree to a plan for self-government, returned with nothing accomplished.

Meanwhile India loyally supported the British cause in the war; and though an Indian National Army was formed to fight on the Japanese side, it was a tiny and futile organization compared with the great Indian fighting machine which withstood the enemies of Britain in East Africa, in North Africa, Italy, and Burma. By 1942 loyal Indian forces totalled a million men.

When peace came the question of self-government was at once reopened. The insistence of the Moslems on their own state of Pakistan (*q.v.*), a demand they backed up with non-co-operation and deeds of violence, reduced to virtually nothing the hope of Britain's handing over power to a responsible Indian government composed of both Hindu and Mahomedan representatives. Elections were held in 1945 for a new Central Legislature, but the Moslems who provided 30 of the 102 members of the Con-stituent Assembly refused to take part in its activities. A second British Cabinet mission went to India in April 1946 and a temporary govern-ment was established, charged with the task of devising some form of self-government which should be acceptable to the whole Indian community. But Mahomedan insistence on an independent realm (Pakistan) foredoomed the plans to failure.

In August 1946 fighting broke out between Mahomedans and Hindus in localities where the Hindus were in the minority. Many hundreds of Hindus in predominantly Mahomedan areas were massacred and their homes pillaged and burnt. This fresh outbreak of religious persecution increased the tension throughout India.

Despairing of finding a solution to the question on the lines pursued hitherto, Britain's Prime Minister, Mr. Attlee, took the extreme step in February 1947 of announcing that the British would quit India by June 1947, whether or not a responsible Indian government had been formed to take over the country's administration. Viscount Mountbatten (*q.v.*), succeeding Lord Wavell as Viceroy, held almost daily meetings with Gandhi

JINNAH, FOUNDER OF PAKISTAN
Leader of the movement for the creation of an independent Mahomedan State in India, Mahomed Ali Jinnah (above, seated nearest camera) became the first Governor-General of the Mahomedan Dominion of Pakistan in 1947.

and Jinnah, and it became clear that nothing could prevent the creation of a Mahomedan state in India. Mahatma (" great soul ") Mohandas Gandhi was not alone in foreseeing the wave of bloodshed that would surely follow such a decision ; but with the Mahomedans and Hindus equally obstinate, bloodshed seemed inevitable, whatever course was followed. So in June 1947 the Indian Independence Bill was introduced into the British House of Commons, setting the date of August 15, 1947, for the creation of the two new Dominions of India and Pakistan. Dominion status, previously refused by all Indian parties, was accepted as a temporary measure while new constitutions were worked out, both countries being free to secede from the British Empire later. Viscount Mountbatten, now created an Earl, became the first Governor-General of the Indian Dominion, with

JAWARHARLAL NEHRU
When the Dominion of India was formed in 1947 Nehru, who had been Gandhi's chief supporter, became Prime Minister. He is seen holding the flag of the new State.

In January 1948 the man who above all others had striven so desperately for a peaceful solution to the difficulties was struck down : on his way to a prayer meeting Gandhi was shot and killed by a Hindu extremist.

While still in the first uneasy stages of self-rule, the Dominion of India declared itself to be, in January 1950, a republic within the British Commonwealth—a " sovereign democratic republic" —a Union of States. Consisting of 27 states and the territories of the Andaman and Nicobar Islands, the Indian Union, with an area of 1,246,880 square miles and a population of 342,105,000, had as its first president Dr. Rajendra Prasad, Jawarharlal Nehru remaining Prime Minister.

The President holds office for five years, but is eligible for re-election. He is aided and advised by a Council of Ministers, who hold office during his

Pandit (" learned man ") Jawarharlal Nehru, who had been Gandhi's chief supporter during India's struggle for independence, as Prime Minister. The post of Governor-General in Pakistan was filled by Mahomed Ali Jinnah, who died on September 11, 1948, Kwaja Nizamuddin succeeding him.

The task of partition proved almost impossibly difficult. Pakistan's boundaries passed through the middle of the Punjab and of Bengal; and since the representatives of India and of Pakistan could agree on nothing, the British chairman of the Boundary Commission, Sir Cyril Radcliffe, had to decide every difficult point personally. The armed forces were divided under the supervision of Field-Marshal Auchinleck. British generals were appointed by both new dominions to command their armies.

Tragic Results of Political Enmity

As Independence Day approached the rioting between Mahomedans and Hindus reached new heights of savagery. The Sikhs, embittered by the failure of the partition plan to meet what they felt to be their just claims, fell upon defenceless villages and streams of refugees, fleeing to the safety of regions where they would be among their own people. Everywhere Hindus and Mahomedans were on the move, desperately trying to reach the regions where they would be among co-religionists. By the end of September 1947, when the orgy of killing began to die down, the number of victims was put at no fewer than 15,000, and possibly twice that figure. At least four million (some said eight) had taken part in these migrations.

The " native states " which had not been included in the measures set down in the Indian Independence Bill, mostly joined together in federations which adhered to one or other of the new Dominions. But in Kashmir, where a Hindu ruler governed a mainly Mahomedan population, fighting broke out and brought the two dominions perilously near to war, until the dispute was referred to the United Nations.

pleasure. The Union Parliament consists of the President and two Houses, known as the Council of States and the House of the People. The Council of States consists of not more than 250 members. The House of the People consists of not more than 500 members. The flag of the Indian Union is coloured saffron, white and dark green.

Pakistan is dealt with under its own heading.

Indiana. Occupying what is, in many respects, the most prosperous portion of the United States, this north-eastern state lies south of Lake Michigan, on which it has about 50 miles of coast, with the state of Ohio to the east, Illinois to the west, and Kentucky forming the southern boundary. It has an area of 36,291 square miles. The surface is mainly undulating plain, and most of Indiana is drained by the Wabash and Ohio rivers.

Level land, rich soil and a favourable climate have made the state an ideal region for farming. Maize is the most important crop, but wheat, oats, rye, tobacco, soya beans, potatoes, onions, tomatoes and fruit are also grown. Stock raising and diary farming are carried on. But Indiana is predominantly a manufacturing state, the lake ports and the steel work of Gary, East Chicago, Hammond and Whiting constituting one of the world's greatest industrial centres.

Mineral resources include coal, limestone and natural gas. Amongst the manufactured products are refrigerators, wireless sets, machinery, cement and furniture. There are oil refineries, machine shops, railway works, meat-packing plants and flour-mills. The capital of the state is Indianapolis, with a population of 386,972; it is a " planned " city, set in the exact geographical centre of the state.

French traders reached Indiana early in the 18th century; at their post of Vincennes, established about 1732, grew up the first permanent settlement, Indiana became a state of the Union in 1816. The population is 3,427,796.

Indian Ocean. Two thousand years ago, when mariners of western Europe were still venturing only on short voyages along the Atlantic coast, the Indian Ocean could already boast established trade routes, and Egyptian Greeks boldly sailed across the open sea between Arabia and Hindustan though they had neither chart nor compass. They knew they had nothing to fear if they avoided the hurricane months from December to April, for they had observed that the monsoon winds blow nearly half the year from the north-east, and the rest of the year from the opposite direction.

Washing the shores of Asia in the north, Africa on the west, and the East Indian islands, Australia, and Tasmania on the east, the Indian Ocean is the third largest of the oceans.

Its length from north to south is somewhat over 6,500 miles, its breadth 4,000 to 6,000 miles, and its area about 28,000,000 square miles. The average depth is over 2,000 fathoms, the deepest sounding so far being 20,340 feet off the south-east coast of Java.

At Cape Comorin, the southern tip of the sub-continent of India, the Indian Ocean meets the Bay of Bengal on the east and the Arabian Sea on the west, the latter branching again into the Persian Gulf. Beyond the Arabian peninsula it connects with the Red Sea. From Asia several great rivers enter it—the Ganges, the Brahmaputra, the Irrawaddy and the Indus; and from Africa the Zambezi and the Limpopo. Its largest islands are Madagascar, Sumatra, Java, Borneo and Ceylon, the rest being mostly groups of small islands.

India Office. Until the Indian Mutiny of 1857, India was governed from London by the Honourable East India Company, the Governor-General and all his subordinates being appointed by the Company, which also controlled the Indian Army. After the Mutiny the control of the government was transferred to the British Crown, the India Office being established in 1858, as a department of the British Civil Service under a Secretary of State. The Indian Office was responsible for all such business connected with Indian public affairs as was transacted in Great Britain.

In 1919 a High Commissioner for India was appointed by the Indian Government, his functions being to take over from the India Office such functions as the payment of Indian officials in England, the education and welfare of Indian students abroad, and the handling of all commercial matters. The India Office remained the channel of communication between the British and Indian governments, and the Secretary of State continued to be the agent of the British Crown. Upon the granting of Dominion status to India and Pakistan in 1947, the India Office was abolished.

Mme. Vassal

INDO-CHINESE ARCHERS

The Mois are a tribe of Indo-China who lead a nomadic life and get their food by hunting. This small boy is having a lesson in shooting with a bow and arrow, so that later on he may do his share in providing the family's dinner.

Indigo. For centuries the much prized blue dye called indigo was obtained exclusively from the indigo plant, and the indigo trade with India and other centres of production was flourishing and prosperous. This natural indigo trade has dwindled to a fraction of its former importance following the discovery of ways to make artificial indigo.

The story of artificial indigo is one of the most interesting in the history of chemistry. It took 17 years of tireless experiment and the expenditure of a vast sum of money to perfect the process. As early as 1880, a German chemist, Adolph von Baeyer, produced synthetic indigo from coal-tar products, but the cost of production was much greater than that of the natural dye. From then until 1897 he and others worked on the problem of making indigo by less expensive processes, finally succeeding in producing it at less than half the cost of the plant dye.

Vegetable indigo is obtained from a shrubby plant 3 to 5 feet high, with rounded leaves and pale red flowers, belonging to the bean family. When three months old and in blossom, the plants are cut down, but soon shoot up again, and yield a second and often a third cutting in one year. The cut stems and leaves are crushed and soaked in water for several hours. Fermentation takes place with the formation of a sugar (glucose), and of a substance called indoxyl. Then the water, which is clear yellow, is run off into another vat and stirred, when atmospheric oxidation of the indoxyl produces a precipitate of indigo.

The best quality comes from Bengal. Indigo plants are also grown in Java, China, Ceylon, Mexico, Brazil and Central America. The scientific name of the plant is *Indigofera tinctoria*.

Indo-China. The name Indo-China suggests a mingling of India and China. And that, in fact, is what Indo-China is. Almost from the beginnings of civilization the south-eastern peninsula of Asia has been a meeting ground for Hindus and Chinese. " Farther India " it used to be called, but the name Indo-China is better.

Several mountain ranges which slope south-east from the Himalayas make Indo-China a bridge between these two vast regions. One of these ranges extends like a long tendril as the Malay Peninsula. Others divide the land into valleys, with deltas at the river mouths.

Protected by these mountains, the valley peoples escaped conquest by their great neighbours. But they did receive a constant trickle of population, particularly from China. And from both neighbours they took their arts and industries. Hence today we find the Hindu temple near the Chinese pagoda, Chinese ploughs used to cultivate rice by Indian methods, and other minglings of Hindu and Chinese.

The peninsula lies inside the tropics and has a monsoon climate. But its range of altitude—from sea level to mountain heights—gives a wide variety of temperature, rainfall, and plant life. Tropical trees and plants flourish in the hot, rain-drenched southern coastal regions and the flooded river plains. Yet some inland regions are virtual deserts. The high hills and mountains have frosts.

In normal times the region is the world's largest exporter of rice, its chief source of tin and rubber, and a rich source of petroleum. Untapped mineral deposits and forests await development. Most of the people are still rooted to the land as peasant farmers.

The people are as varied as the land. The chief groups are the Burmese, Siamese, Malays, Annamese, and Cambodians, with smaller numbers of Shans, Chins, and Kachins. Immigration has brought large numbers of Chinese and Indians.

GIRL OF INDO-CHINA
Four-fifths of the inhabitants of Indo-China are Annamese. Indoors the women wear this costume of loose trousers and a square bodice that leaves the back and arms bare.

Important trade cities have a sprinkling of Europeans. Until European nations took possession of most of the peninsula during the 19th century it was divided into several small kingdoms.

Today it consists of what until recently was known as French Indo-China, Burma (q.v.), Malaya (q.v.) and Siam (q.v.). Together these countries have a total area of about 790,000 square miles and a population of about 57 million. Thus Indo-China is nearly half as large as the subcontinent of India but it has less than a sixth of the population.

What was formerly French Indo-China now comprises a federation of independent territories within the framework of the French Union. This federation consists of the State of Viet-Nam, which was established in 1946, and the kingdoms of Cambodia (q.v.) and Laos. Viet-Nam consists of the former protectorates of northern Annam, Tonking, and Cochin-China. The area of this Federation of Indo-China is about 286,000 square miles, and the population is over 26½ million.

Tonking's chief crop is rice, followed by maize, arrowroot, sugar-cane, coffee, tea ; a

INDO-CHINA: ON THE BANKS OF THE SAIGON
On the Saigon river, about 35 miles from the South China Sea, Saigon is the chief town and port of Cochin-China (Viet-Nam). The town, which has 695,000 inhabitants, is well laid out, with town hall, cathedral, theatre, and shops and houses in European style. But by the banks of the river living quarters are squalid, with rickety dwellings raised on piles to avoid the floods, in striking contrast to the prosperous shopping centre. There is a large harbour.

large quantity of raw silk is produced; and there are rich tin mines. Tonking's exports include coal and iron. Its chief town is Hanoi, and the principal port is Haiphong.

Annam's most important product is rice. Cattle rearing is carried on, and there is a gold mine. Chief exports are sugar, rice, cotton and silk tissues, cinnamon, tea and paper. Annam's former emperor, Bao-Dai, became head of the State of Viet-Nam in 1949.

Fish and rubber are prominent in exports from Cochin-China, which has soap, varnish, tire, rubber and other factories; its chief port is Saigon, on the Saigon river, 35 miles from the South China Sea.

Laos (formerly Lane Xang, " land of the millions of elephants ") cultivates rice, coffee, tea and other crops ; two tin mines are worked; its forests yield teak and other valuable woods ; elephants are hunted; and it has 20 aerodromes, with two regular air-lines.

Indonesia.

For centuries medieval Europe was fascinated by tales about the Spice Islands. It was from this distant unknown region that spices came. Spices were enormously important in the diet of the Middle Ages and sold for high prices. After the Crusades the spice trade became one of the most profitable branches of commerce, and Europeans longed to trade directly with the islands.

In 1488 joy bells rang in Portugal when Bartholomew Diaz returned from finding the beginning of a sea route around Africa to these fabled lands. Four years later Columbus rejoiced to think—though he was wrong—that he had found a westward route to them. Thirty years after Columbus's first voyage Magellan did find this route, and one of his ships sailed around the world for the first time in history.

Thus the Spice Islands were one of the magnets which drew Europe on to its " Golden Age of Discovery." For the next four centuries the seafaring nations of Europe often fought for these rich islands, which came to be known variously as the East Indies or the Malay Archipelago or Indonesia. By the 19th century the Netherlands held most of them.

This is the world's largest group of islands. There are thousands of them, scattered along the equator between south-east Asia and Australia. They range in size from Borneo and New Guinea down to mud flats of an acre or so. All told, they cover more than a million square miles, and have some 90 million people, mostly brown or black. (*See* map in pages 1074-75.)

Since 1945 the term Indonesia has been applied particularly to those parts of the archipelago which made up the former colonial empire called the Netherlands East Indies—about two-thirds of the archipelago and four-fifths of the people. How that empire became an independent republic with the title of the United States of Indonesia is told in the article under the heading East Indies.

The territory now comprised in the United States of Indonesia produced in normal times about a third of the world's natural rubber ; about a fifth of its tin, agave and sisal fibre, and palm-oil products ; three-fourths of the kapok; considerable quantities of tea, coffee and sugar; and almost all of the world's supply of pepper and quinine. Its petroleum, too, is of great value.

About 60 languages are spoken, the most important being Javanese, Sudanese and Madurese; but Malay is understood in most of the islands, and was the second official language with Dutch under Netherlands rule.

With this diversity of race and tongue and religious belief go considerable unrest and strife, and the complete handing over of power by the Netherlands to the Indonesians in 1949 did little, if anything, to pour oil on the sorely troubled waters.

The federal capital of the United States of Indonesia is Djakarta (formerly known as Batavia), in West Java. (*See* Java).

Induction Coil.

In reading about early experiments in high-voltage electricity—for example, those of Hertz and Röntgen, and the later inventors who gave us wireless communication—you will often find the induction coil mentioned. As a scientific curiosity, or a mere plaything, the coil became popular. For example, a boy could connect the terminals from a " shocking coil '' to some metal object, and then ask an unsuspecting friend to pick up that object!

An induction coil is a device for obtaining high-voltage alternating current—up to the thousands of volts required to produce an electric spark—from low-voltage direct current such as is obtained from batteries. It was, at one time, the only method of producing a high-voltage supply without using frictional machines. In the story of electricity there is an explanation of electro-magnetic induction and the way in which an E.M.F. (electromotive force) is induced in a conductor which is either moving in a magnetic field (as in a dynamo); or is stationary in a moving (i.e., changing or alternating) magnetic field, as in a transformer (*q.v.*). An induction coil is, in effect, a " step-up " transformer. It has a *primary* and a *secondary* winding, but the primary, instead of being fed with alternating current, is supplied with interrupted direct current which gives a similar effect, since the current is continually rising and falling, although it does not actually reverse.

The " core " of an induction coil must be laminated and not solid; but, unlike a transformer core, it does not form a closed magnetic circuit. It is frequently made of a bundle of soft iron wires. On this bundle are wound (1) the primary, a small number of turns of comparatively thick wire; and (2) the secondary, a large number (several thousands) of turns of thin wire. Fig. 1 shows the general appearance of such a coil, and Fig. 2 is a diagram of the connexions.

In very large coils the interruption or "chopping" of the primary circuit was done by an external interrupter, sometimes motor-driven, but the simplest method is that shown. The supply from the battery to the primary winding is taken through a pair of contacts variously known as the interrupter, vibrator, trembler, or make-and-break. This consists of a springy piece of metal A, carrying a silver or platinum contact, and a platinum- or silver-tipped screw B. A piece of iron at the end of A is placed so as to be near to the iron core of the coil.

When the battery is connected current flows through the primary winding, magnetising the core, and attracting the iron on A. The movement of A causes the contacts to separate, breaking the circuit and demagnetising the core; this releases A, and causes it to spring back and allow the contacts to touch once more. This process is repeated very

rapidly—so rapidly, in fact, that the eye cannot follow it—and results in a continuous high-speed interruption of the circuit. Since the circuit is highly inductive, the current does not "want" to stop abruptly when the contacts open, but tries to follow across the contact gap in the form of a small electric arc which would rapidly burn the contacts. To prevent this, a condenser is connected across them, as shown. This acts as a sort of buffer, since the "kick" when the contacts open is absorbed in charging the condenser, which discharges again each time the contacts close, thus assisting in starting the current flowing again by helping to overcome the "inertia" of the circuit inductance.

The pulsating magnetic field which is set up in the core induces an alternating voltage in the secondary winding, the actual amount depending on the strength of the field, the speed of interruption, and the number of secondary turns. The secondary winding is connected to the spark gap and, if this is correctly set, a continuous stream of sparks will flow.

Induction coils are commonly known by the size of spark they would produce—a "four-inch" coil means one which will give a spark four inches long, without overheating or damage. Their chief use, apart from laboratory experiments, was in the early days of wireless telegraphy as "spark" transmitters; and in ignition work for petrol and gas engines. For this last duty they were largely replaced by the magneto (a simple form of generator, driven by the engine), but have now largely returned in a modified form, and "coil" ignition is once more popular. Smaller and much less powerful forms of induction coils, commonly called "shocking coils," were used for providing a mild form of electric shock for medical purposes—and, in a cheaper form, are still seen as a plaything.

Indus, RIVER. Rising near the sources of three other great rivers—the Sutlej, Brahmaputra and Ganges—on the northern slope of Mount Kailas in the Tibetan Himalayas, this mighty river of

India flows for the first 500 miles of its 1,800-mile course through deep gorges in the Himalayas. After flowing north-westwardly through Kashmir it turns south-west, and emerges into the plain of the Punjab, which is watered by the Indus and its five tributaries—the Sutlej, Beas, Ravi, Chenab, and Jhelum.

The Indus then flows through the Sind plain—a region which is as much the creation of the Indus as Egypt is of the Nile. The climate here is almost rainless, but an intricate network of irrigation canals enables this region to produce abundant crops of cotton, millet, rice, and wheat. The Lloyd Barrage at Sukkur in Sind, one of the world's engineering wonders, provides water for about 8,000 square miles that were once dry and barren.

In the lower part of its course, except where it runs between walls of rock, the river continually

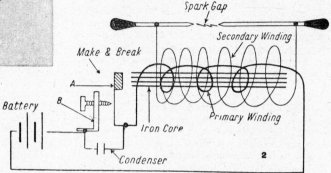

AN INDUCTION COIL AND ITS CONNEXIONS
To obtain high-voltage alternating current from low-voltage direct current an induction coil (upper left) is used. The core of the coil is frequently made of a bundle of soft iron wires, on which are wound the primary and secondary turns. The connexions are shown in the diagram.

shifts its bed, especially in the 130-mile wide delta, through which it finds outlet to the Indian Ocean by means of a great number of narrow channels. Hence there is little navigation, except by native boats. The Indus abounds in fish, and alligators infest most of the lower reaches. Karachi, the capital of Pakistan, stands at the western extremity of the Indus delta, the only other city of importance on its banks being Hyderabad, Sind.

Industrial Revolution. Until about 1750 the world carried on its daily work in much the same way as it had done for more than 2,000 years. Ploughs were still clumsy wooden affairs; reaping was done by hand with sickles and scythes; jointed sticks, called flails, were used for threshing the grain. The tools of the carpenter, smith and mason were not widely different from those shown on old Egyptian monuments; and except for the hand- or foot-driven spinning-wheel, spinning and weaving had shown little progress.

We may sum it all up by saying that there were no *machines* before 1750, such as now perform most of Man's work for him and place at the disposal of the majority goods which only the wealthy could formerly buy. On the other hand, there were no smoke-blackened factory towns with their squalor and desolation; and problems of unemployment, of capital and labour, were few or none at all.

It is to the revolutionary changes which, within less than 100 years, wiped out this age-long condition of affairs and brought about the machine age as we know it today, that the name Industrial Revolution has been given.

The movement began first in Great Britain, and it gradually spread to Europe and North America. In agriculture it came first with better tools and methods of cultivation, particularly the growing of root-crops—turnips and beets—in rotation with grain. Breeds of cattle and sheep were improved, and draining and fertilization made the land more productive and capable of supporting a larger population (*see* Agriculture). At the same time roads were improved and canals were built for transporting heavy goods.

Then about 1750 began the great movement made possible by the new machines for spinning and weaving. These brought the factory system and the application of water- and steam-power to manufacturing, with the long train of inventions which made the steam-engine more and more efficient. The development of England's mineral resources, checked in 17th century for lack of steam power, now proceeded apace, and by 1815 England was exporting 90,000 tons of iron a year. The people began to move from the countryside into the towns, where there was employment at higher wages in the new industries. The population was increasing by leaps and bounds, and to meet the growing demand for food the first imports had to be made from abroad, despite ever-improving methods of agriculture inaugurated by 18th century farming pioneers.

Early in the 19th century the Industrial Revolution was virtually complete in England. Steam and machines had done away with the old hand-work in all the principal industries. Work was done in factories and not in the homes of the people as heretofore, and—unfortunately—masses of men were crowded together in streets of mean houses in the industrial centres.

Trade, in which England kept the lead given her by her inventors for many years, the command of the sea, and her supplies of raw material brought immense wealth into the country, which was shared by relatively few. *See* illustrations in facing page.

Infra-Red Rays. When a red-hot coal is taken out of the fire and held in a pair of tongs the red glow gradually becomes dimmer as it cools down, and finally vanishes. Although no visible light is then being given out heat is still being radiated in all directions, which we can verify by putting our hand anywhere close to the coal. These "heat rays" are very similar to the visible light rays, both being waves which travel through the ether (like radio waves) at a very high speed; the only difference between the two is that our eyes are not adapted to "see" the infra-red, or heat radiation.

Infra-red rays are so called because, if the light radiated from a glowing substance is split up into its constituent wavelengths by means of a spectrometer, then the spectrum so formed will be found to extend *beyond* the red end. No actual visible spectrum will be there, but if an instrument designed to detect heat is placed in the infra-red (i.e. beyond the red) region, it will show that heat radiation is in fact falling on it. An ordinary mercury thermometer with its bulb blackened is quite a good detector; but for accurate scientific work a sensitive electrical thermometer, known as a bolometer, is generally used.

The wavelengths of infra-red radiations range from about $\frac{1}{1000}$ millimetre (near that of red light) up to about $\frac{1}{2}$ millimetre, where they merge into the spectral region of radio waves, which are also another form of electro-magnetic waves. A hot body will give out infra-red rays covering a whole band of wavelengths, but the hotter it is the larger will be the amount of shorter wavelength radiation emitted, until finally it becomes hot enough to send out some visible light, too.

There are a large number of uses to which infra-red rays are put. Rheumatism and associated ailments are often treated by means of the infra-red lamp. This lamp is virtually an electric fire, the heat rays from it being directed on to the limb under treatment by means of a polished reflector. The heating caused within the tissues of the body is responsible for any beneficial effect.

It is possible to make a photographic plate sensitive to some of the infra-red radiations (those closest

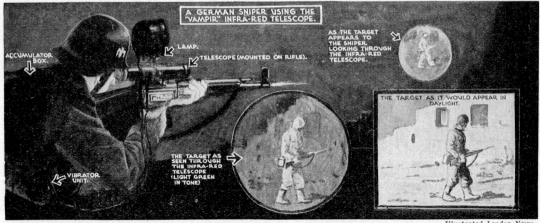

Illustrated London News

INFRA-RED RAYS ALLOW VISION ON THE DARKEST NIGHT
By the use of infra-red telescopes an enemy can be observed on the darkest night and accurate fire opened on him. A sniper's outfit (above) consists of an infra-red telescope and lamp attached to a rifle, the accumulator and other equipment being carried on the man's back. The outfit weighs about 35 lb.

FIRST STEPS IN THE INDUSTRIAL REVOLUTION

One of the most important of the inventions that brought about the Industrial Revolution was that of the spinning mule (left) by Samuel Crompton in 1779. Above, two of the first blast furnaces that used coal to make iron, erected by Samuel Darby at Coalbrookdale, Shropshire, in 1709.

Great impetus was given to the Industrial Revolution by the invention of the steam locomotive and the construction of railways. It then became possible to move heavy goods far more easily and quickly than had been the case when canals and horse-drawn waggons were the only means of transport, and coal could be carried from the pits to the factories with an ease hitherto impossible. This illustration is a drawing of the Liverpool and Manchester Railway as it was in 1833. It shows an engine taking in water at Parkside Station. George Stephenson (1781–1848) built this line on which his engine 'The Rocket,' constructed in 1829, hauled trains. *See* article commencing page 1721.

in wavelength to visible light). If we take a photograph with one of these plates, the result will be as if we are "seeing" in infra-red. Some striking effects can be obtained like this. For instance, green foliage and grass reflect the infra-red strongly, and so they appear almost white on a print, giving a sort of moonlight effect. Photographs taken with infra-red plates from tops of mountains are always much clearer than ordinary ones, since those radiations penetrate mist and haze to a far greater extent than does visible light (*see* page 696). Infra-red radiation is also used in the detection of forgeries, since inks and chemicals which appear to be the same in ordinary light are almost sure to look different in the infra-red.

During the Second World War (1939–45) a great number of devices were developed for "seeing in the dark" by means of infra-red rays. The simpler instruments merely detected the presence of the hot exhausts of enemy vehicles, or even the presence of men themselves, by the heat rays which the machines or the men emit. Other more complicated pieces of equipment included the snipers' infra-red telescope, which proved very effective in night-fighting. This device incorporates a "black" searchlight which is shone on to the target area; an image of this area is formed, in infra-red, by the telescope, which subsequently converts the infra-red image to a visible one by an electrical process similar to that used in television.

Infra-red rays are used as a tool by the research chemist for studying the ways in which chemical molecules are built up. The molecules are often found to vibrate in sympathy with a certain frequency of infra-red radiation, much as the air inside a closed box can be made to resonate with the sound waves from a tuning fork placed on it. By finding these "resonance frequencies," much can be learnt of the ways in which the atoms of a molecule are bound together. (*See* Heat; Light).

Ink. If the ink runs smooth and free from your pen, sinks into the paper without spreading, and leaves a blue-black mark that becomes deeper and deeper in colour when it is exposed to daylight, it is probable that it was made from nut-galls, from which, for centuries past, the best grades of ink have been manufactured.

The nut-galls used are growths on a species of oak found in Asia Minor. The gall-fly, a small wasp-like insect, burrows into the soft twigs and deposits her eggs. The tree throws protective tissues over the spot until a lump, sometimes nearly an inch in diameter, is formed. These lumps, or galls, contain a large amount of tannin, the substance which makes them so valuable for ink making.

Solutions of an aniline dye, the galls, and an iron salt, usually green vitriol (ferrous sulphate), are mixed. When you write, the blue dye makes your writing visible, but this blue colour tends to fade on exposure to light and air. However, light and air change the iron tannin salt to a black and very permanent substance. Such ink is called "blue-black" ink. A thickening substance, often a mucilage known as gum-senegal, holds the colour suspended in solution. Small quantities of various acids keep the ink from coagulating and moulding.

If you are using an inferior grade of ink, it may have been made of logwood from the West Indies,

or by mixing green vitriol with other tannin solutions. Such inks, while they may be satisfactory at first, fade after a few years. Some ancient documents written with ink made of galls are as bright and clear today as when written centuries ago.

If you are writing with a special fountain pen ink, it was probably made from the black aniline dye nigrosine. This ink never thickens and forms no sediment, so that it is peculiarly adapted to the fountain pen, although the colour is not so permanent. All colours of ink can be made with aniline dyes.

Red ink is sometimes coloured with the powdered bodies of thousands of tiny red insects called cochineal, brushed from cactus plants in Mexico, Central America and Peru. Most red ink is made from brazilwood, imported from Central and South America; while not producing such a brilliant scarlet as cochineal, this ink fades less quickly.

Varieties of Invisible Ink

Then there are the secret or "sympathetic" inks, which leave no visible mark on the paper when they are used. In days gone by, many important papers have slipped past an enemy's eyes by this means, to reveal their messages when they have reached their destinations. Some of the favourite secret inks were lead acetate solution, whose invisible marks turn black upon exposure to sulphuretted hydrogen; cobalt nitrate solution, which turns blue when it is treated with oxalic acid; and cobalt chloride or nitro-chloride, which becomes green when heated. But the spy or enemy agent who used such crude methods today would merely write his own death warrant. During the Indian Mutiny letters and orders were sometimes written with rice-water, to be developed later with iodine. A clean pen dipped in lemon juice will produce writing which is invisible when dry, but which stands out sharply in brown when the paper is heated.

Artists use Indian ink or "Chinese ink." This is an early form of ink invented in China probably 2,000–3,000 years before the Christian era, and the best qualities are still made in China and Japan. Lamp-black, made from sesame oil or from tung oil, is mixed into a paste with a glue made from skins of asses or oxen, and then pressed into sticks or moulds. But for drawings made to prepare process-photographic printing blocks, a black ink which photographs better than Indian ink is preferred.

The most interesting ink of all, perhaps, is sepia, which was formerly obtained from the cuttle-fish or squid. This most uncanny sea creature has on the under side of its body a gland containing a deep brown fluid, which it can throw out at will to conceal its escape when it is alarmed. Today sepia ink, which is used by artists, is manufactured from walnut juice or other substances.

Copying inks are made with less water and a larger amount of pigment than ordinary inks; they contain a substance (gum arabic, glycerine, etc.) which will retard the oxidizing effect of the air. Another special ink is the marking ink used for linen and other materials. One kind is made from silver nitrate, suitably treated. It stands all conditions well, but gradually turns pale brown.

Printing inks are quite gummy, adhesive substances. In the "fountains" of the printing presses this ink looks like heavy black or coloured pitch,

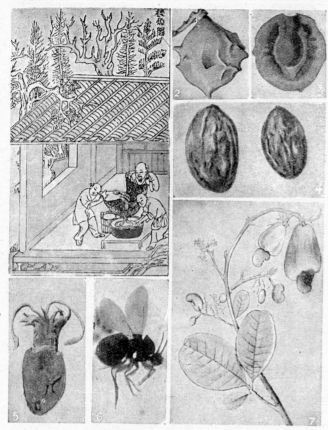

SOME OF THE SOURCES OF INK

(1) Chinese ink-makers straining a mixture of glue and lamp black. Iron-gall ink is made from tannin obtained from Aleppo galls, shown whole (2) and in section (3), or from dried Indian fruit, rather like prunes, called myrobalans (4). The galls are produced on a species of oak found in Asia Minor, by the gall fly (6). Sepia ink comes from the ink glands of cuttle-fish (5); marking inks are sometimes made from semecarpus, an Indian nut (7).

and the oils contained in it give it a distinctive though pleasant smell. A good printing ink must fulfil many requirements. It must distribute freely over the roller, spread sharp and clear over the type, and come off easily from the type to the paper. The best printing inks are mixtures of carbon black or gas-black and linseed oil, and some form of resin oil is generally used, as well as common soap. Gas-black is made by burning gas flames in a scanty supply of air. The flames are thrown against metal slabs or into revolving cylinders, and the soot that accumulates is scraped off and ground.

Inks were used by the Egyptians and the Chinese more than 4,000 years ago. While the exact character of these inks is not known, they were probably simple mixtures of powdered charcoal and glue. The Romans used natural sepia as a writing fluid. Iron-gall inks, however, seem to have been first compounded about the 11th century A.D. From that time forward these inks gradually replaced other types. In those early days they were usually mixed by the writers themselves, and friends circulated recipes for their preparation.

Most makers of fountain pens today supply suitable inks which may be very different from those used to fill ink-wells. The introduction of the stylo-graphic pen or "ink-pencil" brought the need for a less fluid writing medium in a form which would not leak from the pen. So ink manufacture nowadays is a more complex business than it was a few years ago, and inventors and chemists may give us a writing fluid belonging to quite a different "family" from those we knew of old. But still the main object is permanence, along with a pleasant hue.

Innocent. POPES. Of the 13 Popes who have borne this name, INNOCENT I was in office from 402 to 417, and is chiefly remembered because the Goths under Alaric sacked the city of Rome in 410, though the Pope was absent at the time. He was an able and most energetic pontiff, and lost no opportunity of asserting the papal power. INNOCENT II (Pope 1130–43) denounced the French scholar Abélard (q.v.) as a heretic.

INNOCENT III (Pope 1198–1216) was in many respects the ablest and most powerful Pope of the Middle Ages. His character inspired universal respect. He greatly strengthened the power of the papacy, exercising his claim to spiritual overlordship throughout Europe. It was to him that King John (1167–1216) of England made an abject submission, recognizing the Pope as his spiritual overlord. INNOCENT III also put in practice the papal claim to choose or remove emperors of the Holy Roman Empire.

INNOCENT VII (1404–06) was Pope when the Roman Catholic Church was split in two factions, one section supporting the Pope at Avignon (Benedict XIII) and the other Innocent in Rome. Under INNOCENT VIII (1484–92) corruption reigned at Rome. INNOCENT X (1644–55), INNOCENT XI (1676–89), and INNOCENT XII (1691–1700) were all reforming Popes, who combated heresy and sought to improve the administration.

Innsbruck. Standing on the river Inn, its name meaning Inn Bridge (German brücke, bridge), this ancient Austrian town is the capital of the province of Tirol and in normal times is a popular tourist resort. It is pleasantly situated in a valley at the foot of the Alps, and at the meeting point of the little River Sill with the Inn. It lies about 1,900 feet above sea-level, and is surrounded by mountains from 7,000 to 9,000 feet in height.

The seat of a university founded in the 17th century, it had a number of fine public buildings, including the Franciscan church built about 1500 to contain the magnificent cenotaph to Emperor Maximilian I; this consisted of a marble sarcophagus, or tomb, crowned by a kneeling figure of the emperor in bronze, while on either side were 28 bronze statues of royal personages. The Ferdinandeum was a museum with a good Tirolean art, literature and natural history collection.

The manufacture of glass and cotton goods and glass painting are carried on. The town was a target for Allied bombers in the Second World War (1939–45), suffering considerable damage.

Inquisition. To check the waves of heresy (religious opinions opposed to the established or usually accepted doctrines) that swept over Europe in the 13th century, the Roman Catholic Church established a special tribunal called the Inquisition to try persons accused of holding religious beliefs contrary to those taught by the Roman Catholic Church. In 1215 Pope Innocent III sent special delegates to southern France to inquire into the existence of heresy, and in 1216 the religious order of Dominican friars was founded to repress it. The Inquisition proper was established by Innocent IV in 1248 and Dominicans were entrusted with its chief direction.

Arriving in a district, the judges, aided by the local bishop and the State authorities, would announce 30 days' grace for all heretics to confess their crime. When that period was up, the trial of the accused and unrepentant ones began. The names of witnesses were kept secret ; but the defendant was permitted to submit a list of enemies, and none of these might appear against him. Following the frequent practice of the period in criminal trials, torture was often used to force confessions.

At a grand ceremonial, called *auto-da-fé* (Portuguese, act of faith), the names of the guilty were announced and punishments inflicted, ranging from fines and excommunication to imprisonment for life or burning at the stake for incorrigible heretics. Since the clergy were forbidden to participate in bloodshed, the severer penalties were carried out by the State.

The Inquisition reached its height in Spain during the days of King Ferdinand and Queen Isabella, when Fray Tomás de Torquemada (1420–98) was made Inquisitor-General for the kingdom. The Inquisition was sometimes used by unscrupulous persons as a means of revenging themselves upon their enemies, and at times the sincerest inquisitors were misled by fanatical zeal and practised great cruelties. But on the whole the institution was a logical product of its time. In those days the Church and State were united in the closest bonds, and heresy was considered a crime against both, to be compared with high treason and anarchy. To the people of the period it seemed as reasonable to punish a man who " plotted against the life of the Church " as it would in our day to punish a man who plotted against the State.

The Inquisition was chiefly active in southern Europe, and continued in a modified form in Spain until 1820. The Congregation of the Holy Office, established by Pope Paul III in 1542 to review the judgements of the Inquisition courts, still exists. It examines charges of heresy, but imposes only spiritual punishments.

OUR SIX-LEGGED FOES *and* FRIENDS

*M*an *wages a never-ceasing battle with many kinds of insects, and but for his vigilance and their own unending wars they might make the world a very disagreeable place for human beings, so prolific are they.*

Insects. In all places where life is, these six-legged creatures thrive and multiply—flying, creeping, burrowing. Most people pay little attention to them, except when they are bitten or otherwise bothered by some of the bolder members. Yet insect habits and history are stranger than the weirdest tales of fairyland, and these hosts of tiny creatures influence, directly or indirectly, our everyday life to an enormous extent.

Imagine yourself a pygmy one inch high pushing out into the insect world to learn its customs at close range. You would need to have, of course, some magic password to ensure your safety, or you would be killed within an hour. You would learn as your first lesson that in insect land " might is right." Death lurks at every corner. Each hole in the ground or hollow beneath a stone may hide some nightmare monster with yawning jaws waiting for its prey. A dead leaf may conceal a hungry enemy who will pounce upon you as you pass. Or some flying creature may swoop down out of the air to deliver a fatal blow.

We might state the two main laws of insect life thus : " To eat without being eaten is the first law of insect land. The second is to lay eggs and provide for the young." Born with a tremendous hunger, the insect must start at once to labour and fight to satisfy it. And when he is grown he must turn to and work for the next generation as fast and as hard as he can. Were it not for this constant struggle, insects would soon multiply so rapidly that they would cover the whole earth.

All the shapes and colours of insects that seem so horrible, or beautiful, are not accidents. They all mean something in the insect's struggle to live; they are its chief defence against enemies. Anything that is alive, or has ever been alive, is food for one kind of insect or another. There are even some that live on the paste behind wallpaper, others on old shoes, and the paper in books. Others, such as fleas and many other parasites, live at the expense of living men and animals. Still others—a vast and varied host—clean up dead vegetable and animal matter.

But by far the greater number feed upon living plants or upon one another. The caterpillar eats the leaf, the wasp eats the caterpillar, the spider eats the wasp, the bird eats the spider (for though spiders are not members of the insect class, they often fit into the insects' scheme of existence). Then, when the bird dies in some forest tragedy, a beetle comes and buries him, and the grubs emerging from the beetle's eggs eat a part of the body; the rest stays in the ground

PARTS OF AN INSECT
The head (A) ; the first region of the thorax (B), bearing the front legs ; the second region (C), bearing middle legs and front wings ; the third region (D), bearing hind-legs and second pair of wings ; and the abdomen (E), bearing the egg-laying apparatus and the sting.

and makes it rich so that another tree can grow whose leaves in turn another caterpillar will eat.

The character of an insect's mouth-parts depends on what it eats. Some have strong jaws to tear leaves or bite the bark of trees or gnaw one another. Some have a sucking apparatus to draw in honey

The mole cricket is the greatest digger for his size in the world. Look at his front foot (left) and you'll see why. With those powerful spines he cuts and scrapes through the earth, scooping it back with the strong broad palm. That slit at the top of the foot is the mole cricket's ear.

made up of plates of chitin, a horny substance which is tough and strong. Beetles are particularly well protected by it. With many of them it amounts to a solid shell of armour that will blunt the sharpest pair of jaws in insect land. The only places on a beetle where it is vulnerable are its knees and elbows, or in the soft joints of its hind-body. Some beetles can draw their heads and legs so close in that they are quite hidden in neat grooves or folded back on themselves. Besides furnishing an outside armouring, plates of chitin inside take the place of a bony skeleton, acting as supports for the powerful muscles of an insect's legs and wings.

or fruit juices. Some have tiny pointed beaks to pierce the skin of plants or of animals whose juice or blood they drink.

The manner of an insect's life also influences its feet and legs. Some have sharp claws for climbing or clinging to the bottom of a leaf, while others have sucker-like disks on their feet for hanging upside-down on smooth surfaces. Others have broad, flat feet for digging, or huge front legs with great spines for seizing and holding their prey, like the praying mantis.

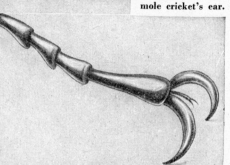

As for weapons, the creature's jaws are very effective against enemies who are near the same size. For larger foes, insects have a wide assortment of piercing jaws and poison stings, with which they can inflict painful wounds on the biggest of creatures—even on Man. The wasps and hornets are examples of single-handed fighters. There are insects which band themselves together to offer battle in organized armies under leaders, making raids and taking prisoners to hold as slaves. We refer to the warrior ants. Here is what Henry Walter Bates (1825-92), author of The Naturalist on the Amazons, said of them:

All insect tribes that are alive today have survived because they have some special tricks for avoiding destruction. These tricks all follow one or more of four systems—reproduction in prodigal numbers, concealment, armour and weapons, and what we may call " frightfulness," which is another name for bluff. All insects, particularly such helpless creatures as the green-fly, or aphids, produce enormous numbers of offspring. You will know from experience in your own garden how hard it is to get rid of these. You can destroy thousands of these, but if one escapes, there will be thousands more produced within a week or two.

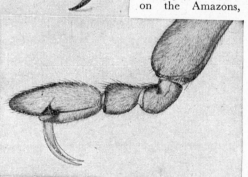

"Wherever they pass, all the rest of the animal world is thrown into a state of alarm. They stream along the ground and climb to the summit of all the lower trees . . . Where booty is plenti-

STRANGE FEET
Second from the top we see the stag beetle's two claws. The third picture shows the foot of the water-skater that flits over the surface of ponds and ditches. The claws are for holding to water plants or to its prey. Right, the foot of the scorpion fly.

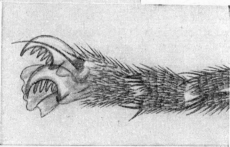

Some insects are geniuses at concealment. The leaf-insect imitates the colour and shape of a leaf so skilfully that other insects may be deceived. There are butterflies that do the same thing, even imitating the stem which attaches the leaf to the twig. Some insects imitate a stick of wood, or the bark of a tree, or a flower blossom.

Then there is the great multitude of armoured insects, from ants to beetles. Their armour is partly

ful they concentrate all their forces upon it, the dense phalanx of shining and quickly moving bodies, as it spreads over the surface, looking like a flood of dark-red liquid. All soft bodied and inactive insects fall an easy prey to them, and they tear their victims in pieces for facility in carriage."

Then there are insects which " bluff " their way through the world—pretending to be fierce or powerful or annoying to their enemies. We all

Above, a willow beauty moth on the bark of a tree. Right, two Indian leaf butterflies, one with wings folded.

Left, a lappet moth, another leaf imitator. Above, a walking leaf insect, probably the best mimic of all.

know how fearsome the earwig looks when it curls up its forked tail, with its pincers. That is bluff, pure and simple. The earwig couldn't possibly hurt anything with that; yet many an earwig owes its life to the terror it inspires.

The stag-beetle and the African rhinoceros-beetle look so fierce with their horns that they scare insects and even birds away. But the stag-beetle cannot pinch hard enough to do any harm to us. There are dozens of such examples. Some harmless insects imitate the shape and colour of the stinging kind and so escape. Certain flies, for instance, mimic bees; and beetles imitate fierce wasps or flies. The record for bluffing is held by the Indian leaf butterfly, the stick insects and the leaf insects. They resemble the objects after which they are named so closely that they are very hard to find when at rest.

Did you ever hear of the bombardier-beetle? He is the real inventor of the poison-gas artillery. When a larger beetle or a bird pursues him he discharges a drop of corrosive fluid from the tip of the hind body. It forms a tiny cloud of gas as soon as it meets the air and, at the same time, makes a cracking sound or pop. This performance enables the beetle to escape its pursuers.

If we have a lot of bluffers, we have also some really dangerous characters which attack even four-footed animals and kill them

This foot-long creature known as 'Gray's Spiny Stick-Insect,' looks so much like the thorny bushes on which it feeds that its enemies have great trouble in finding it.

"single-handed." There is a giant water-bug that can kill small frogs and fish, seizing them in its powerful front legs and plunging in its deadly beak. Even among our English beetles we have the great water beetle that will kill small minnows and goldfish if it gets into an aquarium with them. So much, then, for insect character and behaviour. Now we must say something about that wonderful feature of insect life we call metamorphosis, or change of form. With very few exceptions insects grow from eggs. Most species after hatching from the egg do not resemble their parents at all. They may be smooth, worm-like creatures, such as the maggot of the bee or the fly; or they may be hairy like some caterpillars; or big, fierce-looking grubs like the young of the tiger-beetle and the "ground" beetles (Carabidae).

At this period of its life the insect is called a larva, and its duty is to eat and grow. The period may last only a few days, as is the case with bees and flies, or it may extend over years, as is the case with the cicada or "17-year locust." This period may be spent burrowing in the ground, hiding in holes in the trunks of trees, swimming in the water, or crawling about in the open air.

In due time the insect enters the pupa stage (or chrysalis stage as it is called in the case of butterflies and moths), which is a period of change

CAMOUFLAGE AMONG THE INSECTS
Here are seven examples of how insects protect themselves. Of the two directly above (considerably enlarged), that on the left is a weevil whose 'thorns' make him resemble a bit of dead wood; the ruby wasp (right) is protected by a hard body-covering.

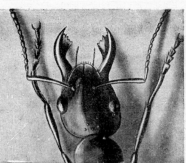

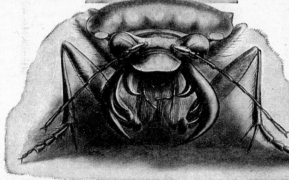

but not of growth. For this purpose many larvae, such as caterpillars, form a sort of silken cradle called a cocoon, made from filament which the insect spins. During this period the whole shape and structure of the creature changes, and when it awakes and bursts out of its old skin it has become for the first time a fully-developed insect like its parents. The caterpillar, for instance, has turned into a handsome butterfly or a moth.

There are strange variations and exceptions to this law of metamorphosis. Some insects, like the oil-beetles, pass through two or more larval forms before they become pupae; and the mayflies cast their old skin even after they have grown their wings. There are, on the other hand, groups of insects, such as the grasshoppers, l o c u s t s, crickets, and all true bugs, in which the young resemble the parents just as soon as they hatch from the eggs, needing only to grow larger and to develop wings if they are of the winged kind. Such young insects are called nymphs and not larvae. During the growing period nymphs shed their skins several times. This is necessary because the chitin covering of an insect cannot stretch. The larva, of course, sheds its skin from time to time, too, as it grows up.

There are exceptions also to the egg stage, for the young of some insects are born alive. Such insects are called viviparous (Latin *vivus,* "alive," and *parere,* "bring forth") to distinguish them from egg-laying insects, which are called oviparous (Latin *ovum,* "egg"). Plant-lice, or aphids, have the curious habit of sometimes laying eggs and sometimes producing living young. Furthermore, there are insects such as aphids and some kinds of gall wasps, which produce fertile eggs without their having been fertilized by the male. Such insects commonly produce only females, and this

INSECT MOUTHS FOR DIFFERENT PURPOSES
The first picture on the left at the top shows the jaws of the stag beetle. Next are the scissor-like jaws with which the leaf-cutter bee does such neat work. On the right of the top row are the powerful jaws with which the wood ant fights and works. The central picture shows the jaws of the sawyer beetle; below it is a head-on close-up of the green tiger beetle. All are considerably magnified.

method of reproduction is known as parthenogenesis (from the Greek words *parthenos,* "virgin," and *genesis,* "birth").

The social groups of insects—ants, wasps, bees, and termites—that live together in colonies or communities rank highest in intelligence. These have learned the lesson of co-operation, which reduces the struggle for existence to its easiest terms. With them, the spirit of the hive or nest rules supreme over the members. From the earliest times men have found inspiration to devotion and self-sacrifice in the lives of these ingenious insects. (*See* Ant; Bee).

In general, it is in the nest-building habits of insects that their highest skill is s h o w n, rivalling many of Man's cleverest accomplishments. The carpenter bee, for instance, bores into the solid wood and builds cells for its eggs, divided by partitions formed of wood dust. The leaf-cutter bee is responsible for the curious half - moon shaped "bites" often to be seen in the leaves of garden rose bushes. With these carefully cut pieces of leaf cells for the eggs are constructed, in burrows in dry soil or rotten wood. The mason wasp constructs a beautiful home of mud, often with a curved porch to keep out the wind. There are spinners of silk and makers of wax, upholsterers, workers in wood-pulp and tree-gums, and other special trades represented in the insect world.

Most of these nest-builders store up food for their young. It may be honey or pollen, or the bodies of other insects killed for this purpose. Some wasps store up living insects, after paralysing them with their stings, so that their young may have fresh food when they hatch from the egg.

What happens to insects in the winter? Most of the adult ones die, leaving eggs or half-developed young to await the warmth of spring underground or in some other protected place. In certain species, like the social wasps, the female sleeps through the cold weather and lays the eggs for the new generation as soon as warm weather comes. The colony life of ants and bees, however, continues all the year round.

The chief distinguishing feature of insects is that all of them have six legs—in the adult state, that is; for many larvae have more than that number if the false " pro-legs " are included. They carry a pair of feelers or antennae and their bodies are always divided up into segments or rings. There are a great many creatures which closely resemble insects, for instance, spiders and scorpions, which have eight legs and no antennae; while centipedes have antennae and many pairs of legs.

All the insects belong to the larger group of creatures with jointed legs called *Arthropoda*. This includes not only centipedes, spiders and scorpions, but marine creatures such as shrimps, crabs and lobsters and their relatives.

The name " bug " belongs only to certain special kinds of insects. Among other peculiarities which distinguish the true bugs—members of the order *Hemiptera*—from other insects is the beak with which they suck plant juices or animal blood.

The body of an insect is divided into three parts—head, fore-body or thorax, and hind-body or abdomen—each of which, in the faraway ancestors of insects, as in the modern larvae, is further divided into rings or segments. The head bears the delicate feelers or antennae, the mouth parts, and the eyes. The sense of smell is situated chiefly in the antennae. There are two sorts of insect eye: the compound kind made up of many separate facets or lenses, and the simple eyes, usually known as ocelli. Many insects have both kinds, the ocelli being situated between the two prominent compound eyes. In certain insects a sense of hearing is present. Thus, crickets and many grasshoppers have organs of hearing on the shins of their fore-legs. Other kinds of grasshoppers, and locusts, have such organs at the base of the hind-body where it joins the thorax.

The mouths of insects are supplied usually with mandibles, or pinching jaws; maxillae, or biting and chewing jaws; certain palps, which help to taste the food and to guide it into the mouth; and a labrum and labium, upper and lower lip respectively. The palps are attached to the maxillae and labium, and are called maxillary or labial palps, as the case may be. The size, shape, and arrangement

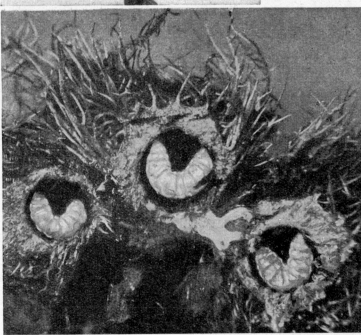

H. Bastin; J. J. Ward

GALL WASPS AND GRUBS AND THE GALLS THEY MAKE

The curious deformities known as galls which we see on all sorts of trees and shrubs are the result usually of the working of certain insects, mostly of the order Hymenoptera. In the top picture, considerably magnified, are two gall wasps laying their eggs in an oak shoot, where later there will be 'marble galls.' Below it, on the left, are three grubs (highly magnified), curled up in the chambers of the 'pincushion gall,' which is shown on the right.

LIVES OF TWO INSECT FRIENDS AND A FOE

H. Bastin; J. J. Ward; A. S. Martin

While some insects do great damage to Man's crops, flowers, and vegetable products, others, by eating the harmful sorts, are indirectly very beneficial. The top row here shows stages in the life of a ladybird, which does much good by eating aphids (greenfly). On the left are the eggs; middle, a ladybird larva is eating the aphids on a rose bud; right, the adult two-spot ladybird. The centre row shows a similar series from the life of the common hover fly; left, an egg; centre, the larva devouring a greenfly; right, the adult fly. Below, removed from its burrow in a piece of ash, is the larva of an American wood-borer, which does much harm to timber; on the right is the adult beetle, near the hole from which it emerged. The larvae reach Britain in imported timber.

Ward; Crawford; Hinkins; Bastin

THE CHIEF ORDERS OF INSECTS

These six photographs show typical members of the most important orders of insects. They are : top row, left, a magpie moth (Lepidoptera) ; centre, top row, a cockroach which has just shed its skin (Orthoptera); right, a potter wasp at its mud nest (Hymenoptera). The central picture shows a daddy-long-legs or crane fly (Diptera). Lower are, left, a cardinal beetle (Coleoptera) and, right, a frog-hopper (Hemiptera). Sizes : life-size ; × ¾ ; × 5 ; less than life-size ; life-size ; × 2½.

the females. Certain species, like the plant-lice, develop wings only under special conditions of diet or weather. Often, as in the beetle tribe, the front wings of insects have become armoured wing-covers, which protect the delicate rear wings when not used in flight.

The abdomen, consisting of a varying number of segments, contains the digestive tract, and in females the egg-laying apparatus, or ovipositor. This is often very complicated, enabling the insect to bore into the ground, or into trees, or through the skins of other insects to lay its eggs. A sting, when present, is situated conveniently at the tip of the abdomen and is, in fact, a transformed ovipositor ; for this reason male insects cannot sting. Mosquitoes and other blood-sucking insects bite with their mouth-parts, and do not sting.

Insects have well-developed brains and nervous systems. A simple contracting tube-like heart provides for the circulation of blood. They have no lungs and do not breathe through their mouths. Air is drawn in through tiny pores, or spiracles, in the body-segments, and passes through an intricate system of branching tubes, or tracheae, carrying oxygen to all parts of the body.

The muscle system in insects is perhaps as delicate and complicated as in any higher animal. Scientists with microscopes have counted as many as 4,000 muscles in the body of a caterpillar.

About one million species of insects have been collected, named and described by scientists. But by far the greater part of the insects which inhabit the world are still unknown to science. Hundreds of new species are discovered every year. Estimates of the number of species run into several millions.

As a class, insects are found in virtually all parts of the world. They flourish best in warm countries. In the forests and other regions of the tropics, insects of every kind swarm in incredible numbers and breed throughout the year.

From Man's point of view, insects may be divided into the harmful and useful classes. Many kinds, like grasshoppers and locusts, plant-lice, scale-insects, cotton-weevils and the caterpillars of certain moths and butterflies do an immense amount of damage to trees, crops, domestic animals, and food stores. Others, such as cockroaches, flies, fleas, mosquitoes and gnats, annoy men and animals

of these mouth parts vary greatly in different species. In the true bugs, the mandibles are modified into sucking lancets and in general the range of modification for different organs is really extraordinary.

The thorax bears the three pairs of legs, and the wings when these are present. The typical insect has four wings; but in many species, such as the house-fly, they are reduced to two, and in others they have disappeared altogether. In some insect groups, the males only have wings, in others only

Insects appeared on earth long before mammals, some scientists claiming to have found insect remains in Devonian rocks (*see* Geology). The forests of the Coal Age contained many insects, some measuring two feet across the wings. From that time on, thanks to their rapid propagation and powers of concealment and defence, they have held their own against later forms, and today they number, as we have said, several million species.

The classification of insects for scientific purposes varies as new species are discovered. In the left column is a common modern classification.

Insurance. In our daily lives we are surrounded by dangers and risks. No one knows when he or she may be the victim of misfortune, so many people are prepared to pay a certain yearly sum of money in return for assurance that they or their dependants will receive a much larger sum in case of misfortune befalling them. This is obtained by joining others who also want the same protection. Each pays a certain amount to an insurance company and when any member of the group dies or his house burns down or he has an accident, the company pays him or his family a certain sum. In the case of death or accident the sum paid is an agreed one, depending on the amount of the premium paid. If a house is damaged or destroyed by fire or flood, the sum paid is that which will make good the damage or loss.

That, in a nutshell, is the fundamental principle of insurance. It rests upon the obvious fact that a burden which would crush one man can easily be carried if distributed among many men.

The earliest forms of insurance were against the loss of ships and cargoes at sea. Possibly insurance was known in ancient times, but the first records date from the Middle Ages, and the first English law on the subject was not passed until 1601. The earliest known life insurance policy was issued in 1583. For nearly three centuries thereafter insurance

and are even instrumental in spreading some of the most dreaded diseases of mankind, such as malaria, yellow fever and bubonic plague.

There is another side of the story which is too often overlooked. If it were not for bees and other nectar-seeking insects, which carry the fertilizing pollen from flower to flower, it would be almost impossible to raise many kinds of fruit and other crops. Bees had to be imported into Australia to make the cultivation of red clover possible. If it were not for the beetles and wasps and others, which destroy every year vast numbers of the harmful insects, our fields and gardens would be overrun with pests of all kinds. Many insects which burrow in the ground do great work as cultivators. Countless scavenger insects help the bacteria in getting rid of refuse for us. Certain insects manufacture substances of great value, such as silk, honey, wax, dyes, and lac (or the raw material of shellac). Only two kinds can be domesticated with profit—the silk-worm and the honey bee.

A. Montgomery

TERMITE QUEEN AT HOME

The queen termite lives in a specially-built cell in the heart of the nest. As you see from this life-size picture, she has an enormous body, and this is entirely filled with eggs, which she lays in immense numbers. Surrounding her in the 'royal cell' are the workers, whose business is to look after her, feed her and remove the eggs as fast as she lays them.

AN INTERNAL COMBUSTION ENGINE OF THE DIESEL TYPE

A six-cylinder engine, this Diesel is started by compressed air which is let into the cylinders to force out the pistons. Once the engine is turning over, ordinary air enters each cylinder in turn through an inlet valve and is compressed by the upward stroke of the piston, thereby becoming hot. At the same time, just before the piston reaches the top of the cylinder, a fuel valve opens and a small quantity of oil is sprayed into the cylinder. At once the heat of the air in the cylinder fires the oil, the expansion of the gases driving the piston down. The burnt gases escape through an exhaust valve, operated by the cam-shaft. When this valve has shut, the air valve opens, and so on.

was limited to the three fields of marine insurance (including ships and cargoes), life insurance (also known as assurance), and fire insurance. One of the oldest and most famous marine insurance companies in the world is Lloyd's (*q.v.*) of London.

The great development of insurance in all its branches coincided roughly with the spread of industrial organization in the second half of the 19th century. Special companies now insure against accidents, ill-health, theft and burglary, damage to motor-cars, or by motor-cars, damage by storms or by aircraft, and losses from bad debts or embezzlement by employees. It is even possible to take out insurance which will compensate one in the event of rain or snow on a specified date. In short, it is now possible to insure against almost any kind of inconvenience, loss or suffering.

The commonest form of insurance policy is the " ordinary life " under which a person pays a fixed annual sum, called a premium, for life in return for which a lump sum (say £1,000) is payable on his death to his dependants. The next most popular form is the " endowment " policy. Here the annual payments are for a limited period only (usually 20 years), and the insured himself is then entitled to the whole sum (say, £1,000); or, if he dies at any time within the limited period, his dependants or beneficiaries receive the whole £1,000.

An interesting development is that by which a person who buys his house on mortgage from a building society is able to protect his dependants against dispossession if he dies without paying all the mortgage repayments. This he does by means of a special kind of policy under which all outstanding payments on his mortgage are automatically wiped off at his death.

" Third-party " insurance covers accidents to a person or persons outside those specifically mentioned in the insurance policy. By law, insurance covering third-party risks must be held by every person driving a motor-car.

No matter what the kind of insurance, the payment made for the protection is called the premium. The size of a premium is calculated according to the law of averages, and the total amount which past experience has shown that the companies are likely to have to provide in compensation or replacement. Life insurance premiums are based on an estimate of the insurer's " expectation of life," in view of his age and occupation; a medical examination is made to find out if any special risk is present which might lead to premature death.

When you insure your house, an examination of the building may be made by a surveyor on behalf of the insurance company. For many years the insurance experts have kept records of losses by fire, not only as to the number of buildings burned but as to the relative loss in various types of construction and kinds of business. Obviously, an ironmonger's building with steel beams, brick walls, and a tile roof is a much better risk than a saw-mill built of wood. A wooden dwelling carries a higher risk than a brick, stone or concrete building.

In Great Britain a National Health Service was inaugurated in July 1948, establishing comprehensive health and national insurance services under the control of the Ministry of National Insurance. Subject to certain exceptions every person in the United Kingdom over 15 and under pensionable age is insured against injury at work, and against ill-health and unemployment, and is entitled to free medical attention.

The STORY of the EXPLOSION ENGINE

No more thrilling tale of progress from small beginnings can be imagined than that of the Internal Combustion Engine. In less than a century it has completely altered the life of the entire world—in peace as in war.

Internal Combustion Engine.

This means an engine which burns its energy-giving fuel internally—as contrasted with one like the steam engine, where the fuel is burned externally, beneath a boiler ; or the hot-air engine, in which the flame which heats the air is applied outside the cylinder. Another point to observe is that the " working fluid "—which fills the cylinder and drives the piston—is the gasefied fuel, after burning. In the steam engine, of course, the fuel escapes as smoke and unburnt gases after heating the water and providing the steam which, in that case, is the working fluid.

We may liken the internal combustion engine to a cannon barrel with its charge of powder and its ball. We apply a match to the touch-hole; the powder ignites and turns into a gas; the gas, enormously increased in volume, exerts a pressure about 6,000 times as great as normal atmospheric pressure; out goes the cannon-ball, which we can liken to a piston. Compare this with the cylinder of a petrol engine, where vaporized petrol, mixed with air to give the needed oxygen, is fired by an electric spark after the gas has been compressed by the descent of the piston.

Here, instead of a projectile being driven forth on its errand of destruction, we have a piston which is linked by a crank to a flywheel, and provides useful and controllable power. " Controllable " is the key-word ; early inventors tried to harness the explosion of gunpowder to drive an engine, and failed.

The first engines to dispense with a boiler were those called hot-air engines. Sir George Cayley designed one in 1807 ; 27 years later John Ericsson made an engine rather like Cayley's, and in 1852 he adapted hot-air engines for ship propulsion. In 1816 a Scottish minister named Robert Stirling built an air engine which embodied many theoretical principles which still hold good today. But, despite these promising beginnings, the only form in which we knew the hot-air engine until very recently was as a toy or model—safe for youngsters to play about with, since there was nothing to explode, and the engine derived its power from the alternate heating and cooling of a quantity of air contained in a closed cylinder.

In 1937 an engineer of the Phillips electrical works in the Netherlands chanced to come across an old Stirling engine, and wondered if the idea might not be utilized for small-power motors. He had a notion that a modernized hot-air engine would be valuable for working radio transmitters in isolated areas where no ordinary source of power was available. During the German occupation of the Netherlands the Dutch engineers continued their researches secretly, and eventually devised a type of engine which may have great value not only as a small power source but as a much larger " prime mover."

To return to the internal combustion engine, while Ericsson was evolving his hot-air engine other inventors were busy with the gas engine. The Frenchman Lenoir took out a patent in 1860 ; but before this two Britons (R. Street, 1794, and S. Brown, 1823) had glimpsed the path towards an internal combustion engine. Two German engineers, Langen and Otto, patented a gas engine in 1866 on entirely new principles, using the now familiar four-stroke cycle. A Frenchman named Beau de Rochas had suggested a similar principle for driving a gas engine in 1862. A score of years later Sir Dugald Clerk patented a "two-stroke" method of operating a gas engine. The four-stroke cycle is explained under the heading Gas Engine; we illustrate here its application to a motor-car engine using petrol.

Diagrams of these cycles may appear complicated, but all that we really need to remember is that there are *four* things necessary : 1, intake of fuel gas, or fuel oil ; 2, compression of the fuel and the air sucked in with it, or forced in separately; 3, ignition by a spark, a flame or, in the case of the Diesel engine, by the heat of compression; and 4, the ejection of the products of combustion. This is the four-stroke cycle ; No. 3 is the power-stroke, during which the exploding gas-air mixture, or the burning oil-air mixture, expands enormously against the piston and drives it downwards. For the rest of the three operations in the cycle it is the flywheel, by its acquired momentum, which moves the piston in and out.

The inlet and exhaust valves are lifted at the proper moments by cams kept moving by linkage from the main driving shaft, once the engine is got moving. The suction needed to draw in the mixture (in petrol engines, for example) is supplied by the engine piston, but some initial force must be supplied from outside for starting. In petrol engines this is obtained by turning a hand-crank slipped over the end of the driving shaft; motor vehicles have an electric starter, driven by the vehicle-lighting batteries, and this is automatically disengaged when the car engine has gathered sufficient speed to run on its own. Large Diesel engines are started by a blast of compressed air

from a supply previously stored in an " air-bottle.' Other oil engines need the flame from a blowlamp to warm up the mixture in a sort of annexe to the cylinder, and require the flywheel to be turned to start the sequence of operations.

In the petrol engine (this is a type in which the fuel is an oil very volatile, and easily vaporized at ordinary temperatures), the air is drawn through a choke tube; the petrol jet is so placed, with its orifice in the throat of the choke tube, that the entering air draws fuel out in the form of minute globules, so that an explosive petrol-air mixture is fed to the cylinders. A float in the carburetter maintains a suitable level of petrol, working something like the float-valve of a water cistern. Petrol flows either by gravity from the petrol tank, or is pumped by mechanism connected with the engine, or by an electric pump driven off the vehicle batteries.

These were for a long time the only methods of feeding fuel to such an engine, but owing to the development of aircraft engines and the need for them to be independent of gravity, various methods of injecting the petrol directly into the cylinders have been used, air being then supplied independently. It is of course the oxygen that is really important in the air supply. By super-charging—forcing in air under pressure instead of merely letting the engine suck in atmospheric air—a greater volume of air (more oxygen, in fact) can be supplied in a given time, with the benefit of greater power. Super-charging has been adopted also for racing cars, and for certain other types of motor vehicles.

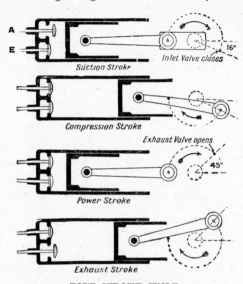

FOUR-STROKE CYCLE
The four " strokes " of an internal combustion engine are shown. Except during the power stroke, the piston is moved only by the fly-wheel; the inlet (A) and exhaust (E) valves are operated by cams.

The electric spark for igniting the mixture is supplied by an induction coil or a magneto-electric generator driven by the engine. The proper timing of the spark is done by cam mechanism connected to the engine. The petrol engine works best at high speed, and the special problems involved in making a vehicle go at various speeds—ranging from a slow one for manoeuvring, to a fast one for open-road motoring—are overcome by the use of a variable-speed gear-box, a device which is described under the heading Motor Vehicles.

In a petrol engine working on the two-stroke system there is an enclosed, gas-tight, crankshaft case which plays a large part in taking in the fuel-air mixture and in transferring it to the engine cylinder at the appropriate time. The mixture, sucked in by the piston on an upward stroke, is drawn into the crankcase below the piston: it is compressed (in the crankcase) by the downward stroke of the piston; and the piston, moving further down, opens the transfer ports seen on the left in the diagram (page 1737), thus forcing the mixture into the cylinder head, on top of the piston.

On beginning to rise again, the piston closes the transfer ports which it had just opened; rising farther, it compresses the mixture in the cylinder above it. Now the piston is forced down by the explosion which takes place at this moment. It uncovers the exhaust port (*see* diagram), and the burnt gases and products of the explosion escape, aided by the peculiar shape of the top of the piston. In its next upward movement the piston uncovers the induction port from the carburetter and sucks in more fuel-air mixture, bringing us back to where we were at the beginning of the cycle. Immediately the sequence starts again.

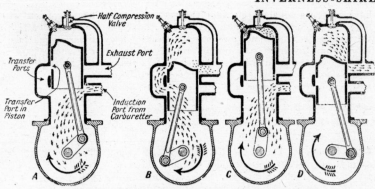

CYCLE OF THE 'TWO-STROKE' PETROL ENGINE
These diagrams illustrate the working of a 'two-stroke' engine—that is, one in which an explosion takes place in the cylinder on every alternate piston stroke. (A) induction and compression of the mixture; (B) transfer to cylinder; (C) explosion; and (D) exhaust. The two-stroke engine has a distinctive 'purring' note.

In examining the two-stroke diagram, remember that A and C show different portions of the up-stroke; while B and D illustrate different portions of the down-stroke. There are four ports: two transfer ports, an exhaust port, and an induction or fuel-inlet port. They are all uncovered or closed by the piston. A transfer port in the piston itself allows the fuel-air mixture in the crankcase below to pass up around the transfer ports in the cylinder and to travel above the piston. The only valve is the half-compression valve, used to ease the compression in starting the engine.

Gottfried Daimler (who had been manager of Otto's factory) produced an engine working on petrol in 1884. Two years later he built a petrol engine which weighed 88 lb. per horse-power. Heavy as this engine seems to us today, in proportion to its power output, it was only about one-tenth as weighty as the gas engines then being built. Daimler's original idea was to use his engine for propelling small boats and barges. The coming of the motor-car spurred on inventors of petrol engines, and the use of aluminium alloys made for reduction in weight. Carburetters were gradually improved. Later came the aeroplane, and we may recall that until the Wright brothers had managed to build a light and efficient petrol engine they could not fly.

Priestman's Paraffin-driven Engine

About the same time that Daimler built his first petrol engine, Priestman invented one to run on a heavier oil—paraffin, or kerosene as it is sometimes named. The oil was sprayed into a vaporizing chamber warmed by a lamp, and the charge of oil vapour and air was fired by a hot tube. The tube had an open end where it projected in the cylinder, and a closed end outside. It was first heated by a lamp to start the engine, and then remained hot enough to fire the charge by itself as the piston compressed the fuel mixture. Early petrol and gas engines also were fired by the hot-tube method, for the reason that electrical apparatus at that day was not yet efficient enough to give reliable spark ignition.

Later came engines—such as the Hornsby-Akroyd—using medium-oil, a heavier fuel than paraffin. For these the hot-bulb system of ignition

was used. This bulb was an extension of the cylinder and was heated by a lamp; here again the heat of compression, when the engine got running, proved enough to fire the charge thereafter.

With the Diesel engine we come to a new type, in which the fuel does not need to be vaporized before the engine can burn it, and only the air needed for combustion has to be compressed. This engine is described and illustrated under its own heading where also are some facts about its relative, known as the semi-Diesel.

These, then, are the lines on which the internal engine has developed, as far as reciprocating engines—those that act by the two-and-fro movement of a piston—are concerned. But there is another class, including the gas turbine and various jet-propulsion devices. These are described under the headings Gas Turbine and Jet Propulsion.

Inverness-shire. The largest county of Scotland, it stretches across the country from the Moray Firth on the east to the Atlantic Ocean. It lies south of Ross and Cromarty, and west of Nairn, Banff, and Aberdeenshire, with Perthshire and Argyll on its southern boundary. It is entirely a mountainous country, except for the low-lying land adjoining the shores of the Moray Firth, in the neighbourhood of the county town of Inverness. The county also includes several islands, among them being the curiously named Rum, Eigg and Muck in the Inner Hebrides, and Harris (the south part of the island Harris and Lewis, which gives its name to the tweeds) and Uist farther out. The largest of them is the lovely isle of Skye.

A very interesting feature is the Caledonian Canal, which links up the waters of Loch Linnhe, Loch Lochy and Loch Ness, thus providing a navigable waterway right across Scotland, over 60 miles in length. Some of the highest mountains in the United Kingdom are within Inverness-shire, including the monarch of all, Ben Nevis (4,406 feet). At its foot is Fort William, a favourite tourist centre. Much of the county is moorland, little of the soil being under cultivation. Sheep breeding is the leading industry, but fishing and distilling are also important.

The town of Inverness, capital of the Highlands, is on the river Ness, and has an ancient history, having been a royal burgh since the 12th century. One of the principal buildings is St. Andrew's Cathedral, a handsome modern structure. Six miles from Inverness (the population of which is 25,000) is Culloden Moor, where the English, under the Duke of Cumberland, inflicted a crushing defeat on Prince Charles and his supporters (April 16, 1746), destroying the hopes of the House of Stuart of regaining the English throne. The area of Inverness-shire is 4,210 square miles and its population about 82,000.

Iodine.

The drug iodine and its compounds are used in the treatment of many ailments. Iodine is used as a disinfectant and antiseptic; and also as a counter-irritant to relieve pain and congestion. Iodoform, which has an unpleasant, sweetish odour, is a compound of carbon, hydrogen and iodine used as an antiseptic in surgical dressings.

Iodine is the essential constituent of thyroxin, the active principle of the thyroid gland; and a deficiency of iodine tends to promote the disease called goitre, in which the gland becomes enlarged. It is believed that a person who receives an exceedingly small quantity of iodine each day will remain free from goitrous symptoms; our food and water we drink often contains sufficient iodine to supply this small quantity, which is probably something like ·000005 oz. Iodine occurs in seaweed, sea water, and fish, and in the air about salt water. There are, generally few goitre cases near sea-coasts or among people who eat considerable sea food.

Most of the world's iodine comes as a by-product from the nitrate beds of Chile. Commercial quantities of iodine are secured from seaweed in France, Scotland, Ireland, Norway, Japan and Java. The seaweed, or kelp, is collected and dried in the open, usually on the shore. It is then burned in shallow troughs lined with pebbles from the beach. The resultant " ash," in the form of brittle slabs, is now the raw material from which iodine can easily be extracted.

Iodine is known in chemistry as one of the four halogens (*q.v.*), the others being chlorine, bromine, and fluorine. Its chief compounds, called iodides, are formed with various metals Pure iodine is a crystalline substance which turns to heavy purple vapour when heated. It was discovered in 1811 by Bernard Courtois, of Paris, who was treating seaweed to get saltpetre for the manufacture of gunpowder for Napoleon's army.

Ions AND Ionization.

The word " ion " was coined by the famous chemist Michael Faraday (1791–1867), and means an electrically charged atom, radical, or molecule. (*See* Chemistry).

If you dissolve some ordinary sugar in water and dip into this solution two separate wires which are connected to the terminals of a dry battery or accumulator, no electric current will pass through the solution, which is therefore a non-conductor of electricity. But if you do the same thing with a solution of common salt (sodium chloride, NaCl) you will find that the solution conducts electricity, and that some bubbles of gas (hydrogen) are formed near the wire connected with the negative terminal of the battery. This strange difference in behaviour is due to the fact that sodium chloride is what we call an " ionized " compound, whereas sugar is not ionized.

Ionization is caused by the way in which atoms combine (*see* Chemistry). When an atom of sodium and an atom of chlorine combine to form a molecule of sodium chloride it is believed that the sodium atom loses an electron which it gives to the chlorine atom, and so the sodium atom becomes a positively charged ion and the chlorine atom a negatively charged ion. Being charged with electricity of opposite kinds, these ions, when in solution in water, conduct electricity by moving towards the wires connected with the battery, the sodium ion moving towards the negative pole and the chlorine ion towards the positive pole. In our experiment using metal wires and a water solution of sodium chloride we do not actually see sodium and chlorine liberated, because sodium metal rapidly reacts with water to form caustic soda and hydrogen (our bubbles of gas), and freshly formed (" nascent ") chlorine attacks most metals, forming the chloride of the metal.

BEAUTY SPOT OF INVERNESS-SHIRE
Alexander B. Beattie
Beauly Firth, near Inverness, a favourite resort of yachtsmen, flows out into the North Sea through Moray Firth. The opposite shore is in the county of Ross and Cromarty. In the distance, above Strathpeffer, can be seen Ben Wyvis, rising to a height of 3,429 feet.

Many compounds, like the sugar of our experiment, are not ionized, and it is thought that this is because their atoms are held together by sharing electrons, and are not, therefore, electrically charged.

Our experiment with the salt solution is an example of a process called electrolysis (*q.v.*), which is the basis of many important industries, such as those for the production of chlorine and caustic soda, magnesium metal, aluminium metal, and for electroplating. These large industries could never have been established if there were no such thing as ionization.

Ions that, during electrolysis, collect at the anode (the positive pole) are called anions; ions that collect at the cathode (the negative pole) are called cations. Thus, hydrogen ions and many of the metal ions are cations, whereas ions of the halogens (*q.v.*). and of radicals, like nitrate and sulphate radicals, are anions.

Svante August Arrhenius (1859–1927), a Swedish chemist, provided ideas about ionization which fit many of the experimental facts. At one time it was thought that inorganic crystals like common salt split up into ions when the crystals were dissolved in water; but we now know that the solid crystals are made up of ions, so that the action of dissolving the crystals does not produce the ions. We do not yet completely understand ionization; but two chemists, Debye and Hückel, have suggested that, when ionic compounds are dissolved in water, the

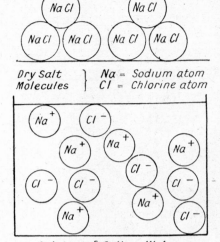

Dry Salt Molecules } Na = Sodium atom Cl = Chlorine atom

Solution of Salt in Water
Na⁺ = Sodium ion Cl⁻ = Chlorine ion

Na⁺ = Sodium ion Cl⁻ = Chlorine ion

BREAKING UP MOLECULES

Shown diagrammatically at the top are molecules of common salt in a dry state, the atoms being in close association. Lower is indicated the breaking up of this connexion by dissolving the salt in water. Each atom carries an electric charge, such electrically charged atoms being known as ions.

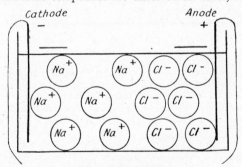

Cathode   Anode

HOW IONS MOVE

The movement of ions in a solution of sodium chloride is shown. The positively charged sodium ions (cations) move to the negative pole or cathode ; the negatively charged chloric ions (anions) move to the positive pole or anode. Ions may also be formed in gases.

ions already present in the crystals merely become separated from one another by the water.

We see therefore that ions exist in some solids, and persist as ions when these solids are dissolved in water. Ions may also be formed in gases, these gaseous ions being molecules or atoms which have lost or gained electrons and which are therefore positively or negatively charged. The ionization of gases has played a very important part in scientific developments, mainly because ionized gases (like solutions of ionized solids) are conductors of electricity.

You may wonder how it is that we know how atoms and ions are arranged in crystals. Sir William H. Bragg (1862–1942) was a pioneer in the use of X-rays for the study of the internal structure of crystals, and to do so he had to measure the angles at which X-rays are deflected after falling on crystals. In order to do this he used an " ionization chamber," that is, a chamber containing a gas. X-rays ionize gases and make them conduct electricity; and by rotating the crystal until the ionization chamber became a conductor of electricity he was able to measure the angles at which the X-rays were deflected, and then to make calculations about the arrangements of the ions in crystals.

The gamma rays and the particles shot off from the nuclei of radio-active atoms, such as radium atoms, also ionize gases. That is why radium can be detected and measured with a simple gold-leaf electroscope. By making these gaseous ions condense water vapour, C. T. R. Wilson, of Cambridge, was actually able to photograph the tracks made by the extremely rapidly moving particles. The instrument known as a Geiger-Müller counter may be considered to be an elaborate form of ionization chamber ; with it we can detect extremely small quantities of radium, and even count the particles as they are hurled out of the splitting atoms.

Gaseous ionization plays a part in other things, such as the transmission of wireless waves, the Aurora Borealis, modern electric street lighting, and the production of very short and intense flashes of light used to photograph rapidly moving objects. Uranium isotopes can be separated by deflecting charged atoms, so that ionization has helped to produce atom bombs. (*See* Electrolysis).

Iowa. Among the finest farming regions of the world, Iowa is the leading agricultural state of the United States. It is bounded on the north by the state of Minnesota, on the east by Wisconsin and Illinois, on the south by Missouri, on the west by Nebraska and South Dakota. The Mississippi river flows along the entire eastern boundary, and the Missouri along three-quarters of the western. Its area is 56,280 square miles, most of it prairie.

Among the principal products of Iowa are maize, oats, butter, eggs, poultry, cattle and fruit. There are no big industrial centres, the various manufactures being dispersed throughout the State, which

National Museum, Naples; photo Brogi

IPHIGENIA AND AGAMEMNON

The Greek hero Agamemnon having killed a stag sacred to the goddess
Artemis, a soothsayer declared that he must offer his daughter Iphigenia as
a sacrifice. In this Pompeiian wall-painting Agamemnon (extreme left)
is mourning, while Iphigenia is being carried away.

pearl buttons and cosmetics. Mineral resources include coal, gypsum, limestone, clay, sand and gravel.

There are 8,800 miles of railway and 83 airports in the State, and 25 universities and colleges. Iowa City, the seat of the State university, was the capital from 1839 to 1857, when it was superseded by Des Moines. The population of Iowa State is 2,538,268.

Iphigenia. (Pron. if-i-jen-ī′-a). According to Greek legend, the Greek fleet destined for Troy was detained at Aulis by a calm sent by the goddess Artemis, who had been offended because the Greek hero Agamemnon had killed a stag sacred to her. A soothsayer declared that Agamemnon must sacrifice his daughter Iphigenia to appease the wrath of the goddess. Iphigenia was sent for, under the pretext that she was to be married to Achilles, but at the moment when the sacrifice was about to take place, Artemis carried her off in a cloud to the country of the Tauri (Crimea), where she became a priestess. Subsequently Iphigenia's brother Orestes and his friend Pylades arrived at the Crimea, where they were taken prisoners and were to be sacrificed ; but Iphigenia recognized Orestes and fled with him to Greece. The story of Iphigenia is the subject of two plays (Iphigenia at Aulis, and Iphigenia among the Tauri) by the Athenian dramatist Euripides (480–406 B.C.), which have been translated by Gilbert Murray ; one by the French playwright Jean Racine (1639–99) ; and one by Johann von Goethe (1749–1832).

has the world's largest cereal, washing-machine and fountain-pen factories. It makes also agricultural implements, furnaces, gas and electrical equipment, bronze, aluminium and copper goods, clothing,

MODERN PERSIA *under* TWO NAMES

Like several of the mighty empires of the past, Persia or Iran (it is known by both names) retains only a memory of its former glory. But now it is developing new industries and may yet experience a great revival.

Iran (Pron. i-rahn′) or **Persia.** One of the many interesting things about this country is its use of two names : Iran for use within its own boundaries, Persia as its official designation abroad. Iran is its name in the Persian language, and it was as Iran that the country wished to be known from March 1935 in external affairs, on the grounds that the name Persia was, strictly speaking, associated only with the small southern province of Pars (or Fars) and did not properly cover the whole country. But mistakes occurred owing to the resemblance between the name Iran and that of the neighbouring country of Iraq, and because of that it

was decided in 1949 to resume the name of Persia abroad. As Iran appears on many maps we continue to use that name equally with Persia in this chapter. Of the great Persian Empire that 25 centuries ago extended from the Indus in the sub-continent of India to the Danube and from the Oxus in Central Asia to the Nile, only the western half of the Iranian plateau remains to Persia—a region three times as large as France.

Today Persia is thought of by most of the world as a country out of which come beautiful things—Omar Khayyam's poems and countless legends and fables; Persian rugs, usually in flower patterns woven of silk or of wool; attar of roses from

---

Extent.—North to south, about 860 miles ; east to west, 1,385 miles. Area about 628,000 square miles. Population estimated at 13,000,000.

Physical Features.—Western half of Iranian plateau (general altitude 3,000 to 5,000 feet), crossed by numerous mountain ranges (Mt. Demavend, 18,600 feet) ; salt and sandy deserts cover about two-thirds of the plateau area. Salt lakes, Sistan and Urmia. Caspian Sea on north, Persian Gulf and Gulf of Oman on south : only navigable river, Karun.

Principal Products.—Wheat, barley, cotton, tobacco, rice, beet sugar, fruit and nuts ; silk, opium, gums ; wool and hides ; iron, copper, tin, lead, coal, petroleum, turquoises, salt, etc. ; rugs and carpets ; attar of roses.

Chief Cities.—Teheran (capital, about 540,000), Tabriz (214,000), Isfahan (205,000), Meshed (176,000), Shiraz (129,000), Resht (122,000), Hamadan (104,000).

stretch oasis towns like stepping-stones—Meshed, the most hallowed spot for Mahomedans in the whole of Iran ; then Tabbas; then Yezd, in the very heart of the country, and important for its silk manufactures and opium trade; then Kerman.

At Kerman are manufactured some of the most beautiful Persian rugs. Forty miles west of Meshed, in a fertile plain, lies Nishapur, the birthplace of the poet Omar Khayyám.

It is in the western part of Iran that you will find most of the great cities, including those that have been capitals in ancient and modern times. Here are Susa and Ecbatana, now Hamadan, the cities one reads of in Xenophon. Susa is the ancient "Shushan," where the story of the book of Esther is laid. Here, too, is Shiraz, the city of wine, rose-water and attar of roses; and 35 miles east lie the ruins of Persepolis, the great city that Alexander destroyed in 331 B.C. These ruins are among the most important that have survived from the ancient days of Iran. Isfahan (or Ispahan), once a capital, lies in the centre of the habitable part of the country, in a pleasant fertile plain.

Tabriz is an important commercial centre and the terminus of the railway from Tiflis. Teheran, the modern capital, lies at the foot of the Elburz Mountains, only 70 miles from the Caspian Sea. The city is at an altitude of 4,000 feet, overlooked by the snowy peak of Demavend, the highest mountain in Iran. The air is dry and bracing, and you can see for almost unbelievable distances. Teheran

the gardens of Shiraz; and turquoises from Nishapur. For the collector it means old porcelains having a rare apple-green glaze, and manuscripts illuminated with delicate miniatures of turbaned princes, flowering trees, and dancing gazelles, so faultless that there may be hundreds of figures in one square foot of battle scene, all of which will stand scrutiny with a magnifying glass.

Persia has been sung by the poets as the land of luscious fruits, and yet the Iranian plateau,

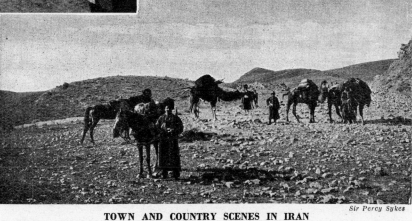

Sir Percy Sykes

TOWN AND COUNTRY SCENES IN IRAN

The city of Kum in Iran is visited every year by thousands of pilgrims who go to worship at the golden-domed shrine of the revered Fatima—the favourite daughter of Mahomet, founder of the Mahomedan religion. The upper photograph shows the gateway to her burial place. In the lower picture are men of one of the nomadic tribes of Turkish origin who spend the warm months in the uplands, moving down to the plains in winter.

which it shares with Afghanistan and Baluchistan to the east, is a high arid region more than two-thirds desert. To enter Iran is like climbing a ladder, whether you come across the Caspian Sea from Russia, or follow the old caravan trail from Trebizond, a Turkish town on the Black Sea, or sail up the Tigris and take the older trail between Baghdad, the capital of Iraq, and Kermanshah.

In one-third of Iran nothing could ever be made to grow. The great salt deserts, or Kavirs, occupy the greater part of the eastern provinces. Across the salt deserts and the adjoining sandy deserts

has a beautiful gate of coloured porcelain tiles, and all the better houses have high-vaulted underground rooms. A city once dull and dismal is being gradually transformed into a real capital.

During the past 50 years the rulers, or shahs, who rule the country through an elected assembly called the Majlis, have made various attempts to modernize Teheran. A tramway line was built, and in recent years several modern buildings have been erected. The water supply is brought by canals from the mountains; it is sufficient in winter, but usually runs short in summer when it is most

IRAN: LAND OF DESERT AND PLATEAU

In one-third of Iran nothing could ever be made to grow. The richest agricultural region is the narrow plain bordering the Caspian Sea. Vast areas of salt or sandy desert have hindered the development of communications.

of exploitation, near Shushtar and Haft-Kel, to a refinery on the island of Abadan in the Gulf. The fields, still far from fully developed, are now being worked by foreign capital, principally British and American. Copper, iron, tin, lead, rock salt and coal are found in large quantities, especially in the mountains of central and western Iran. Although some of these minerals have been mined for centuries, the methods have been primitive and it remains for modern engineering to develop these great resources more fully.

Most of the people are Mahomedans of the Shiite sect, and are inclined to look upon the innovations of western Christians with suspicion. Education was made compulsory in 1943, but this is only gradually being enforced. Doctors are urgently needed. With sewage systems almost unknown, flies everywhere, water supplies unprotected from animals and refuse, it is little wonder that Iran is disease-ridden.

A tradition-bound official class long held back Iran's development, but Riza Pahlevi, who seized power in 1925, was an enlightened Shah. In particular he realized the importance of building roads and railways. Under him Iran made great strides forward; but in 1941 he was forced to abdicate when the British and Russians, dissatisfied with his refusal to get rid of the many Germans in his capital whose presence threatened the Allied war effort in the Middle East, declared war on Iran and conquered it after four days' fighting. At the Teheran Conference of 1943 the leaders of the Governments of the U.S.A., U.S.S.R., and Great Britain guaranteed to respect the territorial integrity, sovereignty, and independence of Iran. For Iran's history *see* Persia, pages 2554-2556.

needed. About one-fourth of the people of Iran are city dwellers, and another fourth are nomads. These nomads tend their flocks and herds in the grassy valleys and on the slopes of the mountain ranges, and prey upon the peaceful communities for agricultural supplies.

Half the people are peasants, tillers of the soil, and this in spite of the fact that only three or four districts of Iran are naturally fertile. The most important agricultural province is Azerbaijan to the extreme north-west; always a centre of unrest, it was granted a measure of home rule in June 1946, but the concession was withdrawn six months later.

In most places the Iranian peasant can wrest crops from the soil only by irrigation, and irrigation is not the simple matter of canals and surface channels that it is in other countries. Having little rain and few rivers he must use the mountain snows as they melt, and must bring the water, often long distances, by tunnel—otherwise this source of supply would evaporate in the dry air.

Beneath this barren land lies buried the key to Iran's future—oil. Vast petroleum fields stretch from the Caspian Sea to the Persian Gulf. There are pipe-lines from the centres

OIL LINE CROSSING THE IRANIAN DESERT

Like the neighbouring country of Iraq, Iran is rich in oil, the fields stretching from the Caspian Sea to the Persian Gulf. Above is a section of a pipe-line through which oil is pumped to a port, whence it will be taken by tankers all over the world. Among other mineral resources, coal, lead, salt and turquoise mines are worked.

A Living LAND of Long-Dead EMPIRES

Of the greatest antiquity is Iraq, though its name is new. Where Babylon and Nineveh flourished and faded, where Greek and Persian and Turk conquered and laid waste, a strong new Arab nation is growing up.

Iraq. That cradle of civilization, the wide plain between the Rivers Tigris and Euphrates, which for uncounted centuries has watched peoples and cities rise to power and vanish, is once more the home of a young nation. This is Iraq, an Arab country formed from the land of ancient Mesopotamia (*q.v.*) and wrested by the British in the First World War (1914–18) from the rule of the Turk.

It is bounded by the Persian Hills on the east, by Turkey on the north, the Syrian mountains on the west, and the deserts of Arabia on the south. The greater part of the country is desert and barren, rolling steppes, relieved only by a fringe of green along the banks of the Tigris and Euphrates which unite to form the Shatt-el-Arab emptying into the Persian Gulf in the south-east. The silt of the two rivers has formed a plain and delta so fertile that here legend places the Garden of Eden.

Centuries of war and the shifting of the river beds have destroyed the irrigation systems which made the plain the seat of scores of cities now long crumbled into ruins. Plans to bring back the old prosperity by new canals, reservoirs, and power-pumps lag because of the nation's poverty. Yet good crops grow where water is available, and Iraq exports four-fifths of the world's supply of dates, as well as barley, wheat, cotton goods, liquorice roots, sheepskins and wool.

Straggling towns dotting the river banks have none of the ancient grandeur of Babylon and Nineveh. Mosul, far up the Tigris, and the rich oilfields of the north were claimed by Turkey, but were awarded to Iraq by the League of Nations in 1926. Iraq is developing this wealth, and one pipe-line runs from Kirkuk across the desert to Tripoli in Syria, and another to Haifa, a port of Palestine. Near Hit, on the Euphrates, are rich bitumen wells which furnish pitch to cover the bowl-like native reed boats. In Baghdad (*q.v.*), the capital, the depressing summer heat, often reaching 122° F., drives the people to the *serdab*, a cellar with a ventilating shaft, whose opening is turned to catch every breath of wind.

Basra, situated on the Shatt-el-Arab 60 miles from the Persian Gulf, is the chief port. Basra and Baghdad are on air service routes between Europe and the East, and one of the country's few railways connects them. The last part of

Area.—116,600 square miles: estimated population (1945), 4,611,350.

Physical Features.—Desert area, relieved only by foothills and the valleys of the Euphrates and Tigris, which unite to form the Shatt-el-Arab.

Principal Products.—Wheat, barley; dates; wool; oil.

Chief Cities.—Baghdad (capital, 340,000); Mosul (98,000); Basra (62,000).

the railway line linking Baghdad with the Bosporus was opened to traffic in July 1940. There are about 4,000 miles of roads suitable for vehicular traffic.

The Arabs, who make up more than 90 per cent of the population, are about equally divided between the Sunnite and Shiite sects of Mahomedanism. Strange religions are those of the Sabians —star-worshippers, who live in riverside towns, for their ritual calls for running water—and of the Yezidis, who are devil-worshippers.

Among the ruins of the old irrigation canals live the swamp Arabs in their reed huts. These people were never conquered by the Turks. They claim descent from the first dwellers of the plain, the Sumerians, and believe that the swamp districts where they live have remained there since the great flood of Biblical times. The swamp Arabs, the city-dwellers and the farmers are all scorned by the

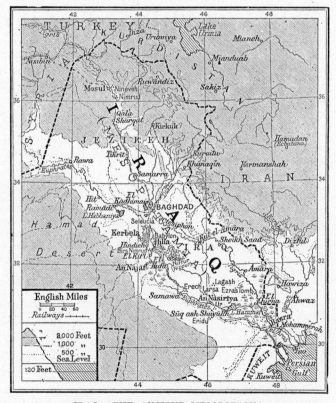

IRAQ : THE ANCIENT MESOPOTAMIA
Freed from the Turks during the First World War (1914–18), Iraq became an independent Arab kingdom in 1932. The most fertile region lies between the Tigris and the Euphrates—the land of Mesopotamia.

Major W. J. P. Rodd

IRAQIS BUYING POTTERY
Just outside Baghdad, the capital of Iraq, is a potters' village, where every sort of domestic utensil is made in forms that have endured for centuries.

desert Arab, who leads a wandering life and is largely a law unto himself.

Freed from Turkish rule after the First World War (1914–18), Iraq became an independent State; and Feisal, an able Arab leader who had directed the Arab revolt against the Turks, was pro-

claimed king in 1921. Great Britain received from the League of Nations a mandate to administer the country until it was ready for complete self-government. In 1932 the mandate was terminated, and Iraq became a member of the League of Nations. Under the terms of a Treaty of Alliance, Great Britain was allowed to retain air bases in Iraq and was granted the right to land troops in emergency.

During the Second World War (1939–45) such an emergency did arise when in April 1941 Rashid Ali el Gailani, a former Prime Minister and a pro-German, seized power and formed an anti-British Government. The British air base at Habbaniya, near Baghdad, was besieged for several weeks. Meanwhile British troops had been landed at Basra and others had crossed the desert from Palestine. After some fighting the Iraqis asked for an armistice in May 1941, and Rashid Ali fled the country.

Iraq declared war on Germany, Italy, and Japan in January 1943, but took no active part in the struggle. In 1945 the country joined the Arab League, the other members being Egypt, Transjordan, Saudi Arabia, Syria, the Lebanon and Yemen. The avowed purposes of the League are to further the political, cultural and economic interests of all Arab countries. Iraqi sympathies were with the Arabs over the question of the division of Palestine between the Jews and the Arabs, and in 1948 Iraqi troops took part in fighting against the Jews who set up a Jewish State. The population of Iraq is 3,560,000.

PAST and PRESENT of the EMERALD ISLE

Here are strange contrasts of a lovely land of rich green pastures (hence 'Emerald Isle'), beautiful scenery and warm-hearted people and a chronicle of centuries of turbulence and distress.

Ireland. A romantic history, alluring scenic beauty, the charm of a warm-hearted and impulsive people, and its political problems of recent times, give to Ireland an importance out of all proportion to its 32,586 square miles of area. It is separated from its sister island of Great Britain by only 13 miles of water (North Channel) in the north, and 47 miles (St. George's Channel) in the south, and its fortunes have been inextricably entangled for more than 1,500 years with those of its neighbour.

In surface Ireland is an inland plain, surrounded by a rim of low mountains. The climate is much like that of England, mild and temperate, but the winters are warmer, and there is more rain. There are numerous rivers, of which the Boyne and Liffey in the east, the Barrow and Blackwater in the south, and the Shannon in the west are the most important. Lough Neagh is the largest lake in the British Isles, and the Lakes of Killarney perhaps the most beautiful.

The population represents two waves of Celtic peoples who came by way of England from the

Continent. About three-quarters of the inhabitants are Roman Catholics. While the northern counties are predominantly Protestant (mostly Presbyterian), the western and southern counties are almost entirely Roman Catholic.

Historic antagonisms even more than religion separate the Protestant Ulstermen from the Catholic south. Economic differences also serve to divide the Emerald Isle. The Ulstermen are hard-headed men of business whose trade and manufactures have enriched their part of the country. They are accustomed of old to the monopoly of political power and to play the part of a ruling class. The south, on the other hand, is made up of a Catholic peasantry who are less progressive than their neighbours to the north. They cherish old traditions and old grievances; but they are essentially a kindly, generous, and talented people.

The land in Ireland is mostly leased in small holdings, averaging not more than 28 acres to a farm. The soil is thin, and the rainfall so heavy that not much grain can be raised. Most

---

Extent.—Greatest length (N.E. to S.W.), 302 miles ; greatest breadth, 174 miles. Total area, 32,586 sq. miles ; total population, about 4,230,000.

Physical Features.—Central plain surrounded by mountains. Highest peaks—Carrantuohill in the Macgillicuddy Reeks (3,414 feet) ; Lugnaquilla in the Wicklow Mts. (3,039 feet) ; Galtee Mts. (3,018 feet) ; and Slieve Donard in the Mts. of Mourne (2,796 feet). Largest lake—Lough Neagh (150 square miles) ; chief river, the Shannon (240 miles long), flowing into the Atlantic.

Principal Products.—Turnips, potatoes, mangolds, flax ; linen goods ; ships ; fish ; cattle, horses ; beer ; whisky ; bread and biscuits ; dairy produce.

Chief Towns.—Dublin (capital of Eire), 495,000 ; Belfast (capital Northern Ireland), 438,000 ; Cork (Eire), 75,000 ; Londonderry (Northern Ireland), 47,000 ; Limerick (Eire), 42,000.

of the country is given over to cattle-raising and dairying; potatoes are the staple crop. The climate makes the raising of flax profitable, and much of the north is given over to this crop which partially supplies the linen manufactures of Belfast. There is almost no iron or coal in the country, and there was no water-power development until the Irish Free State (Eire) carried out the Shannon electrification scheme. Despite these handicaps, the linen and shipbuilding industries of Belfast are world famous.

While the people of England were still barbarians, Ireland for a time possessed one of the most advanced civilizations in western Europe. This was the time of St. Patrick (died A.D. 461 ?) and of a flourishing Irish Celtic Christianity. Henry II of England conquered the Irish in the latter part of the 12th century. But only the eastern portion of the island was much affected by English institutions, or (for centuries) adopted the English language. The rest of Ireland was long occupied by clans who warred with one another and with the English. Irish habits and customs even invaded the English Pale, as the colonized area about Dublin was called, and within a few generations English settlers within the Pale tended to become Irish in outlook and sympathy, in many cases " more Irish than the Irish themselves." The Reformation, which left Ireland unchanged in its Catholic faith while England broke with the Pope and set up a national Church, widened the breach.

The Tudor sovereigns began in the 16th century the policy of enlarging English influence by settling large plantations or colonies of English and Scots in Ireland, dispossessing the Irish peasants of their land and driving them into the west. Further dispossessions went on under the first Stuarts, and whole tracts of north Ireland were taken from a desperate peasantry, to be given to Scottish settlers.

Later, when Charles I of England was busy with affairs at home, the Irish rebelled and put to death thousands of Protestant settlers (1641). Oliver Cromwell (1599–1658) reconquered the country, and with such rigour that his name remains a byword of cruelty there. More land was taken from the peasants and given to the English; and indeed the " Cromwellian Settlement," as it was called, was the cause of most of the later troubles between the real Irish and the imported English colonists, in spite of the measure of prosperity which it created.

Then, when James II was driven from England in 1688, Ireland supported him because of his efforts on behalf of the Catholic religion. But with the aid of the Protestant north and an English army, William of Orange—who had become William III of England—defeated James at the Battle of the Boyne (1690). This meant the triumph of Pro-

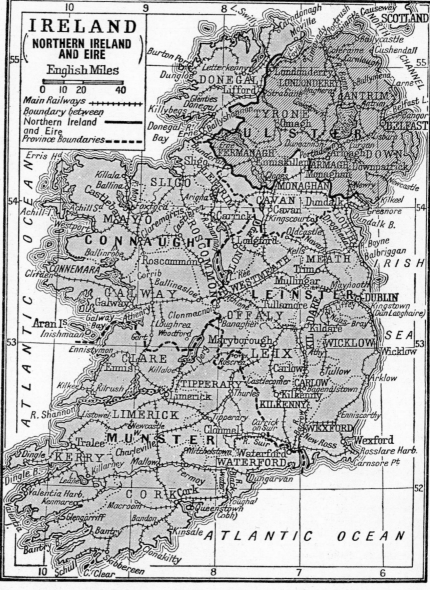

WILLIAM III AT THE BATTLE OF THE BOYNE

On July 1, 1690, the English under William III met the French and Irish under the exiled James II at the Battle of the Boyne, near Drogheda. William led his army in person, and in this painting by Benjamin West (1738-1820) he is seen emerging from the River Drogheda at the head of his cavalry. The lifeless body of Schomberg, William's lieutenant, is being carried off the field. The defeat of James put an end to his hope of regaining the English throne.

testant Ulster, or the Orangemen, who for a century and a half remained all-powerful in Ireland. Catholics were debarred from voting or holding office; Catholic Church services were forbidden under penalty of death. Such legislation only had the effect of intensifying the Catholicism of Ireland.

With the close of the 18th century, Ireland was induced to give up its separate Parliament by the Act of Union with Great Britain (1800), but thenceforth it had representatives in the House of Lords and the House of Commons. In 1829 the last of the penal laws against Catholics—excluding them from Parliament—was repealed.

In 1845 a blight destroyed the potato crop and there followed terrible sufferings of the famine years 1846–47. England suspended and then repealed, when too late, the Corn Laws which hindered the free importation of grain. Thousands died from starvation and famine fever, and millions emigrated. From that time on the people have been leaving Ireland for other lands. Before the great famine the population of Ireland was more than 8,000,000; today the population of Eire is about 2,950,000 and that of Northern Ireland about 1,280,000.

The last part of the 19th century saw an attempt by English statesmen to undo old wrongs in Ireland. In 1869 the Protestant Church of Ireland was disestablished, that is, deprived of its privileges as a State church. The Land Acts of 1870, 1881, and 1885 protected tenant farmers, reduced their rents, and made it possible for them to buy their farms on easy terms. The Home Rule Bills of W.E. Gladstone (q.v.) were defeated in the English parliament, but in 1898 the Conservative party gave Ireland a measure of local self-government, and other measures improved conditions.

In 1912 Asquith, the British Prime Minister, introduced into Parliament his Home Rule Bill. The northern province of Ulster feared that an all-Ireland Parliament would discriminate against its religion and against its industry. The Home Rule Bill became law soon after the First World War broke out in 1914. By another act, however, its operation was postponed until after that war.

The attempt of Sir Roger Casement to bring German aid to Ireland (for which he was condemned and hanged), and the trial and execution of 14 leaders of the unsuccessful Easter Rebellion of 1916, when Irish insurgents seized important public buildings in Dublin and proclaimed a Republic, further widened the breach between England and Ireland. Leadership more and more fell into the hands of the Sinn Fein (pron. shin-fān, meaning "ourselves alone "), a revolutionary party which set up an Irish Parliament in 1919, and tried to make Ireland an independent republic. The passing by the British Parliament of a new Home Rule Bill, establishing one Parliament for Ulster and another for the rest of Ireland, did not satisfy the Irish.

The Ulster Parliament was opened, however, in 1921; and a conference was arranged in London between Irish republican delegates and members of the British Cabinet. A treaty was signed on December 6, 1922, giving Ireland full Dominion status in the British Empire, under the name of the Irish Free State, with its own Parliament and President; while Northern Ireland (six counties in Ulster) still held to British allegiance. In 1937 the Free State was renamed Eire and declared to be an independent, sovereign State. For the history of Ireland since 1921, *see* the separate articles on Ireland, Northern; Irish Free State.

BRITAIN'S REALM *in* IRELAND'S ISLE

The only remaining part of Ireland within the United Kingdom is the small north-eastern corner. This little land shows strong contrasts with Southern Ireland in its industry and people, as well as its political loyalties.

Ireland, NORTHERN. At the beginning of the 20th century, when most of Ireland was demanding Home Rule, six of the nine counties in the province of Ulster opposed all attempts to separate them from the United Kingdom. Two-thirds of the people in this region are Protestants, most of them descendants of the Scottish and English colonists who were "planted" in ancient Ulster in the 17th century. They have remained essentially British, and have preferred to keep their status as part of the United Kingdom rather than to become a small Protestant minority in a predominantly Catholic united Ireland.

At Londonderry is this monument to the Reverend George Walker, hero of the city's siege by James II in 1689.

These six north-east counties—Antrim, Down, Armagh, Fermanagh, Londonderry, and Tyrone—together make up only one-sixth of Ireland. They have an area of 5,237 square miles. The country is rolling, with rounded hills geologically a continuation of the Scottish Highlands. Large sections of land are used for grazing, since stock-breeding is the most important branch of agriculture in Northern Ireland. Cattle, sheep, pigs, and poultry are raised for local and English markets, and dairying is a considerable industry. Although there is little level land, more than a fourth of the total area is devoted to crops, of which hay, oats, flax, turnips and potatoes are the most important.

Agriculture, however, is not the chief industry, as it is in the Irish Free State; for the greatest manufacturing region of Ireland centres about Belfast (*q.v.*), the capital of Northern Ireland and its busiest seaport. Here and in neighbouring towns is concentrated more than half the population of the six counties. Londonderry, the second city, is also a manufacturing centre and a seaport. The chief industry in both cities is the manufacture of linen, which employs about one-third of all the country's factory workers. Some of the flax is home-grown, but in normal times the greater part is imported from Russia and Belgium. Shipbuilding, the other leading industry, is centred at Belfast. There are many small industries, such as flour milling and the manufacture of machinery,

J. Dixon-Scott

PARLIAMENT BUILDINGS OF NORTHERN IRELAND

Belfast, the capital of Northern Ireland, boasts many fine buildings, but its chief pride is the Parliament House which contains not only both houses of Parliament but also a number of Government offices. It stands in Stormont Park, an estate of about 300 acres, just outside the city on the Newtownards Road. The foundation stone was laid in 1928 and the buildings were opened four years later. The photograph shows the imposing façade which overlooks the park.

rope and twine, clothing, tobacco and soap; and liquor distilling. Herring and salmon are the principal fisheries. Clay, chalk, granite, and sandstone are quarried. There is no coal worth mining, all the coal consumed having to be imported.

By the terms of the Anglo-Irish Treaty of 1921, six counties of Ulster remained a part of the United Kingdom, the other three, Donegal, Cavan and Monaghan, joining the Irish Free State. The events leading up to this step are described in the article on Ireland (page 1746).

Ulster's history after 1921 continued to be stormy. Within Northern Ireland itself, fierce dissension arose between the Protestant Unionist majority and the Catholic minority that favoured joining the Free State. Relations between Northern

Ireland and the Irish Free State were difficult. Efforts of Free State leaders to bring the northern counties into the Free State were ill received, and a four-year dispute over boundary lines almost started a civil war. The Free State claimed the counties of Fermanagh and Tyrone and several border towns, which are predominantly Catholic. In 1925, however, this difficulty was settled by agreement, and Northern Ireland retained the disputed territory.

Economic barriers, in the form of import duties, as well as racial and religious differences and political loyalties, have prevented the union of Northern and Southern Ireland. Northern Ireland's leaders are conservative, and they believe that the country's prosperity depends upon continuing to encourage the spirit of private enterprise on which its great industries were founded. Hence they dislike and fear the economic policies of Eire with its experiments in government control.

Northern Ireland has a considerable measure of self-government. It has a parliament consisting of a Senate and a House of Commons. The power of putting laws into force is vested in a Governor-General appointed by the British Crown. The Governor-General is advised by a cabinet of ministers, who are responsible to the local parliament. Certain legislative and financial powers are reserved to the British Parliament, to which Northern Ireland, as a part of the United Kingdom, elects 13 members. The population is 1,280,000.

Iris. Although the yellow and purple-and-yellow " flags " are the only wild irises found in Britain, there are many species, ranging in colour from white and yellow to deep blue and purple, found in other parts of the world. Indeed, to its varied hues the flower owes its official name, for Iris was the Greek goddess of the rainbow who carried messages between the gods and men. There are rhizomatous species (with thick rootstems) and bulbous-rooted species.

From a white form of the iris which grows in southern Europe was derived the heraldic device of the fleur-de-lis, which Louis VII of France in the 12th century adopted as the emblem of the French royal house. The fragrant orris-root, used in making toothpaste and powders, is obtained from the rootstocks of the Florentine species. The purple iris of Japan (*I. laevigata*) has been immortalized in many of the loveliest works of that country's artists. The scientific name of the iris family is *Iridaceae*.

J. Dixon-Scott

IN A BELFAST SHIPBUILDING YARD

Shipbuilding is one of Belfast's most important industries, and many famous vessels have been constructed there. Above is one of the slipways on which big ships are built, with huge gantries for hoisting the steelwork into position. The harbour extends over 2,500 acres, with 10 docks and basins.

RIVALS IN BEAUTY—THE IRIS AND THE MOTH

From photo by LYNWOOD M. CHACE. *Painted by* J. M. ETTWEIN   *See text overleaf*

GARDEN IRISES IN EARLY SUMMER

THE picture above shows the glory of a huge bed of irises, flourishing in all their beauty in a garden border. The tall, straight stems bear a wealth of the spear-head buds, each of which opens into the lovely, soft-petalled flower we know so well. The colour plate overleaf shows a lovely individual iris, one of the types developed from the German species *Iris germanica*. Though most wild sorts are yellow or purple, the breeder's skill has made this one red and pink and orange. Beneath it is a great *Cecropia* moth, a native of North America. That the insect is as lovely in its own way as the iris you can see for yourself, as it hangs, newly emerged, beneath the cocoon.

To face page 1749

A YOUNG REPUBLIC *in the* BRITISH ISLES

The greater part of Ireland is included in the Irish Free State, the birth of which is mentioned in the article on Ireland (see page 1746.) In 1937 it adopted a new republican constitution, changing its official name to Eire.

Irish Free State (Eire). "Home Rule," the dream of generations of Irish people, was realized in 1922, when the Irish Free State (Saorstat Eireann) came into being as a self-governing Dominion of the British Commonwealth of Nations. Perhaps no government born of 20th century struggle started with more handicaps or made greater progress than this new state.

A family of Irish peasants, with the baby in its cradle, at the doorway of their white-washed cottage.

Except the small section in the north-east which comprises Northern Ireland, all of Ireland—that is, the provinces of Leinster, Munster (part), and Connaught, and the three counties of Cavan, Donegal, and Monaghan—is included in the Free State's 26,600 square miles. The people in its 26 counties have a lively sense of their differences from the people of Northern Ireland and of Great Britain. The hills of ancient Connaught and the islands off the west coast shelter the descendants of the former Gaels. And the transplanted English here, unlike those in Northern Ireland, have become thoroughly Irish through adoption of Celtic ways.

The character of the land, its abundant rainfall, and its lack of raw materials for manufacturing, predestined Ireland to become an agricultural country, with stock-raising as the chief industry (*see* Ireland). The area devoted to crops is being constantly increased, however; and so industries dependent on agriculture for their raw materials are being developed by the government in the effort to make the country less dependant on imports. The leading crops are oats, potatoes, turnips, barley, wheat, sugar-beet, and cabbage. Great Britain has always bought much of Eire's surplus beef cattle, sheep, horses, pigs and poultry, as well as dairy products and eggs and bacon. Potato growing and pig rearing go hand in hand on many small farms, for potatoes are good food for pigs.

From the bogs of the central lowlands quantities of peat are cut; peat warms many an Irish home, for imported coal is expensive. Herring and mackerel are the chief products of the deep-sea fisheries, and salmon is the most important fresh-water fish. Shellfish—crabs, crawfish, lobsters, and oysters—are abundant.

Industry has made good progress in Eire, stimulated by the government's desire for economic independence. Lack of coal has always been a serious handicap, but the completion of a large hydro-electric plant on the Shannon in 1929 made electric power available to industrial installations. In 1932 the government gave great impetus to manufacturing by offering loans to help in the building of factories and by imposing import duties on agricultural products from abroad so that industry might depend more on the country's agriculture for raw materials. Increased production of wheat demanded additional flour mills, and by 1934 practically enough flour for home needs was being milled, though a considerable part of the wheat used was imported. Sugar factories using home-grown beets have cut down sugar imports to a minimum. Boot and shoe factories have been established to supply the home market; other industries include brewing and malting and the manufacture of tobacco, and clothing.

Factories are widely distributed through the country, in line with the government's policy to prevent concentration in one or two areas. The population is mostly rural, and the only cities of any size are the seaports. Dublin (in Irish, Baile Atha Cliath), the capital and largest city, and Cork, the second city in size, with its outport Queenstown (Cobh), owe their growth chiefly to trade with Britain. Their industries, however, are increasing. Limerick (Luimneach) is the chief western port.

Education is free and compulsory for children under 14. The government has stimulated a revival of the Irish language, which is taught in the national schools. Dublin, Cork, and Galway have branches of the National University.

A PEASANT TYPE

Wearing a dress of homespun and seated at her spinning-wheel this old lady belongs to the Irish peasantry. Little spinning is now done at home.

The Irish Free State came into existence in 1922 with the ratifying of the Anglo-Irish Treaty (*see* Ireland). A provisional government was established in January 1922. But the Free State experienced great difficulties from the first. Already at odds with Northern Ireland (*see* Ireland, Northern), it was plunged into civil war—remembered by all Irishmen as The Troubles—by the Irish patriot and politician Eamon de Valera and his followers, who were insisting on the formation of a republic. There was fighting in Dublin, ending in the defeat of De Valera's supporters, but the civil war continued for some time in the south and west. The task of restoring order was a difficult one, but the new government was at last free to lay the foundations for the new State. The financial position of the country was unsound, and heavy taxes had to be imposed to meet expenditure. These measures made the government unpopular with the people. The growth of industry was encouraged by the imposition of import duties, and an attempt was made to become independent of English manufactures. In 1923 the Free State became a member of the League of Nations.

At the election of February 1932 the government was defeated by Eamon de Valera's party, De Valera himself becoming President of the Executive Council or Prime Minister. He at once began to take steps leading toward complete independence from Great Britain, although he held that a united Ireland should come before a free Ireland. The oath of allegiance to the British Crown was abolished, and in 1935 Free State citizenship was established to supplant British citizenship. The new government proceeded to map out an extensive programme of social as well as political and economic reform.

The constitution of 1922 had created a parliament comprising the Dail Eireann (house of representatives) and the Seanad (senate), with a president of the council (cabinet). A governor-general, representing the British Crown, gave assent to bills passed by Parliament. In 1936 the senate was abolished, as well as the office of governor-general.

In 1937 a new constitution was proposed by De Valera and approved by a majority of the people, providing for the election of a President, and a new type of legislature: a Dail Eireann and a Senate. The name of the State was changed from *Saorstat Eireann* (Irish Free State) to *Eire* (Ireland), and Eire was proclaimed a sovereign independent, democratic State; but the first President of Eire, Mr. Sean T. O'Kelly, was not elected until June 1945.

During the Second World War (1939-45) Eire emphasized its independence by remaining neutral. Pleading lack of defence against German attacks, it refused the Allies' requests to open its ports to their vessels. In 1941 a few scattered bombs were dropped by German aircraft in Dublin and the provinces, and while neutrality remained the government's policy, thousands of Southern Irishmen joined the British armed forces or went to work in Britain's war factories.

The immediate post-war years found the country in a very favourable position owing to the world-wide demand for her exportable surplus of agricultural produce. In comparison with the war-torn countries of the European continent, she was indeed fortunate. At the General Election of February 1948 Mr. de Valera's party lost its majority in the Irish Parliament, Mr. Costello succeeding De Valera as Prime Minister. So after being Premier and Minister for External Affairs for 16 years, and the personification of the Irish Republican Movement, De Valera ceased to be the political leader of Eire. Population is nearly 3,000,000.

Irish Literature.

For centuries before English became the dominant language in the British Isles, the people of Ireland spoke and wrote a language of their own. This language, Irish Gaelic, is a sister tongue of Scots Gaelic and Manx, and belongs to the Celtic branch of the Indo-European group of languages (*see* Philology). With the emergence of nationalist feeling in Ireland after the formation of the Irish Free State in 1922, the Gaelic tongue was revived. It is now taught in schools and is in official use generally.

In this language the Celts developed an extensive literature. Their stories of gods and heroes—of Cuchulain, of Deirdre, of Finn and Ossian, and of the Shee (fairies)—were long handed down by word of mouth.

The piety and learning which blossomed under St. Patrick in the 5th century turned Ireland into

DESIGNS THAT ADORN THE COINS OF EIRE

These representations of native animals, birds and a fish appear on the coins of Eire. Left to right in the upper row : hen and chickens on the penny ; Irish wolfhound on the sixpence ; pig and litter on the halfpenny ; a half-crown with an Irish hunter. The lower row shows a bull on the shilling ; hare on the threepenny piece ; harp, which is stamped on the reverse side of each of the coins ; leaping salmon on the two-shilling coin ; woodcock on the farthing.

The design of the coins was selected after public competition in which artists of several countries took part. Although Irish artists submitted entries, it was that of an Englishman, Percy Metcalfe of Yorkshire, which was accepted. The designer made not only a beautiful picture of each creature but they are also perfect specimens of their kind. Eire, the ancient name of Ireland, began to appear on the coins after 1937 in place of Saorstat Eireann (Irish Free State).

W. Lawrence

KILLARNEY'S LAKES IN COUNTY KERRY, EIRE

Overlooking the famed lakes of Killarney are the Macgilli- cuddy Reeks, the highest mountains in Eire. Of the three main lakes Lower Lake or Lough Leane is the largest, being four miles long. It is connected with Middle or Muckross Lake at Brickeen and also at the Meeting of the Waters, whence a narrow channel joins the Lower and Middle Lakes with the Upper. The lakes are studded with islands, one being the 'sweet Innisfallen' of the poet Thomas Moore.

the "Island of Saints and Scholars" (see Hebrides; Patrick, Saint.) A flood of manuscripts recorded the old stories and the new religious writings— saints' lives, books of hours, and the like, but all but a handful of these manuscripts perished during the Danish invasions (A.D. 795–1000) or later. Fortunately scribes of the 11th and 12th centuries copied or revised older manuscripts. Most of the later literature came from the bards (minstrels) rather than from the churchmen.

The English occupation of Ireland produced little literature until the 17th century. In the Kildare Poems of the early 14th cen- tury the interest is chiefly philological. But with the steady increase of English domination, especially during the 18th century, most of the old great families died out or allied themselves with English culture. The best-known writers of that period—Jonathan Swift, Oliver Goldsmith, Richard Steele, Edmund Burke, Richard Brinsley Sheridan—belong properly to English literature (see English Literature). More truly Irish in subject and spirit are the novelist Maria Edgeworth and the caricaturist writers Samuel Lover and Charles James Lever, with their tales of peasant life and country squires.

Poetry still lived, in English forms and language. Gay and tuneful rhymes sing in the Irish Melodies of Thomas Moore and the poems of

W. B. YEATS
Poet and dramatist, William Butler Yeats was a potent force in the Irish literary revival of the 20th century.

Francis Mahony (Father Prout). Deeper feeling marks the work of James Clarence Mangan, with his matchless translations and patriotic poems, and of Sir Samuel Ferguson. The poems of Gerard Manley Hopkins stand in a class apart, though in their mystic intensity and beauty of imagery they are redolent of the Celtic spirit.

Late in the 19th century the Gaelic League began to collect and publish the remnants of the native folk literature. Side by side with this revival of the Gaelic tongue grew a literary movement of dis- tinctively Irish writing in English. Although some modern writers—such as Oscar Wilde, George Moore, Bernard Shaw and Lord Dunsany—belong to English literature, present-day Irish literature owes its glory to those who felt the inspiration of the Irish Literary Revival. Stories of Erin's former greatness and her modern struggle for a life of her own stirred W. B. Yeats, Padraic Colum, Katharine Tynan, George W. Russell (" Æ "), and James Stephens. The greatest prestige came to the movement from the romantic tragedies and folk drama, written especially for Irish players by the Abbey Theatre group. Yeats, Colum, Lady Gregory, Sean O'Casey, St. John Ervine, Lennox Robinson, Denis Johnston and Paul Vincent Carroll were members of this group. Foremost of all was John M. Synge, master of beautiful language.

MINING *and* SMELTING IRON *and* STEEL

*Possibly the most important industries in the world, apart from agriculture,
are those that deal with iron and steel in their various stages; for upon
these metals our very life depends in this mechanical age.*

Iron AND STEEL. Steel is a combination of iron usually with carbon, and is the form assumed by the metal when it does its mightiest works. Twentieth-century civilization is built on iron, almost always in the form of steel. Our knives, scissors and razor blades are made of steel, so are the instruments used by surgeons and dentists. Into the construction of every weapon of war steel largely enters. Steel ships carry us across the ocean; we ride in carriages drawn over steel rails by steel and iron locomotives; our great office buildings have steel skeletons; and steel needles make our garments from cloth woven by steel machinery. Steel and iron are at once our servants and our masters.

Iron is one of the commonest of the 92 chemical elements of which the world is made, for only oxygen, silicon and aluminium occur in greater abundance. Its chemical symbol is Fe; its atomic number is 26; atomic weight, 55·84. The melting point of iron is about 1505° C.; its density is about 7·9. Iron, in combination, has been calculated to make up about 5 per cent by weight of the earth's crust. This crust is largely composed of compounds containing silicon and oxygen, and known as silicates; but the core of the earth may be a mixture of metallic iron and metallic nickel. Iron is present, combined with other elements, in many natural substances, such as rocks, plants and blood.

And yet really pure iron is scarcer than gold or diamonds. It is rarely found in Nature except as a visitor from other worlds in the form of meteorites; it is unknown commercially, and is difficult to obtain even in the laboratory. Probably you have never seen the silver-white metal, pure iron.

Why? Because iron has a strong tendency to rust if exposed to air and damp; for iron and oxygen make rust, or red oxide of iron. Hence, while iron does not refuse to make close associations or combinations with many other elements, the oxides and other combinations into which oxygen enters are the most important iron-containing substances in Nature. You may see iron and oxygen in the red dust and clay of the road, in the red brick of houses, in many red paints, and in the red cheeks of a healthy child.

Iron is adroit and versatile, changing its very nature according to circumstances and the company it keeps. By special treatment, and by alloying or combining the element iron with other elements, Man produces substances that may be almost "diamond" hard or almost as soft as copper, brittle as glass or malleable as silver, easily welded

WHERE IRON ORE IS DUG WITH STEAM SHOVELS
One of the largest producers of iron in the world is the United States of America, and above is one of the open iron ore mines of the Mesaba Range in the State of Minnesota. There the iron is so close to the surface that after the top soil or 'overburden' is stripped away the ore can be loaded directly into railway wagons by steam shovels, as seen here.

or unweldable, fusible easily or with difficulty, magnetic or non-magnetic. For range of adaptability, iron stands alone.

Because uncombined iron is practically unknown in Nature, primitive Man used stone and bronze instead of iron for his weapons and tools. Gold and copper were worked long before iron, which has to be released from the grip of other elements in order to take the metallic form. But long before history began to be written some lucky savage, happening on a windy day to back an excessively hot fire with pieces of iron-ore, may have found a lump of strange metal in the coals, and was perhaps inspired to pound its red-hot mass into shape between two stones. Because of this he gained not only a very superior spear-head or sword but much prestige among his fellows. The tales of divine or miracle-working smiths in many lands show the awed esteem in which the new craft was held. "Smith" is one of the commonest personal names in the English and German language groups.

During ancient times and the Middle Ages, the highest output of a furnace was three or four tons of iron a week. Four loads of timber were required to make each ton of pig-iron, and three additional loads to convert the pig-iron into bar-iron, and it took at least two weeks more— not to mention the additional fuel required —to convert the iron bars into steel.

AN OPEN-HEARTH FURNACE
British Iron & Steel Fean.

On each side of the ' hearth ' are sets of heating chambers. Gas and air are led to the hearth through one set, where they burn fiercely ; the hot spent gases then pass to the other chambers to heat them (upper). When the first set begins to cool the gas-flow is reversed (lower).

Today our whole civilization is woven over a framework of iron and steel. The Age of Steel is the result of many innovations, discoveries and inventions. Some are the evolution of centuries, but most are the product of the last 200 years.

The bulk of our commercial iron is produced from four ores, the most important being oxides (hematite, magnetite and limonite), and one (siderite) a carbonate. Pyrites, the sulphide, is in wide use for some purposes (see below), but is often regarded as a sulphur ore rather than an iron ore.

The oxides and carbonates are widely distributed and important ores. Clay ironstone, once an important English ore, is iron carbonate containing clay. Iron pyrites (a compound of iron with sulphur), often called "fool's gold" because of its glittering aspect, is used in enormous quantities in making sulphuric acid. Other iron-bearing minerals occur, but are unimportant as sources of iron.

The ores contain impurities, such as silica, alumina and lime. A rich ore contains more than 50 per cent of iron; an average ore, from 35 to 50 per cent; a poor one, working under favourable conditions, from 20 to 35 per cent. Ores containing less than 20 per cent of iron are considered useless.

Iron ores are very widely distributed over the **face of the earth.** The United States is at present the leading iron-ore producer and consumer, producing about one-third of the world's total output of pig-iron.

Outside the United States the most important ore-producing regions are Russia, France, Sweden, the United Kingdom, and Germany. It was largely the acquisition of part of the Lorraine iron mines at the close of the Franco-German War (1871) that enabled Germany to attain her manufacturing and military greatness. The loss of these ores through the return of Alsace-Lorraine to France in 1918 was a very serious loss to German industry. In recent years the output of iron ore from Russia has been increasing and is now second only to that of the United States; the estimate for 1950 was stated to be 40 million tons.

Britain has relied for many years upon imported ores, as most of those found here are of low iron content, our high grade deposits having been largely worked out. This is one reason why many great British ironworks are found near the coast and adjacent to the coal fields. Here the ships bringing the ore can get close up to the stock yards, and it has been found more economical thus to work high-grade imported ore than to build the expensive plant necessary for preparing and treating our native products. Comparatively recent developments in ore treating and blast furnace technique, however, have made it economic to use the low-grade ores found in Lincolnshire and Northamptonshire, and great integrated works have been and are being built in these districts to exploit them. Taking May 1948 as a typical month, for example, we find that of about 350,000 tons of ore used, 200,000 was home produced and 150,000 tons imported from Newfoundland West and North Africa, Sweden, Spain and elsewhere. It must be remembered, however, that the Fe (iron) content of the imported ore is over twice that of the home produced,

The Times

MOLTEN IRON POURS FROM A BLAST FURNACE

When the tap-hole of a blast furnace is opened a stream of white-hot iron pours down a channel made for it in sand, men directing the flow into moulds or 'pigs.' These pigs are broken up and converted into steel by one of many processes. The finished steel is poured, while still white-hot, into huge moulds where it is allowed to cool, forming great ingots. Frequently the liquid iron is taken to the steel mill to be made into steel before it cools.

so that probably just over one-third of the pig-iron made in Britain is extracted from home ores.

Iron is obtained from its ores by smelting; that is heating the ore in a blast furnace (q.v.) with a mixture of coke and limestone. As this mixture travels downwards from the top to the bottom of the furnace it gets heated, and the iron ore is reduced to metal by the hot gases (which contain carbon monoxide) and by contact with hot coke. The metallic iron takes up much carbon, forming a mixture of iron and carbon which melts at a lower temperature than pure iron. At the same time, the clay and other earthy " gangue," present in the iron ore, form a fusible slag with the lime produced by the action of the heat on the limestone; eventually the iron and slag melt and trickle to the bottom of the furnace, where the melted slag floats on top of the molten iron, the two being separated by running off through holes in the furnace—upper holes for the slag, lower ones for the iron.

In old-fashioned blast furnaces the molten iron was drawn off directly into sand moulds or troughs which bore a fancied resemblance to a family of little pigs lying alongside their mother and feeding. Hence the term pig-iron was applied to the product of the blast furnace.

In modern practice, the liquid iron is frequently taken to the steel mill to be made into steel before it cools, or to the pig casting machine which today takes the place of the old sand moulds. Whether it ever becomes a pig or not, the product of the blast furnace is called pig-iron, the intermediate or semi-raw material from which practically all our iron—cast iron, wrought iron and steel—is made.

Early blast furnaces used charcoal instead of coke, and could not therefore exceed about 30 feet in height, with a correspondingly small output of, say, 10 tons per week. Many of them did not produce the iron in a molten state, but as a "sponge" or viscous mass. This was hammered into shape as wrought iron. Alternatively the iron was cast as pigs and subsequently re-heated to "sponge" in various types of furnaces before being hammered. The most efficient was a late development, the "puddling" furnace, invented in 1784. Many famous structures and a host of common articles, from anchor chains to

The Times

SHAPING A STEEL INGOT FOR A GUN

Immensely powerful hydraulic presses shape the steel ingots. Here, one is being squeezed into the right shape for a naval gun. Before being placed in the press the metal is made almost white-hot to soften it.

CASTING STEEL INGOTS FROM THE MOLTEN METAL

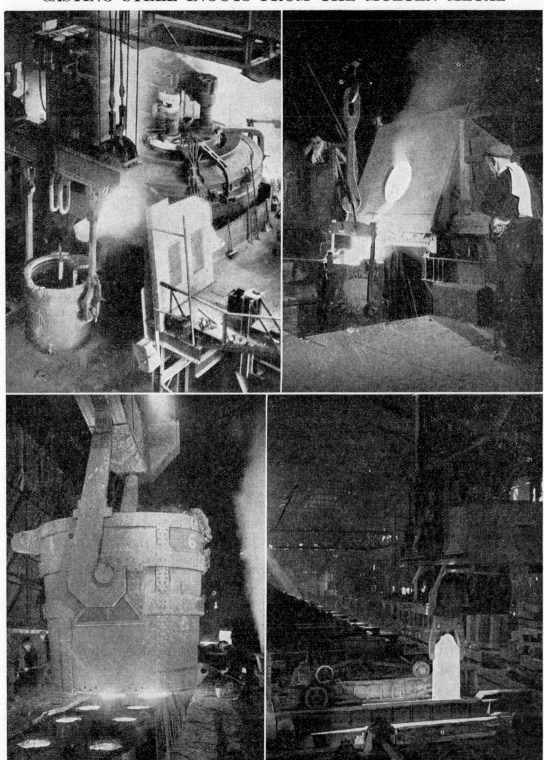

The British Iron and Steel Research Association

At the top left the molten metal is being drawn off from a 30-ton electric arc furnace. The tapping of a 10-cwt. high-frequency furnace is seen at the top right. Arc furnaces produce the bulk of electrically melted steel. For later roll-ing or forging, the steel is poured into ingot moulds (lower left). When the ingots are wanted for use they are re-heated until soft, then withdrawn (lower right) from the furnace in a condition to be dealt with by the rolling mills or forge.

nails and pins, used to be made from wrought iron, which is still manufactured in small quantities for special purposes. About 180,000 tons were made in the United Kingdom in 1946, against twelve and a half million tons of steel, which has superseded it almost entirely.

Even the small iron production of 200 years ago was threatened by shortage of raw materials, and the growing scarcity of wood for making charcoal for a time checked the growth of the iron industry. But about 1735 the step was taken which made possible our modern blast furnaces, producing 400 to 1,000 tons of iron every day; this was the substitution as fuel of coke, manufactured from bituminous coal, in place of charcoal.

Differences Between Iron and Steel

Cast iron, wrought iron, and steel are all mixtures or combinations, in varying proportions, of iron and carbon. The differences among them might once have been simply stated in the following way. Cast iron has a high percentage of carbon—usually about 2 to 3·5 per cent. It melts at a lower temperature than wrought iron and flows readily into moulds, becoming brittle when cold. It is cast into stoves, radiators, gas pipes, water and sewage mains, and machine parts which do not have to withstand severe shocks and strains.

Wrought iron has had most of the carbon burned out, leaving not more than 0·1—0·3 per cent. It does not melt as readily as cast iron, but it softens when heated and can be hammered into shape. It is tough and strong, though not so strong as steel; it welds easily and bends before it breaks.

Steel, until our own time, was defined as iron containing less carbon than cast iron (not more than 2 per cent) and more carbon than wrought iron. Its distinguishing property is that it can easily be made hard and brittle, or tough and malleable at will by careful "tempering"; that is, by heating to a cherry-red, then cooling—in water, oil, air or some special bath. Thus suitable steels may be made for very different uses.

Though these definitions are still true of types of iron and steel, and may well be remembered as such, the addition of new members to the cast-iron and steel groups has criss-crossed the family characteristics confusingly, and made necessary enlargements of the old definitions. A malleable cast iron is now produced by annealing—that is, controlled and gradual cooling after heating. It resists battering and shock, is nearly as strong as mild steel and, because of its cheapness, is much used in railway-carriage castings, reaper-binders, pipe fittings, and so on. The Age of Steel was created by new steels which satisfy the old definition with difficulty or not at all; that is, by so-called mild and medium steels which contain so little carbon that they can never be made hard. In fact, the name of "steel" is now generally applied to any malleable iron obtained from the liquid state. The ancient steel is thus placed in a subordinate class as "high carbon steel."

We have spoken as yet only of iron and carbon, but other elements—especially silicon, manganese, sulphur, nickel, chromium, tungsten, and phosphorus—enter into our manufactured iron and steel. (The wonderful alloy steels are described under Alloys.) In steel and some irons a fraction of one per cent of a single ingredient may make or mar the product. The metallurgist who watches these points is therefore an indispensable man in iron and steel making. The addition of nickel, chromium, tungsten and other metals in small proportions has resulted in high-tensile steels (which have great strength under tension) of the greatest value to armaments firms and machine-tool makers.

Steel was once made by packing bars of wrought iron on to powdered charcoal, sealing them in a clay chest, keeping the whole red-hot in a furnace for a week or 10 days, then letting it cool for another week or so. This was the cementation process; its product was spring steel or shear steel. Then in 1740 a Sheffield watchmaker produced an improved steel by smelting cemented steel in a clay crucible. Ever since, the incomparable Sheffield steel for fine cutlery has been made in that way, though an increasing proportion is now made by electric and other methods.

About 1847 an American named William Kelly noticed that a draught of air striking the molten iron in his Kentucky iron works made the metal seethe and boil. Why did cold air heat instead of chilling the metal? He remembered that the molten iron still contained carbon and other combustible material, and guessed that the oxygen of the air captured and carried away the excess carbon as a gas. A few years later Sir Henry Bessemer (q.v.) also observed it, and independently worked out the "fuelless" process which he patented in Great Britain in 1855.

How Phosphorus is Eliminated

The original Bessemer process failed to remove any phosphorus that might be present in the iron. This meant that no ores containing more than 0·1 per cent of phosphorus could be used as the basis of the pig-iron worked up by this process into steel, for steel containing a small percentage of phosphorus is brittle. Thus the Lorraine ores, and most British ones, which contain phosphorus, were useless for Bessemer steel. But, in 1878, a new process (the basic Bessemer process) was invented, which makes many phosphorus iron-ores available for Bessemer steel. By lining the Bessemer converter with a kind of limestone, and adding some lime to the charge of pig-iron, the phosphorus is removed from the iron and forms "basic slag," an important phosphoric fertilizer. Thus the phosphorus now provides a valuable by-product instead of being a nuisance.

The next great advance in steel-making was what is called the Siemens-Martin process, after its inventors. In this process the molten iron is placed in a basin or open hearth played over by intense flames which are obtained by an ingenious device called the regenerative furnace. For about half an hour gas and air enter through the ports or valves on one side, and burn in the furnace over the top of the "bath" of pig-iron and steel scrap. The hot gas produced by the combustion escapes through the ports on the *opposite* side. Then the valves are reversed and the gas and air admitted through the heated chambers on *that* side. This periodic reversal produces a continually rising heat until the charge is ready to "tap," the name given to the process of running the ready-molten metal into giant ladles, from which it is run into moulds.

With the open-hearth process steel can be made from iron of any composition, and it has the further

HOW RED-HOT STEEL IS WORKED INTO SHAPE

The British Iron and Steel Federation

Ingots cannot be dealt with by the various finishing mills without first being reduced in size. This is done in a cogging mill (top left). The red-hot steel is passed to and fro through rollers and pressed into slabs (top right). At lower left, a billet for a motor-car axle is being shaped under a steam hammer. In a continuous rolling mill (lower right) the steel billet can be rolled down quickly to the finished product in one forward operation by successive sets of rolls.

The Times

FORGING SHEFFIELD STEEL
One of the centres of the British steel industry is Sheffield in Yorkshire, and there every sort of steel article, from razor blades to locomotives, is produced. This steel billet is being forged under a 10,000-ton hydraulic press, which is the customary process with the largest forgings; steam hammers and rolling mills treat the smaller ones.

exert a force of up to 7,000 tons. For every ton of steel forged, thirty tons are nowadays rolled. A rolling mill is a series of large mangles, through grooves in the rollers of which hot steel is passed at speed to take the cross-sectional shape of the grooves. The process was invented by Henry Cort for rolling wrought iron in the 18th century, and has so vastly developed that a modern continuous rod mill will take a three-inch square billet 30 feet long and almost white hot. In a matter of seconds the steel will be whipped through perhaps eight or 10 pairs of rolls, emerging at over 40 miles per hour nearly half a mile in length and half an inch in diameter. Some such mills can produce 25,000 tons of material in a month.

There are also cold rolling mills for steel at "room temperature," to give it the accuracy and finish demanded in the manufacture of such things as clock springs and razor blades, which last are usually 0·006-inch thick, or even thinner. Tube making, wire drawing and other fascinating processes have been brought to a high stage of technique for the production of steel in the myriad forms that modern industry demands. "Stainless steel" and "rustless iron," forms of alloy steel, are taking important places in commerce. Stainless steel, which contains some chromium and nickel, is used extensively for cutlery. It resists corrosion and appears valuable in resisting heat. Bridges and general construction may some day be built from alloys of this type. Some motor-car manufacturers use rustless iron for hub caps, lamp frames and radiators. It takes a high polish and does not stain. (See Alloy).

advantage of permitting physical and chemical tests of the product at any time during the "heat." On the other hand, while a Bessemer converter will make 25 tons of steel in a single "blow" of 15 or 20 minutes, an open-hearth furnace requires about 13 hours to make 125 tons of steel. Both processes have their advantages, therefore, and in 1946 about a million tons of Bessemer and 11 million tons of open hearth steel were made in the United Kingdom. It seems probable that the proportion of Bessemer steel will increase as modern technique enables closer control to be maintained over the Bessemer process. There are also electrical processes of steel-making which have been in commercial use since the beginning of the 20th century. But the bulk of the world's steel is made by the open-hearth and the Bessemer processes. World production averages round about 120,000,000 tons annually.

The earliest method of shaping iron and steel was by hammering. Water-power superseded hand-power, and James Nasmyth's steam hammer, an instrument of astonishing precision invented in 1839, in turn superseded water-power. Large steam hammers of up to 100 or 125 tons are used in forging innumerable shapes demanded by the engineer; but the largest forgings are now usually formed in gigantic hydraulic presses, which may

Iron Mask, MAN IN THE. There are many mysteries in history that puzzle and interest us, although we are never likely to solve them. One is the identity of The Man in the Iron Mask. The person so called was a political prisoner in the Bastille, the fortress-prison in Paris, in the days of Louis XIV (1638–1715). His face was always covered with a mask, not of iron but of black velvet. He had been brought to the Bastille in 1698 from another prison, and he died there in 1703.

One theory, perhaps the most likely, is that the mysterious prisoner was Count Mattioli, the chief minister of the Duke of Mantua, the ruler of a district in north-east Italy. Mattioli had promised, for a large bribe, to betray an important frontier fortress to Louis XIV, but had broken his word.

Louis thereupon had him kidnapped and imprisoned for life in the Parisian fortress.

Another theory has it that the prisoner was the chief of a great conspiracy against the king; others say that he was a son of Charles II or of Oliver Cromwell. Voltaire (who had himself been an inmate of the Bastille on two occasions) suggested that the prisoner was a brother of Louis XIV. When the Bastille fell in 1789 the room that had been occupied by the mysterious prisoner was ransacked, but nothing that threw any light on his identity was ever discovered. We shall probably never know for certain the name of the person whose face was hid behind that black mask; but of this there can be no doubt, that he supplied Dumas with the name and inspiration of one of his most thrilling historical romances in Le Vicomte de Bragelonne.

Irving, SIR HENRY (1838-1905). The first actor to be knighted—an honour which both recognized his leadership of the English stage and put an end to the old idea that actors and actresses had no social position: the man who gained this honour for himself and his profession was born on February 6, 1838, the son of a small shopkeeper at Keinton Mandeville in Somersetshire, and he won fame entirely by his own merits and exertions. In his youth he worked as a clerk, but his heart was set on the stage, and in his spare time he studied elocution, dancing, and fencing, and read plays in which he hoped one day to act.

At the age of 18 he obtained his first engagement as an actor, and for the next few years played with many provincial companies, sometimes earning as little as 25 shillings a week, out of which he had to contribute to the support of his parents. He obtained his first London engagement in 1866, but he did not achieve fame until 1871, when, as Mathias in The Bells, an English version of Erckmann-Chatrian's Le Juif Polonais, he gave a memorable performance. That play remained in his repertory until his death.

Irving is best remembered by his actor-managership of the Lyceum Theatre, London (1878-1902), where, with Ellen Terry as his leading lady, he had a long series of successes, staging Shakespearean plays and poetical and romantic dramas. His greatest financial success was an adaptation of Faust, he himself playing Mephistopheles and Ellen Terry playing Marguerite. His greatest artistic triumph was achieved in Lord Tennyson's Becket, produced in 1893. In 1905 he went on a provincial tour, and after playing in Becket at Bradford, Yorkshire, collapsed on leaving the stage and died after being taken to his hotel. He was buried in Westminster Abbey on October 20, 1905. A statue of Irving stands at the back of the National Portrait Gallery near Trafalgar Square, London.

Irving, WASHINGTON (1783-1859). Essayist, historian, and writer of stories, Irving was the first of the great American writers, and is best known as the creator of Rip Van Winkle. Irving was born in New York City on April 3, 1783, and it was from there that he drew much of the material for his stories and sketches, nearly all of which deal with the romantic past. Never a very strong child, he spent more time with dog and gun, rambling about the country regions which he later described, than he did in school. Sometimes, too, he wandered into

the Dutch part of the city and listened to the quaint stories told by the descendants of the original Dutch settlers. While at home he spent a great deal of time reading in his father's large library. He was always cheerful, kindly, and good-natured, though a great part of his life was a struggle against ill-health, grief, and uncongenial work.

Irving began the study of law, but his delicate health was further impaired by grief over the death of his fiancée. His family, therefore, sent him abroad, where he travelled in England, the Netherlands, France, and Italy. When he returned, he wrote a humorous miscellany entitled Salmagundi, and in 1809 appeared his burlesque History of New York from the Beginning of the World to the End of the Dutch Dynasty, published under the pseudonym of Diedrich Knickerbocker.

The young author soon went abroad again on business for his brothers, and met famous writers in England and gained new inspiration. He now set about writing in earnest, and the first result of these labours was entitled The Sketch Book of Geoffrey Crayon, Gent., which, through the influence of Sir Walter Scott, met with a good reception in England. Irving remained abroad for many years travelling, writing, and in the diplomatic service of his country. While he was minister to Spain (1843-46) he became interested in Spanish history, and his studies there furnished his lively imagination with plenty of material for The Alhambra and his life of Christopher Columbus.

The Sketch Book is the best and most widely known of Irving's works. It contains the stories and sketches of Rip Van Winkle and The Legend of Sleepy Hollow in which Irving used material gathered from the descendants of the old Dutch

IRVING IN THE BELLS

One of Sir Henry Irving's most famous parts was that of Mathias in The Bells. This was the rôle of a murderer, in whose ears rang the bells of his victim's sleigh—until he was tortured by his conscience into confessing to the crime.

settlers; the mysterious tale of the return of Hendrick Hudson and his men; and a ghost story concerning a headless horseman.

Isabella OF CASTILE (1451–1504). It was the happy fortune of Queen Isabella I of the Spanish kingdom Castile and Leon to give to Europe a new nation and to the world a new continent. The first event came through her marriage in 1469, while Queen of Castile and Leon, to King Ferdinand of the neighbouring and rival kingdom of Aragon, thus uniting the two chief kingdoms in the Spanish peninsula. Her second claim to fame came through her support of the explorer, Christopher Columbus.

Isabella was a woman of remarkable energy and talent, beautiful, and possessed of winning grace, although at times proud and ambitious. She was always present at state meetings, and her name was placed with that of Ferdinand at the end of all official documents. Her part in the founding of a national Spanish inquisition under royal control, with its persecution of the Moors and Jews, shows the intolerance in religious matters which she shared with her husband and most of her contemporaries.

History relates that Columbus, when he applied at the court of Spain for help in his projected voyage of discovery, failed to receive the sanction or aid of Ferdinand and the learned council. Columbus, discouraged, was about to leave for France, when he succeeded in interesting Isabella in his plan. The king remained indifferent and pleaded want of funds. The queen, so the story runs, in her earnestness exclaimed, " I pledge my jewels to raise the money ! " Columbus succeeded at last, and to Queen Isabella belongs much of the honour; for even though the story of the jewels has no basis in fact, it is true that Isabella's interest and support ᴍade possible the voyage of Columbus.

Isinglass. Consisting of the dried swimming bladders of several varieties of fish, this substance contains from 86 to 93 per cent gelatine and sometimes more. The Russian variety, which is supposed to be the best, is made principally from sturgeons' bladders. Isinglass is used for the same purposes as gelatine, in soups and jellies, and for clarifying fermented liquors. (*See* Gelatine).

Isis. (Pron. i'-sis). The "queen of the gods" in Egyptian mythology was Isis, the sister and wife of Osiris, the god of the sun, resurrection and eternal life. She represented the moon, as Osiris did the sun, and was believed by the Egyptians to have taught them agriculture. The old legends tell of her weeping for her slain husband, and it was said that her tears caused the overflow of the Nile. The cow was sacred to her, and she is often represented with the horns of this animal. The worship of Isis was introduced into Greece about the 3rd century B.C., and later into Rome. The cult extended into Asia Minor, where Isis was regarded as the bestower of dreams and also as the inflicter of diseases and the restorer of health.

British Museum
GODDESS ISIS
The ancient Egyptian goddess of the moon carried a moon-like disk between the horns on her head. She wore horns because the cow was sacred to her.

Isotope. Isotopes are elements which although chemically identical with one another have different atomic weights. Until about 1913 chemists thought that all atoms of the same element had exactly the same weight, but F. Soddy and others, after studying the manner in which radio-active elements undergo changes and produce other elements, came to the conclusion that some of the elements must be chemically identical but of different atomic weight.

The elements uranium and thorium are believed to be the parents of all the *natural* radio-active elements, and they each produce, by a series of disruptive changes, a distinct series of radio-active elements, the final product of each series being lead. It was suggested that the atomic weights of uranium-lead and of thorium-lead should be different; and in fact T. W. Richards determined the atomic weights of lead from different sources and obtained different results, thus demonstrating that isotopes exist. This discovery completely exploded the idea that the weights of all atoms of the same chemical element are the same, and provided an explanation of the fact that many atomic weights are not whole numbers (*see* Chemistry).

Thanks to the work of J. J. Thompson and F. W. Aston at Cambridge, the mass-spectrograph was developed. This instrument separates atoms of different weights, and has enabled physicists and chemists to show that most of the elements have isotopes. Chlorine, for instance, has a fractional atomic weight (35.46) largely because it is composed of a mixture of atoms of weights 35 and 37.

Because isotopes are, for practical purposes, chemically identical, they cannot be separated from one another by chemical processes, but they can be separated by physical methods. For example, the rates at which gases pass through a membrane vary with the densities of the gases (*see* Gas), and these densities depend on the weights of the atoms. Gaseous isotopes can therefore be separated by using a suitable membrane. If a volatile compound of a solid element which contains isotopes can be made, then a similar method for separating the isotopes can be used.

One way of making atomic bombs uses the uranium isotope of mass 235 ; but ordinary uranium contains less than one per cent of this isotope, and, as we have seen, isotopes are for practical purposes chemically inseparable. To produce the bombs, the uranium 235 was separated by making use of the principle of Aston's mass-spectrograph, and by preparing volatile uranium compounds which could be treated more or less by methods similar to those already mentioned for gaseous isotopes. The production of uranium 235 by these methods was enormously expensive, and only justified by wartime needs during the Second World War (1939–45).

These great wartime developments also supplied us with the means whereby radio-active isotopes of some of the

E.N.A.

ISTANBUL SEEN FROM ACROSS THE GOLDEN HORN

The capital of Turkey until 1923, when it was superseded by Ankara, Istanbul lies on the shores of the Bosporus, an inlet of which, called the Golden Horn, provides a fine natural harbour (above). In the foreground is Pera, the foreign residential quarter, and across the harbour is the 200-feet high Seraskerat Tower, with blocks of barracks on the horizon to the right. On the extreme right is the mosque of Solyman the Great, with four beautiful minarets.

common non-radio-active elements can be prepared in appreciable quantities and used for medical purposes and scientific research.

By bombarding atoms of some ordinary elements with highspeed particles, such as neutrons, either in the " atomic pile " or by some other means, we are able to transform them into radio-active isotopes of, for example, carbon, phosphorus, iodine, sulphur, and iron. These radio-active isotopes have been named " tracers," because they are being used to " trace " the movements of elements during physical, chemical, and biological changes. If we add to a non-radio-active element a small quantity of its radio-active isotope, then, as these two are chemically the same element, where one goes the other goes, and the radio-activity can be used to trace the movements of the element, merely by using a Geiger-Müller counter. (See Ions and Ionization).

The use of " tracers " is a comparatively new development. They have many possible applications, a few examples being the study of wear on internal parts of machinery, the study of chemical changes taking place in live animals and plants, the detection of cancerous tissue in cancer of the thyroid gland, the study of the uses that plants make of fertilizers, and maybe for inexpensive and safe radio-active treatment of some diseases.

Istanbul (CONSTANTINOPLE). Founded by the Roman Emperor Constantine the Great in A.D. 330, Constantinople occupied the site of the Greek city of Byzantium, founded by the Greeks in 667 B.C.

It was in turn the capital of the Roman, Byzantine and Turkish Empires. (See Byzantine Empire).

In 1923, when Turkey became a republic, Constantinople ceased to be the capital, and the seat of government was transferred to Ankara in Asia Minor. In July 1932 the name of Constantinople was officially changed to Istanbul, and it was decreed that the use of the old name would be punishable by law and that letters addressed to Constantinople would be returned to the senders.

In the days of her greatest prosperity the riches of the most distant countries of the world came into her secure and capacious harbour, the Golden Horn. Situated on her seven hills on the shores of the narrow Bosporus, between the Black Sea and the Sea of Marmara, with the narrow Hellespont (Dardanelles) leading thence to the Aegean, her port could easily be closed to the fleet of an enemy in time of war, and opened in peace to commerce. When the Turks captured Istanbul in 1453 they were able to cut off the trade of Europe with the East, and so gave occasion for Columbus, Vasco da Gama, and other explorers to search for new routes to the Orient.

The city presents a magnificent appearance from the sea, especially in that section where the rose and white of the former church of St. Sophia, which under the Turks became first a mosque and then a museum of Byzantine art, and the golden gleam of many minarets, are visible. Another showplace is the old Seraglio, which was for 400

VENICE : THE ITALIAN PORT AT THE HEAD OF THE ADRIATIC

Once one of the most powerful States in Europe, Venice is still a city of great beauty. In this view we see the domes of St. Mark's Cathedral in the left foreground, with the campanile or bell-tower on the farther side of the piazza. The cathedral was begun in the 10th century and grew in glory with the rise to power of the Venetian Republic. The discovery of the route to the East round the Cape of Good Hope in 1486 terminated the overland trade with the East upon which Venice depended for her prosperity.

years the private home of the Sultans of Turkey and has now been restored to its original condition and is known as the museum of Top Kapu.

The city is really made up of three smaller cities. To the south lies Stamboul, or Istanbul, the Mahomedan quarter. Galata on the east is the business section; and Pera, to the north, the foreign quarter. Stamboul is separated from Galata by the Golden Horn, an inlet that is one of the most distinctive features of Istanbul, for it provides a fine natural harbour capable of floating the largest ships. Across the Bosporus is Scutari, or Usküdar, which is practically a suburb of Istanbul. Typical products are the rugs, carpets, and embroideries which are made by hand in small shops and in the homes. There are cement, tobacco and munitions factories, shipyards, and motor-car assembly plants. The population of Istanbul is about 845,000.

Through SPACE and TIME in ITALY

Famed for sunshine, beautiful scenery and picturesque cities, Italy has for long been a favoured touring-ground for leisured travellers. Here we survey the country, its people, and its history, most fascinating of any land.

Italy. The peninsula of Italy dips down into the blue waters of the Mediterranean like a tall high-heeled boot, walking off towards Spain and kicking along the islands of Sardinia and Sicily in its path. The very top of the boot is rimmed with the snowy peaks of the Alps, and bejewelled with bright lakes—Maggiore, Lugano, Como, Iseo, and Garda. Here also lies the flat fertile valley of the Po, containing the richest of farm land. The leg of the boot is ridged by the Apennine Mountains; and scattered along its length are the plains of Tuscany, the Campagna di Roma, Apulia, and the fertile Campania which accounts for much of the prosperity of Naples.

On the Adriatic side lies the misplaced " spur " of Mt. Gargano, partially enclosing the Gulf of Manfredonia; in the hollow of the foot lies the deeply indented Gulf of Taranto. Many short rapid streams dart down the mountain slopes. The chief rivers besides the 420-mile Po are the Adige, Arno, Volturno, and the Tiber, the historic river of Rome. The " boot " is about 700 miles long and 350 miles in extreme breadth.

Its climate ranges from the ice-bound Alps and chilly winters of the north, to a nearly tropical warmth in the southernmost section, where orange and lemon trees grow abundantly and the hills are " o'er-smoked by the faint grey olive trees." So blue are the skies and so warm the air of most of the peninsula, so pleasant the life and so storied the land, that poets have sung of Italy for centuries.

It is in the north that the manufacturing industry of the country is centred. In fact, we may think of Italy as divided into three sections—north, south, and central—so different are the interests and traits of these parts. By northern Italy is meant Lombardy, Piedmont, Venetia, Emilia, Liguria, Tuscany, and the Trentino.

Here, more than elsewhere, is the hum of manufacturing, the bustle of modern cities, such as Turin and Milan, the trade through busy ports like Genoa and Venice. Here fine silks are woven, white marble is quarried, motor-cars and machinery made, wines pressed out, Leghorn hats woven, beautiful jewelry designed and fashioned, mirrors and glass-ware of world fame manufactured. Here farms produce grain, poultry, cheese, potatoes, flax, and (in the wet areas) rice. Here the people are better educated, more prosperous and progressive and cool-blooded; many have fair hair and blue eyes, and contrast in their cool realism with their warmer-blooded brothers from farther south.

Central Italy includes the provinces of Umbria, the Marches, Abruzzi and Molise, and the Romagna. Many of the greatest artists, musicians, and professional men of Italy come from the central section. The district is chiefly agricultural, having but two large cities, Rome and Naples.

The south includes Campania, Apulia, Basilicata, Calabria, Sicily, and Sardinia. The peasants plod along over the brown hills behind their great oxen, working for 16 and 17 hours a day. There are few cities in the south, and the people seem content in their hard life, following their old traditional ways.

All Italians, whether of the north, centre, or south, are usually possessed of charm and natural courtesy, a combined simplicity and cynicism, a quick temper and a kind heart. Swarthy men and women of the Mediterranean race inhabited Italy in the Stone Age, and a substratum of that population exists to this day. The Latins, who founded Rome, were one of a group of fairer Indo-European peoples, who came into the peninsula before recorded history begins. Etruscans, Greeks, and Carthaginians, Goths, Vandals, Lombards, Saracens, and Normans —all left traces of their blood in the Italians of today.

Following the downfall of the Roman Empire in the West (*see* Rome: History) and the fleeting rule of the barbarian kings, Odoacer the Herulian and Theodoric (*c.* 454–526) the Ostrogoth, came an equally fleeting reunion of Italy with the East

Extent.—Greatest length of peninsula, about 700 miles ; average breadth, 200 miles. Area (including Sicily, Sardinia and other islands), 116,000 square miles. Population, about 45,637,000.

Physical Features.—Mountains : Alps and Apennines. Volcanoes : Mt. Vesuvius (near Naples), and Mt. Etna (in Sicily). Rivers : Po, Adige, Arno, Volturno, Tiber. Lakes : Maggiore, Lugano, Como, Iseo, Garda.

Cities.—Rome (capital, 1,574,000), Milan (1,268,000), Naples (978,000), Turin (713,000), Genoa (649,000), Palermo (458,000), Florence (374,000), Bologna (324,000), Venice (303,000), Catania (277,000), Bari (253,000), Messina (215,000).

Products.—Agricultural : grapes, olives, lemons, oranges, and other fruits ; wheat, maize, oats, barley, and rye ; beans, potatoes and other vegetables ; forage crops ; sugar beets ; dairy products. Manufactures : textiles (cotton, silk, rayon, and wool) ; wines, olive oil, sugar ; clothing (including hats, gloves, shoes), leather, paper, steel, machinery, and motor-cars ; chemical products ; glass and pottery. Mining : marble, sulphur, mercury, zinc, lead, and iron. Fishing : tunny, sardines, and anchovies.

ITALIAN PENINSULA ALMOST BRIDGING THE MEDITERRANEAN

At the northern end of Italy lofty Alps rise above the broad fertile plain of the River Po. The rugged Apennines, from which short rivers flow east and west, extend down the narrow peninsula to the tip of the toe. At the end of the Second World War (1939–45) certain Alpine valleys on the western frontier were given up to France, and most of the Istrian Peninsula at the head of the Adriatic Sea, with the ports of Pola and Fiume, became part of Yugoslavia. Trieste is a Free Territory, ruled by a Governor appointed by the United Nations. Sicily and Sardinia belong to Italy.

Roman or Byzantine Empire. The Frankish conquests of the Lombards by Charlemagne, and his coronation at Rome as Holy Roman Emperor in A.D. 800, checked for a time the breaking-up of Italy, but it was resumed with the rise of feudalism.

The refounding of the medieval empire by the Saxon Otho I (in 962), and his assumption of the Iron Crown of Italy, brought only nominal union of that land with Germany in the Holy Roman Empire. Even the rise of the powerful city-states —Florence, Venice, Genoa, Milan, and their fellows —helped on the division and weakness by adding yet another important factor to the age-long conflict of Papacy and Empire. The epoch of French and Spanish rivalries over Italy began with the triumphal raid of Charles VIII of France through the

GLIMPSES OF THE ITALIAN SCENE

E.N.A.

The photograph at the top of this page shows a scene in Northern Italy, where the ancient city of Arco forms a semi-circle at the base of a rock 930 feet high. The town lies on the River Sarca, which follows a serpentine course through the mountains. In the south of Italy is the magnificent Bay of Naples, seen in the lower photograph. The city's buildings form an amphitheatre on the hills, while across the bay is the cone of Vesuvius, perhaps the world's most famous volcano.

H. W. Nicholls

NARROW LANE IN OLD SAN REMO

San Remo is a favourite winter resort on the Italian Riviera, for it has an exceptionally mild climate, being backed by a semicircle of hills and faced by a bay of the Ligurian Sea. The old town has tall houses crowding together along narrow streets. The arches that span the street shown above are a safeguard against earthquakes.

D. McLeish

A GEM OF THE ITALIAN LAKES

Lake Orta, one of the smaller of the northern Italian lakes, lies west of the more
famous Maggiore.   This photograph was taken from above the village of Orta on
the shore of the lake, looking towards the island of San Giulio.   On the left of the
island is seen the church founded in A.D. 379 and from which the island takes its name.

SMILING BEAUTY OF THE ABRUZZI

The women of Abruzzi e Molise, a department of central Italy, are noted for their beauty. This girl is a native of Clociaria, a region of mountain and forest. She is wearing the traditional costume of the district. The pattern of her skirt resembles a Scottish tartan, and over her arm she carries a plaid shawl.

peninsula to Naples, in 1494. It closed with the recognition of the Spanish rule of Charles V over Sicily, Naples and Milan, in 1544.

Thenceforth the bustling cities of Italy, in which the Italian Renaissance had flowered in master-pieces of literature, art and science stood still under petty ducal houses. French Bourbons supplanted Spanish kings in Sicily and Naples in 1738; then the French Revolution and the conquests of Napoleon for a time overwhelmed the peninsula like an avalanche. But Bourbons and petty dukes alike came back in 1815, with the added incubus of Austrian rule in Lombardy and Venetia. As Metter-nich, the Austrian statesman, truly said, Italy had become nothing but a mere geographical expression.

A secret society called the *Carbonari* (charcoal burners) flourished in the early part of the 19th century, with the overthrow of native and foreign despotism as its object. Not merely rude peasants but fiery patriots of the best families were among its members.

Revolts in 1820 and 1831 were crushed by Austrian troops. Then the idealistic republican Giuseppe Mazzini (1805–72), organized his new revolutionary society called Young Italy. And while King Charles Albert of Sardinia-Piedmont in the stirring days of 1848 battled unsuccessfully against the Austrians at Custozza and Novara, Mazzini drove out the Pope and set up a brave but ill-starred republic in Rome. French soldiers of Napoleon III, however, soon conquered it, and Italy was, as before, a dark realm of Austrian and Bourbon tyranny in the north and south, with the temporal power of the Papacy between. Only Sardinia-Piedmont under its new king, Victor Emmanuel II, kept its constitution and independence and the Italian tri-coloured flag.

But this, as it proved, was the seed from which Italian unity and liberty were to grow. Under the able leadership of that shrewd diplomat Count Cavour (1810–61), the great minister of Victor Emmanuel, Sardinia-Piedmont grew strong in resources and in alliances. Cavour had learned that, genuine as was Italian patriotic fervour, Italy would never be unified with-out help from abroad. Therefore he cleverly won the support of Napoleon III of France, and in the spring of 1859 Austria declared war against France and the kingdom of Sardinia-Piedmont.

France and Sardinia-Piedmont defeated the Austrians at Magenta and Solferino, and so won Lombardy for United Italy. But Napoleon hurriedly arranged an armistice with the Austrians, allowing them to retain Venetia. Cavour and Victor Emmanuel were clever enough to veil their disappointment and wait. At once the small states which chequered north-central Italy—Tuscany, Modena, Parma, and the Romagna—cast out their absolute princes and joined the new kingdom of Italy. Napoleon III consented to the arrangement, in return for the cession by Piedmont of the provinces of Savoy and Nice to France.

The second stride toward a United Italy came the following year, when the famous soldier of fortune Giuseppe Garibaldi (1807–82) gathered about him his volunteers, stormed the island of Sicily, and then the mainland part of the kingdom of Naples. The people everywhere hailed him as a liberator, and drove out the hated Bourbon king. There remained only the Papal States and Venetia to be joined to the new-made Italian nation, when (in February 1861) Victor Emmanuel of Sardinia (1820–78) was proclaimed king of Italy. Venetia was gained in 1866, after Austria was defeated by Prussia. Rome alone was now outside the Italian kingdom, and the lack of that central strip of territory was a very real handicap.

French troops still guarded the Pope's sov-ereignty, and Victor Emmanuel was too intelligent a pupil of Cavour (who had died in 1861) to attack the French and thus, perhaps, undo all that had

E.N.A.

MAKING ITALY'S STAPLE FOOD

Macaroni is the almost universal diet of the Italian people, and much of it is home-made (above). Wheat flour, kneaded into a paste with water, is the basis of macaroni, vermicelli and spaghetti.

been accomplished. Once more he let " the stars in their courses work for Italy." In 1870 the Franco-Prussian war forced France to withdraw her soldiers from Rome. The Roman people welcomed the army with which Victor Emmanuel marched into Italy's ancient capital. Pope Pius IX, excommunicating the invaders, withdrew into the Vatican; there he and his successors remained " voluntary prisoners " until the Con-cordat of 1929 between Italy and the Holy See recognized the temporal power of the Pope as sovereign ruler over a tiny Vatican territory.

Giant tasks lay before the new Italy. Though staggering under a load of debt and heavy taxa-tion, it built up a strong army and navy, and developed railways, ports, schools, and a mercantile marine. Manufacturing industries sprang up, bringing with them labour troubles and social

ITALY

unrest. In 1878 King Humbert (b. 1844), son of the first king, Victor Emmanuel II, succeeded to the throne; he was assassinated by an anarchist in 1900. His son, Victor Emmanuel III (1869-1947), was not a strong character. His reign went on uneventfully until the First World War (1914-18), except for disastrous earthquakes in Messina and central Italy in 1908 and 1915.

Meanwhile Italian statesmen were attempting to gain territory in Africa for colonial expansion. On the east coast they obtained two colonies of doubtful value, Eritrea and Italian Somaliland, and on the north coast they won Libya after war with Turkey (1911-12). The First World War (1914-18) added large tracts of land formerly under Austrian rule, including the Trentino in the north, and the peninsula of Istria at the head of the Adriatic. When she entered the war, Italy had been torn in two by the advocates of neutrality and the pro-war faction. At that time a young revolutionary, Benito Mussolini (q.v.), editing the Socialist newspaper Avanti, in Milan, was discharged from his position and expelled from the Socialist party because he preached with fiery words that Italy ought to join the allies (Britain, France and Russia) in the war. He enlisted, was wounded, and was decorated for valour. He returned a hero and an enemy of Socialism.

After the First World War Socialism tended to drift towards Communism. Returning soldiers were mocked in the streets. Patriotic receptions of the troops were prevented. Strikes paralysed industry. Bands of former service men roamed the country, angry, embittered, dangerous, eager to strike a blow against the evils which menaced their land. In these bands Mussolini saw his opportunity. With his gift of eloquence he soon organized them into groups in each community, armed them with sticks, and set them to preserving order. Each group was called a Fascio (which means bundle or bunch), in token of the close union of its members, and in allusion to the fasces, ancient emblem of office of the Roman lictors. Those belonging to the organization were called Fascisti. These groups Mussolini formed into a political army to fight Socialism. (See Fascism).

In 1919 the soldier-poet Gabriele d'Annunzio (1863-1938) organized an attack on the seaport of Fiume (which was awarded to Italy by treaty in 1924) and stirred the whole nation to a high degree of national fervour.

When the Radical element called a general strike in 1920 the Fascisti were strong enough to end it, and to break up a Socialist reunion in Rome the year after; also strong enough in 1922 to call a Fascist congress in Naples. The Government, which had been too weak to control the Radicals, was powerless to oppose the men who had put fear into the Radicals. It offered the Fascists any portfolio in the Cabinet except that of Minister of the Interior. Strangely enough, Victor Emmanuel concurred in the surrender to Fascist audacity, when to the rest of the world it seemed that a bolder front would have made Mussolini's movement collapse. Through the years of turmoil and unrest which followed, the king showed the same lack of initiative. In October 1922 the victorious Fascisti made their famous march on Rome. The Cabinet resigned;

M. O. Henchoz

ITALIAN PEASANTS DRYING THEIR CROP OF MAIZE
In certain parts of Italy, especially in the south, maize is the main crop, and villagers spread out the grain to dry on the stones in front of their houses (above). When the sun has done its work the harvest will be stored until it is needed. Most of the peasants are very hardworking, but owing to the smallness of their farms have difficulty in earning a living.

YESTERDAY & TODAY RUB SHOULDERS IN ITALY

1. Two cypresses guard the village church at Oria on mountain-girt Lake Lugano, which lies partly in Italy and partly in Switzerland. 2. This Roman theatre is part of the ruins of Hadrian's villa in Tivoli, a suburb of Rome. The gardens, baths and terraces of the villa covered acres. 3. As Pan piped, so pipes this Calabrian boy in his fur jacket. 4. Now the city hall, the 14th century Palazzo Vecchio in Florence once housed the government of the Florentine republic. Savonarola was imprisoned in its tower. 5. The Arms of Venice, showing the winged lion of St. Mark with his paw on an open book and the motto, "Peace to you, Mark, my evangelist," surmount the balcony on the side of the Doges' palace in Venice. The Palace of the Doges, or Ducal Palace, dates from the 14th century, when Venice was a great power. 6. The monastery of St. Francis, with its two churches, was built in the hill town of Assisi in 1228, two years after the death of St. Francis, and contains the crypt of the saint. Art treasures in the churches are delicately coloured frescoes by Giotto and Cimabue. 7. Sardinian women bake bread in outdoor ovens.

THE BEAUTIFUL CITY OF THE DEAD IN GENOA

In Italy a cemetery is known as Campo Santo (Holy Field), and this is a corner in one of the most famous of them all, the Campo Santo at Genoa. The Italian people take so much pride and delight in the cities of their dead that the French writer, René Bazin (1853–1932), calls them 'funereal pleasure-grounds.' Of the parts of the cemetery occupied by the tombs of the wealthier Genoese he says : ' Nowhere is the stone made so supple, required to represent so many family scenes, so many trained and ruffled gowns with marvellous imitations of lace. These Italian cemeteries are like a great album of departed generations.' On the tombs are frequently kept burning ' tall night lights in coloured glass ; and always the bust, with spectacles if the dead man wore them ; or the photograph, framed and protected by glass.'

as Prime Minister, Mussolini formed a new one, took the portfolios of the Interior and of Foreign Affairs, and became the virtual dictator of Italy.

Within a few years Mussolini had made such drastic changes in the Government that no semblance of popular sovereignty remained. His methods were ruthless. The Fascists held that the individual existed only for the State, and had no rights as against the State. They rejected popular government and majority rule. There was only one political party and no opposition was tolerated.

To meet the needs of its increasing population, the Italian government promoted agriculture in various ways. Only about half of the country is adapted to farming, hence all available land was reclaimed by irrigation and drainage. Enormous tracts were drained in the Maremma, or swamp lands, of Tuscany, in the Roman Campagna (Agro Romano), in the famed Pontine Marshes (Paludi Pontine) and in districts of Sicily and Sardinia. The Pontine region, from which malaria had once driven all inhabitants, became the fertile Littoria province in 1934. There are four entirely new towns—Littoria, Sabaudia, Pontina, and Aprilia—in this reclaimed region; much of this valuable work, however, was undone during the Second World War (1939–45).

Despite its best efforts, Italy could not grow enough food for home use. It tried to build up its manufactures so that it can pay for its imports not only of wheat but also of cotton, coal, iron and steel, machinery, and oil, by its exports of cotton goods, silk fabrics, rayon, wool fabrics, raw silk, fruits, and wine. Industry was handicapped, however, by the lack of minerals and other raw materials. There is a little iron, chiefly on the islands of Sardinia and Elba, on the Tuscan mainland and in the high Alps in the province of Aosta; and some coal is mined. To make up for the lack of coal on the Italian mainland, there has been a tremendous development of water power, furnished by the many mountain rivers. In hydro-electric power, Italy leads all Europe.

But the cost of government mounted enormously under Fascism. Great sums were spent on a unified educational system, in the effort to end illiteracy and to get all the people to use the official Tuscan language instead of the 15 provincial dialects. Public works—like the building of the magnificent arterial roads known as *autostrade*—also absorbed large sums. The greatest expense of all was incurred in building up a powerful army, navy, and air force, and in the military training of youth. The internal debt rose to staggering heights.

As a way out of these many difficulties Mussolini decided on colonial expansion in East Africa, at the expense of Abyssinia. Once before, in 1896, Italy had attempted this, but had been disastrously repulsed at Adowa. He planned now with one bold stroke to wipe out the memory of this defeat and gain new territory which would supply raw materials and furnish an outlet for surplus population. A clash between Italian and Abyssinian troops on the border of Somaliland afforded the pretext, and on October 2, 1935, bombing planes, troops and tanks from Eritrea and Italian Somaliland began the invasion. Four days later Adowa fell.

The League of Nations imposed sanctions (penalties) against Italy as an aggressor nation, but the all-important supply of oil, without which Italy's war machine would have been paralysed, was not cut off, owing to disagreement among other League Powers. The Italians reached Addis Ababa in seven months; Abyssinia was annexed in May 1936, and the King of Italy was proclaimed emperor of the new Italian Empire in East Africa.

In April 1939, on Good Friday, Italian forces invaded Albania, and the King of Italy added King of Albania to his titles. When the Second World War broke out in September 1939 Mussolini was less daring. He waited until the French were on the point of collapse before declaring war on France and Britain, on June 10, 1940, and marched into southern France against negligible resistance. An armistice was signed on June 24; Italy regained Nice after 80 years.

For the rest, the Italians made a poor showing. The Greeks held them, even pushed them back, until taken in the rear by the Germans. After

THESE HORSES HAVE BEEN PRANCING FOR 2,000 YEARS

There stand in Venice four famous bronze horses (above) over the entrance to St. Mark's Cathedral. They were made at Corinth, Greece, nearly 20 centuries ago. The Roman Emperor Nero (37–68) took them to Rome; the Byzantine Emperor Constantine the Great (c. 288–337) removed them to Constantinople (Istanbul); thence they went to Venice. Napoleon Bonaparte (1769–1821) took them to Paris, but after his defeat at Waterloo in 1815 they returned to St. Mark's.

SPLENDID MODERN ARENA IN ANCIENT ROME
Unlike the ancient Roman Colosseum which was built for gladiatorial contests, the Forum (above) built in Rome by Benito Mussolini (1883–1945), the Dictator of Italy from 1922 to 1943, is used for such peaceful purposes as athletic meetings.

In North Africa, after a crushing defeat at the hands of General (later Lord) Wavell's British, Australian, Indian and New Zealand divisions, the Italians became little more than cannon fodder at the disposal of the German generals whose arrival narrowly saved them from annihilation. Finally beaten in Africa in May 1943, they asked for an armistice when the Allies' invasion of Sicily had been followed by that of the Italian mainland in September 1943.

German strategy saw to it that Italy should not escape becoming a battlefield. Mussolini had by now been deposed and imprisoned; but German parachutists rescued him, and he formed a new government in the north. Two and a half years of bitter fighting laid waste many a splendid building, many a picturesque village, before Italy knew peace. During this time the pro-Ally government

some initial success in East Africa, including the capture of British Somaliland against a tiny garrison, the Italians were out-fought by the British and South Africans, who overran Italian Somaliland and Eritrea and restored Ethiopia to its Emperor.

M. O. Henchoz

GONDOLAS ON ST. MARK'S CANAL, VENICE
Venice is a city whose roads are waterways, traversed by steam-boats, launches and gondolas. There are some 150 canals, and in this photograph we are looking across the Canal of St. Mark to the island of St. Giorgio Maggiore. Gondolas are long, narrow, flat-bottomed boats, with high-curved prow and stern; the gondoliers stand to wield their sweeps.

which had taken power in the south completed their renunciation of the Fascists by joining the war on the Allied side; and in the north Italian partisans were active behind the lines.

Peace brought unrest to Italy after the Second World War as after the First. In 1946 the King abdicated in favour of his son Humbert; and he too abdicated a month later after a vote of the people went in favour of a republic. Communism was rife, there were strikes, riots, outbreaks of violence; but out of it all a new constitution took shape.

Italy today is described officially as " a democratic republic founded on work." The government consists of a Senate, of whose members 237 are elected on a regional basis for a term of six years and 107 are appointed by the Chamber of Deputies; and a Chamber of Deputies, with 574 members elected for five years by the vote of all men and women who have come of age. The president is elected by the Senate and the Chamber in joint session, and holds office for seven years; it is a condition that he must be at least 50 years old.

ITALIAN ART *through the* CENTURIES

Italy has produced more ' old masters ' than any other land, and it is on their principles and practice that painting has developed. We read here of the long procession of painters that is her greatest glory.

Italy, ART OF. For a space of almost 2,000 years, from the later days of the Roman Republic to the 17th century, there came from Italy a high proportion of the finest works of art in the world. It is obviously impossible here to do much more than indicate the names of some of the greatest of the artists, not painters only, but architects, sculptors, and workers in gold, jewelry and other substances. You will find the early work under the heading Rome : Art and Architecture ; here we start with the lovely mosaics that, from A.D. 300 onwards, were used in Rome for the decoration of churches and other buildings, and show the influence of Byzantine art.

Paintings and mosaics were at first preferred to sculpture. The mosaics are not limited to panels but cover the entire interior of the Orthodox Baptistry at Ravenna. These date from the 6th century and for the most part illustrate Biblical subjects and incidents in the history of the Church. The mosaics of the church of San Vitale, also at Ravenna, are especially famous for the representation of Emperor Justinian (483–565) and his wife the Empress Theodora, each attended by their courtiers. After the Justinian period mosaic art began to decline. The lower walls of St. Apollinare in Classe at Ravenna show inferior work.

There was, too, a strong school of mural painters at Rome, whose work is of great merit, especially during the 8th century ; but it was with the coming of Cimabue, in the 13th century, that painting was really revived in Italy. It was through him that painting became a new, living art, divorced from the strained and artificial formalism of the Byzantines. It is known that he did frescoes and numerous altar-pieces, but perhaps nothing now remains that can be definitely assigned to him.

It is to his pupil, Giotto di Bondone (c. 1266–1337) that many people would ascribe the sure foundation of the new art. Usually referred to as " the father of the Italian Renaissance," this great master drew his inspiration largely from Nature, painting " like the life " and giving to his masterpieces, such as the series of paintings of the life of St. Francis of Assisi, a liveliness and a human quality that were lacking in his previous works (*see* illus., page 1384). Giotto's numerous followers, who include many of the best Italian painters of the 14th century, were called *giotteschi* after him.

Giotto gave form to a specifically Florentine spirit and after almost a century of painters had used variations upon his subjects the Florentine spirit was revived in the great innovator, Masaccio (1400–38). Chief among Giotto's immediate disciples, and one of the most influential masters of the succeeding period, was Andrea Orcagna (c. 1308–c. 1368), better known as a sculptor and architect, who did some very fine frescoes.

Contemporary with these painters there was another great school, working at Siena. In this the influence of Byzantine art is more obvious, but there is the same novel air about it that marked the work of the Florentines. The three foremost Sienese of the period were Duccio (c. 1260–1318), Simone Martini (1283–1344), and Lippo Memmi (d. 1356).

Returning to Florence we find in the next period, that of the Italian Quattrocento or 15th century, Fra Angelico (1387–1455), famed for the religious intensity and the moving beauty of his paintings. Within his lifetime lived Masaccio, the first man to make his figures really living people, and considered by many people as the real innovator of all later paintings. In the church of the Carmine at Florence one may admire a series of frescoes begun by Masolino, the teacher of Masaccio, continued by his pupil and finished after a lapse of years by Filippino Lippi (1457–1504). A follower of Masaccio was Uccello (1396–1475), who if he did not actually invent perspective at least studied it to such an extent that many of his works are exercises in this type of drawing.

Andrea del Castagno (c. 1410–57) and Fra Lippo Lippi (1406–69) were other painters of this time, the latter executing very tender and beautiful religious paintings. He must not be confused with his son, Filippino Lippi. Verocchio (1435–88), more sculptor than painter, was the teacher of Perugino and of Leonardo da Vinci, and a master of figure drawing. Another great name of this time is that of Sandro Botticelli (1444–1510), the pupil of Fra Lippo Lippi, and one of the artists whose works have captured the imagination of the world, and who took for his subjects the scenes and myths of classical antiquity. The art of Botticelli is extremely individual; he was most concerned, as was almost every painter of the Quattrocento, by the Florentine preoccupation with plastic form, but his own genius was related to that of the Sienese

ELABORATE DECORATION IN THE OLD PALACE, FLORENCE

The Palazzo Vecchio, or Old Palace, was built in the 14th century to house the government of Florence ; today it is used as the City Hall. In contrast with the severe grandeur of the exterior, the courtyard of the palace is elaborately decorated in the later Renaissance style. The figure of a boy on the fountain is the work of the great sculptor Andrea Verrocchio (c. 1435–88). The coat of arms of the Medici is above the centre pillar in the right background.

painters. Before the end of this period in Florence, Ghirlandaio (1449–94), a pupil of Baldovinetti (1425–99), was executing vigorous and sincere paintings. He was a prolific fresco artist and portrait painter, and left a vivid record of his time.

During this century another school flourished in Umbria, whose masters produced more simple, restrained and peaceful work than that of the Florentines. Piero della Francesca (c. 1423–92) was a member of this school; Perugino (1446–1523) and Pinturicchio (1454–1513) were others. Yet another school, destined to outlast all of these, was that of Venice. Of the Venetians it has been said that they appreciated better than anyone else the pictorial value of a painting. They were influenced at first by the great painter of Padua and Mantua, Andrea Mantegna (1431–1506), whose work has a character all its own—grand in conception and execution and with a curious hard brilliance. He went to Venice in 1455, and became highly sensitive to the colour and opulence of the Venetians. His realism and his treatment of space make his work compellingly solid, and characteristic of Northern Italy.

The real masters of Venice at this time were the Bellini. The first of these was Jacopo (c. 1400–70), but his sons, Gentile (c. 1429–1507) and Giovanni (c. 1430–1516), were better painters. The Bellini, though not the first painters to work in oils in Italy, were the first really to profit by the adoption of this medium, which was brought from Flanders by Antonello da Messina (c. 1430–79). Contemporary with them worked Cima (1449–1517) and Carpaccio (c. 1460–1520), the one tranquil, lovely and unsophisticated, the other vigorous, rough, yet technically brilliant.

The Venetian school reached its greatest heights in the next century, with the work of Giorgione (c. 1477–1510), Titian (1477–1576), Tintoretto (1518–94), and Paolo Veronese (1528–88). Giorgione, a pupil of Giovanni Bellini, is known now by only a few works of beauty; a set of four small panels claimed to be by him were bought by the National Gallery, London, in 1937. Apart from four masterpieces all other works attributed to him have been disputed. Titian, one of the mightiest figures in all Italian art, is famed for his tremendous vitality, glorious colour, perfect draughtsmanship and generally magnificent atmosphere. In vitality he is rivalled in some ways by Tintoretto, the master of El Greco (c. 1544–1614) of the Spanish school, who is also remarkable for the size of his paintings, which were done at great speed and with a sureness of touch that amazed his contemporaries.

Paolo Veronese, who also executed many enormous canvases, was a fine designer, giving as much attention to the settings of his subjects as to the figures themselves. The Venetian school was continued much later by Tiepolo (1696–1770), the greatest of baroque decorators, and by Canaletto (1697–1768), Bellotto and Francesco Guardi (d. 1793) of whom Guardi, especially, executed some extremely lovely paintings of Venice during the last period of her greatness. Tiepolo owed his inspiration to Veronese ; many of his ceiling

Anderson

It is as painters of religious subjects that the Italian masters excel above all ; and, as a religious artist Raphael (1483–1520), whose real name was Raffaelo Sanzio or Santi, was perhaps the greatest of them all.   No subject seems to have attracted him or called forth the very best of his art so much as the Madonna and Child, and this lovely Madonna del Gran Duca is one of many such paintings by him.   It shows how well he deserves his great reputation as an artist of wonderful grace, tenderness, and technical ability. Even in his own day he enjoyed tremendous popularity.

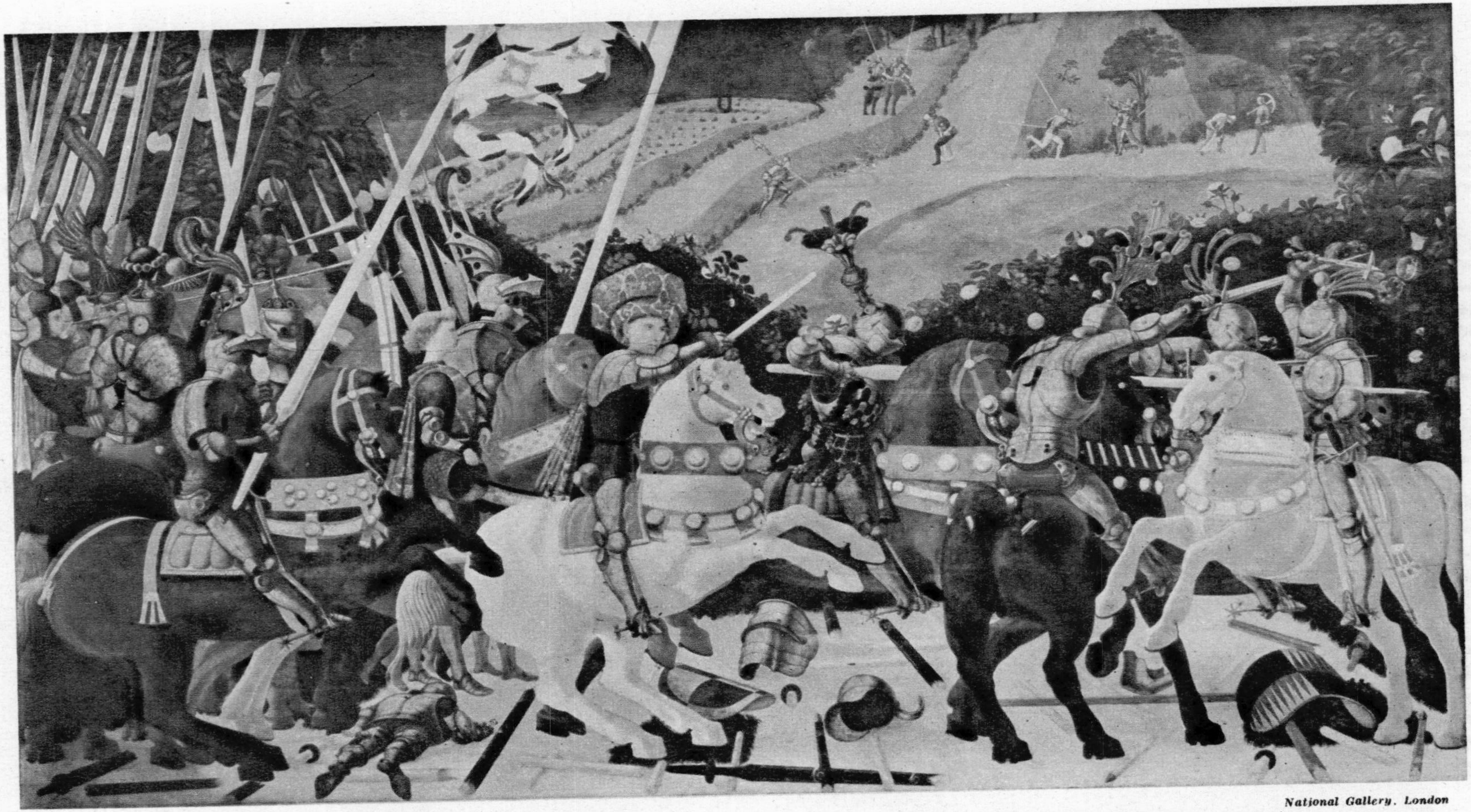

National Gallery, London

'THE ROUT OF SAN ROMANO'—AN EXERCISE IN PERSPECTIVE BY UCCELLO

Although he may not have been the actual re-discoverer of perspective the Florentine painter Uccello or Paolo Di Dono (*c.* 1397–1475) became famous for the attention which he paid to this branch of drawing, and many of his finest subjects, such as that above, seem to have been chosen mainly from the point of view of problems in this difficult art. The scene depicted here is the defeat of the army of Siena by the Florentine forces in 1431, for these two great cities of northern Italy were political as well as artistic rivals. Full of action and with a childlike, fairy-tale atmosphere, the battle seems more like play than war. But a close study of the picture will show how cunningly the problems of perspective are dealt with by a master-draughtsman who made these his special interest. This painting was one of a series done by Uccello for the Medici palace at Florence.

CHRIST'S NATIVITY PAINTED BY BOTTICELLI

Beautiful and unusual, this painting is not a straightforward representation of the Nativity (Birth) of Our Lord, but is rather an allegory. The inscription at the top explains this, and states that it was done in 1500. Kneeling on the right are two shepherds; in the sky is the 'multitude of the heavenly host.' Like other painters of his time, Sandro Botticelli (c. 1444–1510) clothed his figures in the costume of his own period.

SAINT CHRISTOPHER AND THE CHILD

Ducal Palace, Venice; photo Anderson

Tiziano Vecelli, better known as Titian, created this fresco, which illustrates the legend of how St. Christopher, carrying a small child across a river, nearly stumbled, and exclaimed, 'Had I borne the whole world upon my back, it could not have weighed heavier than thou!' 'Marvel not,' the child replied, 'for thou hast borne upon thy back the world and Him who created it.'

VENETIAN CONTRASTS IN SUBJECT AND STYLE

This fine painting, ' The Family of Darius before Alexander,' is a typical work of the painter Paolo Veronese, or Caliari, who specialized in large, colourful pictures, in which the setting is often as important as the design. Here the captive family of the Persian king is being presented to the young Macedonian conqueror, Alexander the Great, by one of Darius's ministers. Actually, these principal figures are portraits of the Pisani family, for whom it was painted.

Although the Venetian school continued to produce fine painters when most others in Italy had long passed away, their work was very different from that done in the heyday of Italian art. Typical is this ' Scene on the Lagoon,' by Francesco Guardi (1712–93), who is famous for such peaceful, lovely paintings in which Venice is portrayed with delicacy of touch as well as of colour—usually silvery greys, blues and greens. In style Guardi resembles his master Canaletto.

DIGNITY IN THE PORTRAIT OF A DOGE OF VENICE

National Gallery, London; photo Mansell

The founders of the Venetian school were the members of the Bellini family, one of whom, Giovanni (c. 1430–1516) painted this portrait of Leonardo Loredano, Doge of Venice in 1501. When they turned their hand to portraiture, the Italians brought to it the same strength and technical skill that made them pre-eminent in other types of painting. What power and dignity has this face, and with what skill and cunning are the details of the costume rendered ! The office of Doge, chief magistrate (the word is a form of Italian duce, 'leader'), was created in Venice about the year 700.

1782

Anderson

Whether as sculptor or painter, Michelangelo (1475-1564) stands out for his tremendous power and dynamic energy, and even a seated figure such as this wonderful statue of Moses, from the church of St. Peter ad Vincula in Rome, impresses one by its restless energy. Moses is here shown with horns, which, on account of an ancient misreading of a passage in Exodus xxiv, he is supposed to have had when he returned from Mount Sinai with the tablets of the Law. This figure forms part of the tomb of Pope Julius II, on which Michelangelo worked at intervals for 40 years.

FINE RENAISSANCE SCULPTURE AND METALWORK

Top, Venice, photo, Anderson; bottom, photo, Wolfram

Verrocchio, sculptor of the monument to the Venetian soldier of fortune Bartolommeo Colleoni (upper) was famous also as a painter, but this monument is generally considered his greatest masterpiece. As an expression of power and dignity it stands among the world's finest sculptures. The glorious salt-cellar (lower) is the work of Benvenuto Cellini, the finest goldsmith the world has ever had. Done by him for Francis I of France, it is made of pure gold, and represents Poseidon (Neptune) and Aphrodite (Venus) reclining above a sea full of dolphins.

paintings may be found in Venetian churches, and he decorated also many palaces, one of his most famous works, Antony and Cleopatra, being in the Labia Palace at Venice.

An isolated figure, in that he worked largely at Milan and belongs to no school, is Leonardo da Vinci (1452–1519). He is classed with the 16th century artists although he lived chiefly during the previous one. Not many of his pictures are extant, but those remaining show him as a master of portraiture, of fresco and of art in its highest sense. Yet his influence was less than that of Michelangelo (*q.v.*), the painter of the Last Judgement, one of the world's masterpieces, who regarded himself as a poor painter. His interest was in sculpture, and that is why his figures have such solidity and force.

For centuries, indeed, Italy led the world in sculpture and painting. Among sculptors Michelangelo (1475–1564) stands supreme; few others have equalled him in breadth of vision and power. It was not only in these arts that Italy held first place. The finest of all metal workers, Benvenuto Cellini (1500–71), a pupil of Michelangelo, was the greatest goldsmith of his age. Luca Della Robbia (*c.* 1400–82) discovered a method of enamelling terra-cotta with a milky-white glaze to which he added an exquisite blue. He is best known for his Madonnas and children. His nephew Andrea Della Robbia (1435–1523) executed some remarkable reliefs for the cathedral of Florence.

The third big figure in Italian painting at this time is that of Raphael (1483–1520), whose finest paintings have unique spiritual beauty. He worked at Perugia, Florence, and at Rome, where he executed superb frescoes for the Vatican.

Besides these three giants there were innumerable other fine painters during the 16th century. At Florence worked Piero di Cosimo (1462–1521), who was influenced by Leonardo and by Andrea del Sarto (1486–1531), the faultless painter, whose technique was perfect although his figures lack power. At Bologna, the Caracci did what the Bellini had done earlier at Venice, founding a very distinct school and rising to great heights themselves. The greatest was Annibale Caracci (1560–1609), who is especially interesting as perhaps the first Italian to paint landscape for its own sake,

not merely as a background. Domenichino (1581–1641), Guido Reni (1574–1642), and Guercino (1591–1666) were notable followers of this school.

Considerably earlier than any of these painters was an artist who came from Parma, named Correggio (1494–1534), and who became famous after his death. His most marked qualities were a certain joyousness of expression, and a remarkable fondness for foreshortening, and light and shade—an aspect of painting which also attracted Caravaggio (1569–1609), a painter of the Roman school, who aimed at a violent realism. His scenes of everyday life have deep shadows and sharp lights. Of his religious pictures one of the most famous is the Death of the Virgin, in the Louvre.

Salvator Rosa (1615–73), one of the founders of romantic landscape, belonged to the Neapolitan school. He excelled in tempestuous landscapes and had a strong influence on later landscapists.

Italian painting, which had exerted the greatest influence on European art from the 13th century, gradually declined in the 18th century. There were many painters of talent, but few of outstanding genius. The ancient centres of culture, Siena, Bologna, Mantua, Verona, and the works of older masters, became objects of aesthetic pleasure and curiosity rather than parts of a living art. The galleries of museums all over the world were filled with examples of every Italian school, and Italy herself became a storehouse of artistic treasures.

By the beginning of the 19th century there remained only the traditions of the various schools, and a knowledge of these was considered indispensable to the education of cultivated persons throughout Europe. The initiative passed to France during the latter half of the 17th century, and during the 19th and 20th centuries many important movements were launched in Paris; these had a permanent influence on the development of painting in all countries. Italy as a whole contributed little to modern development, but in 1910 the writer F. T. Marinetti (1876–1944) launched the Futurist school of painters.

Futurism preached the renovation of Italian art, declaring that art could live only by freedom from the past. It failed to survive the First World War (1914–18), though Surrealists of the 1930's used its mannerisms.

Topical

A GUERCINO MASTERPIECE
The leading Bolognese painter of the 17th century, Guercino was among those who contributed to a type of religious painting lacking simplicity but having studied grace or pathos. This work, Elijah Fed by the Ravens, shows his use of strongly-contrasted light and shade.

GREAT WRITERS *in the* ITALIAN TONGUE

The history of Italian literature begins late—just before the Renaissance, or revival of art and learning, in the 14th century—but it contains some of the world's greatest names. Who they were is told here.

Italy, LITERATURE OF. The Italian language has descended in the direct line from ancient Latin, which it most resembles of all the Romance (derived from Latin) languages. The sonority and rhythm which French has lost, the delightful clearness which has become rather blurred in Spanish, all remain in melodious Italian, the ideal language of poetry, in which it has always excelled.

Yet modern Italian, being to a large extent a forced bloom, suffers in many respects from its artificial growth. For in the Middle Ages, while literary Latin of a sort continued to be used as the learned and cultured language, the mass of the people of Italy, mingling the old Low Latin of popular speech with imported foreign elements, contrived to form it into a score of different dialects.

Then came the great Dante (1265–1321), who selected the dialect of Tuscany for his literary work, and revealed its strength and beauty. Petrarch (1304–74) and Giovanni Boccaccio (1313–75) followed him, and wrote immortal lines in Tuscan —beautiful verse in the one case, and prose stories in the other. Thus this dialect became the fixed literary language of Italy, and is today so recognized.

But the many other dialects still exist, and their words tend to creep in, not always elegant or well-conceived; and it is here that the struggle between the classic but often cramped Tuscan and the cruder but more vigorous popular dialects places the Italian writer at a loss. This artificiality and limitation of Italian, in spite of its rich sweetness, is therefore to be reckoned with in explaining why Italian writers of all times, and especially the present, are not so numerous as in other countries. But it has with equal truth been said that " Italian writers must be weighed, not counted." If they have been few, they have also been worthy to rank among the greatest.

Latin long remained in Italy more nearly a living tongue than elsewhere, hence a written literature in the vernacular, or people's language, was slow in arising—hardly existing before the beginning of the 14th century.

Late as it was in starting, this literature attained its greatest glory almost immediately, far outshining all other literatures of the period. Dante wrote his Divine Comedy a century before Chaucer and three centuries before Shakespeare. Petrarch followed with his immortal sonnets to the Laura who inspired him to write poetry; and Boccaccio with the stories of the Decameron.

But with the great revival of interest in the ancient Greek and Latin literatures, which was a feature of the Renaissance, the new Italian literature declined. The brightest spirits sought their inspiration in antiquity, and the newly formed Italian tongue suffered through an affected and elaborate striving for Latin elegance.

It was not until the 16th century that Italian writers returned to a natural and spontaneous style. This century has been called the "golden age of Italian literature " because of the large number of pleasing and competent writers who appeared. The best known of these are Ludovico Ariosto (1474–1533) with his masterpiece entitled Orlando Furioso, and Torquato Tasso (1544–95), whose Gerusalemme Liberata (Jerusalem Delivered) is a reaction against the worldliness of religion in his time, expressed in thunderous verse, telling the story of the First Crusade.

Alinari

PETRARCH AND HIS FRIEND BOCCACCIO
The writings of Petrarch, Francesco Petrarca (1304–74), left, had much to do with the revival of learning in Europe. Although a writer of admirable Latin verse and prose, he is remembered primarily as a lyric poet. About 1350 he developed a friendship with Giovanni Boccaccio (1313–75), right, author of The Decameron.

Tasso's claim to immortality rests on two works alone—the wonderful epic that has just been mentioned and his pastoral play Aminta. He was engaged on the former from 1563 till 1575. His life was full of tragedy—a hopeless passion having disturbed his mental balance. He had to be put under restraint at different times, finding a final refuge at Rome, where he died in 1595.

Ludovico Ariosto, both in temperament and outlook, differed from Tasso. He was born in 1474, and came of an ancient and noble family. He had been studying law for five years when he found his vocation for poetry. Whilst acting as an attendant gentleman to Cardinal Ippolito d'Este he pursued his fancy and in 10 years he had completed 24 cantos of his great Orlando Furioso.

The poem first appeared complete in 1532. Whilst the volume of his output was not great, his work reached a very high standard, and he has five comedies and many graceful sonnets to his credit. To the same era belongs Niccolo Machiavelli, author of several volumes of history, and of the work entitled The Prince, in which he maintained that the State is supreme, and all means to preserve it are justified.

During the 17th and the first half of the 18th century Italy suffered from a grandiose literary style and a lack of literary ideas. It was not until the advent of Count Vittorio Alfieri (1749-1803) with his tragic plays, in the second half of the 18th century, that Italy was aroused to a sense of the emptiness of its recent literature. Alfieri also started a wave of Italian patriotism—the desire to be rid of the petty tyrannies and foreign control which had torn the land for centuries.

Out of this new patriotism grew many romantic dreams, touched with intense political reactions, which give the Italian literature of the 19th century —the century of Italian unity and freedom— a new vigour. Among the poets of this period were Ugo Foscolo (1778-1827) and Giacomo Leopardi (1798-1837). The writer Alessandro Manzoni (1785-1873) created a school of Italian historical fiction, and his novel I Promessi Sposi (The Betrothed) stands at the head of Italian fiction.

With the awakening of Italian national consciousness came a reaction against the imitation of foreign literature, and a desire to depict the life and thoughts of the Italian people.

Giosuè Carducci in verse, and Matilde Serao and Antonio Fogazzaro in prose, wrote of Italy and things Italian, with a really native point of view, expressing the new patriotism. None excelled the novels and short stories of Giovanni Verga (1840-1922), the Sicilian. Maestro-Don Gesualdo is his masterpiece; and his Cavalleria Rusticana supplied the plot of the famous opera by Pietro Mascagni (1863-1945).

Overshadowing all other Italian writers in the first quarter of the 20th century was the romantic figure of Gabriele d'Annunzio (1863-1938)— poet, novelist, dramatist and airman. Of Luigi Pirandello's (1867-1936) plays and stories, Six Characters in Search of an Author, widely translated, has scored successes in Great Britain and the United States. Benedetto Croce (born 1866) is one of the world's leaders of philosophical thought.

After the Second World War (1939-45) there was a revival of Italian literature, with an auto-

E.N.A.

GABRIELE D'ANNUNZIO

Poet, dramatist and novelist, Gabriele d'Annunzio was the leading Italian literary figure at the beginning of the 20th century. He served in the Italian Air Force during the First World War (1914–18), and is here seen (in foreground) in his motor-boat on Lake Garda.

biographical tendency. Il Demiurgo, by Filippo Burzio, contains an original conception of spiritual perfection. Fontamara, Ignazio Silone's bitter satire on Fascism, won perhaps even greater popularity abroad than in Italy. Alberto Moravia's Gli Indifferenti is an outstanding novel. Ungaretti and Quasimodo are notable modern poets.

Ivan. GRAND DUKES AND TSARS OF RUSSIA. Six rulers of Russia have borne the name Ivan, the Russian for John. Some of them ruled before the country was called Russia, and were known as the Grand Dukes of Moscow. The foundation of Tsarist Russia was the work of the third and fourth rulers of the name.

IVAN III, who ruled from 1462 to 1505, freed his country from the Tartars by refusing to pay tribute to their Great Khan. He conquered the wealthy city of Novgorod and annexed it with other cities and states to his dominion. He adopted the double-headed black eagle as the Russian emblem, fostered art and learning, encouraged industry, and was responsible for the introduction of civil laws. Because of the importance of his work he is known as Ivan the Great.

IVAN IV earned the title of the Terrible because of the insane cruelty he manifested at times during his reign from 1547 to 1584. Once in a fit of anger he killed his own son. But Ivan IV, like Ivan the Great, was also a man of great energy. He extended his dominions south to Astrakhan on the Caspian Sea and north to the White Sea, and on the east he added western Siberia. In 1547 he formally assumed the title of Tsar (Caesar), and laid the foundation of the autocratic government under which Russia was ruled by the Tsars for nearly four centuries.

Ivory. True ivory is obtained only from the tusks of the elephant, generally the male. In the ivory trade elephants' tusks are properly called teeth, because they are the animals' upper incisors. The tusks grow during the animal's entire life, usually attaining a length of several feet and a weight of from 150 to 200 lb. or more a pair. The tusks of the Indian elephant are inferior in quality and size to those of the African species, and the female Indian elephant seldom has any tusks at all.

Ivory used for commercial purposes is also obtained from the teeth of the hippopotamus and wild boar; and even from the fossil remains of prehistoric animals, such as the mammoth, which are still found in the far north of Asia and America. Among marine creatures whose teeth or tusks yield ivory are the walrus, narwhal (species of porpoise), and sperm-whale. But all this ivory is inferior to elephant ivory.

From ivory are made billiard-balls, piano-keys, toilet articles, handles for knives, umbrellas and

R. B. Matson

FIVE-LOBED IVY LEAVES

A climbing shrub of the natural order *Araliaceae*, ivy has thick, glossy, dark-green leaves with five lobes which vary greatly in depth. These plants grow in cool regions of the Northern Hemisphere. They bloom in late summer or autumn, the greenish flowers being succeeded by berries.

doors, and ornamental earrings. It is very elastic and flexible so that riding-whips have actually been cut in one piece from a single long tusk. It has a peculiar marking, a cross-section showing many lines of different colours running in arcs. By this means it is distinguished from imitations, which are unmarked. Ivory is classified as hard and soft, the former having a more glassy and transparent appearance and being more difficult to cut with the saw. Hard ivory comes mostly from West Africa. Soft ivory contains more moisture than the hard variety, and is able to stand variable conditions better without cracking.

So valuable is ivory that no part of it is wasted. Sacks full of cuttings and shavings are sold, to be used for inlay work. Even the dust is used for polishing and, when suitably treated, for the preparation of Indian ink. The most valuable ivory—that of the African elephant—is required for billiard-balls, three balls of best quality usually being obtained from one tooth. Ivory for piano-keys, the other most important use, is of the soft variety.

The use of ivory can be traced to prehistoric times. We read in the Bible that King Solomon "made a great throne of ivory." There still exist examples of inlaid Egyptian ivory, and in the British Museum, London, are many Assyrian ivory carvings made in Nineveh nearly 1,000 years before Christ. In ancient Greece ivory was used for carvings, sculpture, and various objects of luxury. The sculptures in ivory of the Gothic art of the 13th and 14th centuries are distinguished for their beauty; much of this work is done in walrus ivory, which is now less popular. Walrus ivory is also used for fine oriental sword handles. Ivory mirror-cases, caskets for jewelry or toilet purposes, and other articles used to be carved with scenes from real life or illustrations from the romances, which set forth vividly the dress and customs of the times they represented.

Vegetable ivory is a material resembling ivory, obtained principally from a genus of palm (*Phytelephas*), native to tropical South America. Other palms (*Attalea*) from Central America also supply a certain amount. The fruit, as large as a man's head, contains numerous nuts or seeds, called corozo or tagua nuts, which, when ripe, are so hard that they make a valuable substitute for ivory. These hard nuts are usually about the size of a large plum. They are much used for buttons, umbrella handles, and similar purposes. There are also various artificial compounds which resemble ivory, such as celluloid and xylonite.

Ivy. One of the best-known of all our plants, with its creeping, climbing stems and rich dark-green leathery leaves, is ivy.

There are about 50 species growing in the Northern Hemisphere. They climb by means of sucker-like disks which attach themselves to walls and trees, or by means of tendrils. The leaves of the English ivy are evergreen. The small greenish flowers are succeeded by berries which later turn black. Contrary to common belief, ivy does not ordinarily injure its means of support, for it is a climber and not a parasite. But it will worm its way into the interstices of masonry, sometimes forcing the blocks apart; and when ivy makes much growth about the limbs of a tree the latter may eventually be killed by it. The plant belongs to the genus *Hedera*. The berries are poisonous.

The ivy has always been a symbol of the clinging love of woman. The altar of Hymen, the Greek god of marriage, whose blessing was invoked at every wedding, was kept green with this plant. When Isolde, the bride of King Mark of Cornwall, in the old Welsh or Cornish legend of Tristan and Isolde (immortalized in Wagner's opera) died lamenting the death of her lover Tristan, King Mark in his anger buried them apart; but an ivy plant growing from the breast of Tristan met another growing from the grave of Isolde, and the two plants, entwining, convinced the king that the union of the lovers was pure and undying, and caused him to repent of his anger and rebury them, together.

J

Jackal. Eastern Europe, southern Asia, and northern Africa are the home of the jackal (*Canis aureus*), a dog-like animal closely related to but smaller than the wolves. It has a pointed muzzle, and a bushy tail about one-third the length of the body. The common jackal of southern Asia is the best known. It is greyish-yellow in colour, darker above, and lighter on the underside. In Africa, one species has a kind of saddle of silvery black, while the rest of the body is bright tan.

During the day jackals remain concealed in burrows, caves, and jungles, coming out at night to hunt, usually in packs. They utter a piercing cry, and the howling of a pack at night makes an appalling chorus, familiar in Oriental villages. They feed on smaller mammals, poultry, and, when living food is unobtainable, on carrion, waiting for them to die; and they devour the unfinished kills of larger carnivores. When running in packs they attack sheep and antelopes. They probably represent one of the breeds from which the domestic dog is descended.

Jackdaw. A member of the crow family and common in Great Britain, the jackdaw is a fairly large bird—though not so big as his cousin, the rook—black for the most part, with grey on the neck, so that the black on the head looks like a little cap. In towns the jackdaw builds in chimneys, in ruins, belfries and similar places. Out in the country hollow trees, cliffs, and even rabbit holes are used as sites for the nest, built untidily of sticks. The eggs are pale blue, with black spots.

W. S. Berridge
JACKAL : RELATIVE OF THE DOG
Whether the modern jackal is an ancestor of our dogs is a moot point, but you can see here how very dog-like he is in general appearance. In colour this animal is a greyish- or yellowish-brown. Jackals hunt at night, in packs, attacking sheep and antelopes as well as smaller animals.

The jackdaw (*Corvus monedula*) is a useful bird, for it spends most of its time, except the breeding season, wandering over the fields with the rooks, picking up harmful insects and slugs. And you may see a jackdaw sitting on the back of a sheep, not, as people have thought, waiting to peck out its eyes, but actually ridding it of its parasites. At the same time, the jackdaw's reputation for cunning and mischief is not without foundation, and although the famous Jackdaw of Rheims, in the Ingoldsby Legends, was perhaps an exception, there is no doubt that they are great thieves. They can be easily tamed and make amusing pets. The cheerful, noisy call of "tchak, tchak" suggests the origin of the jackdaw's name.

M. H. Crawford
PERKY JACKDAW
A lively and noisy member of the crow family, the jackdaw can be recognized by its greyish neck and black ' cap.'

Jackson, THOMAS JONATHAN ("STONEWALL") (1824–63). In the history of the American Civil War (1861–1865) no figure stands out with greater vividness than that of " Stonewall " Jackson. His strength of will was probably the result of his Scottish-Irish descent, and of his fight with adverse circumstances. He was born at Clarksburg, West Virginia, on January 21, 1824, and was left a penniless orphan at an early age. After attending a small country school in Virginia he decided to enter the army. He set out for Washington, travelling part of the way on foot, and when he arrived in that city he presented himself before the Secretary of War, and asked for an appointment to the military academy at West Point, New York.

The secretary was so impressed by the boy's determination that he gave him the appointment. After his graduation in 1846, Jackson served in the Mexican War and won such distinction that in seven months he was promoted to the rank of major. After the close of that war he became a teacher in the Virginia Military Institute, and though he was not a success in the class-room he left an indelible impression upon the Negroes of the community, for whom he established a Sunday-school and to whom he was unfailingly kind.

In 1861, when the quarrel between the Northern and the Southern states over the abolition of slavery came to a crisis, he threw in his fortunes with his own people. He wished to see the unity of the United States preserved, but he did not believe that the North should force the South to remain a party to a compact which had become hateful. At the battle of Bull Run, when some of the Confederates (southern troops) were thrown into confusion, one of their generals called to the men, "There stands Jackson like a stone wall; rally behind the

Virginians!" The cry was taken up by the soldiers, and "Stonewall" Jackson was the name by which he was known thereafter.

In 1862 he won victory after victory as general of the Confederate forces. In May 1863, after winning the battle of Chancellorsville, he and his escort were mistaken in the dusk by his own outposts for a detachment of Federal (Northern) cavalry. They were fired upon, and Jackson fell wounded. His right arm had to be amputated, and then pneumonia set in. He died on May 10. The loss of this brilliant general more than offset the Confederate gain in their victory.

On the march he always carried with him his Bible and Napoleon's Maxims of War. To the study of the latter he owed his success as a general, to the study of the Bible his greatness as a man. He interpreted literally the injunction to pray without ceasing, and even while he was directing operations on the battlefield his lips were often seen moving in prayer.

After the painting by Nast

'STONEWALL' JACKSON
One of the heroes of the American Civil War (1861–65), Thomas Jonathan Jackson gained his nickname of 'Stonewall' at the battle of Bull Run when he 'stood like a stone wall' and rallied the men of the Southern Army.

Jacobins. Originating at Versailles, near Paris, in 1789 this prominent political society of the French Revolution took up its quarters in an old disused monastery of the Jacobin, or Dominican, monks, and received its popular name from this meeting-place. At first it organized a network of branches throughout the country to assist in preserving and defending the monarchy. Gradually it became more republican in its aims and more and more powerful, and the more moderate members left it or were expelled and formed other clubs. The attempt of King Louis XVI to escape from France in 1791 turned its whole influence against the monarchy and in favour of a republic. The leadership passed to men like Robespierre and Danton, until the word "Jacobin" came to mean a person of extreme revolutionary sentiments.

For a short time the Jacobins were the rulers of France, and it was they who had King Louis executed in 1793. After the fall of their leader Robespierre in July 1794 their sway came to an end, and the society was abolished in the following November.

Jacobites. The chief interest felt today in the Jacobite party arises from the fact that the devotion of the Highlanders to the Stuart or Jacobite cause has added many beautiful songs to the minstrelsy of Scotland.

The name Jacobite comes from *Jacobus*, the Latin form of James. It was given to the supporters of James II of England and his descendants. James,

having roused almost the whole of England against him by his ill-advised efforts to re-establish the Roman Catholic religion, fled the country after the landing on these shores of William of Orange in 1688. James made an effort to regain the throne of England when he landed in Ireland in 1689, but the defeat inflicted on him by William at the battle of the Boyne in the following year compelled him to flee again to France.

James Edward Francis (1688–1766), son of James II and his second wife, Mary of Modena, was known as the Old Pretender; he attempted a rising in England and Scotland in 1715. His followers were defeated, and James III, as he styled himself, returned to France.

His son, Charles Edward Stuart (Bonnie Prince Charlie, 1720–88) made another and final effort to restore the Stuarts in 1745.

On his landing in Scotland, an army of Highlanders flocked to his standard but they were defeated by the English at Culloden in 1746, and this finally extinguished the hopes of the Jacobites. Charles Edward was enabled to escape because of the devotion of some of his followers, notably Flora Macdonald. He was known as the Young Pretender.

In St. Peter's, Rome, is a monument by Canova, put up by King George IV, to the memory of " James III, Charles III, and Henry IX "—the Old Pretender, Young Pretender, and the latter's brother Henry, a Cardinal of the Roman Catholic Church, respectively. On Henry's death in 1807 the Stuarts' claims passed to a distant branch of the family. (*See* illustration on opposite page).

Jacquard Loom. Until the beginning of the 19th century only simple designs were able to be woven on a loom. These simple patterns were woven by connecting groups of warp threads (*warp* is the lengthwise thread of a fabric, and *weft* is the crosswise thread) to one or more of the heddles which, operated by the worker's feet through pedals, lifted these warp threads and so opened what the weaver calls a "shed" though which the shuttle carrying the weft could be thrown, sideways. These terms are explained in our story of the Loom. When more complicated patterns had to be woven, three persons were needed for each loom: one who "read " a master design, and called out to a second person which warp threads to lift in order to secure the desired pattern; and directed a third person (the actual weaver) what coloured threads to employ in shooting his shuttles through the opened shed.

The pattern-weaving loom invented in 1804 by Joseph Marie Jacquard (1752–1834) altered all this, and enabled complicated designs to be woven automatically—as far as the pattern went—by a single operator. Moreover, the guiding mechanism, in the forms of cards punched with series of holes and strung together in a long chain, could be used over and over again to repeat patterns.

But credit must be given also to another Frenchman, Jacques de Vaucanson (1704–82), who had invented a means of automatic pattern control by a cylinder perforated with holes in regular lines. He attached a lifting thread to every warp thread: the opposite end of the lifting thread went to a framework in which were needles pressed by springs against the face of the perforated cylinder. Around this cylinder was wrapped a sheet of card perforated with holes according to a master design; a hole in the card would let a needle pass through and go into a corresponding hole in the cylinder beneath, thus causing the lifting thread of a warp thread to pull up its warp.

Vaucanson was a mechanical genius whose automatons (self-working figures) were celebrated. He paved the way for Jacquard's later invention. But the Vaucanson device was only suited for small pieces of weaving, since the entire design had to be contained on the card wrapped around the cylinder; mechanical difficulties prevented this cylinder being made very large in diameter. Jacquard, while using a modified form of Vaucanson's warp lifting device, did away with the card around the cylinder. Instead, he used perforated rectangular sheets of card, and hinged them together on the longest edges. A comparatively small piece of design could be worked by joining the first and last cards so as to make an endless chain, which passed continuously through the " Jacquard box " above the loom. A longer series of cards could be dealt with by folding them over and stacking them as they came down.

When the weaver pressed his foot on a pedal, a member known as the " griffe," in the overhead box, engaged with and lifted the hooks attached to the lifting threads—provided that plungers linked with these threads could pass through perforations in the card then in the box, ready in position. Where the card *had* holes registering with any plungers, such plungers would pass through and allow warp threads to be lifted; where holes were *absent* from the card, the lifting hooks were not engaged, and the griffe slipped past them, so that corresponding warp threads stayed down.

Jacquard's loom revolutionised figure weaving, and in its modernised forms is highly important today. Moreover, the punched-card method of controlling automatic machines is much used today—for example, in such widely differing appliances as the piano player and the calculating machine. Joseph Marie Jacquard built better than he knew when he produced his first successful pattern-weaving apparatus. In our story of Lace is an illustration of card-punching for a design—an adaptation of the Jacquard system.

Painting by John Pettie, R.A.

CHARLES EDWARD, JACOBITE LEADER
The landing of Charles Edward, the Young Pretender and grandson of James II, at Moidart, Scotland, on July 2, 1745, marked the beginning of the last real attempt to restore the Stuarts to the British throne. His handsome appearance gained for him the designation of Bonnie Prince Charlie. (*See* article on facing page).

Jaguar. (Pron. jag′-ū-ar). The largest member of the cat family found on the North and South American continents, the jaguar (*Felis onca*) is the tiger of the New World. The head is large and the legs massive, and the length may be four feet

Fox

JAGUAR AND HER KITTEN
The largest member of the cat family found in the New World, the jaguar is a more
massive beast than the leopard.   It is usually yellowish-brown in colour, with black
markings arranged in rosettes.   From two to four cubs are born at a time, and they
are able to follow the mother after some 15 days.

without the tail. There is much variation in
colour, but in general the animal is yellowish-brown,
with black markings, each of which takes the form
of a rough rectangle or ring, with a lighter spot in
the centre. The tail has a black tip.

The jaguar inhabits all South America, except
Patagonia, and is found as far north as Texas in the
United States. It lives chiefly in trees, from which
it springs upon its prey; but sometimes it hunts
upon the plains, killing horses, cattle and sheep.
The jaguar is also expert at catching fresh-water
turtles, even pursuing them into midstream.

Jam. As explained in the story of Food Preservation (page 1341), the principle of preserving
fruits to make jam is to boil them with sugar. This
drives off much of the water contained in the fruit;
the rest of the water is bound into a syrup.

In ripening fruits, a substance known as pectin
develops, by the action of an enzyme (q.v.); when
fruit is boiled along with water, and sugar and an
acid are present, the pectin causes a jellying action,
and the jam "sets," as the housewife terms it.
Some fruits contain more pectin and acid than others
—for example, apples, damsons, gooseberries and
black or red currants; the plums come next, along
with blackberries,
loganberries and
raspberries. Poorest
of all in setting
property are pears
and cherries, so that
it is usual to add
pectin artificially
prepared in order
to make them set
better. Such pectin
can be made from
the residue of sugar-
beet, or from the
inside part of lemon
or orange peel.

After the jam
has been made it

is put into jars and the mouth
of the jar sealed, first with a
waxed paper disk and then with
a cover of paper-lined metal,
prepared paper, or cellophane.
This keeps out air and prevents
the formation of mould.

Fruit jellies are made from
juice strained from the cooked
fruit pulp. Then the juice is
boiled with sugar, much as in
jam-making. Marmalade is a
kind of jam made with oranges
and lemons, the shredded peel
being added to the fruit during
the boiling process. Jams and
jellies are wholesome foods,
especially valuable to young
people, whose natural appetite
for "sweets" is thereby satisfied
in an excellent manner. Such
fruit preserves enable us to store
up summer sunshine and enjoy
its beneficial products during the
winter months. (*See* Sugar).

Jamaica. With its palm-fringed coves and
cloud-capped mountains rising out of the blue
waters of the Caribbean Sea, Jamaica is a lovely
land of perpetual summer. But Jamaica (whose
Indian name *Xaymaca* means " island of fountains ")
is not merely a wonderland bright with orchids, iris,
passion-flowers, poppies, sparkling streams and
jungle-lands of palms, bamboos, and giant ferns,
where humming-birds, parrots, and many coloured
butterflies flutter.

It is also a land of rich commercial resources, with
luxuriant lowland plantations, fruit trees, and mountain forests of logwood, satinwood, mahogany, rose-
wood and ebony. Jamaica exports chiefly bananas,
coconuts, logwood (used for dyeing), logwood extract, sugar, coffee, rum, cocoa, allspice or Jamaica
pepper (the berry of an evergreen tree), and the
famous Jamaica ginger. The largest and most important of the British West Indies, it is singularly
free from venomous snakes and dangerous animals,
for only a few wild pigs and an occasional alligator
are found there.

Jamaica lies about 90 miles south of Cuba on the
main ship route between the Panama Canal and
Europe and the Atlantic ports of the United States.

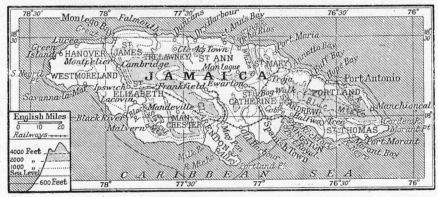

JAMAICA : LARGEST OF BRITISH WEST INDIAN ISLES

STEALTHY PROWLERS OF THE AMAZON FORESTS

For size and ferocity jaguars rank in the cat family next to tigers and lions. Not only do they stalk their prey on the ground, but they also pounce on their victims from overhanging branches of trees. Their mottled coats mimic the play of sunlight and leaf shadows in the forest and render them almost indistinguishable at a short distance, while their complete stillness when waiting for their prey aids this disguise. The scientific name of the jaguar is *Felis onca*

Fox

BABY JAGUAR

JAGUARS hardly ever breed in captivity, and even when young are born they seldom live long in the cage. This lively youngster, however, seems to be as well as one could wish, when photographed for the first time, at the age of two months. But he had a twin which died at birth, and other jaguars born in captivity have usually met the same fate. Already, you see, this jaguar cub is giving some indication of the fierce and unruly nature of his kind, for jaguars are notoriously bad-tempered animals.

FEROCIOUS YAWN

WHEN the jaguar yawns you see the full array of his teeth, as fine a set as anyone could wish to possess. Of all the great cats, jaguars are the most difficult to keep in captivity, and it is seldom that one sees so fine a specimen as this anywhere but in its native haunts. The average length when full-grown is four feet from nose to the root of the tail, the head being noticeably large.

It is 144 miles long, 40 miles wide, with an area of 4,404 square miles, and has good harbours, of which Kingston, the capital (population, 109,000), has the best. Other towns are Spanish Town, Port Antonio, and Montego Bay.

In the early days the island was a haunt of pirates. During the 18th century more than 600,000 Negroes were imported to work on the plantations as slaves. Slavery was finally abolished and the slaves liberated in 1834. The inhabitants now are about 77 per cent Negroes, 20 per cent half-castes, less than two per cent whites, the rest being East Indian coolies, imported as plantation labourers, and Chinese. The government is in the hands of a Governor, an Executive Council, and a House of Representatives. Attached to

Central Art Gallery; Elders & Fyffes, Ltd.

IN BRITAIN'S COLONY OF JAMAICA

King Street (lower) is the principal thoroughfare of Kingston, the capital and chief port of Jamaica. Situated on the south-east coast, the town stands at the head of an excellent land-locked harbour. Bananas are among the island's main exports ; in the upper photograph bunches of the green fruit are awaiting transportation to the docks.

Jamaica as dependencies are Turks and Caicos Islands, Cayman Islands and certain very small islands of the West Indies.

Jamaica was discovered by Christopher Columbus on his second voyage to the West Indies, in 1494, Spanish settlements being established there 15 years later. A British expedition captured the island in 1655, and it remains a British possession. In November 1940, during the Second World War (1939–45), sites on the island were leased to the United States for military purposes. The population of Jamaica is 1,237,000.

James. KINGS OF ENGLAND. Only two rulers of England have borne the name of James. The hatred which was felt for the second of these, because of his attempt to rule despotically and restore the Catholic religion, is probably the reason for its disuse as a royal name.

JAMES I, who was king of England from 1603 to 1625, was already King James VI of Scotland when he came to the English throne as the first of the Stuart line and the first Sovereign of Great Britain (though the two kingdoms were not united until 100 years later). He was the son of the unfortunate Mary Queen of Scots and of her second husband, the dissolute James Stuart, Lord Darnley. Born in Edinburgh Castle on June 19, 1566, he became king of Scotland the following year when his mother was forced to abdicate. During his minority a regent ruled in his stead, and the boy-king became a prize fought for by rival lords who coveted that office. In 1582 he was seized by the Earl of Gowrie and held captive for a year. On his escape he began to govern in reality, and succeeded in making the nobles subservient to the throne.

As a boy the young king was sickly, and he never outgrew a weakness of the legs which made it impossible for him to stand without support until he was seven. He became a bold rider, although for years he found it necessary to be tied in the saddle. He was well educated, especially in theology; although born the son of a Catholic mother, he was a staunch Protestant.

When James succeeded to the English throne in 1603, on the death of Queen Elizabeth, he was a man of 37, and prided himself on what he called his " king-craft." In reality he so lacked political discretion that a French statesman once characterized him as " the wisest fool in Christendom."

Nearly everything that James did displeased some section of the English people. He aroused their jealousy by a vain attempt to bring about a closer union of his two kingdoms of England and Scotland. He lost the support of both the Puritans and the Catholics, each of whom had expected concessions from him. Some of the Catholics engaged in the Gunpowder Plot, engineered by Guy Fawkes, to blow up Parliament and the king and to place a Catholic ruler on the throne of England. Only one of his acts pleased the Puritans, and that was the new translation of the Bible, which forms the Authorised Version.

James I also quarrelled with Parliament over taxation and political matters. He believed in the " divine right of kings "—that is, that they receive their powers from God, and are responsible to Him alone and not to their subjects. He was of the opinion that Parliament owed all its powers and privileges to the graciousness of the king, while Parliament claimed that these were the " birthright and inheritance of the subjects of England."

He quarrelled with it, too, over foreign affairs. He wanted as an ally the Catholic country of Spain, and to marry his son Charles to a Spanish princess. Parliament wanted to fight Spain at sea and thus aid the German Protestants in the Thirty Years' War (1618–48). Not until James's plans for a Spanish alliance failed and he decided to make war upon that country did he and his Parliament agree. The year after the war had begun James I died, relinquishing to his son Charles I the problem of settling the differences between Crown and Parliament that he himself had been unable to solve.

JAMES II, who reigned from 1685 to 1688, was a grandson of James I. His ideas of the divine right of kings were the same as those of his grandfather, and of his father, Charles I. He still attempted to carry out his ideas in spite of the fact that his father had been beheaded for this by Parliament. It has been said of James II that he alienated " not only the classes which had fought *against* his father, but also those that had fought *for* his father."

When James II came to the throne the great majority of the people welcomed him, and fought for him against a rebellion led by the Duke of Monmouth. But the cruelty shown by Judge Jeffreys and others to the followers of Monmouth at their trial—called the Bloody Assize—turned many against the king. Then James angered the nation by trying to restore Catholicism as the religion of England. When he came to the throne he had promised to maintain the Church " as by law established." The people took this to mean the Established Church of England, and rejoiced that they had " the word of a king, and of a king who was no worse than his word."

But they soon learned that James put a different meaning on his word. He set aside or " dispensed " with the laws against Catholics and Dissenters. Seven bishops protested against reading one of his dispensing proclamations, and James sent them for trial, but they were acquitted. He appointed many Catholics to office, and even named some as bishops in the Church of England. If some of his acts indicated a toleration that was in advance of his age, they were merely to aid his fellow Catholics.

At first there was no organized opposition. Waiting seemed wiser, for James was 52 years old when he came to the throne, and his only children, Mary and Anne, by his first wife, were both Protestants. But in 1688 a son was born to him, by his second wife, who would be the heir to the throne and would be educated as a Catholic and so would prove another Catholic king. Protestant nobles claimed that the child was not really the son of James and the queen, but had been smuggled into the palace. They therefore invited James's daughter Mary and her husband, William of Orange, to come from the Netherlands and take the throne of England. When William landed practically everyone, even his daughter Anne, deserted James, and he fled. This was the " glorious revolution of 1688."

James went to France, where he was cordially received by Louis XIV, who had been furnishing him with money to carry on his fight for absolute power, both civil and religious. The French king now gave James a pension and support in trying to recover his throne. But James was defeated in Ireland at the battle of the Boyne (July 1, 1690) and the French fleet was defeated by the English at La Hogue in 1692.

After these two reverses James realized that he was no longer wanted in England. He abandoned all active attempts to regain the English throne, which by his obstinacy he had forfeited, and led a life of exile in France, where he died in 1701.

Hampton Court Palace, photo Mansell; by gracious permission of His Majesty the King

JAMES I IN HIS ROBES

Even in these magnificent robes James has the ungainly appearance which visitors to his Court always noticed. He was already King of Scotland when he ascended the English throne in 1603. This portrait was painted by Van Somer.

ISLAND KINGDOM *of the* RISING SUN

Within less than 100 years this former Hermit Kingdom of the East was transformed from a medieval State into a modern Empire dominating the Far East. Here is an outline of its achievements and its downfall.

Japan. Of all the remarkable changes that took place in the 19th century perhaps none was more notable and more unexpected than the transformation of Japan—called by its inhabitants *Nippon*, The Land of the Rising Sun. In 1850 it was an obscure Asiatic country, which for 200 years had shut itself off from the rest of the world. Foreigners were not allowed to enter the kingdom, and subjects were forbidden to leave it.

Suddenly came the awakening. In July 1853 Commodore Matthew Perry appeared off the coast with a squadron of ships of the United States Navy, sent to induce Japan to enter into trade relations with the nations of the West. Then a treaty of friendship was signed (in February 1854) by which Japan agreed to open certain ports to United States vessels. European countries, which for some time had been seeking to open up Japan, followed this lead.

After a few years of hesitation Japan unlocked the doors of its Empire, and began rapidly to adopt Western civilization.

It was in the year 1868 that a political revolution took place by which the Shogun (a sort of viceroy), who for 250 years had been the real ruler of Japan, was deposed and the power of the Tenno, or Emperor, was restored.

In a little over half a century Japan evolved from a feudal nation, utterly closed in, to one of the important trading countries of the world, its ships being found in every port and carrying a large part of the traffic of the Pacific Ocean. The Japanese became proficient in science and engineering and created a great modern army, navy and air force. Then, in conflicts with China, Russia and Germany the Japanese doubled the area of the empire. The greed for more territory seemed insatiable, and led to Japan entering the Second World War in December 1941 on the side of Germany and Italy. For three and a half years she ruled or controlled a vast expanse of lands seized in that war, until her defeat by the Allies in 1945.

The four principal Japanese islands are Honshu, Hokkaido, Shikoku and Kyushu. In addition there are innumerable smaller islands in the archipelago,

many of them uninhabited specks. Before the Second World War the Japanese Empire included within its boundaries the southern half of Sakhalin, known as Karafuto, taken from Russia in 1905 ; the island of Formosa (Taiwan) taken from China in 1895; and Korea (Chosen) annexed in 1910. Japan also ruled the Kurile Islands, which trail north towards Kamchatka, and the Bonin group. Far out in the Pacific it held hundreds of the small islands of Micronesia—the Carolines, Marianas and the Marshalls—mandated to Japan after the defeat of their former ruler, Germany, in 1918, at the end of the First World War. Dai Nippon, as the Japanese Empire was called, covered about 260,000 square miles, and was the home of about 100 million people. During the Second World War (1939–45) it was greatly expanded, only to lose all its outlying territories in 1945.

Nature in Japan is arresting and beautiful. The islands are crowded with mountains of more than average height, whose soft contours, caused by erosion and volcanic force, are responsible for a landscape that is as unusual as it is lovely. Probably in no other part of the world are flowers so greatly appreciated as in Japan, and they enter largely into public festivals. The most famous and lovely of Japan's wonders is Fujiyama (12,395 feet high), the sacred mountain of the land. A dormant volcano, it has been inactive for more than two centuries. It stands alone in a plain about 70 miles from Tokyo. From very early times Japanese poets and painters have made it their theme, and many thousand pilgrims ascend each year the shrine-bordered paths to its summit.

There are many charming waterfalls and lakes in the mountain districts, and streams and bridges are to be seen everywhere. The island-studded Inland Sea south of the main island is world-renowned for its lovely scenery; as are also the Pine Islands in north-eastern Japan—800 of all shapes and sizes, each with its crown of twisted pines, arising out of the blue waters. Japan's numerous volcanoes furnish hundreds of hot mineral springs, visited continually by crowds of ailing Japanese.

Among Japan's mountain ranges are more than 200 volcanic cones, of which no fewer than 50 are

---

Extent.—Length of island chain, north to south, about 1,300 miles. Area (Honshu, Hokkaido, Kyushu, Shikoku, and adjacent small islands) 144,000 square miles ; Population 79,000,000. Area of the Japanese Empire before its defeat by the Allies in August 1945, about 260,000 square miles; population about 100 million. In 1895 Japan took Formosa and the Pescadores Islands from China ; Korea was formally annexed in 1910 ; the territory of Kwantung, the southern part of the Liaotung Peninsula on the Japanese mainland, was taken from Russia in 1905 at the end of the Russo-Japanese War ; the southern part of the island of Sakhalin was also surrendered by Russia in 1905. Included in the Empire were certain Pacific islands which were German territory until the termination of the First World War (1914-18), when they were administered by Japan under a mandate from the League of Nations. These groups were the Marianas Islands, the Caroline Islands, and the Marshall Islands.

Physical Features.—About 3,000 islands, largely of volcanic formation, with numerous high mountain ranges and more than 200 volcanic peaks, about 50 of which are active. Highest point, Fujiyama, the "sacred" mountain (12,395 feet). Climate humid ; it varies from tropical in the south to cold in the north.

Products.—Rice and other cereals, raw silk, tobacco, tea ; sugar ; fish ; coal, copper, petroleum ; silk, cotton, and woollen goods ; chemicals, steel, paper, matches, toys, earthenware, lacquer ware, and mattings.

Principal Cities.—Tokyo (capital, 6,800,000) ; Osaka (3,300,000) ; Nagoya (1,300,000) ; Kyoto (1,000,000) ; Kobe, Yokohama (over 900,000).

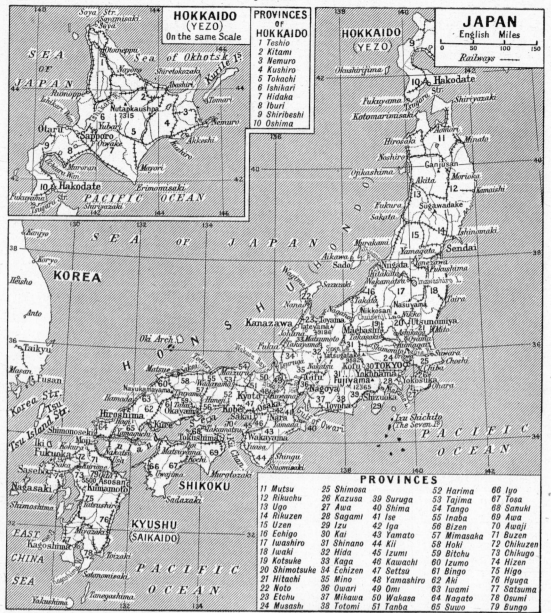

JAPAN: A COUNTRY CONSISTING OF MANY ISLANDS

The length of the island chain of which Japan is comprised is about 1,300 miles. The four principal islands—Hokkaido, Honshu, Shikoku and Kyushu—separate the Sea of Japan from the Pacific Ocean. The total area of Japan now is 144,000 square miles, and the population is 79 million. Inset is a map of Hokkaido, the most northerly of the main islands.

known to be active. Japan has an average of four earthquakes a day, not counting the minor vibrations felt only by delicate instruments. The worst on record is that which destroyed Tokyo and Yokohama in 1923; both cities had to be virtually rebuilt, and 150,000 lives were lost. Equally great harm to life and property is inflicted by floods, caused by swollen mountain streams and tidal waves. Occasionally, too, typhoons or hurricanes do considerable damage on land and sea.

Japan has a coastline out of all proportion to its area, and good harbours are to be found nearly everywhere, but especially in the east. Here, con-

sequently, are most of the large cities. Tokyo is the capital and largest; and on the same bay is its port, Yokohama, which handled more than one-half of Japan's foreign trade. Farther south is Osaka, the nation's industrial centre and second largest city; and Kobe, its port, which is to Osaka what Yokohama is to Tokyo. About 26 miles from Osaka is Kyoto, which for more than 1,000 years was the capital of Japan. It is the centre of the Buddhist faith, and its beautiful temples are visited every year by many pilgrims.

The remarkable extent of Japan from north to south affords great variety of climate and a resulting variety of crops, much of the country producing easily two harvests a year. Despite the mountain ranges, which permit only about one-eighth of the land to be cultivated, agriculture has always been Japan's most important industry. More than half the arable land grows rice. Everywhere in the lowlands are found the little square rice-fields, surrounding small villages of brown-thatched cottages of wood and oiled paper, where the farmers live. The people still do all the work by hand or with crude implements; and women and children, as well as men, are seen in the fields. Labour is cheap, and the great and increasing population of Japan necessitates an intensive system of agriculture; even the steep hill-sides are terraced with fields.

As the country slopes upwards from the plains the rice-fields disappear. Wheat and barley take their place, or sweet potatoes, daikon (a large radish), and egg-plants. These form the food of most of the agricultural class; rice is usually sold to the cities or to foreign countries. Much rice of cheaper quality is also imported in normal times from other Asiatic countries. Tea is the national drink of the people, and the tea plant is widely cultivated, especially near Kyoto. Tobacco is also raised extensively. And over two million of the Japanese people are engaged in fishing.

Since the average farm of each family does not exceed three acres, it is only by double crops and home industries that the peasant can make a living. The chief home industry is silk-worm culture and

Rev. W. Weston

GATEWAY TO JAPAN'S HOLY MOUNT

Lofty ornamental gateways or torii stand at the entrance of every road leading to the sacred mountain of Fujiyama. This gate at Omiya marks the beginning of the ancient route by which thousands of pilgrims annually climb the sacred peak, which can be seen in the background.

silk production. Rows of dwarf mulberry trees are often seen forming a hedge around the up-land fields, their leaves supplying food for the silkworms. Piles of cocoons are set out in the sun to dry, and the cottages hum with the sound of silk-winding. Raw silk is one of the chief exports of Japan.

Bamboo is widely raised and, next to rice, plays the chief part in Japanese life. Not only is it used for building and furniture, but the tender young sprouts of the plant are eaten.

Forests cover nearly 6o per cent of the land, and many valuable products are obtained from them. For instance, lacquer, one of Japan's most prized

MOUNTAIN-CLIMBING—JAPANESE FASHION

Over two-thirds of Japan is mountainous, and mountain-climbing is a favourite sport. Japan-ese ladies of the upper class, however, do their mountaineering in palanquins borne by coolies. Most of the mountains are thickly wooded except where they have been terraced for farming.

and characteristic products, is made from the resin of the lacquer tree. The great timber tree, however, is the Japanese cypress, *Cryptomeria japonica*, one of the finest of all conifers, which is sometimes seen in gardens in Britain.

The fibres which are obtained from the paper mulberry are used for making "Japanese paper"; and other trees which grow in abundance furnish wood for match-making and for toy-making.

But all over the land the old way of life is passing and is being replaced by the whirr and rush of modern industry. In all sorts of places, amid the low, picturesque bamboo buildings of old Japan, you come upon great factory compounds, surrounded by high board fences, where several hundred people live and work. This industrial expansion was accompanied by an intensive drive to open up foreign markets. The wealth of Japan was owned and controlled by no more than eight rich families, called the Zaibatsu or "wealth clique." By the use of cheap labour Japan was able to compete with the established exporting countries and even under-sell them in the home market; and before her heavy industry was destroyed in the Second World War she had won Great Britain's former place as the world's leading exporter of cotton textiles. Wool exports and iron and steel industries were expanding, and the world's markets were flooded with cheap knicknacks, bicycles, electric light bulbs and other electrical equipment. Other exports were rubber goods and machinery, including cheap motor-cars. These exports nearly balanced the imports.

With the adoption of western methods and machinery the output of Japan's mines increased enormously, though she remained the poorest in minerals of the world powers. Coal is abundant, but of a low quality. Iron ore and copper are produced, and a little gold and silver. Sulphur for chemicals and kaolin for pottery are plentiful.

In old Japan baggage was carried by men or packhorses, and heavy goods went from port to port by boat. Later the streets were thronged with bicycles, rickshaws, taxis and trams. Motor-cars were cheap, but hampered by lack of good roads. The railways are narrow-gauge, single track lines, with an average speed of 18 miles per hour. The first railway from Tokyo to Yokohama (18 miles) was built by British engineers in 1872. Today there are more than 15,000 miles of railway track, much of it being electrified.

The rivers of Japan are short and broken by falls and rapids, and are of little value as means of communication, but there is much coastal traffic. In 1853 the 200-year-old law prohibiting the construction of ocean-going ships was repealed, and 30 years later Japan had become the third nation in the world for merchant shipping. Little of its mercantile marine survived the country's defeat in the Second World War.

Although most Japanese who work in modern businesses wear European clothes, they change into kimonos and live in the ancestral manner when they return to their houses in the evenings. That Japan was able to take a place so speedily among the great commercial nations is due to the national quickness of its people and to their skill in adaptation; they are not outstanding inventors. The government early sent many young men to study abroad, and it also dispatched missions to study trade conditions and factory systems all over the world. Modern educational methods, modern machinery and inventions were adopted wholesale. Japan was a flourishing market for gramophone records of classical music, and before 1941 was the world's second largest maker of films. Elementary education, modelled on European lines, is compulsory; and there are six imperial universities.

One religion of Japan is Shintoism, a combination of nature worship and ancestor worship. The chief deity, the sun-goddess Amaterasu, was looked upon as the ancestress of the imperial family, while lesser gods are associated with mountains, streams, forests, etc. Every home has its miniature shrine, where homage is paid to ancestors and local gods. From 1930 to 1945 Shintoism was compulsory, because of its element of emperor-worship. Buddhism ranks with Shintoism in importance, and among the upper classes Confucianism has many disciples. Christian missions made considerable progress until about 1940.

The royal ancestry of the Tenno, as the Japanese emperor is called (only foreigners use the poetical name Mikado) is perhaps the most ancient in the world. Japanese tradition fixes the foundation of the dynasty in the year 660 B.C., and 122 rulers of the imperial line are counted since that time, 16 of whom were women. The most important event in early Japanese history was the adoption of Buddhism from Korea in the 6th century of the Christian era.

New York Times Photos

REBUILDING JAPAN'S CITY OF NAGOYA
During the Second World War (1939–45) nearly all major industrial centres of Japan were heavily bombed by Allied aircraft. Work of reconstruction effected some big changes, as can be seen from this photograph of modern buildings in Nagoya, a city on the island of Honshu.

Acme

JAPANESE POTTERY WORKS
In Nagoya is a pottery factory which made parts for aeroplane engines during the Second World War, and when this photograph was taken was still camouflaged (above). At the left, teapots are being prepared for the final baking.

Although the emperor has always been the nominal ruler in Japan, his power was usurped in the 12th century by a military class whose leader was called the Shogun. The emperor came to be regarded as a divine ruler, who had no part in the practical work of government. A system developed closely resembling the feudalism of medieval Europe, in which the fighting barons and knights (*daimios* and *samurai*) were separated by a wide gulf from the commercial and agricultural classes. These caste lines have not yet all disappeared. There was also a group, the *eta* class, whose members were social outcasts and were employed as slaughterers and public executioners.

Marco Polo, a Venetian who travelled extensively in the East in the 13th century, first brought reports of Japan to Europe; and Cipango, as he called the country, was one of the objects of Columbus's search. Three Portuguese sailors, blown out of their course from the coast of China, were the first Europeans actually to visit the islands (1542).

The great Jesuit missionary, Saint Francis Xavier, began his labours in Japan in 1549. For some years the Dutch and English had trading posts in Japan, and Japanese sailors traded with Mexico, the Philippines, China, and India. Then, in 1614, the Shogun ordered all foreign priests to be expelled and all their churches destroyed,

on account of plots against him in which Christians were said to be involved. By relentless persecution Christianity was stamped out, Japanese were forbidden to leave the islands on penalty of death, and until the middle of the 19th century Japan pursued its policy of isolation.

The reign of a single emperor, the benevolent Mutsuhito (1867–1912), covers almost the whole period of Japan's marvellous transformation into a modern nation. Coming to the Tenno's throne 13 years after Perry's treaty, he overthrew the Shogun the next year (1868). In his famous Charter Oath, he urged his subjects to seek knowledge and wisdom in all parts of the world, so that they might help to place the empire upon a firm foundation. Embassies of Japanese statesmen and students set forth to visit every civilized nation. Some of them had learned a little English by careful study of a grammar. They were garbed in the dress of old Japan, in kimonos with plaited overskirts of heavy silk, and they wore their hair in pigtails knotted on top of their heads. In appearance they were men of old Japan, but their minds were alert to receive new ideas.

Those who studied political systems were influenced by the German idea of government, and so drafted a constitution (proclaimed in 1889) on that pattern rather than one according to the British idea of democracy. They also chose the German army and navy as models. France and Italy gave them ideas of art and architecture; England and the United States their systems of education and industrialisation.

The changes that stand out as most important since that time relate to the territorial growth of the country. In the war with China in 1894-95 came the first test of Japan's new strength. The Japanese navy, built in the best shipyards of Europe, speedily sank the Chinese fleet; and the Japanese army, drilled and equipped in modern fashion, overwhelmed China's out-of-date forces.

Russia, Germany, and France intervened, however, and forced Japan to accept the island of Formosa as compensation in place of Port Arthur

PRIESTS OF JAPAN'S OLDEST RELIGION
Combining nature worship and ancestor worship, Shintoism, which is the most ancient religion of Japan, in a sense was formerly a worship of Japan itself. All Japanese were believed to be descendants of the sun goddess Amaterasu and to belong to one family headed by the Emperor, whom the people regarded as divine ; but the Emperor officially denied his divine origin in December 1945. Though the sun goddess is the chief deity there are lesser gods of the mountains, streams and forests.

and other places on the mainland which China had agreed to give up. Then Russia took Port Arthur for herself, and Germany followed suit with Kiaochow (Tsingtao). Japan accepted the situation—and waited.

Nine years later Japan settled accounts with Russia in the Russo-Japanese War (1904-1905), in which the fleets and armies of the Tsar were thoroughly beaten. This victory brought to Japan Korea, half of Sakhalin, together with Russia's rights in Port Arthur, Liaotung and Manchuria.

When the First World War began in 1914, Japan in fulfilment of a treaty of alliance with Great Britain, attacked and captured the strongly fortified German position in Kiaochow. At the close of the war the Treaty of Versailles left Kiaochow and all the former German concessions in the province of Shantung in the hands of Japan. But later Japan withdrew and accepted the Washington or Nine-Power Treaty (1922), guaranteeing the territorial integrity of China.

In 1931 Japan began the aggression that finally developed into war for the mastery of the Pacific. Manchuria was occupied, and the puppet state of Manchukuo set up there in 1932. Protests from the League of Nations were answered by Japan's withdrawal from the League, and in 1934 she announced herself " guardian of the peace of the Pacific." In 1937 without a declaration of war the invasion of China began, and was resisted by the Chinese with unexpected determination. Peking, Shanghai and Nanking fell, and in 1940 a puppet government was set up in Nanking to administer the occupied territory. The " China Incident " (as the Japanese called this war) dragged on, but China fought back despite huge losses in land, population and men. A year after the outbreak of the Second Great War (1939-45), with Germany and Italy enjoying their temporary triumph in Europe, Japan signed an alliance with them in which she was assigned dominance of " Greater East Asia." Later, with Russia, Japan's old enemy, fully occupied against Germany in the west, came the opportunity for which Japan had waited.

On December 7, 1941, Japan without declaring war, sent an air fleet and submarines to attack the United States' main Pacific base, Pearl Harbour in Hawaii, hoping thus to cripple the Americans with one treacherous blow. A declaration of war followed. Forces built up in the Pacific, in China, and in French Indo-China (which Japan had pretended needed " protection " from Allied attacks) were unleashed in drives against Burma, Malaya, and the islands of the Western Pacific and the East Indies. America was unprepared; the forces of Britain and the Netherlands were hopelessly outnumbered; and within less than a year Japan had occupied enormous regions in pursuance of her plan for an Empire of " Greater East Asia."

In 1944 the tide turned. Step by step the United States and British Commonwealth forces drove the Japanese out of New Guinea, the Marshall Islands, Guam, Leyte, Manila and Okinawa. Burma was recaptured. On August 6, 1945, a new and fearful chapter in the history of warfare was opened when an American bomber dropped the first atomic bomb on the Japanese town of Hiroshima. This killed 78,150 of Hiroshima's 350,000 inhabitants. A second bomb was dropped, on Nagasaki, three days later.

These devastating blows hastened the inevitable end, and on August 15, 1945, Japan surrendered to the Allies. Japanese forces in Indonesia, Borneo and other regions laid down their arms. An occupation force of American and British Commonwealth forces took over the administration of Japan; and a Parliamentary form of Government elected by the people was established. The Emperor in a proclamation on December 31, 1945, specifically denied that he was divine, or that the Japanese had any right to dominate other people.

COLOUR IN THE JAPANESE SCENE

W. Hill

As the traveller wanders through those towns and countryside of Japan which escaped the ravages of the Second World War (1939–45), he meets with charming and colourful expressions of Man's taste for beauty matched with the loveliness of Nature's making. Some suggestion of what he sees is shown in this colour-sequence. Above, as a commencement, we glimpse beyond the green and mauve of leaf and flower the many-storeyed Yasaka Pagoda of Kyoto, the old-time capital of Japan and centre of the Buddhist religion.

Rev. W. Weston

IN A JAPANESE GARDEN

When the cherry blossom has died, the Japanese look forward to the flowering of the wistaria. In this lovely garden the blossoms hang like a canopy above many a path and pool of a temple precinct. No Japanese garden is really complete without an artificial pool, and here the purple wistaria blossoms are reflected in the still water.

Rev. W. Weston

WHEN THE IRIS IS IN BLOOM

Another favourite flower of the Japanese is the iris, and the Japanese variety is large and of a lovely mauve. June is the month of the iris, and at that time of year the people of Tokyo make a special trip to see the acres of these blossoms in the famous Gardens of Hori-Kori, much as Londoners go to Kew Gardens in bluebell time.

PAGEANT OF PRAYER IN A GREAT SHINTO TEMPLE OF JAPAN

A national religion of Japan is Shintoism, a faith of unknown origin and very primitive in type. The chief temple is at Nikko, to which throughout the year pilgrims come from all parts of Japan. The chief deity is the sun goddess Amaterasu. There are no idols or images, but the goddess is invoked through inferior beings, the majority of whom are deified men. Gaily decorated litters, supposed to contain these intangible beings, are carried from shrine to shrine. Until 1946, the Emperor was regarded as divine.

Rev. W. Weston

A JAPANESE SERVANT OF BUDDHA

In Japan there is complete religious freedom, no faith being State-supported. After
Shintoism, Buddhism is the prevailing faith and has many institutions and temples.
This abbot of a Buddhist monastery sits for hours on his heels in silent contempla-
tion.   He is of the Zen sect, which closely resembles the Buddhism of Ceylon.

The print reproduced above is a portrait of Ujiyama, a famous Japanese beauty of the 18th century. It is the work of Hosoda Eishi (1746-1829), one of the most distinguished print-makers of his time. His work is notable for the beautiful composition of figure subjects, and for the subtle colour combinations which he achieved with wood-blocks

ONE OF HOKUSAI'S BEAUTIFUL WATERFALLS

The great charm of Japanese art lies in its decorative value and in colour harmonies so delicate that they defy description. It cannot be judged by Western standards, for it has its own principles and rules of composition. Hokusai Katsushuka (1760-1849), the artist of this example, is one of the most famous of the Japanese colour-print makers.

Rev. W. Weston

SNOW-CLAD BEAUTY OF FUJIYAMA

Above the still waters of a lake stands the stately peak of Fujiyama, Japan's greatest volcano, rising to a height of 12,395 feet, far above the snow line. In ancient times great streams of lava flowed from its crater. Some of them dammed the rivers on the north and west sides. forming a series of lakes, from the shores of one of which this photograph was taken. Its last recorded eruption occurred in 1707.

ARTISTIC GENIUS *of a* STRANGE PEOPLE

*As a race the Japanese are very appreciative of beauty and delicate craftsman-
ship. Even in the poorest home there is usually some object that is prized
for its artistic worth alone and placed in a prominent position.*

Japanese Art. The love of the beautiful in Nature and Art seemingly inborn in the Japanese people is in puzzling contrast to the ruthlessness with which they wage war and the cruelties they can perpetrate in cold blood. That the Japanese have artistic genius cannot be denied; but the traditional forms followed in their painting, architecture, sculpture, pottery and metal work are based on the older art of the Chinese and Koreans.

The Japanese artists, however, have not been content to remain mere slavish imitators and have stamped their painting with unique delicacy, charm, and imaginative quality. The painstaking skill of Japanese craftsmen has transformed many of their humbler wares into pieces valued for graceful design and exquisite detail.

Japanese bronzes are famous: this temple lantern is in the Victoria and Albert Museum, London.

In the Japanese language there is only one word —kaku—for writing, drawing, and painting. From this it is plain to see that writing has always been looked upon as one of the fine arts. From 1,500–2,000 characters must be learned for daily use. The student who wants to become a scholar must learn twice as many. Instead of placing his roll of paper upon a table as an English boy or girl would, the Japanese student holds it in his left hand; he, therefore, must write from the shoulder and elbow as well as the wrist. He uses a brush dipped in Indian ink, and his writing paper, being porous, absorbs it immediately, thus producing strength, precision, and grace.

After the art of writing has been learnt, painting is the next step. The Japanese child, no matter how young he may be, looks forward with eagerness to the time when his fingers will be sufficiently skilled to paint the beauties of the cherry blossom season, the moon rising over a pine tree, or the grandeur of Fujiyama, the sacred mountain of Japan. Many a laborious hour does the young artist spend in learning how to make a single stroke. Over and again he strives to gain mastery of the few bold strokes that represent a river, or the straight lines picturing rain, blades of grass, or shoots of bamboo. But the painstaking labour is not so tiresome to a Japanese child as it would be to his English counterpart.

The potter's wheel, according to tradition, was introduced into Japan from China in the 8th century A.D. Five centuries later a Japanese potter discovered the art of glazing. Small jars of stoneware with brown glazes flecked with black were his first production. In 1598 the Prince of Satsuma invaded Korea and returned with 17 skilled potters, who taught the making of a ware which was called " Satsuma " in his honour. This is a glazed earthenware of firm texture, much like porcelain, decorated in colour, and with the surface " crackled " just perceptibly. This so-called Satsuma ware is now made in a number of Japanese cities and is very popular for export trade.

At the close of the 16th century a Korean potter at work in Japan discovered on Mount Izumi (in Hizen province) a peculiar clay needed to reproduce the blue and white porcelains of China. This " Hizen " ware, known also as " Arita," from the town of its manufacture, and " Imari," from the place of exportation, is today one of the finest wares made in Japan. The two centuries from 1645 to 1845 were the golden age of Japanese pottery. During that time the work was carried on under the patronage of noblemen and gentlemen of wealth.

In the museums of Nara and Kyoto may be seen also some wonderful examples of the ancient wood-carver's art. Japanese sculptors used chiefly wood and metal, seldom stone. The wooden statues at Nara represent Indian Buddhists in dignified pose, and they date from the eighth century. At the end of the 16th century (a period of war and chaos) there was a new development in wood-cutting, in the carved decorations of temples, coloured in gold and vermilion, the favourite Buddhist colours. These carvings represent flowers, birds, angels, and dragons. One of the finest examples of the wood-carver's skill is the " netsuke," a little figure which is used to fasten the cord on a man's sash or

Victoria & Albert Museum

JAPAN'S ARTISTRY

At the top is a sword-guard showing a garden scene inlaid in gold and silver ; lower, a bottle and bowl of Satsuma ware.

the string of his tobacco pouch. The faces of these tiny netsukes are carved with wonderful expressiveness.

One of the most notable bronzes in Japan is the Daibutsu, or Great Buddha, at Kamakura —nearly 50 feet high. The image was formed of sheets of bronze cast separately and finished off with a chisel. In ancient times the bronze-maker, who now makes ornaments for sale, devoted himself almost entirely to the art of making images and temple adornments.

Instead of idols the ivory-carver today makes statuettes, fans, and umbrella handles; instead of fashioning Samurai sword-hilts, the worker in damascene is devising fashionable jewelry. In the ancient art of inlaying steel and iron with silver and gold, as in the enamel-ware known as cloisonné, the Japanese workman has no superior in the world.

The history of Japanese art, as distinguished from Japanese archaeology, begins with the introduction of Buddhism in the sixth century A.D. With the new religion came the knowledge of Chinese ideo-

Victoria & Albert Museum

JAPANESE EMBROIDERY

Here is a lovely piece of Japanese needlework of the 19th century. It is an embroidered cover of black silk velvet, known as a fukusa, used for wrapping a ceremonial present conveyed in a lacquered box.

graphs (word characters) and the art of the calligraphist. As in China, dexterity by the use of the brush greatly influences the manner and method of Japanese artists; both calligraphy and painting are classified according to the nature of the brush strokes. While Japanese art inherits from Chinese, the Buddhist art which Chinese pilgrims carried back with them from India to the Far East was in its turn influenced by the Greek civilization introduced by the successors of Alexander the Great.

Paintings are of three different forms. These include the tall, hanging picture for display on walls, singly, or in screens or sets of two or three. It is mounted on brocade or paper, at the lower end of which is an ivory-tipped stick around which it is rolled when not on exhibition. There is a long roll for the representation of processions and serial pictures. And there is the picture which is framed but not glazed.

The principal Japanese schools of painting include the following : Chinese or Buddhist, dating

A TYPICAL EXAMPLE OF JAPANESE COLOUR ENGRAVING

Perhaps the most beautiful of the various kinds of picture that can be produced by engraving is the colour print. This is made by printing a series of wood blocks one over the other. Each block carries a different coloured ink, and this over-printing can create delicate effects unobtainable by any other means. During the 18th and 19th centuries colour printing was developed to a remarkable degree by Japanese craftsmen. Reproduced above is a splendid example of the work of their master Hiroshige (1797–1858). Called Full Moon on Kanazawa, it is in the British Museum.

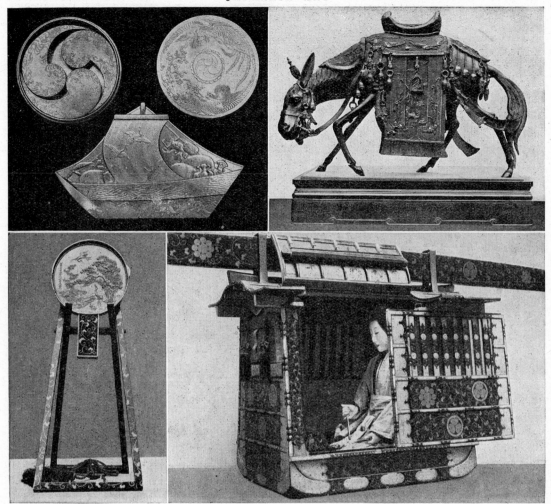

Victoria & Albert Museum

SUPERB JAPANESE ARTISTRY AND CRAFTSMANSHIP

The diversity of Japanese art is well illustrated here. The bronze hand-mirror with decorated back (lower left) dates from the 19th century. The sedan chair (lower right) is lacquered gilt and black and mounted with engraved and gilt metal. The perfume box and its cover (top, upper left) belong to the Iyemetsu period (1622–49); the box is lacquered on the outside with gold, and the cover is enriched with mother-of-pearl. The sweetmeat box in the form of a ship (lower, upper left) is of wood covered with gold lacquer. The richly draped bronze mule (upper right) is an incense burner.

from the sixth century, whose subjects were almost wholly religious. The Yamato and Tosa, dating from the 11th century, influenced by the Chinese, but executed with a lighter touch and representing subjects connected with Japanese history, legends, and court ceremonials. Kano, founded by Kano Monotobu (1476–1559), depicting figures, landscapes, birds, and flowers. Ukiyoye, founded by Iwasa Matahei (1577–1650), which corresponds to European genre painting. Korin, named after the eminent artist Koyetsu (1552–1637), aimed at imaginative treatment of Nature without employing the formal manner of the Kano school. Shijo, dating from the 18th century; its founder Okyo (1733–95) closely imitated Nature, and used washes and subdued tones instead of sharp lines and bright colours.

The essence of all Japanese art lies in its power of suggestion, and during the latter half of the 17th century it was individual artists rather than schools that gave Japanese painting fresh impetus. The

19th century, which brought revolutionary changes, produced painters who, after 1868, worked in the Western style; but towards the end of the century a return was made to the old, native style, even when depicting European subjects. This essentially Japanese style has assimilated the finer Western methods, and shows a discriminative selection in all that is best in Occidental art.

Lacquer is an art product in the making of which Japan cannot be excelled. The lac used is made from the poisonous resin of a tree belonging to the sumac family. It is applied to the wood in thin layers, and after being dried in a steam chest is carefully rubbed down and polished. The whole process is repeated over and over again.

Of all Japanese arts, that of colour printing is the most readily understood and admired. It unites the dexterity of the wood-carver and the skill of the painter, to form an art with power in every line and grace and lightness of touch. The artist first

JAPANESE IVORY CARVER TURNING A TUSK INTO ELEPHANTS

By the wizardry of his skill the ivory carver on the right has caused a procession of elephants to emerge from a single tusk ; the other craftsman is making exquisite figures. In ancient times the ivory worker devoted himself almost exclusively to the production of idols and sword hilts, but now he fashions statuettes, fans, umbrella handles and ornaments for commercial purposes. Years of training make Japanese craftsmen extremely dexterous.

draws his picture on transparent paper. Then the wood-carver pastes the drawing on a cherry-wood block, and cuts away between the lines. The printer mixes his vegetable colour with a rice-paste and applies it to the engraving. A sheet of paper is placed on the inked block, and pressed down by rubbing with a pad. A separate block is made for each colour, and colour after colour is printed until the original conception reappears in the completed print.

Although wood-block printing had been known to the Japanese as early as the 8th century it had never been used as a separate medium until the 17th century. Moronobu (1645–1715) recognized its usefulness for book illustrations and single sheets. These early prints were in black-and-white. About 1740 printing in colour replaced hand-coloured prints. The supreme triumphs of colour printing belong to such men as Harunobu (1725–70); Toyokuni (1769–1825); Hiroshige (1797–1858); and Hokusai (1760–1849). Not until the 1870's did collections of Japanese prints find their way to Europe, where they had a strong influence upon the art of France and England, notably Impressionism, and the decorative arts at the beginning of the 20th century.

Jasmine. Noted for the fragrance of their blossoms, the jasmines, of which there are many species, are native to the warm regions of the Old World. The Chinese yellow jasmine, *Jasminum nudiflorum*, blooms profusely during the winter, long before the leaves appear. The yellow-flowered evergreen jasmine (*J. fruticans*) is native to southern Europe, where another yellow species, *J. humile*, grows.

The most popular species grown in Britain is the white jasmine, *J. officinale*, native of Persia and India. It is usually grown against the house or garden wall, because it is a profuse grower with long, slender and very weak stems —this last feature being characteristic of most of the jasmines. The height of this plant may exceed 15 feet. In the south of France and elsewhere an oil used in the perfumery trade is extracted from jasmine blossoms. The Chinese species is used in the Orient for scenting tea.

J. E. Tyler

WINTER JASMINE

The Chinese yellow jasmine blooms in Britain during the coldest months, while the plant is without leaves. The more commonly cultivated white variety, flowering in summer, is a native of India and Persia. Jasmines are usually grown against a house or wall.

SEA-GIRT PEARL *of the* EAST INDIES

*The island of Java is a 'pearl' for two reasons : not only is it a place of
great natural beauty but it is one of the world's richest tropical areas.
With the small island of Madura it about equals England in size.*

Java. Third largest of the Sunda group, ranking after Sumatra and Borneo, this long and narrow island of Indonesia may be pictured as a ridge of mountains with low coastal plains. Its extreme length is 632 miles, the width varying from 35 to 120 miles. With the adjacent island of Madura, it has an area of 51,032 square miles. Each side of Java has a wet and a dry season, so for part of the year the people enjoy some relief from the steaming tropical heat.

In the mountainous interior there are active and also extinct volcanoes, and these have contributed to Java's riches, because volcanic ash makes excellent soil.

As a result of its moist warm climate, fertile soil, and the variations in altitude, Java has rich and varied plant life. Up to about 2,000 feet the vegetation is tropical, with palms, figs, bamboo and vines. Above this is a sub-tropical level, with magnolias, orchids and ferns. At 5,000 feet there are forests of chestnut, oak and maple, with azaleas and rhododendrons. Some of the peaks rise above 10,000 feet, the highest being Mount Semeru (12,060 feet). In the drier eastern region there are grassy plains, with trees along the rivers.

Among the many birds are weavers, parrots, ducks and peacocks. One kind of swift constructs a gluey nest, which the Chinese use for making soup. There are huge butterflies; and some of the spiders are large enough to prey on birds. The reptiles include pythons, cobras, crocodiles and various lizards.

The most dangerous mammals are the tiger, the one-horned rhinoceros, and the leopard. Other large animals are the banteng (wild ox), wild pigs, and d e e r. There are also apes, monkeys, rats, hares, squirrels, and scaly ant-eaters. Insect pests are, of course, innumerable. Fish and shellfish abound in sea and rivers, and are important articles of diet.

Nearly two-thirds of the island is cultivated. Plantations in the lowlands grow rubber, cotton, sugar-cane, coconuts and tobacco ; on the subtropical uplands t e a, quinine and coffee are chief crops. Nearly half of the cultivated area is irrigated for rice. Sheep, goats, poultry and cattle are raised. The most important minerals are oil, tin and coal. There are factories for the production of textiles, soap and margarine, cigars and cigarettes, paper, glass and chemicals.

The largest city of Java is Djakarta (formerly known as Batavia), in the north-west. It has a population of 260,000 and it is the seat of government of the United States of Indonesia. Second largest is Sourabaya, population 250,000. This city, near the eastern end of the island, was developed by the Dutch as a naval base and sugar exporting centre. Bandoeng, in the west, has a population of about 167,000 ; Jogjakarta, in south central Java, about 140,000. In the island there are 3,000 miles of rail and tramways and 5,500 miles of motor roads.

Although most of the people are of Malayan origin, they are divided into the Sundanese in the west and the Javanese in the east. The Sundanese are practically pure Malay, with light yellow skins and oblique Mongolian eyes. The Javanese are darker, and show many traits of physique, language, and character inherited from the Hindus who long ruled the island.

Hindus conquered Java early in the Christian era, and there developed the highest civilization in all the East Indies. Some of their immense temples remain, the most imposing one being that at Boro Budor, which was built between 750 and 850 (*see* illustration page 1814). The Mahomedan Malays overthrew the Hindus in the 15th century, and little is known of the history of the island until the arrival of the Portuguese early in the 16th century. They were soon supplanted by the Dutch, who governed Java until its occupation by the Japanese in 1942, during the Second World War (1939–45).

On the surrender of Japan to the Allied Nations in August 1945, a powerful Indonesian nationalist movement set up an Indonesian Republic centred on Java. The Dutch refused to recognize the republic and fighting broke out between the J a v a n e s e and the Dutch, in which British troops were involved. A truce was signed in 1946 and a

ROADSIDE COOK OF JAVA
Though the meals which this man cooks would not perhaps be very agreeable to Western tastes, they are thoroughly enjoyed by the natives. When customers run short he can sling his kitchen over his shoulder and move to a new pitch.

One of the great architectural marvels of the world is the great Buddhist temple at Boro Budor, built between the 8th and 9th centuries of the Christian era. Strictly speaking it is not a temple but a hill surrounded with terraces of stone, in which are cut in relief thousands of figures portraying the Buddhist way of life. On the lowest terraces are scenes of ordinary life—men fishing, playing music, and so on. As the pilgrim ascends he sees the principles of the Buddhist religion depicted in symbolic figures until at the top he comes to an image of Buddha himself.

As a result of its moist warm climate and fertile soil, Java has an exceptionally rich and varied plant life. The above view, taken near Djakarta (formerly known as Batavia), gives some idea of the density and luxuriance of the vegetation. Great palms rise from the river bank, and farther back grow teak and upas trees and bamboo. Because of its many canals Djakarta has been called the Venice of the East. It is the seat of government of the United States of Indonesia. On the north coast of west Java, it exports coffee, sugar, tea, rice and spices. The town consists of two parts: the old town, and the modern part containing the European residential quarter.

Republic of Indonesia, which at first included Java, Sumatra and Madura, was established. Later the Indonesian Republic was confined to eastern Java, the western portion forming a separate state known as West Java; Sumatra and Madura also established their own governments. In 1949 all the Netherlands East Indies, except Dutch New Guinea, were given independence by the Netherlands and became the Republic of the United States of Indonesia. The population of Java, with Madura, is about 45 million. *See map on page* 1074.

Jay. Members of the crow family, jays are natives of Europe, Asia, Africa and North America. The typical species is the common jay (*Garrulus glandarius*), which is found in British woodlands and over the greater part of Europe. About the size of a jackdaw, it is one of the most handsome of British birds, its general colour being cinnamon with a grey crest streaked with black, and a white throat. On each wing there is a large patch of brilliant blue, barred with black.

The jay destroys snails and insects, but is also very fond of fruit; and gamekeepers wage war on them because they steal game-birds' eggs and kill nestlings. The cup-shaped nest of the jay, constructed of twigs, is placed in a tree or bush, and contains from three to seven eggs of a greenish tint and dotted with brown spots. This bird is no songster: its call is harsh and disturbing.

Jazz. In its true form jazz is folk music, the music of the Negro slaves of North America who inherited from their forefathers the subtleties of rhythm of their many drum languages. Work songs lightened the burden of monotonous labour on the cotton plantations—songs that were rhythmical, making use of a recurrent beat that stressed the regular phase in the actual work being done. It was from these that the songs of misery, love, joy, despair and hope developed to form the essence of jazz, called the "blues."

The forerunner of jazz was ragtime, which came into being shortly before the outbreak of the First World War (1914–18). It originated in the attempts of Negro pianists to copy the brass bands' tricks of shifting the accent from strong to weak beats when playing marches. This was the introduction of syncopation—in other words, the accented note very often did not fall where one expected. Ragtime died out at the end of the First World War, but jazz continued. About 1929 a form of jazz called swing was developed in the United States. In swing, effects were striven for just for the sake of novelty.

Probably the most lasting contributions to this type of music have been made by Negro musicians and certain masters of such instruments as the saxophone, trumpet, clarionet and tap-drum. One of the most celebrated musicians of the jazz era was George Gershwin (1898–1937), the composer of Rhapsody in Blue.

Jeans, Sir James Hopwood (1877–1946). Only a few years ago astronomy and astro-physics, the sciences which deal with the Heavens, were as closed books to all but the most advanced mathematicians. There was little opportunity for the ordinary person to glean much knowledge of the universe beyond the names of the planets and chief stars and constellations. There his information stopped, until such writers as James Jeans made it possible for even young people to obtain a comprehensive idea of the universe.

Jeans, whose father was a Londoner, was born on September 11, 1877. After a brilliant career at Trinity College, Cambridge, he was elected a fellow of his college and in 1904 appointed lecturer in mathematics. From 1905 to 1909 he was professor of applied mathematics at Princeton University, U.S.A., returning to fill the Stokes lectureship in the same subject at Cambridge, 1910–12. From 1919 to 1929 he was Secretary of the Royal Society, of which he was made a fellow (F.R.S.), and in 1923 he was appointed research associate of Mount Wilson Observatory in California. In 1934 he became President of the British Association; in

THE GAILY-PLUMAGED JAY
A handsome bird, the jay's general colour is cinnamon with a grey crest streaked with black, and a white throat. On the wings there is a patch of bright blue, barred with black. These birds, which live in British woodlands, are unpopular with gamekeepers because they eat the eggs and young of the pheasant.

SIR JAMES JEANS
The famous astronomer Sir James Jeans (left) is here seen examining a giant telescope built at Mount Wilson Observatory in California, United States. A writer of popular books on astronomy and physics, he was knighted in 1928 and was awarded the Order of Merit by King George VI.

January 1939 the King honoured him with the award of the Order of Merit.

Jeans wrote much, of course, for his fellow astronomers and mathematicians—such technical works as Problems of Cosmogony and Stellar Dynamics, or Atomicity and Quanta. He also wrote books for popular reading: The Universe Around Us, The Mysterious Universe, and The Stars in their Courses. In The New Background of Science (1933) Jeans presented a fascinating speculation on the nature of the universe. Sir James Jeans died on September 16, 1946.

Jefferies, JOHN RICHARD (1848–87). If you have any interest in literature, or in natural history, in the English countryside, or in the English classics, you will sooner or later come across the works of Richard Jefferies.

He was born near Swindon in Wiltshire on November 6, 1848. After having published a few novels which had little success, he became a journalist, specializing in articles on natural history and rural life. His name was made by a series of essays in the Pall Mall Gazette, which, appearing as The Gamekeeper at Home, brought home to Londoners, perhaps for the first time, the beauty and variety of the countryside. The same characteristics distinguished his Wood Magic, which came out in 1881. In this he made his characters—the animals—speak and think and experience emotion

like human beings, and he created the charming character of Bevis, the child to whom their life was fully revealed.

The style of this book, as of some of his others, is a most effective mingling of prose and poetry, for, while written in prose, it rises to heights of poetic beauty and reveals imaginative power seldom surpassed in his century. His contemporaries, however, gave Jefferies little encouragement, and it was not until about 1900 that he really came into his own. His later novels and The Story of My Heart, an engrossing autobiography, earned him little money, and his last years were clouded by physical suffering and poverty. His other books include The Life of the Fields, Red Deer, and Amaryllis at the Fair. He died at Goring, Oxfordshire, on August 14, 1887.

Jefferson, THOMAS (1743–1826). Known as the Father of American Democracy, Jefferson was born at Shadwell, Virginia, on April 13, 1743. A bold and fearless thinker, he read deeply in the English and French political philosophers. Elected to the Virginia House of Burgesses (parliament) in 1769, he won fame as the draughtsman of the American Declaration of Independence against the sovereignty of Great Britain six years later.

In 1800 Jefferson became the third President of the United States, and tried to put into practice his ideas of democratic simplicity. In general the four years of Jefferson's first administration were years of prosperity; the greatest event was the Government's purchase of the State of Louisiana from Napoleon Bonaparte, whereby a million square miles of territory were added to the United States. Jefferson was re-elected in 1804 by an overwhelming majority. An important event of his second term as President was the passage of a law forbidding the slave trade after January 1, 1808. But overshadowing all else were the difficulties in foreign affairs which finally led to the second war with Great Britain.

Jefferson died on July 4, 1826, just 50 years after the adoption of the Declaration of Independence. In accordance with his request this epitaph was inscribed on his monument: " Here was buried Thomas Jefferson, Author of the Declaration of American Independence, of the Statute of Virginia for Religious Freedom, and Father of the University of Virginia." He is remembered as one of the greatest Presidents of the United States.

Jellicoe, JOHN RUSHWORTH JELLICOE, EARL (1859–1935). The Commander-in-Chief of the British Grand Fleet at the Battle of Jutland in the First World War (1914–18), was born in Southampton, his father being a captain in the Mercantile Marine. After a period of schooling at Rottingdean, Sussex, he entered the Navy as a cadet in 1872. On the Britannia he passed first in all the examinations. Promoted to lieutenant in 1880, he had his first taste of active service two years afterwards in the Egyptian war, on H.M.S. Agincourt.

When he proceeded to the Royal Naval Academy in 1883, he again showed great ability, and won the special £80 prize for gunnery. After a spell of work as assistant to Captain John Fisher (later Lord Fisher of Kilverstone), who was then Director of Naval Ordnance, Jellicoe became commander of the Victoria, the flagship of Admiral Sir George Tryon. When this battleship was rammed by the Camperdown off Tripoli, North Africa, he was lying seriously ill in his cabin, and had an almost miraculous escape from drowning. Jellicoe became Sir Edward Seymour's Flag-Captain and Chief of Staff in the expedition to relieve the legations at Peking (1900) when they were besieged by Chinese troops. He commanded the Naval Brigade, and was wounded at the battle of Peitsang.

In 1908 Jellicoe returned, as Third Sea Lord and Controller of the Navy, to the Admiralty, where he remained until his appointment in 1910 as Commander of the Atlantic Fleet. In 1912 he became Second Sea Lord, a position which he held until he was given the post of Commander-in-Chief of the Grand Fleet at the outbreak of the First World War (1914–18). For his services at Jutland (fought May 31, 1916), in which the German High Sea Fleet was driven back into port, Jellicoe was promoted Knight Grand Cross of the Royal Victorian Order, and awarded the Order of Merit. In November 1916 he relinquished the position of Commander-in-Chief and was succeeded by Sir David (later Earl) Beatty. He was First Sea Lord from November 1916 to December 1917. In the following year Sir John was raised to the peerage as Viscount Jellicoe of Scapa in the county of Orkney. For his valuable services he received a grant of £50,000, and in 1919 he visited the Dominions and India to advise on naval matters. In the next year Viscount Jellicoe was appointed Governor of New Zealand, and in 1925 was created an Earl. He was President of the British Legion from 1928 to 1932. The admiral's two volumes, entitled The Grand Fleet, 1914-16 and The Crisis of the Naval War, are valuable contributions to the study of the First World War. Jellicoe died on November 20, 1935, and was buried in St. Paul's Cathedral. On October 21 (Trafalgar Day), 1948, bronze busts of Lord Jellicoe and Lord Beatty were unveiled in Trafalgar Square, London.

Jelly-fish.

These are amongst the strangest of sea creatures, for they are almost entirely composed of jelly—in some of them there is actually 99 per cent of jelly, while in none is there much more than a tenth of any other matter. They have no relationship to the fishes, nor do they resemble them in any way whatever. With the hydra (q.v.) and other similar simple creatures, they help to make up the group Coelenterata. They vary a good deal in size, form and shape; some are seven feet across, others are almost microscopic.

An adult jelly-fish is a rounded, umbrella-shaped object, with a number of tentacles hanging down inside the rim of the umbrella, and, within them again, a loose ring of tissue guarding the entrance to the mouth and called the manubrium; the mouth is in the middle of the underside. The tentacles are armed with stinging organs that can paralyse the jelly-fish's prey, which are then swept into the mouth. Some jelly-fish can inflict painful stings on swimmers who come in contact with them.

Russell, Southsea
JELLICOE : VICTOR OF JUTLAND
Commander-in-Chief of the British Grand Fleet from August 1914 to November 1916, during the First World War (1914–18), Earl Jellicoe was in command at the battle of Jutland (May 31–June 1, 1916) in which the German Fleet was driven back to port.

There are few other organs of interest—except to scientists—but it is strange that in this lowly form of life there should be eyes, and actually, in one or two species, eyes of such advanced development as to have most of the features found in those of the vertebrates. To swim, jelly-fishes contract and expand muscles on the underside of the body, much like the opening and closing of an umbrella, although they are largely carried along by currents. Many jelly-fish are luminescent, and at night their glow can be seen in the dark water.

The development of a jelly-fish is a complicated business. In those forms that belong to the division Scyphozoa the fertilized egg may develop into a medusa (adult free-swimming jelly-fish) or it may form a polyp, which becomes fixed to the sea bottom. This polyp can produce root-like growths (stolons), whence also polyps are budded. In the other great division, Hydrozoa, from the point of view of reproduction the young medusa is less important than the polyp form, which becomes a colony of branching individuals. Each polyp is a tubular body, round the free end of which are a number of tentacles. Sooner or later buds of a new type appear, from which numerous little medusae are produced. The fertilized eggs

JELLY-FISH
The upper part of this jelly-fish (known as the Portuguese man-of-war) acts as a ' sail.' Below hang stinging tentacles.

of the medusae become new polyps, which in their turn establish fresh colonies.

The most complex of all jelly-fish are members of the *Siphonophora* group. These also live in colonies but, unlike the ordinary polyp colonies, they are unattached and float or swim in the seas, free medusae hardly ever occurring. On the other hand, the colony may consist of a large number of very varied types of polyp all strung together, usually in groups, each group containing three or four different sorts. At the end of the long stalk to which all these are attached is a large body known as the float, which drifts along on or near the surface and which supports all the rest of the colony. The float is the most conspicuous part of the organism; the best-known example of its functions is in the famous Portuguese man-of-war (*Physalia*). Here the float acts as a sail above the surface of the water, while the whole colony, which may be a brilliant blue or orange in colour, floats underwater. Below the float are groups of various organs, and from each group hangs down a long " fishing-line," covered with stinging cells, which kill the creature's prey. In this species the stings may be powerful enough seriously to injure a human being.

Adult Jellyfish
(Aurelia)

Strobila
stage of
growth

Polyp about to
develop into
Strobila

HOW JELLY-FISH ARE BORN AND GROW UP
The business of becoming a full-grown jelly-fish is a complicated process. Here we see the life history of one of the commonest forms, the Aurelia. First, the egg swims about as though it intended to stay just as it is. But soon it becomes attached to the bottom of the sea and begins to grow like a plant. This is the polyp stage. Soon the top of the polyp, carrying the arms, moves up, and another cup-shaped segment is formed, then another and another until there are 13 in all. This is the strobila stage. Then the top segment breaks off and swims away, and in time turns into a real jelly-fish. Meanwhile the second segment of the strobila grows tentacles and splits off, and so on until 13 new jelly-fish have appeared.

Jenner, EDWARD (1749–1823). How a chance remark may alter profoundly the course of scientific thought is well illustrated in the life of Jenner, an English physician to whom mankind must ever remain indebted.

"I cannot take smallpox, for I have had cowpox." This remark, made by a country girl who was waiting in a doctor's consulting-room at Chipping Sodbury, near Bristol, led to the introduction of vaccination, and so lessened the incidence of the scourge of smallpox which had ravaged mankind for 800 years, causing the deaths, on an average, of one million people each year.

Dr. Edward Jenner, who was born at Berkeley, Gloucestershire, on May 17, 1749, happened to hear that remark in his master's consulting-room, when he was a surgeon's apprentice, and he found that there was a tradition in Gloucestershire that people who had contracted cowpox through milking diseased cows were afterwards immune against smallpox.

After many years of study, he made the first experiment of vaccination (from *vacca*, Latin for cow) in 1796. He inoculated a boy from a cowpox sore on the hand of a girl. When the boy's arm healed he inoculated him with the germs of smallpox; but, as he anticipated, without any ill effects. The inoculation of animal cowpox virus had produced a definite degree of immunity against the human disease of smallpox.

He then pursued his investigations, as he himself put it, " with redoubled ardour." Jenner

Alinari

JENNER'S FIRST EXPERIMENT

Edward Jenner's discovery of the possibility of securing immunity from smallpox by vaccination made his name world-famous. This piece of statuary by an Italian sculptor, G. Monteverde, is in the Palazzo Bianco at Genoa, Italy.

met with many disappointments and much abuse, but the beneficent nature of his discovery was soon proved, and he lived to find himself one of the most famous and honoured men in Europe, and to see smallpox disappearing with the spread of vaccination. (*See* Antitoxin).

Jerboa. Though its body is but eight inches in length, the jerboa moves in great bounds, covering as much as four feet at each leap. It is, in fact, almost a miniature kangaroo, and it provides an interesting example of what scientists call independent evolution. For though it is no relation of the kangaroos, it has evolved, on its own account, the same form for the same purpose: a smallish body, tiny front legs that can be tucked up close to the chest, and long hind legs and tail. The tail is longer than the body, and, like that of the kangaroo, it can be used as a support for the animal when it is at rest. The hind legs, nearly as long as the body, propel the jerboa over the ground at a great rate. It lands on all fours, tips its body upright, and leaps again, so that each "stride" is a complicated process.

The forelegs are used for digging, and the animal lives in a burrow excavated in the sand of the deserts which it inhabits, often in large colonies. Being defenceless, it generally feeds by night. Besides the common jerboa (*Jaculus aegypticus*), which is found all over the desert regions of the northern half of Africa, there are several other

species. Sometimes called desert rats, jerboas live on roots and seeds, and birds' eggs. They often do great damage to crops.

Jerusalem, PALESTINE. "If I forget thee, O Jerusalem, let my right hand forget her cunning !" So sang the psalmist as he thought with passionate devotion of the holy city from which he was exiled. In the Middle Ages the Crusaders, who had toiled the long weary way from their homes in Europe to redeem the city of Christ from Mahomedan rule, knelt in the dust and wept with joy as they beheld from afar the city of their dreams. In normal times Jerusalem is still visited by hosts of pilgrims.

Standing on a rocky plateau, 2,500 feet above sea-level, in the mountain region of Palestine between the Mediterranean and the Dead Sea, Jerusalem, as seen from the neighbouring hills, is still as the Bible describes it, "beautiful for situation, the joy of the whole earth." Though the name Jerusalem means "city of peace," it is a natural fortress, and few cities have suffered more terrible sieges. Had it not been for the lack of water within its walls, it would in ancient days have been well-nigh impregnable, for deep-cut ravines protect it on three sides.

Separating it from the Mount of Olives on the east and north-east is the Valley of Kidron. On the west and running to the south is the Valley of Hinnom, or Gehenna. This ravine was deemed accursed in ancient times, for here human sacrifices were made to the Phoenician god Moloch, and later the bodies of criminals were thrown there. For this reason the name of Gehenna came to mean Hell.

The walls surrounding Jerusalem have been many times destroyed and rebuilt. Those standing today were built by Sultan Solyman the Magnificent in the 16th century and are pierced by eight gates. Of the splendid Temple, which was the centre of worship for all Israel, no part remains standing today. The "Wailing Wall," where every Friday Jews still gather to mourn and pray, may be part of the wall that surrounded the Temple erected by Solomon, or may, as many think, belong to later times. A Mahomedan place of worship, the Dome of the Rock, now stands on the holy spot. Eight gateways open into its

W. S. Berridge

JERBOA : A DESERT RODENT

Sometimes called the desert rat, the jerboa is remarkable for its long hind legs and tail. Propelled by its muscular hind legs the small light-brown rodent covers the ground in bounds, travelling as much as four feet at each leap. The forelegs are used for digging, the jerboa living in a burrow.

Rising above the garden and overlooking the whole city from the east is the Mount of Olives.

The streets of old Jerusalem are narrow and crooked, but in the suburbs that have grown up outside the walls in recent years there are wide tree-lined thoroughfares, gardens and modern houses. The largest new quarter lies west of the Jaffa Gate.

The recorded history of Jerusalem goes back to about 1400 B.C., when it was occupied by the Egyptians. At the time of the Israelites' entrance into Palestine it was held by the Jebusites, a Canaanite tribe. David conquered the city and made it the capital of his kingdom about 1000 B.C. It reached its greatest splendour under Solomon.

courtyard, within which, in the centre of a group of buildings, is the mosque, an octagonal shrine surmounted by a dome. It covers the traditional altar of burnt offering on Mount Moriah.

The place in Jerusalem most visited by Christian pilgrims is the Church of the Holy Sepulchre, built over the supposed tomb of Jesus. No man can point with certainty either to Golgotha, the place of the crucifixion, or to the place of Christ's burial; but for ages men have made long pilgrimages to visit these "holy places," have suffered and struggled and died for possession of them, so we cannot look without feelings of awe on the reputed spots.

Franciscan friars tend the place which they believe to be the Garden of Gethsemane. Here ancient olive trees are pointed out as the very ones in whose shadow Jesus knelt and prayed.

Dorien Leigh; American Colony in Jerusalem

JERUSALEM : HOLY CITY OF PALESTINE

The Holy City (lower) is here seen from the tower of the ruined citadel of David, near the Jaffa Gate. The site of Solomon's Temple is occupied by a domed mosque (middle distance), known as the Dome of the Rock. In the background is the Mount of Olives, surmounted by the Russian Church. The Wailing Wall (upper) may be part of the wall that once surrounded the Temple, and here Jews gather on Fridays to mourn the vanished glories of Israel.

It was the capital of Judah until destroyed by the Romans under the Emperor Titus in A.D. 70.

About A.D. 130 the Roman Emperor Hadrian rebuilt the city and named it Aelia Capitolina. Its history from that time is obscure until the 4th century, when Constantine the Great, after his conversion to Christianity, gave orders for the recovery of the holy places and the erection of two magnificent churches. In 687 Jerusalem was captured by the Mahomedans. It was captured by the Crusaders under Godfrey de Bouillon in 1099 and held by them until 1187, when it was reconquered by the Saracens.

Except for brief intervals Jerusalem remained in the hands of Mahomedans until 1917, when General Allenby (q.v.) captured it from the Turks. Then it became the capital of the mandated territory of Palestine. When Britain relinquished the mandate in 1948 war broke out between the Jews and Arabs, and Jerusalem suffered some damage. The independent State of Israel was proclaimed by the Jewish National Council in May 1948, and the following year an uneasy peace was made between the Jews and Arabs. In 1950 Jerusalem was proclaimed capital of Israel, the Israeli Government transferring its offices thereto from Tel Aviv.

The STORY of CHRIST the SAVIOUR

The greatest story of the world, told in the world's most wonderful Book, never loses by repetition any of its beauty or its message for mankind. Nor will the first Christmas and the first Easter ever be forgotten.

Jesus Christ. The story of Jesus Christ is an account of One Who lived long ago but Whom the world cannot forget; Who was born in a manger and died upon a Cross; Who, during His earthly life, was despised and rejected, but Whose name today is above every name, and Who is worshipped and adored by multitudes of the human race as their Saviour.

Long before Jesus appeared upon earth men foretold His coming. Even in what are called pagan lands there was a dim expectation of someone nobler than the sons of men appearing. Especially amongst the Jews was there such an expectation. They believed in the coming of One Whom they called the Messiah, and Whom one of their prophets called Immanuel—God with us.

But when Jesus was born they failed to recognize Him. They expected someone far different, someone who would come with outward pomp and glory, and, sitting upon a throne, would rescue Israel from her enemies and make of her a mighty nation.

Nothing could exceed the lowliness of Jesus's coming into the world. When Joseph and Mary, His earthly parents, went down to the little town of Bethlehem, about six miles from Jerusalem, to be included in the census the Romans were taking, they found that every house was full, nor could they find a room even in the village inn. So they had to take shelter in a stable, and there, that night, Jesus was born, and His mother laid Him in a manger. In all the world no one knew what a wondrous thing had happened, save a few shepherds watching their flocks, who heard the music of the Angel Host heralding the birth of the Son of God.

That night, too, a new star appeared in the sky. There were men who watched the stars in a country far away and said they could tell from the movements of the stars what was going to happen. These wise men were called Magi. They noticed this star, and after a while set out to journey to the place over which it shone, taking with them presents, for they were rich men and they expected that the star was meant by God to announce the coming of a King.

When they came to Jerusalem, King Herod of Judaea heard about them and was told they had come to seek for the young Christ who was born King. This news startled King Herod, who was a cruel man and thought that people were always plotting against him. When he learnt that Christ was to be born in Bethlehem, he sent for the wise men and told them to go to Bethlehem, and if they found the Christ to return and tell him. Herod meant, of course, to kill the Christ Child.

So the Magi went to Bethlehem, where they found Mary and Joseph and the Child in a very humble house. They knelt and worshipped Him, and offered Him their gifts, intending

CHRIST IN THE BETHLEHEM STABLE
Carved in marble by Mino da Fiesole in 1463, this sculpture of the birth of Christ is from part of a panel in the Church of St. Maria Maggiore in Rome. It shows the crib with the Child beside the manger.

next morning to return to King Herod. But as they slept they dreamt that they were not to tell the king that they had found Jesus, and they returned to their own country by another road.

When King Herod heard of this he was very angry, and gave orders that all the children in Bethlehem under the age of two years were to be killed. This is known as the Massacre of the Innocents. Jesus would have been killed also if Joseph, having been warned by an angel in a dream, had not fled with Mary and the Child to Egypt.

And now, for a long time, we hear very little about the life of Jesus. He returned with His parents to Nazareth when Herod was dead, and there in that little village amongst the hills, He increased in stature and in favour with God and Man.

Happy would we be if we could know something about the childhood and boyhood of Jesus, but all that is hidden from us. Yet we must believe that in His secluded home, where He was patiently preparing for His mighty work, His life was full of peace and content. In His parables and talks we see how much He loved Nature, how He rejoiced in flowers, and how all the visible world contained revelations of truth and beauty.

There is one glimpse which lightens for a moment those early years; it is a glimpse of Jesus in the Temple. Joseph and Mary had gone on a pilgrimage to Jerusalem, and, returning, they missed Him.

They found Him standing in the midst of a group of learned men in the Temple, asking and answering questions, so that all were astonished at His learning.

At 30 years of age Christ began to teach and preach. First of all, He was baptized by his cousin, John the Baptist, in the River Jordan. Then he suffered the temptation in the wilderness. Jesus knew quite well what His powers were; He knew that if He liked He could get great fame or glory or riches; and the devil tempted Him with those things, but Jesus was bent on doing good to others, so He told the tempter to be gone. Then He collected round about Himself a band of men, called disciples, who were his assistants, and with them He went about the country preaching to large numbers of people and performing miracles.

Jesus spoke out against the priests and the scribes and the sect called the Sadducees. Although the common people heard Him gladly, these others feared Him and His works. Multitudes followed Him, and He preached to them beautiful words of comfort—as in His Sermon on the Mount—and showed them what life really was, besides healing many of wasting diseases and other illnesses.

For three years Christ went about the country healing, and speaking parables—that is, telling stories from which a moral may be drawn—and preaching the Gospel of Love—for that was what He was continually saying: that we should love one

JESUS AMONG THE LEARNED MEN IN THE TEMPLE

" And when they had fulfilled the days, as they returned, the child Jesus tarried behind in Jerusalem; and Joseph and His mother knew not of it. And it came to pass . . . that after three days they found Him in the Temple in the midst of the doctors, both hearing them and asking them questions. And all that heard Him were astonished at His understanding and answers." This passage from the New Testament (Luke ii, 41–47) is here illustrated by Hofmann's painting.

FAMOUS PAINTING OF JESUS BLESSING THE CHILDREN

Formerly ascribed to Rembrandt (1606–69), this picture (in the National Gallery, London), entitled Christ Blessing Children, is now held to be the work of one of the famous Dutch painter's pupils. The scene is so beautifully described by the evangelist Mark (x, 13–16), that no painting can convey its ideality in such perfection. Jesus has rebuked the disciples for holding back the children and shows the latter that they are truly blessed.

JESUS BEING TRIED BEFORE PILATE, THE ROMAN GOVERNOR

The trial that preceded that most appalling of judicial crimes, the Crucifixion of Jesus, is dramatically represented in this picture, Christ before Pilate. Our Lord's answers in the Hall of Judgement to Pilate's questions must have reassured the Roman Governor that no rival to the authority of Rome stood before him. But the chief priests had so agitated the people that they would listen to no suggestion in favour of Christ, and Pilate had no alternative but to condemn Him to death. The Hungarian painter Michael Munkacsy, whose real name was Lieb, achieved immense success at the end of the 19th century with his religious pictures, of which the above is a typical example.

another. All the time the hatred of the priests increased, until at last it was hardly safe for Jesus to show Himself.

When He went to Jerusalem to keep the feast of the Passover, He knew that the end was near. Enemies were close around Him on all sides, plotting to take His life, and, alas! there was a traitor even among His disciples. This was Judas Iscariot. Of his character we know little, but when the enemies of Jesus approached Judas and tempted him with a bribe of 30 pieces of silver to betray his Master, he consented.

In a quiet upstairs room in Jerusalem, with the door shut and the lamps burning brightly, Jesus took His last supper with His disciples, and had His last opportunity of talking privately with them. The things He had said then will never be forgotten; they are the greatest in the world. After breaking the bread and passing the cup of wine, He said to Judas who was to betray Him, "What thou doest, do quickly." Judas went out; and when Jesus, a short time afterwards, also went out, to pray in the Garden of Geth-semane, Judas had his plan of betrayal ready. Coming from the garden Jesus was met by the servants of the High Priest, who insulted Him and smote Him, and at length led Him to the Judgement Hall, where He had to undergo a mock trial before the High Priest. This person had not the power to pass any sentence on Christ, so was compelled to send Him on to the Roman Governor, Pontius Pilate, who was greatly perplexed and at first much inclined to let Christ go free. The multi-tude, however, incited by the High Priest and his party, shouted "Crucify Him!" and Pilate at last yielded, and Christ was led out to be crucified.

Thus was the purest Being that ever lived on earth crucified upon the Cross. His enemies stood round and mocked Him, but Jesus in the midst of His agony prayed for them. "Father, forgive them," He said, "for they know not what they do!"

Mansell

'THE LIGHT OF THE WORLD'
This painting by William Holman Hunt (1827-1910) repre-sents Jesus Christ knocking at the door of the human heart, overgrown with the brambles of sin. The original painting hangs in the chapel of Keble College, Oxford, and a larger replica is in St. Paul's Cathedral, London.

With this prayer of forgiveness Jesus yielded up His spirit to God, His Father; and on the third day He rose from the dead and appeared to His disciples before ascending to Heaven. The Resurrection and the Ascension are sometimes spoken of as if they were a happy ending. It is both true and untrue. The ending *is* happy, because it tells us that human life is worth living, that it has pur-pose, that sacrifice is fruitful. And yet " happy ending " is a trivial, even a false, description. The Christian belief does not in the least mean that all problems have been solved and all victories won. They have all still to be met in each fresh generation, and in each fresh life.

The fact is that the Resurrection and Ascen-sion are not really an ending at all; they are a beginning. And we have in the 20th century come only a small part of the way towards the recognition, not to say the possession, of the re-newal, the illumination, and the consecration which they give to the life of Man. But we have come far enough to know that the thing is a reality.

What it does for us can be described in a very simple way. One of the verses in the ac-count of the Resurrection which is as worthy as any to be remembered and repeated over and over again is one of the simplest: " Then were the disciples glad when they saw the Lord." It was written a long time ago. But it can still be true. The Ascension, which seems to take the Lord away, and does, indeed, take Him away from some, really brings Him near to all.

Jesus lives in the hearts of all who love Him, and the influence which He wields increases from generation to generation. Countless missionaries have left home and kindred to spread the knowledge of His name in heathen lands, in every corner of the globe. Jesus left no writings; but from re-collections of His teachings His followers later put together the record of His ministry, as we have it in the New Testament.

Jet Propulsion. The old proverb that "there is nothing new under the sun" has a good deal of truth in it. The idea of propulsion by means of a jet is more than 200 years old; for in 1729 one John Allen proposed to drive a ship in a calm by such means. Allen's idea was to work his engine by the explosion of gunpowder; he even took out a patent for the scheme.

A little over 50 years later James Rumsey, an American, made a trip on the Potomac River in a boat driven by hydraulic jet propulsion. Water was sucked in at the bow of the boat by a steam pump, and forced out in a jet at the stern. The boat was driven *forward* by the reaction of the body of water shot *backward* from the jet orifice. Rumsey came to England, and in 1793 another of his jet-propelled boats made a run on the Thames; meanwhile the inventor had died, in 1792, and the success of paddle-wheel boats had robbed his scheme of its prospects.

A British armoured gunboat, H.M.S. Waterwitch, was fitted with jet-propulsion engines in 1866; a speed of 9¼ knots was obtained, but no advantage over screw propellers was gained, despite the 700 horse-power generated by the steam plant. Some 30 years later, steam lifeboats were driven by hydraulic jets, but then this method of propulsion almost died out; it was tried for steam trawlers during the First World War (1914–18), with the

object of getting a silent engine. A jet-propelled ferry boat was built for the Port of London Authority at the Royal Albert Dock in 1925 and is still in use.

Anyone who has dropped a garden hose when the water was turned on fully and has watched the loose end squirm about on the ground has seen jet propulsion at work. The same pressure that drives the water out of the nozzle pushes back upon the hose—by its reaction. So when the hose is free to move it backs away from the jet as best it can. Another illustration from the garden is the lawn sprinkler, which has four bent nozzles through which water is forced from a hose. As the arms carrying the nozzles are pivoted, the reaction from the jets spurting from them drives the arms in the opposite direction, and the grass gets sprinkled over a radius from the appliance. The squid (*see page 946*) propels itself backwards by squirting out a jet of water from beneath its head, so that Nature really invented jet propulsion.

All this may seem a long way from the jet-propelled aircraft of today, but the principle is the same. If we take as our next examples the rocket and the catherine-wheel we shall come very close indeed to the flying bomb (*q.v.*), the rocket-driven motor-car, the rocket device for assisting an aircraft at take-off, and the jet-propelled aeroplane itself. You will notice the similarity of principle between **the catherine-wheel and the lawn sprinkler: the**

burning gunpowder of the firework generates high-pressure gas which gushes out from the lighted end of the coiled tube, and spins it round upon the pin by which it is pivoted. In the rocket, loosely held upright in the ground by a stick, gas pressure is generated again by gunpowder : reaction from the jet of hot gases drives the rocket upwards.

More scientific rockets were made with the object of sending mails to places difficult or inaccessible by road; men even dreamed of sending gigantic rockets to the moon. Liquefied gas (for example

Science Museum; Port of London Authority

JET PROPULSION APPLIED TO SMALL VESSELS

The idea of jet propulsion is by no means new. Indeed, it is about 200 years old. At top left is a model of a steam lifeboat which in 1889 was propelled by jets of water forced out of an orifice at the stern by a steam pump. It never came into general use. Since 1925 a jet-propelled ferry-boat (lower) has been continuously in use at the Royal Albert Dock, London, and has proved reliable and handy to manoeuvre on a stretch of water that is often very congested.

Fox; P.A.-Reuter

JET UNITS FITTED TO CIVIL AND MILITARY AIRCRAFT

Though jet-propelled aircraft were used by several of the combatant nations during the Second World War (1939–45), jet engines were not extensively tested in civil aeroplanes until after the cessation of hostilities. In July 1948 a Viking airliner (lower), with two Nene jet engines, flew from London to Paris in 34 minutes seven seconds. A gas turbine engine—a jet unit driving a propeller—is used in the Balliol (upper), a Royal Air Force trainer.

air, oxygen) was tried as the propellant instead of gunpowder. Fritz von Opel propelled a motor-car by igniting in series a battery of rockets fixed at the rear of the vehicle; in 1930 a rocket-propelled aircraft on Opel's system was tried out. The German fighter aircraft known as the Messerschmitt 163, used during the Second World War (1939–45), was driven by a rocket engine; the necessary oxygen fuel was carried in liquid form in tanks.

During the Second World War jet-propelled aircraft were built by several of the combatant countries. The Italians demonstrated one in 1941; the German Messerschmitt 262 was another. Britain produced the Gloster fighter with a single jet; a later type of this aircraft (twin-jet) set up a record with a speed of 606 miles per hour in November 1945. The German pilotless aircraft known as the flying-bomb made its appearance in 1944, and was the pioneer of the intermittent-impulse jet engine. The explanation of this machine, given in pages 1330–32, should be referred to, as should the story of the Gas Turbine. In the flying bomb there is a series of explosions in the combustion chamber; in other types of jet engine the explosion is continuous, once the engine has started. The exploded mixture of hot air and enormously expanded gases can only move rearwards, through the jet orifices at the back of the aircraft.

What are the advantages of this method of driving aircraft? High speed, and the maintenance of great power at high altitudes where, with internal combustion engines of the piston type, power begins to fall off. The fuel may be one such as paraffin oil, instead of the more inflammable motor spirits such as petrol. Already jet-propelled aircraft have travelled faster than the speed of sound waves. This speed varies with the altitude, and with the altering density of the atmosphere. At sea level the speed of sound waves—air waves, in fact—is about 760 miles per hour. As one climbs higher the speed of sound grows less, until at 40,000 feet it is only about 660 m.p.h.; at levels higher than 40,000 feet it is believed that the temperature of the atmosphere remains constant, and the speed of sound also.

At normal speeds the aircraft thrusts back the air in waves as it flies through the atmosphere; when the forward movement of the aircraft approaches the speed of sound, however, the machine " catches up " with the air waves it has caused to form in front of it, and now compresses

Planet News Ltd.

JET ENGINE FOR A SPEED-BOAT
Sir Malcolm Campbell (nearer the camera) is here seen inspecting the Goblin jet engine which he fitted to the hull of his record-breaking motor-boat Blue Bird II (*see also illustration in page 485*).

the air. Moreover, the ordinary steady flow of air over the wings breaks down, and the aircraft may stall (*see* Aeroplane), or collapse in pieces. Until many brave test pilots have risked their lives in this perilous region of aeronautics we shall lack information on all these matters.

In jet engines the power is expressed as " thrust " measured in pounds, rather than as horse-power.

We also often find mention of the " Mach number " (named after an Austrian scientist, Ernst Mach—1838–1916). This number expresses speed in relation to the velocity of sound, so that a Mach number of 1 indicates the same speed as that of sound; a lower Mach number would indicate a slower speed, and a higher number would mean a speed greater than that of sound. Not only the altitude but the prevailing temperature of the atmosphere also affects this speed; for this reason the Mach number system (utilising the ratio of aircraft speed to the velocity of sound) is convenient. (*See* Rocket Bomb).

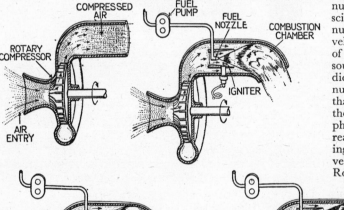

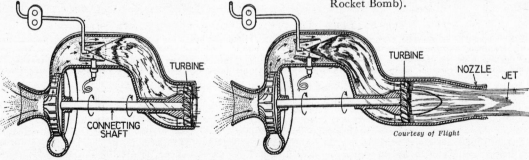

Courtesy of Flight

JET PROPULSION : A POWER UNIT FOR AIRCRAFT

The working cycle of a jet propulsion engine for propelling an aircraft is illustrated. Air enters the intake (upper left), is compressed and passed to the combustion chamber (upper right) where fuel is squirted in and continuous combustion takes place. The mixture of combustion gases and air rushes at high velocity through the turbine, rotating it and driving the compressor (lower left). The gases then pass out through the nozzle into the open air (lower right).

Jews. A people scattered over the length and breadth of the earth for almost 19 centuries, and still remaining a distinct race, though mingling with the people of many lands, the Jews have well been called the "eternal people." We cannot speak of the Jews merely as an ancient people as we do of the Assyrians and Babylonians, for they are still a living race, and a vital force in the world today. Though they number only about 11 millions, virtually every important field of human activity includes Jews among the great names.

The same intensity of character that made Israel an important nation in ancient times has given the Jews distinction in every department of modern life. For in mental and moral traits, and even in form and feature, the Jew of today is much the same as his forefathers of the days of Solomon and David. No race has endured greater sufferings and misfortunes; and no race in proportion to its size can boast of higher achievements and culture.

The history of the Jews begins in a far-distant past, when their ancestors were wandering Semitic tribes of the Arabian desert, slowly drifting into Palestine. According to the Bible, the great forefather of the race was Abraham, who, about 2000 B.C., led his people from Ur of the Chaldees (in the country now called Iraq) into Palestine at the Divine call to found a nation dedicated to the service of the one God. Because he came from beyond the Euphrates, Abraham was called "the Hebrew" (meaning to "cross over").

SCROLL OF THE LAW
This is the Scroll of the Law used in synagogues (Jewish places of worship). On the right is the breastplate worn by the rabbi (priest), on the left the pointer with which he follows the text. In reading, the scroll is unwound from one roller and rewound on the other.

Isaac, who succeeded Abraham as patriarch of the people, had twin sons, Esau and Jacob. Jacob, whose name was changed to Israel, gained the leadership. He was followed by his 12 sons, who became the heads of the 12 tribes known as the Israelites. Esau founded the Edomites. Jacob's fondness for his son Joseph aroused the jealousy of the other brothers, and they secretly sold him as a slave to some merchants on their way to Egypt. But Joseph rose to the position of ruler of Egypt.

After a time, because of famine in Palestine, Jacob and his sons arrived in Egypt to buy grain. Through Joseph's influence they and their families were given land, and there they remained for generations, enjoying prosperity and increasing in numbers. But in after years, according to the Biblical account, the Egyptians became jealous of the Israelites and made them slaves.

From this oppression they were delivered by Moses and led back to Palestine, or Canaan, "the Promised Land," which was then inhabited by a highly civilized Semitic people called the Canaanites. Before this time the Israelites had been a wandering shepherd people; now, under the laws established by Moses and the influence of Canaanite civilization, they gradually grew into a strong nation.

Moses was succeeded by Joshua, who led the Israelites across the River Jordan, taking possession of the land of the Canaanites and dividing it among the tribes. Levi, the priestly tribe (whose members were called Levites), was given no land, for its members were to dwell among the other tribes as religious leaders. Joshua won victories against the Canaanites, but the Israelites were still sorely harassed by them and other warlike tribes, especially the Moabites, the Ammonites and the Philistines.

To lead the people during those troublous times, officers known as judges were appointed. Among the most famous of these were the warrior Gideon, the woman-judge Deborah, and Samson, who performed marvellous feats of strength. In the time of the prophet Samuel the people decided that they must have a stronger form of government, and demanded a king. For this office Saul was chosen. He united the tribes of Israel to form a strong kingdom, and won brilliant victories against neighbouring tribes, but he and his son Jonathan both fell in battle against the Philistines (c. 1010 B.C.).

David (c. 1030–990 B.C.) was then proclaimed king, and peace was established throughout the land. Under his son Solomon (died c. 937 B.C.) the kingdom reached its greatest prosperity and glory. When Solomon's son Rehoboam ascended the throne the 10 northern tribes revolted and made Jeroboam (died c. 915 B.C.) king. Only Rehoboam's own tribe of Judah, together with the little tribe of Benjamin, remained faithful to the house of David. From that time on (about the 10th century B.C.) the land of the Hebrews was divided into two kingdoms—the northern one being known as Israel, and the southern as Judah.

Feeling was bitter between the two kingdoms and border wars were frequent. Israel was rich and prosperous; its land was fertile, and its people lived in towns. The land of Judah was stony and sterile; Jerusalem was its only large town, and most of its people still clung to their old shepherd ways of life.

Jeroboam forbade his people to worship at the temple in Jerusalem, and introduced idolatrous practices. Under his successors the country went from bad to worse. In 721 B.C. the Assyrians captured Samaria, the capital of Israel, and, driving off the mass of the people into slavery, put an end to the kingdom of Israel. The 10 tribes were thus lost to history. Their place was taken by Assyrian colonists, who, mingling and intermarrying with such Israelites as were left, formed the people known as the Samaritans.

The little kingdom of Judah endured for more than 100 years longer, though its position between the powerful states of Egypt and Assyria exposed it to repeated invasions. For the most part it remained

American Colony in Jerusalem

BLOWING THE RAM'S HORN

To remind Jewish people of the approach of the Sabbath (Saturday), the shofar or ram's horn is blown on Friday evenings. This photograph shows a Yemenite Jew of Jerusalem performing that duty. The Yemenites are a Jewish sect which settled in Arabia and claim to be descendants of the tribe of Gad, which originally lived on the east bank of the Jordan.

Judea, by the Persians, and in this position was able to do much for his people. During this period the writings contained in the Hebrew Bible were collected.

After the conquests of Alexander and his death (323 B.C.), the Ptolemies of Egypt ruled Judea for about 100 years, and then it fell into the hands of Syria. The Syrian king Antiochus Epiphanes outraged the feelings of the Jews by setting up idols and ordering the people to worship them. The aged priest Mattathias then raised the flag of revolt, and under the leadership of his five sons, known as the Maccabees, the Jews defeated the Syrian army and won their independence (130 B.C.).

Before long, however, the people became divided into parties, or sects, such as the Pharisees and the Sadducees. A dispute arose between two claimants to the throne; and Rome, with whom an alliance had been formed, was called upon to act as arbiter. The Roman general Pompey (106–48 B.C.) took advantage of the situation to make himself master of Jerusalem and force the Jews to pay tribute. When Julius Caesar (102–44 B.C.) came into power he placed a foreign ruler, Antipater of Idumea (mountainous region south of the Dead Sea), over Judea. Antipater's son and grandson ruled from 37 B.C. to A.D. 39. Under the Roman governors who followed there were frequent insurrections, culminating in the great Jewish war of A.D. 66. After a long siege the Roman general Titus, afterwards emperor, took Jerusalem in A.D. 70, burned the temple, massacred thousands of Jews and enslaved thousands of others.

The Jewish nation was destroyed, but not their spirit. Dispersed throughout the world, they established synagogues wherever they went, and their rabbis, or doctors of the law, continued the teaching of the Mosaic law. The fact that they were dwelling among strangers made them cling with greater tenacity to the very letter of this law, following it in every detail of their lives.

It was at the cost of terrible suffering that the Jews remained faithful to their religion. Their history is, for the most part, a long succession of persecutions. In many places they were forced to live in crowded quarters called *ghettos*, and compelled to wear a distinguishing dress. They were not allowed to own land. Trading and money-lending were the only pursuits open to them. The shrewdness which many of them developed became a reproach to the whole race. For a long time they were deprived of political and educational privileges in most European countries, and were exposed to the violence of mobs that time and again rose against them, massacring men, women and children. Wherever small Jewish colonies existed they dreaded a sudden outburst of hostile feeling.

In Germany in 1933 there began a most violent persecution of the Jews, and many fled the country. After the outbreak of the Second World War (1939–

faithful to the ancient religion. Under King Hezekiah, Jerusalem was strengthened, and an attack of the Assyrian army under Sennacherib (reigned 705–680 B.C.) was driven back. King Josiah was slain in a battle with the Egyptians, and Judah was forced to pay tribute to Egypt. The weakened kingdom finally fell a prey to the Babylonians or Chaldeans, who had become the great world power. Jerusalem was captured by Nebuchadrezzar in 586 B.C., most of the people being carried away into exile in Babylon, and the once flourishing kingdom of Judah became a wilderness as the prophets had foretold.

It was now that the word Jew, which originally meant an inhabitant of Judea, was applied to all the members of the Hebrew race.

After about 70 years the Babylonian Empire was overthrown by the Persian king Cyrus (*c.* 600–529 B.C.), who permitted the Jews who so desired to return to Jerusalem. Later, Ezra the Scribe led another band back to Jerusalem and brought about a great religious awakening. In 444 B.C. Nehemiah, a Jew, was appointed governor of

45) the leaders of the German people resolved on the extermination of the Jews in all countries occupied by German forces. They practised mass-deportation of Jews, followed by mass-murder. It has been estimated that nearly six million Jews perished in central and eastern Europe, including hundreds of thousands deported from the Netherlands and France.

The persecutions the Jews have suffered caused many of them to look with longing eyes to their former home in Palestine, and Jewish settlements were established there after the end of the First World War (1914–18) when the country was ruled by Great Britain under a mandate of the League of Nations. Great Britain surrendered the mandate in 1947—and fighting broke out between Jews and Arabs for possession of Palestine, a Jewish State of Israel being established over a part of the country in 1948. The United Nations tried to solve the problem, but without success. In the spring of 1949 armistices were made between Israel and the Arab States, and Palestine was divided into the two States of Israel and Transjordan. The latter then changed its name to the Hashimite Kingdom of the Jordan.

During the 19th and 20th centuries the Jews produced an exceptional number of philosophers, scientists, and artists, including Karl Marx (1818–83), Albert Einstein (born 1879), and Henry Bergson (1859–1941). In Britain there have been many distinguished Jews in trade and politics.

Jinnah, MAHOMED ALI (1876–1948). Creator of the Dominion of Pakistan (*q.v.*) and its first Governor-General, Jinnah strove for years for the foundation of a Mahomedan State in India, declaring that it was impossible for Mahomedans to live in a land ruled by Hindus—as would be the case if the sub-continent of India had one Government when the British granted self-government to the country.

Jinnah (*see* photograph in page 1716) was born on December 25, 1876, at Karachi, on the Indus delta, and studied law in England before practising in Bombay. By sheer personality and political ability he established himself as the recognized representative of Mahomedan opinion in India, being for many years the leader of the Mahomedans in the Central Legislative Assembly (parliament). In March 1940 he demanded that India should be divided into two self-governing States—one Mahomedan and one Hindu—when the British left the country, and he maintained his attitude through the seven years of tension that followed.

In the end the Hindu leaders yielded, and on the transfer of power in India from the British to the two Dominions—of India and of Pakistan—on August 15, 1947, he was sworn in as Governor-General of Pakistan. Jinnah, who bore the title of Quaid-i-Azam, or Great Leader, died at Karachi on September 11, 1948.

SAINT *and* SOLDIER—MAID OF ORLEANS

People will never grow tired of disputing the truth of Joan of Arc's claim to have heard the voices of angels. But there is no dispute about her courage and achievements as a young fighter for France.

Joan of Arc. (1412–31). This is the immortal story of Joan of Arc—Jeanne d'Arc, as the French call her—the girl heroine who saved France from conquest in the first half of the 15th century. Her home was at Domrémy, in the valley of the River Meuse, in north-eastern France; and her father, Jacques d'Arc, was a well-to-do peasant proprietor. His daughter did not work in the fields, but helped her mother in the home with the spinning, weaving and other duties.

Energetic, good-tempered, and kind-hearted, Joan was a general favourite in the village. But often her heart was troubled by what she heard of the sad plight of her beloved land. For many years it had been wasted with war, and now the whole northern half was in the hands of the English and their ally, the Duke of Burgundy. Its young prince, Charles VII—called the Dauphin because he had not yet been crowned king at Reims—was without money, armies or competent generals, and, moreover, he expected shortly to lose that part of France which still remained in his hands.

When Joan was 13 she became devoutly religious. Loving quiet and solitude for meditation, she often took the dog and watched her father's flock of sheep, while she worked an altar cloth with the exquisite embroidery which, afterwards, was to occupy her dark days in prison.

On the breezy hillside, in the orchard, and as she knelt before an image of the Virgin in the village church, Joan began to hear heavenly voices and to see visions—of Saints Margaret and Catherine, and of the archangel Michael, patron saint of the soldiers. Their message was that she should go to the Dauphin, lead his troops to victory, and free France of the invaders. Her family and the village priest tried to dissuade her, thinking her distracted, but she was determined to obey the voices. She overcame the opposition of officials, bishops, and nobles, reached the Dauphin, and won his belief in her mission. Now, clothed in armour, and with the golden-lilied banner of France waving above her head, she led an enthusiastic army to the relief of the walled city of Orléans, which the English at that time were besieging. Cutting boldly through the enemy, she and her troops entered the city, and in four days of masterly sallies and attacks, sent the enemy flying. This was in May 1429, when she was not yet 17. In July, Joan was able to conduct the Dauphin in triumph to Reims Cathedral for coronation at the altar where the kings of France were always crowned.

Joan now regarded her mission as finished, and begged permission to return to her home. She declared her unfitness to remain at the head of the army, since her heavenly " voices " had deserted her. The king, however, persuaded her to remain, and she marched to drive away the Burgundians who were besieging Compiègne. Here she was defeated, taken prisoner, and sold as a prize of war to the English. For months she was kept in prison in the Norman city of Rouen, and was subjected to shameful indignities and a long trial.

Delivered to her enemies, and abandoned to her fate by an ungrateful king and courtiers, she defended herself at her trial with great skill and courage. In the end she was convicted of witchcraft and heresy, and was burned at the stake in May 1431. On May 16, 1920, nearly 500 years later, she was canonized, i.e. enrolled in the list of Catholic saints. The immortal deeds and piteous death of " the Maid of Orleans " have inspired sculptors, painters, and poets for five centuries, while to France she has been for long the nation's best-loved heroine.

JOAN RECEIVES THE SWORD OF ST. MICHAEL
Reproduced from a French painting, this picture illustrates the story that Joan of Arc received a sword from the Archangel Michael, with the message that she should lead the French troops to victory against the English.

Job. The most sublime treatment of the great mystery of human suffering is given in the Book of Job in the Bible. In dignity and beauty of phrase the prose of the prologue and epilogue must for ever rank among the masterpieces of literary composition. The hero is a wealthy chieftain of Uz, somewhere between Palestine and the Euphrates, who is noted as a God-fearing and upright man. But to test whether his righteousness will remain strong in suffering as in prosperity, God allows Satan to inflict upon Job a series of terrible misfortunes and afflictions.

His friends tell him that this suffering has come through sin. But Job refuses to believe it is punishment for wrong-doing; he cries out to God for some other explanation. Filled with pain and doubt as Job is, he still has not lost his faith in God. " I know that my Redeemer liveth," he says; and at last God, speaking out of a whirlwind, answers him. Job bows in submission, realizing that the great mysteries of life are beyond Man's understanding.

Joffre, JOSEPH JACQUES CÉSAIRE (1852-1931). One of the most beloved French Commanders-in-Chief was " Papa " Joffre (pron. zho'-fr), " the Victor of the Marne," who in the First World War (1914-18) halted the overwhelming rush of the German armies in 1914 and saved Paris and France. Marshal Joffre was of humble origin, his father being a maker of wine casks in the south of France. The boy was sent to the famous École Polytechnique in Paris, where he prepared himself for a military career. But before he had finished his education he was called to arms in the Franco-Prussian War of 1870-71, and at the end of the disastrous siege of Paris he saw the victorious Germans march into his beloved city.

The young soldier spent the next 40 years in making himself and France ready, should the Prussian foe strike again. Joffre saw many years of service in the French colonies in Africa and Asia and when the First World War broke out in 1914 he was made commander of all the French forces on the Western front. In the face of the crushing onslaught of the German army through Belgium, he ordered his troops to retire mile after mile into France. Then the call went forth (September 6, 1914): " Soldiers, we are attacking. Advance as long as you can. When you can no longer advance, hold your position. When you can no longer hold it, die!" The result was the victory of the Marne. Created a Marshal of France, Joffre was removed from the active supreme command in 1916 as the result of the necessity of trying other tactics and other men in the supreme task of defeating the German armies.

COUNTRY GIRL WHO LED A KING TO VICTORY

Painted specially for this work by DUDLEY TENNANT

Joan of Arc, whom the world honours as one of the greatest women of all time, was a simple country girl, born and bred in a French village. At that time a large part of France was in the hands of the English, and it was to expel them that she felt her call. After many difficulties she was given her opportunity. Clad in armour, she placed herself at the head of the French army and raised the siege of Orleans. Joan was taken prisoner by the English and burned as a witch, but not until she had fulfilled her ambition and seen Charles VII of France crowned at Reims.

MEMORIALS TO JOAN OF ARC

JOAN OF ARC was born at Domrémy, a village of Eastern France, in the department of Vosges; it is now known as Domrémy-la-Pucelle (la pucelle being French for 'the maid').

Domrémy's present population is only a little over 250, but every year thousands of sightseers make pilgrimages there to see the house in which Joan was born in 1412; the actual room is shown below. Over the door are the Royal Arms of France and the inscription ' Vive Labeur: Vive le Roi Louys' (Long live work: long live King Louis). It is a very humble house, judged by our modern standards, for Joan's parents were but peasant-farmers who never in their wildest dreams saw Joan regaining the throne for her king and leaving a name that is one of the most illustrious in history. In the centre of the room in which she was born is a statuette of the Maid. The statue of Joan on the left, the work of Princess Marie of Orleans, stands outside the Town Hall of Orleans.

Johannesburg, SOUTH AFRICA. Few cities have developed so rapidly, and in so orderly a fashion as this " City of Gold " in the Transvaal. Peaceful Boer farms occupied what today is the most thriving hive of industry in Africa. Situated 5,760 feet above sea-level on the famous Witwatersrand (Ridge of White Waters), one of the world's richest goldfields, Johannesburg exists primarily for the mining industry. Mining engineers have determined the existence of a gold reef (gold-bearing seam of rock) 61 miles long and, apparently, limited in depth only by Man's ability to reach the deepest levels.

Johannesburg, which has an area of 89 square miles, has broad straight streets, many handsome public, business, and private buildings, and delightful suburbs. These lie, in general, to the north and east of the city, while the mining area is in the south. It is the largest commercial and industrial city in South Africa.

Of its buildings, among the most attractive are the Town Hall and Municipal Buildings, which were opened in 1915, the University of the Witwaters-

rand, the Municipal Art Gallery, the Law Courts, and the Post Office, with a clock tower 106 feet high.

Founded in 1886 and named after Johannes Kissik, then surveyor-general of the Transvaal (the name meaning Johannes' town) following the discovery of the Rand gold reef in the previous year

South African Railways

JOHANNESBURG'S IMPOSING BUILDINGS
Centre of South Africa's gold-mining industry, Johannesburg is in the Transvaal. One of its finest thoroughfares is Kissik Street (lower). The University of the Witwatersrand (upper) was constituted in 1922, developing from a School of Mines.

by a mason employed by a Dutch farmer, Johannesburg grew with astonishing speed. At first a part of the independent Boer Republic of the Transvaal, after the Boer War (1899–1902) it became a Crown Colony under the British flag, and later, in 1910, a part of the Union of South Africa.

The population is about 767,000, of whom less than half are whites.

John, KING OF ENGLAND (1167–1216). Vicious, shameless, and ungrateful, King John holds the title of the worst English king. He was nicknamed " Lackland " because his father, King Henry II, gave him no possessions on the Continent, although all his elder brothers had received such grants. Later he was endowed with castles, lands and revenues on both sides of the Channel. John showed his characteristic ingratitude and spite by joining his brother Richard the Lion-Hearted in conspiring against their father, and it was the discovery of this treason that brought the old king to his grave. When Richard became king he confirmed John in his possessions and added others ; but again John showed his treacherous character by conspiring against Richard during the latter's absence on the Third Crusade.

On Richard's death in 1199 the barons chose John to be king, despite the claim of his nephew Arthur, the son of another brother, Geoffrey, who had died some time before. Two French provinces took up arms in young Arthur's support, but he fell into the king's hands and was murdered by John's

KING JOHN OF ENGLAND
In Worcester Cathedral this effigy of King John surmounts his tomb. The youngest son of Henry II, he succeeded his brother Richard I in 1199, his reign marking one of the least honourable periods of English history. He died at Newark, Nottinghamshire, on October 19, 1216.

command. In a war with the king of France, John lost all his French possessions except Aquitaine.

Then came a quarrel with Pope Innocent III over the nomination of Stephen Langton as Archbishop of Canterbury. John's resistance was broken at last by the Pope's threat to depose him and by the growing disaffection of his subjects. He not only received Langton as archbishop, but he abjectly agreed to hold England as a fief from the Pope and to pay a yearly tribute. While John was absent on the Continent, seeking to regain his forfeited fief of Normandy, the barons of England united to resist the tyrant's rule. John met the barons at Runnymede on June 15, 1215, and was forced to put the royal seal upon the Great Charter of liberties. (*See* Magna Carta).

But John raised an army and harried with fire and sword the estates of the barons, who in despair offered the crown to Louis, son of the French king. Louis landed with a great army, and received the submission of a large part of England. But while the issue was still doubtful, John died suddenly of a fever at Newark.

John, AUGUSTUS EDWIN (born 1878). One of the best known of modern British painters, Augustus John was born at Tenby, South Wales, on January 4, 1878. He studied art at the Slade School, London, and in Paris, and between 1900 and 1914 he assumed the leadership of the younger painters.

John's work may be divided into four groups: gipsy scenes, portraits, landscapes and etchings. Two most characteristic works, The Smiling Woman, and the portrait of Madame Suggia, both in the Tate Gallery, London, are brilliant examples of his spirited style (*see also* illustration in page 1192). He had a masterly sense of design, and in his etchings (32 of which have been presented to the Fitzwilliam Museum, Cambridge) was influenced by the Spanish painter and etcher Goya (1746–1828).

John Bull. Used as a personification of the English nation, and for the typical Englishman, this name and character were first popularised in 1712 by John Arbuthnot in the History of John Bull. In this satire on the struggle of the nations for power in Europe, France appears under the name of Lewis Baboon, Spain as Lord Strutt, and the Low Countries (Holland and Belgium) as Nicholas Frog, who attempts to equal John Bull in size.

Johnson, AMY (1904–1941). On May 5, 1930, a young woman, who had started flying only 18 months before, stepped into a second-hand aeroplane, called Jason, at Croydon Aerodrome, near London, and without ostentation started on a solo flight to Australia.

After having taken her degree of Bachelor of Arts at Sheffield University, Miss Amy Johnson found teaching and secretarial work slow and monotonous, so she took up flying, and was the first Englishwoman to gain a ground engineer's licence. She then decided that she would attempt to beat a record of Bert Hinkler, who in 1928 had flown from England to Australia in 15½ days. In that she was not successful, but she reached Port Darwin in 19 days—a most remarkable achievement in the circumstances, and one which immediately brought her world-wide fame. She received the congratulations of the King and Queen on "her wonderful and courageous achievement," and was made a Commander of the Order of the British Empire.

The daring airwoman was well ahead of the record until she reached Rangoon, where she missed her way, and had to make a forced landing. Her little Moth plane toppled into a ditch, and she was compelled to wait until the damage to the machine was repaired. Afterwards she encountered gales and tropical rain, which forced her aeroplane so low when crossing the shark-infested Java Sea that it almost touched the waves. Then she had to climb over cloud-capped mountains before she sighted the Timor Sea. At last, on the afternoon of May 24, 1930, Miss Johnson had completed the first woman's solo flight from England to the Antipodes, over 10,000 miles.

In 1931 she flew to Japan and back with a companion. In 1932 she flew from England to Cape

AMY JOHNSON
Her solo flight from England to Australia in 1930 first brought fame to Amy Johnson. In November 1932 she flew to South Africa in four days six hours; in 1933 she made a flight across the Atlantic with her husband, J. A. Mollison. She was killed on January 5, 1941, when her aeroplane fell into the Thames.

Town alone in 4 days 6 hours and in 1936 made a there-and-back flight in just under 11 days, a double record. She married J. A. Mollison in 1932, and flew the Atlantic with him in July 1933. She crashed in the Thames on A.T.A. (Air Transport Auxiliary) duty, on January 5, 1941.

Johnson, SAMUEL (1709–84). The unique position which Samuel Johnson held among English men of letters and scholars of discernment was due

DR. JOHNSON
For much of his life Samuel Johnson held a position unique in English literature, his word being unquestioned among the learned.

as much to intellectual integrity as to wide erudition; his was in large measure a triumph of vigorous and upright personality. In the words of Lord Brougham, " Johnson was a good as he was a great man; and he had so firm a regard for virtue that he wisely ' set much greater store by his worth than by his fame."

As a boy in Lichfield, Staffordshire, where he was born, Johnson gave early promise of the

powers of mind which were one day to make him the literary dictator of his times. He " gorged " the books in his father's bookshop. The days of his early manhood, however, were filled with disappointment and failure. His father lost most of his

From the painting by E. M. Ward
JOHNSON SLIGHTED
During his early struggles, Dr. Johnson called on Lord Chesterfield to ask for his assistance but was left neglected in the anteroom, as shown here. When success came Chesterfield offered his support, which Johnson refused.

money, and the son found that the family poverty made it impossible for him to continue his studies at Oxford and take his degree. He fell in love and married, at the age of 26, Mrs. Porter, a widow 20 years older than himself, who died in 1752. With the aid of his wife's small fortune Johnson set up a school near Lichfield. But the school failed, and he set off for London to seek his fortune. With him went David Garrick, his favourite pupil.

The early days in London were so full of hardship that years later Johnson is said to have burst into tears on recalling them. He wrote Parliamentary reports. He made translations for the press. He made catalogues for booksellers, one of whom he knocked down for reproving him for negligence. Hard worker as Johnson was he barely made a living for himself and his wife.` Often he walked the streets at night for lack of a few pence for a lodging. But even in those pinching times he would put pennies into the hands of poor children sleeping in the streets.

Gradually Johnson's reputation grew; he became well-known to the publishers and booksellers of London. One, Robert Dodsley, suggested that an English dictionary would be well received by the public. Johnson had already dreamed of such a work, and when a combination of booksellers offered him a considerable sum for the undertaking, he accepted. But when one considers that the Dictionary took almost eight years to complete, and that Johnson had to pay his assistants out of his own pocket, one can see that he was not yet free from money worries. Nowadays Johnson's Dic-

WHERE JOHNSON WAS BORN
In this house at the corner of Market Street, Lichfield, Staffordshire, Dr. Johnson was born on September 18, 1709. The house is now a Johnson museum.

A. M. Broadley, Dr. Johnson and Mrs. Thrale, John Lane

DR. JOHNSON AT THE THRALES'
During the lifetime of Mrs. Thrale's first husband, Johnson
(left) was a frequent visitor at their house in Streatham
(now a London suburb). In this engraving by Isaac
Cruickshank he is seen at breakfast with the Thrales.

When Johnson had first come to London he had
found dinners for sixpence, and coffee-houses where
by paying threepence he spent long hours talking
to his friends. Good company and good dinners
he loved more than anything on earth. " I look
upon a day as lost," said he, " in which I do not
make a new acquaintance." He ate enormously
of such dishes as roast pork or veal pie stuffed with
plums and sugar. His tea-pot held two quarts—
as well it might, for he boasted of having drunk 25
cups at a sitting. To take dinner with Dr. Johnson
in one of the London taverns, and to hear his
brilliant, witty table-talk was considered a great
distinction, marking the recipient as a person of
intelligence, for it was well known that the great
literary " lion " did not tolerate fools or boors.

Thus grew up his famous Literary Club, which
included Garrick the actor, Reynolds the artist,
Gibbon the historian, Sheridan the playwright
and politician, Goldsmith the man of letters, Burke
the statesman, and others. There were women, too,
who enjoyed an evening of conversation with the
great man. They could hear him talk at the home
in Streatham of Henry Thrale, a wealthy brewer,
who was always a generous friend to him. There
he met " little Burney " (Fanny Burney) who wrote
the novel Evelina, and there he formed the friendship with Mrs. Thrale.

In 1763 James Boswell, a young Scots lawyer, met
Dr. Johnson and became his admirer and friend.
No words of his idol escaped him. He put them all
down on paper, and published them for the world
to read after Johnson's death. And they are well
worth reading. We see him as the tender-hearted
friend, the generous almsgiver, for in the last years
of his life he used his pension mainly for the poor.
We see his independence of thought and his stubborn prejudices. Boswell records such gems as :
" While you are considering which of two things you
should teach your child first, another boy has
learned them both"; "Life is a pill which none
of us can bear to swallow without gilding"; and
"It is better to live rich than to die rich." Boswell's
Life of Johnson preserves the picture of this
strange, uncouth, great-hearted man—so eccentric
that some were afraid of him, so learned and
brilliant in his talk that the proudest and best were
glad to gather at his feet. During
the years 1748–59 Johnson lived at
17, Gough Square, off Fleet Street,
London. His house is open to the
public as a museum of Johnson
relics. It was here that he compiled his Dictionary.

In addition to the Dictionary
(1748–55), Johnson wrote a novel,
Rasselas (1759) ; a play, Irene
(1737); some poems and essays in
the Rambler and the Idler.

tionary seems old-fashioned and unscientific; it
was, however, far better than those which preceded
it, and paved the way for the better ones which we
have today.

The Dictionary brought Johnson such fame that
the University of Oxford conferred upon him the
degree of Doctor of Laws (LL.D.).
But it did not bring him much
relief from poverty. In the 18th
century men were often given pen-
sions in recognition of literary
work or as a mark of political
favour. In 1762 the government
decided to bestow a pension of
£300 a year upon him. The
author of the Dictionary was
rather hesitant about accepting the
money. Had he not defined " pension " in his own pages as " pay
given to a state hireling for treason
to his country " ? Had he not
defined patriotism as " the last
refuge of a scoundrel " ? The
Prime Minister, Lord Bute, reassured him, saying the money was
being given him in recognition of
what he had done, not for what
he was to do.

Portrait by Van Dyck
INIGO JONES
Introducer of the Palladian style (an
adaptation of classical) into England,
this great architect died in 1652.

Jones, INIGO (1573–1652). Of
architects there are few whose
names survive their works, and
among these in England one of the
greatest is Inigo Jones. Born in
London on July 15, 1573, he
met as a young man a wealthy
patron who provided him with
the means for a European tour.

After visiting Venice, where he studied the work of Palladio, and Copenhagen, where he is said to have designed two royal palaces, he returned home in 1604, and was employed by the Prince of Wales as architect and designer for the court masques. He visited Italy again, 1612–13. In 1615 he was appointed surveyor-general; he designed the Queen's House at Greenwich in 1617, and in 1619 the Banqueting House at Whitehall.

His other principal works were the water-front of old Somerset House; Ashburnham House, Westminster; Wilton House; and Amesbury Abbey, Wilts, executed from his designs by his pupil John Webb. Jones was the first to introduce the Palladian style into England; in this style, the dignity and solidity of the finer classical architecture were combined by him with the direct, simple and more typically English manner. In the Civil War he was taken prisoner by the Roundheads, and was heavily fined. He returned to his profession in 1646. He died, like so many great men, in a state of poverty, on July 5, 1652. As a designer of masques he had as rival Ben Jonson, who refers to him in several satires.

Donald McLeish

INIGO JONES'S WORK IN WHITEHALL

In 1612 Inigo Jones was commissioned by King James I to design a new palace in Whitehall, London; the Banqueting House (above), which was intended as one side of a quadrangle that was never completed, was erected in 1622. A splendid example of the Palladian style, it now houses the museum of the Royal United Service Institution.

Jones, JOHN PAUL (1747–92). This American naval hero was born at Kirkbean, Kirkcudbrightshire, on July 6, 1747, went to sea at the age of 12, and soon rose to be skipper of a Whitehaven slaver. When 26 years old, Jones left the sea and settled in Virginia on a plantation. In 1775 he joined the American navy. That he was a born fighter is shown by his famous expression: " I do not wish to have command of any ship that does not sail fast, for I intend to go in harm's way."

In 1777 his exploits around the coast of Britain gained him fame as a daring commander. He destroyed the fort at Whitehaven, and captured the English frigate Drake. Returning to France, then an ally of America, he asked for, and received, a naval vessel which he named the Bonhomme Richard in compliment to Franklin, the American minister to France. With this vessel Jones fought a naval duel with the Serapis on September 23, 1779. After several hours of such fighting as had rarely been seen on the seas, the English commander called upon Jones to surrender; but although his ship was sinking, that intrepid commander retorted, " I have not yet begun to fight! " and in a short time he actually compelled the English ship to surrender to him.

Jones died in Paris, on July 18, 1792, and was buried in a Protestant cemetery in that city, but in 1905 his body was taken to America and interred at the United States Naval Academy at Annapolis. The name of Paul Jones is perpetuated in the dance introduced into England by American sailors at the end of the First World War (1914–18).

Jonson, BEN (1573?–1637). To have been a bricklayer at the building of Lincoln's Inn, London, and to be buried in Westminster Abbey under a slab bearing the words " O rare Ben Jonson," are facts showing that here was an exceptional man. It is true that even as a bricklayer with a trowel in his hand "he had a book in his pocket," but it was neither study nor learning which made Jonson famous. It was his amazing personality. He had run away from home as a boy, led a hard life in times of war as a private in the army, been in prison, killed a rival actor in a duel; yet he became one of the most famous poets, dramatists, and wits of his time, and the friend of Shakespeare.

He wrote the comedy, still regarded as a masterpiece, Every Man in his Humour, in which Shakespeare himself took a part at its first performance. In 1603 Shakespeare's own company performed Jonson's first tragedy, Sejanus, at the Globe Theatre, on Bankside, London.

For years Ben Jonson's pen produced comedies, masques, dramas, tragedies, poems and songs (including Drink to Me Only with Thine Eyes), as well as prose works. He was, moreover, one of the social idols of his day, and one of the leaders of the convivial clubs which were such a feature of London tavern life in the 17th century. One of his favourite resorts was the Mermaid Club in the Mermaid Tavern, in Cheapside, London, where he impressed younger writers with something of the power which Dr. Samuel Johnson was to exercise over a later generation. Here Shakespeare, Jonson, Beau-

After Gerard Honthorst
'O RARE BEN JONSON'
After Shakespeare and Marlowe, Ben Jonson ranks as the greatest of the Elizabethan dramatists. His plays, however, brought him no great monetary reward, and he died in poverty. As a scholar he towered far above the rank and file.

mont, Fletcher, and other great literary men of the time were wont to foregather. For his satire on the Scots he was imprisoned, but he contrived to reinstate himself in favour and later became Poet Laureate and was granted a State pension of £200 a year.

Jordaens, JAKOB (1593–1678). Considered the greatest contemporary Flemish painter after Peter Paul Rubens (1577–1640), Jordaens was born at Antwerp on May 19, 1593. He painted his masterpiece, The Triumph of Prince Frederick Henry of Nassau, as wall decorations for the house of Princess Amelia of Orange, near The Hague, the Netherlands. He died at Antwerp on October 18, 1678.

Jordan. Until quite recently the kingdom of Transjordan (*q.v.*) lay wholly east of the Jordan river (which then formed the frontier between Palestine and Transjordan), but now the country claims a large part of Arab Palestine. This would extend it to both banks of the river. In 1949 the Emir Abdullah, ruler of Transjordan, changed the name to the Hashimite Kingdom of the Jordan.

JOSEPH AND BENJAMIN
The French artist, J. James Tissot (1836–1902) depicts Joseph, in the wig and girdled skirt of the ancient Egyptians, speaking to his brother Benjamin, while his elder brothers kneel before him.

Joseph. The story of Joseph in the Old Testament is one of the masterpieces of literature. The patriarch Jacob gave Joseph, first-born son of his favourite wife, Rachel, a " coat of many colours " as a token that Joseph should succeed him as chief of the tribe of Israel. Jealousy flamed among the 10 elder brothers, and as Joseph tended his sheep at Dothan in the land of Canaan his brothers sold him to Ishmaelite traders, who carried him into slavery in Egypt. The brothers dipped the coat in the blood of a kid, and Jacob cried when he saw it: " An evil beast hath devoured him! " Potiphar, an officer of Egypt's Pharaoh, bought Joseph, and made him master of his household. Potiphar's wife, by false charges, caused him to be cast into prison, but Pharaoh made him his Prime Minister when Joseph interpreted his dreams to mean that Egypt faced seven years of plenty and then seven years of famine. In the years of plenty Joseph stored up great quantities of grain. In the years of famine Joseph's 10 elder brothers and Benjamin, younger than Joseph, went to Egypt to buy grain, and Joseph eventually installed his father and Jacob's whole tribe in Egypt.

Josephine, MARIE ROSE, EMPRESS OF THE FRENCH (1763–1814). In Martinique in the French West Indies is the statue of a woman. It is that of Josephine, daughter of Joseph Tascher de la Pagerie, a native of Martinique, who was raised by her second husband, Napoleon Bonaparte, to the position of Empress of the French.

When, as Madame de Beauharnais, a widow with two children, she married Bonaparte, he was a little-known artillery officer. She gave him a social acquaintance he had not had before, for she was a conspicuous figure in Parisian society. By cleverly pretending to hold republican principles, she had barely escaped the guillotine on which her first husband, General Beauharnais, had perished during the Reign of Terror. Thereafter she had made her way in society by use of her wits and charm.

It was with reluctance that she had been induced to marry the rising young commander, who was then desperately in love with her. But within 10 years he had made her Empress of the French, a position for which she was fitted by the charm and graciousness which concealed a limited education.

Napoleon's love, however, cooled. In 1809, in spite of her tears and entreaties, she was forced to consent to a divorce. Napoleon wished to secure an heir to his throne and to ally himself with the royal families of Europe, and soon afterward he married Marie Louise of Austria. After the divorce

JOSEPHINE CROWNED EMPRESS BY NAPOLEON
Born on June 24, 1763, on the island of Martinique in the French West Indies, Josephine married Napoleon Bonaparte in
1796, two years after her first husband had been executed as an enemy of the French Revolution. This painting depicts
Napoleon crowning Josephine Empress of the French in 1804 ; five years later he divorced her.

Josephine lived at La Malmaison, near Paris, where
she died on May 24, 1814. During her later years
she exerted every effort to secure peace.

Josephine's two children by her first marriage
were Eugène and Hortense. Eugène proved an
able and loyal general under Napoleon, and was for
a time viceroy of Italy. Hortense married Napoleon's brother, Louis, King of Holland, and became
the mother of Napoleon III (*q.v.*).

Joule, JAMES PRESCOTT (1818–89). The
science of heat, as we know it today, was established
by three men : Count Rumford (*q.v.*), Sir Humphry
Davy (*q.v.*), and James Joule, the Manchester
physicist. For practical purposes, the work of
Joule had the greatest bearing on the utilization of
heat for mechanical power.

Born at Salford on December 24, 1818, Joule
studied under the great John Dalton (*q.v.*), founder
of the atomic theory. Later, he investigated the
phenomena of magnetism and electricity, and it
was in the course of experiments to find a method
of measuring electricity that Joule in 1843 first
ascertained the mechanical equivalent of heat.
For 40 years he studied and experimented on the
problem of translating heat energy into terms of
mechanical work. What is now known as Joule's
Law is based on this work and states that the heat
required to raise one pound of water by $1°$ Fahrenheit ($=$ 1 British Thermal Unit) is equivalent to

the mechanical force needed to raise 778 lb.
through a distance of one foot. (*See* Heat).

Joule made innumerable experiments, extending
over a period of six years. At length he obtained his
sought-for equivalent by causing a kind of paddle
wheel to rotate in a vessel of water, and measuring
the rise in temperature of the water recorded on a
delicate thermometer. At the top of the paddle
spindle, above the water vessel, was a drum upon
which was coiled a cord. The end of this cord was
led over a pulley and attached to a weight. Joule
disconnected the cord from the spindle, and raised
the weight to the highest point; then he connected
the cord to the spindle, and let fall the weight.
The latter pulled on the cord, turned the spindle,
and caused the paddles to turn round in the water.
By observing the distance the weight fell in causing
a given rise in temperature of the water, Joule
obtained the value of 772 foot-pounds for the
mechanical equivalent of heat. When later
investigators, with better apparatus and more
delicate measuring instruments at their disposal,
made similar experiments, they established the
equivalent at 778 foot-pounds, which is the value
accepted today. Joule's work, in his day, was a
triumph of patient and careful experiment.

Joule received many honours, being elected
F.R.S. in 1850 and receiving in 1860 the Copley
medal of the Royal Society. He collaborated

with Lord Kelvin (*q.v.*) in researches into the properties of gases. It was then that Joule realized the value of surface condensation in increasing the efficiency of steam-engines. The Royal Society supplied him with money to pursue his investigations, and the result was the improvement of condensers, a most important advance in marine steam-engines. He died on October 11, 1889. The joule, the unit of " work," is named after him. It is equivalent to 10,000,000 ergs. One calorie is equivalent to 4·186 joules.

Jujitsu. According to a Japanese dictionary, this Japanese art of self-defence, which is also called Ju-Jutsu or Judo, was invented by the Chinese as a form of torture and improved by the Japanese for self-defence and physical training more than 2,000 years ago. It enables the weak to overcome the strong by the scientific use of leverage and balance, much as heavy weights can be controlled by a lever operated by a man who without it would have no power over them. Leverage is applied to the assailant's limbs, which can be broken by anyone of average strength. Joints can be dislocated and muscles torn by forcing the limbs into unnatural positions, called locks.

In this form of wrestling the nerves are pressed against bones, causing great pain and also a feeling of numbness akin to the sensation known as pins and needles. Arteries are knocked and pressed, and unconsciousness can be produced.

Jujitsu locks can be applied in a standing position or when prone on the ground. The expert uses strategy when defending himself or seeking an opportunity to apply a lock. He will give way to his opponent momentarily, the better to obtain victory. He may suddenly throw his hat or handkerchief in his opponent's face, temporarily obscuring his vision, and thus secure a lock or throw him.

The throws in jujitsu are very violent, the object being to pitch the opponent on to his head, shoulder or spine. When an attack is made the jujitsu exponent may retreat, and then, as his assailant advances and brings forward his leg, the exponent taps it with the sole of his foot at the knee or ankle, causing the other to trip. The throws by leverage on the body are effected with the thighs, hips and shoulders. In tripping and throwing his opponent the wrestler makes good use of his enemy's coat collar, lapels and sleeves to obtain the grip he wants or to throw him off his balance.

A jujitsu expert rarely gets hurt in falling or being thrown, because he will have practised the breakfall, the object of which is to save falling (or being thrown) on a joint or on the head. To break the force of a fall, the expert straightens his arm quickly and strikes the floor sharply with the palm of the hand a second before the body touches the ground. When falling or being thrown straight forward on to the face, the expert keeps his body and legs straight and the head in a line with the tensed muscles of the neck ; the ground is struck with the forearms and palms of the hands, the arms being bent in the act of falling. The breakfall is useful in other directions, as on the football field.

Jung, CARL GUSTAVE (born 1875). Few doctors have devoted themselves so entirely to the study of mental life, usually called psychology, as has this brilliant Swiss scientist. Born at Basle, Switzerland, on July 26, 1875, Jung graduated in medicine at the university there, then went to Paris to continue his studies. At this time Freud (*q.v.*), the " father of psycho-analysis," was expounding his new theories of mental action, behaviour, and abnormal impulses, and Jung was irresistibly drawn to him. He joined Freud, and devoted himself to the study of mental diseases.

Returning to Switzerland, Jung became physician at the Psychiatric (mental diseases) Clinic at Zürich, Switzerland, and lecturer in the same subject at the university. Here he discarded the chief theories of his master, Freud, and invented his system of analytical psychology, based on an ingenious theory that divides people into two main groups— introverts, or those whose mental processes are governed from within their own consciousness ; and extroverts, or those whose impulses are influenced largely by their environment.

Thus, introverts are unsociable and outwardly unemotional, prone to think and read in solitude ; while extroverts are lively, essentially sociable and readily free to express their emotions, and generally are fonder of music, pictures or anything possessing sensuous beauty than of study. These extreme cases are, of course, comparatively rare.

His chief works include Psychoanalysis (1912), Psychology of the Unconscious (1916), Studies in Word Association (1916), Analytical Psychology (1917), Psychological Types (1923), and Modern Man in Search of a Soul (1933).

Juniper. Peculiar among conifers is the juniper, on account of the fact that its cones are round and berry-like with blue-black fleshy scales.

Natural History Museum

TWISTED JUNIPER TREE
Frequently growing on bare hillsides, the juniper is a tree that is often bent into strange shapes by the force of the wind. The wood is red like that of the yew, and the whole plant has a strong odour of turpentine. The berries are used as a flavouring.

The needle-like foliage is dull green, and the wood red, like that of the yew. The whole plant has a strong odour of turpentine.

There are several species, widely distributed throughout the cooler parts of the Northern Hemisphere. The one known in Europe is the common juniper (*Juniper communis*), which grows specially on limestone hills. It is often more like a shrub than a tree. The berries are used to flavour a certain kind of gin.

Juno. The chief Roman goddess and the wife of Jupiter was Juno, identified with the Greek goddess Hera. Juno, Jupiter and Minerva formed a trinity which was believed to watch over the Roman State. Juno was looked upon especially as the deity of women and marriage, and on March 1 of each year married women celebrated in her honour the festival of Matronalia, at which gifts of flowers were offered in her temple on the Esquiline Hill in Rome. In Roman art, Juno is often

British Museum
JUPITER, CHIEF ROMAN GOD
Although identified with the Greek god Zeus, Jupiter was regarded by the Romans as the father of the State. He is here seen with the three-headed dog Cerberus and an eagle, which signify that he is the ruler of the world below ground and the world above.

depicted riding in a chariot drawn by sacred peacocks.

One of the minor planets between Mars and Jupiter is named Juno. It has a diameter of about 120 miles and takes just over four years to go around the sun.

Jupiter. In Roman mythology, this deity was identified with the Greek god Zeus. Jupiter was first associated with the heavens, and with rain, thunder, and lightning, and with the growth of the fruits of the field. He then came to be regarded as the god of hospitality, truth, and justice in local and international relations. A further development of his functions was that of a war god and giver of victory. His temple on the Capitoline Hill, the shrine of Jupiter Optimus Maximus (best and greatest), was regarded as the heart of the Roman State.

The name Jupiter is also given to the largest of the major planets, which has an equatorial diameter of 88,770 miles. The average distance of the planet from

From the drawing by G. F. Morell
JUPITER, THE GIANT OF THE SOLAR SYSTEM
Were the planet Jupiter as near to us as the moon, it would appear as awe-inspiring as it does in this picture. Its colossal size may be gauged by comparison with the moon (marked M) and the constellation of Orion (right). Jupiter has 11 satellites, one of which (Io) is 261,000 miles from the planet, so this view of Jupiter is very similar to that which an inhabitant of Io might see. The dark streaks and white spots on Jupiter's disk are storms passing through its atmosphere.

the sun is 483,900,000 miles, and it travels around the sun once in about 12 years. The planet Jupiter is curiously marked with dark and light bands, and it has 11 satellites.

Jura Mountains. (Pron. jŏŏ′-ra).

The same titanic upheaval which crumpled the earth's crust and formed the Alps produced the comparatively low Jura Mountains, on the border of France and Switzerland. These mountains cannot boast the grandeur and beauty of the Alps, and the area covered by them is but a small part of that of the Alps. The highest peak, Crête de la Neige, is 5,654 feet, and the average height about 2,600 feet.

The Jura range is 156 miles long by 38 miles broad, and is situated between the Rhine and the Rhône valleys. Except in its central portion the range is pierced by deep ravines and valleys. On the west the mountains descend by gentle slopes to the fertile plains of France, but the eastern side is precipitous.

At the extreme north end of the range is the Belfort Gap, a broad pass in low rolling hills between the Vosges and Jura Mountains. This pass may well be called the " front door of France," for it opens on the most beautiful, fertile, and prosperous section of the country and is the natural highway between eastern France and central Europe. In 1870 this was one of the roads by which German forces invaded France.

The peasants pasture their flocks on the grassy uplands of the Jura, and some farming is carried on. There are vineyards in the more sheltered valleys. Mining is of little importance. The mountains are sparsely wooded, though the south-west section is noted for wooden toys manufactured from boxwood which grows in the mountains.

Jury. A jury is a body of men, or of men and

women, sworn to try any matter of fact and to declare the truth according to the evidence given before them and as directed on law by the presiding judge. The jury sits in an enclosed space at the side of the judge in the court-room. They listen to the evidence tendered by the witnesses, to the statement of the case by the lawyers, and to the accused's defence, in criminal cases, or the arguments on behalf of defendants in civil actions, and to the judge's instructions to them on the law and the evidence in the case. Then they retire to a private room where they are locked in. The judge may keep them there as long as he thinks there is a reasonable hope of their agreeing. When they return to the court they have usually all agreed, and in criminal cases the fate of the prisoner depends upon the verdict of "guilty" or "not guilty," read by the "foreman," whom they have chosen. And in civil actions their verdict will decide which side has to pay damages and, perhaps, the costs of the proceedings. The jury in England is the sole judge of the facts; they must take the law from the judge. They are absolutely independent. If they have not agreed they are dismissed and a new trial is held.

Qualification of Jurymen and Women

In all criminal cases an acquittal is conclusive. If, however, the evidence is clearly insufficient to establish guilt, the judge may direct a verdict of not guilty or, after a verdict of guilty, may grant a new trial if it appears that legal error was permitted in the conduct of the case. In criminal cases the jury's verdict must be unanimous in England. Such a jury is a " petty jury." In England a majority verdict may be agreed on in civil cases. Under Scottish law a majority verdict is allowed, and there is a choice of three verdicts— " Guilty," " Not Guilty " and " Not Proven."

The general qualification of a juryman or woman is that he or she be between the ages of 21 and 60, and owns a certain amount of freehold or leasehold property ; or that he or she is a householder. A juryman summoned cannot refuse to serve and can be punished severely for failure to appear when summoned.

Until 1933 the " grand jury " was in general use throughout England. Its duty was to decide after hearing the preliminary evidence against a man, whether the State should accuse him of a crime and hold him for trial. When it was first instituted, probably in the reign of Henry II (1154–89), the grand jury system enabled a charge to be brought against an evil-doer by a group of persons, without fear of vengeance such as might be wreaked upon an individual accuser. This grand jury, or great jury, usually had 23 members, though the number varied, at times being only 12. Whatever the number on the grand jury, 12 members had to agree. If they thought from the evidence which they

JURY LISTENING TO A JUDGE SUMMING UP

Trial by jury, like many other popular institutions and legal rights established in almost every civilized country in the world, derives from England, where it is still regarded as one of the safeguards of the liberty of the people. Here a jury is listening to a judge's summing-up of a case before retiring to consider their verdict.

TRIAL BY A JURY OF THANES IN THE DAYS OF KING ALFRED
Until 1933 the grand jury was in general use in England, and this picture by C. W. Cope (1811–90) portrays an Anglo-Saxon institution which resembled it. The twelve senior thanes (class of soldiers and landholders) of a district heard the charges against any man accused and determined whether the evidence warranted holding him for a test of his guilt.

had heard that the accused was probably guilty, they indicted him or "brought in a true bill," and then he was tried by a petty jury. Cases usually came before a grand jury as a result of activity by the police, sheriff, or coroner. The grand jury—the oldest and probably the original type of jury—was abolished generally in 1933, and is now used only for certain types of cases in London and Middlesex.

Coroner and Procurator Fiscal

Besides the petty and grand juries there is also the "coroner's jury," consisting of a minimum of seven or a maximum of 11 jurymen. This is summoned by the coroner in case of a sudden or violent death to decide whether the death was due to murder, suicide, accident, or natural causes, and therefore whether some person under suspicion of causing the death should not be held for further investigation. In Scotland there are no coroners and so no coroner's juries; this function is performed in that country by an official known as the Procurator Fiscal.

In civil cases—that is, in controversies between individuals—juries are widely used to decide questions of fact. The judge applies the law to the facts as the jury finds them to be, and renders judgement. In certain circumstances the judge can direct a verdict, or if a verdict is manifestly improper he can set it aside. Usually juries in such cases are not confined during the trial, as they are in important criminal cases.

The right of trial by jury is one of the most cherished rights of the Anglo-Saxon nations. Of all our institutions—legislatures, courts, etc.—the jury is one of the oldest, and its development one of the chief gifts of England to the rest of the world. The Normans made use of the most primitive form after they conquered England in 1066. The men who served at these "inquests," as they were then called, had to know the facts themselves instead of learning them from witnesses. This sworn inquest was used chiefly by the king in transacting the business of the kingdom, but it represented also a notable participation by the freemen in the most important matters of government. Not until the reign of Henry II in the latter half of the 12th century were jurors changed from those who decided on the ground of what they knew to men who would decide solely on the evidence that they heard in court.

But how, you ask, were the trials conducted when they did not use a jury? In Anglo-Saxon times, when a man accused of a crime could bring into court a sufficient number of his neighbours who were willing to swear to his innocence he was released. In this trial by compurgation the number of compurgators depended upon the rank of the men who took the oath, and the importance of the case.

Then there was the trial by ordeal, which was really an appeal to God for a miracle to "make manifest the innocent and confound the guilty." In the ordeal by hot water or by hot iron, the accused plunged his hand into boiling water or carried a red-hot iron a certain distance; if the hand healed in three days, the accused was innocent. In the ordeal by cold water the accused was thrown into running water with hands and feet tied together; if he floated he was guilty, but if he sank he was innocent and was quickly hauled out.

Also there was the trial by combat, or judicial duel, in which a man proved his case by defeating his adversary in battle. As late as 1817 a man in England appealed to the old forgotten law of trial by combat, which was still on the statute book. His accuser refused the challenge, and the man was freed. But trial by jury had been in use for centuries before that, and the old law was repealed the next year.

Justinian I, EMPEROR OF THE EASTERN ROMAN EMPIRE (483?–565).
Most illustrious of all the emperors of the Eastern Roman or Byzantine Empire, Justinian earned the title of " the Great." To him the world today owes a greater debt than to any other of the long line of emperors of the Eastern Empire, for through him we received the Roman law in a usable form. At his direction the Code, containing the decrees of the Emperors, was com-

Alinari

JUSTINIAN THE GREAT
Emperor of the Eastern Roman or Byzantine Empire, Justinian I is commemorated by some remarkable mosaics at Ravenna, Italy. The above portrait is in the Basilica of St. Apollinare Nuovo.

piled; this was followed by the Digest or Pandects—a summary of the opinions of lawyers and judges who had interpreted these decrees; and there was the Institutes, a text-book for students of law. These works form the basis of the civil law of several European nations, including France and Italy.

Justinian's parents were peasants, but he received a good education through his uncle, the Emperor Justin I, whom he succeeded as emperor in 527.

Justinian's ambition was to restore the grandeur of the empire, and he had the rare faculty of choosing the most competent people as his helpers. His wife, the Empress Theodora, was a brilliant woman, who increased the splendour of the court while she tyrannized over the nobles and magistrates. When Justinian would have fled during an insurrection her firmness kept him on the throne. In Belisarius and Narses the Emperor found commanders well qualified to lead in the great work of conquest. They reconquered both North Africa and Italy.

As a builder Justinian constructed churches, aqueducts, forts, and hospitals throughout his empire. The greatest of his buildings was the domed cathedral of St. Sophia in Constantinople, his capital city. Unfortunately, his people were burdened with heavy taxes to pay for all this magnificence, and he left at his death on November 14, 565, an empire well on the way to decline.

Jute. Sacking of various kinds is made from fibres obtained from the stalks of the jute plant, which is grown in the sub-continent of India, chiefly in Bengal and Assam. There are two varieties, both members of the genus *Corchorus*. The stalks are cut while the plants are still in flower, and, placed in stagnant water, are left until the bark can be easily separated from the tough fibre. The fibre is dried in the sun, pressed into bales, and taken to factories where it is spun into jute yarn or woven into gunny cloth or sacking. The best grades of fibre are used in cheap tapestries, stair carpets, carpet backings, and stiff linings. Jute is, in effect, a coarser flax or hemp, and is inferior to hemp in strength and durability. Calcutta and Dundee are the two main centres of the jute industry.

JUTE WAREHOUSE IN BENGAL
Most of the world's jute comes from the sub-continent of India. The bulk of it is grown in Bengal and sent to Calcutta to be woven into coarse cloth, called hessian, or sacking. Jute is soaked in water to enable the fibres to be separated from the stalk, and in this shed the dried fibre is being sorted prior to going to the mills.

K

Kaleidoscope. Since its invention by Sir David Brewster in 1817, the kaleidoscope has given pleasure to millions. It is one of the most interesting of scientific toys, presenting a beautiful and ever-changing series of bright and coloured patterns. The simplest form is a tube about 12 inches long and 3 inches in diameter. Through this tube run three mirrors which form a hollow triangle inside the tube.

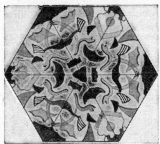

A KALEIDOSCOPE PATTERN

At one end there is a little compartment with bits of coloured glass of various sizes and shapes. The outer end of this compartment is clouded glass, and the inner end is clear glass. At the top of the outside tube is a small eye piece. When the tube is turned, the coloured bits fall into different positions and, being reflected and multiplied in the mirrors, give rise to an endless variety of regular patterns.

Kamchatka. (Pron. kam-chat'-ka). This peninsula of eastern Siberia stretches into the Pacific, between the Bering Sea on the east and the Sea of Okhotsk on the west, for a distance of 750 miles. It covers an area of 105,000 square miles, but the population is under 10,000.

Fishing and hunting constitute the chief occupations, and furs are the most valuable production. The peninsula contains volcanoes, both extinct and active, one of which reaches 16,000 feet. Kamchatka was annexed by Russia at the close of the 17th century.

Kangaroo. When Captain James Cook was exploring the coast of Australia in 1770 his men were amazed by a strange animal. At times it stood upright, braced on its hind legs and huge tail. It moved by prodigious leaps. Thus white men first met the great gray kangaroo.

More than 100 species of the kangaroo family live in the open spaces of Australia, New Guinea and near-by islands. They belong to the marsupial order (animals that carry their young in pouches). Kangaroos are distinguished by a remarkable adaptation of body form for jumping.

The great gray kangaroo reaches a weight of 200 lb. and a length of 10 feet from nose to tip of tail. The tail alone is about four feet long, and the powerful muscles at the base make it nearly as thick as the animal's body. On each of the hind feet are four toes. The second from the outside is much stronger and longer than the others and ends in a huge claw. This toe and the shorter outside toe are used in the leaps that can carry the kangaroo at 40 miles an hour. The two slender inside toes are closely joined by a growth of skin and are used only for scratching. Three-fourths of the animal's bulk lies in its hindquarters. The front legs are short and slender, with small five-toed paws. These are used like hands in grasping food, but are drawn up against the breast in jumping.

The female has a large pouch on the abdomen, formed by a fold in the soft furry skin. When the single, inch-long, naked young is born, it finds shelter in this pouch. There it attaches itself to one of the mother's nipples, which swell inside its mouth so that for several weeks the young kangaroo cannot loosen its grip. It is unable at first to draw out milk for itself or to swallow it. The mother is provided with muscles for pumping her milk down the tiny throat. After about four months the young kangaroo is able to lean out of the sheltering pouch and nibble grass when its mother bends over to

Australian National Travel Association

A KANGAROO SHOWS ITS PACES

You have heard how a kangaroo can hop, but you are not likely to see many photos like this one showing it in action. Notice the tremendously long hind legs and the great thickness of the tail, which acts as a balancer when it leaps and as a support when it rests. The front legs, with clawed feet, are held tucked up to the chest, while the small size of the body assists 'streamlining.'

graze. Presently it climbs out and learns to hop around in search of food, but continues for several weeks longer to climb back into the pouch for sleep and safety. If a sudden danger threatens while the young kangaroo is some distance away, the mother will start towards it at full speed, gather it up in her forepaws as she passes, and tuck it into her pouch without seeming to check her flight.

Nearly as large as the great gray kangaroo are the red kangaroo and the more stocky wallaroo. Next in size are various species popularly known as wallabies. These larger types are usually found in small groups that move from place to place, feeding on grass, shrubs, and the leaves of small trees. Their keen noses, ears and eyes warn them of danger from hunters or from dingoes or wild dogs—their only important foes. Kangaroos are hunted because of the damage they do to crops and for their tender flesh; their skins produce fine flexible leather, suitable for gloves and light shoes.

Timid as it is, the kangaroo fights desperately when cornered. It stamps its hind feet and growls. With its front paws it tries to push attackers down within reach of a forward-slashing blow from the terrible claws on its back feet. It can rip a dog to death with a single stroke. When pursued by a pack, a kangaroo sometimes takes to the water, and if a dog swims out in pursuit the kangaroo seizes it and holds it under the surface until it is drowned.

The smaller kangaroos, such as the rock wallabies, the hare wallabies, and the rat-kangaroos, live in secluded retreats among cliffs or dense thickets. A few species have become adapted to tree life. These tree kangaroos have much shorter hind legs and longer forelegs than the others of the family. They do not hop but climb among the branches like small slender bears. Some of these smaller kangaroos eat berries and small insects as well as grass and leaves.

Fossil remains of about 30 different kangaroo species have been found in Australia. Among them were several giant types, one of which is estimated to have stood fully 10 feet tall. Kangaroos constitute the family *Macropodidae* of the marsupial order (*Marsupialia*). The great gray kangaroo is *Macropus giganteus*.

Kansas, United States. Occupying the geographical centre of the United States, Kansas is a land of undulating prairies, with no mountains, no marshes, few navigable rivers and only a few small lakes. It is bounded on the north by Nebraska, on the east by Missouri and the Missouri river, on the south by Oklahoma, and on the west by Colorado. It has an area of 82,276 square miles. The State is liable to blizzards and tornadoes, and to droughts, but by careful irrigation has attained fourth position amongst the wheat-producing States.

Besides wheat, the principal crops include maize, rye, barley, flax, sugar-beet and fruit. In the western part of the State, where insufficient rainfall does not permit the cultivation of cereal crops, there is ample pasture for millions of cattle and pigs bred for the meat-packing industry. The chief minerals are coal, natural gas, oil, zinc, lead, salt and limestone. The industries include meat-packing, and manufactures of steel, aeroplanes, motor-cars, agricultural machinery, and cement. Topeka is the capital. The population of Kansas is 1,801,000.

Central Press

HOW THE KANGAROO CARRIES HER BABY

The kangaroo belongs to the strange group of animals called, on account of the pouch in which they carry their young, marsupials. In this picture you see the pouch in use; in it is comfortably housed the baby kangaroo, its head looking out to survey the world. Even with this weight the mother kangaroo can hop many feet at a time and keep up a great speed.

Kant, IMMANUEL (1724–1804). Just as the study of Nature and the wonders of creation has been the passion and the life-work of many of the

IMMANUEL KANT
Born at Königsberg, East Prussia, in 1724, Kant became professor of logic and metaphysics at the university there in 1770. His great service to philosophy was his endeavour to find a bond of union between materialism and idealism.

did this great modern philosopher obtain an education. His life was devoted to study, to lengthy writings on philosophy, and to his duties as lecturer and professor at the university of his native city. He died at Königsberg in 1804. The best-known works of Kant are Dreams of a Visionary (1766); Critique of Pure Reason (1781); Prolegomena (1783); Critique of Practical Reason (1788); and Critique of Judgement (1790).

Kapok. The seed-hairs contained in the pods of certain plants give some of our most valuable fibres for weaving into cloth; cotton is an example. The pods of the kapok tree furnish fibre unsuited for weaving, but most useful because of the air-spaces which make these fibres into tubes. Life-belts and life-saving jackets for seamen are filled with the soft, downy fibre, which has six times the supporting power of cork. The same reason—air content—makes kapok useful in a hundred other ways: airmen's clothing is lined with the fibre as an insulation against cold; refrigerator casings are packed with kapok to keep out the heat; mattresses and cushions are stuffed with kapok because the air entrapped in the delicate tubular fibres gives springiness to the mattress or cushion. Children's cuddly toys are filled with the fibre; they can be squeezed, and will return to the original form again.

Kapok comes from a tree (*Eriodendron anfractuosum*) of the natural order *Malvaceae*, which includes

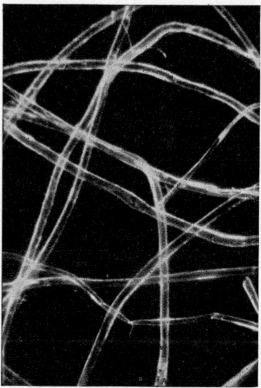

Dry Zero Corporation
KAPOK FIBRES MAGNIFIED
Clearly seen as air-filled tubes, these kapok fibres are magnified 110 times. The inner-air space accounts for their buoyancy and insulating properties. Kapok is used in life-saving equipment instead of cork.

greatest intellects, so also the study of the human mind, the subject to which Immanuel Kant devoted his great gifts, has attracted the deepest thinkers in all ages. But while the average man can follow the researches of naturalists, he is generally somewhat perplexed by abstract philosophy.

The chief propositions of Kant's theory of knowledge, as they emerge through the maze of words, are the following: We cannot know things as they really *are*, but only as they *appear* to us, since they are modified by the "categories" (*i.e.* mental "frames" or divisions, into which all objects of thought might be classified), and by passing through the medium of space and time. Experience alone supplies us with the knowledge, and it is impossible, by the exercise of thought, to attain to the knowledge of anything beyond such material. On this basis Kant builds his theory. The person who would read and understand the philosophy of Kant must be at least familiar with logic and metaphysics. And to appreciate Kant's finer shades of meaning the reader should be able to read him in German.

Immanuel Kant was born at Königsberg, in East Prussia, on April 22, 1724. He was the son of a saddler, and only by the self-denial of his parents

the hollyhock and the mallows. It grows in tropical or semi-tropical climes, reaching a height of about 40 feet or more. The seed capsules are

Leaves and flowers of the kapok tree, with a seed-pod on the right.

filled with the fluffy down, composed of the innumerable hairs attached to the seeds. A mature tree yields about 60 lb. of cleaned fibre every year; about double this weight of seeds is obtained, and they are pressed to extract the oil, which is made into soap. Java and Central America supply most of the kapok fibre of commerce. The greater part comes from wild trees; in plantations, the seedlings anchor themselves by a long tap-root and begin to bear useful pods in five to seven years. It is the smoothness of the fibres which prevents them being spun into yarn for weaving, thus differing from those of the cotton plant.

Karachi, (Pron. ka-rah'-chi), Pakistan. Capital of the Dominion of Pakistan, and the seaport of the province of Sind, Karachi stands at the western end of the Indus delta on an arm of the Arabian Sea. Cotton goods are manufactured, and there is a trade in salt; but the city is important chiefly as the outlet for the rich crops, mainly wheat, of the Punjab and Sind. The wharves and docks of the modern port are on the island of Keamari, which is joined to Karachi by the three-miles-long Napier Mole. The port lies on air routes from Europe to the East and Australasia. The population is 359,500.

Kashmir. In the north of the sub-continent of India, reaching from the plains of the Punjab northward over the western Himalaya ranges to the borders of Tibet, lies the mountainous state of Kashmir (or Cashmere). It is a region of wild and gorgeous scenery, of snow-crowned summits, cut by deep gorges and valleys filled with rich and varied vegetation. It is traversed by the River Indus, and in the south-west the valley of the upper Jhelum widens out to form the Vale of Kashmir—about 20 miles wide and encircled by mountain spurs which rise 14,000 and 15,000 feet above sea-level. Here rice, buckwheat, and barley are grown. Within the vale lies the summer capital and largest city of Kashmir, Srinagar. It stands on both sides of the Jhelum, 5,000 feet above sea level. The winter capital is Jammu, near the Punjab border.

Although Kashmir has an area of 82,258 square miles, much of it is wild, uninhabited mountain country, and the greater part of the population is gathered in the south-western part. Its cool, healthy climate makes it a summer resort in normal times. From the wool of its goats, yaks and wild sheep are made the celebrated "Cashmere" woollen goods, especially shawls. Carpet making has to some extent replaced the shawl trade, and the most thriving industry today is that of silk weaving. The rose fields of the Vale of Kashmir give the finest attar, and Srinagar is noted for its silver work and wood carving. The natives are a fair, handsome race; most of them are Mahomedans, but there

are also a number of Hindus, Sikhs, and Buddhists. The ruler is a Hindu maharajah officially called by the title of the maharajah of Jammu and Kashmir.

Possessing no railways, and connected with the sub-continent of India by roads which are often blocked with snow during the winter months, Kashmir has always been a backward State. But the construction of hydro-electric installations at Jammu, the establishing of salt factories, and the introduction of compulsory education have contributed to progress.

After the creation of the Dominions of Pakistan and India in August 1947 the Maharajah and the non-Mahomedan section of the people wished to join the Dominion of India, while the Mahomedans were in favour of union with Pakistan. Fighting broke out, and in October 1947 tribesmen from Pakistan invaded Kashmir to help their fellow-Mahomedans. The Government of Kashmir accused Pakistan of assisting the raiders and of preventing food and other necessities reaching the country. Kashmir's accession to India was announced on October 27, 1947, and troops from the Dominion of India went to aid the Maharajah's forces. The matter was referred to the Security Council of the United Nations, but a settlement had still to be reached in early 1950.

Fox

A GARDEN IN KASHMIR
Perhaps the most famous garden in the sub-continent of India is the Shalimar Bagh (above) on the shores of the Dal Lake in the Vale of Kashmir. It is laid out with terraces and ornamental waters, and there are about 150 small fountains like those shown here.

Keats, JOHN (1795–1821). " Here lies one whose name was writ in water." That is the epitaph which the English poet John Keats wrote for himself in the melancholy days when he felt his death approaching and despaired of winning that fame for which he so ardently longed. Keats lived only a little more than 25 years, and his whole poetical career was but seven years long ; yet during this brief period he wrote some of the greatest poems in the English language, crowded with musical lines of exquisite and haunting beauty.

John Keats was the son of a livery-stable keeper. He passed his early years not close to Nature as did most of our poets but in the City of London. There was born in him an intense love of beauty, surpassing that of many other poets. " A thing of beauty is a joy for ever " is the first line of his Endymion, and in his Ode on a Grecian Urn, in which he seems to have caught much of the ancient Greeks' worship of beauty, he declares:

> Beauty is truth, truth beauty—that is all
> Ye know on earth, and all ye need to know.

Beauty was all in all to Keats. Unlike his great contemporaries Shelley and Wordsworth, he had no desire to reform the world or to teach a lesson. He was content if he could make us see and hear and feel with our own senses those marvellous forms and colours and sounds that his imagination produced.

Keats was apprenticed to a surgeon in early youth, but his heart was elsewhere. " I find I cannot exist without Poetry . . . without Eternal Poetry," he declared. In 1816 he became acquainted with Leigh Hunt, Benjamin Haydon the painter and, through Hunt, with Shelley. In the following year he gave up his apothecary work and devoted the rest of his short life to poetry. In 1818 his first long poem, Endymion, appeared. It was bitterly attacked by the reviewers, who overlooked its beauties and failed to see that its faults were due to immaturity. Other troubles crowded upon the young poet. He was in money difficulties, and he was tormented by a hopeless love affair. His health had begun to fail, and he rapidly developed consumption. In the autumn of 1820 he went to Italy, and early in the following year he died at Rome, where in the old Protestant cemetery he was buried. During the Second World War his tomb escaped damage, as also did the house in which he used to live.

Keats's chief poems are Endymion, Isabella, or The Pot of Basil, The Eve of St. Agnes, La Belle Dame Sans Merci, Ode

Will F. Taylor
KEATS'S HOUSE AT HAMPSTEAD
In 1818 John Keats went to live at Wentworth Place in Hampstead, London. Financial worries and an unhappy love affair tormented the poet while he was there. His health began to fail, and he developed consumption.

to a Nightingale, and a number of sonnets among which are On First Looking into Chapman's Homer. All were published between 1817 and 1820, at the time when Keats was living at Hampstead, London, first in Well Walk, then at a house called Wentworth Place (later Lawn Bank). This house is now preserved as a Keats Memorial House.

Kelvin, WILLIAM THOMSON, IST BARON. (1824–1907). Every English and American schoolboy knows the romantic story of the laying of the first successful transatlantic cable between Valentia Island, Ireland, and Newfoundland in 1865 (*see* Cable). Not everyone may know that it was largely the genius of William Thomson that made that epoch-making event possible. But for the delicate and sensitive receiving instruments he devised for the cable, the weak currents then able to be sent through its long mileage could not have been made to give any practical signals for the eye or ear of the operator.

Born in Belfast on June 26, 1824, young Thomson matriculated at 10 years of age, and entered Peterhouse, Cambridge, in 1841, when only 17. Four years later he was second wrangler and first Smith's prizeman. For about a year he studied in Paris under Regnault, the French physicist, but returned in 1846 to take the chair of natural philosophy at Glasgow University, being then only 22 years old.

For 53 years, until his retirement in 1899, he held this professorship with such distinction that

After the painting by W. Hilton, National Portrait Gallery
JOHN KEATS
In the last four years of his short life Keats wrote poems which are among the most beautiful in the English language. Endymion, his first long poem, which appeared in 1818, met with little success. Keats died in Italy in 1821.

he received practically every honour which the scientific world had to bestow. During this period, and even after his retirement, his output in theoretical science and practical inventions was prodigious. It is amazing to reflect how, in his spare time, he could occupy with complete success such an onerous post as electrical engineer for English, French, American, Brazilian, and West Indian cable companies, and also invent the mirror galvanometer, the siphon recorder, a new mariner's compass, the navigational sounding machine, and electrical measuring and recording machines.

It was Kelvin's investigation of the discharge of the Leyden jar (q.v.) in 1853 that partly gave Hertz the key to his electro-magnetic researches which resulted in the discovery of Hertzian waves and made wireless telegraphy possible (see Hertz). In his collaboration with Joule (q.v.) on expansions, pressure-temperature changes, and other phenomena

LORD KELVIN
Among the greatest scientists of the 19th century, William Thomson, Baron Kelvin invented or improved many scientific instruments. Knighted in 1866, he was made a peer in 1892.

of heat, Kelvin produced the absolute scale of temperatures (1848); and in 1851 his theory of the dynamic nature of heat.

Kelvin was knighted in 1866, made a peer in 1892, and given the Order of Merit in 1902. He was elected President of the British Association in 1871, of the Royal Society in 1890–95, and Chancellor of Glasgow University in 1904. Even after his retirement he worked on the theory of matter and electricity and magnetism. He died on December 17, 1907.

Kemal Ataturk

(1880–1938). Few men have led so full a life and survived so many dangers and difficulties as this man who became the first President of the Turkish republic. Mustapha, which was the name given him by his parents, was born in Salonika, Greece. He entered the army in 1904 and, brilliant at mathematics and all military work, soon found favour with his superiors. The name Kemal was given him at this time by one of his masters whose own name chanced to be Mustapha. Kemal means "perfection," so the name both distinguished the young man from his teacher and showed what the latter thought of him. As a soldier young Mustapha Kemal rose rapidly, but he took part in politics and became a leader of the revolutionary or Young Turk party, which comprised almost all the younger officers who wished to introduce western ideas into Turkey. He was arrested—and discharged—several times.

Shortly before the First World War (1914–18) he made plans for an elaborate defence of the Dardanelles. Thus it was that when the Turkish High Command had given up hope of preventing the Allied armies reaching Constantinople, Mustapha Kemal was given the task of checking their advance. This he succeeded in doing, and eventually the Allies evacuated the Gallipoli Peninsula. Against the Russians in the Caucasus, and then again against the British in Mesopotamia (now Iraq), he fought brilliantly, and although he was unable to save the situation in the latter country he made good what would otherwise have been a disastrous retreat. No sooner was the First World War over than Kemal was fighting the Greeks, who claimed part of Asia Minor, and against them he turned the whole tide of the war once he obtained the supreme command, being responsible in person for the Turkish victory at Smyrna in 1921.

All the while, Mustapha Kemal had two ideas at heart: the complete liberation of the Turkish nation from the despotic rule of the sultans and the placing of himself at the head of the people. Though he then held no political appointment he had a great deal of influence, and it was mainly at his instigation that the Turkish National Assembly (parliament) abolished the Sultanate in 1922.

Turkey was declared a Republic on October 29, 1923, with Kemal as its first President. He em-

KEMAL ATATURK
Founder of the Turkish Republic, which he established in 1923, Kemal Ataturk, here seen in civilian clothes, introduced reforms into his country and was the maker of modern Turkey. Formerly called Mustapha Kemal, in 1934 he took the name of Ataturk, meaning Father of the Turks.

barked at once on a policy for the modernisation of the country, ruling as a Dictator. The wearing of European hats and clothes was made compulsory; the practice of a man having more than one wife was abolished, and the wearing of veils by women was banned. In 1928 the Latin alphabet replaced the Arabic script which the Turks had used for centuries. In 1934 women were allowed to vote, Kemal taking the name of Ataturk (meaning father of the Turks) in the same year. He died on November 10, 1938, and was succeeded as president by Ismet Inönü.

Kemsley, James Gomer Berry, 1st Viscount (born 1883). Youngest of the three famous Berry brothers, Gomer Berry was born at Merthyr Tydfil, South Wales, on May 7, 1883. Some account of this family's achievements is given in our article on Lord Camrose (*see* page 675); and there, too, is told how, when the Berry Group of papers had grown to such an extent that a division of interests had become desirable, Lord Camrose took over the complete ownership of the Daily Telegraph and sold to his brother his shares in Allied Newspapers Ltd., whose title was changed to Kemsley Newspapers in 1943. Thereby Lord Kemsley assumed control of the Sunday Times, Daily Sketch and the Sunday Graphic, as well as numerous provincial journals. Created a baronet in 1928, Gomer Berry was raised to the peerage in 1936, when he chose the title of Baron Kemsley of Farnham Royal—the Buckinghamshire village in which he has his home. He was made a Viscount in 1945.

A knight of St. John and High Sheriff of Buckinghamshire in 1929, Lord Kemsley is known not only as a highly successful newspaper proprietor but also as a supporter of many a deserving charity.

Kenilworth. Situated in the heart of Warwickshire, this historic town is chiefly noted for its magnificent ruined castle, the walls of which enclose about seven acres. The castle, which dates back to the early 12th century and has a long and stirring history, is a prominent feature in Sir Walter Scott's Kenilworth. In this novel the story is told of how Queen Elizabeth came to the castle to visit Robert Dudley, Earl of Leicester (who had received the castle at the Queen's hands in 1562), and how the tragic heroine Amy Robsart met her mysterious death.

Amy had been secretly married to Leicester, who, however, had indulged in hopes of becoming the Queen's consort and so kept the marriage secret and his bride a prisoner at Cumnor Place, Berkshire. Amy escaped to Kenilworth and appealed to the Queen, but at this critical moment Robert Varney, Leicester's attendant, claimed her as *his* wife, saying that she was distraught. In Scott's version of her death Amy fell through a trap-door at Cumnor, as she was hastening, misled by Varney's imitation of Leicester's whistle, to meet her husband.

In spite of this tragedy, Elizabeth continued to favour Leicester, and in 1575 she was his guest at Kenilworth for 18 days, when there took place the entertainment described by Scott.

Kent. The south-easterly corner of England is one of the most historic localities on British soil. It abuts on the Strait of Dover, and its nearness to the Continent has repeatedly meant that here invaders have first sought a footing.

Kent, with an area of 1,525 square miles, is a beautiful and fertile county, with a mild climate. A striking physical feature is the range of chalk hills which crosses it from east to west, known as the North Downs. The River Medway divides the county into East Kent and West Kent, and such is local pride and tradition that a man born east of the Medway is called " a man of Kent," while one born west of the river is known as " a Kentish man." On that part of the Kent coast west of Margate the sea is constantly making inroads on the land, while at other low-lying points the land is being gradually extended by deposits left by the sea.

Possessing a fertile soil, and long famous for its fruit, Kent is known as the Garden of England. Market-gardening and sheep-raising are among the important industries. Its hop-fields are unrivalled, and the district known as the Weald, and those districts along the banks of the Thames and Medway comprise some of the finest farming country in England. Coal is mined near Dover. Besides the south-eastern suburbs of London, which are now very important industrial areas, Kent has a number of large towns within its borders, including Maidstone, the county town ; Ashford, a market town and railway centre ; Gravesend, a paper-milling centre ; Whitstable, famous for oysters; Canterbury, with its great double cruciform cathedral; and

W. F. Taylor

KENILWORTH CASTLE IN WARWICKSHIRE
Founded by Geoffrey de Clinton in the 12th century, Kenilworth Castle, the present walls of which enclose about seven acres, was added to at various times, Caesar's Tower (above) with walls 16 feet thick being all that remains of the original stronghold. Amongst the ruins of later structures are a gatehouse, and a great hall with beautiful windows, built by John of Gaunt (1340–99).

Dell & Wainwright

THE PILGRIMS' WAY IN KENT

An ancient road running from Winchester to Canterbury, known as the Pilgrims' Way, dates from many centuries before the time when pilgrims flocked along it to Becket's shrine. Parts of the road, indeed, date from the Stone Age, when the plains below were covered with forests, and the only safe path was along the top of the Downs. This view was taken near Wrotham.

natural gas, lead and limestone. There are forests of oak, maple, ash, walnut, pine, beech and cedar. Among the industries are flour-milling, lumbering, printing and publishing, meat-packing, and the manufacturing of clothing and cotton goods. The capital is Frankfurt; but Louisville, on the River Ohio, and the centre of the tobacco industry, is much larger, having a population of 319,000.

In the centre of Kentucky are 9,000 square miles of underground caverns, the most famous being the Mammoth Cave and the Colossal Cavern. At Covington is the smallest church in the world, seating only three worshippers. The population of the State is 2,845,620.

Chatham and Rochester, both great industrial areas; the Channel ports of Dover and Folkestone; Ramsgate and Margate, popular watering places.

Towns of note in the Weald of West Kent include Tunbridge Wells, an inland spa; Tonbridge, on the Medway, with its castle and public school; and Sevenoaks, near which are historic Knole House and its park, and Penshurst Place. East of Maidstone is Leeds Castle, a fine example of a medieval fortress. In the far south is Romney Marsh. Kent forms the background to much of Dickens's Pickwick Papers and David Copperfield; while the pilgrims of Chaucer's Canterbury Tales travelled along what is now the Dover Road and was once Watling Street. The Pilgrims' Way itself runs from west to east across the county to Canterbury. Charles Darwin lived and worked at Downe. The population of the county is 1,219,270.

Kentucky. Lying between the northern and southern States of the U.S.A., Kentucky shares in the characteristics of both regions, having the manufacturing centres of the North and the plantations of the South. It is bounded on the south by Tennessee, on the west by Missouri and Illinois, on the north by Indiana and Ohio, by West Virginia and Virginia on the east. Its area is 40,395 square miles, and it has almost every type of scenery within its boundaries. In the east and south-east are the Cumberland Mountains; to the south and west stretches a succession of hills and plains; in the centre and north is the Blue Grass region.

Kentucky is largely an agricultural State, the most important crops being tobacco, maize, hay, wheat and fruit. Livestock-breeding is an extensive industry, and the State has long been noted for its horses. Mineral resources include coal, iron, oil,

Kepler, JOHANN (1571–1630). The son of a German soldier of fortune, cradled in poverty and neglect, from childhood crippled in the hands, so that manual dexterity with instruments was impossible for him, too dim-sighted to make keen observations, too delicate of constitution to bear long exposure to night air—surely never was a great astronomer so handicapped as Johann Kepler. He was educated at the University of Tübingen for the ministry, but with his appointment to the chair of mathematics and astronomy at Graz (Austria) came the call to his life-work.

Astronomers of that day were mostly astrologers and fortune-telling charlatans, but Kepler bent all his energies to extracting from observations of the stars some real knowledge of the universe. All that was yet known of planetary motion was what Copernicus had established—that the planets move, not around the earth, but about the sun (in circles, it was then supposed). Two other great men, Galileo, an Italian, and Tycho Brahe, a Dane, were seriously studying the heavens at this time. Kepler became acquainted with them through correspondence, and in 1600 accepted an invitation to become Tycho Brahe's assistant in his observatory near Prague (Bohemia). Brahe's death the next year opened the way for Kepler's appointment to succeed him as mathematician and astronomer to the Emperor Rudolph II. One theory after another was tried and abandoned, until at last he hailed with delight the three laws which brought order out of the chaos of astronomy, and prepared the ground for Newton's discovery of the law of gravitation. (See Astronomy).

To the end of his life Kepler was dogged by misfortune—by war, which interrupted his work;

by illness, domestic calamity, and poverty—his salary was always in arrears. Nor was his position improved when, in 1628, he left the emperor's service to enter that of Wallenstein, the great general of the Thirty Years' War.

The laws of planetary motion, which are still known as "Kepler's laws," may be stated as follows: (1) The path of every planet in its motion about the sun forms an ellipse, with the sun at one focus. (2) The speed of the planet in its orbit varies, so that the line joining the centre of the sun with the centre of the planet sweeps over equal areas in equal times. (3) The *time* taken by any planet in its revolution about the sun has a definite relation to its *distance* from the sun, the "square" of its time being in exact proportion to the "cube" of its distance. These three laws give us the principle "by which the universe is balanced,"

JOHANN KEPLER
Making an enormous number of astronomical observations, Johann Kepler laid the basis of modern astronomy. He produced a vast amount of work, and died on November 15, 1630.

and enable astronomers to tell the position of a planet at any given time. The laws were enunciated in Kepler's Harmonices Mundi—Harmonics of the World—(1619).

Kerry. Most westerly and one of the largest counties in Eire, Kerry is a land of mountain and lake, of sea loughs, and headlands reaching out into the Atlantic Ocean. Here are the Lakes of Killarney, the Macgillycuddy range of mountains, with Carrantuohill, 3,414 feet and the highest peak in Ireland, the beautiful bay of Tralee, and Valentia Island, the starting-point of the first trans-Atlantic cable which was laid in 1866.

Kerry, which is in the province of Munster, is rich in historical and literary associations. Agriculture is the chief industry, deep-sea and coastal fishing and the tourist trade coming next. Kerry cattle, a small, black hardy breed, are noted for the large amount of milk they yield. Tralee (population, 10,000) is the county town. The area of Kerry is about 1,815 square miles and the population is 136,000.

Kew Gardens. Covering an area of 302 acres near Richmond, Surrey, the Royal Botanic Gardens at Kew were opened to the public in 1841, and came under Government control in

The Times

IN KEW'S ROYAL BOTANIC GARDENS
The building in the background of this beauty-spot in Surrey is a museum which was built in 1848 and now displays examples of dried ferns and grasses and their economic uses. The statue on a white pedestal is of a man leaning on a spade (appropriate symbol for Kew Gardens !) and is entitled 'Out in the Fields.' The flower-beds are filled with flag iris.

the same year. They contain glasshouses, museums, a laboratory where research work of an experimental nature is carried on, a library, and vast collections of plants from all parts of the world.

Kew Gardens as they are now were laid out by William Aiton (1731–93). He was assisted by Sir Joseph Banks (q.v.) who started the Gardens' long tradition of collecting plants from all parts of the world, propagating them and distributing them, if necessary, to other parts of the world. Thus, it is through Kew that the rubber plant was introduced into Malaya in 1875, and the quinine plant (cinchona) was first sent to India in 1860.

In the Temperate House —more than an eighth of a mile in length, and probably the largest glasshouse in the world — are acacias from Australia; camellias of Japan; tree ferns and rhododendrons from the Himalayas and Java; and plants from tropical America. The Palm House, which took four years to construct and was completed in 1848, is 360 feet long and 66 feet high. In the Victoria Regia House are specimens of a gigantic South American water-lily, with leaves from four to 10 feet in diameter and flowers 18 inches across. The Orchid Houses contain a collection of dazzling beauty; and in the Cactus House there is a wonderful array of these weird plants. The grounds contain, among other notable features, a flagstaff consisting of a single pole of Douglas fir, 215 feet in height; Kew Palace (rebuilt in 1631), where George III (1738–1820) often stayed; Queen's Cottage, built by George III for Queen Charlotte; a Chinese pagoda, and a replica of a Japanese gateway.

Fox; New York Times Photos

GIANT WATER-LILIES AND A PAGODA AT KEW
Erected in 1761, the Pagoda (lower) in the Royal Botanic Gardens at Kew, Surrey, is an eight-sided building, has 10 storeys, and is 163 feet high. It stands in the south-east corner of the grounds, at the end of Cedar Vista. In a glasshouse (upper) grows an enormous South American water-lily (Victoria regia) with leaves up to 10 feet in diameter.

Kharkov, (Pron. har'–kof), RUSSIA. Standing on three small streams which flow into the Uda, a tributary of the Donetz, and about 450 miles south of Moscow, the city of Kharkov is the second largest in the Ukrainian Soviet Socialist Republic. Around Kharkov is one of the richest agricultural regions in the world, wheat, buckwheat, sugarbeet, sunflowers, cotton and flax being cultivated. To the south and southeast are the vast coalfields of the Donetz basin, and to the south-west are rich deposits of iron ore at Krivoi Rog. Its industries include iron-smelting, and the manufacture of tractors, machinery, machine tools, electrical equipment, rope and chemicals. Kharkov is an important railway junction, and has air services to Moscow, Kiev and Odessa.

The city was founded as a fort in 1654, becoming

the seat of the Government of the Ukraine in 1765. Industrial development in the Donetz coal-field and in the Krivoi iron ore district in the 19th century led to its expansion. During the Second World War (1939–45) the city was heavily bombed in 1941 by the Germans, who captured it in October 1941. The Russians retook it in February 1943, were compelled to withdraw in the following month, but in August succeeded in driving the Germans out again. The population is 833,430.

Khartum. (Pron. kar-tōōm′). Capital of the Anglo-Egyptian Sudan, this city stands at the junction of the White Nile and the Blue Nile. It is connected by railway with Sennar and El Obeid in the south, with Port Sudan on the Red Sea, and with Wady Halfa in the north; and it is a stopping-place on the air route between Britain and South and East Africa.

The main portion of Khartum is on the south bank of the Blue Nile, which is spanned by a bridge. Rebuilt after its destruction in 1885 by Sudanese tribesmen who were led by the Mahdi, a religious fanatic, the city is planned on modern lines. The chief buildings, which are on the embankment along the river and on Gordon Avenue, include the Cathedral. The palace of the Governor-General of the Sudan occupies the site of one in which lived General Gordon (killed by the Mahdi's followers on January 26, 1885). The trade of the Sudan passes through here, carried by river and by railway. The population is 44,950.

Kidd. WILLIAM (1650?—1701). Of all the reckless sea-rovers who flew the Jolly Roger at the mastheads of their pirate ships, made their victims walk the plank, and buried their ill-gotten treasures on lonely isles, Captain Kidd is the most notorious—though one of the least typical, despite the legends that have grown up about his name.

William Kidd, son of a Scottish minister, followed the sea from youth. In the war between the English and the French, during the reign of William and Mary, he became known as the bold captain of a privateer in the West Indies. British commerce then suffered greatly from marauding pirates; and at the request of the British governor of New York, Kidd received two commissions from the king addressed to " our trusty and well-beloved Captain Kidd "—one for suppressing piracy and the other recognizing him as a privateer against the French. With his 30-gun ship Adventure, and his crew of 155 men, he set sail for Madagascar and the Red Sea region, chief haunts of the pirates.

His troubles now began. No pirates were found, cholera killed off many of his crew, the ship grew leaky, and supplies began to give out. Then, apparently, Captain Kidd followed the advice of his discontented crew and himself turned pirate. He took several small Moorish vessels, was defeated in a battle with a Portuguese man-of-war, and then in his turn captured a Portuguese and an Armenian vessel.

But the day of reckoning came. In 1699 he deserted the leaky old Adventure, boarded one of his prizes, and headed for America. Learning that he had been proclaimed a pirate, he sent to the governor a part of his booty. He was arrested in Boston, where he landed, and was sent to London for trial. There he was convicted of murder by killing a mutinous sailor. After a trial in which the evidence was inconclusive and during which he kept protesting that he was " the most innocent person of them all," he was pronounced guilty also of piracy. He was hanged at Execution Dock, Wapping, London, and his body hung in chains.

Kidneys. The kidneys of the human body constitute the main purifying and filtering plant for the blood. The pure blood remains in the system,

MODERN KHARTUM
Destroyed by the Mahdi's army in 1885, Khartum was rebuilt on modern lines, as can be seen above. Capital of the Anglo-Egyptian Sudan, it is situated at the junction of the White Nile and the Blue Nile, about 1,300 miles south of Cairo. Here General Gordon was killed in 1885.

Sudan Railways

and the poisonous waste is filtered off through the direct agency of this pair of organs.

The kidneys are bean-shaped, about $4\frac{1}{2}$ inches long, $2\frac{1}{2}$ inches wide, and $1\frac{1}{2}$ inch thick, one situated on each side of the spinal column, directly under the " small of the back." The right kidney is placed slightly lower than the left, to make room for the liver above, but the upper part of each lies against the lowest rib. The function of the kidneys is to collect waste matter from the blood and excrete it via the bladder in the form of urine.

The kidneys, which are protected by a mass of fat, consist of numerous minute tubes gathered into groups. These groups, it has been discovered, do not act all at once but in relays. The cells which line these tubes collect the waste from the blood as it passes over them. They have also a remarkable power of leaving untouched the valuable proteins of the blood stream, picking out the toxic material, and filtering back again into the blood stream the fluids which had held the poisonous matter in solution. Ordinarily the kidneys throw off some three to four pints of urine daily, in which is carried spent material that would otherwise be harmful;

anything, therefore, which interferes with the activity of these organs means the accumulation of poisonous waste matter in the body and immediately brings on serious sickness or even death.

It is this fact which makes disease of the kidneys so serious. " Bright's disease," for instance, is an inflammation of the kidneys which interferes with their normal activity and causes them to let pass the valuable proteins. Unless this condition is cured, the waste poison called *urea* accumulates in the blood with fatal results. Sometimes chalk-like stones (calculi) are formed in the kidneys, and these may block up one or both ureters, as the tubes leading from the kidneys to the bladder are called. A blocked ureter is a dangerous condition because the kidney above becomes paralysed in function. If both ureters become blocked the danger is increased and death is inevitable unless the obstructions are removed at once.

The outside coat of the kidneys manufactures some substance which is of much importance in maintaining the arterial blood pressure; sometimes too much of this substance is secreted, leading to high blood pressure.

Almost all diseases have some effect upon the kidneys, and one of the methods most relied upon by the modern physician in determining the general health of a patient and detecting unsuspected trouble is to subject the urine to chemical analysis.

Kiel Canal.

The peninsula forming Schleswig-Holstein in Germany and Jutland in Denmark was long regarded as a hindrance to navigation between the North Sea and the Baltic, and the possibility of a canal had been discussed at least 500 years before the Kiel Canal was first opened in 1895.

The canal extends 61 miles, between the estuary of the Elbe on the North Sea and Kiel Bay on the Baltic. As the size of battleships, for which it was primarily built, increased, the German Government decided to widen and deepen it. The work was completed in 1914, the depth of the waterway being increased to 36 feet, with a surface width of 331 feet. During the Second World War (1939–45) the canal was frequently bombed by Allied aircraft, the locks being damaged and the fairway blocked with sunken shipping. It was reopened to traffic at the end of 1945.

Kiev,

(Pron. kē'-yef), RUSSIA. One of the most fascinating cities in Russia was ancient Kiev, on the River Dnieper, capital of the Ukraine Socialist Soviet Republic. The exact origin of the city is lost in legend, but it is certainly one of the oldest settlements in eastern Europe. Despite its ancient aspect, Kiev was modern, too, with busy wharves, smelting works, flour mills, sugar refineries, distilleries, and tobacco, leather, glass and other factories.

There are three distinct parts of Kiev—the low-lying business section, called the Podol; old Kiev, crowning the highest of the hills; and, on Pechersky Hill, the world-famous monastery, or Lavra, with its caves of cells, founded in the 11th century.

Formerly the Lavra was a city in itself, with walls and towers, streets of cells, inns, churches, printing press, and schools. Thousands of Russians made annual pilgrimages to it before the Bolshevik Revolution of 1917. In old Kiev stood the lovely 11th century cathedral of St. Sophia, with its golden-topped bell tower.

Kiev is said to have been founded in the 5th century. Late in the 10th century it was the capital of the Grand Duke Vladimir, who was baptized a Christian and made Kiev the home of the Greek Church in Russia. In the Second World War (1939–45) the city was captured by German troops in September 1941, after the Russians had destroyed the bridges over the Dnieper and many of the public buildings. On November 6, 1943, it was stormed and retaken by Russian troops, after the Germans had demolished and set fire to most of the remaining buildings of any importance. The population is 846,290.

Kildare.

In the central plain of Ireland, this rich pastoral county of Eire in the province of Leinster includes the Curragh, probably the foremost centre of racehorse breeding in the world. Much of the land is given up to grass, and cattle, sheep, pigs and poul-

STEAMING ALONG THE KIEL CANAL

Cutting the peninsula that lies between the North Sea and the Baltic, the Kiel Canal was formerly of enormous value to Germany as an outlet, under her own control, to the high seas. After the Second World War (1939–45) the canal was included in the British zone of occupation in Germany. At Levensau the waterway is spanned by a bridge (above) about 140 feet high.

KINGFISHER—MOST BRILLIANT OF BRITISH BIRDS

W. S. Berridge

All the members of the kingfisher tribe are birds of brilliant plumage, and Britain's own representative is one of the most gorgeous. Blue and green and chestnut, with patches of white, are its chief colours ; and the back feathers glitter in the sun so that when the bird flies by it is as though a flash of blue were passing above the stream which is the kingfisher's haunt. Short wings and tail are notable features, as is the long, straight, sharp-pointed bill—an admirable ' tool ' for catching small fish, which form a large portion of its diet. Total length of this expert diver is about seven inches.　*See article in page 1857.*

Above, Arthur Brook; left, Fox

KINGFISHERS AND THEIR
BANK-SIDE HOME

HERE are two splendid photographs of
the kingfisher, finest in plumage
of native British birds. Above, a lusty
family of seven youngsters on the branch
of a tree, certainly not distant from their
home for they are not yet able to fly far.
Notice that their tails, never large in this
species, are as yet hardly developed.
Young kingfishers often sit like this, but
you have to be very quiet if you want to
get such a good view without frightening
them. On the left is a kingfisher outside the entrance to its home. It is
strange to think that such a brilliantly-
plumaged bird nests in deep, dark holes
in the river's bank excavated and deserted
by, perhaps, a water-rat or rabbit, at the
end of which a bare chamber forms the
nest, which is constructed largely of
layers of fish-bones.

try are raised in great numbers; oats, barley, turnips, and potatoes are the chief crops produced. Fine specimens of the ancient round towers— probably towers of refuge against invaders—are found throughout the county, the one in Kildare town being 108 feet high. Kildare is the county and market town, with a population of about 2,000. The area of County Kildare is about 654 square miles and the population 64,560.

Kilkenny. In the province of Leinster and forming the south-eastern end of the great central plain, Kilkenny is one of the most interesting counties in Eire, and one of the few to possess mineral wealth—though on a small scale. Anthracite coal is worked at Castlecomer, iron and manganese ores are found in several places, and at Knocktopher copper is mined. There are also black marble and limestone quarries. Marl, a mixture of clay and lime carbonate possessing high fertilizing value, is plentiful.

Agriculture is the chief occupation, and barley, oats, potatoes, and turnips are the main crops. Stock-raising is an extensive industry, cattle, sheep, pigs, and poultry being reared in large numbers. Subsidiary manufactures are marble polishing, brewing, distilling and flour-milling. Kilkenny, the county town, with a population of 10,000, is a cathedral city. The cathedral of St. Canice, dating back to 1255, is the largest, next to St. Patrick's pro-cathedral, Dublin, in the country. Kilkenny county has an area of about 800 square miles, and a population of 68,000.

The saying " to fight like Kilkenny cats," that is, till only their tails are left, may have originated in disputes that raged for centuries between the two divisions of the city, Englishtown and Irishtown.

Kincardineshire. Known also as the Mearns, the Scottish county of Kincardineshire is 383 square miles in extent. It lies on the east coast between Aberdeenshire and Angus, and is in

ROUND TOWER OF KILDARE
This old round tower near the cathedral at Kildare is 108 feet high. It is in good condition, but has been rather spoilt by the addition of a modern battlement. Towers such as this were built as refuges during time of war.

general a rugged, picturesque region of mountain, forest, and moor, the Grampian Mountains occupying much of the central and western districts. Stonehaven is the county town and chief fishing port; inland, near the River Dee, is Banchory, noted for its shortbread. The estimated population of the county is 28,000.

Kingfisher. One day, as you walk by a stream or river, you may hear a sudden shrill cry almost like a mechanical whistle; then, if you keep alert and are fortunate, you may see a sudden brilliant flash of blue and green and chestnut darting down the watercourse. It will be a kingfisher (*Alcedo ispida*). This is Britain's most brilliant bird, and a wonderful diver. By his diving he gets his living. From a perch above the water he swoops in a sudden dive, seizes a fish in his long beak, flies back to his perch, tosses the fish into the air and swallows it. Should the fish be rather too large to swallow intact, the kingfisher will fly with it to a stone or stump and there pound its prey a time or two to make it more easy to swallow. As this may happen many times a day, and the little fish may be trout, the kingfisher is apt to be unpopular where fish are preserved. But aquatic insects, luckily, and other creatures form a large part of the diet.

The British kingfisher burrows a hole in the river bank, laying its round pink eggs in a nest at the end of the long tunnel; the nest is very dirty, unlike that of most other birds. The eggs usually number from six to eight and often there are two broods. The bird's total length is about seven inches. Foreign kingfishers include the

KINGFISHER'S CATCH
The camera caught this kingfisher in the act of returning to its perch on a dead branch and holding in its beak a small fish, which was unwise enough to show itself as the bird sat poised above the stream. Kingfishers often have favourite perches above the water in which they fish.

American belted kingfisher and the famous " laughing jackass " of Australia.

Many legends are connected with the European kingfisher, which was anciently called the halcyon. An old belief was that the seven days preceding the shortest day of the year were used by these birds to build their nests which, it was thought, floated on the water, and the seven days following were devoted to hatching the eggs. During this period, " the halcyon days," the ancients believed the sea was always calm. Hence " halcyon " (from Greek name of the bird) to describe calm and peaceful days.

'King Lear.' By many judges this tragedy of Shakespeare is ranked as the finest piece of dramatic literature in the world, but it is rarely acted because it is harrowing throughout. Lear,

City Art Gallery, Leeds

KING LEAR COMFORTED BY CORDELIA

There is unrelieved tragedy in Shakespeare's play King Lear, but the deep devotion of Lear's daughter Cordelia to her father breaks through the gloom like a ray of sunshine piercing a grey sky. This illustration, reproduced from a painting by G. W. Joy, shows Cordelia comforting her father in the prison to which he and she had been taken after the defeat of their armies by that of her sisters Goneril and Regan.

a headstrong old sovereign of ancient Britain, divides his realm into three parts, and then calls on his three daughters to receive each her share according to the love she professes for him.

Goneril and Regan so insult reason with their extravagant avowals of love that the youngest daughter, simple and honest Cordelia, disgusted with them, states her own dutiful love too modestly to please the proud old king. He casts her off penniless, so that she would have been poor indeed had not the King of France claimed her as his bride. The elder daughters, secure in the possession of his wealth, now treat Lear with contempt and cruelty. Shorn of every kingly dignity, denied even the respect due to a father, the old man rushes out into the night, mad with rage and grief. In the pauses of the tempest we hear his curses and the bitter chatter of his faithful fool.

One gleam of peace breaks upon his sin and suffering. This is when Cordelia and poor sick

Lear are reunited. But their armies are defeated, and Lear is next seen bearing the dead body of Cordelia from prison, where her sister has caused her to be hanged. The guilty daughters perish and their party is overthrown, but Lear dies of a broken heart. Shakespeare is believed to have written this play between 1600 and 1608.

Kingsford-Smith, SIR CHARLES EDWARD (1897–1935). The disappearance of this fine airman in November 1935, while attempting to crown all his previous records, was a sad loss to the flying world. Kingsford-Smith was an Australian, a native of Brisbane. He served in the First World War (1914–18) and afterwards took up commercial flying. His first outstanding feat was to fly round Australia in 1927. World-wide fame came in June 1928, when, with three companions, he piloted the Southern Cross over the Pacific from the U.S.A. to Australia, and also flew over the Tasman Sea to New Zealand and back. In the following year, and in the same machine, he made a record flight from Australia to England. The year 1930 saw a triumphant crossing of the Atlantic, also a record flight back to Australia in a light machine. In 1931–32 he commanded the first experimental all-Australian mail plane to England and back.

Another record flight to Australia followed in 1933, and the first crossing of the Pacific to the U.S.A. in 1934. This brilliant career was cut short when Kingsford-Smith—who had been knighted in 1932, and had reached the honorary rank of Air Commodore in the Royal Australian Air Force—was lost in the Bay of Bengal while attempting an even faster flight in a small single-engined machine without wireless equipment.

Kingsley, CHARLES (1819–75). Known chiefly in his own day as a Radical writer and clergyman, Charles Kingsley was also novelist, naturalist, professor and poet. The son of a clergyman, Kingsley was born on June 12, 1819, in Devonshire. He attended King's College in London after his father had obtained a rectory in that city. Later he entered Cambridge University. In 1842 he went as curate to the parish of Eversley, in Hampshire, and soon was appointed rector. He died on January 23, 1875.

Deeply interested in social and economic problems, Kingsley risked his position in the Church by his speeches and writings on behalf of the working classes. Yeast (1849) and Alton Locke (1850) are two of his novels dealing with social problems.

Though Kingsley's years (1860–69) as a professor of modern history at Cambridge were unremarkable, he wrote several novels on historical subjects for which he is chiefly remembered. Westward Ho ! (1855) tells the story of a Devonshire knight making history in the stirring days of Elizabeth. Hypatia (1853) deals with the former glories of Alexandria, in Egypt. Hereward the Wake (1866) is a tale of Saxon England and the struggle with the Normans. For his children Kingsley wrote delightful Nature stories. Among them are Madam How and Lady Why (1869) and The Water Babies (1863). The latter is a fairy story and Nature story combined.

Kipling, RUDYARD (1865–1936).

On December 29, 1865, while Queen Victoria was ruling the Empire and the United States had just come to the end of its Civil War, a boy was born in Bombay who was to win fame as " the spokesman for the Anglo-Saxon breed."

The first five years of Kipling's life were spent in India. Much of the vividness and realism of his Jungle Books is probably due to the impressions that came to him, before he could talk, of the strange primitive country that lay beyond the cities and the highways of British India. He and his sister had a native nurse, and her tales of the jungle animals lingered in his memory, to crystallize later in Mowgli and Shere Khan and the grey wolves. Like most English children born in foreign lands, he was sent to England to be educated. Too young for a boarding school, he was left in the care of a woman who seems to have been the worst possible guardian for a sensitive boy accustomed to sympathy and understanding. Nearly everything that a small boy wanted to do was to her a " sin." As a punishment, even reading was forbidden, and Kipling almost ruined his eyes by devouring in secret every book he could lay his hands on. Those six years in that " House of Desolation " in which—he says rather sadly— " there was so little love and so much Bible," are described in a story called Baa Baa Black Sheep.

At last his parents came home from India on leave, and they remade his world. Glasses helped his weak eyes, and he was carried off for a summer in Devonshire with his father and mother and his lively young cousins. Then his father took him to Paris, a trip which awoke his life-long love for France. At the end of this holiday he was sent to the United Services College, a school for sons of army officers, at Westward Ho, in Devonshire. His years there are recorded in Stalky & Co, in which Kipling is the character known as Beetle. "How we, the originals of Stalky, McTurk and Beetle, came together I do not know,"

he says. "But our triple alliance was well established before we were 13." His first poems, published privately by his father, were written there.

When he was just short of 17, far more mature than most boys of his age, he returned to his family in Lahore, wearing proudly a small moustache which his mother promptly ordered him to remove. He became a reporter on the one daily newspaper in the Punjab, the Civil and Military Gazette. In his autobiography Kipling calls this interval " Seven Years' Hard." To get material for his newspaper articles, he travelled round India and came to know the country as did few other white men.

It was then that Kipling began to write the poems and short stories about the British soldier in India that were to establish his reputation as a writer. Plain Tales from the Hills, Soldiers Three, and Barrack Room Ballads are known wherever English is spoken. The slim little volume called Departmental Ditties (1886) he edited, printed, published, and sold himself.

In 1887 Kipling was transferred to a larger and more important newspaper at Allahabad, the Pioneer. There he had more time for creative writing, and he made the most of it. In 1890, eager to find a publisher for his tales and aware that he had earned a holiday, he set sail for England, going by way of Japan, China and North America. At length the dramatic stories and singing verse fired the public imagination and the books sold rapidly.

Two years later he married an American girl, Caroline Balestier, and started off with her on another holiday trip, this time round the world. After their honeymoon Kipling and his wife settled down in Vermont, U.S.A. In that house their first child was born, and there Kipling wrote the tales that were to make up his Jungle Books. After four years in America the Kiplings decided that their real home was in England. They rented a house in a Sussex village near his uncle, Edward Burne-Jones, and his cousin Stanley Baldwin. There in August 1897 their only son, John, was born.

The story that we know as Kim had been in Kipling's mind for years. Now, stimulated by his father's keen interest, he began to write it. Long visits to South Africa, where they formed a friendship with Cecil Rhodes, varied their life. In 1902 Kipling bought an old house on the edge of the Sussex downs. One day, his cousin, Ambrose Poynter, said to him: "Write a story about Roman times here." So Puck of Pook's Hill and Rewards and

KIPLING IN HAPPY MOOD
Rudyard Kipling was not seen much in public life, for he was shy from his boyhood up. But in October 1923 he was elected Lord Rector of St. Andrew's University ; here he is acknowledging the students' cheers. Behind him (right) is his cousin, Mr. Stanley (later Earl) Baldwin.

Fairies were begun. Each story of England's past is complete in itself. Together they form a chain of "scents and sights and sounds" that reach to the very heart of England.

In 1907 he was awarded the Nobel Prize for literature and he and his wife went to Stockholm to receive it from the Swedish king. The First World War (1914–18) brought him personal tragedy. His only son was killed fighting in France with the Irish Guards. In John's memory Kipling wrote a history of this famous regiment, and the dedicatory poem has a refrain that is like a song once heard and never quite forgotten:

Old Days! The wild geese are flighting!
Head to the storm as they faced it before!
For where there are Irish there's bound to be fighting,
And when there's no fighting it's Ireland no more!
Ireland no more!

With the social and political changes that followed the war Rudyard Kipling had little sympathy. More and more he withdrew from the active scene, spending the greater part of the year in his Sussex house. When he was nearly 70 years old he sat down to write his autobiography, Something of Myself. It was published after his death. Kipling died on January 18, 1936, in the same month as King George V, and was buried in Westminster Abbey, London.

His principal works include Plain Tales from the Hills (1887) ; Soldiers Three, Story of the Gadsbys, Wee Willie Winkie (1888–89) ; The Light That Failed (1891) ; Barrack Room Ballads (1892) ; The Jungle Book (1894) ; The Second Jungle Book (1895) ; Captains Courageous (1897) ; Stalky & Co. (1899) ; Kim (1901) ; Just So Stories (1902) ; Puck of Pook's Hill (1906) ; Rewards and Fairies (1910) ; Songs From Books (1913) ; The Years Between (1918) ; Inclusive Verse (1919) ; The Irish Guards in the Great War (1923) ; Something of Myself (1936).

RUDYARD KIPLING'S STORY OF MOWGLI

SUPPOSE that you were a small boy of Eastern India whose home was on the edge of a great jungle. Suppose that you were sitting one night before a camp-fire with your mother and father, and that suddenly, out of the dark, came a tiger, black and tawny and very fierce. Would you have been frightened? Mowgli wasn't.

Shere Khan, the Tiger, was hungry, and when he saw Man-flesh he jumped, forgetting the fire. That is how he burned his toes. And because he burned his toes, and had to stop to lick them, the baby's mother and father had time to run. Left to himself, and just old enough to walk, Mowgli crawled away through the long grass.

Father Wolf was stretching himself after a nap when he heard a rustling outside his cave. "Look!" he called to Mother Wolf, "a Man's cub." Then with careful teeth that did not even scratch the soft skin, he picked it up and carried it into the cave.

"A Man's cub went this way," roared Shere Khan, his massive head and shoulders blocking the entrance to the cave. "Give it to me."

Mother Wolf sprang forward, her eyes blazing in the darkness like two green moons.

"The Man's cub is mine. He shall live to run with the wolf pack and to hunt with us; in the end he shall hunt thee! Go!"

Mother Wolf was very fierce when she was angry, and Shere Khan skulked away, but in his heart was hatred.

"The Man's cub must be shown to the Pack," said Father Wolf, when the brown baby had settled down to the rough-and-tumble play with the wolf-cubs. "Wilt thou still keep him, mother?"

"Keep him!" she gasped. "He came naked, by night, alone and very hungry; yet he was not afraid! Certainly I will keep him. Lie still, little frog. O thou Mowgli—for Mowgli, the Frog, I will call thee. The time will come when thou wilt hunt Shere Khan!"

On the night of the Pack meeting, when the three young wolf-cubs were old enough to run about a little, Father and Mother Wolf took them to the Council Rock. The Council Rock was a bare hill-top where the wolves met, and where the cubs must be shown to the Pack before they could be accepted by the Free People. Into the centre of the circle which they formed Mowgli was thrust forth.

"Ye know the Law! Look well, O wolves!" Akela, the Lone Wolf, who was their leader, cried in recognition of the new cub.

A roar came from behind the rocks. It was the voice of Shere Khan, demanding his prey. Fearful of the great tiger, one of the young wolves spoke up, asking why this Man-cub was taken into the tribe.

Now there is a Law of the Jungle that says, when there is a dispute concerning the acceptance of a cub two members of the jungle who are not its mother or father must speak for it.

Up rose Baloo, the Brown Bear, teacher of the wolf-cubs, and he spoke for Mowgli. Then came Bagheera, the Black Panther. He quoted the Law that allows a price to be paid for any cub that is objected to by the Pack. In payment for the Man-cub Bagheera gave a bull, newly killed. This was good meat for the young wolves. So Mowgli was taken into the Pack. Mother Wolf had nursed him with her own babies ; Baloo, the sleepy Brown Bear, taught him the Law of the Jungle; and Bagheera the Panther was his friend.

As he grew up Mowgli learned to hunt and to protect himself, and to climb trees like a monkey for nuts and fruit and honey. Baloo taught him the Stranger's Hunting Call that he must use when he sought food outside his own grounds; the Master Words of the Jungle, that he might claim protection with the Birds and Snake People and all four-footed beasts. He could swim as well as he could run, and climb as well as he could swim. So he grew strong and brown and wise.

"Little Brother," said Bagheera the Panther one day in Mowgli's 12th year, "how often must I tell thee that Shere Khan the Tiger is thine enemy?" But Mowgli only laughed.

"The young wolves are following Shere Khan, who gives scraps from his kill," Bagheera con-

By courtesy of Macmillan & Co., Ltd

MOWGLI DEFEATS HIS TIGER FOE

From the time of his adoption into the wolf pack, the boy Mowgli (the hero of Rudyard Kipling's Jungle Book) had been dogged by Shere Khan, the tiger. Shere Khan persuaded the Pack of the Jungle Free People to expel Mowgli. But the boy, encouraged by his friend Bagheera, the Black Panther (who is seen in the foreground of this picture), went to the village and took some of the Red Flower (fire). Dipping a branch into this he beat the tiger with it, until it slunk away, defeated. Then Mowgli left to join his human brothers, swearing that he would return later and lay out Shere Khan's hide on the Council rock. And this, indeed, he did, and the manner of it is shown overleaf.

S. TREGILIAN

By courtesy of Macmillan & Co., Ltd

MOWGLI LEADS THE CHARGE OF THE BULLS

How Mowgli took his revenge on Shere Khan, the tiger, is told in the story entitled Tiger! Tiger! While living with men, Mowgli was often sent out to watch a herd of water-buffaloes, and one day the wolves, Akela and Grey Brother, came to tell the boy that Shere Khan was lying asleep in a steep-sided and narrow ravine. This was Mowgli's chance! The wolves divided the buffalo herd, driving the cows and calves to the bottom of the ravine and the bulls to the top. Then Mowgli mounted Rama, the bull leader, and the bulls charged furiously down the ravine. Shere Khan, prevented by the cows from escaping, was trampled to death beneath the hoofs of the frenzied beasts.

tinued. "Akela the Lone Wolf is growing old; when he misses his kill—and the time is very near—he will no longer rule the Pack. The others will kill him, for that is the Law. Then they will turn on thee, Little Brother. Shere Khan is urging them."

At this Mowgli's black brows came very close together, because he knew this was the truth.

"I have it!" said Bagheera. "Go thou down to the Man's huts in the village and get some of the Red Flower. Thus wilt thou be master."

Now the Red Flower is Fire, of which all animals live in deadly fear and which only Man can tame. That same night Mowgli went down into the village. Pressing his face close against a window, he watched the boy who lived there put some of the glowing coals from the hearth into a basket lined with clay. Mowgli walked in, took the basket from him, and disappeared into the dark.

When the Pack met at the Council Rock, Akela, for 12 years leader of the Free People, lay still, for

"Listen!" he called, staying his hand. "Akela goes free, to live as he pleases. Ye shall not kill him because that is not my will. I go to the village to my own people. When next I come to the Council Rock, I will come with Shere Khan's hide on my head." He strode off to say good-bye to Mother Wolf and his foster brothers. As he walked he wept and because he wept he thought he must be dying, for he had never wept before.

The dawn was breaking when Mowgli went down the hillside, alone, to meet those things that are called men. In the village he made signs to show that he was hungry. The priest was called and a great crowd gathered. He was taken home by a kindly woman, who fed and clothed him and made him sleep in a house. But the house frightened and angered him, for it seemed like a trap. He was sent to herd buffalo with the other village children.

As he sat wearily making grasshopper houses and watching the wallowing cattle, Gray Brother, one of Mother Wolf's cubs, came to him.

"Listen, you wolves! . . . I, the Man, have here a little of the Red Flower which ye, dogs, fear."

he had missed his kill, and the Law said that he must die. Mowgli sat up very straight, the pot that held the Red Flower clasped between his knees, Bagheera the Panther at his side.

"He is my prey," snarled Shere Khan. "Give him to me!"

"Yes, give the Man-cub to Shere Khan," repeated the young wolves. Restlessly they circled round him; and Shere Khan roared hungrily.

"Now is the time," whispered Bagheera the Panther, and Mowgli rose, holding the fire-pot in his hands.

"Listen, you wolves. Ye have said often that I was a Man. I thought myself your brother, and would have stayed with ye always. But now that ye have turned against me, it is not yours to say what shall be done. I, the Man, have here a little of the Red Flower, which ye, dogs, fear.

"Shere Khan waits for thee by the village gate this evening. But he has eaten and is slow and drowsy from too much food."

"Then we shall catch him," said Mowgli. "Tonight I shall have the skin of Shere Khan." With the help of Grey Brother and Akela, Mowgli divided the buffalo into two herds. One herd was driven to the foot of the ravine where Shere Khan lay sleeping. The other went to the head of the ravine. The two herds formed a rough circle, with Shere Khan in its centre. Down they dashed from either end. When Akela and Gray Brother separated them Shere Khan lay dead.

After Mowgli had stripped the tiger's body of its skin, he and the wolves herded the buffalo and drove them back to the village.

"Sorcerer, wizard, enchanter! Get thee hence!" cried the townspeople as Mowgli neared the gates.

The children who herded with him had told the village folk how the wolf-boy had killed the terrible tiger, and how the wolves obeyed him. So with stones and vile words the village people drove Mowgli back to the jungle.

On the great skin of Shere Khan which lay spread on the Council Rock, Mowgli stood in the light of the full moon. Around him the wolves circled, begging him to be their leader.

"No," said Mowgli, for he was of Man's blood and wise. "I will not lead ye, now that ye are hungry and sore, for when ye are full-fed once more ye will turn on me. I will stay in the Jungle, but I will hunt alone."

So Mowgli hunted only with the four wolves, his brothers, and lived a long life in the Jungle.

Compiled from Kipling's Jungle Book, by permission of, and special arrangement with, Mr. Kipling's executors and Messrs. Macmillan Ltd., holders of the copyright.

Kirkcudbrightshire. (Pron.
ker-kōōb'-ri-shēr). Situated on the Solway Firth, lying between Dumfries and Wigtown, and forming part of the Galloway district, this Scottish county has an area of 900 square miles, and is for the most part mountain and moorland. There are areas where fine farms are to be found, particularly along the river valleys, and the county is noted for its cattle, the Galloway breed, and for its sheep. The Dee, a splendid salmon stream, is the principal river. The county is rich in historical and romantic associations. It was at the wild and picturesque Glen Trool that King Robert Bruce of Scotland defeated the English in 1307.

The county town, Kirkcudbright (population, 2,311), stands on the estuary of the Dee. The county's population is about 30,000.

Kish. The once
majestic city of Kish is today only a mound of desolate ruins on the Mesopotamian plain it ruled some 5,000 years ago. It lies between the Rivers Tigris and Euphrates, 100 miles south of Baghdad, the capital of Iraq. Inscriptions found in the ruins state that it was "the first city founded after the Flood." As the earliest-known capital of the Sumerians (the inhabitants of the lower Euphrates plain, later known as Babylonia), Kish is believed to be the birthplace of civilization in the Near East.

Until as late as the time of the Babylonian King Sargon (about 2750 B.C.) Kish dominated the Near East. Then it declined, for the Euphrates changed its course, Kish's position being taken by Babylon.

Excavations made on the site of the city have shed new light on the history of mankind. Remains of several cultures, dating from Neolithic times to the Christian era, were found, and there were indications that Kish had been flooded about 3200 B.C. Many take this to be evidence of the great Flood described in Genesis. Equally astounding was the discovery, below the flood stratum, of a four-wheeled chariot, the earliest-known wheeled vehicle.

Kitchener OF KHARTUM, EARL (1850–
1916). It was a blazing day on the edge of the Egyptian desert. A detachment of the British Army, which was vainly trying to rescue General Gordon, besieged by the Mahdi's forces at Khartum, had captured two Arabs and hoped to get from them some much needed information. But the men pretended to be deaf, and Major Horatio Herbert Kitchener, who questioned them, got no reply.

An hour later a third Arab was thrust into the tent with the other two. Presently the three men were exchanging confidences in voluble Arabic. After a time the third Arab called the guard and demanded to be taken at once to headquarters. It was Kitchener himself, who, in disguise, had used his expert knowledge of Arabic to learn from the two obstinate natives all that he wished to know.

The attempted rescue of General Gordon failed, Khartum falling on January 26, 1885, two days before the arrival of the relief force. (*See* p. 1487).

Thirteen years later Kitchener, then Sirdar— that is, commander of the Anglo-Egyptian army— defeated the tribesmen at the battle of Omdurman (September 2, 1898), and a few days later he marched into Khartum and held a memorial service for Gordon. This feat, which earned him a place in the English peerage with the title Baron Kitchener of Khartum— or K. of K., as he was popularly called—was no sudden spurt but was the crowning of many years of unceasing effort in organization. He saw war as a great profession, in which the better organized and equipped forces won, and he succeeded because of his attention to these details.

Kitchener was born at Ballylongford, county Kerry, Ireland, on June 24, 1850, and was educated at the Royal Military Academy at Woolwich. In 1871 he fought as a private for France against Germany—anticipating the time, 43 years later, when he was to be an ally of France against the same enemy, as Britain's Secretary of State for War. He later served in Cyprus and Egypt.

Imperial War Museum
EARL KITCHENER OF KHARTUM
At the outbreak of the First World War (1914–18) Kitchener was made Secretary of State for War and created an Earl. He raised a large British army, and in August 1915 went to Gallipoli, the peninsula west of the Dardanelles, where he is seen (centre) discussing the situation.

When the Boer War broke out, in 1899, Kitchener was sent to South Africa as lieutenant-general and chief-of-staff to Lord Roberts, the Commander-in-Chief of the British forces. Later, he succeeded Lord Roberts as Commander-in-Chief, a position he held until the victorious end of the struggle in 1902. After the Boer War Kitchener served for seven years as Commander-in-Chief in India; later he made a tour of inspection of the forces of the Empire; and afterwards he was for three years the representative of the British Government in Egypt.

The outbreak of the First World War (1914–18) found him in England in consultation with the War Office. He was created an Earl and made Secretary of State for War. In this capacity he at once took steps to raise a large new British army of 70 divisions. On June 5, 1916, the cruiser Hampshire, on which he had sailed for Russia, struck a mine laid by a German submarine and sank with all but 10 men ; Kitchener was amongst those who perished.

Kite. A bird of prey belonging to the same family (*Accipitri-diiae*) as the eagles and the hawks, the kite is extremely rare in Great Britain, where it was formerly very common.

Reddish brown on the upper parts, reddish with blackish stripes on the lower, with a deeply forked tail, this particular kite (*Milvus ictinus*) differs from most birds of prey in preferring dead to living food, and it lacks, therefore, the dash and courage of smaller birds such as the peregrine falcon, the hobby, and the merlin. In this respect it resembles carrion birds. Moreover, although a bird of prey, it was itself one of the principal quarries in the days of falconry, and much smaller birds were hawked at it. One of the attractions, in this case, was that the kite, which has superb powers of flight, offered no easy victory to its pursuer. As a soaring bird the kite is the match of any in Britain. Besides the common European species there are others in all parts of the world, especially in hot countries, where they act as scavengers, even in populous cities.

Kites. .For years, the official daily weather forecasts were based upon reports from professional kite-flyers at the Government weather bureaus until aeroplane and balloon replaced the kite for that purpose. Great box kites carrying instruments for recording conditions in the upper air were sent up from one to three miles high. To reach a height much over a mile several kites were used. A train of 10 kites with eight and a half miles of wire has raised instruments for making atmospheric soundings to a height of more than four miles.

This was only one of many practical uses of the kite. Long before Benjamin Franklin (1706–90) with his famous kite and key drew electricity from a storm cloud, kites had been used for mechanical

W. S. Berridge
RARELY-SEEN KITE
Though its food consists largely of carrion, this bird of prey catches young rabbits, hares, rats, mice, moles, nestling birds, snakes, frogs and fish. It is about 20 inches in length.

purposes. Ancient Korean and Chinese stories tell how kites carried cables over streams and chasms and so enabled them to be bridged.

In Eastern countries kite-flying is an ancient custom and popular pastime. Korean men, women, and children, from the highest in the land, fly kites during the first days of the new year, and in China 'Kites' Day'—the ninth day of the ninth month—is a holiday. In China and Japan this toy is made to represent gorgeously coloured birds, insects or flowers, and is also used in highly decorated geometrical forms. In s o m e parts of the East kite-fighting is a sport. The strings near the point where the kite is attached are covered with glue and bits of glass, so that a player who has manoeuvred his kite to windward of his opponent's can cut the cord of the other kite with a sudden jerk.

Kites are of two general classes, the plane surface and the box kite. Each has several varieties, and there are also combination kites using both the plane and box construction. Compound kites may have their several members on the string, or on individual lines connected to the main line. The box kite consists of one or more box-like compartments or "cells," rather like those of the early aeroplane in some types. The covering is of paper or cloth.

The flying of a kite depends upon the same principle as the sailing of a boat or the flight of an aeroplane. The principle is this: The current of air, moving horizontally, strikes the face of the kite, tending to drive it backward. The *inclined surface* of the kite converts part of this force into a thrust upward and, in addition to this thrust, the rush of the wind around the sides of the kite creates a partial vacuum on the upper side. Hence the kite steadily rises. (*See* Aeroplane).

Knighthood. Originating amongst the pagan Germanic tribes, with whom it was customary for the young warrior first to prove himself in battle, then to attend a tribal ceremony at which his chieftain presented him with a sword and shield, knighthood with the spread of Christianity acquired a religious significance. The Crusades against the Saracens, with their religious basis and emphasis on the use of cavalry, gave further impetus to knighthood.

The age of chivalry flourished before the time of guns and gunpowder, when battles were won by hand-to-hand conflicts of heavily armoured knights. Fighting and alarms were almost an every-day occurrence, and the common people generally could not protect themselves against invaders, so in times of danger they fled to the castles or strongholds owned by the nobles. To obtain this protection the poorer folk became the serfs or villeins of their powerful neighbours, who in turn were the vassals of others still more powerful; and closely connected with this feudal system, as it was called, we find the institution of knighthood.

The education of a knight began at the age of seven, when he was taken from his home and sent to the castle of some nobleman, perhaps his father's lord. Here, until he was 14, he served the lord and the lord's wife as a page. It was his duty—and he esteemed it a privilege—to accompany them at all times. He waited on them at table and went with them to the chase. He received religious instruction from the chaplain, training in arms from the squires, and was taught by his mistress and her ladies to honour and protect all women. He also learned to sing and to play the lute (stringed instrument), to hunt and to hawk. Above all else, he learned to ride a horse.

At the age of 14 he became a squire. He now learned to handle sword and lance, and to bear the weight of heavy armour. In addition to other duties, he had now to carve the meat at table and to accompany his knight to war. He saw to it that the knightly sword and other arms were polished until they shone. He stood by to give aid in conflict should his lord be overmatched, to lend his horse should the master lose his own, and to bear his master's body away when wounded or killed in battle.

At the age of 21, that is, if as page and squire he had acquitted himself well, the young man was made a knight. This was an occasion of elaborate ceremony and solemn vows. After the bath of purification (origin of the present knighthood of the Bath) the candidate for knighthood knelt or stood all night in prayer before the altar on which lay the sword which he would don on the morrow.

In the morning there was a religious ceremony, with, perhaps, a sermon on knightly duty to protect the weak, to right wrongs, and to honour women. Then, in the courtyard, in the presence of the assembled knights and ladies, a knight's armour was buckled on the candidate, piece by piece, a sword was girded about his waist, and spurs were attached to his feet. He then knelt to receive the accolade. This was a light blow upon neck or shoulder, given by the officiating lord or knight with his fist, or, more usually, with the flat of a sword. As he gave it he said, " In the name of God and St. Michael and St. George, I dub thee knight; be brave and loyal." This ceremony was usually followed by exhibitions of the newly-made knight's skill in arms.

Sometimes on the occasion of a knighting the lord at whose castle the ceremony took place gave a tournament, often a very gorgeous and extravagant entertainment. Knights for miles around were invited to come and take part, while many persons of distinction came to witness the events.

In the morning, after attending Mass, the knights would go to the tourney field or lists, where the

KNIGHT TEMPLAR
Deriving their name from the palace in Jerusalem known as Solomon's Temple, the Knights Templars were established in 1118. Above is an effigy of a member of this powerful military order.

combats or jousts between the knights were fought. Sometimes two knights fought a duel, sometimes whole companies met in combat. When all were assembled, the heralds announced the names of the contestants. The combats which took place were not without danger. The points of the lances were usually encased in blocks of wood to make the encounter less harmful, but the sport was so rough and the knights fought so strenuously that many were wounded, and not a few, occasionally, killed. About each knight's helmet was tied the favour his lady had given him, and he fought to do her honour quite as much as to do himself credit. Each encounter was attended by much excitement, with the blowing of trumpets, the clash of steel, the shouts of heralds, and the applause of the spectators; and it continued until one or other of the knights was overcome. The defeated knight yielded his horse and armour to his adversary.

Sometimes a tournament lasted for several days, with feasting, dancing and hawking filling the hours not given to fighting. Hawking was a sport indulged in by the ladies and the squires as well as by the knights, and almost every lady had her own hawk or falcon, which, when unhooded, was trained to rise into the air and attack game birds. (*See* Falconry.)

After the festivities attending the conferring of knighthood, the young knight was free to go forth with his squire, in quest of adventure. As a knight-errant he sought a maiden in need of a champion, or a strange knight with whom to fight. Sometimes he stationed himself at a bridge or cross-roads to challenge to combat any knight who happened to pass that way. Usually he was sure of hospitality at any castle to which he came. After a time he might return to his father's castle, or join the following of some great lord, or become one of the Crusaders who went to Palestine to rescue the Holy Sepulchre from the Saracens. Everywhere he took with him the three watchwords of a knight: Religion, Honour, Courtesy.

With the advent of the longbow and crossbow, whose missiles could pierce the finest armour, and the invention of gunpowder and cannon rendering useless the feudal castle, the knight in armour passed out of existence. Knighthood then came to be merely a title of honour conferred for valuable service to the Sovereign or State. Two kinds of knighthood are conferred by British sovereigns ; knights who belong to one of the various orders, and knights bachelor, who do not belong to an order. There are nine orders : the Garter, the Thistle, St. Patrick, Bath, Star of India, St. Michael and St. George, Indian Empire, Royal Victorian Order, and the British Empire. A knight is entitled to the prefix Sir before his first name, and his wife is called by courtesy Lady, her legal title being Dame.

KNIGHTS TILTING IN THE TOURNAMENT

British Museum, Cotton MSS.

The tournament assuaged in times of peace the knightly appetite for battle. It originally included fights on foot as well as jousts, and was often serious enough until the introduction in the mid-15th century of the tilt or longitudinal barrier, seen in this miniature, made direct collisions impossible. In the picture the knight on this side of the barrier has unhorsed his opponent with his lance.

Royal College of Arms Westminster Roll

The noble traditions of chivalry that were born in the hard days of the Crusades expired amid the superficial splendours of the jousting field in the 15th and 16th centuries; and for use in these knightly tourneys plate armour assumed its most sumptuous and least practical forms. This illumination shows King Henry VIII tilting in the jousts held at Westminster, London, in honour of the birth of a son to his first wife, Catherine of Aragon, who watches the combat from a canopied couch.

A YOUNG KNIGHT'S VIGIL

THOUGH a young knight might win his spurs on the field of battle for bravery in the face of the enemy, in the early days of chivalry at least he had to be good as well as valiant. There was a religious element in the initiation of the early knights, and among the formal services of the Church was one for the making of a knight. The religious ceremony began with an all-night vigil of the aspirant before the altar on which his arms were laid. He then took a ceremonial purification in a bath—from which practice arose the still existing order of Knights of the Bath. This prepared him for the celebration of Mass, after which there was a sermon.

Knighthood was a military guild, and there was a freemasonry among knights of all nations that did much to humanize a rough age. In 1165 John of Salisbury thus described the ideals of knighthood: "To protect the Church, to fight against treachery, to reverence the priesthood, to fend off injustice from the poor, to make peace in your own province, to shed your blood for your brethren, and if need be to lay down your life."

This picture by John Pettie, R.A., showing a novice with drawn sword keeping his vigil, is in the Tate Gallery, London.

To face page 1865

Knights Templars.

Originating during the Crusades, when Hugh de Payens and Godfrey de St. Omer and seven other knights established it in 1118, ostensibly to protect pilgrims on the roads in the Holy Land, this religious and military order derived its name from the palace at Jerusalem known as Solomon's Temple, where the headquarters were.

Their power speedily increased and, having declared themselves defenders of the Christian faith and the Holy Sepulchre, they received recruits from all over Europe. Soon the strength and influence of the Templars rivalled that of the Knights of St. John of Jerusalem, or the Hospitallers, a contemporary order. The Saracens drove the Knights Templars out of the Holy Land in 1291, but by this time the order was immensely wealthy, its members considering themselves above kingly authority.

Philip IV of France and Pope Clement V led an attack on the knights, on the alleged grounds that they worshipped the devil and practised sorcery. This persecution extended throughout Europe, until in 1312 the possessions of the knights and of the order were confiscated almost everywhere, except in Germany, and the order was banned. In England the order was suppressed without violence. The Templars were placed under arrest during the reign of Edward II (1307–1327), and in 1309, after they had been convicted of various crimes, all their possessions passed into other hands.

The Temple Church (damaged by German bombs during the Second World War), close to Fleet Street, London, and the peaceful and picturesque locality around it known as The Temple, are present-day links with the Knights Templars. In page 1864 is a reproduction of one of the effigies formerly in the Temple Church.

Knitting Machines.

In hand knitting, a single continuous thread is formed into loops on a long eyeless needle; two needles are used in the simplest form, flat knitting, and the second needle casts a new row of loops into those already formed on the first. These loops are slipped off the needle in the process. Thus we get a piece of fabric connected together by the loops, the size of which depends on the diameter of the needles. Being formed of a single continuous thread, the piece of material can be unravelled by pulling upon the loose end.

Here is the difference from a woven fabric, which is made from at least two sets of threads—warp and weft—which cross and intersect one another at right angles, and lock the successive rows. The turn of the weft thread at each end of every row makes a " selvedge," and prevents unravelling.

We all know the varied and pleasing patterns which can be made by hand knitting, using various " stitches." In the knitting of tubular articles such as socks or stockings, four needles are needed, pointed at both ends. The loops are cast on three to form a circle of fabric. The first known knitting machine, called a knitting frame, is fairly ancient; it was invented by William Lee, of Calverton, in Nottinghamshire, and first used in 1589. Various improvements were made during the next 200 years, and in 1758 Jedediah Strutt added a ribbing machine to the frame. Stockings were the main articles made by these machines. Up till now the frame was worked by pedals, but in about 1828 a rotary frame was invented, and then steam power could be used. Stockings were made first in a flat piece of fabric, and then seamed up the back.

Moses Mellor is credited with the turning of the frame into a rotary machine. Methods of narrowing, or " fashioning," the fabric were next introduced ; and later still seamless stockings could be produced. William Cotton's rotary frame set the style for machines which developed into the modern type. In 1856 a needle carrying a small hinged latch was introduced. Warp knitting machines, forming vertical rows of loops, intersected between threads which are stretched horizontally something like the warp

Hand Stocking Frame

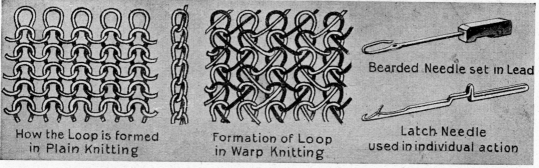

How the Loop is formed in Plain Knitting   Formation of Loop in Warp Knitting   Bearded Needle set in Lead

Latch Needle used in individual action

KNITTING MACHINE, NEEDLES AND STYLES OF KNITTING

Early methods of machine knitting and two kinds of needle used in the work are shown in the lower pictures. The upper illustration is of an old hand-frame, of a type that was mainly used for making stockings. The old machines produced a flat piece of fabric, which required to be sewn up at the back. Tubular machines, to turn out seamless stockings, came later. Both are used today, and 'fashioned' stockings are knitted flat, to be seamed up afterwards.

of a woven fabric, gave to knitted fabrics some of the characters of a woven one. As you may read in our story of Lace, it was an adapted knitting frame on which the first machine-made lace was made.

The working of modern automatic knitting machines is complicated; it will help us to understand machine knitting if we look first at the method used in the earliest frames. The thread was laid along a row of horizontal needles made of spring wire and hooked at the ends. The thread was pressed by the aid of " sinkers " into loops hanging between each of these needles, and at the same time the thread was slipped under the beards or hooks of the needles. Next the loops of the previous row were pushed over the closed hooks, and thus over the ends of the needles, joining these loops to the next row, and ultimately forming a continuous flat web of fabric which could afterwards be sewn up into tubular and other shapes. We can see how, by adding fashioning or narrowing mechanism, the width of the flat piece of knitted material could be varied so that, when seamed up later, a stocking could be formed, with its characteristic shape—its swell at the calf and its decreasing at the ankle.

Courtesy of I. & R. Morley, Ltd.

KNITTING MACHINES FOR MAKING FULLY-FASHIONED STOCKINGS

There are two complete 28-unit machines shown in the lower photograph. Each unit produces one stocking, and the average time taken to make a set of 28 is 50 minutes. In the course of a normal 45-hour week such a machine will turn out 55 dozen pairs of stockings. Top, a close-up view of one unit : the width of the fabric lessens and increases automatically to give the ' fashioned ' shape from leg to foot when later seamed up. *See text for explanation.*

Courtesy of I. & R. Morley, Ltd.

KNITTING SOCKS FOR MEN

Each sock needs 2½ miles of Cashmere thread ; the machine knits at the rate of 160 rows per minute, and there are more than 200 needles. A pair of seamless socks is completed in about 9 minutes.

Let us look now at a machine for making men's socks, or "half-hose" as they are named in the trade. A typical machine is illustrated in this page. It uses about 200 needles, and knits at the rate of 160 rows per minute. About 2½ miles of cashmere thread are consumed in knitting a pair of socks, and nearly 500 separate stitches are made every second; a complete pair of socks is turned out in nine minutes. All that remains to be done after this machine has finished its work is the linking of the toe, a highly skilled job done by women on another machine.

Women's stockings are made on a different type of machine, set up in long rows of units comprising 28 separate machines in effect, though they all work together. In page 1866 we show a near view and in another photograph are seen two complete machines, each with 28 sections. Each unit or section produces a fully-fashioned stocking, in this case of what is known as 45-gauge. The average time taken to make a set of 28 stockings is 50 minutes; in a working week of 45 hours, the possible production is 55 dozen pairs.

As the piece of hose fabric is being knitted, the width is lessened at the proper places by a narrowing machine which takes loops from the outside needles and transfers them inwards. In the heels and toes also the narrowing is varied so as to give the close fitting and "tailored" shape to those parts, as well as to the leg. Strengthening threads are introduced at the ankle, the heel, the side panels of the foot bottom, and the toe, to give reinforcement. The control of all these variations in width and thickness is brought about by automatic disks and by inclined studs which are set out beforehand on what is known as a "pattern chain."

So much for hosiery. Underwear and other knitted garments are made on machines working on similar principles. Machine-knitted garments have brought much comfort and convenience to men and women, and in the case of children's garments have supplanted the heavy and clumsy underwear of half a century ago. We owe a big debt to the devisers of the early knitting frames, and to the long line of inventors who have made possible cheap and plentiful knitted wear.

Knives and Forks. In Queen Elizabeth's time (1533–1603) etiquette ruled that one should not use more than three fingers when conveying food to one's mouth, and the use of forks at table was laughed at as a new-fangled fad as late as 1608. Table-knives, too, were rare, and large portions of food were cut up with the knife which each person habitually carried with him stuck in his stocking or in his belt.

But though table-knives are comparatively recent, knives for general purposes were one of the first inventions of early Man. Many implements, whose use and general form was that of a knife blade, have been found dating back to the Stone Age. Spoons, too, have been in use a long time. In museums we may see spoons of wood, stone or ivory, which were found in ancient Egyptian tombs.

National Museum, Florence; photo. Alinari

ANCIENT CUTLERY

Here are a pair of beautifully chased carvers, and one dinner knife, made in Italy in the 16th century, when forks at least were still uncommon.

The Greeks and Romans used spoons of bronze or silver, and during the Middle Ages spoons of bone, wood or tin were common; the wealthy had spoons made of beaten silver. Forks came along after knives and spoons, and were long used only in cooking or for holding the joint of meat while it was being carved. The first forks were two - pronged affairs, much like our carving-forks, and were made of iron, bone, or hard wood.

The use of the fork at table seems to have been introduced into Europe from the Orient through Venice. A story of the 11th century tells of the wife of a Venetian ruler who was "luxurious beyond belief," because "instead of eating like other people, she had her food cut up and ate the pieces by means of a two-pronged fork."

When the custom of using a dining-fork was brought to England in 1608 by a traveller who had observed it in Italy, it caused a great deal of excite-ment. He was laughed at by some, and railed at by others, one person declaring that it was an "insult to Providence, who has given us fingers." Even today forks are not used in many parts of the world, food being prepared in such a way as to render them unnecessary, as in China and Japan where chop-sticks are used.

ALL *the* KNOTS *and* HOW *to* TIE THEM

N̄ot only Boy Scouts and sailors need to know how to tie knots. All of us at some time or other are faced with occasions requiring ability to make a reef or slip or other reliable knot, or perhaps a splice.

Knots, HITCHES AND SPLICES. It is important to know how to tie knots properly. Such knowledge saves much time and trouble, and in some cases even lives depend upon it. The sailor aloft in a ship's rigging, the cowboy roping a wild steer, the steeple-jack dangling high in the air, all of them know what will happen if a knot slips.

Some knots are valuable because of the speed with which they can be made. But the best are those that hold firmly without slipping, yet do not bind so tightly that it is hard to untie them when their work is done. Most of the simpler knots which are described here meet this requirement.

When a rope is bent in a loop, the looped part is called the bight. The long portion of the rope is known as the standing part, and the short part used in forming the knot or hitch is known as the end. The simplest is the overhand knot (Fig. 1). It forms a part of many other knots. It is used to keep the end of a rope from ravelling, to provide a hand-hold on a halter or bell-rope, to prevent the end of a rope from running through a pulley, or a sewing thread

from pulling through cloth. The square knot, known also as the reef or sailor's knot (Fig. 2A), is the commonest of all for fastening ropes or strings together. When correctly made it is as perfect as a knot can be, for it is reliable, and unties easily. If we tie our shoe-laces correctly, we use this square knot, although the ends are not pulled right through but are looped and drawn tight. When a reef knot is tied without a single or double bow, it is called a "hard" knot. Its one disadvantage is that it will not hold so well when made with ropes of different sizes. This knot is always used when the sailor reefs a sail, for even with stiff wet ropes it can be loosened easily by pushing the free ends back against the knot, and completely untied by pulling at the loops which appear. Surgeons use the reef knot when tying arteries.

Sometimes when we are tying our shoe-laces we make a mistake, and instead of forming a reef knot we get the troublesome granny or lubber's knot, which slips easily and gives way under a strain (Fig. 2B). Many people go through life with their

Fig. 1.—OVERHAND KNOT
Standing part of the rope is held in the left hand and the end is passed back over it, and put through the loop just formed.

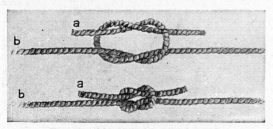

Fig. 2A.—SQUARE OR REEF KNOT
Here is shown the proper way to tie two pieces of rope together. The ropes are passed once around each other. The ends are then brought up and the process repeated, care being taken that on each side the standing part and free end (a, b) come out on the same side of the loop. When drawn tight, the free ends will lie parallel to the standing parts.

Fig. 2B.—GRANNY KNOT
This unreliable knot results when the second twist, instead of following the square knot rule, is made in the reverse direction, so that the parts (a, b) are separated from each other by a part of the loop. When this is drawn tight the ends stick out at right angles to the knot.

Fig. 3.—WEAVER'S OR SHEET-BEND KNOT
This also begins like a square knot, but one of the ends thrusts back under itself and comes out at right angles to the knot. Weavers use it to tie ends of threads.

Fig. 4.—RUNNING OR SLIP KNOT
A bight is first formed and an overhand knot made around the standing part.

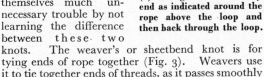

Fig. 5.—BOWLINE
Make a loop (a) and pass end (b) through it. Now carry end as indicated around the rope above the loop and then back through the loop.

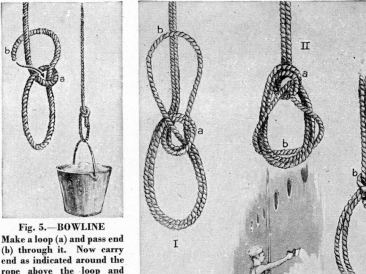

Fig. 6.—BOWLINE ON A BIGHT
Make a loop (a) and pass the end of the bight (b) through it as in I. Now hold the loop in the left hand and pull the bight down and around the hanging part as in II. Now raise the bight (b) up above the loop (a) and draw it down tight as in III. This is much stronger than the bowline.

shoe-laces always dangling without realizing that they are giving themselves much unnecessary trouble by not learning the difference between these two knots. The weaver's or sheetbend knot is for tying ends of rope together (Fig. 3). Weavers use it to tie together ends of threads, as it passes smoothly through the heddle. One of the simplest "eye" knots is shown in Fig. 4, and is known as the running or slip knot.

The bowline is one of the best and most useful of all the knots; indeed, it is often called the king of knots (Fig. 5). It will not slip and is widely used —on the farm, in construction work, by mechanics, and in nearly every branch of industry. It is the safest knot to put round an animal's neck. It is often

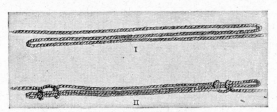

Fig. 7.—SHEEPSHANK
Fold rope back on itself forming a double loop of the required length (I). Then weave a clove hitch (Fig. 11) with the standing part of the rope over each end of the double loop (II), and draw tight. This is one way of shortening a rope.

used in fastening a rope to a bucket to hoist material such as tools or mortar, to workmen on a scaffold. When tying an animal or fastening a rope to a bucket, the end (b) is first passed round the animal's neck or round the bail of the bucket, before going through the loop (a).

A close relative of this knot is called a bowline on a bight (Fig. 6). Being made with a loop or bight of the rope, it is much stronger and does not require the use of either end of the rope in tying it. With this knot a man can be lowered in safety from a great height. Sailors swing comfortably in the loop of this knot. It is used also to hold ships to their mooring posts.

Although there is no sharp distinction between knots and hitches, the name hitch is usually applied to those temporary devices which are not, as the

sailors say, "made fast." A knot is thus the more permanent fastening. Another difference is that a knot may be made in the rope itself without requiring anything else for its security. A hitch, on the other hand, usually takes the form of self-binding loops round some solid object, and will come loose as soon as the strain is removed. The sheepshank is

Fig. 8.—SLIP KNOT HALTER TIE
Put the end of the halter rope through a ring or hole in the manger, then tie a slip knot as in Fig. 4, except that the end of the rope is not pulled all the way through but is left to form a loop (right).

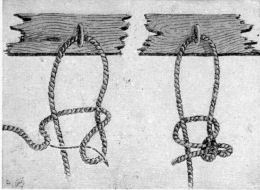

Fig. 9.—'FIGURE EIGHT' HALTER TIE
The difference between this knot and plain halter tie lies in the extra twist given the first loop, before the second loop passes through it.

the most practical way of shortening a rope without cutting it, and often proves of use to sailors (Fig. 7).

The halter-hitch has many uses, the most common one being to fasten the halter ropes of horses or cows to the manger or to a post or hitching ring (Fig. 8). When a halter-hitch is properly made it will become very tight if any strain is put upon the rope, and therefore should never be used round an animal's neck. An even better halter tie is shown in Fig. 9. This is called the figure eight tie, and no matter how tight it has been drawn by the animal it can easily be untied by jerking the loose end of the rope.

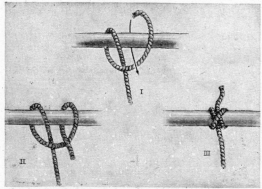

Fig. 10.—CLOVE HITCH
To put a clove hitch on a stake or other support, the top of which can be reached, make a half-hitch or loop (I), passing the right hand part of the rope under the left. Now hold the first loop in the left hand and make another one exactly like it with the right (II). Slip the right hand loop over the left-hand one, drop the loops over the stake and draw them tight. When a clove hitch is put round a tree or high pole, the end has to be passed around and woven under and over to get the same effect (III).

The clove-hitch, best known of all the hitches, is easy to make, and the harder the pull against it the tighter it holds. The foundation of it is the half-hitch (Fig. 10, I). It is, in fact, sometimes called the double half-hitch. It will serve as well as a fastening whenever the rope is to have a constant and steady strain upon it. It is always easy to loosen, even when made with a hard wet rope. Note that when the clove hitch is put around a

tree or high pole, the end has to be passed round and woven under and over in order to get the same effect. In Fig. 11 the clove hitch is used to make a running noose.

Few people know how to splice a rope, yet knowledge of splicing is valuable in many ways. A worn or broken rope can be neatly mended by this means, and a good splice is always stronger than a knot. Splicing is necessary if the rope is to pass through pulley blocks where knots cannot be used. The simplest type is the short splice. In making this the strands of each rope are spliced into the strands of the other rope. First the strands of each rope are untwisted (Fig. 12).

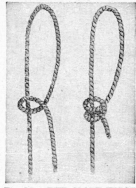

Fig. 11.—THE CLOVE HITCH SLIP KNOT
In this knot the rope is looped over and a clove hitch is made around the standing part.

Then the ends are brought together so that strands *a, b,* and *c* alternate between strands *d, e,* and *f.* When they have been spliced together as far as they will go (II) they may be tied with a string to hold them in place during the remainder of the operation.

Taking one of the strands (*a,* III), it is passed over the twisted strand nearest to it and under the next to it. The same thing is done with strands *b* and *c* in one direction, and with *d, e, f* in the other direction. The process is repeated (IV) until all the six loose strands have been woven over and under into the

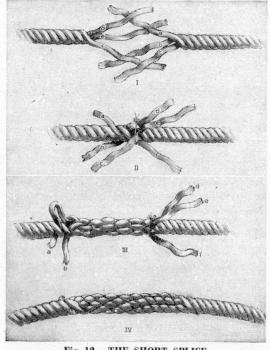

Fig. 12.—THE SHORT SPLICE
A worn or broken rope can be neatly mended with a splice, a good splice always being stronger than a knot.

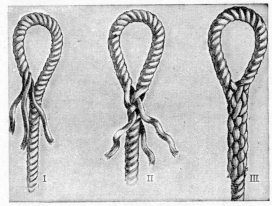

Fig. 13.—THE EYE SPLICE
Except that the end of the rope is woven back into itself, the eye splice is made in the same way as the short splice.

solid body of the rope. One must be careful that the separate strands do not unravel during the splicing. A properly-made splice will give practically the same strength as the original rope, provided that a sufficient length of strands is spliced. The short splice makes the joint much thicker than the rest of the rope. In splicing hard-twisted ropes, a pointed peg or marlinspike is often used for making the openings under the twisted strands so that the loose strands can pass through more easily.

The eye splice is made according to the same principle as the short splice, except that the end of the rope is woven back into itself, forming a loop, which in this instance is called an eye (Fig. 13). The rope is untwisted for six or eight inches, and the untwisted ends are doubled back against the main part of the rope to form a loop of the size desired (I). Each of the loose ends is then passed over the nearest strand and under the next (II) until the splice is completed (III). It will be noticed that here, as in the short splice, the loose ends are woven round in the reverse direction from the twist of the body of the rope. The long splice is used when a rope must pass through a block, the joint being the same thickness as the original rope.

Knox, JOHN (1514?–72). Seldom has a man so imprinted himself upon a nation as did the religious reformer John Knox upon the people of Scotland. Nowhere was the Church of his day more corrupt and oppressive than in Scotland. Cardinal Beaton, the Chancellor of Scotland,

matched the scandal of his private life with the zeal with which he persecuted heretics. His murder, in May 1546, is attributed to revenge for his burning of the reforming preacher George Wishart. Seizing the cardinal's castle of St. Andrews, his murderers were besieged there, and among the sympathizers who flocked to their aid was John Knox. Here he became preacher to the Protestant reformers.

In June 1547 the castle surrendered to a French fleet, for Scotland was then in close alliance with France. Knox and other captives were taken to France and condemned to labour at the oars in the convict galleys. Released in 1549 he took refuge in England, but with the accession in 1553 of Mary Tudor, who was a Catholic, England ceased to be safe for Protestants. The next five years he spent chiefly in Geneva in contact with John Calvin, the French religious reformer.

The French regent of Scotland, Mary of Guise, believed herself strong enough in 1559 to forbid the teaching of the Protestant religion. When Knox arrived in Edinburgh, in May of that year, he was outlawed. He escaped to Dundee and Perth, where his sermons against Roman Catholicism led to civil war. To counterbalance the French alliance, on which the regent relied, the Lords of the Congregation, as the Protestant leaders were

Tate Gallery, London; photo Mansell

KNOX PREACHING TO THE PROTESTANT LEADERS
When the Scottish religious reformer John Knox returned to Edinburgh from exile in France in 1559 he was outlawed by Mary of Guise, the Catholic Regent of Scotland. But there was so much agitation against this decree that he was allowed to preach for six months. This picture by Sir David Wilkie (1785–1841) depicts Knox preaching to the Lords of the Congregation, as the Protestant chiefs were called.

called, successfully appealed to England, where Elizabeth now reigned in place of Mary. Mary of Guise died almost at the moment of Protestant victory. A treaty signed on June 6, 1560, led to the withdrawal of the French troops and left the Lords of the Congregation the masters of Scotland.

Knox's power was now at its height. Parliament abolished the Pope's authority in Scotland and forbade the celebration of Mass. When young Mary Queen of Scots returned from France to Scotland in 1561 only the protection of her half-brother, Lord James Stuart, enabled her to attend Roman Catholic services in her private chapel. Loud and bitter were the protests of Knox, and Mary humbled herself in repeated interviews with the stern reformer. So began a contest which ended only when the queen, as a result of her own criminal folly in marrying her husband's murderer, had fallen from her high estate and become a fugitive and a prisoner in England.

After preaching the coronation sermon of Mary's baby son by the Earl of Darnley, James IV of Scotland, Knox retired from public life, and died three years later on November 24, 1572.

Koala. With its fat body, short legs, small ears and snub nose, this little animal closely resembles a "teddy bear." It is about the size of a small bull-terrier dog, and at one time was common in parts of Australia, especially the south-east. But hunting koalas for their fur—which is very soft, and of a pleasing grey or brown colour

Australian National Travel Association
KOALAS OF AUSTRALIA
An expert climber, the koala is commonly called the native bear by Australians. It is a member of the marsupial group, to which kangaroos also belong. A thick-set animal resembling a teddy bear, it spends most of its time in eucalyptus or blue gum trees feeding on the leaves and shoots.

—resulted in a serious reduction of numbers, so that they are now protected by law. The koala's home is in the tops of tall eucalyptus trees, where it eats the young buds and shoots. It is nocturnal in its habits, but at no time is it very active. And because it is specially adapted to clamber about tree-branches it makes but slow progress on the ground, to which it occasionally descends.

The koala, whose scientific name is *Phascolarctus cinereus*—Australians call him "native bear"—is a member of the group of animals known as marsupials, all of which have a pouch in which the young live for weeks after birth. The kangaroo and opossum are the two best-known members of this group. The koala has no tail.

Koran. On the sacred book called the Koran (derived from the Arabic word *qur'an*, meaning "that should be read") is founded the religion of about 225 million Mahomedans or followers of the prophet Mahomet (*c.* 570–632), a native of Mecca, Arabia. It is used in public worship, is the chief text-book in Mahomedan schools, and upon it are based the Mahomedan legal code and way of life.

The Koran is regarded by Mahomedans or Moslems ("the faithful") as the word of God revealed to the prophet Mahomet through the angel Gabriel. Its various parts were dictated by the prophet, from time to time, and inscribed on dried palm leaves, bits of leather, whitened shoulder-blades of sheep, or whatever else was at hand. In the reign of the Caliph Abu-Bekr (573–634) these fragments were made into one volume, of which many copies were made. The text is in rhymed prose and is recognized as the finest production in Arabic literature.

The Koran is about as long as the New Testament, and is divided into 114 *suras*, or chapters. Each of these begins with the words "In the name of God, the merciful and compassionate." The book consists of history, legends, prophecies, moral precepts, and laws. The histories are chiefly about Old Testament characters, and many of the doctrines and laws are the same as those of Judaism or of Christianity. Moses, Jesus and Mahomet are named as the greatest of the line of prophets sent by God to lead mankind in the path of truth.

The fundamental doctrine is the oneness of God expressed in the simple statement, "There is no God but God (Allah)"; and submission to His will (Islam) is the highest virtue. Much emphasis is laid also on the Last Judgement, when everyone shall receive reward or punishment for his deeds. The Mahomedan is commanded to pray five times a day, turning his face toward Mecca, to fast at stated times, to give alms, and to make at least one pilgrimage in his lifetime to Mecca, the sacred city, if his financial circumstances allow him to do so. (*See* Mahomet.)

Korea. Occupying a peninsula extending south from the east coast of Asia, between the Sea of Japan and the Yellow Sea, Korea is separated from Manchuria and Siberia by the Yalu and Tumen rivers. Most of the country enjoys a sub-tropical climate, but the winters in the north-east are very cold.

About three-quarters of Korea is mountainous or hilly; in the north some peaks, notably Pei-shan,

Will Taylor; Dorien Leigh

PICTURES OF LIFE IN KOREA

Above is a palanquin, which travels on its single wheel on smooth ground and is carried over rough ground. Top right, a Korean woman in full dress, showing her wonderful sash. Lower right shows an outdoor stove from which heat is carried into the house through a channel.

rise to over 8,000 feet. A range runs down from the north, with spurs extending to the south and west. The coastal plain in the east is narrow but fertile ; between the western spurs lie deep valleys. Tigers, leopards, bears, foxes and deer are found; and the fur-bearing animals include martens, otters and beavers.

Although only about a fifth of the total area of 85,000 square miles can be cultivated, some three-quarters of the people are farmers, earning their living from tiny plots of land averaging about four acres. The most important crop is rice, others being barley, wheat, millet, soya beans, cotton and tobacco. Most of the work in the fields is done by hand.

The Japanese, who ruled Korea from 1910 to 1945, developed the resources of the country. Paper and pulp mills were built; coal, iron and gold were worked. There are also deposits of silver, lead, tungsten and molybdenum. A vast dam completed on the Yalu river in 1941 furnishes hydro-electric power for electro-chemical industries. There are 3,000 miles of railway and 19,000 miles of roads. The largest city is Seoul, on the Kan river, others being Heijo, the old capital, Gishu, Fusan, Chinampo and Jinsen.

The Koreans are of the Mongol family and are physically a fine race, taller than the Japanese. Years of misgovernment and oppression have made them lazy and servile, and they show little capacity for political or industrial organization.

Before the beginning of the Christian era the people of Korea possessed a high degree of civilization, and literary and religious culture. The kingdom was founded in 1122 B.C., and in the fourth century under the influence of Buddhism the Koreans began to imitate Chinese ideas and culture. From 1592 to 1598 the Japanese pillaged

the land, and from that time on the Koreans hated the Japanese. For the next 200 years Korea remained isolated from the world; and it was not until 1876 that Japan was able to force the Koreans to open their ports to foreign ships.

In 1910 Japan annexed Korea and in 1919 incorporated it in the Japanese Empire. When Japan surrendered to the Allied nations in August 1945 (during the Second World War) troops of the Soviet Union occupied the northern half of Korea, and United States forces garrisoned the southern half. A Korean Republic, with its capital at Seoul, was established in August 1948 in the American-occupied zone, Mr. Syngman Rhee becoming the first President. The population of Korea is 24,326,000.

Kosciusko, TADEUSZ (1746–1817). Like

Lafayette, the French soldier who aided the American colonists against Britain during the American War of Independence (1776–82), this gallant Polish general and patriot won fame as a champion of freedom on two continents.

Kosciusko (pron. kos-yus'-ko) was born in Lithuania on February 12, 1746, the son of a Court official, and entered the Polish army. An unhappy love affair led him when a young captain of artillery, in 1777, to leave Poland and offer his sword to the new republic of the United States, and there he served with distinction as an engineer in the War of Independence.

Poland meanwhile was succumbing to external aggression and internal anarchy. Kosciusko returned in time to fight valiantly but unsuccessfully at Dubienka (1792) and elsewhere against the Russian invasion which preceded the second partition of Poland between Russia, Prussia and Austria in 1793. When the Poles rebelled in March 1794 Kosciusko became dictator and commander-in-chief.

His victory over the Russians at Raclawice, won in part by peasant forces, was followed by the capture of Warsaw. His engineering skill successfully defended the city against siege by the combined Russian and Prussian armies. But the defeat of his army of 7,000 Poles by 16,000 Russians at Maciejowice (October 10, 1794) ended Poland's chance of withstanding her powerful neighbours.

Taken prisoner by the Russians, Kosciusko was released in 1796, and visited England, France and America. His remaining years were spent in Switzerland, where he was killed through his horse falling over a precipice on October 15, 1817.

Kossuth, Louis

(1802–94). A brilliant Hungarian lawyer and a fiery orator, Kossuth (pron. kosh'-oot) was born at Monok, Hungary, on September 19, 1802, and studied law at Budapest University. He entered the Hungarian Parliament in 1825, where his revolutionary ideas soon attracted attention and eventually led to his imprisonment in 1837.

From the study of the Bible and Shakespeare during his confinement he gained a wonderful knowledge of the English language. In 1847 he was again elected to Parliament, where he fearlessly denounced Austrian domination of Hungary. In 1848 Hungary revolted against Austrian rule, and Kossuth became the virtual dictator of his country. But owing to his vanity he was unable to get on with the other Hungarian leaders, and the rebellion was suppressed in 1849.

Kossuth was compelled to flee into Turkey for refuge. Austria and Russia demanded that he should be given up for execution, but Britain prevailed on the Turkish government to refuse. In 1851 he arrived in England, where he remained for the greater part of the next 17 years. When his rival Deák brought about the reconciliation of Hungary with Austria (1867), Kossuth, then in Italy, refused to return to his native land. He died in Turin on March 20, 1894.

Kyoto.

For more than 1,000 years Kyoto (Kioto) was the political, intellectual, and artistic centre of Japan. Rich in history and legend, a city of ancient temples, beautiful palaces, and rare treasures of art, the city represents all that is most admirable and interesting in old Japanese civilization. Wooded hills encircle it, and the River Kamogawa, for the greater part of the year little more than a rivulet, meanders through its midst. On surrounding hills are picturesque Buddhist and Shinto monasteries, shrines and pagodas, surrounded by gardens, persimmon orchards and tea plantations.

W. Wimbledon Hill

BEAUTY SPOT OF KYOTO

On the Japanese island of Honshu, Kyoto contains more than 1,000 temples. The highly-ornamented gables shown above are part of the famous Kiyomzu-Dera temples which stand on a hill above the city. The artistic centre of Japan, Kyoto is noted for its pottery, bronze and lacquer ware.

Kyoto tea is considered the finest grown in the whole of Japan. Indeed, it is thought to be far too good for export, so practically the whole crop is consumed by the Japanese themselves. In the manufacture of pottery, bronze, and ivory wares, of cloisonné, silk, embroidery, brocade, fans, and lacquer dusted with gold or silver powder, Kyoto surpasses all other cities in Japan. Proud of their products the craftsmen handed down from father to son the secret processes of their handicrafts.

Kyoto is still the goal of devout pilgrims from all parts of Japan. Within its borders are nearly 1,000 temples and shrines, many of which appear in the most unexpected places—in the heart of the business district, in Theatre Street, and in secluded gardens. Fires have repeatedly devastated the city, which was founded in 794, but each time it has been rebuilt. During the Middle Ages, when Kyoto enjoyed its greatest prestige, the population is estimated to have been about 500,000. But as Tokyo (the northern capital) grew, Kyoto declined in size and importance, and in 1868 the Imperial Court was moved to the northern metropolis. Kyoto was the only major Japanese city that was not bombed by Allied aircraft during the Second World War (1939–45). The population is estimated to be about a million. (*See* illus., page 1801.)

L

Labour and National Service, MINISTRY OF.

Established in 1916 as the Ministry of Labour, this department of the British Government took over all the affairs previously under the Labour Department of the Board of Trade. Its responsibilities included national business affecting unemployment and insurance, administered through labour exchanges, friendly societies, and trade unions; industrial arbitration; and employment and training of juvenile workers. During the Second World War (1939–45) the Ministry took over the organization of manpower, including registration for military service. Its name was changed to its present form in December 1939. The main London office is in St. James's Square, S.W.1.

Labour Movement.

After the introduction of the factory system as a result of the Industrial Revolution in the 18th and 19th centuries, most of the former independent handworkers became wage-earners completely dependent on their employers. Competition forced them to accept low wages, and it also in many instances made them endure a working day of 12 to 14 hours in unhealthy conditions.

When working men protested separately against these conditions they seldom gained their demands and, indeed, often lost their positions. At that period there was a surplus of men, and once a worker lost his job he might be for months unemployed. Accordingly, workers in industrial countries began to unite for self-protection in trade unions and other labour organizations. Today about 6,671,000 workers belong to registered labour unions in Great Britain.

The first trade unions were formed in England by the tailors and wool-workers, who found that they could improve their conditions only by bargaining as a united group with their employers. Previous efforts of labour to organize had been discouraged, from as early as the 14th century, by scores of Court decisions; and labour unions did not receive full legal recognition until the Trade Union Acts of 1871 and 1876.

As labour gained power through organization, political parties arose in most of the industrial nations to represent the workers in government. In England two significant movements were forerunners of the later political organization of workers. The Owenites, followers of Robert Owen (1771–1858), Socialist and reformer, sought among other aims the betterment of working and living conditions for the masses; and the Chartist Movement, started by the London Working Men's Association in 1837, urged political reforms. Later, Socialist groups, organized locally, sought to gain a voice in governmental matters. Notable among these were the Fabian Society, 1884, and the Scottish Labour Party, formed under the leadership of Keir Hardie in 1889.

When local efforts to elect labour candidates to Parliament failed—mainly because of lack of money to pay for the expenses—various labour groups united to form the Independent Labour Party in 1893. The trade unions and Socialist organizations united in 1900 to form the Labour Representation Committee, which became the Labour Party in 1906. In 1924 a Labour government took office for the first time, with Ramsay MacDonald (1866–1937) as Prime Minister. A second one, again led by Ramsay MacDonald, held office from 1929 to 1931. A third took office in 1945, Mr. Clement Attlee succeeding Mr. Winston Churchill as Prime Minister. (*See also* Socialism).

Labrador.

This most easterly part of the North American continent consists of a triangular strip of the Canadian mainland from 10 to 475 miles wide and about 800 miles long. The territory forms a dependency of Newfoundland, and in 1927 the boundaries between Labrador and the Canadian province of Quebec were fixed, Cape Chidley and Blanc Sablon marking the northern and southern limits respectively. The estimated area is 110,000 square miles.

A barren land of brief summers and cold stormy winters, Labrador has an average annual temperature below freezing point. Its ports are ice-locked until midsummer by the cold waters of the Labrador current flowing down from the Polar regions. The country is townless and almost roadless. Goose Airport, near the head of Hamilton Inlet, is on the shortest air route between North America and Europe.

The Cree Indian trapper of the south, the squat sturdy Eskimo of the north, and the scattered groups of white settlers are well supplied with firewood, lumber and game. Trapping is the chief winter occupation; fur-bearing animals include ermine, marten, fox, beaver, mink, otter, muskrat

Georg Haeckel

LABRADOR ESKIMO
In the northern part of Labrador are scattered bands of Eskimos. This young woman is wearing a sealskin costume as a protection against the cold, which is intensified by bitter winds.

Georg Haeckel

SUMMER ON THE COAST OF LABRADOR

For the fisherfolk of Labrador the months of August and September are the busiest of the year, because these comprise the cod-fishing season on which many of the inhabitants depend for their livelihood. The people scatter along the coast, living in tents (above), while they split, dry and salt the fish.

In the interior of this vast region there is an untapped source of almost limitless water-power on the Hamilton river, some 250 miles from its mouth. The potential provider of this power is Grand Falls, 316 feet high and 200 feet wide, whose roar can be heard 20 miles away. If these falls were used to generate electric power it has been estimated that they would develop energy equal to 1,700,000 horsepower, capable of operating a large proportion of Canada's factories and railways.

After John Cabot visited the coast of Labrador in 1497 fishermen from England, France, Spain and Portugal flocked there, attracted by the excellent cod-fishing. The territory has been British since 1793, but the interior was little known until 1840. Newfoundland and Canada for long disputed over their respective boundaries in Labrador, and in 1927 the British Privy Council, the supreme court of the British Commonwealth, awarded Newfoundland the whole area east of the Height of Land, which divides the east-flowing rivers from those with their outlets in Ungava Bay on Hudson Strait. The estimated population is about 5,000.

and lynx. In the summer nearly everyone goes fishing for salmon and cod. Exports of dried cod, salmon, trout, herring and cod-liver oil are the country's chief source of income. Furs, lumber and eider-down are also sent abroad. There are vast forests of birch and fir, and valuable mineral deposits in the interior.

DAINTY LACE *and* HOW *it is* MADE

One of the most beautiful handicraft products, lace has been to most a joy to see and to many a pleasure to make for hundreds of years. The main kinds and their characteristics are described here.

Lace. It is probable that lace-making developed gradually from two other crafts—one utilitarian, that of net-making, and one decorative, that of embroidery. Formerly the production of lace fabrics was a slow process, demanding great skill and infinite care. Also it was an expensive handicraft to patronize. At the Paris Exhibition in 1867, for example, there was a dress of filmy lace which was valued at £3,500. To make the cobweb-like fabric of this dress 40 women toiled day after day for a period of seven years.

This is only one example of the extreme costliness of lace, and the painstaking toil required in its making before the invention of lace-making machines made possible the mass production of cheap lace. On these machines many thousands of yards of lace can be woven in less time than half a hundred workers can produce a few inches of hand-made lace of the same pattern. Some of these machine-made laces are so exquisite in beauty of design and perfection of finish that it is difficult for the inexpert to distinguish them from hand-made laces.

The lace-making machine is one of the marvels of the engineering world. Imagine a machine carrying on its reels, which are placed one above the other, fine threads set so close together that a sixpence can only just pass edgeways between them. The power is turned on, and shining little flattened bobbins dance in and out between the close-set threads. Sometimes they dart swiftly over one thread and under the next; sometimes they stop and vibrate rapidly a fraction of a second before they go on.

This vibrating movement twists sometimes the warp threads fastened to the reels and sometimes the bobbin threads, and the patterns are made by these twisted threads. Combs quickly press down through the threads to the completed pattern to make it more compact, and more quickly still are up and out of the way. Sixty pieces of lace are often made at once.

As in the case of so many other labour-saving machines, the development of the lace machine to its present perfection was a slow process. In the year 1764 a stocking maker of Nottingham, examining the lace on his wife's cap, believed that he could make a similar fabric on his stocking-knitting frame (*see* Knitting Machine), and produced an open-mesh fabric, which, however, was a knitted fabric made of one thread passing from one end of the piece to the other, and which unravelled if the thread broke.

In 1809 John Heathcoat perfected his bobbin-net machine, for making a plain hexagonal net. It got its name because the individual threads were wound upon bobbins, and was a fundamental

in lace. Our illustrations show various stages in producing machine-made lace: making from the original design a pattern sheet from which the Jacquard cards are punched; punching these cards; and a machine on which the lace is woven. Nearly every design and mesh of hand-made lace has been mechanically produced. The machine-lace industry of Europe is carried on in Paris, Lyons, Calais, Puy, St. Gall, Nottingham and Plauen.

Millions of yards of plain net are made every year —for dresses, millinery, as a basis for embroidery, and for more prosaic uses such as mosquito netting and so on. Machines have thus made beautiful lace accessible to all, repeating some of the finest designs originated by hand workers. It is distinguishable generally by its greater regularity and by the absence of the little differences and variations which lend character and individuality to hand-made lace.

Hand-made laces are still worked all over the world, but their production in quantities for commerce is confined to France, Belgium, Spain, Ireland, Italy and England. Because of the infinite care and pains and the great amount of time that have to be taken in its production, hand-made lace will always remain one of the dearest articles of commerce. Some hand-made laces, it is true, are produced easily and cheaply, but on the most delicate, finely wrought designs years of labour may be expended.

Hand-made lace is of two main types—needle-point and bobbin or pillow lace. Needle-point is made with a needle and a single thread. The pattern, drawn on parchment, is stitched to a piece of heavy linen for the purpose of holding it straight. Threads, sometimes three or four in number, are laid on the many lines of the pattern and are lightly fastened through to the linen. The entire figure is then worked, filling and open-work mesh by mesh, and when it is completed the stitches holding it to the linen are cut and the lace comes free.

In bobbin lace, the design is drawn out on stiff parchment, stretched over a

departure from the adapted knitting-frame just mentioned, utilizing, in its working, one main practice of the hand lace makers. Then an invention by a Nottingham mechanic named John Leavers laid the foundation of the modern lace-making machine.

Leavers's machine had (1) a series of vertical threads; and (2) a bar carrying many small bobbins, on each of which a thread was wound. These bobbins could be moved from side to side in such a manner that patterns could be formed by twisting one set of threads around the other set. There might be as many as 5,000 tiny bobbins.

After Joseph Marie Jacquard invented his pattern-weaving apparatus in 1804 (see Jacquard Loom), a modification of this was adapted to enable patterns to be made automatically

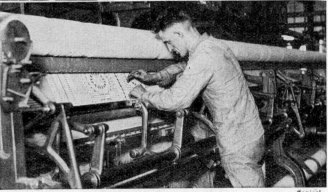

Topical

LACE-MAKING BY MACHINERY

In the top picture an operator is making a pattern sheet from the original design. From this will be punched Jacquard cards (centre), which control the design when the lace-making machine is running. In the lower picture a 'fault' in the weaving is being corrected. These photographs were taken in a lace curtain factory at Nottingham, England.

EXQUISITE EXAMPLES OF NEEDLE-POINT AND—

Hayward's (Bond Street) Ltd.

Lace made by working with a single-threaded needle is known as needle-point : four specimens are shown above. Limerick lace (top left) has a running design worked on fine net. At top right is a piece of needle appliqué. In the centre, Point de France, dating from the time of Louis XIV (1638–1715), a forerunner of many machine-made laces. Lower, raised Venice point ; the outlines are first heavily padded, the design being connected with threads.

Hayward's (Bond Street) Ltd.

Another form of hand-made lace is made on a ' pillow '—a small cushion on which the design is marked with pins—with the thread wound on bobbins. At the top left is a specimen of Maltese silk lace, the border showing a design of Maltese crosses. Top right, Mechlin, another type of pillow lace, one of the many produced in Belgium. Centre, a delicate variety of guipure made with bobbins. Lower, detail from a handkerchief border in modern Bruges lace.

LACE

"pillow," a round or oval board stuffed to form a cushion, and placed on the knees of the worker. The pattern is picked out along the outline of the drawing, and small pins are stuck at close intervals. Around these pins threads wound on bobbins of varying size are twisted and crossed to form the various meshes and openings. The pattern, or "gimp," is formed by interweaving a much thicker thread. Needle-point lace is the heavier lace, and has the appearance of greater strength, but pillow lace is very supple and drapes well.

It is probable that lace, as we understand it today, was first made when Europe, emerging from the severe and formal Middle Ages, began to bedeck itself in a graceful and beautiful manner,

although specimens of woven fabrics of lace-like character have been found in ancient tombs.

During the first two centuries of lace-making, men used more lace on their dress than women. It was used for ruffs, cuffs, collars, scarves and cravats, while ruffles of lace at the top of heavy boots were not unusual. The most famous laces of this early time were those of Venice, Milan and Genoa. Venice was celebrated for her points, and Genoa and Milan produced almost exclusively pillow laces. Such lace as was woven in the 16th and 17th centuries cannot be made in a commercial way today. The modern hand-made lace is often more artistic in design, but it cannot be compared in fineness of execution and thread with the old pieces preserved in our museums.

As the industry developed in those early days, the workers broke away from the stiff geometrical designs which mark the early laces. The various towns of Italy, France, Belgium, Spain, and elsewhere, sought to make a product of exclusive pattern that would gain them prestige in the few great centres of commerce of that day. This explains the various names that were given to types of laces hundreds of years ago, and which still persist.

Well-known hand-made laces are as follows.

Alençon is a fine needle-point lace named from the town in which it was first made. It has a characteristic closeness, firmness, and evenness.

Best-known variety of Brussels is an appliqué lace —a lace made by sewing completed patterns on a

New York Times Photos

LACE-MAKING MACHINES IN A FRENCH FACTORY

The town of Puy in France is noted for its lace, and in this factory (lower) machines are making the fabric in a continuous narrow strip, which emerges from the dome-shaped opening in the centre. Spaced around the circumference of the machines are the bobbins; in front of the two nearest units are the automatic control frames which govern the design. In the upper photograph a worker is mending a broken thread on one of the bobbins.

LACE OF FINEST THREAD AND EXQUISITE DESIGN

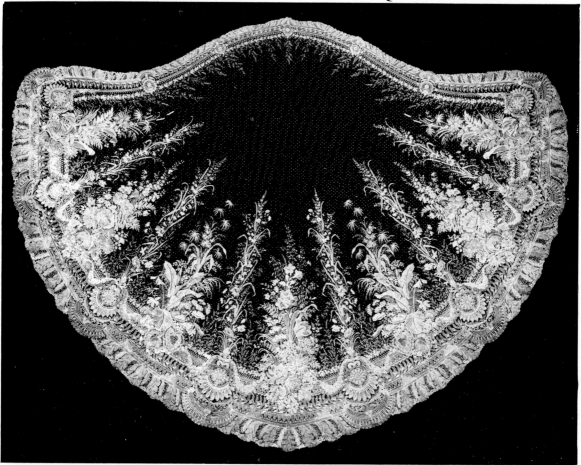

These four specimens of lace represent perfect examples of the old handicraft of lace-making. The top photograph shows the veil worn by the bride of King Farouk of Egypt at her wedding in January 1938. Made in Brussels some 70 years before, it is a magnificent piece of needle-point. Below (left) is a specimen of lace produced at Honiton, Devonshire, which has been a lace-making centre for 300 years. To the right are (upper) Valenciennes lace and (lower) Italian filet lace of the 18th century.

LACE-MAKING IN AN ENGLISH VILLAGE

THIS is one of the oldest of village industries, and the pillow lace made in the cottages of Buckinghamshire and Bedfordshire is world-famous. The photograph shows a piece of Buckinghamshire lace being made by an expert worker. Across the pillow a perforated parchment pattern is stretched. In the perforations pins are placed, and the threads, wound on bobbins seen hanging down on the side of the pillow, are worked round the pins to reproduce the pattern. Beside the lace-maker is the machine used for winding the thread on the bobbins. Many of the parchment patterns used in making these laces are 200 or 300 years old and have been handed down from mother to daughter for generations. The bone bobbins on which the thread is wound are often elaborately carved, and the older specimens are greatly valued by collectors.

To face page 1881

hand-made or machine-made net. Cluny is a plaited lace made in silk, linen, or cotton. The patterns are mostly birds, animals, or flowers.

Filet lace is darned net lace. Irish is chiefly a point lace made at Limerick entirely by the needle with very small meshes. Honiton pillow, made in Honiton, Devonshire, is celebrated for the beauty of its figures and sprigs. Valenciennes is a solid and durable pillow lace having the same kind of thread throughout for ground and pattern; it is the most beautiful of all French pillow laces.

Lacquer AND SHELLAC. Nearly everyone has seen those highly polished boxes, trays, cups and other articles called lacquer-ware. The shiny black or red finish was produced by some painstaking Oriental, by one of the longest and most skilful of all artistic processes. He covered the wood with cloth or paper, brushed on the lacquer, and, when it was dry, carefully rubbed it down with fine charcoal and water. In high-grade work possibly 18 or 20 preliminary coats of lacquer were applied before the box was ready for decorating with colours or inlaying.

This kind of lacquer, which dries so hard that even hot water will not soften it, is made from the "lac" or sap of the varnish tree (*Rhus vernicifera*). The tree grows abundantly in China, where the art of lacquering was discovered more than 3,000 years ago. The Japanese borrowed the art from their neighbours, and imported the varnish tree, which they cultivated in large groves. Their artists so surpassed the Chinese that by the 17th century lacquering was known as "japanning" in England. English cabinet-makers produced japanned screens and chairs, but these were far inferior to the real lacquer-ware of the Orient.

The Japanese, besides lacquering furniture and even their temples, produce some exquisite work on figured vases, gold and silver trays, leather boxes, and other decorative objects. The characteristic Japanese lacquer-ware is the gold or silver finish. In China, however, carved lacquer has been the object of greater attention, and the Japanese have never really competed in the best of this type of work. The Chinese, too, use far more brilliant colours, while they developed the use of iridescent sea-shells also to a greater extent than the Japanese. In both China and Japan the art of lacquering is now declining.

The lac from which shellac is made is different from the lac used in making lacquer-ware. It is a resin produced by tiny insects, which bite into the twigs of several species of East Indian trees and suck the sap. The insects are called lacs (*Coccus lacca*) from Hindustani *lakh*, a hundred thousand, perhaps because it requires thousands of them to produce even a small quantity of shellac, perhaps because the insects are themselves so very numerous.

Shellac is used in making gramophone records, and as size or stiffening in felt hats ; it holds the bristles in your hairbrush and the glass electric light bulb in its brass base; it is widely used in sealing-wax. Toothbrush handles, imitation ivory toilet articles, billiard balls, and mouthpieces and reeivers of telephones may contain a portion of shellac, but nowadays the synthetic resins called plastics are often substituted. Huge quantities of shellac are used every year in electrical work, principally as a binder and insulator, and it goes

Victoria & Albert Museum

SUPERB EXAMPLE OF CHINESE LACQUER WORK

In most of the arts requiring great patience and attention to the minutest detail, and in those involving difficult processes that need care, the Chinese are supreme. An example of typical Chinese industry and ingenuity is this magnificent screen of lacquered wood ; it is decorated on both sides with incised ornament, painted and gilt on a black ground, this side showing a mountain scene. The height of the screen is 8 feet 10 inches, and its width 21 feet.

into oilcloth, glue, linoleum, cements, certain kinds of ink, shoe dressings, and varnishes for paper, and leather and furniture polishes. Unlike Japanese lacquer, shellac varnish is not suited to withstand water, which turns it white.

Shellac makes a smooth, glossy coating when properly applied, and is widely used on floors and other surfaces where a quick-drying, tough, hard finish is most commonly desired. Also it is used in the " French polish " of the furniture maker.

In India, Burma and Siam these little lac insects, in compact colonies of many thousands of females and a few males, attach themselves to the tender shoots of the fig and certain acacia trees, and suck the sap with their tiny beaks. They give off through their pores a resinous substance which hardens when it meets the air, and forms a protective shell about the lac insect. They afterwards become glued to the twig by this superfluous excretion, and after a time die, forming with their bodies little domes over their myriads of eggs. Generation after generation dwells upon the same twig until it is enveloped in a coating often half an inch thick. This substance, gathered and refined, is what we call shellac.

The natives cut twigs that are coated with these bumpy shells to a depth of an inch or more, or they scrape off the shells, and in this form lac is called stick-lac. The stick-lac is cracked by a mill in a factory and sieved and washed to remove fragments of wood and dirt and the natural red colour, which

in ancient times was used to dye cloth, and which is the true " lake " of the artist's colour-box. Cheap aniline dyes have now replaced this primitive product. (*See* Dyes).

The lac is now anything from a dark to a clear golden yellow, and this is raw shellac. The raw product is now melted, and filtered by squeezing the melted substance through cloth bags; it is then stretched into thin strips. Sometimes it is formed into little round cakes and stamped with the maker's initials. In this form it is called button lac. It is now ready to be packed and shipped to the western world, where more than half the total supply is marketed. Besides being used with other ingredients, shellac itself is used for making ornaments, being dyed in a large variety of colours.

Two crops of stick-lac can be harvested each year. The natives induce the insects to spread by tying a few twigs coated with lac eggs to other trees, where the young, upon hatching, immediately shift for themselves and start new colonies.

The name lacquer is used for a quick-drying, durable coating applied to metal such as brass in order to prevent it tarnishing. The metal has to be chemically cleaned first. Still another kind of lacquer—the kind that is used to produce a quick-drying finish on motor-cars and furniture, and is called cellulose-lacquer—is made from cotton that has gone through a complex series of chemical treatments. Varnishes and lacquers now often contain synthetic resins (plastics), made from coal-tar chemicals. (*See* Coal Tar).

A TUSSLE IN LACROSSE
Originally played by the Red Indians of North America, lacrosse is very popular in Canada and the United States, and is played to a certain extent in Britain. The ' crosse ' is the curiously shaped stick (with net) which the French colonists in Canada fancied resembled a bishop's crozier or crosse.

Lacrosse. Of all the games now played in the United States there is probably none so truly American as lacrosse. Before Europeans landed in America this was the favourite game of the most active tribes, who used it as training for war. As played by the Indians there were sometimes several hundred persons on a side. The goals were placed half a mile or farther apart, the size of the playing area was almost limitless, and games sometimes lasted for many hours. "Baggataway" is the name the Ojibwa Indians gave to the sport. Lacrosse is the name given to it by the French colonists, since the stick used reminded them of a " crosse," or bishop's crozier. They learned the game from the Indians and revised its rules.

Lacrosse became very popular among the white people, and was accepted as the national game of Canada. In that country, as in the United States, it has been developed on most strenuous and exacting lines. It demands of the player great agility, speed and endurance, also skill and dexterity in handling his stick. The game was introduced into the British Isles in 1876, and became fairly popular. It is played principally in girls' schools, though an English Lacrosse Union exists.

Lacrosse is played with a solid rubber ball 2½ inches in diameter, which is caught and carried in or thrown from a " crosse," 40 to 50 inches long and not more than a foot across at the bent end.

The stick is shaped like a fish-hook, with the curved part filled with a strong netting of raw-hide or catgut. The ball is caught and thrown from this netting, which extends nearly half-way up the handle of the stick. The player usually places one hand on the end of the stick and the other round the middle near the netting. The playing field is

LADYBIRD WITH WINGS EXPANDED
The ladybird is not often seen in flight. This photograph shows the
delicate texture of the wings which, when at rest, are folded away beneath
the horny wing-covers. Each wing-cover has a single black spot.

J. J. Ward

about 100 yards long and 50 yards wide, with a goal
6 feet square, like a hockey goal, at each end.

There are 12 players in a team, and the object is
to carry the ball to the vicinity of the opposing
team's goal and throw it into the goal. It is a foul
for a player to touch the ball or another player with
the hand—except for a goal-keeper, who may not
throw the ball but may stop it by hand. A player
may run with the ball, as far as possible, but
opposing players may knock the ball out of his stick
or run in front of him and " check " him with their
bodies. In lacrosse there is no offside rule, nor is
the ball out of play when it has passed behind
the goal-line outside the goal.

Ladybird. There are in Britain several
species of these beetles of the family *Coccinellidae*.
Most people think of them simply as little, rounded,
red-backed insects with black spots, but they vary a
great deal, really. Some of them conform to the
type, at least when they are normal; a good
example is provided by the two-spot ladybird,
which has ordinarily just the two spots, one on each
wing-cover. But sometimes these two black spots
are so large that the beetle looks as if it were all
black, with two little red markings. And at other
times the spots can hardly be seen at all, and the
beetle appears entirely red.

Besides the two-spotted our other very common
ladybird is the seven-spotted. There are others
whose spots number as many as 24. Some of these
are black with red spots, some are yellow with
white spots, and one has black spots each surrounded with a yellowish ring on its red wing-cases.

All the ladybirds are most useful little creatures,
for they spend their time, as larvae and as adults,
in devouring harmful pests, chiefly the aphids or
greenfly which infest our roses and potatoes and
other plants (*see* Aphis). So good are they at
this that in certain parts of the world millions of
ladybirds are collected and bred every year and then
sent by post to other parts where their enemies are
doing particularly well on cultivated crops.

On the approach of winter, ladybirds assemble in
great numbers and take shelter behind the bark of
trees, in cracks in rocks, frequently in window

frames or in nooks and crannies in a
garden shed or outhouse. Those which
survive lay eggs in the spring, and from
these hatch the larvae.

These larvae are little violet-grey or
blackish creatures, soft, and quite unlike
their parents. They eat a great number
of aphids every day, seizing them in their
strong jaws and sucking out their inside
juices. If you examine a rose-tree where
there are ladybirds at work you can see
the empty skins of the aphids lying all
around. When it is full-grown the grub
turns into a rather soft, curious-looking
pupa, coloured orange and marked with
black, attached by the tail to the surface
of a leaf. From the pupa emerges the
adult ladybird, soft and pale in colour at
first but gradually hardening and then
flying away. In a year when there are
large numbers of aphids the ladybirds
breed very rapidly, and there may be
several generations in one summer.

Lady's Slipper. This is one of the
rarest of our British wild flowers. And together
with its relations it is among the most popular of all
orchids for indoor cultivation. Its name refers to the
curious third petal of all the orchids of this genus,

M. H. Crawford
LADY'S SLIPPER FLOWERS
The name of this plant refers to the curious third petal
which suggests a miniature slipper. A member of the orchid
family, it is now extremely rare in Britain.

Cypripedium, which, instead of being, as in most common orchids, thrust forward as a flat lip, is curved round and inwards on both sides to form a sort of vessel which suggests a miniature slipper.

The English lady's slipper (*C. calceolus*) was at one time less rare than it is now, being found in many localities in deep, moist woods in the limestone districts of the north of England. The greed of collectors began to reduce the plants, and they were wiped out in many places. Now there are only one or two spots in all England where the lady's slipper grows wild. The flowers of this species are green and yellow, on slender yet stiff stems, wrapped round with typical orchid leaves, smooth and pale green, with veins running lengthwise and parallel.

Lafayette, MARQUIS DE (1757–1834). Only the name of George Washington among the heroes of the American Revolution ranks above that of Lafayette, a young Frenchman who helped the American colonists in their fight for freedom. He was born at Chavagnac, Haute-Loire, France, on September 6, 1757, the son of a noble family. When he was 19 and a captain in the French army, news arrived that the American colonies had declared their independence of England, France's ancient foe. "At the first news of this quarrel," Lafayette wrote, "my heart was enrolled in it!"

So he disobeyed the commands of his king and his angry father-in-law, purchased a ship, and after many difficulties sailed for America in 1777. He offered to serve without pay, and Congress gave him the rank of major-general. Lafayette's services were of great value to the colonists. Of particular importance was his influence in inducing the French government to sign a treaty of alliance with the colonies, in 1778.

Lafayette's love of liberty naturally led him to join those French noblemen who favoured the Revolution of 1789 in his own country. On the day after the storming of the Bastille (July 14, 1789) he was made commander-in-chief of the new National Guard, organized to safeguard the Revolution. It was he who proposed for the Revolutionary armies the famous tricolour—" the red, white and blue."

Lafayette rescued Queen Marie Antoinette from the mob that stormed the palace of Versailles on October 5, 1789, and issued orders to stop King Louis XVI when he sought to escape from France. But gradually he became dismayed at the growing excesses of the Revolution. As the head of an army raised to defend France against Austria, he planned to overthrow the Jacobins (body of extreme revolutionaries, who ruled France from 1791 to 1794) and support a monarchy with limited powers. He was therefore proclaimed a traitor, and to escape arrest and the guillotine he fled to Belgium, where he was imprisoned by the Austrians until his release was obtained by Napoleon in 1799.

Lafayette took no further part in public affairs until after Napoleon's overthrow in 1815. When Charles X (1757–1836) attempted to take away from the people many of the rights they had won during the Revolution he led the opposition, and in 1830 took part in his third revolution as commander of the army of National Guards that drove Charles X from France and placed on the throne Louis Philippe, the so-called citizen-king. Lafayette died in Paris on May 20, 1834.

La Fontaine, JEAN DE (1621–95). Strangely enough, some English-speaking people are better acquainted with the famous fables of La Fontaine in their native French than in an English translation, for they are among the few really popular books one meets in French lessons at school.

The son of a forest ranger, La Fontaine was born at Château-Thierry, France, on July 8, 1621, succeeding his father as ranger of the duchy in 1647. From about 1660 he lived chiefly in Paris, and it was comparatively late in life that La Fontaine turned to literature. Having secured a pension from the statesman Nicolas Fouquet, the chief literary patron of the age in France, he began to write light verses and translate some of the less edifying classical works. The first volume of his Contes et Nouvelles en Vers (Tales and Novels in Verse) did not appear until 1664, though three years earlier he had produced the well-known Elégie aux Nymphes, and in 1663 his Voyage en Limousin. In 1668 there appeared a

British Museum

LAFAYETTE IN PRISON
Though he supported the French Revolution, Lafayette came into conflict later with the Jacobins (extreme revolutionaries). He was obliged to flee to Belgium where he was arrested and imprisoned, but he returned to France in 1799. This contemporary engraving shows him with his captors, who are riveting shackles upon him.

LA FONTAINE'S FABLE OF KING FROG AND KING STORK
Reproduced from a drawing by J. J. Grandville (1803–47), this is an illustration of La Fontaine's fable in which the stork is made king of the frogs. At first the old log in the foreground was their ruler, but as he did nothing they grumbled. When the frog-eating stork became their new king they soon found they were much worse off.

country; the result, entitled The Wonderful Adventures of Nils (1907), became a children's classic, and was translated into seven languages before its 10th birthday.

The life of Selma Lagerlöf has almost the romance she gives to her stories. She was born at Marbacka, Sweden, on November 20, 1858, and as a small child she was unable to roam about the picturesque country surrounding the old homestead. But by the fireside she listened to often-repeated weird tales with which the Northland abounds. When not listening she read, or wrote wild strange stories for her own amusement. At 33 she was an unknown school-teacher. Then in 1891 her first published book, Gösta Berling, brought her swift fame. Within 20 years she was known and loved throughout Europe and America, not only as the winner of honours rarely bestowed upon women—among others the Nobel prize for literature—or as one of the foremost women writers of the age, but as a teller of fairy tales that are read by young and old alike. All her books have been translated and published in English. She died on March 16, 1940, at Marbacka, home of her childhood.

second series of Contes, and the first six books of the famous Fables which were to prove their author's most enduring monuments; a second series of Fables followed in 1679, a third in 1693.

Among his contemporaries the Fables were highly appreciated, and in 1684 La Fontaine was elected a member of the French Academy. He had a genius for friendship, and with Molière, Racine, and Boileau formed a quartet notable in literary history. La Fontaine is, with Molière, the most widely read French writer of the 17th century. His Fables, rendered in wonderfully easy and varied verse, are regarded as among the glories of French literature. They were based on those of Aesop (q.v.), and in them La Fontaine demonstrates a wide knowledge of Nature, and a deep perception of the workings of human hearts and minds. He died in Paris on April 13, 1695.

Lagerlöf, OTTILIANA LOUISA SELMA (1858–1940). The big forests, rocks and rivers of southwestern Sweden are poor in wealth, but they are rich in folklore. There, among tales and legends which the centuries have woven like mists about the lakes and valleys, a girl learned the old stories and by them changed the commonplace region into fairyland. With an art all her own, Selma Lagerlöf (pron. lah'-ger-lêf) carries us into far fantastic worlds, where through strange eyes we catch glimpses which give daily happenings a meaning we quite miss in the busy workaday world. She speaks to both head and heart.

To make a school-book she called to her aid the elf of Northland myth. Together they seated the boy Nils on the back of Morten Goosey-gander, and sent him with the wild geese to learn of the geography, plants, animals, industries, and folklore of his

Lakes. Technically, a lake is an inland body of water larger than a pool or pond, and surrounded by land. Actually, however, the name is given also to the widened parts of rivers, and to bodies of water which are in direct connexion with the sea. Some inland waters like the Caspian and Dead Seas are in reality lakes. Like the Great Salt Lake of Utah in the United States those seas are salty because they have no outlet to the ocean, but lose their water by evaporation, which leaves an excessive amount of mineral matter behind. The Caspian Sea is the largest salt lake and inland body of water in the world, while Lake Superior, between Canada and the United States, is the greatest freshwater lake.

Lakes are found in any depression of the land surface where there is a sufficient supply of moisture. These depressions may be due to various causes. (1) Hundreds of thousands of lakes owe their origin to the great glaciers which in ancient times filled many river valleys with their deposits, or created new hollows by gouging out rock or distributing their debris unequally. (2) Many lakes are formed by obstructions in river channels caused by lava flows, landslides, or tributaries that bring down sediment which blocks the main stream and forms a lake. The abandoned meanders or windings of a river often become the sites of lakes. (3) Occasionally the warping of the earth's crust creates depressions, as in the case of Lake Geneva, which was formed by the subsidence of part of the Alps. (4) Sometimes " sink lakes " are formed by the sinking of land due to the washing away of underlying soluble rocks. (5) Lakes are often found also in craters of inactive volcanoes.

Many European lakes show signs of having been inhabited by prehistoric lake-dwellers, whose houses were built on wooden piles driven into the lake bottom along the shore. (A reconstruction of a lake-dwellers' village is given in page 1237; *see also* plate facing page 2081.) The idea behind this mode of living was to ensure safety from wild animals and from enemies. *See also* Physiography, and separate articles under the names of different lakes.

Lamb, CHARLES (1775–1834). As long as the English language is spoken or read, Charles Lamb will be remembered as one of the greatest and most lovable figures in its literature.

He was born in the heart of London, in the Inner Temple, on February 10, 1775, his father, whom he described as " of incorrigible and losing honesty," being a poor lawyer's clerk. At the age of seven Charles was sent to Christ's Hospital, the famous Bluecoat school. Here he met Samuel Taylor Coleridge, who became his life-long friend, and another important figure in the literary world.

In 1792 Lamb became a clerk in the accountant's office in East India House, the head office of the East India Company, and here he remained until he retired on a pension 33 years later.

National Portrait Gallery
CHARLES LAMB AND HIS SISTER MARY
One of the most delightful of children's books is the Tales from Shake-speare of which Charles and Mary Lamb were the authors, Charles writing the stories of the tragedies and Mary those of the comedies. Mary was 70 and Charles 59 when this picture by F. S. Cary was painted.

When he was 21 his beloved sister Mary fell a victim to the insanity that was hereditary in their family, and killed their mother. She was confined in an asylum, where she recovered temporarily and upon her brother giving a solemn promise to care for her for the rest of her life she was released. Thenceforth, Charles Lamb sacrificed everything for his sister. When her malady recurred he would take her by the hand, and brother and sister would walk mournfully to the asylum. But in the intervals, which he called " between the acts," there was much that was cheerful and beautiful in their life. They wrote together the Tales from Shakespeare which have given pleasure to so many children.

Although he began his literary career by writing poetry, and first won distinction by his literary criticism, Charles Lamb's fame today rests chiefly on the essays written under the name of Elia. In these essays he has taken the most trivial subjects, chosen apparently at random, and put into them his own whimsical, pathetic, quaintly humorous personality. Whether he writes A Chapter on Ears, Imperfect Sympathies, The Praise of Chimney-Sweepers, Old China, or a Complaint on the Decay of Beggars, he says something worth while, and says it in his own inimitable way. Probably no essay in the English language has aroused more laughter than his Dissertation on Roast Pig, and none is more full of pathos than his Dream Children. He died at Edmonton, Middlesex, on December 27, 1834.

Lamprey. There are gruesome stories that in the days of the Roman Empire wealthy masters sometimes punished their slaves by chopping them up and feeding them to lampreys in their fish-ponds. Whatever the truth of these stories, we know that lampreys were considered one of the greatest delicacies in Roman days, and that the millionaires of the time kept them alive in special ponds where they were carefully fattened for the banquet table. King Henry I (1068–1135) of England is said to have died from indigestion caused by lampreys, which were his favourite dish.

These eel-like creatures, which inhabit today almost all oceans, seas, and rivers, are able to fasten themselves with their cup-shaped mouths to other fish and suck the blood of their hosts. Salmon and shad are sometimes caught with lampreys attached to them, and much damage is done among valuable food fishes in this way. Lampreys also feed upon small water creatures.

Belonging to the order *Cyclostomata* (round-mouthed), the lamprey differs from the true fishes in having neither scales, paired fins, nor jaws, as well as in various points of internal anatomy. The colour is olive brown, spotted and mottled with dark brown and greenish olive. The average length is about 16 to 20 inches. There are two principal species —the sea lamprey (*Petromyzon marinus*) and the river lamprey (*P. fluviatilis*).

Lamps.

Probably nothing has helped modern science and industrial progress more than good and ample lighting, for study and for work. In the day of James Watt and the Stephensons a candle or a crude lamp burning vegetable oil was all that could be had to light their work during the long winter evenings, or to enable them to study such books as then existed on engineering. In the feeble illumination afforded by rushlights, candles, or even the glow from the dying fire, workmen who wished to advance themselves by study would peruse treatises on simple science ; boys who later became some of our notable inventors learned by slow and painful home study in the same way. Much ingenuity was devoted to improving lamps, but until a plentiful and cheap supply of mineral oil became available, about 1860, with the exploitation of American petroleum, little could be done.

Gas lighting was introduced at the beginning of the 19th century, but did nothing to help people in villages or small towns until many years later. It was another half-century before electricity, in the form of the arc lamp, came into use, and then mainly for lighthouses. The "subdivision of the electric light "—i.e., the making of small lamps which could be used in rooms—had to wait until Edison and Swan independently had invented filament lamps (see Electric Lighting), about 1879 ; before these lamps could be used generally, a practical means of generating and distributing electric current had to be developed (see Grid). So people had to go on using portable lamps for many more years. Candle-lamps were even used in horse-drawn carriages almost up to the time that motor vehicles got into their stride. There is still a big field for paraffin oil lamps, though the improved forms use a mantle like that which Carl Auer von Welsbach invented for the gas lamp between 1885 and 1893, and they burn vaporised oil.

Torches and camp fires gave early Man his only light. Later he used the bodies of animals or fish; Shetland islanders threaded a wick through the body of a storm petrel and lighted it ; North American Indians who live along the coasts where

Science Museum, South Kensington

RUSHLIGHT

Made from the pith of rushes, a rushlight, here shown in its holder, gave very little illumination ; but poor people were glad enough of it.

Science Museum, South Kensington

BIRDS USED AS LAMPS

The bodies of fish and birds were long used as illuminants. Shetland islanders, off the north coast of Scotland, threaded a wick through the oily body of a storm petrel and so made a lamp : two are shown, with feet embedded in clay.

fatty fishes of the salmon tribe are plentiful still dry these fish and use the bodies as lamps. Oil-containing nuts were used by South Sea islanders to make torches; all over the world, oil expressed from fish was used for burning in torches or in crude lamps. In Arctic regions today people burn fish oil, or the fat from whales, in simple saucer-like lamps made from a hollowed-out stone or a sea shell; the wick is a piece of moss or vegetable fibre. In many churches you may see simple votive lamps made from a glass vessel in which floats a wick-holder, and which burn usually vegetable oil.

Well-wrought terra-cotta lamps have been found in the long-buried cities of Mesopotamia ; also lamps made of gold. Three thousand years ago, saucer-type lamps were in use in China, Greece and Egypt. A channel for the wick came much later; and the lamp with a closed top was developed later still. The Romans made lamps with several wick-spouts, and hung them by chains. Then some of these improvements were lost sight of, and the open saucer became common again. A lamp on the principle we use for the bird fountain (in which the liquid flows from an inverted container to a lower spout, and the flow is regulated by a sort of air valve) was invented by the Italian scientist, Jerome Cardan (1501–76). Leonardo da Vinci (q.v.) is said to

ROMAN LAMP

Lamps of terra-cotta or metal (above), with a handle at one end and a spout for the wick at the other, were used by the Romans. This one was hung from the ceiling.

have used a metal chimney above a lamp flame to improve the draught; in the 18th century a Frenchman invented the glass chimney.

As we have said, much ingenuity went to improving lamps, making them burn longer, and providing a steady flow of oil. The bird-fountain principle was used with many variations: one was to use a reservoir which slid on a pillar and could be clamped at a convenient height; the lamp with its chimney projected from the reservoir, and was fed by a tube from the lower part of the oil container. Pump devices to feed the oil, or clockwork apparatus for the same purpose, were other variations.

Benjamin Franklin (q.v.) introduced a duplex burner, with two wicks side by side in a tube on the top of the oil container. Flat wicks were adopted, with a serrated wheel to raise them by turning a milled screw. A Swiss, Aimé Argand (1755–1803), gave his attention to providing a better air supply to the wick. His lamp had a tube running clean through the oil reservoir from the bottom to the top, where it acted as the inner wall of the wick tube; the wick was a flat one, but it was bent around the inner tube we have mentioned, and was enclosed by an outer tube which communi-

cated with the reservoir. So air was drawn up through the inner tube and found its way to the centre of the flame, as well as coming through a perforated cover at the outside of the wick tube.

Argand's invention was the first big improvement, and gave a striking increase in illuminating power. It was later adopted for gas lamps, and held its own until the Welsbach mantle came into use for gas.

The introduction of mineral oil (paraffin oil or kerosene) proved a blessing, but brought many tragedies. Previously colza oil, made from cole or rape seed, had been commonly used. This oil was safe because it had a high "flash-point" and did not easily take fire. Mineral oil as first introduced had a much lower flash-point, and needed more accurately made burners. Until governments introduced regulations to prevent low flash-point oil being sold, there were many accidents and conflagrations due to lamps taking fire or exploding. Then, too, many lamps had reservoirs of glass to avoid casting a shadow, or for

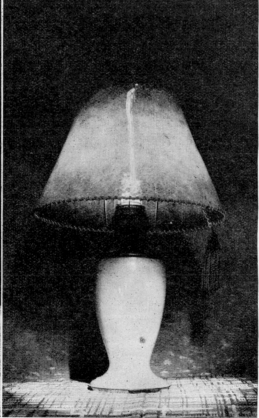

Science Museum, South Kensington

OIL LAMPS OF YESTERDAY AND TODAY

The colza lamp (top left) burned oil obtained from cole or rape seed. To avoid throwing shadows, lamps were made as much as possible from glass; at top right is a lace-maker's glass lamp. The paraffin-oil lamp (lower left, a Victorian one) gave a much improved light; but the modern paraffin-vapour type (lower right) far surpasses it.

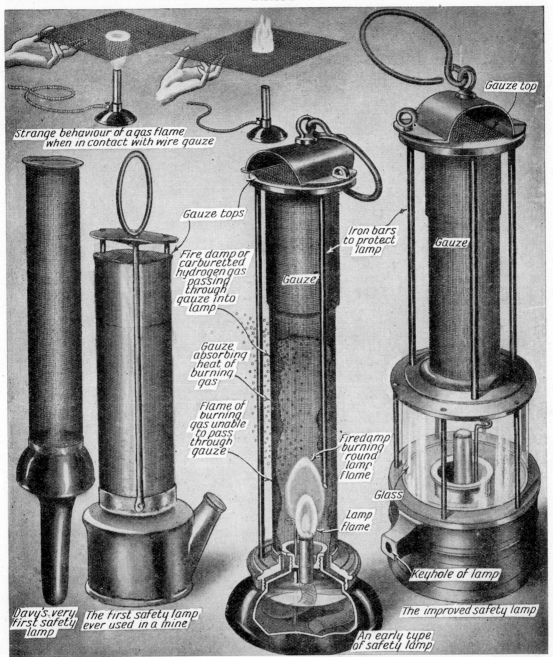

Strange behaviour of a gas flame when in contact with wire gauze

Gauze tops

Fire damp or carburetted hydrogen gas passing through gauze into lamp

Gauze absorbing heat of burning gas

Flame of burning gas unable to pass through gauze

Gauze top

Iron bars to protect lamp

Gauze

Gauze

Firedamp burning round lamp flame

Glass

Lamp flame

Keyhole of lamp

Davy's very first safety lamp

The first safety lamp ever used in a mine

An early type of safety lamp

The improved safety lamp

EARLY SAFETY LAMPS FOR COAL MINERS

Lamps which could be used with safety in coal mines where the dangerous fire-damp (carburetted hydrogen) formed were invented in the 19th century ; that of Sir Humphry Davy came into general use. The principle of the Davy lamp is shown in these diagrams. Fire-damp is able to pass through the wire gauze which encloses the lamp burner and burn harmlessly inside, but ordinarily the flame cannot pass out and fire the gas outside the gauze, which conducts the heat away too quickly for ignition. Considerable improvements have since been effected in safety lamps.

improved appearance; they got knocked over, and broke, spilling the inflammable oil. However, these difficulties were overcome, and today the oil lamp is safe and efficient, if given proper attention and the burners regularly cleaned. The introduction of the vaporising principle, and the use of a mantle as the actual illuminant, have given a portable lamp which rivals gas or electric light.

Safety lamps for the use of miners were devised by many inventors. Best known are those of Sir Humphry Davy and George Stephenson. The flame is protected by a cylinder of metal gauze which conducts the heat away very rapidly and ordinarily prevents ignition of inflammable gases present in coal mines. Considerable improvements have been made in safety lamps since those days.

Lanarkshire. The fact that Glasgow (*q.v.*) is situated within its borders is in itself sufficient to distinguish this county (also called Clydesdale) as one of the most important in Scotland from an industrial and commercial point of view.

The prosperity of the county, which has an area of 879 square miles, is founded largely on its extensive coal-fields and iron-ore deposits. This circumstance led to Lanarkshire becoming the centre of the Scottish iron and steel industry, with numerous blast-furnaces, and a considerable number of steel-works and iron-foundries, furnishing employment to many thousands. Agriculture is another important industry, with Lanark, the county town (population, 6,178), as the chief market-town. Fruit-farming is carried on extensively, the centre of the industry being at Carluke, where many jam factories are situated.

This county is the most populous in Scotland, containing, besides those already mentioned, important industrial towns such as Motherwell, Coatbridge, Airdrie, Hamilton, and Wishaw. The most important river is the Clyde (*q.v.*), which the enterprise of the citizens of Glasgow transformed from a shallow, muddy creek into one of the leading waterways of the British Isles. There is much picturesque scenery in Clydesdale, which is also noted for its breed of horses. The population of Lanarkshire is 1,643,000.

Lancashire. The great cotton industry of Lancashire, although it met with severe competition, particularly from Japan, between the First and Second World Wars, is still an important factor in the industrial life of England. In this county, which has an area of 1,875 square miles, the modern factory system had its birth. Lancashire is also known for the very distinctive dialect spoken by its inhabitants.

There are numerous large cities and important manufacturing towns within the county, including Liverpool (*q.v.*), Manchester (*q.v.*)—connected with Liverpool and the Irish Sea by the Manchester Ship Canal—Accrington, Blackburn, Blackpool (the greatest pleasure resort and amusement centre in the North), Bolton, Bootle, Burnley, Bury, Preston, Rochdale, Oldham, St. Helens, Salford, Southport, Widnes, Wigan, and Lancaster. The last-named, with a population of 47,000, is the county town.

In the southern part of the county extensive coal-fields are worked. In the northern Furness district beyond Morecambe Bay the iron-ore mines led to the growth of the industrial town of Barrow-in-Furness (*q.v.*). In the North, too, are mountains of the Cumbrian group, where Coniston Old Man rises to 2630 feet; in the centre are some of the heights of the Pennine Chain, Pendle Hill, 1800 feet, being the highest point. Coniston Lake is included in the county. The level areas are in the south and along the coastline. The largest rivers are the Mersey, on the estuary of which Liverpool lies, the Ribble and the Lune. The population of the county is 4,659,000.

Landor, WALTER SAVAGE (1775–1864). Gifted English poet and man of letters, Landor was born at Ipsley Court, Warwickshire, on January 30, 1775. He came of a wealthy family, and probably inheritance and easy circumstances contributed to the uncertain temper and pride which were prominent features of his character.

He was a strange mixture. Endowed with great intellectual gifts, and a distinguished classical scholar, he was expelled from Rugby School, and in after life contrived to quarrel with and openly despised many of the writers of his time. Yet to others he was generous and devoted ; among the friends whom he valued most was Robert Southey (1774–1843).

Landor's writings have little interest today, except to scholars and people who delight in literary style. He assuredly did not write for the great reading public, and was not in any sense a popular writer. On the other hand, Landor's prose, as well as his verse, is often characterized by a singular sweetness and perfectly balanced literary expression. His greatest achievement is his Imaginary Conversations. These contain nearly 150 dialogues put into the mouths of eminent figures in history. He died in Florence, Italy, on September 17, 1864.

Landseer, SIR EDWIN HENRY (1802–73). "Where is my curly-headed dog boy?" the teacher of the Royal Academy school used to ask, when he missed young Landseer from his classes. The answer would be "At the Zoo," for this boy divided his time between the two places, and at either was sure to be found studying animals or making pictures of them. Dogs were his favourites, and his first drawing to be engraved and published was of a great St. Bernard.

Landseer could draw rapidly and easily. A story is told of how he once drew a stag's head

J. Dixon-Scott
LANCASTER CASTLE GATE
County town of Lancashire, Lancaster's most notable building is the Castle, mainly built in the 11th century by John of Gaunt. This view is of the Gateway Tower.

with his right hand, at the same time drawing a horse's head with his left. Although lacking confirmation, the probability is that the story is quite true, for he could draw almost equally well with both hands.

He was born in London on March 7, 1802, and from boyhood, when at the age of 11 his drawings won a silver palette from the Society of Arts in London, Landseer's life-story is of one success after another. He was made a member of the Royal Academy in 1826; enjoyed the patronage and friendship of Queen Victoria; was knighted in 1850; and the presidency of the Royal Academy was offered to him in 1865. Upon his death on October 1, 1873, he was buried in St. Paul's Cathedral.

Of his many dog pictures, Dignity and Impudence is perhaps the best-known. His stags were quite as popular as his dogs, and of these the Monarch of the Glen was favourite. Besides his pictures of animals Sir Edwin Landseer painted many portraits of celebrated people. The sculptures of the well-known lions in Trafalgar Square, London, are also his work.

Language AND LITERATURE. We know little of how the first words were born, whether people imitated sounds of water and wind and beasts, or by what means they assigned a certain significance to a sound. But, like many things that Man has made, language has grown with the human race, changed with its history, its tastes, and its fancies, and accurately reflected the image of the people who made and used it. Primitive people have a limited language and small vocabulary. A crude, dull person uses a language of the same quality as his mind. Clever races with quick, keen minds develop a language of subtlety and clarity.

Languages, of which there are some 1,500 in use today, live, grow, and die, as do people. They record the march of history. The conquering Romans spread their Latin speech throughout their empire, so that it lives today in French, Italian, Spanish, Portuguese and Rumanian. Many a foreigner today twists his tongue round the strange and difficult language of the English because those enterprising people were the first settlers in many parts of the world.

North Americans speak English rather than French or Spanish, because the vast majority of the colonists who settled in North America came from the British Isles. But there are about three million persons of French origin in Canada ; and more than a quarter of the Canadian population speak French as their native tongue.

In a world linked ever more closely by railways, aeroplanes, steamships, cables, wireless, telegraphs and telephones, language barriers between peoples become an increasing nuisance. People have tried to create artificial languages, such as Esperanto, easy to learn, without the grammatical difficulties of a natural tongue, for the use of all nations. But an artificial language, like a wax doll, lacks life and strength and conviction.

Only a race producing writers of spiritual depth and possessing a language capable of interpreting the finest shades of meaning can produce a great literature. Poems, plays, and tales are the products of their own age, in the same way as architecture and painting. A rough age never produces elegant

Mansell

' DIGNITY AND IMPUDENCE '
This is Sir Edwin Landseer's most famous painting, now in the Tate Gallery, London. Though once the most popular of all works of art Landseer's animal paintings are today little admired, his portraits being more esteemed.

literature, nor a shallow era anything but trash. Intellectual movements and trends in taste sweep from one country to another in all the arts, like wind over a wheat field. Language and literature are the best record of the growth of human knowledge throughout the centuries.

Lapland. The homeland of the Lapps is an undefined district in the north-west of Europe, extending from the White Sea, on the north coast of the Soviet Union, to the Atlantic coast of northern Scandinavia. In the west this region consists of the barren plateau and moorland of Norway; east of this are the lake-dotted lowlands of Sweden and north Finland; then comes the low Murman coast on the Arctic Ocean.

The Lapps are of Asiatic origin and speak a language something like that of the Finns. They are a short, thick-set race, with Mongolian features, and spend their lives fishing, hunting and tending their herds of reindeer. Many of the Lapps lead a semi-wandering life following their herds, which supply them with meat, milk and clothing, from pasture to pasture. Others have established permanent settlements along the coast or on the banks of rivers, where they fish and breed cattle.

In the north-western part of Finnish Lapland live the Scolt Lapps. Although they are of Tibetan origin, they are part of Europe now and are almost certainly the oldest inhabitants of Scandinavia. They have never been warriors, so that their more warlike neighbours have pushed them farther and

Wide World Photos

LAPP FAMILY AND REINDEER

Inhabiting the extreme north of Norway, Sweden, Finland and European Russia, the Lapps hunt and fish. They obtain milk, meat and clothing from their reindeer, which also draw their curious boat-like sledges. They are a short sturdy people of Asiatic origin, the Scolt Lapps having come from Tibet.

leaving its branches bare in winter, the common larch (*Larix europaea*), found in the mountainous regions of Europe, is a tree reaching a height of 80 to 130 feet. It flourishes also in Asia, where it grows at higher latitudes than in Europe. It is ornamental and graceful, its slenderness of form being accentuated by the dainty pale green foliage; the leaves are arranged in tufts on all but the youngest shoots. In spring they are a beautiful pale green, and together with the crimson female and yellowish male flowers and grey-brown old cones, make the trees a lovely sight. The mature cones are small, with paper scales which distinguish them from those of any other conifer. The timber is noted for its toughness, and is resinous and durable. It is used for pit-props, scaffolding and garden rustic work.

The Japanese larch (*L. kaempferi*), is easily distinguished from the common species by the faintly blue-green colour of the leaves. American species include the American larch, tamarack, or hackmatack (*L. laricina*), and the western larch (*L.*

farther north. Now, having reached the shores of the Arctic Ocean, they can go no farther. Their language is much purer than any Tibetan dialect spoken at the present time. Fishing is their main occupation, reindeer herds supplying most of their requirements.

The Scolt Lapps are an exceptionally happy and contented people. Crimes of theft are unknown, and their simple life, lived in intimate contact with Nature some 300 miles north of the Arctic Circle, appears to have allowed them to retain powers of which other races have only faint recollections. For instance, they seem to be able to read a person's thoughts as easily as most of us can read a book, and they are said to be able to arrange appointments with friends in their dreams—or, at any rate, without getting into communication with them by any obvious means. Every object is a friend to them, and they believe that the dead dance in the Aurora Borealis. They hunt only the wolf, and the glutton or wolverine (member of the weasel family) which sucks the blood of its victims. They maintain that many animals are inhabited by human spirits, and they have other strange beliefs concerning them.

The Lapps number possibly 20,000 in Norway; 7,000 in Sweden; and 2,000 each in Finland and in the Soviet Union. During the Second World War (1939–45) most of the Norwegian Lapps migrated into Sweden to escape annihilation by the German forces, who destroyed their principal town, Ivola, and heavily damaged many of their settlements. They returned to Norway towards the end of 1945. There is a colony of Lapps in Alaska, where they tend reindeer herds owned by the United States Government.

Larch. Peculiar among conifers in that its needle-like leaves are shed completely each year,

H. Bastin

EVER-GRACEFUL LARCH

So fine are the needles of the larch that even in summer, when this photograph was taken, the tree has a light and airy appearance. Unlike most conifers it loses its leaves in winter, but even then its spire-like form and the upward trend of its branches make it easy to recognize.

occidentalis), which is the largest species, attaining a height of 180 feet. The species *L. laricina* grows in the Great Lakes and New England states, and throughout Canada east of the Rocky Mountains as far north as the Arctic Ocean. In its northern range it thrives on well-drained uplands, but in the United States it is found more commonly in swamps. It is a slender, graceful tree, about 60 feet high, with dainty threadlike needles. Longfellow mentions this larch in The Song of Hiawatha:

> " Give me of your roots, O Tamarack !
> Of your fibrous roots, O Larch Tree !
> My canoe to bind together
> That the water may not enter,
> That the river may not wet me."
> And the Larch with all its fibres,
> Shivered in the air of morning,
> Touched his forehead with its tassels,
> Said, with one long sigh of sorrow:
> " Take them all, O Hiawatha ! "

Its strong, tough resinous wood is used for railway sleepers, fence posts, telegraph and telephone poles, and boats.

Lark. Almost exclusively birds of the Old World, and especially its more temperate countries, larks are members of the Alaudidae family. There are about 100 species, usually streaked brown above and white and brown beneath. The only species found in North America is the horned lark. Like its more famous cousin, the skylark of Europe, it sings its wild, joyous song on the wing.

The skylark, *Alauda arvensis*, is the poet's bird. " On the wings of song " he soars until he fades from view, and only his melody, wafted downward, tells of his flight. Then, still fluttering and singing, he comes again into sight, swinging in wide circuits until, his song ended, he drops to the earth, where among the grasses his mate is sitting on the nest. This is usually a simple affair of fine grasses, well concealed among the herbage, or even partially under a stone or a tuft of grass. The eggs, from three to five in number, are dull grey mottled with olive-brown. Two or three broods may be reared in a season. In winter the British larks are augmented by vast flocks from farther north, which assemble chiefly on the coast of East Anglia.

Besides the skylark, which is found throughout Britain, we have another species, the less common woodlark (*Lullula*

I. M. Thompson

A LARK AND ITS HUNGRY BROOD
The skylark is one of our best-known birds, although most people know its voice better than its appearance. Here is a cock lark—you can tell him by his crest—just arrived back at the nest with a beakful of caterpillars, dinner for his hungry brood. The nest, as you see, is simply constructed of grass, harmonizing well with its surroundings.

arborea), which likes open woodlands and has also a beautiful song. The titlark, a bird which is sometimes confused with the skylark, is actually the meadow-pipit. (*See* Pipit).

Larkspur. This plant with charming clustered blue, white or pink blossoms belongs to the genus *Delphinium*. The blossoms, with their long up-tilted spurs, grow compactly around a stalk from 12 inches to five feet high. They rest lightly on the ends of tiny stems that crowd close together on a central stalk, which lower down bears also large, deeply divided leaves.

The structure of the flowers is interesting, for there are five petal-like sepals with the rear one prolonged into a slender curved spur (which resembles the rear toe-nail of a lark's foot, hence the name larkspur) and two united petals with spurs that project into the spur of the sepals. In spite of this curious arrangement the larkspur (*D. ajacis*) is a member of the buttercup family, Ranunculaceae. There are annual and perennial species of larkspur, found in both the Old and the New Worlds in temperate regions north of the equator.

Larva. In biology, this term is applied to the young of many animals which, on hatching from the egg, are markedly different from the adult. It is especially applied to insects, most of which hatch as larvae; but frogs and toads also have a larval stage in the fish-like tadpoles, which hatch from the eggs; and many fish have a so-called larval stage, such, for example, as the leptocephalus larva, or elver, of the eel.

The larvae of beetles are usually known as grubs; of flies, as maggots; of butterflies and moths, as caterpillars. The true larva must go through

R. A. Maltby
LARKSPUR
Varying in colour of flower-spike, and differing in habit of growth, larkspurs comprise annual and perennial species, all adapted to British gardens.

another stage, called the pupa, before it becomes a fully developed insect. Larvae live only to eat and grow, often causing great harm to vegetation. As some larvae grow they shed their skins (moult). The caterpillar, for instance, moults four or five times, other larvae as often as 20 times, before they are full-grown. (*See* Butterflies and Moths; Caterpillars; Insects).

La Salle, RENÉ ROBERT CAVELIER, SIEUR DE (1643–87). The son of a rich merchant of Rouen in Normandy, La Salle was born on November 22, 1643. In 1666 he went to Canada to seek his fortune. There he heard Indian tales of a great river called the Ohio, and in 1669 he set out in search of it. He probably reached the falls of the Ohio, and perhaps the Mississippi; but his records were lost, and no one can say just where he went. In 1671 he reached the Illinois river before turning back. Early in August 1679 he launched on the Niagara river, above the Falls, a little vessel, called

the Griffin, which he hoped would bear him through the Great Lakes to the site of the city of Chicago; but the vessel was lost.

In February 1682 he followed the Illinois and Mississippi rivers to the Gulf of Mexico, giving the name of Louisiana to the entire Mississippi valley and claiming it for France. After his return to Quebec in 1683 he resolved to go to France and get men for a colony which he wished to establish at the mouth of the Mississippi.

Having gained the assent of Louis XIV (1638–1715) to his project, he sailed with four vessels early in July 1684, in search of the Mississippi river by way of the Gulf of Mexico. Losing his way, he missed the mouth of the Mississippi and landed in Spanish territory, at Matagorda Bay, 400 miles to the west. He attempted to make his way back overland to Canada for supplies, but had not gone far when he was assassinated on the bank of Trinity river, Texas, in March 1687, by his followers.

The MOTHER-TONGUE *of* CIVILIZATION

Far from Rome—and for many centuries after her downfall—Latin was the speech of learned men of all races; and, in debased form, of the multitude also. In it were written the majority of the ' classics.'

Latin LANGUAGE AND LITERATURE. The idea of an international language spoken by all the peoples of Christendom seems visionary to us. But such a language really existed for many centuries—from just before the dawn of the Christian era until about the 9th century. This language was Latin. It began as a tongue spoken by the victorious Roman legions, and was carried by them through most of Europe, and into Asia and Africa.

Reconstruction by Niemann
EARLY HOME OF LATIN BOOKS
It was at Ephesus that the first large Roman library was founded, in 39 B.C., and later most of the larger towns had them. There was a central reading-room (on the lines shown above), with smaller rooms and manuscript-presses around it.

In the mouths of the unlearned and careless majority, the Latin of everyday life kept steadily changing in pronunciation, grammar and vocabulary. Thus various dialects grew up in different localities, which in the course of a few centuries developed into the group of related tongues called the Romance languages—Italian, Spanish, French, Rumanian and Portuguese. But written Latin, which remained the language of religious and political life as well as of scholars, underwent little change.

In the Middle Ages scholars, priests, and statesmen could travel the length of Europe without learning the languages of the various countries, since in every community there were sure to be men of learning who spoke Latin; and state documents and scholarly and scientific works were written exclusively in Latin.

Many English authors have written in Latin, for they knew that this would render their books accessible to a wider public than if in English. Bede, in the 8th century, wrote his famous History in Latin; Roger Bacon, in the 13th century, composed all his works in Latin; Francis Bacon and William Camden, in the 16th century, employed Latin in some of their books; and in the following century, when Sir Isaac Newton described his great discoveries to the world, he did so in the Latin tongue.

Even today Latin is something of a world language, though in a different way. In the sciences Latin terms are used—for example, *Rosa canina* for the dog-rose, *Felis leo* for the lion—in order that they may be understood by scientists of all nationalities. In the practice of English law many Latin phrases are in current use.

About a quarter of the English that we write is borrowed from Latin, and we can hardly speak a sentence without using some such words as " mile," " city," " army," " justice," " religion," and thousands of others that we have inherited from the ancient Romans (*see* English Language). In the

Romance languages of Europe the proportion of Latin words is far higher than in English.

At the time when Greece was creating poetry for all time, Latin was still only a dialect spoken by a few tribes in the vicinity of Rome. It was not until the 3rd century B.C. that it superseded the other Italic dialects ; and not until the 1st century B.C. that it developed into a superb literary language, a marvellous instrument for prose and poetry.

Just what Latin literature might have become if it had been left to itself, as the Greek was, we shall never know. Certainly it would have been very different. Before the increased influence of Greek literature that followed the Roman capture of Tarentum (272 B.C.), the greatest of the Greek colonies in southern Italy, the Romans had developed a metre of their own and the beginnings of a literary form. Their so-called Saturnian verse was apparently based upon accent, as our verse forms are, and was a vigorous, rough-and-ready line capable of adaptation to a variety of poetical purposes. The Greek measures, which Latin afterwards imitated, were based not on accent but upon long and short syllables.

In the languages of many uncivilized peoples nowadays the first written book is a translation of the Bible. In Rome the first book seems to have been a translation of the Odyssey, an epic poem reputed to be by Homer. This was made in the latter half of the 3rd century B.C. by a Greek, Livius Andronicus, who was brought to Rome as a slave after the capture of Tarentum. Andronicus translated some Greek plays as well. The next poet, Gnaeus Naevius (died about 200 B.C.), went on translating or imitating Greek drama, often using subjects from Roman history and introducing allusions to contemporary politics. He made use also of the pattern given by Andronicus's Odyssey to write an epic of the First Punic War. Thus, from the very beginnings, Roman literature was based on Greek models.

On this foundation Quintus Ennius (239–169 B.C.), the most important Roman writer before the age of Cicero, reared the stately edifice of his Annales—a tremendous epic history of the Roman state, which unfortunately is known to us by only a few fragments. In this poem Ennius remoulded the still rude and clumsy Latin to fit the stately flow of the Greek hexameter verse form, thus influencing the whole later history of the language.

The first Latin writer whose works have survived in any considerable body is Titus Maccius Plautus (c. 251–184 B.C.), the greatest comic dramatist of Rome. His plots—which he borrowed from the later Greek comic poets—have in turn furnished a rich mine for later playwrights, including Shakespeare and Molière.

Though Plautus got the substance of his plots and characters from Greek sources, his manner and spirit were essentially Roman. His great successor Terence, who was born about the year 194 B.C.,

Bardo Museum, Tunis; from Monuments Piot

VIRGIL INSPIRED BY THE MUSES

The Aeneid is without question the greatest glory of Latin poetry, and Virgil was always the most highly regarded of Roman poets, both in his own day and since. This mosaic from a Roman villa at Carthage shows him with the manuscript of the Aeneid on his knee, with Clio, the muse of history (left) and Melpomene, muse of tragic poetry, standing beside him.

devoted himself to copying his Greek originals more closely. His merit is that he thus brought into Roman literature the Greek standards of elegance, artistic perfection and moderation. His six plays, which all survive, have served as models of classical perfection to every generation of playwrights since.

In addition to these poets we have Cato the Censor (234–149 B.C.), who was the first writer of prose history in Rome to use his native tongue, and whose published speeches Cicero sincerely admired ; and Lucilius (about 180–103 B.C.), who wrote the first satires in the modern sense of witty social criticism.

The Golden Age, as the period when Latin literature reached its greatest splendour is called, covers about a century (80 B.C.–A.D. 14), from the beginning of Cicero's rise as an orator to the death of the Emperor Augustus, under whose patronage arts and letters flourished as never before in Italy. Cicero brought Latin prose as an instrument for oratorical, philosophical, literary and epistolary (for correspondence) expression to such a pitch of perfection that the adjective Ciceronian is a synonym for " classically perfect," " polished." Different from, but not inferior to, the stately sonorous periods of Cicero was the simple straightforward style of Julius Caesar, whose commentaries on the Gallic War, recording his campaign in Gaul, and on the Civil War, describing his actions in Italy itself, will ever remain models of prose narration.

The other chief writers of the Ciceronian period are Sallust, Lucretius and Catullus. Sallust (86–34 B.C.) is placed in the front rank of Roman historians by the accounts he has left us of the Catiline

LATIN

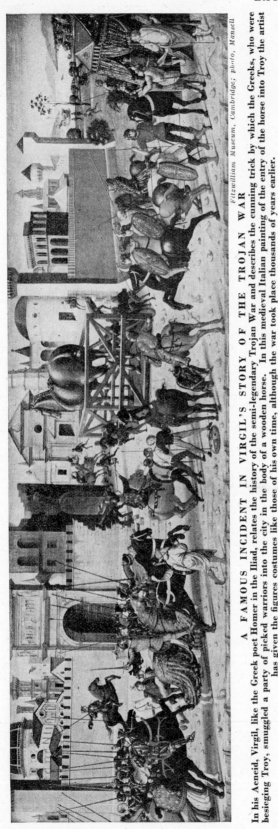

A FAMOUS INCIDENT IN VIRGIL'S STORY OF THE TROJAN WAR

In his Aeneid, Virgil, like the Greek poet Homer in the Iliad, relates the history of the semi-legendary Trojan War and describes the cunning trick by which the Greeks, who were besieging Troy, smuggled a party of picked warriors into the city in the body of a wooden horse. In this medieval Italian painting of the entry of the horse into Troy the artist has given the figures costumes like those of his own time, although the war took place thousands of years earlier.

Fitzwilliam Museum, Cambridge; photo, Mansell

conspiracy to murder the Senate and the war with Jugurtha, ruler of the North African kingdom of Numidia. The philosophical epic *De rerum natura* (Concerning the Nature of Things) of Lucretius (*c.*98–55 B.C.) is perhaps the most original and certainly, next to the Aeneid, the greatest poem in Latin. Catullus (*c.* 84–54) was the greatest lyric poet of ancient Rome, and one of the greatest of all time. He wrote love poems that bring the joy and pain of the passing moment vividly before us.

With these names we pass from the literature of the Roman Republic to that of the Empire. First of these both in time and genius was Virgil (Publius Vergilius Maro), 70–19 B.C. His national epic, the Aeneid, is one of the supreme masterpieces of the world. In his hands the Latin hexameter became what the English poet Lord Tennyson described as "the stateliest measure ever moulded by the lips of Man," and the unforgettable pictures he wrought —of the last agony of Troy, of the wanderings of the "pious Aeneas," of the tragic passion of the ill-starred Dido—have moved to sympathy generation after generation of readers as nothing else in all literature has been able to do.

In the field of light and satiric verse, the genial and accomplished Horace (Quintus Horatius Flaccus, 65–8 B.C.) was as pre-eminent as was Virgil in that of the epic. He embodied his philosophy of "idealized common sense" in phrases of such unforgettable charm that many of them have become as familiar as proverbs. In his mildly ironical Satires and Epistles he left the most complete and vivid picture we have of life in the Augustan age.

There was nothing of Horatian self-restraint and calm in the brief erratic life of Sextus Propertius (*c.* 49–16 B.C.), who delighted the Roman world as a boy of 20 with a volume of passionate poems celebrating his love for the capricious Cynthia. A gentler and more refined young poet of the same time was Tibullus (59–18 B.C.), in whom grace and melodiousness took the place of Propertius's fire.

Gay and Cynical Poems of Ovid

These two poets both used the metrical form called the elegiac, which their brilliant contemporary Ovid (43 B.C.–A.D. 18) polished to the same perfection to which Virgil brought the hexameter and Horace various lyrical forms.

A facile and copious writer, Ovid became the uncrowned laureate of the later Augustan age, whose glittering coldness and cynical worldliness he so perfectly embodied in his Art of Love. For us the most attractive of his many works is the romantic Metamorphoses—a fascinating narrative poem as long as the Odyssey—in which he has interwoven a vast number of stories derived from ancient mythology.

The Augustan age was pre-eminently the Golden Age of Latin poetry, but to this time belongs also the most famous of the Roman historians. Livy (Titus Livius, 59 B.C.–A.D. 17), is noted for the splendour of his rhetoric. He preferred literary effectiveness to historical accuracy, so that his narrative of Rome from its founding is more like a prose epic, a series of splendid pictures, than a critical history.

After Ovid and Livy the decline of Roman literature set in rapidly; but in the so-called Silver

Age that followed the reign of Augustus there are still several writers who deserve attention.

The satirist Juvenal (A.D. 60–140) and the epigrammatist Martial (A.D. *c.* 40–*c.* 104) belong to this later period. Juvenal's savage castigations of Roman life have been translated and imitated by many English poets, especially Dryden. These men are chiefly interesting to us for the picture they give of Roman life in the days of the Empire. The tragedies of Seneca—Nero's tutor—were the chief models for tragedy, as Plautus and Terence were for comedy, among the early writers of English drama. Today they are read as curiosities, though we can still enjoy Seneca's philosophical studies written in the form of letters.

Tacitus, Rome's Great Historian

Tacitus (A.D. 55–120), whose terse, pungent, and vivid style has sometimes been compared with that of Carlyle, gives us a number of valuable historical pictures. His Germania is our only account of Central Europe under the early Roman Empire. His Agricola is a very beautiful piece of biography and describes Agricola's campaigns in Britain. And what remains of his Annals and Histories is our chief source of knowledge of the events of the first century of the Roman Empire. He mentions briefly the first Christians in Rome, but was obviously unable to foresee the importance which they were to assume. The historian Suetonius (75–160), a writer of much less distinction than Tacitus, had the advantage of being one of Hadrian's private secretaries, and could therefore write his very gossipy Lives of the Twelve Caesars from documentary sources.

Perhaps the most interesting writings of the Silver Age are the letters of Pliny the Younger (61–*c.* 113). The most famous is the one telling of the death of his uncle, Pliny the Elder, in the

Uffizi Gallery, Florence; photo, Brogi

POET OF LOVE AND LEGEND

Ovid is most familiar to us as the author of the delightful Metamorphoses, which tells in beautiful verse many of the old tales of Roman legend. He was also the great love poet of his age, and perfected what is called the 'elegiac' metre.

eruption of Vesuvius that buried Pompeii. As a whole these letters give a racy picture of the time that is also described by Juvenal and Tacitus. Pliny the Elder (23–79) was the author of a Natural History, which is a priceless storehouse of information about the science of ancient times. Two other works of the Silver Age strike a more modern note, the literary criticism of Quintilian and the Satyricon, the prose novel of Petronius Arbiter.

Decline of Latin Literature

With the gradual breakdown of the Roman Empire which followed the death of Marcus Aurelius (A.D. 180), literature almost disappeared. Although there were brief flickers of activity from time to time, the genuine Roman spirit was dead. Latin continued to be written for 1,500 years, throughout the Middle Ages and beyond it; but though many important books, like St. Augustine's Confessions, and much poetry—many of our oldest hymns, for example—were written in Latin, Latin literature after the 2nd century never reached the heights to which it had attained in the Augustan and Silver Ages.

As Latin has never ceased to be spoken as a learned language, its pronunciation has been corrupted by the pronunciation of the various European languages. Thus the name *Cicero* is pronounced *Chichero* in Italy, and *Sisero* in Britain. But in the teaching of Latin in many British schools the consonants *c* and *g* are always given their hard sound, *v* is pronounced as *w*, and the "continental" vowel sounds are taught, *Cicero* being kik'-ār-ō ; *Augustus*, ow-goos-toos ; *Vergilius*, wār-gil'-i-oos ; and *Horatius* hor-ah'-ti-oos.

National Museum, Naples; photo, Anderson

WRITING A LETTER IN LATIN

This wall-painting from Pompeii shows a Roman girl thinking over her theme before she begins to write. In her left hand she holds her wooden tablets, and in her right her 'stylus,' or pen, with which she will scratch her words in the wax that coats the surface of the tablets.

Latitude and Longitude.

(Pron. lat′-i-tūd; lŏn′-ji-tūd). To indicate accurately the position of a place on the surface of the earth, geographers imagine the globe to be covered with a network of lines regularly spaced. Those running east and west—parallel to the Equator—are called "parallels," and the distance between them is measured in "degrees of latitude." Those running north and south—from pole to pole—are called "meridians," and the distance between them is measured in "degrees of longitude." Instead of marking each degree, which would make a confusing network of lines on the map, every fifth or tenth degree only is usually marked.

In numbering the parallels, we begin with the Equator as zero and count north and south. Thus the first degree north of the Equator is one degree north latitude, usually written "lat. 1° N."; and the first degree south of the Equator is one degree south latitude, or "lat. 1° S." Since the distance from the Equator to either of the poles is one-fourth of a circle round the earth, it will measure one-fourth of 360 degrees (the number of equal parts into which a circle is divided), which equals 90 degrees. Thus 90 degrees north latitude marks the position of the North Pole, 90 degrees south latitude that of the South Pole.

In numbering the meridians all countries by agreement have chosen as the point of departure the meridian passing through Greenwich, where the British Royal Observatory was established in 1675.

PARALLELS AND MERIDIANS
The imaginary lines encircling the Earth parallel to the Equator are the parallels of latitude; those intersecting at the Poles are the meridians of longitude.

Beginning with this as 0°, the first degree east of Greenwich is called one degree east longitude, or "long. 1° E."; the first degree west is "long. 1° W."; and so on until 180 degrees (half of 360) have been measured off eastward and westward. The 180th meridian is on the other side of the earth, exactly opposite to the one which passes through Greenwich, and, with it, forms one of the great circles which pass through the poles round the earth. This meridian is neither "east" nor "west," for both the east and west reckonings end here. Other meridians which before 1884 were used in calculating longitude are the ones passing through Washington (U.S.A.), Ferro (Canary Is.), and Paris.

As you can readily see, the circles forming the parallels decrease in size from the Equator to the poles. The meridians all meet at the poles, therefore the North Pole cannot be said to have longitude. It has only latitude (lat. 90° N.), and from there the only direction is south, just as from the South Pole the only possible direction is north. A degree of longitude measured on the Equator is a little more than 69 miles. This distance decreases until at 30° it is a little less than 60 miles, at 60° about 34½ miles, and at the poles zero.

A degree of latitude measured from the Equator to the first parallel north or south is about 68¾ miles; but between lat. 45° and lat. 46° it is a little more than 69 miles. If the earth were a perfect sphere the degrees of latitude would, of course, all be an equal distance apart; but the earth is flattened at the poles and bulging at the Equator, which accounts for the difference which we have just noted.

The determination of both latitude and longitude depends upon astronomical observations. Latitude is found at sea by measuring with an instrument called a sextant the sun's angular distance above the horizon when it is at the highest point or "culmination"—that is, at exact noon. From astronomical tables which give the "declination" of the sun (its distance north or south of the Equator for that day) the latitude is then found.

One of the easiest ways of computing longitude at sea is by noting the difference in time between that given by the observation of the sun at noon, and that given by a chronometer or watch set to Greenwich time. The longitude is the amount by which noon by Greenwich time is earlier or later than noon at the observer's point; one hour's difference in time, therefore, means 15° difference in longitude.

Other imaginary lines on the earth's surface are the two tropics—the Tropic of Cancer (23½ degrees north of the Equator) and the Tropic of Capricorn (23½ degrees south of the Equator). These two parallels mark off the belt round the middle of the earth in which the sun, at some period of every year, is directly overhead.

The polar circles are the same distance from the poles that the tropics are from the Equator. The

Topical

'ZERO HOUR' OF LONGITUDE
All countries now calculate longitude from the meridian of Greenwich. In the grounds of Greenwich Observatory stands this tablet which shows longitude 0°. Greenwich time is set from the moment at which the sun passes over this imaginary line.

Latvian Government, Riga

LATVIAN SUMMER FESTIVAL
The feast of St. John's Day, June 24, is a holiday for the people of Latvia to welcome the arrival of midsummer, and the country folk decorate themselves and their houses with garlands of foliage, generally oak leaves.

Arctic Circle, therefore, is 66½ degrees north latitude, and the Antarctic Circle is 66½ degrees south latitude. They mark off the regions around the poles where each year there is at least one day when the sun does not set, but is visible above the horizon for the full 24 hours.

Latvia. A republic of the Soviet Union, it is bounded on the north by Estonia, on the east by the Russian Soviet Federal Socialist Republic, on the south by Lithuania, on the west by the Baltic Sea and Gulf of Riga. Latvia possesses about 340 miles of sea-coast and there are good harbours at Riga, Liepaja (Libau), and Ventspils (Windau).

Much of the surface of the country is very low, and there are many marshes and peat-bogs ; but part of the province of Vidzeme consists of wooded hills, deep valleys, and charming lakes. Latvia is mainly an agricultural country, rye, barley, oats, potatoes, and flax being the main crops ; other industries include light engineering, woodworking, and the manufacture of textiles and chemicals. The principal exports are fish, dairy produce, flax, and timber. Riga, the capital, with a population of 393,210, is the chief seaport.

The Letts, who make up about 76 per cent of the population, are, like the Lithuanians, akin to the Slavs. In the 13th century what is now Latvia was a part of the territory conquered and Christian-

ized by the Teutonic knights. For some centuries the country was divided between Poland and Russia, but in 1795 it came under the rule of the Tsar, remaining a part of Russia until it was established as a separate republic in 1918. Latvia was admitted to the League of Nations in 1921.

In June 1940 the Russian government demanded free passage for Soviet troops through Latvian

Area.—25,000 square miles (including inland lakes). Population, 1,950,000.
Physical Features.—A flat region, largely forest. Chief river, the Daugava (Dvina).
Principal Products.—Rye, barley, oats, wheat, flax ; timber ; butter and other foodstuffs.
Chief Cities.—Riga (capital), 393,210 ; Liepaja (Libau), 57.000 : Daugavpils (Dvinsk), 45,000.

territory and the formation of a government acceptable to them. Two months later the Latvian Parliament voted in favour of incorporation in the Soviet Union. The country was overrun by German forces when Germany invaded Russia in June 1941, but was liberated by Russian troops in 1944. The population of Latvia is 1,950,000.

Laud, WILLIAM (1573–1645). The son of a clothier, this remarkable man rose to the highest position in the Church in the reign of Charles I. Laud was born at Reading on October 7, 1573, and was educated there and at St. John's College, Oxford. He entered the Church in 1600, and was Bishop of London from 1628–33, being noted for the severity with which he enforced discipline in the Church. He was appointed Archbishop of Canterbury in 1633 and was a member of the Court of Star Chamber, which was hated for the savage sentences it inflicted as well as for its high-handed procedure.

Laud unsuccessfully attempted to combat the spread of Presbyterianism in Scotland, and it was

From the painting by P. Delaroche

LAUD BLESSING STRAFFORD
While Laud was lying in the Tower of London under sentence of death, the Earl of Strafford, who was also condemned to death for treason, sent a message to the Archbishop begging him to be at his window and give him his blessing as he passed to the block. This painting shows Strafford receiving the blessing outside Laud's cell.

felt in England that the spirit of religion was being submerged by rules and ritual. He was suspected of inciting King Charles to defy Parliament, and on December 18, 1640, he was arrested on a charge of high treason and imprisoned in the Tower of London. Condemned to death, he was beheaded on Tower Hill, London, on January 10, 1645.

Laundry AND DRY-CLEANING. Washing clothes, always a highly unpopular task in the home, is a big, thriving industry. Collected from homes and taken to a power laundry equipped to make short work of what is a back-breaking job for the housewife, the soiled pieces, identified by indelible marks or tags, are sorted and dropped inside the cylinder of a huge washer. The cylinder, of wood or stainless steel, can sluice as much as 600 lb. of clothes at one time. It rotates inside a water-filled shell, whirling the clothes through thick suds and dipping them into the bath hundreds of times. The clothes are given 10 to 12 washings in suds, rinsing water and blueing water.

Then they go into a centrifugal water-extractor in the shape of a whirling metal basket. " Rough wash " is dried by hot air and then sent home. " Finished service " is starched when necessary, and sent to the ironers. All " flat work," such as towels, table cloths and sheets, passes between a polished,

LAUREL AND SWEET BAY

The large and leathery leaves of the common or cherry laurel (lower) distinguish it at once from the sweet bay or ' victor's laurel ' (top). The foliage of the sweet bay is much smaller and is aromatic, and in a dried state is used for flavouring in cookery. The leaves of the cherry laurel when bruised smell very strongly of bitter almonds ; a deadly poison is distilled from them.

W. B. Johnson

steam-heated surface and a series of soft padded rollers. Clothing is finished on steam-heated presses and by electric hand-irons. It requires the most careful work to remove spots and stains, and to bleach the clothes without damaging them.

Silks, velvets, woollen suits and dresses, felt hats, and fine rugs should be dry-cleaned. Cleaners may remove grease or dirt with volatile solvents, e.g. benzine or petrol, but these are now being replaced by various chemical solvents, such as chlorinated hydro-carbons. Garments are agitated in a metal washer with a clear solvent, then with a soapy solvent. Next they are rinsed in cleaning fluid and dried. Then stains are removed by expert spotters, and finally the article is pressed.

Laurel. Many people think of the laurel as the tree whose leaves, woven into a wreath, adorned the victor at the ancient games of the Greeks and Romans. But this tree, in Britain, is known as the sweet bay, its scientific name, *Laurus nobilis*, showing that it is not a member of the laurel family (*Prunus*). It is not often a large tree, although at times it may exceed 30 feet in height, sending up a mass of long, straight shoots rather than a single stem. It is seen more often in garden shrubberies and churchyards than anywhere else, but it is not really a native of Britain. It is also sometimes grown as a neat, rounded bush on a long, straight stem, in an ornamental tub. The wood, though hard, of good colour and fine grain, is seldom large enough to be of value.

The sweet bay is found growing wild in the Mediterranean districts of Europe. It belongs to the family which includes the camphor and other trees remarkable for their aromatic qualities. From the berries and other parts of the sweet bay is distilled an oil used in the manufacture of toilet waters. The dried leaves are used for flavouring in cookery. The tree was sacred to Apollo, and the nymph Daphne, when pursued by Apollo, was, in answer to her prayers, changed into a " laurel," the Greek name for which is daphne.

The trees which are commonly known as laurels in Britain and often are grown to form garden hedges are no relation of the bay but are members of the same genus as the cherries and the plums, *Prunus*, and of these laurels the commonest is the cherry laurel (*P. laurocerasus*). This tree, which has been grown in Britain for several hundred years, comes from the Caucasus in Russia. It has large, leathery leaves, shiny on the upper surface and rather like those of the rhododendron. Its flowers are white, and the fruits black. The leaves, when cut up or bruised, smell very strongly of bitter almonds (prussic acid or hydrogen cyanide). When distilled, they yield the oil of hydrocyanic acid, which is a deadly poison.

The Portugal laurel (*P. lusitanica*) has leaves spotted with yellow. The spurge laurel (*Daphne laureola*) is a small shrub with long, narrow dark green leaves, and tiny green flowers which open early in the year.

Lava. Terrible things happen when a volcano erupts, and of these perhaps the worst is the flow of lava. This is more or less completely melted rock discharged from the volcano. Molten lava is a very thick fluid saturated with gases and steam. Its fluidity depends on its temperature, the amount of vapour it contains, and its chemical composition. Those lavas which contain not more than 58 per cent of silica come from the deeper levels of the earth and are called basic lavas. They melt at about 2,250° Fahrenheit. Lavas containing 66 per cent or more of silica are acid lavas and remain more or less pasty even at 3,100° F.

The rate of flow of basic lava is faster than that of acid lava, and the cones of volcanoes producing it are generally low, with gentle slopes. Mountains which erupt acid lava tend to have high steep cones. Newly ejected lava may flow as fast as 50 miles an hour, but it usually slows down to less than a mile an hour.

If acid lava cools so quickly that there is no opportunity for the constituents to crystallize, it forms glass-like obsidian. Lava which has large crystals embedded in a ground mass of small crystals is called por-phyry. The top of lava is often frothy from bubbles of gas, and is then called scoriaceous. Pumice is rock froth so light that it will float on water. There are other rocks composed of lavas, which indeed have done a tremendous amount to make the face of the earth what it is today. (*See also* Geology).

LAVA ROCKS ON THE SIDE OF VESUVIUS
One can see that these twisted rocks, now hard and solid, were once part of a stream of molten matter that flowed from the volcano Vesuvius, near Naples, Italy, for they have the appearance of a fluid suddenly solidified. The normal rate of flow of a lava stream is about one mile an hour.

Lavender. Known for its delightful fragrance, *Lavandula vera* is a bush about 18 inches high, and the erect spikes of mauve bloom rise above the leaves another 18 inches. The flowers and their stalks should be picked when the sun is on them if the full fragrance is to be retained after they are dried. The flowers yield by distillation about one per cent of the essential oil which is the basis of lavender water. The stem is thick, and ragged-barked; the leaves are downy, grey-green and slender. The plant is a native of southern Europe, and grows best on chalky soils, in sunny positions. It belongs to the order *Labiatae*.

Lavoisier, ANTOINE LAURENT (1743–94). "The Republic has no need of scientists," declared the president of the tribunal that sent Lavoisier (pron. lav-waz'-yā), "father of modern chemistry," to the guillotine in May 1794, when the French revolutionary terror was at its height. This fanatical declar-ation drew forth from Lagrange, the great French mathematician, the retort, " You have in a moment cut off a head whose like may not be seen again for a century ! "

LAVENDER HEADS
From the mauve flowers of the sweet-scented lavender plant is dis-tilled the essential oil which forms the basis of lavender water.

Lavoisier was born in Paris on August 26, 1743, the son of a well-to-do merchant, and had a good education. He early showed an aptitude for science, and in 1766 he won a prize for an essay on the best means of lighting the streets of Paris. At the age of 25 he took up an appointment at the Academy of Sciences. Interested by the recently published discoveries of Joseph Black (1728–99) on the nature of heat, he decided to make chemistry his main study; though he ranged over a wide field later, including physics, meteorology, agri-culture, gunpowder manufacture, economics and currency.

It was a misfortune, in a way, that Lavoisier's wide knowledge and his flair brought him government appointments, since at the outbreak of the Revolution he thus fell under suspicion. Then, too, he had been a " farmer-general "—one of those financiers who, on payment of an agreed sum to the State, were allowed to collect and retain the taxes in certain areas. The un-scrupulous methods of some farmers-general had long aroused the hatred of the people; this position of Lavoisier, in particular, brought him under the suspicion of the revolu-tionaries; he was dismissed from his appointments in 1792, and two years later was guillotined.

Lavoisier founded what led to the modern theory of the chemi-cal elements. He destroyed the "phlogiston" theory, which pre-supposed that an inflammatory, unknown principle resided in combustible bodies, and so he paved the way for a true science of heat. He gave the name oxygen ("acid producer") to that gas, and showed, with Laplace, that water is formed by the combustion of oxygen and hydrogen.

Science will always honour this martyred genius, for, in the words of Liebig, the German chemist, "his merit, his immortal glory is that he infused into the body of science a new spirit."

Lavoisier's greatest work was his Traité élémentaire de Chimie, 1789. Mémoires de Chimie, published by his widow in 1805, was completed just before he was guillotined. Between 1862 and 1893 the complete works of Lavoisier in six volumes were published by the French Ministry of Public Instruction.

Law AND LAWYERS. We use the word law with at least three fundamentally different meanings. In its widest sense, law expresses the relation between cause and effect. Students of the sciences found, after long observation, that natural objects and forces can be depended upon to act in certain ways; these ways are natural laws. Thus the chemist speaks of the law of the conservation of matter; the physicist, of the laws of motion; the biologist, of the laws of heredity.

In a narrower sense the word law refers to the social life of Man. Thus we speak of laws of etiquette, laws of honour, and the moral law. Historians tell us that when people first began to live in groups they had no rules or laws, but they soon realized that each man had to pay attention to the needs and welfare of his neighbours in order to make life not only pleasant but possible for the greatest number. These rules or customs were at first unwritten, and were not always observed. When law in this second sense failed, when ridicule or ostracism were not effective checks, the state stepped in, making law in a third sense.

The word law is now most commonly used in this stricter or more positive sense of rules or codes which the state enforces through its political organization. The earliest code of laws that has come down to us is that of Hammurabi, the Babylonian monarch, who lived about 2100 B.C. Sometimes laws proved unsatisfactory and were changed, as for example in Athens when the harsh laws of Draco, in the 7th century B.C., were displaced by the more humane code of Solon.

The Romans, with their genius for government, gradually built up a remarkable body of law based on long established custom, modified and increased by judicial decisions and legislative enactments, which the Emperor Justinian codified in what came to be called the Roman Civil Law. So logical and just were its principles that it has been called "crystallized reason." In the latter part of the Middle Ages the study of this Roman law was revived in the universities of Europe. It has determined the general character of the laws of every nation in western Europe except England. And even in English law there is abundant evidence of Roman influences.

Before the Norman invasion of England, each manor, borough, or shire had its rules based on established custom— laws of tradition. After the Normans conquered the island, judges appointed by the king moved from place to place to administer these local laws, and gradually popular custom gave way to judicial decisions. In medieval England a custom was held to be law if it had been in force (in the old phrase) "from a time when the memory of Man runneth not to the contrary." As time went on, the decisions of the judges, constantly modified as they were by later decisions, were accepted as the body of English "common law."

Statute law, or legislation, is another kind of law which grew up because conditions arose to which judge-made or common law did not apply. This

Donald McLeish

THE HIGH COURT OF JUSTICE, LONDON
At the east end of the Strand, London, stands the High Court of Justice (commonly known as the Law Courts), built between 1874 and 1882, where some of the English courts of law have their seat. Before the erection of this structure they were housed in Westminster Hall, beside the Houses of Parliament.

is law made by legislative bodies, such as parliaments, congresses, and legislatures; and by bodies, such as County Councils, authorized to make laws (by-laws) by the central legislative body, or Parliament. Furthermore, two chief types of law came to be recognized: civil law, which sets forth the rights of persons, with methods for maintaining or regaining them; and criminal law, which deals with the nature of actions harmful to the public and the private good, with punishments for offenders. Constitutional law is the basic law of a nation or state, and it sets forth in general terms the nature of the government established under it.

In some countries, such as the United States and France, the Constitution is a written instrument. In England the law

BARRISTERS IN PROCESSION
At the opening of the Michaelmas term at the Law Courts, London, judges and barristers attend a service at Westminster Abbey or Westminster Cathedral, and are entertained by the Lord Chancellor at the House of Lords. The top photograph shows King's Counsel, in full State dress, entering the Law Courts; the lower, Junior Counsel entering the House of Lords. Notice the difference in their wigs and gowns.

under the Lord Chancellor. Military law is the set of rules used for governing a military organization. Martial law is the suspension of civil laws in time of emergency, such as invasion or insurrection, and the enforcement of military law on the civilian population. Parliamentary law is not "law." It is merely a body of rules to regulate the procedure of a deliberative group.

The legal profession is crowded, but many persons with legal training enter business in which they find their knowledge of great value. In recent years women have entered the legal profession. Law has become so complex that it is almost impossible for one to become an expert in all its branches. Laws are constantly changing and are so voluminous that only a specialist can keep himself fully informed.

Barristers and solicitors, who plead in the courts as advocate or counsel, or otherwise act as a client's legal agent, form the two great branches of the profession.

To qualify for call to the English Bar takes at least three years, and the candidate must become a student of one of what are called the four Inns of Court in London—the Inner Temple, Middle Temple, Lincoln's Inn and Gray's Inn. A large proportion of law students who now enter the Inns have taken a University degree. An interesting feature is that a certain number of dinners must be attended in the hall of an Inn to "keep terms." This requirement survives from the days when after dinner the student received instruction in law from a Reader. Now instruction is organized as in a university and the "eating of dinners," though obligatory, has only a social side. The higher grades in the profession—king's counsel (K.C.) or judge—are open only to those who have established a good practice.

To become a solicitor (once called an "attorney"), the usual method is for a young man to be articled to a member of the profession for five years; or he may serve in a solicitor's office as an ordinary clerk for 10 years. There are three examinations

of the Constitution is unwritten. The characteristic of a written Constitution is rigidity; of an unwritten Constitution, flexibility.

Canon law arose in the Middle Ages to deal with Church matters. It was administered in separate Church courts, with the Pope at the head; and there were numerous conflicts of jurisdiction between the Church and the secular courts. The new code of the canon law is a collection of all the disciplinary laws of the Roman Catholic Church. In England, Canon law is restricted to the regulation of church affairs and nowhere conflicts with or concerns itself with Civil law.

"Equity" is the name that is applied to a body of legal principles which arose in England to remedy the injustices which were done by a strict application of the letter of the law. For a long time (until 1873) the English Courts of Justice were distinct from the "equity" tribunals, which were

(controlled by the Incorporated Law Society, Chancery Lane, London, W.C.), but the preliminary is often excused. Passing the intermediate and final examinations, and the payment of certain fees, admit the candidate to practice. The Finance Act, 1947, reduced the stamp duty payable by the student becoming articled to a solicitor from £80 to 2s. 6d.; it abolished the £25 stamp duty payable on qualifying, and reduced from pounds to shillings the cost of a practising certificate for the first three years. The same Act abolished the stamp duty of £25 payable by the Bar student on joining his Inn of Court, and the £50 stamp duty payable on call to the Bar. The fees payable to the Inn of Court are £183. The standard required has been made exceedingly high.

Barristers are disciplined by the " Parliaments " of their Inns; solicitors by the Law Society. (*See also* Courts of Justice).

Law, INTERNATIONAL. " The law of nations," or international law, is the group of rules and principles which by general agreement the states of the civilized world observe in their relations with one another. Rome had a code of laws, called the *jus gentium*, governing its relations with foreigners, in which we find some of the early beginnings of international law as it is practised in modern times.

With the growth and intercourse of the modern states at the close of the Middle Ages, the need of an accepted body of principles governing their relations began to be felt; and a number of writers, foremost of whom was Hugo Grotius, a Dutch scholar, published treatises on the subject. In Grotius's book De jure belli et pacis (Concerning the Laws of War and Peace), published in 1625, we have the basis of much of the subsequent work on the subject, including the following principles : (1) war should be carried on only for a just cause, and for the purpose of defence; (2) do no more injury to the vanquished than is strictly necessary; (3) force alone ought not to regulate the relations of peoples, for there is justice between states as well as between individuals; (4) to observe treaties is the wisest practice and greatest strength of sovereigns.

In a strict sense international law is not "law." It is only a body of customs and conventions which the nations have agreed to accept, and its force depends on the good faith of the states that accept it. Treaties, ordinances of states, decisions of international tribunals, and the opinions of prominent jurists are studied to determine what rules have been most generally accepted. In recent years international congresses have been held to determine and interpret various phases of international

The Times

SWEARING-IN THE LORD CHIEF JUSTICE AT THE HIGH COURT

When a new Lord Chief Justice of England is sworn in (takes the oath of allegiance to the King) the ceremony takes place at the High Court, London. Here the Lord Chief Justice is seen standing and reading a document, with the Lord Chancellor seated on his left. Behind the Lord Chancellor and on his right are the mace-bearer and purse-bearer. The Lord Chancellor is the highest judicial functionary in Great Britain, the Lord Chief Justice ranking next to him.

law, the most important of these being The Hague Peace Conferences held in 1899 and 1907. After the First World War (1914–18), in 1919, there was established at The Hague the Permanent Court of International Justice. The International Court of Justice, which held its inaugural meeting at The Hague in April 1946, is the judicial body of the United Nations (*q.v.*).

International law recognizes that a sovereign state has complete authority within its own borders and, in the case of maritime states, a jurisdiction over the sea for a distance of about three miles from its coast. The freedom of the high seas, or that part of the ocean which lies beyond territorial waters, is possessed by all.

In reducing the sufferings of war, international law made considerable progress in the 19th century, but the practices of the First World War (1914–18) violated many cherished principles, and the Second World War (1939–45) revealed the impotence of such law in face of an aggressor nation. For example, the invasion of Czechoslovakia by Hitler in March 1939 was in total defiance of International law; and thereafter, until the end of the War of 1939–45 it remained virtually without force. In the wars in China, Japan, and Spain in the nineteen-thirties principles which, it had been fondly believed, were well established were shown to rest on the flimsiest foundations.

International law becomes increasingly important as science advances and devises ever more terrible methods of destruction. The atom bomb, and its use at Hiroshima against the Japanese, revealed to humanity the urgent need for the universal observance of laws made for the preservation of human life on earth. By 1948, the organization known as United Nations, which might be called a re-formed League of Nations, was seen to suffer the double handicap of dissension among member nations, and the lack of appropriate means to enforce its will—that is, to apply international law. Nevertheless, by that year it was clearly recognized that without a workable system of international law able to bring force (" sanctions ") against offending nations, the danger of unbridled force and cruelty in war must continue.

A GAME *of* WORLD-WIDE POPULARITY

An offshoot of real or 'royal' tennis, lawn tennis is played all over the world. Though it was formerly considered a summer game, the introduction of hard courts now enables it to be enjoyed the year round.

Lawn Tennis. A modern development of the much older game of real tennis (*q.v.*) which is now but little played, lawn tennis was devised by a Major Wingfield in England about 1874. A lawn tennis court is marked out on a closely cut, level grass lawn, or on a hard surface such as gravel, asphalt or concrete; it is 78 feet long and 27 feet wide. A hard court is, of course, usable throughout the winter season. When four persons play the game the court is 9 feet wider, the extra width being afforded by two side strips each 4½ feet wide. It is divided in halves by a net 3 feet high in the centre, and 3 feet 6 inches at the posts which support the ends. White lines or tapes indicate the base lines, side lines, service lines, and half-court line within the court. The length of the service court is 21 feet from the net, a line parallel to the side lines dividing the court in halves.

The object of the game is for the player on one side of the net to send the ball into his opponent's court in such a manner that it cannot be returned. The ball is a hollow sphere of rubber covered with white felt, not more than 2½ inches in diameter. The racket is a flat net of tightly-strung gut in a frame, with a handle a little more than a foot long; the whole is about 27 inches in length and usually weighs from 12 to 14 ounces, though there is no restriction in the rules regarding the size or weight.

At the start of a match of singles—as the game is called when two persons play—one player serves while the other receives. The server stands with both feet behind the base-line, throws the ball into the air, and by striking it with the racket sends it over the net into his opponent's service diagonally opposite. Any breach of the service law is a " fault," two faults losing a point. The receiver, or striker-out, must hit the ball on the first bound, attempting to send it back over the net so that it will fall within the court. If he fails to return it over the net or sends it outside the court, he loses the point. After the service has been returned either player may hit the ball before it has bounced, i.e., volley it.

The ball frequently passes to and fro across the net several times before one of the players fails to return it. The service alternates, first from the right then from the left court, and a player continues to serve until he wins or loses a game, when the service passes to his opponent. The doubles game on the larger court—with two players on each side of the net—is played in the same manner, except that the partners alternate in serving, and different tactics must obviously be employed.

The first point won makes the score 15, the second point 30, the third 40, and the fourth wins the game unless each side has scored 40. In that case the score is deuce, and in order to win the game thereafter one side or the other must take two points in succession. The scores " 15 to 0 " and " 30 to 0 " are called as " 15 love," " 30 love," etc., the opposite being " love 15," and so on. The first of

TENNIS COURT MARKINGS

The standard plan and dimensions of a lawn tennis court for singles and doubles play are shown.

Court labels: 18 FT. — HALF COURT LINE, 42 FT. — NET — SIDE LINE, 78 FEET — SERVICE LINE, 27 FT. — BASE LINE, 36 FEET — 4½ FT.

LAWN TENNIS

the two points after deuce is called advantage in (also van in, vantage server, or vantage So-and-so) if this is won by the server, and advantage out, etc., if it is won by his opponent, the striker-out.

At the end of each game the player who has served becomes striker-out while his opponent serves. The play continues until one player wins six games, which gives him the "set." If, however, the score should become five games all, one player or the other must win two further consecutive games to win the set. Sides are usually changed at the end of every odd game. A match is the best of three or five sets.

The principal strokes used in returning the ball are the forehand drive, the backhand, the volley, the half-volley, the lob, the drop-shot, and the smash. If the player is right-handed, and the ball falls to the right of his (or her) body, he stands sideways to the ball, with his left foot forward, and uses the forehand drive by hitting the ball with a smooth forward swing near the top of its bounce. If the ball falls to his left, he advances his right foot, swings

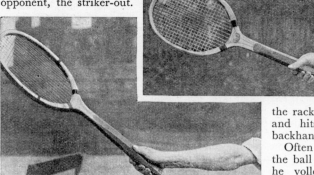

HOW TO GRIP THE RACKET
Above are the handgrips adopted by the majority of lawn tennis players for (upper) the forehand drive, and (lower) the backhand. Note that the racket is held at the very end of the handle to give a smooth swing.

the racket across his body, and hits the ball with a backhand stroke.

Often when he can reach the ball before it bounces, he volleys by hitting it while it is still in the air. If his opponent has run in close to the net he sometimes lobs by sending the ball high over the opponent's head. The overhead smash is employed in "killing" any weak return that his opponent may send high above the net, and the drop-shot is used to send the ball gently just over the net.

Service gives opportunity for many skilful strokes. There are two styles of service in lawn tennis—the overarm and the underarm—although the underarm is rarely used by modern exponents of the game, as sufficient speed cannot be given to the ball with-

Sport & General

LAWN TENNIS ON THE CENTRE COURT AT WIMBLEDON
To play in the All-England Championships at Wimbledon, Surrey, is the hall-mark of a first-class lawn tennis player. To win is the highest lawn tennis honour that he or she can achieve. Every summer in normal times the finals are fought out on the Centre Court (above) in an atmosphere tense with excitement. For these matches there are linesmen and ball-boys, in addition to an umpire who has a raised seat by the net. The governing body of the game in Britain is the Lawn Tennis Association, which organizes also the Hard Courts and Covered Courts Championships.

out sending it out of the court. With the overarm service the full striking force of the arm can be used, and the style can be varied. To an inexperienced player "spin" or "swerve" services are difficult to take, but the first-class player relies as much on speed as on finesse.

To the annual Championships of the All-England Lawn Tennis (and Croquet) Club held at Wimbledon, Surrey, players come from all over the world. Many of the men play for their country in the International Lawn Tennis Championship for the Davis Cup. The nearest approach to this gruelling competition in women's tennis is the Wightman Cup, played for annually by teams representing Great Britain and the United States.

The Lawn Tennis Association, the governing body of the game in Britain, organizes two other important events—the Hard Courts Championships, held at Bournemouth, Hampshire, and the Covered Courts Championships at Queen's Club, London. There is also a long succession of tournaments which attract a large entry of aspiring players of both sexes. There are also special events for juniors.

There is much discussion as to the relative merit of the greatest men players in the history of lawn tennis. Some veterans of the game say that no modern player, despite the all-round speeding-up and higher standard of play, would have been able to beat the brothers R. F. and H. L. Doherty, who "reigned" at Wimbledon in the '90s and in the early part of the present century. The Renshaw twins were earlier champions, W. Renshaw winning the men's singles on seven occasions—six of them consecutive. After the Dohertys and A. W. Gore came the first of the invaders from a-broad, such players as N. E. Brookes (Australia) and A. F. Wilding (New Zealand) being worthy champions of the game. The year 1919 saw the introduction of the "cannon-ball" service, used with deadly effect by G. L. Patterson (Australia). The greatest of all American players, W. T. Tilden, won the first of his three victories in 1920. Later there came France's "Four Musketeers"—J. Borotra, R. Lacoste, H. Cochet and J. Brugnon—the first three of whom became singles champions. F. J. Perry was the next British player to win at Wimbledon—and did so three times running, in 1934, 1935, and 1936—and J. D. Budge

(U.S.A.) won in 1937 and 1938. From 1939 (outbreak of the Second World War) to 1945 there was no play at Wimbledon.

In women's tennis, Mlle. Suzanne Lenglen (died 1938), of France, first won the Wimbledon crown in 1919, at the age of 20, and proceeded to win again in 1920, 1921, 1922, 1923 and 1925. Other great women players include Mrs. G. W. Hillyard, six times champion; Mrs. Lambert Chambers, seven times champion; and Mrs. Helen Wills-Moody, compatriot of Tilden, who equalled this record. During the Second World War (1939-1945) more serious matters engaged the attention of everyone in Britain, and "form" was not easily regained when play again started.

Lawrence, THOMAS EDWARD (1888–1935). A motor-cycle accident on an English country road brought to a dramatic close one of the most remarkable and romantic careers of the 20th century. "Lawrence of Arabia" had become famous the world over because of his amazing exploits as leader of the Arab revolt against the Turks in 1916–18, during the First World War; and his dislike of publicity, which led him afterwards to change his name twice and hide himself in the ranks of the Royal Air Force, has made him an almost legendary figure.

Lawrence was born on August 15, 1888, in North Wales, and was educated at Oxford High School and at Jesus College, Oxford, where his unusual personality began to show itself. His attendance at classes were irregular; he spent his nights roaming about the city; he read continuously, skimming over thousands of books on a variety of subjects.

Daily Mirror

'LAWRENCE OF ARABIA'

His exploits as leader of the Arabs against the Turks in the First World War (1914–18) won for Thomas Edward Lawrence the title of Lawrence of Arabia. He is here seen in Arab dress. He was killed in a motor-cycle accident in 1935.

He became specially interested in the Middle Ages, and this interest resulted in a journey to the Near East to study the castles of the Crusaders. He tramped all over Palestine, Syria, and Mesopotamia (now Iraq) becoming acquainted with the Arabs, and thus laying the foundations of his great life-work.

When the First World War (1914–18) broke out Lawrence was recalled to England to carry out mapping work, but was transferred to the British intelligence service in Egypt. Soon afterwards he was sent to Arabia, with the rank of colonel, and there he began to take an active part in the revolt of the Arabs against their Turkish oppressors. He arrived at a time when the Arabian forces were scattered, weakened, and discouraged. With tireless energy he rode all over Arabia, winning the confidence and admiration of the tribes, and constantly urging Arab unity. Soon Lawrence had organized the Arabs into a formidable fighting force, and by a series of lightning manoeuvres he time and again outwitted the Turks.

As the campaign continued, Lawrence, working closely with the British commander General Allenby and the Arabian Prince Feisal, moved steadily north. He won battle after battle, until in one last magnificent push his forces completely destroyed the Fourth Turkish Army and captured Damascus on October 1, 1918.

Lawrence's major task was over. But Arab independence was still close to his heart, and he looked after Arab interests at the Peace Conference in 1919. By his influence Prince Feisal was made King of Iraq and Feisal's brother Abdulla was placed on the throne of Transjordan. This work ended, he retired from public life, to write his account of the revolt in a book entitled The Seven Pillars of Wisdom. An abridged edition was later issued, with the title of Revolt in the Desert.

In search of privacy he enlisted in the Royal Air Force under the name of Ross, transferring to the Royal Armoured Corps in 1923. Rejoining the R.A.F. in 1925, he went to India, returning to England in 1929. Having again changed his name, this time to Shaw, he retired in 1935, and died in Dorsetshire, after an accident, on May 19, 1935.

Lead. The great weight and softness of lead and the ease with which it is extracted from its native ores have made it one of the handiest metals since very ancient times.

Lead was known to the Egyptians and is mentioned several times in the Bible. The Romans used metallic lead for making water-pipes, tanks, weights, and rings, and lead compounds for cosmetics and paint. The great resistance of metallic lead to attack by most acids has given it a high place in modern chemical trades and industries. A form of specially acid-resistant lead, known as tellurium lead, and containing about 0·05 per cent of tellurium, is more resistant to vibration and repeated bending than is ordinary lead.

Pure lead is used chiefly today for making water-pipes, coverings for electric cables, chemical tanks, and electrical storage batteries. Mixed with a small amount of arsenic, it is made into small shot and shrapnel bullets; with about 30 per cent of tin and a little antimony it gives plumber's solder. The principal lead compounds employed in the arts and manufactures are white lead (a form of lead carbonate), used for making paints; red lead (minium), one of the lead oxides, also used for making paint, particularly for ironwork to prevent rust formation; and litharge (PbO), sometimes used during the manufacture of varnishes and paints, to cause them to dry more quickly, and in the making of flint glass. The so-called lead in pencils is a form of carbon called graphite (q.v.).

Before the invention of high-power explosives had compelled the use of tougher metals, all rifle bullets were cast of lead. The small shot of olden days was made in high shot-towers (some of which are still to be seen near the Thames in London), from the top of which molten lead, passing through a sieve, fell in tiny drops and plunged into water tanks at the bottom, thus acquiring a globular shape.

Lead in its pure state is greyish-white in colour. A fresh-cut surface will glitter brilliantly, but soon becomes dull on exposure to the air. Because it lacks rigidity and tensile strength it is unfit to support any great strain, either pull or pressure. It melts at 327·4 degrees Centigrade (621 degrees Fahrenheit). Its chemical symbol is Pb (from the Latin *plumbum*); its atomic weight is 207·22; atomic number 82; density 11·37.

Lead is mined chiefly in the form of galena (lead sulphide), which usually contains some silver. The process of extraction is simple, the ore being nowadays usually roasted to burn away sulphur and form lead oxide, which is then converted to metallic lead in a small blast furnace.

All the compounds of lead are poisonous. Special caution is required in occupations where quantities of this metal are used, such as glazing, painting, plumbing, and printing, for lead is a cumulative poison; that is, succeeding amounts accumulate in the body, gradually producing graver symptoms, extending from colic to nerve paralysis, blindness, convulsions, and death. The cold water pipes in our homes and other buildings are often made of lead, but we do not get lead poisoning if the water is " hard," for a coating of insoluble salts is formed on the insides of the pipes. Lead pipes should not be used for " soft " drinking water, as soluble poisonous compounds may be formed.

League of Nations. Long before the League of Nations was established in 1920 efforts had been made to solve international problems by discussions. They all tended to confirm the opinion that representatives of nations can harmonize national with common interests and settle disputes without war.

Innumerable international meetings had been held—in a single year as many as 160—to consider special aspects of world problems; and since the organization of the International Postal Union in 1874 an increasing number of permanent official international bodies were set up with administrative and other powers. The Permanent Court of Arbitration, established at The Hague, The Netherlands, by the conferences of 1899 and 1907, was the most important attempt to create a court where justice in the varied fields of international relations could be determined; where even threats of war could be changed into agreements.

To President Woodrow Wilson (1856–1924) of the United States belongs the chief credit for forming the League of Nations. In his famous Fourteen Points (January 8, 1918) he named the formation of the League as part of the peace programme, subsequently accepted by the Allies and by Germany under the terms of the armistice which terminated the fighting in the First World War in November 1918. " A general association of nations," read Point Fourteen, " must be formed under specific covenants, for the purpose of affording guarantees of political independence and territorial integrity to great and small states alike." His insistence made the League a part of the Versailles Treaty. Many offered suggestions for the organization of the League, the one most closely followed being that of General Jan C.

PALACE OF THE LEAGUE OF NATIONS AT GENEVA

The magnificent home of the League of Nations at Geneva, Switzerland, replaced a disused hotel in which the affairs of the League had previously been conducted. The building, which covers an area of four acres, was begun in March 1931, first occupied in February 1936, and cost £2,000,000. The staff of the Secretary of the League occupied one wing in which was also the Council Hall accommodating about 2,000. In April 1946 the League of Nations was replaced by the United Nations, who took over the palace as headquarters for permanent technical bodies of their organization.

Smuts of South Africa. The efficiency of the League of Nations was, however, greatly impaired by the absence of the United States, the American nation refusing to agree to America's intervention in non-American controversies. Germany was admitted to the League in 1926 and left it in 1935, when Japan also withdrew. Russia was admitted in 1934; Italy withdrew in 1937.

The machinery of the League consisted of an Assembly, a Council and an international Secretariat. The Assembly, which met usually once a year, was composed of three representatives from each of the member countries, and each State had one vote. The Council met at least three times a year. It normally consisted of 14 members, of whom five were permanent, nine being chosen annually in rotation.

The Council selected the permanent Secretary General for the League, who, with his staff, formed the Secretariat. New member states were admitted upon the consent of two-thirds of the Assembly. They had to be self-governing countries, including dominions and colonies. Withdrawal required two years' notice and fulfilment of all obligations. With few exceptions all votes in both Council and Assembly were required to be unanimous. Geneva, Switzerland, was the seat of the League.

The purposes of the League were stated thus: To prevent wars by insisting upon arbitration and judicial decision to settle disputes; to secure a reduction of natural armaments; to prevent international traffic in arms, drugs, women and children; and to obtain fair and humane conditions for labour. All treaties entered into by member States had to be registered with the League Secretariat.

Certain States responsible to the League were given mandates to rule the former German colonies and certain portions of the old Turkish Empire, and other territories. In Article 10, the members undertook " to respect and preserve as against external aggression the territorial integrity and existing political independence of all members of the League." The chief weapon to be used against offending states was an economic blockade. This part of the League machinery broke down completely in 1936, when it was found impossible or inexpedient to employ a blockade against Italy during her campaign against Abyssinia, a fellow League member that Italy had herself proposed for membership. The League had previously failed in the Chinese-Japanese dispute of 1934, when Japan wrested Manchuria from China.

The first meeting of the Executive Council was held in Paris, on January 16, 1920. On November

15, 1920, the full Assembly of the League met in Geneva for the first time, with 42 countries represented. Fifty-eight States were members in 1938. Britain's share of the cost of upkeep was the highest.

An important adjunct to the League was the Permanent Court of International Justice, or World Court, of 11 judges and four deputy judges to hear cases voluntarily submitted by disputing States, concerning interpretations of treaties, questions of international law, breaches of international obligation, and reparations for such breaches. The judges were elected for terms of nine years by separate majority votes of the Council and the Assembly from a list of nominees. Sittings were held in The Hague Peace Palace.

The International Labour Office also had its headquarters in Geneva. The governing body consisted of 12 Government, eight employers', and eight workers' representatives. Learning from the experience of the League, the United Nations at San Francisco in 1945 adopted a Charter which superseded the League and both greatly widened the scope and strengthened the organization for world peace. The 21st and final meeting of the League took place in April 1946, its work being taken over by the United Nations (*q.v.*).

Lear, EDWARD (1812–88). If you haven't yet made the acquaintance of the works of Edward Lear, a great treat is in store for you. For he was the writer and illustrator of two of the most famous humorous children's books in the world—The Book of Nonsense, which consists of limericks, and The Nonsense Book. These are books of pure nonsense. Lewis Carroll's " Alice " books are nonsense, too, but they are deliberately witty and well thought out, often almost scientific; they have not the spontaneous " craziness " which characterizes the work of Lear.

Born in London on May 12, 1812, Lear was employed by the Earl of Derby, for whom he drew series of sketches of the menagerie at Knowsley, Lancashire, and for whose children the Book of Nonsense was written. Later Lear lived in Rome, travelling widely in the Mediterranean region, and he died at San Remo, Italy, on January 30, 1888. By profession he was a serious water-colour painter, and his Illustrated Journals of a Landscape Painter enjoyed as much popularity for their illustrations as for their text. But his fame rests principally on the books previously mentioned, popular alike with children and with adults.

In his preface to The Book of Nonsense, Edward Lear gives a summary of his life together with some verses about himself:

> How pleasant to know Mr. Lear!
> Who has written such volumes of stuff!

he begins; and he goes on to tell us that

> His mind is concrete and fastidious,
> His nose is remarkably big;
> His visage is more or less hideous,
> His beard it resembles a wig.

And here is one of his Limericks :

> There was an Old Person of Anerley,
> Whose conduct was strange and unmannerly;
> He rushed down the Strand,
> With a pig in each hand,
> But returned in the evening to Anerley.

Limericks we hear nowadays usually contain a fresh rhyme in the last line. The origin of the term Limerick is doubtful; some suggestions are given in the article under that heading.

How HIDES *and* SKINS *become* LEATHER

'There's nothing like leather' is an old saying and a true one, for despite Man's ingenuity he has found no satisfactory substitute. This article tells leather's story from its beginning as some creature's covering.

Leather. Long ago, primitive Man learnt how to make the skins and hides of animals soft and pliable, and to prevent decay, by cleaning them of flesh and treating them with such things as salt or oil or, later, with the juice from certain astringent barks such as oak bark. The name tanning comes from a French word for oak, and oak bark is still used for the purpose. At first the skins were used as garments with the fur still on, giving added warmth.

Hides were prepared with the hair on, almost in the natural state except that the flesh was removed from the inside. Later, various crude methods of making them pliable and stopping putrefaction came into use.

Most leather comes from the skins and hides of domestic animals. The skins of the larger animals are called hides. Those of smaller animals, such as sheep, goats, pigs, dogs, etc., are known to the trade as skins. The deer, kangaroo, buffalo, antelope, and water animals such as the alligator, walrus, and seal (not the fur-bearing

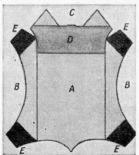

PARTS OF A HIDE
The various sections of a hide are : **(A)** the butt, **(B)** belly, **(C)** cheek, **(D)** neck, **(E)** shanks.

seal, but a quite distinct species), also furnish leather. In recent times all sorts of lizards, snakes and crocodiles and even sharks have been made to yield their coverings as leather for fancy articles, such as handbags, and for women's shoes. Among birds, the skin of the ostrich also makes a good leather.

Before the hides are ready for use as leather they have to go through a good many processes. Some of these processes are much the same today as they were among the ancient Egyptians. The first step is to remove the skin from the animal, whole and without blemish. With modern tools this is done very skilfully and quickly; sometimes air is forced under the skin with a bellows to make removal easy. If the hides are to go at once to the tanning process they are left untreated or " green." If there is any delay they must be dried, or be " green salted," that is, have salt rubbed into the fleshy side in order to prevent the process of decomposition, which would soon set in and ruin the skin otherwise.

LIME VATS TO LOOSEN HAIR ON HIDES

When the raw hides reach the tannery the hanging parts, such as ears and tail, are trimmed off, and all remaining bits of flesh removed. After the hides have been soaked for several days in a brine bath to soften and cleanse them, a machine takes off the last traces of fat and tissue. Then the hides are put into lime vats (above) to loosen the hair, which is scraped from the hide by another machine. After further washing and trimming the hides are ready for tanning.

At the tannery the skins and hides are trimmed to remove flesh and useless parts, and put into " soaks "—large tanks of brine. Here they are left for from two to four days to be plumped, softened, and cleansed. The fleshing machine next removes all fat and tissue remnants. The hair is loosened by a chemical bath, and is scraped off by another machine or sometimes by hand.

After thorough washing and trimming the hides are ready for tanning. The purpose of tanning is to stop decomposition, to give the hides greater strength, toughness and pliability, and to make them proof against water. There is a choice of processes, upon which will depend the grade and special quality of the finished leather. The chief processes are vegetable tanning, oil tanning, and mineral tanning. When it is desired to tan skins without removing the fur or hair—for example, for use as furs or rugs—they are " tawed " or dry-tanned by packing in moist salt and powdered alum.

For the heavier leathers and some of the lighter kinds, the tan-bark process is in most general use. Originally the bark of oak-trees was employed almost exclusively, and in parts of Britain large areas were covered with trees grown for this purpose. Modern methods no longer depend on this source of raw material. Barks, leaves, nuts or wood of several kinds of trees containing tannin are now used,

and the manner of their use and the choice of barks largely determine the kind and quality of the leather. Most heavy leathers, such as sole and belting leather, upholstery, harness, bag, and strap leathers are tanned with hemlock and oak. In Australia the mimosa or wattle-barks are much used. Tannin is also found in the bark and leaves of most forest trees,

Topical

OAK BARK IN A SUSSEX TANNERY

At Battle, Sussex, seven miles from Hastings, hand-made leather is still tanned in the old-fashioned way with oak bark, a stack of which can be seen above. The bark, which contains a quantity of tannin, is powdered before being made into the tan-liquor.

but the only other ones which furnish enough to be of value are certain willows, chestnuts and birches.

Other tanning materials of importance are quebracho, a widely distributed tree of South America; myrobalans, the fruit of an Indian tree; divi-divi, the dried seed-pods of a South American tree; galls, abnormal growths found on oaks, caused by the gall-wasp laying eggs in the plant; gambier, the product of a shrub cultivated in Singapore and the Malay Archipelago; mangrove, from the mangrove trees of Borneo; valonia, the acorn cup of the Turkish and Greek oak; and sumach, the ground leaves of one of the sumach trees (*Rhus coriaria*) grown in Mediterranean regions.

The skins are suspended in vats containing tanning solutions made of various ingredients, singly or in combination, and are removed from one vat to another, each succeeding vat containing a stronger solution. They are then dried by artificial heat, oiled, and ironed by large rollers.

Vegetable tanning requires from 90 to 100 days, while the process of mineral tanning takes less than a third of that time. This process was invented in 1884, and is now the most general mode of dressing light leathers. It is also used for heavy leathers where great strength is needed. The liquid used for this purpose is a solution of chromium salts, obtained from chrome iron ore.

Oil tanning is used for making soft glove leathers such as chamois, buckskin, and piano leather. The process is called "shammying" (*chamoising*) and consists of working oil into the skins to make them spongy and soft. Many of the soft leathers—the chamois leathers—formerly treated in this way are now chrome-tanned.

The finishing processes are varied according to the use for which the leather is intended. The leather, as it dries after tanning, is stiff and rough. Rubbing oil into it to make it soft and pliable is called currying. Sometimes the currying and finish-

Topical

MAKING LEATHER BY HAND IN SOUTHERN ENGLAND

At the top left, skins are being taken out of a lime pit in a Sussex tannery (*see* also illus. page 1911). The hair, loosened by immersion in lime, is scraped off with a bow-shaped knife (top right) before the hides are suspended in vats containing tanning liquid. At intervals they are removed from one vat to another (lower left), each succeeding vat containing a stronger solution. After tanning, marks are erased by rubbing with a wooden roller (lower right).

'AT THE END OF THE PROCESS—OILING AND DRYING

After the hides have been tanned, they are coloured, seasoned, and oiled. Left, we see two workmen applying the oil with soft cloths. The right-hand picture shows men hanging up the hides to dry. Once dry, the finished leather is sorted according to weight. The heaviest and strongest skins are collected and classed as 'first grade,' and the others graded accordingly. Since leather is sold by the square foot, each hide is measured in a machine and its size marked upon it. Then they are put into big bundles which are sent to factories for making into leather goods.

ing are done as a separate industry, the currier buying the rough leather from the tanner.

Dull leather, such as is used in cheaper grades of shoes, may be simply oiled and worked to make it pliable. Harness leather and sole leather is put in great presses to make it hard and durable. If a lustre is desired a dressing is applied to the grain side of the leather and then it is run through pressure rollers which polish the surface; if a dull polish is desired a revolving brush is passed over the surface. Grain leather may also be given a pattern, as is done in box calf or imitation alligator skins.

The colouring of leather is an art in itself, requiring great care to bring about a uniform result. Different skins going through the same colour bath will be of different shades, and portions of the same skin may take the colour unevenly, so that the leather may appear spotted.

Something may now be said on the subject of the chemistry of tanning.

The skin (see diagram under the heading Skin) consists of an outer layer known as the *epidermis*, a second layer known as the *dermis*, *corium* or *true skin*, and a *fatty layer*. The first layer is thin, and it is the next one which is important from the tanner's point of view, being formed of what the anatomist calls connective tissue. The epidermis is mainly keratin

KINDS OF LEATHER
These four varieties of 'fancy' leather are (left to right) morocco and pig-skin (upper), calf and heavily-grained crocodile (lower).

(see Horn), a protein, and the dermis also consists chiefly of protein. Untanned skin absorbs water, swells up and stretches, the fibres becoming plastic; on drying out the water, the skin hardens into a horny mass useless for the purposes of leather and very liable to decay. Tanning combines the protein with the tanning agent, softens the skin, and protects it from decay.

In vegetable tanning, a colloid (q.v.) is deposited upon the fibres as a precipitate, and the protein is made to coagulate or solidify. The interstices between the fibres become filled with tannin, some of which is taken out in further processes which follow, in order that the leather shall be pliable and not crack upon bending. In chrome tanning, the chromium salt is deposited upon the skin as a precipitate from the tanning solution; the fibres, after tanning is completed, repel water, whereas before they would have absorbed it greedily.

The spaces between the fibres are not filled, as they are in vegetable tanning, so that chrome-tanned leathers remain soft and supple. Before drying, the leather is treated with an emulsion of oil (such as cod liver or neats-foot oil), this process being known as fat-liquoring. This prevents the fibres from sticking together, and allows the leather to flex. Fat-liquoring is used for vegetable-tanned leather as well as chrome-tanned, but is more important for the last named.

Leathers are distinguished by names according to their material and treatment. The most numerous and useful are made of cowhide and calf-skin. Box calf is calf leather. Wax calf is heavy calf-skin with a wax finish. Suède is calf-skin (or sometimes kid) finished by buffing or grinding the face on an emery wheel. Glazed or glacé kid is a common form, having a smooth, highly polished surface. Undressed kid is a skin dressed only on one side, used chiefly for gloves. Morocco was originally a sumach-tanned goat-skin, made in Morocco and stained red; the term is also applied to imitations of morocco, and to any heavily tanned goat-skin. Morocco makes good book-covers.

Russia leather was originally a very high-grade calf-skin made in Russia and dressed with birch oil, giving it a peculiar fragrance; it was dyed a deep red. So-called Russia leather is now made throughout Europe and America of heavy skins of various kinds, and finished in tan, brown or black. Red russia is now chiefly used for binding fine books, as the leather is watertight and strong and repels insects. Patent leathers are made from any firm, soft leather, free from grease and with no tendency to stretch. Successive coats of black varnish are applied, until the surface is covered with a heavy coat of enamel, and the last coat is baked on.

Cordovan is horse-hide, very durable and watertight; the name comes from the Spanish city of Cordova, which had an ancient reputation for making fine shoes. Imitations are now made from calf. Chamois is properly the dressed skin of the Alpine chamois, but the genuine article is very scarce; most of the so-called chamois is chrome-tanned sheep-skin. Buckskin, originally tanned deer-skin, is nowadays usually suède-finished calf-skin or kid. It is a buff or cream-coloured leather, almost as soft and pliable as cloth, and is widely used in glove-making.

The GREEN GARMENT of the TREES

What is the function of leaves? Why do those of some trees fall when autumn comes, while other trees and shrubs are 'evergreen'? These and other questions are part of a fascinating story in plant physiology.

Leaves. Most people look upon leaves merely as the brilliant costume of the trees, without realizing their immense importance to human as well as to plant life. By far the largest part of the food we eat is manufactured originally by the leaves of plants—even such things as bacon and eggs if we follow them back far enough. Indeed, we shall see that leaves are the mouths, the lungs, the stomachs, the pores, and the " eyes " of the plant, without which the plant could not live. Moreover, they are the factories in which, by chemical synthesis, plant food is made.

We can learn many important facts about leaves by examining any ordinary leaf from a tree or bush. From the stem a network of veins branches out to all parts of the leaf. Those veins act not only as the fibre skeleton which holds the leaf spread out in shape, but as the " blood-vessels " which connect every portion of the leaf with the deepest rootlet far underground. In between the veins the leaf is filled with a spongy mass of green-coloured cells, held in place by a thin skin or membrane on the upper and lower surfaces. (These cell layers are seen in diagram at right.)

Now let us follow the leaf through a day's work as it hangs upon the tree. First, we find that the upper surface of a leaf tends to face the sunlit sky. If a tree is growing close against a high wall, very few leaves will be found on the dark side. That is because the leaf needs sunlight to do its work. (This is called phototropism, or heliotropism —from Greek words meaning " light " and " turn "; and " sun " and " turn.") A strange thing is that leaves arrange themselves so as not to shade one another; this means that the leaves turn so that ultimately they are at an angle to the light rays, not directly facing them. There are a few interesting exceptions to this light-seeking movement, such as the compass plant, which grows on the open prairie in North America. Its leaves are turned on edge pointing roughly north and south. This is an adaptation to avoid the intense heat of such regions.

As the sunlight strikes through the smooth transparent membrane on the upper surface of the leaf, small quantities of air enter through thousands of tiny *stomata*—mouths— mostly on the under side. Some of these are water-stomata, which enable the leaf to get rid of water by transpiration. Other stomata are the organs by which the gaseous exchange is effected between the plant and the atmosphere. Two stomata are shown in the diagram at left. Usually at the side of the stomata there are guard-cells, which open or close the

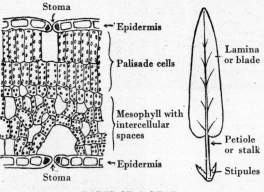

PARTS OF A LEAF

In the left-hand drawing the inside of a leaf is shown, highly magnified. On the upper and lower surfaces are two stomata (plural form of stoma or breathing pore) ; some stomata serve as water openings for transpiration, others enable gas interchange to be effected between the plant and the air. The palisade cells add strength, the mesophyll conducts solutions. The drawing on the right shows some essential parts of a typical leaf.

stoma more or less, as is required by differing conditions of temperature, season and weather. Under the influence of sunshine a strange thing takes place. The green colouring matter (*chlorophyll*) of the leaf takes from the air the gas carbon dioxide, and mixes it with water which has reached the leaf, via the plant's transpiration system of "water-pipes" or vessels, extending up from the distant roots. Then, with the aid of the sunlight, the leaf manufactures out of this mixture the carbohydrates—s u g a r s a n d starches—which are the basis of plant food, and turns out into the air again through those same "mouths" the surplus oxygen. The s u g a r s and starches then pass back through the veins and stem of the leaf, and unite with other chemicals in the sap to nourish the plant and build up the hard woody material (cellulose) of the stem and branches. Again, this same transpiration water carries up from the soil nitrates out of which the leaf manufactures proteins, another important class of food stuffs.

But in land plants the leaf performs another important function. When they are not drawing in air to make food, the stomata act as pores, and transpire or sweat away excess water. This may help to keep the leaf cool and healthy.

Leaves of some plants—especially those which live in dry localities—store water in specially adapted cell tissue. The common stonecrop (*Sedum acre*) is a familiar example of such "succulent" plants. The strange cactus plants are other water-storers.

The leaves of some plants are sensitive to touch as well as to light, in almost the same way as the tendrils of climbers. One of the mimosas (*Mimosa pudica*), for example, is called the sensitive plant because its leaves react so strongly to touch and take up the "sleeping" posture. Other plants unfold perianth leaves (*see* Flower) during the day and close them at night. Leaves of some plants make autonomic (spontaneous) movements. For example, the telegraph plant (*Desmodium gyrans*) has leaves composed of three leaflets; the two lower leaflets move jerkily up and down, the entire movement taking s e v e r a l minutes to complete. Leaflets of some clovers move up and down in warm weather, but here the movement t a k e s several hours to complete.

Plants show a wide range of leaf shapes, each suited to particular needs. But there are three main t y p e s of

VEINS IN A LEAF
The manner in which the veins are arranged in a leaf is known botanically as 'venation.' In this leaf of a poplar tree continuous branching from the stout midrib forms a fine network.

arrangement of the main ribs of their skeleton: (1) those with several main ribs branching out finger-like from the stem, called palmate (from the Latin *palma*, palm of the hand); (2) those with a single large middle rib from which smaller ribs branch out feather-like on each side, called pinnate (from the Latin *pinna*, feather); and (3) those in which the ribs do not form a branching network at all, but run from stem to tip, called parallel-veined.

These terms refer only to the venation (veining), not to the shape of leaf, where the terms palmate and pinnate have a much more restricted meaning. For instance, the round nasturtium leaf, the slightly indented leaf of the scarlet geranium, the ivy leaf with its sharp lobes, and the leaf of the horse-chestnut, which is divided down to the stem—all have the palmate system of venation. Yet, considering the shape and not the vein arrangement, the leaves of the first are referred to as round, those of the second as lobed, and those of the third alone as palmate—and even for the horse-chestnut this word is not always used. Similarly, the beech leaf, the oak leaf, the elm leaf, and even the locust leaf, which consists of groups of pairs of small leaflets arranged around the main stalk, are all good examples of the pinnate type of venation. Y e t t h e beech leaf is ovate, the oak leaf lobed, the elm leaf often o b o v a t e, and the locust leaf alone is truly pinnate (t e r m s e x p l a i n e d later). Lilies, tulips and almost all grasses illustrate the third or parallel-veined type of leaves.

Leaves are arranged generally to get the greatest amount of light, as seen in the photograph on the left, where leaves of the horse-chestnut fit into each other like a sort of mosaic. They may be in pairs (opposite), or in spirals or zig-zags about the branch (alternate), or in whorls, many springing from one point,

The normal form of the leaf is broad and thin, but there are many modified leaves—the needles of the pine tree, the long ribbon-like grasses, the finely divided compound

SPECIAL FORMATIONS
Leaves of the horse chestnut tree (lower) are so arranged that overshadowing is largely avoided ; thus the most is made of sunlight. The fleshy leaves of a cactus plant (upper) growing in the hot desert are specially adapted to act as water-storers.

leaves of the tribe *Umbelliferae*, the hollow traps in which the pitcher-plant catches insects.

Most leaves consist of two distinct parts: the petiole or stalk attached to the stem, and the thin expanded portion called the blade. Sometimes there is no petiole and the blade is attached directly to the stem, when it is said to be sessile. Many leaves grow from between a pair of small appendages, called stipules, attached either to the base of the petiole or to the stem. Some stipules remain attached during the life of the leaf. In the grasses the lower part of the leaf folds round the stem for some distance and is called the sheath.

Some of the different kinds of leaves have just been mentioned, but there are really a large number of quite well-marked types of blade to which you will find reference made again and again. Starting from the narrowest, we have, first, linear, the parallel-sided leaf like a blade of grass; lanceolate, ranging from a narrow leaf which is not linear, to a longish, quite broad leaf which comes to a sharp point; ovate, which is broader near the base than the top; obovate, which is broader near the upper part of the leaf; cordate, a heart-shaped leaf; peltate, in which the petiole comes up into the centre of the blade, as in the nasturtium; hastate, in which there are lobes running back on either side of the leaf-stalk; sagittate (arrow-shaped), in which the lobes running back are almost or quite as large as the main part of the leaf; trifoliate, a three-lobed leaf like that of the clover; palmate, in which a number of lobes radiate from the base of the leaf; perfoliate, where the actual stem runs through the middle of the leaf; spatulate (or spathulate), spoon-shaped; and pinnate—feather-like—where there are a number of opposite leaflets all the way up the midrib, as the main central vein is called. Opposite leaves are sometimes joined at their base (connate).

Besides these terms describing the leaf itself, there are others which refer to the margin. This may be entire, or quite unbroken; serrate, with a saw-like edge; dentate, in which the margin is toothed rather than saw-like; crenate, with rounded serrations; and lobed, as in the oak leaf. Finally, if the leaf has a single blade, it is called simple; if the blade is divided deeply, right down to the mid-rib, so that there are several distinct leaflets, it is said to be compound. Thus, the horse-chestnut leaf is described as a compound leaf, palmately

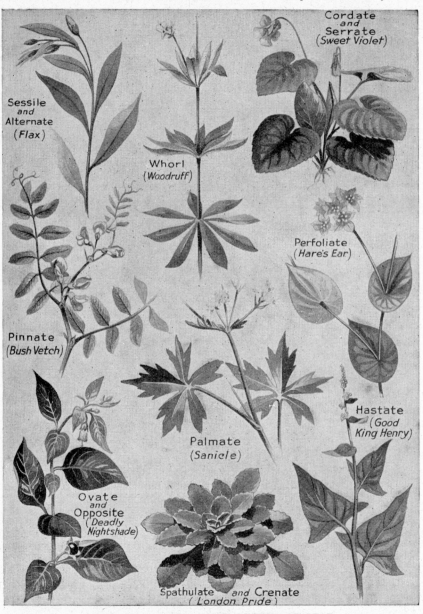

SOME OF NATURE'S MANY DESIGNS OF LEAF
Plant leaves exhibit almost infinite variety, but they may be conveniently classified into a number of groups according to the way in which they are attached to the plant stem, their shape, and their structure. Here some of the principal types are represented by a number of common plants characteristic of the flora of the British Isles.

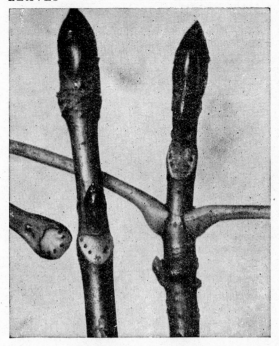

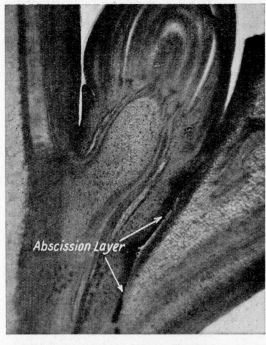

Abscission Layer

WHY LEAVES FALL IN AUTUMN, AND THE SCARS THEY MAKE

When winter approaches and a tree has no further need of its leaves, a layer of corky cells is formed across the base of the leaf-stalk. This is called the abscission layer (right, enlarged) and chemical changes here take place by which the attachment of the leaf is weakened. When the leaf falls the 'wound' is healed by a scar. On the left, below the new buds, can be seen the horseshoe-shaped scars of the horse chestnut; the scars are different in every type of tree.

veined, with from seven to nine leaflets; and these leaflets, in turn, are practically sessile, obovate, with serrate margins, or acuminate, the term used for a leaf which narrows suddenly and runs into a more or less long point. All pinnate leaves, of course, are compound, and sometimes the primary leaflets are divided up again, when the leaf becomes bi-pinnate; nor does it necessarily stop here, for there may be tri-pinnate, or even more compound leaves of this type.

Lest you may become impatient with this long list of terms, let us explain that they are necessary for the accurate description of plants. Moreover, if you seek to identify wild flowers, for instance, you will find that books give a " key " in which these terms are quoted, in order to enable you to distinguish one species from another.

Even the sepals and petals of a flower are modified leaves, though they have come to play a very different role from that of the true leaves. The leaves of water plants show many interesting differences from those of land plants.

In the autumn the leaves of deciduous trees— that is, those that lose their foliage every year—deck themselves in gorgeous crimsons, purples, browns, and golds. These remarkable displays of colour are the result of life changes taking place in the trees themselves. A layer of denser cells, known as the abscission or " cut-off " layer, forms at the base of the leaf petiole; chemical changes in the cells of this layer weaken the attachment to the tree, so that when autumn comes it is held on only by some strands of vascular (vessel) tissue. The autumn and winter winds, and the frosts, helped by the

force of gravitation, break off the leaves. The wounds they leave are healed—and sealed against the loss of vital plant fluids—by the formation of layers of cork cells, or by changes taking place in other cell layers. On branches which have died, the leaves wither but do not break away, since the cut-off layer has not formed in such cases. Such is the wonderful mechanism of the " fall," by which the leaves are shed when no longer needed as foodstuff gatherers and manufacturers.

Not all trees thus shed their leaves completely. Evergreen trees and shrubs, although they, too, lose leaves, do this gradually, and at other seasons than autumn. Holly, for example, sheds some of its leaves in the spring, but the tree is never leafless; the new leaves which form then may last three or four years. To this habit of the evergreens we owe the beautiful appearance of the countryside even in winter, if many conifers and other evergreens grow in the region. (See also Flower; Plant Life; Trees).

Lee, GENERAL ROBERT EDWARD (1807–70). " Massa Robert," as the great military leader of the Confederate (Southern) States in the American Civil War (1861–65) was affectionately called by the people of the South, was born at Stratford, in Virginia, on January 19, 1807, and educated for the army. On the eve of the Civil War he held the rank of colonel ; in 1861 President Lincoln offered him the command of the Federal (Northern) forces. But Lee was a Southerner, and so chose to fight on the opposite side.

He was made one of the five generals in the Confederate service, and in the spring of 1862 was

GENERAL LEE SURRENDERS

The last dramatic incident of the American Civil War (1861–65) which brought the conflict to an end is shown in this picture. General Lee (holding his horse's reins, left) was given supreme command of the Confederate (Southern) forces only when it was too late. On April 9, 1865, he surrendered to General Grant (saluting, right) at Appomattox Court House, Virginia.

placed in command of the armies operating in defence of Richmond, the capital of Virginia. The masterly strategy which he displayed in the Seven Days' Battles showed him to be a commander of the highest ability. Lee then gathered together all his available forces and marched northward, his campaign ending with the battle of Gettysburg, which took place in the first three days of July 1863. On the first two days of this battle the advantage seemed to rest with Lee's army, but on the third day he staked the issue on a grand charge, which was completely repulsed, and he was compelled to retreat.

Early in May 1864, General Grant took the field against Lee in person. He attempted to turn Lee's flank, near the Wilderness, in Virginia, where occurred a two days' indecisive fight. In the spring of 1865 General Lee was compelled to abandon both Petersburg and Richmond. He was hotly pursued by Grant, and a few days later at Appomattox Court House in Virginia his entire force surrendered, and the civil war came to an end. He died on October 12, 1870.

Leeds, ENGLAND. For centuries England has been noted for the quality of its woollen cloths, the manufacture of which centres in Leeds, Yorkshire —the sixth largest city in England.

Leeds has been important in English trade ever since woollen manufacture was introduced in the 14th century. It owes its commercial supremacy to two chief factors: its transport facilities and its situation on the edge of the great Yorkshire coal-fields. The River Aire connects it with the east coast, while the Leeds and Liverpool Canal provides cheap transportation to the west coast. The iron manufactures are nearly as important as the woollen. In the manufacture of boots and shoes, felt, ready-made clothing, artificial silk, glass and pottery, Leeds also ranks high. Linen manufacture is another important industry.

A trace of the interesting history of Leeds, which goes back for 13 centuries, is found in the celebrated ruins of Kirkstall Abbey, a Cistercian foundation of the 12th century. Leeds is noted for its university, its Civic Hall opened by King George V in 1933, and for the music festival which is held there every three years. The population is 481,570.

There is another Leeds, a village in Kent, four miles from Maidstone. Leeds Castle, standing on a small island in a branch of the River Medway, has some portions dating from the 13th century.

Legend. Students of folklore have found it convenient to distinguish myths (*see* Mythology), which are explanatory stories invented to show how the world and the things in it came to be, from legends, which are popular history containing an element of historical truth or, at least, the names of historical people. Sir Walter Scott (1771–1832) used the word rightly in A Legend of Montrose, for that novel, though not historically accurate in details, deals with historical people.

The story of how St. Patrick at a single stroke cleared Ireland of snakes is a legend, and similar marvellous stories grew up around many early saints. One of the first books printed by William Caxton (c. 1422–91), The Golden Legend was a collection of these stories. Legends have also been told of other great figures, such as the story of King Alfred burning the cakes.

CIVIC CENTRE OF LEEDS

This fine modern building is the home of the municipality of Leeds, in Yorkshire, and its handsome façade is seen to great advantage on account of the wide open space on which it stands. It was opened by King George V in 1933.

An early and interesting legend tells us that Jesus visited England in the company of His friend Joseph of Arimathea, who was a merchant, and may have come to Britain to buy tin. It is to this legend that the poet Blake refers in his lines:

> And did those feet in ancient time
>   Walk upon England's mountains green?
> And was the holy Lamb of God
>   On England's pleasant pastures seen?

Legion. The Roman legion was a division of picked soldiers, numbering 3,000 to 6,000, and including cavalry. The name is from a Latin verb, *legere*, to choose. In Roman times the legion was the major fighting unit of the armies, and from those days to this, for over 2,000 years, legions of one sort or another have been prominent in wars all over the world. Originally the *legio* or legion was a citizen levy; later it came to be a highly-organized army. The legionary soldier was equipped with helmet, shield, breast-plate, sword, dagger, and sometimes a javelin.

In the Middle Ages the word fell more or less into disuse, but gradually it came into use again, chiefly for groups of mixed troops, often mercenaries, fighting first for one country then for another. From these developed the " foreign legions " of more recent times, such as those which served during the wars of the 18th century and early 19th century in Europe. These were still more or less mercenary bodies, and often consisted of Scottish and Irish troops. The most famous of all modern legions of this type, the French Foreign Legion was at one time actually sold to Spain.

About a century ago the French Foreign Legion became organized, under the name of the *Régiments étrangers*, much on the same lines as today. It consists of eight battalions of infantry and one cavalry regiment, a regiment of artillery, 'and a battalion of engineers, stationed principally in Morocco. Life in " the Legion " is notoriously hard, and for that reason discipline is a mixture of severity in barracks and apparent laxity off duty. The Legion attracts adventurers from many lands.

Another modern foreign legion was the International Brigade which fought on the Government side in the Spanish Civil War (1936–38).

Still another use of the word legion is found in its application to associations of men or women—e.g. those who served in the First and Second World Wars, such as the British Legion and the American Legion. These seek to maintain contact between members, to help them to obtain work, and to keep alive their countries' traditions.

The Legion of Honour is a French order of merit, founded by the first Napoleon in 1802. The badge is a five-branched cross bearing a symbolic figure of the Republic and crowned by a laurel wreath.

Leicestershire. Almost in the centre of England, Leicestershire in many ways is a typical English county, and the fact that it contains within its borders market-towns with such old English names as Market Harborough, Lutterworth, Ashby-de-la-Zouch and Melton Mowbray indicates its links with the past. The soil is good and there are many rich dairy farms. Cattle and sheep are reared and wheat is grown.

With an area of 823 square miles, Leicestershire is a famous hunting district; this sport has its centre

HERE LAY A ROMAN LEGIONARY
This gravestone stood above the grave of a Roman legionary. It shows him armed with his javelin, shield, and the short sword which was so deadly a weapon in his hands against the barbarian. By such legionaries the Roman empire was built.

at Melton Mowbray. The county has become the centre of the hosiery industry. Leicester (population, 254,000), the county town, has been a cathedral city since 1926. Boots and shoes are made there as well as hosiery. Loughborough, the only other borough, is noted for its technical college and athletic training school, and for its bell foundries. The Loughborough war memorial consists of a carillon of 47 bells, which were cast in the local foundries. Near Market Bosworth was fought the great battle between Richard III and the future Henry VII in 1485. The population of the county is about 567,000.

Leighton, FREDERICK LEIGHTON, LORD (1830–96). Though neither an inspired draughtsman not a great painter, Leighton's works reveal a love for beauty of line and form. Born at Scarborough on December 3, 1830, he studied for many years on the Continent before settling in London. He produced numerous black-and-white drawings for the most famous wood engravers of the time. Some of his Biblical subjects, like Cain and Abel, are among the finest book illustrations ever printed in Britain. (*See also* page 1921).

His paintings are notable for dignified and rhythmical design, but he lacked colour perception. He was an accomplished sculptor, and many of the ablest critics of his day awarded him the highest position in that branch of art. He was elected President of the Royal Academy in 1878, and was knighted the same year; he was created Baron Leighton in 1896. He died on January 25, 1896, and was buried in St. Paul's Cathedral, London.

Leipzig. Before the 11th century there was a small settlement at Leipzig, on the River Elster in the middle of the German plain at the junction of two ancient trade routes. In later centuries its location was destined to turn Leipzig into one of Germany's most important cities. It became the cultural and commercial centre of central Germany and the capital of the State of Saxony. The medieval market held there survived as the Leipzig Fair, attracting buyers from all over the world.

The city also became the heart of the German book trade, noted not only for the book treasures in its libraries and Museum and its book publishing

LEIPZIG'S GREAT BOOK MUSEUM
As befitted a city which was one of the centres of German learning Leipzig was rich in libraries and museums, among the most interesting being the National Museum of German books (above). The collection included a series of specimens of books printed prior to 1471. The city suffered heavy damage from Allied air raids during the Second World War (1939–45).

industry but also for its State institution for teaching book production and the art of book decoration. As a music centre Leipzig won world fame. It was the home of Robert Alexander Schumann (1810–56) and of Johann Sebastian Bach (1685–1750), and the birthplace of Richard Wagner (1813–83). The University of Leipzig, founded in 1409, developed into one of the most important centres of German education.

Leipzig suffered six sieges during the Thirty Years' War (1618-48), and Napoleon Bonaparte was defeated there in 1813. The city, badly damaged by Allied air raids during the Second World War (1939–45), was occupied by United States forces on April 20, 1945, after heavy fighting. Leipzig came within the Russian zone of occupa-

tion in Germany, the Soviet authorities dismantling and removing nearly all important industrial equipment. The population in 1933 was 714,000.

Leitrim, COUNTY OF EIRE. Situated in the north-west corner of the province of Connaught, or Connacht, bordering Donegal and Fermanagh, Leitrim is one of the most varied counties in Eire. Picturesquely mountainous in the north, level and well-wooded in the south, where Lough Allen gives rise to the river Shannon, it is, however, a comparatively poor county. A few coal seams, of low quality, are worked. The soil is not very fertile, except in a few small valleys, and grain crops are difficult to cultivate. Potatoes and roots are the staple crops. Cattle, pigs and poultry are reared; and coarse linen and pottery for domestic uses are manufactured in a small way. The area of the county is 589 square miles, and its population is 46,220. The county town is Carrick-on-Shannon, with a population of approximately 1,000.

Leix, (Pron. lēs), COUNTY OF EIRE. Formerly known as Queen's County, and given its present name when the Irish Free State came into being in 1922, this fertile, gently-undulating county, with its dry, healthy climate, lies in the west of the province of Leinster where it borders Tipperary.

On the east or Kilkenny boundary Leix embraces a large part of the Leinster coalfield, and here mining forms a valuable subsidiary industry to agriculture. The dairy farms and creameries of Leix are notable, even in a country so completely agricultural as Eire. Wheat, oats, barley, roots and potatoes are the main crops; fruit-growing and market-gardening are not unimportant. Leix is remarkable among Irish counties in that its arable (or tilled) area is more than one half the area that is given over to pasturage or grazing.

The name of the county is taken from the ancient district of Leix, where a small market-town, Abbey Leix, south of Portlaoighise, the county town, possesses the remains of a famous Cistercian monastery of the 12th century. Leix is 664 square miles in extent and the population of the county is 49,950. Portlaoighise (pron. port-lē'-sha), formerly called Maryborough, has a population of 12,000.

Lemon. One of the most important of all fruits in the summer time, because of the refreshing drinks which its juice and crushed flesh provide, the lemon has long been appreciated, and in Italy,

'RETURN OF PERSEPHONE' PAINTED BY LEIGHTON

The versatile British artist and sculptor Lord Leighton (1830–96) interpreted in this picture the joyful welcome that Demeter (q.v.), the Greek goddess of agriculture, gave her daughter Persephone when the latter was returned to her from the Realm of the Dead. Persephone is escorted by Hermes (Mercury) who acted as guide to and from the kingdom of Hades. The picture might equally well have been called The Return of Spring for, according to the legend, it was only when Persephone was with her that Demeter would allow the earth to produce its fruits. The original of this painting, executed in 1891, hangs in the Art Gallery in Leeds, Yorkshire. Leighton was knighted in 1878 and was created Baron Leighton in 1896, the day before his death on January 25.

Sicily, Corsica, and particularly in Spain and Portugal, its culture has been a large industry for many years.

The lemon (*Citrus limonum*) is a close relative of the orange, but the straggling branches of the lemon tree show no resemblance to the compact dense foliage of the orange, and the purplish flowers have not the agreeable fragrance of the white orange blossoms. If lemons ripen on the trees they lose their keeping quality, and so they are picked green before there is any sign of the golden yellow colouring. Each picker carries a ring 2¼ inches in diameter, and the fruit is cut when it can just slip through the ring. In dark storehouses, well ventilated but free from draughts, the lemons are spread out and slowly ripened. When ripe they are washed, dried, and wrapped in tissue paper. In this condition they will keep for months, which is a very good thing for the growers, as most of the fruit ripens in the winter and the great market demand takes place in the summer.

The lemon is used in more different ways than any other of the citrus fruits. From the rind, lemon oil or extract, used in flavouring and in perfumery-making, is obtained either by crushing or by distillation, and candied lemon peel is made. The pulp yields lemon juice, which contains citrate of lime and citric acid. Besides its use in flavouring foods and drinks of various kinds, lemon juice may be employed as a bleach in the printing of some cotton fabrics.

W. S. Berridge

RING-TAILED LEMUR

This variety of lemur gets its popular name from the fact that it has a bushy tail marked with alternate bands of black and white. These creatures live mostly in trees, their long hind legs enabling them to make prodigious leaps from branch to branch.

Right, Hinkins; lower, L. Bastin

THE LEMON, INSIDE AND OUT

Like other citrus fruits the lemon has a thick, pithy skin around the juicy central part. The section at the right shows this, together with the arrangement of the inside. Botanically the lemon is classed as a 'berry.'

Lemurs. Small monkey-like animals, with big eyes and rather sharp, foxy faces—such are the lemurs. The name comes from the Latin *lemures*, meaning spirits of the dead, and is given to them because of their nocturnal habits, and silent, ghost-like movements.

Lemurs are the lowest of the Primates, the group which includes monkeys, apes and Man. Most of them have tails, but they cannot hang from trees by them as some monkeys can. With their numerous relatives, lemurs form the group known as the *lemuroids*. The largest of the species reach the size of a cat. All are restricted to the southern regions of the Old World—Africa, the sub-continent of India, Ceylon, and the Malay Archipelago—but only in Madagascar are the true lemurs found. The better-known species of these curious little creatures include the beautiful but noisy ring-tailed lemur (*Lemur catta*), whose bushy tail is marked with alternate rings of black and white; the large indri (*Indris brevicaudata*) or babakoto ("little old man") of Madagascar; the dark iron-grey gentle lemur, which frequents the bamboo jungles; and the aye-aye of Madagascar, so named from its cry. The ring-tailed lemur, which, like most of its genus, comes out more by day than by night, makes an excellent pet. The aye-aye (*Chiromys madagascariensis*) is a funny little creature, whose enormous canine teeth and long middle fingers are adapted to extracting grubs from their tunnels in timber. The Indo-Malayan group of lemurs includes the various species of loris, such as the slow loris (*Nycticebus tardigradus*), all of which move about in a curiously deliberate manner. Fossil remains of lemuroids are found in many lands, including North America. Lemuroids in general eat leaves, fruits, insects, small reptiles, birds, and birds' eggs.

Lenin, NIKOLAI (1870–1924). When the Bolsheviks (*see* Bolshevism) were suppressing opposition to their revolution in Russia in 1917–18, a short stockily-built man, bald-headed, with steel-grey eyes, sat within the Kremlin at Moscow directing the activities of the Soviet government, of which he was the head. The man was Lenin, whose real name was Vladimir Ilyitch Ulyanov.

Born at Simbirsk (renamed Ulyanovsk) on the Volga on April 22, 1870, the son of an inspector of schools, he had been a revolutionary since his youth. When he was 17 years old his brother was hanged for plotting to kill the Tsar Alexander III, and when he was 26 Lenin himself was arrested for the production of illegal newspapers and was exiled to Siberia. On the expiration of this sentence, being forbidden to reside in any of the large cities of Russia, he lived in Munich, Brussels, Paris, London, and Geneva. He became widely known through his authorship of several works on economic topics. After 1903 he was the recognized leader of the wing of Russian Socialists who called themselves Bolsheviks.

When the government of the Tsar was overthrown early in 1917 Lenin returned to Russia from Switzerland, and at once organized the Bolshevik opposition to the moderate Socialist government which had taken its place. Relying for support on the Soviets (councils) of revolutionary-minded workers in Petrograd and Moscow, he and Trotsky (1877–1940) and their Bolshevik colleagues at length on November 7, 1917 (October 25 in the calendar in use in Russia at that time) overthrew the Socialist government and proclaimed in its place a Soviet Republic of Workers, Soldiers and Peasants. As President of the Soviet of People's Commissars Lenin held the supreme position in the State, becoming Dictator of Russia. In the resolve to create this new order in a Russia on the verge of complete collapse, Lenin showed himself a man of determination and iron courage, free from self-seeking.

Lenin furnished the brains of the Soviet rule, and his numerous writings show him as a man of learning with a remarkable grasp of the theories of revolutionary Socialism. His driving energy finally wrecked even his strong constitution, and he died on Janu-

NIKOLAI LENIN
A revolutionary for the greater part of his life Lenin led the Bolsheviks in the Russian Revolution of 1917, becoming Dictator of the country. A man of tremendous determination and driving power, he maintained his position until his death on January 21, 1924.

ary 21, 1924, at Gorky, near Moscow, after an attack of paralysis. Lenin's granite tomb outside the Kremlin at Moscow became a national shrine, the objective of pilgrims from all over Russia. There his embalmed body rests in what appears to be a state of excellent preservation.

Leningrad. When Peter the Great (1672–1725) founded this city as the capital of Russia in 1703 he called it St. Petersburg, after his patron saint. During the First World War (1914–18) the Russians disliked the German ending of the name, and changed it to Petrograd, *grad* being a form of the Russian word for town, *gorod*. In 1924 the Bolsheviks changed it again to Leningrad, in honour of Lenin (*q.v.*).

The site of the city, at the mouth of the Neva on the Gulf of Finland, has been important as a trade outlet from ancient times. The country, however, was a desolate marsh, and the idea of building a city there seemed absurd. But Peter the Great was determined. " I want a window to look out upon Europe!" he said. In 1703, the "window" started to take shape. Thousands of peasants died of disease and hardship as they sank the piles for the city's foundation. So many perished that the city is said to be " built upon bones."

Peter the Great had travelled in western Europe, once working for a while in England as a shipwright

Intourist

SOVIET SYMBOLS IN THE HEART OF LENINGRAD
The name of Leningrad commemorates the founder of Soviet Russia whose portrait is shown above ; and this square in the midst of that fine city commemorates the victims of the Revolution to which the Soviet Union owes its existence. The flower-beds are designed in the form of the badge of the country, the hammer and sickle, and in the centre is the five-pointed star. The fine old buildings of the pre-Revolution era still surround the modern square.

for the sake of the experience, and he wanted his capital to be magnificent. The major portion was to stand on a peninsula where the Neva curved to the northward and then turned south-west to the Gulf of Finland. On the left or south-east bank of this last portion rose the Admiralty in a magnificent square. Adjoining this square stood the Winter Palace, and across the river on an island lay the fortress of St. Peter and St. Paul. The principal streets radiated from this centre, and included the Nevsky (later October 25) Prospekt, meaning " view of the Neva." The islands in the river were linked by bridges, and canals helped to drain the site.

The palaces and the houses of the aristocrats were converted to other uses after the Bolshevik Revolution of 1917. Some are museums and others are hospitals, schools, day nurseries, or club rooms. The colossal Winter Palace—the largest palace in Europe—became the Museum of the Revolution. Adjoining it is the Hermitage, Russia's leading museum and picture gallery, which has one of the finest art collections in the world. There are also the Russian Museum, with records of the history, art and culture of the U.S.S.R., and museums of Children's Welfare, People's Health, Home Industry, and many more.

LENS AS BURNING-GLASS
On a hot summer's day, when the sun's rays are focused through a magnifying glass upon dry paper or other inflammable material they are powerful enough to set the material alight. It is the invisible (infra-red) heat rays which set the paper on fire.

After 1918 Leningrad decreased in importance, Moscow becoming the capital ; but later a drastic effort was made to revive the city. The government erected a number of new factories, and the population increased. Production of textiles, rubber goods and shoes grew enormously. Metal and machinery manufactures increased. Chemicals, clothing, paper, furniture, matches, tobacco, leather goods and alcoholic liquors were manufactured. Exports in normal times include timber, tallow, grain, flax, hemp, linseed, copper, bristles, vegetable oil, furs, leather and skins.

Though the Neva is frozen for six months in the year, Leningrad is now the chief base of the Baltic Fleet. Its population in 1938 was 3,191,000.

During the Second World War (1939–45) the city was besieged by German forces from September 1941 to January 1944, and was completely isolated from the rest of Russia for half the time, for only in winter could convoys cross the ice of Lake Ladoga to reach the city. Starvation and cold killed hundreds of thousands of the inhabitants, but the fact that Leningrad held out was a major contribution to the defeat of the Germans on the Russian Front.

Lens. The sort of lens with which we are most familiar is the ordinary magnifying glass, used to enable us to read small print without having to peer at it too closely. However, lenses are used for other purposes, and their appropriate types form the components of telescopes, microscopes, cameras, spectacles and many other optical instruments. All lenses work on the same principle, depending on their ability to bend rays of light by varying amounts.

With the aid of a magnifying glass you can perform some simple experiments to show how it works. First, go into a dark corner of a room and let the light from the window shine through the lens upon a piece of paper, or on the wall if it is of a light colour. By moving the lens backwards and forwards, you can find a position where an inverted image of the brightly-lighted window and the objects outside will be thrown on to the paper or wall. This illustrates the main property of a lens—its ability to form an image of a distant object, at some fixed distance from the lens. This distance (the distance between lens and piece of paper, in our case) is known as the focal length of the lens.

The same experiment can be carried out using the sun, instead of the bright window, as your distant object. In this instance a very small image, almost a point of light, will be formed on the paper, and, since the magnifying glass focuses both the visible light and the invisible infra-red heat radiation, the paper will probably catch fire because of the great concentration of heat in the image.

Hold the lens at arm's length, and look through it. Again an upside-down picture of the scene in front will be viewed, and it will appear quite small. Here we are looking at a similar image to the one thrown on the piece of paper, only this time the image *exists in space !* A piece of ground glass, which is a kind of translucent screen, if placed where the image exists in space, will show it up properly, and here we see how a camera works. If the ground glass (or piece of paper, in the previous experiment) were replaced by a photographic plate, and the lens and plate boxed in, it would make a simple camera.

The manner in which the magnifying glass forms an image is shown in the first diagram on page 1925, where AB is an object, and F is the centre of a lens, whose sectional view is shown. Light rays are spreading out from all points of the object, in all directions, and some of them will strike the lens. Rays such as AF and BF will go straight through it without being bent, because the surfaces of the lens at the central point are approximately parallel. However, all other rays will be bent in varying degrees. The rays from A and B parallel to the lens axis will both pass through C, which is called the focal point of the lens; and it is seen that both rays leaving A meet again at E, and those leaving B meet at D. The lens is so constructed that all the rays from A, in between those shown,

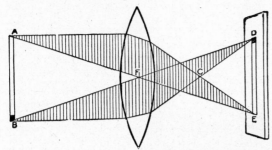

How an inverted image is produced (see text).

also meet at E, which is thus the optical image of A. Similarly, all points on the object AB have corresponding image points on DE, and we see from the diagram that the image is an inverted one. The plane in which the image lies is called the focal plane, and it is here that we should put our photographic plate or film. The human eye is another example of a simple lens forming an image of the object in front of it, and in this case there is a light-sensitive layer, the retina, in the focal plane.

The action of the lens as a magnifying glass is somewhat different. Here the lens is so close to the object that it merely bends the rays of light leaving the object, so that they appear to have come from a different direction. This leads to an apparent magnification of the object, as shown in the drawing on the right. No proper image is formed, so the image is termed a virtual one.

The magnifying glass is only one of many forms of lens. Its two sides are sections of equal spheres, and such a lens, which is always thickest in the middle, is known as a double-convex lens. Other lens may have both sides concave, and thus be thickest at the edges. These are known as double-concave lenses. Again, one side of the lens may be flat and the other concave or convex, in which case the lenses are called plano-concave and plano-convex respectively.

In general, the concave lenses, instead of converging the rays of light to a point, spread them out or disperse them in just the opposite way. For this reason objects seen through a double-concave lens appear right-side up and smaller than normal. The images that these lenses produce are always virtual, and cannot be thrown on to a screen. By varying the curvature of the lenses, differences in focal lengths are obtained, as is also the case when different types of glass are used to make them. Lenses can be ground to throw distorted images, as in the case of spectacle lenses, which are adjusted to combine properly with

MAGNIFICATION WITH A LENS
The normal eye cannot clearly focus objects nearer than about 10 inches from it. By using a magnifying glass we can bring the object nearer, as shown : the lens bends the light rays emanating from the object to a wider angle, and we get an apparent magnification.

the lenses of the eye. If the eye suffers from the distortion known as " astigmatism," the spectacle lens distorts in the opposite manner, and the combination forms a normal image on the retina. This is accomplished by combining in one form a spherical and a cylindrical lens in what opticians call a compound cylinder. (See Spectacles).

The general optical law which governs the construction of lenses is that of the refraction of light, which may be summed up as follows : When a ray of light passing through a lighter (less dense) medium (air) strikes the surface of an optically denser medium (glass) at an oblique angle, the ray is bent or refracted *towards* the perpendicular to that surface; when it passes out again from the denser glass to the lighter air, it is bent *away* from the perpendicular.

Lenses are combined in optical instruments for various purposes. For instance, the enlarged image produced by one magnifying glass may be passed through a second lens and enlarged again, giving us the principle of the microscope.

In almost all optical instruments the lenses used are not simple ones like the magnifying glass, but are made up of several separate components, either mounted very close together or in some cases cemented together. It is necessary to do this so that a perfect image, free from distortions and from colour aberration, may be produced. Colour aberration causes the image to appear coloured at the edges, and is due to the fact that a simple lens, like the magnifying glass, has a slightly different focal length for each colour. It is corrected by combining two or more lenses made of different types of glass.

The manufacture of high-grade lenses is one of the most delicate of all mechanical operations, and the accuracy of a finished surface is made true to a hundred-thousandth of an inch. Glass is, of course, used for most lenses, but recently some of the new plastics, notably " Perspex," have been used successfully. Lenses made from " Perspex " can be moulded from a master-pattern, and so are easily made; but they suffer from the fact that they are easily scratched. Glass lenses have to be ground and polished, the former process being accomplished by using an iron mould and emery powder. When the lens has been ground with the finest powder it is then polished with pads of cloth impregnated with red iron oxide, or jewellers' " rouge," which puts on the highly-polished finish. (See also Camera ; Photography).

Lentil. Akin to the bean and pea, and belonging to the order *Leguminosae*, this food plant (*Lens esculenta*) is said to be one of the oldest cultivated by Man, and is still an important article of food in Egypt, Syria and Mexico. The seeds, which are round and flat and less than half-an-inch in diameter, are made into soup or eaten boiled. The reddish little lentils usually seen in Britain are split seeds. The pottage for which Esau sold his birthright (Genesis, chapter 25) is said to have been made of these seeds. The vines, as the plants themselves are called, make excellent fodder for cattle and sheep.

Leo.

POPES. The first of the 13 popes of this name is known as LEO THE GREAT (Pope, 440–461), because of his learning and the important part which he played in the religious controversies of the time.

LEO III (Pope, 795–816) is chiefly remembered because it was he who placed the imperial crown on the head of Charlemagne (742–814), on that memorable Christmas Day of the year 800. (See Charlemagne).

LEO X (Pope, 1513–21) was a member of the rich Medici family of Florence. He was elected Pope at the age of 38 on the death of Julius II. His reign saw the beginning of Martin Luther's revolt against the Church in Germany, increasing danger to eastern Europe from the Turks, and a continuance of the political struggles and wars involving the Papacy begun by his predecessor. But Leo X is chiefly remembered for his part in the Italian Renaissance, as the liberal patron of Raphael and other artists, and of numerous scholars and poets. It was he chiefly who made Rome the successor of Florence as the literary and artistic capital of Europe.

LEO XIII (Pope, 1878–1903) the latest to bear this name, became Pope at a time when the Papacy had recently been deprived by the Italian Government of its political authority as ruler of Rome and the surrounding country. Like his predecessor, Pius IX, he refused to come to terms with the new kingdom of Italy, and chose to become a voluntary prisoner in the Vatican, which remained Papal territory.

Leonardo da Vinci (1452–1519).

If you can imagine many geniuses residing within one personality you may then have a faint idea of the magnitude and versatility of this most extraordinary man. Of the three Italian giants of the Renaissance—Michelangelo, Raphael, and Leonardo da Vinci (pron. lē-on-ahr'-dō dah vin'-chē)—Leonardo stood for much more than a mastery of art. In the realms of mathematics, science and engineering his mind was one of the keenest the world had known. Curiosity and the love of the uncommon were the ruling passions of his life.

He was insistent on the need for experimenting when investigating the phenomena of Nature. " We must begin by experiment," he wrote, " and endeavour by its means to discover general principles." He declared that " theory is the general of an army, and experiments are his soldiers."

Born at Vinci, near Florence, Leonardo died near Amboise, in France. During his lifetime he visited most of the great cities of Italy—Florence, Milan, Venice, Rome—working in all of them at painting or architectural projects. He served his artist's apprenticeship as the favourite pupil of Andrea del Verrocchio. When 20 years of age he became a member of the painters' guild, and for the next 10 years he practised his art in Florence, in the golden days of Lorenzo the Magnificent of the house of Medici. Much of his later life was spent in Milan in the service of Ludovico Sforza, a short period in that of Caesar Borgia, while his last years were passed in the employ of Francis I.

Anderson

LEONARDO PAINTED BY HIMSELF
In this self-portrait we have the likeness of Leonardo da Vinci, one of the greatest figures the modern world has known. Eminent alike in art and science, Leonardo was as handsome as he was brilliant. One of his most famous paintings is the Mona Lisa in the Louvre, Paris.

Leonardo made great changes in the technique of painting, for to him light and shade were as important as colour to other artists. But what makes Da Vinci's art unique is his ability to express the whole range of hidden emotion. He shows also a rare knowledge of Nature.

Two of Leonardo's paintings are among the masterpieces of the world—the Mona Lisa, a portrait in oils, which is one of the treasures of the Louvre (see illustration under Louvre, page 2033), and The Last Supper, a large wall painting on plaster in " tempera." This latter picture, which is reproduced in page 189 of this work, was painted on the wall of the refectory of the convent church of Santa Maria delle Grazie at Milan. The disciples, with the Master in their midst, are represented at one side of a table, their faces to the spectator. The words, " One of you shall betray Me," have just been spoken.

As a painter, etcher or draughtsman, Leonardo was perfecting the work of others, carrying their ideas further and putting his own theories into practice. But as a scientific investigator he worked on his own account, a pioneer in a land where no man had travelled. He made discoveries of primary importance in both applied and theoretical science. In his theories about dynamics, engineering and even aeronautics (see Aeroplane, page 44), he was hundreds of years ahead of his day. He did work of great value in anatomy and optics.

Even as a child his knowledge of mathematics was profound. As his mind matured he inquired into the composition of explosives, into the possibility of the use of steam as motive power in ships, and studied magnetic attraction.

He made plans, on paper, for all sorts of mechanical appliances including water-mills, engines of war, a paddle-wheel for boats, a mincing machine, and a conical rifle bullet; but while many of his principles were sound, an attempt to apply them as he proposed would often have shown up errors and could seldom have produced real working machines. In any case, the mechanical skill and knowledge, and the availability of materials suitable for the machines, were lacking to the extent which would have enabled Leonardo to have produced, for example, any realistic sort of " flying machine."

While giving all due credit to the activities of this remarkable man we must not belittle the difficulties which hindered practical inventions in his day.

Leonardo understood the impossibility of perpetual motion, and recovered Archimedes' knowledge of the pressure of liquids. He began the study of the motion of liquids and the propagation of waves over their surfaces, thus passing to the problem of waves in the air and the phenomena of sound. His notes include a treatise on aviation, illustrated with sketches analysing the flight of birds. He recognized that parts of the earth have been laid down through geological ages by deposits in water.

Leonardo dissected human bodies and made drawings accurate in all details, those of the heart suggesting a knowledge of the function of the valves. He described the action of the blood as it circulates and makes and re-makes the tissues of the body; and he constructed a model of the optical parts of the eye, showing how an image is formed on the retina. Even in philosophy Leonardo proved his greatness. Much of his system anticipated later developments, and in his insistence upon the will as the energy of life he foreshadowed the theories of some modern philosophers. The full list of his achievements will probably never be known, yet what is known is remarkable enough.

It has only been in the last 100 years or so that any attempt has been made to publish his manuscripts, or to discover just how far Leonardo got in his innumerable researches. Only his famous treatise on painting was published under his own name within a comparatively short time of his death.

Leopard. It is sometimes difficult to distinguish between a jaguar and a leopard (*Felis pardus*), but the leopard is a smaller animal and the rosette-like black markings are without the black central spot which are found in the jaguar. This member of the cat family inhabits Africa, Asia, and the large islands of the Malay Archipelago. It is much smaller than the tiger, which it resembles in ferocity, being about four feet long with a tail three feet in length. There is considerable variation among leopards as to size and colour. They are usually pale fawn or tawny with dark spots, the under-surface of the body being somewhat lighter in shade. The larger types of southern Asia are commonly called panthers. The leopard lives in forests, and is an expert

Mansell

A SUPERB LEONARDO CARTOON
This lovely ' cartoon '—the chalk drawing for a picture—by Leonardo da Vinci, hangs in the Diploma Gallery of Burlington House, London. Known as The Madonna with St. Anne, it is typical of Leonardo's religious work, the faces of the sitters being immediately recognizable, by the natural sweetness of expression, as coming from the master's hand. The finished painting is in the Louvre, Paris.

tree-climber. It is very agile and a remarkable jumper. It attacks antelopes, young cattle, pigs, and, occasionally, Man.

The cheetah or hunting leopard (*Cynaelurus jubatus*) of the sub-continent of India belongs to a different genus and is tamed and trained to hunt antelopes. The ocelot (*F. pardalis*) is another leopard-like cat, with spotted fur, but is found only in tropical regions of America. It is a very handsome creature, but not so fine as the rare clouded leopard

Topical; Gambier Bolton

LEOPARD AT REST : CHEETAH AT SPEED
Found in Africa and Asia, the leopard (lower) is distinguished from the jaguar by the fact that its black markings are solid, not ringlike. In the sub-continent of India the cheetah is trained to hunt gazelles ; in the top photograph a cheetah is seen racing with a greyhound.

(*F. nebulosa*), found in the Himalayas and Malaya. Another is the ounce, or snow leopard (*F. uncia*), a fierce Himalayan cat which is also rare. It has long, thick fur.

Leopold, BELGIAN KINGS. There have been three Kings of the Belgians of the name of Leopold. LEOPOLD I (1790–1865), prince of Saxe-Coburg, a German state, was the brother of the British Queen Victoria's mother, and his first wife was Princess Charlotte, the only child and heiress of King George IV of Great Britain. Leopold married her in 1816, after he had returned from serving in the war against Napoleon Bonaparte, but a year later she and her new-born son died. Throughout his life Leopold was the trusted adviser of the young Queen Victoria, and it was on his advice that she married his nephew and her cousin, Prince Albert of Saxe-Coburg. Leopold was elected King of Greece in 1830, but abdicated after a few months. Then in July 1831 he was elected first King of the Belgians by a national congress, and until his death on December 10, 1865, he ruled that country wisely.

He was succeeded on the throne by his son LEOPOLD II (1835–1909), during whose reign Belgium grew in wealth and prestige. Leopold II was remarkably shrewd, and in politics and in finance he was almost always highly successful. When Stanley (*q.v.*) returned from Africa after having explored the Congo Basin, Leopold was clever enough to grasp the value of his discoveries, and courageous enough to back the explorer with

money and necessary means for developing the great tracts of the Congo basin in western Africa. As a result of this personal speculation the Congo Free State (now Belgian Congo) became King Leopold's private property, and from it he made an enormous private fortune.

In 1908 Leopold agreed to hand over his private interests to Belgium, and the Congo Free State became a colony of Belgium. He died on December 17, 1909, and, as he left only daughters, was succeeded by his nephew Albert (*q.v.*), the king who defended Belgium's soil against Germany from 1914 to 1918. He in turn was followed by his son, LEOPOLD III.

Born on November 3, 1901, King Leopold III was educated at Eton College, Buckinghamshire, and served with the Belgian Army in the field towards the end of the First World War (1914–18). Formerly known as the Duke of Brabant, he came to the throne on February 17, 1934. On August 17, 1935, his wife and Queen, who before her marriage was the Swedish Princess Astrid, was killed while motoring with him in Switzerland. There are three children of the marriage: Princess Josephine (born 1927), Prince Baudouin (born 1930), and Prince Albert (born 1934).

On August 29, 1939, war between Germany and France and Great Britain seeming imminent, King Leopold III made with Queen Wilhelmina of the Netherlands a joint offer of mediation, which was refused by Adolf Hitler, the German leader. On May 11, 1940, the day after the Germans invaded Belgium, the king took command of the Belgian Army. He surrendered on May 28, when his army, outnumbered and exhausted, faced extinction.

After his capitulation the Germans tried to obtain the king's co-operation, but he withdrew from public life, living as a virtual prisoner at Laeken, near Brussels. The Germans sent him to Germany after the Allied landings in Normandy in 1944, and he was liberated, at a castle near Salzburg, by United States forces on May 8, 1945. In the meantime, on September 20, 1944, his brother Prince Charles had been elected Regent during the king's enforced absence.

Leopold's return to Belgium was opposed by the Government on the grounds that he had collaborated with Hitler. A Commission appointed to inquire into his conduct during the war issued a report in June 1947 justifying his actions. Leopold announced that he would return to Belgium and resume his duties when it was publicly recognized that his honour was unblemished. In 1941 he had married Marie Lilian Baels, who was given the title of Princess of Réthy. A son, Alexander, was born in 1942.

Leyden Jar. In the story of Electricity we explain the way in which a condenser can take an electric charge, owing to the dielectric (the insulating material between the plates) being placed in a state of electrical strain which is relieved when the condenser is discharged.

The Leyden jar—named after the town of Leyden (or Leiden) in the Netherlands—is the earliest form of condenser. It consists of a glass jar with a coating of tinfoil inside and outside, to act as the " plates." It was not realized for some time that the charge resides in the dielectric (the glass), and that the plates or coatings serve only to distribute the charge over the surface of the glass. This was appreciated only when a jar was made with removable lining and outer coating. When charged, the coatings could be removed and shown to be free of charge, but upon re-assembling them the jar was found to be still charged with electricity.

The manner of the discovery is amusing. Peter van Musschenbroek (1692–1761) and Cuneus, of Leyden University, observed during their experiments with frictional electricity in 1746 that electrified bodies soon lost their " electric virtue " (owing to surface leakage), and thought that it had something to do with exposure to the air, and could be prevented if the electrified body were surrounded by insulating material. Musschenbroek tried, therefore, to electrify water in a glass bottle—and failed, of course, because although the water acted as an inner coating, he had no outer coating to distribute the charge on the outside. Cuneus, trying the same experiment, held the bottle in his hand, which acted as a partial outer coating and, on touching the connector to the water, received a smart shock. Musschenbroek then repeated the experiment, and the credit for the discovery is usually given to him, although Von Kleist, Dean of the cathedral of Camin, is now recognized as having performed similar experiments in 1745.

For a long time it was considered that the human body played an essential part in the process, and the use of the jar was confined to giving shocks. The electric shock, in fact, caught the popular imagination so that travelling showmen with frictional machines and " the Leyden phial " reaped a rich harvest at fairs. In the presence of the King of France a shock was administered to 180 of the French Guards, standing holding hands

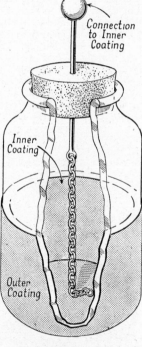

Connection to Inner Coating

Inner Coating

Outer Coating

LEYDEN JAR
The construction of a Leyden jar, a simple form of electrical condenser, is shown.

in a circle. The Abbé Nollet went one better and applied the shock to an entire regiment of 1300 men. In 1747 a Dr. Watson conveyed, by means of a wire supported on insulators, a shock across the Thames at Westminster.

The exaggerated ideas held by the early experimenters of the power of the shock obtained from one small jar are also amusing. Musschenbroek wrote to the physicist, René de Réaumur : " I felt myself struck in arms, shoulder, and breast . . . I lost my breath . . . It was two days before I recovered from the effects of the blow and the terror . . . I would not take another shock for the kingdom of France." By contrast, Benjamin Franklin (*q.v.*) mentions some experiments (with a battery of jars), in which six men were knocked down—without any permanent ill-effect.

Batteries of Leyden jars (connected in parallel) were used in connexion with frictional machines for much of the experimental work carried out on static electricity. Towards the close of the 18th century, Cuthbertson built a " giant Leyden battery " of 100 jars, each with an area of $5\frac{1}{2}$ square feet of coating. This, we are told, rent in pieces blocks of boxwood four inches square and melted iron wire into red-hot globules.

Liberals. Always notable for their advocacy of reform in politics, economics and social affairs generally, Liberals were at one time called Whigs. Perhaps the greatest Liberal Prime Minister was W. E. Gladstone, who was four times Premier under Queen Victoria.

The names of other great Liberals are Charles James Fox, Richard Cobden, John Bright, H. H. Asquith, and David Lloyd George.

After the First World War (1914–18) the Liberal Party fell upon evil days and its place as the progressive party was largely taken by the Labour Party, which was founded in 1900. Another factor making for its decline was the settlement of many of the questions, *e.g.*, financial policy, home rule for Ireland, and the granting of the right to vote to more people, with which 19th-century Liberalism was identified. It is claimed, however, that there is a large body of Liberal opinion in the country which cannot make itself felt owing to the fact that the present electoral system in Britain was designed for two parties and not three. (*See* Government).

Liberia. Situated on the west coast of Africa, with British Sierra Leone to the north and the French Ivory Coast to the south, this Negro republic was founded in 1822 by the American Colonization Society as a refuge for liberated slaves from the United States. Its constitution and flag are modelled on those of the United States, and Monrovia, its capital, is named after President James Monroe of the U.S.A. (1758–1831).

The Liberians proper—the civilized and Christian descendants of American Negroes—number about

LIBERIA

20,000 and live in settlements on the coast or a few miles inland. There are also about 60,000 Negroes of the coastal regions who are partly civilized, and between 1,000,000 and 2,000,000 Mahomedan or pagan tribes living in the forests of the interior.

Area.—43,000 square miles; total population, between one and two millions.
Physical Features.—Mountainous and forested in the interior; coastal lowland.
Principal Products.—Rubber; coffee, cocoa; palm products; piassava fibre.
Chief Town.—Monrovia, capital (10,000).

The country has about 350 miles of coast-line; its area is 43,000 square miles. Five-sixths of it is covered with dense tropical forests, from which are obtained the country's chief exports—palm oil, palm nuts, piassava fibre (used for making brushes and brooms) and rubber. Coffee and cocoa are cultivated and exported.

Liberia possesses great natural wealth, including iron, gold, copper, and other minerals, but there is little mining. There are no railways and few roads, and owing to the difficulties of communication the interior of the country is as little known to the Liberians as to the world at large. In 1943, during the Second World War, the United States obtained permission from Liberia to build and operate air, land and sea bases. In 1944 a United States Commission was appointed to develop a seaport and to increase production of rubber and other crops.

Library. To obtain books from a public library in the United Kingdom for home reading one must secure a member's ticket, either by signing a pledge to obey the rules or by obtaining the signature of some responsible person who acts as guarantor. In the boroughs of London and other cities there are usually two types of tickets available: non-fiction, for books on travel and autobiographies and similar works; and fiction, dealing with classical and modern novels.

There are a few simple devices which serve as keys to the library's contents. The most valuable is the card catalogue, alphabetically arranged under author, title, and subject. If you wish for a particular book and know the author, look for his name in the card catalogue and you will find after it a list of all his works that are in the library.

Perhaps you wish to gather information on some large subject, such as aeroplanes. Look under that heading and you will find a list of books from which to choose. A number will be written after the title of each book, and this

LIBERIAN WOMAN
Occupying scattered villages along the coast of Liberia, West Africa, are the Kru, a Negro tribe to which this woman belongs. They are partly civilized and are fond of wearing European clothes, often very brightly coloured.

LIBRARY

will correspond with the number on the volume on the shelves, enabling it to be identified quickly.

Libraries—by which is meant either collections of books or the places where they are kept (from Latin *liber*, meaning book)—are almost as old as civilization. More than 600 years before Christ, King Ashurbanipal of Assyria gathered a collection of clay tablets—for such were the books of that time—for the great library in his palace at Nineveh; and excavations at Nippur in Babylonia (now Iraq) laid bare another library which even in Ashurbanipal's day would have been considered ancient, for it dates from about 2500 B.C. The greatest of all ancient libraries was that at Alexandria in Egypt, established by the Greek ruler Ptolemy I near the end of the 4th century B.C.

Before the hordes of barbarians descended on Rome and sacked it in the 5th century of the Christian era, and destroyed so many books, Rome had 28 libraries. If Constantine the Great (288–337) had not changed the seat of government from Rome to Constantinople over a century earlier, and formed a fine library there of manuscripts of the classics and of Christian literature, we should probably not have nearly so many remains of ancient literature as we have now. When the Turks overthrew the government of Constantinople about 1,000 years later, the manuscripts in that city were sold and scattered all over Europe. Many manuscripts were also preserved in monasteries, where the monks would spend laborious days copying them.

None of the ancient libraries or those of the Middle Ages were public libraries. In the medieval monastic and cathedral libraries, books were often fastened to the reading desks by chains. The great public libraries of today did not come until comparatively recent times. Public libraries often include not only a lending section, but also a reference library (from which books cannot be borrowed) and a newspaper and magazine room. The National Central Library exists as a kind of central "pool" for the public libraries, who draw books from it.

One of the largest libraries is the Bibliothèque Nationale in Paris, the national library of France. Its vast collection has accumulated since its foundation in the 14th century. The library of the British Museum in London, with its huge circular reading room for students (*see* illustration in page 585), is even larger, and is said to surpass the Bibliothèque Nationale in the value of its contents. Every new book or publication finds a place on its shelves. This is also true, amongst other libraries, of the famous Bodleian at Oxford. The new Cambridge Univer-

1930

CHAINED BOOKS IN A LIBRARY AT FLORENCE

To prevent theft many of the old libraries used to chain their books, as you see in this view in the famous Laurentian Library in Florence, Italy. The reader sat on the bench, chose a book from the lower shelf of the two-storey lectern, and read it on the sloping desk above. This library was completed in 1571 from designs drawn by the artist Michelangelo (1475–1564).

sity Library, opened in 1934, contains 1,500,000 volumes. The Vatican Library at Rome, founded in the 15th century, is rich in manuscripts and books of great historical value. Other noteworthy collections are the Public Reference Library, New York, and the Library of Congress at Washington in the United States, the State Library in Leningrad, and the All-Union Lenin Public Library at Moscow.

Libya. Formerly an Italian colony, this region of North Africa is bounded on the west by Tunisia and Algeria, and on the south by French West Africa and French Equatorial Africa, on the east by Egypt and the Sudan, on the North by the Mediterranean Sea. It has an area of 680,000 square miles, and the vast desert hinterland is one of the hottest and most barren regions in the world. Most of Libya is a great limestone tableland, covered in parts with drifting sand.

The western portion, Tripolitania, has a narrow coastal plain where cereals, cotton, tobacco and fruit can be grown with the help of irrigation. Cyrenaica in the east has no such fertile strip, but dates, olives and barley are cultivated. The sub-desert approaches close to the coast, and there little grows but esparto grass which is exported for paper making. In southern Tripolitania there is a group of oases called the Fezzan, and there dates, olives, figs, almonds, and some grain are grown. In southern Cyrenaica is a similar group called the Kufra oases, also under cultivation.

Industries other than farming are few. The sponge and tunny fisheries are important, and salt and sulphur are mined. Manufactures include tobacco, carpets, leather articles and embroidered fabrics. The chief towns are Tripoli and Homs in Tripolitania, and Benghazi and Derna in Cyrenaica.

The earliest rulers in western Libya in historical times seem to have been the Carthaginians, whose capital was situated on the coast of what is today the French colony of Tunis. In the 7th century B.C. the Greeks founded the city of Cyrene on the north-east coast of Libya, and the region called Cyrenaica became one of the great centres of Greek culture. Both Tripolitania and Cyrenaica were conquered by the Egyptians in the 4th century B.C., and later were included in Rome's North African possessions. The Romans built several fine cities in Libya, and extensive ruins of Leptis Magna have been found.

In the 7th century of the Christian era the whole country was overrun by the Arabs. In 1510 King Ferdinand of Spain seized the city of Tripoli, and from 1530 to 1551 it was occupied by the Knights of St. John (religious order of chivalry). Then the Turks took possession of the region but made little atttempt to rule it, and the ports of Tripoli became nests of pirates. In 1835 Turkey established firmer control over the country, which she retained until the Italo-Turkish War (1911–12), when she surrendered it to Italy. After the First World War (1914–18) the Italians began to develop the country;

E.N.A.

STRETCH OF A THOUSAND-MILE ROAD IN LIBYA

After the First World War (1914–18) the Italians began to develop Libya, which they acquired in 1912. They seem to have inherited some of the genius of their Roman ancestors for road-making, and above is a stretch of high- way they constructed from near the Egyptian frontier at Sollum all along the coast to the Libyan boundary with the French possession of Tunisia, a distance of 1,000 miles. The words on the board at the right mean oasis of Saiad.

roads were built linking the chief towns; settlers were established in colonies in the coastal area, and new towns were founded for immigrants.

In the Second World War (1939–45) Libya became a major theatre of operations, German and Italian forces using it as a base for the invasion of Egypt. Here took place the epic siege of Tobruk, defended by the Imperial garrison for 200 days. Fighting continued from 1940 to 1943, when the British 8th Army swept across the whole width of Libya to join the British 1st Army in Tunisia. At the conclusion of the war Cyrenaica was placed under British control, while Tripoli was adminis- tered by France. The population of Libya in 1938 was 888,400.

Lichens. (Pron. li'kenz). On tree trunks, rocks, old boards, and also on the ground we often see queer patches of variously coloured plant life which we call " lichens " (from Greek *leikhenes*). They are not single plants, but each lichen is formed of a tiny fungus and an equally small alga living together so intimately as to appear like a single plant. The lichens furnish one of the best illus- trations of *symbiosis* (living together), as the scientists call this intimate association of two different kinds of organisms.

Algae (plural form) are mostly water-living plants, and include seaweeds and pond weeds, as well as a host of tiny one-celled plants, among them the dia- toms of the ocean, and the green, globular *Volvox*, which lives in ponds. The fungus makes the bulk of the lichen's " body " with its interwoven threads, and in the meshes live the algae. The special

fungi which take part in this arrangement are almost never found growing separately, but the algae *are* found growing free.

Fungi do not possess chlorophyll, the green or yellow substance by means of which plants, in the

H. Bastin

A LICHEN USED AS FOOD

Known as reindeer moss, this species of lichen provides fodder for the animal whose name it bears. It is even used as food by Man, and in Scandinavia it is also utilised for the manufacture of a spirit that resembles brandy.

presence of sunlight, are able to manufacture food carbohydrates from carbon dioxide taken from the air. The alga does possess chlorophyll, and in partnership with an alga the lichen is able to get foodstuffs made by its ally. If the fungus is unable to find an alga near, when it thrusts out its threads in search, it soon dies. But if it finds the right sort, it enmeshes it with its threads, and then continues to grow around its partner.

Lichens have a peculiar and effective method of propagation. Upon the surface of the body there are commonly seen minute granules which give the body a dusty appearance. These granules (called *soredia*)· each consist of a few cells of the alga surrounded by threads of the fungus. When these soredia are blown off and settle down they start new lichen bodies.

The combination of fungus and alga produces a structure which is able to exist where neither member could live alone. As a consequence lichens are able to grow in the most unfavourable places. About the last plants one finds in the far north or up on a high mountain are the lichens; and they are about the first plants to be found upon rocks brought above the surface of

A. W. Dennis

'PIXIE CUPS' OF LICHEN

Among the lichens occurring in Britain is *Cladonia fimbricata*, sometimes referred to as 'pixie cups,' an apt enough designation. It is shown magnified here about three times. It grows on heathy land, on rocks and walls, and about the roots of trees. Lichens are found all over the world at all levels from seashore to mountain tops, and are generally grey, greenish, yellow or red.

R. M. Adam

STRANGE FORM OF TREE-HAUNTING LICHEN

One of the most remarkable lichens is that known as 'old man's beard,' and botanically as *Usnea barbata*. As you see, it grows on trees, hanging from the branches in long, hair-like wisps and giving them a weird and grotesque appearance. This fine specimen was growing on a rowan tree or mountain ash in Glen Affric, Scotland.

the ocean or newly exposed through landslides, cliff falls, etc. In this way lichens play a very important part in the first stages of soil formation on bare rocks.

Certain kinds of lichens, such as those called "Iceland moss" (*Cetraria islandica*) and "reindeer moss" (*Cladonia rangiferina*), —illustrated in the opposite page— are used as food by reindeer and even by Man. Other kinds produce dyes, drugs, etc. One of the finest species occurring in Britain is the "old man's beard," *Usnea barbata*, which makes long, grey, hair-like festoons on the branches of trees. Another is *Cladonia*, species of which make the familiar "pixie cups" of heathy land. (*See* Algae; Fungi).

Lichfield. Chiefly a market-town, Lichfield is of great interest on account of its 13th–14th century cathedral and its associations with Dr. Johnson (1709–84), the British man of letters.

The cathedral (*see* picture in page 726) is not large but it is very beautiful, being built of the local red sandstone. The west front is elaborately carved, and instead of the three towers which figure on so many English cathedrals it has three graceful spires. The interior is imposing and dignified, and there is some lovely stained glass. Dr. Johnson (*q.v.*) was born in a room in his father's bookshop at the corner of Market Street, the house now being a Johnson museum. Next door is the Three Crowns Inn, where Johnson and Boswell (Johnson's biographer) stayed during their visit to Lichfield in 1776.

The actor David Garrick (1717–79) was born at Lichfield, but his birthplace no longer stands. Both he and Johnson are buried in Westminster Abbey, but there are memorial busts to them in the cathedral at Lichfield and statues in the market-place. Notable buildings are the bishop's palace and the theological college. The town is situated in Staffordshire, and its population is 11,000.

McLeish

LICHFIELD'S STATUE OF DR. JOHNSON

In 1838 this statue was put up in Lichfield's market-place to Dr. Johnson, who was born in the city. Nearly 100 years later, James Boswell, without whose Life of Johnson we should not know that great character, was commemorated in the same way.

Lie, TRYGVE (born 1896). The close of the 19th century was a time of unrest in Norway. The workers were demanding more pay and better conditions, and there was rioting in the streets of the towns. It was amid such events that Trygve Lie (*pron.* Lee) was born, a son of the working-classes, destined to become the Secretary-General of the United Nations.

His father was a journeyman carpenter in Grünerlökka, a busy quarter of Oslo (then called Christiania). When Trygve was barely six his father went to America, and his mother took the little boy to Grorud, an industrial town near Oslo, and there opened a working men's café. At school, Trygve was a splendid footballer and runner, and specialized in the study of history. At 15 he was already interested in politics, joining the Labour movement.

Encouraged and helped by one of his schoolmasters, he went to Oslo University and studied the law; and in 1919 he qualified as a barrister. From then until 1922 he was secretary to the Norwegian Labour party; in 1922 he was appointed legal adviser to the Norwegian Trade Union movement. When the Norwegian Labour party split in 1923, Trygve Lie was one of the majority that allied itself with the Communists, and he visited Moscow as secretary of the Norwegian delegation to the Third International.

In 1935 Trygve Lie became Minister of Justice, and in 1939 Minister of Trade, Industry and Shipping. When war came to Norway in 1940 he was chosen as Minister of Supply; and when the Norwegian government was driven to take refuge in London he was made Minister of Shipping —one of the most important posts in the cabinet, since her great merchant fleet was Norway's principal contribution to the Allied cause. In August 1940 he took over the post of Minister for Foreign Affairs.

" We shall never achieve security," he said in a speech, " until we have a firmly based system of cooperation with all nations that share our ideals." No words could better express the aim of the United Nations. And at the first meeting of the General Assembly of the United Nations at Westminster, London, on June 29, 1946, Trygve Lie, the carpenter's son, was elected its first Secretary-General for a term of five years.

Liechtenstein. Lying between Switzerland, to which it is closely allied, and Austria, the Principality of Liechtenstein occupies a narrow valley 15 miles long between the Rhine and the Austrian province of Vorarlberg, with an area of 65 square miles. The capital and seat of government is Vaduz, with a population of 1,700. Agriculture, cotton weaving and spinning, and the making of leather goods and pottery, are the main industries. The currency and postal system are Swiss, but the Principality issues its own postage stamps. The Principality was created in 1719, but the ruling house dates back to the 12th century. The population of the country is 11,100.

Liége, (Pron. lē-āzh'), BELGIUM. In the wars of Europe from medieval times to the First and Second World Wars, few towns have figured more prominently and frequently than this Belgian city. Even in the Middle Ages Liége was one of the arsenals of Europe. Today the rich coal mines in the valley of the Meuse, on which Liége is situated, make it the chief manufacturing centre of Belgium. It is noted for the manufacture of guns and firearms, together with locomotives, motor-cars, machinery, hardware and textiles.

The history of Liége goes back to St. Monulph, who travelled through the Meuse valley in the 6th century. The chapel which he built was the beginning of the present city, and also of its rule by the bishop, which lasted until 1795. For many centuries the city was famous as a centre of religion and learning, long before its mineral wealth was suspected. Today Liége is the centre of the Walloon culture, which is akin to that of the French.

At Liége was fought the first great battle of the First World War, the battle lasting from August 4 to 9, 1914. The resistance of its girdle of strong forts enabled the French and British to prepare the defences which stopped the Germans on the Marne. In the Second World War (1939–45) Liége was occupied by German forces within three days of the invasion of Belgium on May 10, 1940, though the fortifications held out for several days longer. The city was liberated by United States troops on September 8, 1944, but suffered considerable damage from German flying bombs during the winter of 1944–45. The population is 152,500.

Lifeboat. When storms rage round our coasts we think of the brave lifeboatmen battling against the elements—in the darkness of night, maybe, and at the risk of their lives—to succour those in danger at sea.

The lifeboat, which is now such a familiar institution to all who live on our coasts, or who take their holidays at the seaside, is a comparatively modern invention. Archdeacon Sharp, of Northumberland, had the management of a large estate of which the proceeds were to be devoted to charity. He thought that no better use for some of this money could be imagined than in rescuing sailors in peril. He got the help of a London coachbuilder, Lionel Lukin, and sent up to him a fishing coble, which Lukin converted into what he called an " unimmergible " boat.

Stationed at Bamburgh, in Northumberland, this was the first to be used as a lifeboat (1786). Then, three years later, the members of a club whose place of assembly overlooked the mouth of the Tyne, where they often saw ships wrecked, determined *they* would do something. They offered a reward of two guineas for the best idea for a boat to be used in rescue work.

A local house painter and teacher of music named William Wouldhave sent in a scheme for a self-righting lifeboat—one which, if it were capsized, would turn right way up again. But Wouldhave got only half of the award! And his self-righting scheme was not used.

A model was made, and then a ship's carpenter, Henry Greathead, built a boat; she was named the Original, and launched at the end of 1789. On January 30, 1790, she rescued her first sailors from the sea. Things began to move more quickly now. Lloyd's gave £2,000 to provide more lifeboats, and Greathead built 30 in the next 14 years. Then, in 1823, Lt.-Col. Sir William Hillary, from his home at Douglas, Isle of Man, launched an appeal for a national lifeboat service. In the following March a meeting of the many supporters was held in London, and the society which later became the " Royal National Life-Boat Institution " was founded. Hillary himself, until he was over sixty years of age, went out with the lifeboat from Douglas. He took part in the saving of more than 300 lives, and three times won the gold medal for gallantry.

A quarter of a century went by, with the lifeboat service gradually extending its work; in 1849 it gave rewards for the rescue of more than 6,000 from the sea. But public support fell off. In 1851 the fourth duke of Northumberland—a rear-admiral and sometime First Lord of the Admiralty—became president of the Institution. He whipped up interest again, and offered a hundred guineas for the best model of a new life-saving boat. Out of 280 models or plans, that of James Beeching, of Great Yarmouth, was chosen. It incorporated the self-righting principle. This was the type which for the next forty years was used around our coasts.

Essential Features of a Lifeboat

From twenty lifeboats maintained in 1849 the number grew to 293 by the year 1889. In 1887 George Lennox Watson, designer of the famous yacht Britannia, had become the consulting naval architect of the Life-Boat Institution. He designed a large sailing lifeboat in 1888, not of the self-righting type. Watson's boat was the first of the " modern " fleet. Today, out of 156 maintained by the Institution, only 26 are " self-righters." There had been much controversy about these last, for the quality of turning right way up again was obtained by providing air chambers at bow and stern, by providing a much heavier keel than usual, and by making the vessel narrower than she would otherwise have been. Such boats were more likely to capsize in heavy weather, and were less easy to handle. Some lifeboatmen called them " roly-polies."

What makes a lifeboat? It must be strong, built of English oak, Canadian red cedar, Burma teak and African mahogany—each where its special qualities will serve best. Again, a lifeboat must be able to free itself of water taken in. This it can do in a quarter of a minute by metal flaps, or scuppers, which open outwards in its sides. Thirdly, a lifeboat must be unsinkable. All her empty spaces are filled with boxes made of red cedar and covered with glue, stretched calico, and paint, so that there are 100 to 160 such air-cases which give it buoyancy, even if its sides should be holed and it should fill with water!

Experiments were first made with motor-driven boats in 1903. During the next forty years there were many difficulties to be overcome, for the engine must be made watertight; it must run automatically, for in a gale no one would have time to fiddle with a fussy engine; the controls must be simple, and lubrication must be unfailing. While the engine must continue to work even if the seas should turn the boat on end, it must stop at once should the boat capsize: if a self-righter, when it came up again, had its engine still running, the boat would go on its way leaving the crew in the water. These conditions were satisfied, and today all but two of the modern lifeboat fleet are motor-propelled.

The largest motor-lifeboat is 53 feet long by 13½ feet, and with crew and gear on board weighs 26½ tons. She is a twin-screw boat, driven by two 60 horse-power petrol engines which are in a watertight engine room and are themselves watertight; they will continue running even if the engine room be flooded. The speed is nearly nine knots, and the boat carries fuel enough to travel 180 miles at full speed. She has a cabin, and can take aboard a hundred persons in addition to her crew of eight. There is an oil spray at the bows to make smooth the water around a wreck; she carries a line-throwing gun or pistol, and has an electric search-light. Radio-telephony transmitting and receiving apparatus is fitted.

A new lifeboat for St. Helier, Jersey, launched in 1948, carries enough fuel to travel 230 miles at full speed without refuelling, and is the first lifeboat to have means on board for cooking food—she has a paraffin cooker in the deck cabin. She is the first to have all her superstructure—the deck cabin, the shelter for the mechanics, the mast and the ventilators—made of aluminium alloy instead of wood or mild steel; this means a saving in weight of over a quarter-ton. She is the first to have the engine exhausts carried up the mast, enabling the exhausts to escape well above the heads of the crew.

Such a lifeboat costs about £20,000 to build and equip, and needs £800 for maintenance every year. But no amount of money could pay for the gallant service freely given by the lifeboatmen. Only the motor mechanic at each station is a paid servant; all the rest are men who earn their living in other ways, most of them as fishermen.

On November 15, 1928, the Rye lifeboat went out to the Latvian vessel Alice in distress; the crew of this ship were taken off by another vessel, but the lifeboatmen did not hear the recall signal. On her way back, when almost within the harbour mouth, the Rye lifeboat capsized, overwhelmed by the suddenly increasing tempest, and her crew of seventeen were drowned. Another great tragedy was the loss of the entire crew (eight) of The Mumbles lifeboat on April 23, 1947, when going to the aid of the steamer Santampa.

During the First World War (1914–18) lifeboats of the R.N.L.I. rescued 4,131 persons; during the second world conflict (1939–45), 6,376 lives were saved. In all, between the years 1824 and 1948, the lifeboats saved, in round numbers, 76,000 lives. The funds for carrying on this grand work are provided from pence and silver we put in the collecting boxes at seaside resorts, and from other sums which generous persons send to the Institution, or leave to it as legacies.

Lifts AND ESCALATORS. Until electrically driven passenger lifts came into use, about 1890, there was only the hydraulic lift, and a few special ones driven by a steam engine. The winding gear and cages at a colliery form a lift system, but in the present pages we are considering only passenger-carrying lifts.

If you have read our article on Hydraulic Machinery you will know that water pressure can be employed to force out the piston from a cylinder. Early lifts used a vertical hydraulic cylinder, of

Royal National Life-Boat Institution

NEW LIFEBOAT FOR ST. HELIER, JERSEY

Launched in 1948 and stationed at St. Helier, Jersey, this vessel of the Royal National Life-Boat Institution is 46 feet 9 inches by 12 feet 9 inches and weighs 20 tons. She has twin screws and is driven by two 40-h.p. water-tight Diesel engines in a water-tight engine room. The radio-telephone is in the deck cabin, with a remote control, or extension, in the roof of the engine-room canopy, where the motor mechanic has it close by his head as he sits at his engine controls.

which the piston rod had to be as long as the distance through which the lift car had to be raised : the car rested, in fact, on the end of the piston, or " ram." This meant also that the cylinder had to be sunk in the ground below the lowest point to which the car had to descend. This system is suitable for lifts which travel only short distances, and is used for some lifts still.

In order to overcome the difficulties of the long piston rod, the suspended hydraulic lift was devised. Here the vertical cylinder is fixed in the lift shaft; the piston bears at its top end a pulley sheave around which the rope is wound, one end being fixed to the pulley frame and the other passing around the lift-driving sheave or sheaves at the top of the shaft in which the lift goes up and down, and being attached to the top of the car. Multiplying sheaves rather like those of a pulley block (see Pulley) are used to move the lift several times as fast as the ram travels, and much farther than the stroke of the ram. An early lift of this sort was installed at the Royal Albert Hall, London, to take people up to the gallery.

The electric lift has a motor for its winding engine (see the simplified diagram on the right). The car, like that of the hydraulic lift, runs between guide rails. Most of the weight is balanced by a number of heavy castings in the counterweight frame, which runs up and down in its own guides. Thus the motor has only to raise a weight equal to the difference between that of the car, with its passengers, and that of the counterweight.

Safety Devices of Many Kinds

Elaborate safety devices prevent the lift being moved unless the doors are shut, the landing doors are shut, and the car floor is level with the landing floor. Other devices prevent the landing doors to the lift shaft being opened unless and until the car is stopped and in its proper position level with the landing. Still other mechanisms shut off the power and apply brakes if the car overshoots its normal stopping position at top or bottom. If the hoisting cables, of strong steel wire in many strands, should break, then automatic brakes come into action on the motor drive; and steel jaws below the car dart out and grip the guide rails. All such passenger-carrying machines are designed with a "factor of safety" which endows them with strength many times in excess of their ordinary breaking or failing strength.

Though large lifts are operated by an attendant who rides in the car, the great majority are worked by automatic control. You push the button numbered for the floor to which you desire to ride; if the landing door and car door are properly closed, the lift will start, and run up or down to the indicated floor, where it will stop. You can then open the doors and step out. Unless you close these doors properly the lift will not answer another summons. After the car has been " called " by someone pushing the button at a landing, any other " calls " are rejected until it has answered the earlier summons. Similarly, after you have depressed one of the buttons inside the car, no other " call " will be answered until the present duty has been carried out.

It is not possible without a good deal of space and many technicalities to explain how all this

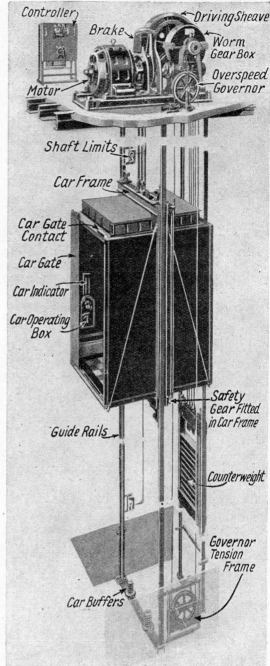

ELECTRIC PASSENGER LIFT
The working of an electric lift is shown. The weight of the car, which carries the passengers and runs on steel guide-rails, is balanced by a counter-weight moving on its own guides and here seen just below the car. The electric motor above has, therefore, only to exert the power necessary to raise the additional weight of the passengers.

automatic working is carried out. All we can say is that there is a complex assembly of selector-switches, resistances and relays, linked up with the safety devices we have mentioned. Some foolish people attempt to " beat " these safety

POWER UNIT OF AN ESCALATOR
On the right is the electric motor which drives the cog-wheels over which the endless band of steps goes at the top and bottom of an escalator. Here we have a view of the turning point at the upper end, as seen from underneath.

precautions. Nothing could be more dangerous. If you ride in a lift, do not tinker with the controls.

The escalator or moving staircase has largely taken the place of passenger lifts where very many persons have to be raised or lowered in a short time. It is simply a stairway running over two pairs of cogwheels at top and bottom, and working in an inclined tunnel. The "treads" (level members) of the stairs are hinged to a jointed chain-like framework so that they will lie flat when passing idle under the escalator; as they come into position at the foot of the escalator they are caused to take up the normal horizontal attitude by means of guides at the side. These guides (*see* diagram below) themselves slope up at the point where the "stairs" begin, and flatten out at the level "landings" at top and bottom. Separate cogwheels move the handrails, endless belts which travel at the same speed as the stairs.

AN ESCALATOR : SIMPLIFIED DIAGRAM TO SHOW THE MECHANISM
The working of an escalator is shown in this diagram. It consists of a series of steps, similar to that seen enlarged on the left, having two small wheels or rollers on each side. The pairs of wheels are out of line with each other and run on separate sets of guide rails. All these steps are linked together and move on an endless chain, passing over two cog-wheels. At the lower end of the escalator the guide rails slant upwards and are farther apart, the treads becoming separated. When they pass from the inclined section to the short horizontal length at the top they flatten out again.

WONDERLAND *in a* FLASH *of* LIGHT

*Like heat, light has mystified Man from the time when he first began to notice
his surroundings, and even today scientists have different theories about it.
However, its ' laws ' are well established.*

Light. Of the five human senses the scientist regards seeing as the most important, for all his measurements, or observations, make use of the agency of light to communicate the course of events to his brain. Thus it is not surprising that the study of light, the great message-bearer, should have interested the earliest of the natural philosophers, such as Newton, in their search after scientific truth. Although better known for his Law of Gravitation, Newton was also a great pioneer in attacking the problem of what light is; by showing how white light can be split up into a spectrum he laid the foundation of the theory of colour.

Light is something which travels very quickly. This was soon realized when it was found impossible to measure its speed directly with a stop-watch. A Danish astronomer named Ole Roemer (1644–1710), showed that light does not travel instantaneously, and he made quite a good estimate of its speed by noting discrepancies in the predicted and actual times at which Saturn's moons became eclipsed. This time-difference was accounted for by the period in which the light was travelling across space to the earth; for, of course, when we " see " a star or planet we are really receiving light which has been given out some time before.

Measuring the Speed of Light

Although various other astronomical estimates of the speed of light were subsequently made, it was not until the middle of the 19th century that it was found possible to measure it directly on the earth. Armand Fizeau (1819–96), a French professor, was the first man to do this successfully. He chose two high towers, or " stations," a little more than five miles apart, in his native town of Paris. On the first was placed a bright lamp, shining in the direction of the second tower, on which was mounted a mirror. This mirror reflected the light directly back to the first station. A toothed wheel was put in the path of the light beam coming from the lamp, so contrived that the light passed through the opening between two teeth, and was reflected back through the same opening when the wheel was at rest. When the wheel was revolved rapidly enough, the light that returned from the second tower found that a tooth of the wheel had moved into the place of the opening; thus no light could then be seen reflected from the second tower.

The time which the light took to travel from the first station to the second and back was thus the time that it took for a tooth of the wheel to move to the place of the opening. By doubling the speed of the wheel, Fizeau could again see the reflected light, because a second opening had moved into the line of sight. From a speedometer he could get the number of revolutions, and thus calculate the time that it took for the light to travel between the stations and back.

The values obtained for the speed of light indicate that it travels at the high speed of approximately 186,000 miles per second. In fact, it is the fastest moving agency in the universe. Even so, the distances between the heavenly bodies are so enormous that light often takes years to travel between them. The light from the Sun takes about eight minutes to travel the 93 million miles separating us from it; and that from the nearest fixed star takes just over four years. There are many stars in the heavens whose light, which we are receiving, must have been emitted thousands of years ago, before the time of Pharaoh. Since then anything may have happened to them; some may no longer exist! Astronomers find it convenient to measure the enormous stellar distances in terms of light-years, because this provides a suitably large unit.

What else do we know about light other than it travels very fast? It is common experience that it can be reflected by mirrors, and in fact all objects reflect light to a certain extent, for this is the way in which we recognize the shape, size and colour of them. The way in which light is reflected is similar to the way in which a ball bounces from a wall. Put precisely, as a scientific law, *the angle of incidence equals the angle of reflection, and both angles lie in the same plane.* This means that a ray of light will depart from a reflecting surface at the same angle as that at which it arrived. A coloured object does not reflect all the light, as does a perfectly white one, but absorbs some of the colours which go to make up white light, *e.g.* a piece of blue cloth, illuminated by white light, absorbs all the green and the red part of the spectrum, and only reflects back what is left, giving a blue sensation to the observer.

The Phenomenon of Refraction

Some substances, like glass or water, offer very little hindrance to the light rays and let them pass right through. Such substances are termed transparent. The light travels through them almost as easily as through space, which enables us to see objects on the other side. In actual fact, the light travels a little slower through the transparent substances than through space and, as we shall see, this leads to a bending of the rays of light at the surface of the transparent medium. The bending of the rays is termed *refraction.*

When a straight stick is thrust into water it appears to be bent at the surface because the light reflected from the stick is bent, or refracted, in coming from the water to the air. Glass will also bend light rays, but this is not noticed in window glass, for example, where the two parallel surfaces bend the light in opposite directions as it goes through. The second refraction cancels the first, so to speak. In prisms and lenses, however, where the surfaces of the glass are not parallel, and not always flat, the refraction of the light rays is the function for which they are used, as in the microscope, telescope, lighthouse lantern, and prism spectroscope.

Some experiments in reflection and refraction are illustrated in page 1940. They will help us to understand the principles. Take an ordinary hand torch and fit over it a cardboard tube with a small hole in it, as shown in Fig. 1. Then take it into a darkened room and shine it on to a mirror. The direction of the reflected beam can often be seen by virtue of dust particles in the air, but if a little smoke is blown into the surrounding air this will show it up better. Now imagine a perpendicular (shown by a dotted line in the figure) rising from the mirror where the *incident beam* strikes. This line always lies midway between the two beams, so that the angle it makes with the *incident ray* is equal to the angle it makes with the *reflected ray*, and all three lie in the same plane. Fig. 2 shows what happens when the mirror is tilted. The angles of incidence and of reflection are still equal. Fig. 3 shows how the eye sees an object by reflection in a mirror. The key appears to be behind the

mirror, in the dotted position, since the rays from it have been bent at the mirror. The image is known as a *virtual* one, and differs from the actual object in being back-to-front, but is the right way up.

Refraction can be studied with the same apparatus, with the addition of a shallow water-tank, such as a square-sided aquarium. Into this is poured water, and a drop of milk is added so that the light beams show up better. Put the mirror in the bottom of the tank, turn on the light, as in Fig. 4, and note the path of the beam. Imagine two perpendiculars, or " normals," drawn at the points where the beam enters and leaves the water. It will be noticed that when the light passes from the lighter to the denser medium (from air to glass) it is bent *towards the normal*, and when from the denser to the lighter medium (as from glass to air) it bends *away from the normal*. This is the

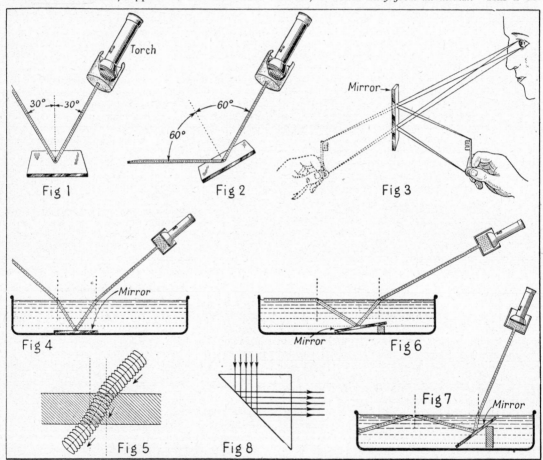

EXPERIMENTS IN REFLECTION AND REFRACTION OF LIGHT

A full explanation is given in the text. Fig. 1 illustrates the law of reflection ; a perpendicular to the surface of the mirror lies always midway between the incident ray and the reflected ray ; the angles with these two rays are equal. Even if the mirror be tilted (Fig. 2), the angles of incidence and of reflection are still equal. How the human eye sees an object by reflection in a mirror is demonstrated by Fig. 3 : the key seems to be behind the mirror, in the dotted position, because the rays have been bent at the mirror. Refraction can be studied with the same apparatus, plus a shallow water tank (Fig. 4). Fig. 5 shows how light rays passing from a lighter medium to a denser one are bent towards the

normal ; and when rays pass from a denser medium to a lighter medium they are bent away from the normal. If the mirror in the tank be tilted sufficiently, a point is reached where the beam cannot quite get out of the water. The angle which the beam then makes with the normal is called the critical angle (Fig. 6). If the mirror be tilted further (Fig. 7), the critical angle is exceeded, and the beam is reflected back—a phenomenon called total internal reflection. A prism is substituted for the mirror in Fig. 8 ; the angle of incidence of this prism is 45 degrees, and since the critical angle for glass is about 42 degrees, we again get total internal reflection. Hence the use of prisms in binoculars.

Law of Refraction, and its action is explained in Fig. 5. Here imagine the light ray to consist of a succession of disks, all of which must be forced "broadside on " through any medium traversed by the ray. Remember now that the light travels more slowly in denser mediums than in lighter ones. Obviously then, when the ray strikes slantwise on the surface of the water, the portion striking first will not travel as fast as the portion still in the air. This second portion will turn around the first, as round a pivot, until it, too, has sunk into the glass; this " wheeling " causes the ray to travel in a new direction through the glass. The reverse action takes place when the ray leaves the glass; the disks " wheel " in the opposite direction, owing to the change in speed.

If the mirror in the bottom of the tank is tilted, as in Fig. 6, a point is reached when the beam cannot quite get out of the water. The angle between the normal and the beam in the water is then known as the *critical angle.* By tilting the mirror further, as in Fig. 7, this critical angle is exceeded, and then the beam is reflected back. This is known as *total internal reflection.* A prism of the shape shown in Fig. 8 is often used instead of a mirror because of this. For glass the critical angle is about 42 degrees, and as the angle of incidence in the prism is 45 degrees, we get total internal reflection.

How then are we to explain these various properties of light? Newton thought of light as consisting of high-speed particles, or " corpuscles," which travelled faster or slower according to the medium in which they were moving. But it was then difficult to give a satisfactory explanation of why light was sometimes reflected and sometimes refracted at a surface, on this theory. Another great mathematician and scientist, Christian Huygens (1629–95), who lived at about the same time as Newton, put forward an alternative theory which had much greater success in explaining the behaviour of light. Huygens was watching the ripples on a Dutch canal when he realized that light might well travel in a similar sort of manner, by means of waves spreading out in ever-widening circles from their point of origin. The light waves would not, of course, travel in a material substance like water, but there would have to be some kind of weightless fluid which must pervade all matter, and even pervade a vacuum. This substance came to be called the ether (*q.v.*). The only way we may know of its existence (which is by no means universally accepted) is by the waves which travel in it.

But most types of waves, such as sound waves and water waves, can spread around corners (otherwise we could not hear noises going on round the corner of a building). Light, on the other hand, travels in straight lines only. How is this to be explained? The answer lies in the extreme shortness of the wavelength of light; for a certain shade of yellow, called " sodium light," the wave-length is only 579 millionths of a millimetre. With such a short wavelength (the distance between two successive crests or troughs), the spreading effect at the corners is

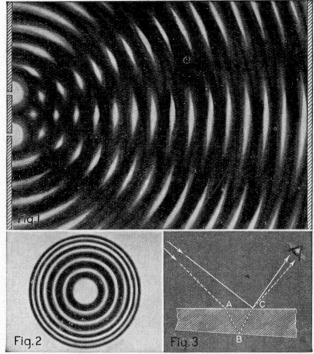

Fig.1

Fig.2

Fig.3

'INTERFERENCE' AND ITS EFFECTS

These three diagrams are explained in the text. Fig. 1 illustrates the experiment made by Thomas Young (1773–1829) which led scientists to adopt the undulatory theory (movement in waves) of light. Sir Isaac Newton (1642–1727) made the experiment of which the result is seen in Fig. 2 ; called Newton's rings, this striking effect is produced when light passes through a thin convex lens laid on a piece of plane (flat) glass. Fig. 3 shows the cause of iridescence, as seen on a bird's feather. Rays striking a wedge-shaped piece of glass are differently refracted, some of the refracted rays interfering with others.

very slight, but is nevertheless detectable. If the shadow of a straight edge is thrown on to a screen, and the light source employed is sufficiently small (a " pin-point " of light) the shadow cast will not be sharp, but will exhibit a number of parallel black and white fringes at the edge. This is due to the spreading, or *diffraction* of the light waves at the edge.

A beautiful instrument, the " interferometer," has been invented which enables us to measure the wave-length of light waves. In this instrument two beams of light, travelling different lengths of path, can be brought together to produce darkness—that is, to annul one another. It is difficult to imagine adding two material things and getting " nothing," but if we think of adding two motions, one *up* and the other *down*, we can then get no resultant motion. This is what happens in the interferometer, which brings the light beams together in such a way that the crest of one wave falls in the same position as the trough of the other, producing darkness. This is known as the " interference of light." The principle is explained in the group of diagrams (Figs. 1-3) above. The top picture here illustrates Thomas Young's experiment in interference which led scientists to believe in the wave theory of light. The dark lines represent the " troughs " of light waves radiating from the two pinholes on the left, the crests lying in between the troughs. Only along three lines in the picture do "troughs" fall on "troughs" and "crests" on "crests," giving rise to three separate diffracted beams. Fig. 2 shows "ring interference," called "Newton's Rings" from the experiment Sir Isaac Newton made by laying a convex lens on plane glass. Fig. 3 shows the cause of iridescence, or shimmering colour, as in an opal, films of oil, and certain bird feathers. If light strikes a thin, wedge-shaped film, certain rays, as at A, will strike in, be reflected from the bottom of the film, as at B, and emerge with further refraction, as at C. All rays reflecting directly from C, except those of one colour, will interfere with the ray ABC—so only that colour is seen. As the shape of the wedge, or the observer's position, changes, so does the colour which "gets through." Hence the shimmering play of colour.

Each colour has its own characteristic wavelength, so that when Sir Isaac Newton sent white light through a prism and produced the coloured spectrum, he was really splitting up the light into its constituent wavelengths. The wavelength of the red light is about one-third longer than that of yellow ; and the wavelength of violet light is about one quarter shorter. Note that all these coloured lights travel at the same speed through empty space, although they may go faster or slower than each other in material substances, such as glass. The property of the material giving rise to this change of velocity is termed its *dispersion*.

It is now known that visible light makes up only a very small part of a large spectrum of electro-magnetic waves. At one end of this spectrum there are X-rays and cosmic rays, whose wavelengths are thousands and even millions of times smaller than those of visible light. Ultra-violet rays, used in medical treatment and for killing bacteria, have wavelengths just shorter than the visible violet light, while infra-red, or heat rays, lie just on the other side of the visible spectrum. The electro-magnetic spectrum extends beyond the infra-red into the realm of wireless waves, which have wavelengths ranging from a few centimetres up to hundreds of metres.

There are a number of ways whereby light may be generated, the chief source being from hot bodies, such as the sun and stars, or from the glowing tungsten filaments of our electric lamps. This is a very inefficient way of producing light, since by far the larger proportion of the radiation emitted is in the form of infra-red, or heat, rays. Much greater efficiency is obtained by discharging electricity through a gas to make it glow. This is how the light is produced in neon signs and in mercury vapour street lamps, as well as in the fluorescent strip-lights (*see* Electric Lighting) which are so widely used today. All these latter forms of light are obtained practically "cold" ; and in Nature there are also examples of cold light being produced, such as that given out by glow-worms and fire-flies. The so-called phosphorescent substances which are used in luminous paints also glow in the dark without giving out measurable quantities of heat.

There is another interesting property of light called polarisation. Certain crystalline substances (*e.g.* tourmaline) cut off some of the light vibrations, and light passing through such crystals is said to be polarised. The waves in an ordinary ray of light do not just go up and down, like the waves on the surface of water, but can go crosswise, diagonally, or in fact in any plane at right angles to the direction of motion of the wave. Looked at end-on, the waves would appear to be like the spokes in a bicycle wheel, all starting from the centre of the wheel and vibrating *up and down the spokes*, with the direction of motion of the waves *along the hub*. When such a ray of light goes through a thin slice of tourmaline, it is as if it were passing through a narrow slit which cuts off all the rays but those vibrating in the direction of the slit. Let us see what happens when this polarised light, whose waves can only vibrate in the one direction, strikes another slice of tourmaline. The light will get through only if the "slit" of the second tourmaline is parallel to that of the

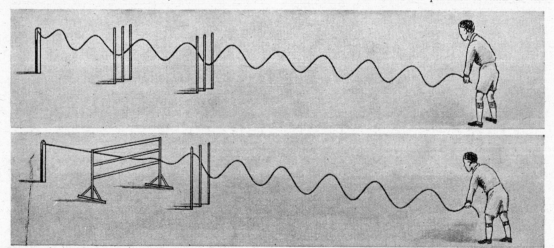

SIMPLE ANALOGY WITH A POLARISED RAY OF LIGHT

Light travels in waves which are at right angles to the direction in which the light beam is moving. Certain crystal substances cut off some of these waves, the reason being explained in the text. When a rope is given an up-and-down wavy motion the undulations are able to pass between posts (upper), but if horizontal bars are placed behind the posts (lower) they will stop the waves. The same thing happens when light rays pass through a 'slit' in one crystal (e.g. a slice of tourmaline) and strike another of which the 'slit' is at right angles, placed behind the first.

first, but will not do so if the slit is at right-angles; so two crossed pieces of tourmaline block the light.

Many other crystals polarise light to a certain degree, and light reflected from a glass surface also suffers partial polarisation. The polarising filters used in photography are designed to cut out this reflected light, so that photographs may be taken through shop windows, or through picture-frame glasses, without the usual interference of the unwanted reflections. Mineralogists use polarised light in their microscopes for the examination of very thin sections of rock. The different mineral formations then stand out more distinctly than otherwise. Again, polarised light is useful in the examination of sugar solutions. Some types of sugar twist the plane of polarisation of the light, as it passes through it, in a clockwise direction, and others in an anti-clockwise direction. The two types of sugar are thus known as dextro-rotatory and laevo-rotatory—from the Latin *dexter*, right ; and *laevus*, left—and the distinction is important in indicating how the atoms in the two chemically-similar sugar molecules are arranged.

There are further properties of light, of relatively recent discovery, which indicate that Newton's idea of light corpuscles was not altogether wrong. If certain metals, such as caesium, are illuminated with a beam of light, electrical particles called electrons are knocked out; and if these are collected on another metal plate, an electric current can be made to flow. The current, of course, only flows when the light is shining. This is the principle of the photo-cell, or electric eye, thousands of which are in everyday use in controlling automatic machinery. The light " bullet " which knocked out the electron from the caesium is known as a " photon," and it was in the attempt to justify its existence in terms of the wave theory of light that the Quantum Theory (*q.v.*) was born.

The wave theory of light also breaks down when we try to detect the presence of the ether, in which the waves must flow. Because of the presumed spin of the earth through the ether, light travelling from east to west should seem faster than light travelling from west to east. Failure to observe this led to the theory of Relativity (*q.v.*).

Lighthouses AND LIGHT-VESSELS.

Bonfires to guide the mariner into his harbour, or to warn him off a dangerous shore, were the earliest fore-runners of the lighthouse. Then there came the iron basket, fixed on top of a stone post, in which a fire was burned as a guide or a warning. A similar basket might be slung from the end of a pole in some lofty perch. It was much later that masonry towers were erected for the fiery beacon. There seems to have been such a tower at Cape Sigeum, in the Dardanelles, as far back as the 7th century before Christ. The Pharos of Alexandria, built on an island in the bay in the 3rd century B.C., gave its name to later light-towers; the modern French word, *phare*, for a lighthouse, is derived from it.

At Boulogne, on the French side of the English Channel, the Romans built a great tower 190 feet round, and 200 feet high, which guided mariners for more than 1,400 years. The idea of a lighthouse built on an isolated rock as a warning came some centuries later. The Eddystone (*q.v.*), on a narrow rock 14 miles off Plymouth, is described under its own heading; first a wooden structure 120 feet high, designed by Winstanley, it lasted only five years (1698–1703), until a hurricane demolished it in 1703. Its successor, built by Rudyerd in 1709, was burnt down in 1755. Then Smeaton built a massive granite lighthouse 95 feet high (1759). In 1877, as a fissure had developed in the rock, it was taken down and the upper sections transferred to Plymouth Hoe. Smeaton introduced the method of dovetailing the joints of the stones for greater strength, and this became the standard way of building lighthouses. The fourth Eddystone was completed in 1882, on a site 40 yards from the previous one. It was of granite, and was 168 feet high, above low water level. We have given the story of the Eddystone in this detail because it illustrates

ANCIENT LIGHTHOUSE BUILT TO GUIDE ROMAN SHIPS

Crude as it appears to us, this lighthouse fulfilled its purpose successfully at Boulogne on the north coast of France for 1,400 years after it was built by the Romans about 40 A.D. The powerful flashing lights in use today were then unknown ; the warning light was simply a bonfire that was lit on top of the tower, but for sailors it was better to have even that flickering signal than to grope blindly for the way to port on a stormy night. This picture is from an old print.

A LIGHTSHIP WITH CREW

Besides sending her warning message to ships by flashing light or fog-horn, this lightship at the entrance to Dublin Bay, Eire, sends out wireless and underwater signals. The latter set up vibrations in the water which can be picked up by the special receiver fitted to many vessels. From the difference in the times of arrival of the wireless and underwater signals the distance from the lightship can be calculated.

to the danger spot, the men being relieved periodically, and fuel and provisions conveyed by a relieving tender. Until the period of the Second World War (1939–45) it was international practice that lighthouses and lightships were not harmed by ships and aircraft of warring countries. But in 1940 German warships and aircraft began to attack lightships. On January 29 of that year the East Dudgeon lightship was bombed from the air. Its crew of eight took to their boat and tried to row to the coast, reaching it after 19 hours' toil only for the boat to capsize in the surf. Seven were drowned, and one struggled ashore.

Lightships having crews were then withdrawn, and their place was taken during the rest of the war by crewless floats with automatic light and bell, or explosive fog signal, able to work unattended for two to six months. It was at East Dudgeon, off the Norfolk coast, that the second of the earliest lightships to be posted was installed, in 1736. The first had been moored at the Nore Sand in 1731. Besides serving as warnings of danger, light-vessels serve of course as navigation lights. In addition to the Eddystone, other famous British lighthouses include the Bell Rock off the Scottish coast; the Fastnet, off S.W. Ireland; the Lizard (Cornwall); Bishop Rock, in the Scillies; and Beachy Head, off the Sussex coast.

Those in England and Wales come under the supervision of the organization known as Trinity

the development of the lighthouse built on an isolated rock away from the shore. At many harbours you will see lighthouses of a different sort—lower structures built on a pier or on the shore. Here the difficulty is much less, and today such structures are often built of a steel or concrete framework in lattice form, with the lantern and keepers' watchroom at the top.

On shoals or other dangerous points where it is not necessary or practicable to erect a lighthouse, a light-vessel may be moored. Other danger points may be indicated by a light-buoy (*see* Buoy). The lightship is a sturdily-built vessel upon whose mast is a lantern of the same general type used in lighthouses. Most lightships are manned, and carry a crew to tend the light, fog signal, and other navigational aids. Some in sheltered positions may be unattended, the light working automatically for many weeks. Lightships are moored close

Central Press

LIGHTSHIPS THAT NEED NO CREWS

Owing to repeated German aircraft attacks on lightships off the east coast of England during the Second World War (1939–45) lightships with crews were withdrawn, their place being taken by crewless floats (above). Craft of this sort, equipped with automatic light and bell, or explosive fog-signal, operate unattended for from two to six months.

THE GIANT SENTINEL OF THE ENGLISH CHANNEL

Painted specially for this work by G. H. DAVIS

The majestic Eddystone Lighthouse stands on the danger-ous Eddystone Rocks, 14 miles south-west of Plymouth. It had three predecessors. The first, a wooden building, was destroyed by a hurricane in 1703, and the second was burned down in 1755. The third, a granite structure 95

feet high, was dismantled in 1877; its base is seen to the left. The present tower, also of granite, and built in circular sections, was completed by Sir James Douglass in 1882. It stands 168 feet above low water, and the flashing light from the lantern can be seen for nearly 18 miles.

BIRTH AND GROWTH OF A MODERN LIGHTHOUSE

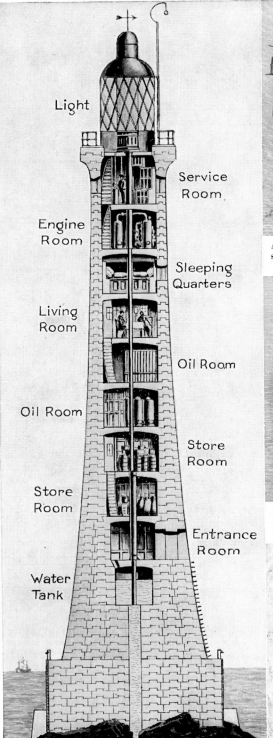

Light

Service Room

Engine Room

Sleeping Quarters

Living Room

Oil Room

Oil Room

Store Room

Store Room

Entrance Room

Water Tank

A raised platform may have to be set up beside the lighthouse site while the foundations are being laid, operations being conducted from that temporary stage.

Sometimes the materials for building a lighthouse have to be delivered along overhead cables strung from near-by cliffs to the temporary stage. Here a great block of stone is on its way.

The interior of a lighthouse of the stone masonry type is shown. Notice how thick the walls are at the bottom, where they have to withstand the heaviest shocks. The massive stone slabs are so shaped that they are locked together. The light may be provided by oil, gas or electricity, and be increased by lenses, prisms and reflectors.

Workmen as well as materials must make a dizzy trip along the overhead cables when such lighthouses as the Beachy Head light on the Sussex coast of England are being erected. This structure took the place of the old Belle Toute Lighthouse, which may still be seen on the cliffs. Smeaton, builder of the third Eddystone Lighthouse, introduced the tapering shape.

To face page 1945

House, already a guild of mariners of some importance when Henry VIII granted it its first charter in 1514. Trinity House is the premier pilotage authority in the United Kingdom, besides being the General Lighthouse Authority for England and Wales and the Channel Islands, with control over local lighthouse authorities. Lighthouses in Scotland and the Isle of Man are supervised by the Commissioners of Northern Lighthouses, a body which came into existence by an Act of Parliament passed in 1786. Trinity House looks after about 60 manned lighthouses, 40 " minor " lights, and between 30 and 40 lightships. The Commissioners of Northern Lighthouses control n e a r l y 90 first-class lighthouses, a manned light-vessel, and about 70 " minor " lights.

So far we have said little about the light itself. How is the intense beam produced, and projected far across the sea? Coal fires were used for the South Foreland lighthouse until about 1793, and it was not until well into the 19th century that those in the Isle of Man began to burn oil. Even a ring of tallow candles was once used, as at first in the Eddystone. The oil was a vegetable or animal product, for (as you may read in the story of Lamps) petroleum oils did not become available until about 1860. The French inventor Aimé Argand made some improvements in oil lamps by using a tubular wick and admitting air to the centre; he also used a glass chimney, which improved the draught. Carcel, another Frenchman, devised clockwork pumping mechanism to feed oil to the burner steadily.

A famous early lighthouse was that of the Tour de Cordouan, on a rocky islet in the mouth of the River Gironde; in 1782 it was lit by 24 oil lamps each with a spherical reflector behind it, made of polished metal. The result can be judged by the fact that local seafarers asked the authorities to scrap this lighting plant, and to go back to the former primitive method of burning coals in an iron basket! As we explain in our story of the Mirror, a spherical reflector gathers up only a small portion of the light, and does not send much in the required direction. Then reflectors having the form of a parabola—the kind of curve that you get if you slice through a cone sideways—began to be used; the parabolic reflector sends out its light in the form of a cylindrical beam, for all practical purposes, and this is therefore the type which is used at the present day for motor-car lamps and searchlights.

Augustine John Fresnel, a French scientist (1788–

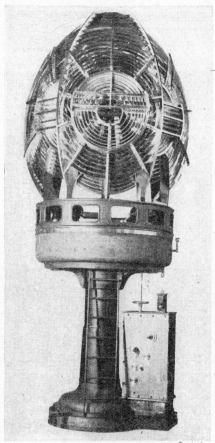

Topical

LIGHTHOUSE LANTERN
At the lower right is the clockwork mechanism which rotates this lantern so that its light can be seen at certain intervals, thus enabling sailors and airmen to identify the lighthouse.

1827) conceived the idea of placing a lens and prisms in front of the light so as to refract and reflect (see Light) the rays from the lamp and send out the greater quantity in a parallel beam. His idea, briefly, was to make the lens of stepped form —as if a number of circular lenses, each wider than the last, were cemented together around one another except that, in actual practice, he did away with the overlapping portion of the lenses. Also, above and below the lens so made, Fresnel placed a number of concentric ring-shaped prisms in order to catch and project yet more light rays, which otherwise would have been wasted.

Fresnel did much to improve the oil lamps of the day, and his system was installed in the Tour de Cordouan in 1823; it was said to give results eight times better than the existing reflector system. After this, lens-panels built up of concentric prisms came generally into use. In our own day, because of advances in optical science, and in the manufacture of lenses and the material from which they are formed, the light from a lighthouse lantern depends quite as much on the lens system as upon the intensity of the light-source.

One of the first uses of the electric arc-lamp, and of the generator which Holmes had produced (improving on a design of Professor Nollet, of Brussels), was to light the lantern of the South Foreland lighthouse (1858). It was mainly because of a favourable report on Holmes's machine by Michael Faraday that Trinity House took this bold step. Electric light in the form of electric filament lamps is used today for lighthouses which are so placed that current can be generated at the site or taken to them conveniently, and also on light-vessels. Most lights, however, including those in isolated situations and sometimes on light-vessels, are produced by petroleum oil, vaporised and burnt in incandescent mantles (see Lamp), or by acetylene gas. This gas, compressed in steel cylinders, is used for automatic lights, being turned on and off and ignited by clockwork mechanism or by devices actuated by the presence or absence of sunlight.

Lightning. When we think what a terrifying thing a lightning flash—with its accompanying peal of thunder—can be, it is hardly surprising that the ancients held it to be a supernatural thing, a sign of the displeasure of the gods. Nowadays we know that it is a natural display of static electrical discharges between charged clouds and the earth. Benjamin Franklin proved that in 1750.

with his famous kite-flying experiment, when he drew sparks from the wetted string to which the kite was attached.

Although it is so long ago since the electrical nature of a discharge was proved, there is still no complete agreement between scientists as to the theory of lightning discharges; the following may be taken as a general idea of what happens.

A cloud accumulates a charge of static electricity (*see* Electricity) by the action of rising currents of air on little drops of moisture. When this charge has built up to a certain amount (which may be as high as a thousand million volts) one of three things may happen : (1) If two portions of a cloud are at different potentials, a discharge may take place within the cloud itself. This is frequently known as " sheet " lightning (although a good deal of so-called sheet lightning is no more than the reflections of flashes far beyond the horizon). (2) If the cloud has a heavy positive charge, it will discharge to the earth. (3) If the cloud has a heavy negative charge, the flash will take place from the earth to a cloud.

A lightning stroke does not occur all at once as a plain spark discharge. First there come—in rapid succession—a series of " streamers " or " leaders," each one ionising (*see* Electro-Chemistry) a path through the air, and each one getting a little nearer to the earth (in the case of a positive stroke), until the path is prepared for the main stroke. Some of the leaders wander off by the shortest route, as they find paths where the air is " weak." These often die out without ever reaching the earth and are responsible for the branching tree-like appearance of a lightning flash. The whole takes only a few microseconds (millionths of a second) to accomplish, so that one's eye seems to see everything at once.

The current in a lightning flash is very high (from 10,000 to 100,000 amps.), and the heating effect is so tremendous that the air in the path of the stroke suddenly expands and flies outwards, leaving a partial vacuum. The noise made by the air rushing back to fill this causes the sound known as thunder. Although it happens instantaneously, we hear a long-drawn rolling noise because the sound from the far end of the flash has to travel a mile or more, and sound is comparatively slow, taking about five seconds to cover a mile. We can use this fact if we wish to measure roughly how far away a distant flash is, by counting the seconds in the interval that elapses between flash and thunder.

During weather suitable for thunderstorms balls of fire sometimes appear on high trees, on lightning conductors, or on the masts of ships. This luminous blue flame is known as " St. Elmo's Fire " and is a glow caused by the concentration of electrical stress at the point.

When a lightning flash strikes a bad conductor such as a tree or a house, it has a shattering effect ; for this reason it is usual to provide tall buildings with a " lightning conductor " of heavy copper wire to provide a low-resistance path to earth for the stroke, and so prevent damage. The power in a lightning stroke is very considerable, running into millions of kilowatts; but since it lasts only a matter of microseconds the actual energy is not as high as has been sometimes thought. An average flash would represent something like 3–4,000 kilowatt-hours

R. Bates

FIERY PATTERN OF THE LIGHTNING FLASH

In forked lightning (above) the ' branches ' are really a series of separate flashes passing from cloud to cloud or from cloud to earth and following at intervals so short that the eye registers them as one. The violent expansion of the air when raised to a very high temperature by lightning is the cause of thunder.

of electricity—enough to run the average all-electric house for about three months.

In order to study lightning in the laboratory for testing purposes, what are known as "surge generators" are used. These consist usually of a number of large condensers which are charged in parallel and discharged in series (see Electricity). By their use, strokes up to two or three million volts can be produced—puny when compared with Nature's efforts, but of very great value in experimental work intended to improve the behaviour of electrical machinery.

Lilac. With its scented creamy white or pinkish purple, crimson or violet inflorescences this shrub makes a delightful show in spring.

The lilac (*Syringa vulgaris*) has been grown in England for well over 300 years; it was first introduced in 1597 from Persia. *S. persica* is the true Persian lilac, and there are other oriental species. The lilac is a relative of the privet and the ash, and, like them, a member of the order *Oleaceae*. When it is not in flower it can be recognized by its smooth, pale green, heart-shaped leaves, and when these have fallen, the buds, arranged neatly in opposite pairs on the shoots, and bright green in colour, easily distinguish it. There are many cultivated varieties, both single and double, ranging in height up to 20 feet. The wood of the common lilac is fine grained and is used in inlaying.

Lille (Pron. lēl). The largest and most prosperous city of northern France, Lille stands on the River Deule, seven miles from the Belgian frontier. Lille is noted for its thriving textile and iron manufactures, its historic old churches, its Palais des Beaux Arts, one of the finest picture galleries in France, and its wonderful library.

For centuries Lille has been famed for the making of fine lawn, linen and damask cloths, and flax thread for lace-making and for sewing; "lisle" thread gets its name from the city. Cotton manufactures are important, as is the making of ribbons and velvet. The city has locomotive and bridge-building works, and manufactures beet sugar, chemicals, tobacco, and soap. Among its educational institutions is the university.

In the 12th century Lille was one of the principal commerical cities of Flanders, and after belonging successively to Flanders, Burgundy, Austria and Spain it was captured by Louis XIV of France in 1667. In the War of the Spanish Succession it was taken by Marlborough and Prince Eugene, but the Treaty of Utrecht restored it to France. In 1792 the Austrians bombarded Lille continuously for nine days and nights, but they were unable to capture the city.

In the First World War (1914–18) Lille was taken by the Germans in October 1914, remaining under German occupation for four years. In the Second World War (1939–45) it was again in German occupation, from May 29, 1940, to September 4, 1944, when the Germans evacuated the city. Allied air raids inflicted damage on railway and industrial installations. The population is 201,500.

Lily. Since so many of its members are used for food, including asparagus, onions, leeks, garlic and chives, the lily family (*Liliaceae*) is one of the important groups of plants. The white lily stands for purity, and artists have for centuries pictured the

E. J. Tyler

BEAUTIFUL LILAC BLOSSOM
Not all lilacs are the colour that their name implies. The fine spray of clustered blossom seen here is one of the specially developed white species. While quite hardy, it is often forced into early flower in a heated greenhouse.

angel Gabriel coming to the Virgin Mary with a spray of lilies in his hand, to announce that she is to be the mother of the Christ-child; hence one species, the white *Lilium candidum*, is known as the Madonna lily. This plant grows wild in Southern Europe and is hardy enough to thrive in British gardens. It was long used as the Easter lily for Church decorations, but since its flowers often failed to appear in time for the festival its place for that purpose has been largely taken by the Bermuda lily (*L. longiflorum*).

Among popular varieties of coloured lilies are the tiger lily, a native of Japan, which bears dark-red purplish-spotted flowers; the Turk's cap, whose orange flowers have red spots; the Siberian coral lily, which has brilliant scarlet flowers; and the golden-rayed lily of Japan, with yellow-banded purple-spotted white flowers. The giant lily of India, which has huge funnel-shaped purple-stained flowers, grows from 10 to 14 feet high, while the other species range from two feet upwards.

The genus *Lilium* is marked by an erect stem, narrow sessile (attached without any obvious projecting support) leaves with alternate, scattered, or whorled arrangement, and large showy bell-shaped or trumpet-shaped six-parted flowers, enclosing six

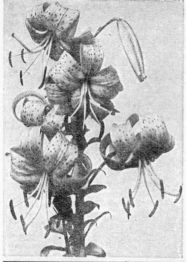

E. J. Tyler; R. Malby

HARDY LILIES FROM THE GARDEN

The unusual and striking beauty of Liliums when in full flower would lead one unfamiliar with them to imagine that they are essentially greenhouse plants. But many of them are hardy species and can be cultivated outdoors in England. These include (1) the orange-red tiger lily (*L. tigrinum*); (2) the regal lily (*L. regale*), white inside, wine-coloured outside; (3) the white, crimson spotted *L. speciosum rubrum*; and (4) the white Madonna lily (*L. candidum*).

stamens and a seed-vessel. The lily of the valley (*Convallaria majalis*) is a member of the *Liliaceae* family, as are the hyacinth and tulip. The water-lilies are not true lilies, and belong to a different family (*Nymphaeaceae*). The so-called arum lily or calla lily (*Richardia ethiopica*) is not a lily at all.

Lima. (Pron. lē′-ma). In the capital of Peru a rain storm is as much feared as an earthquake, because though the houses, with walls of adobe (sun-dried clay bricks) four to six feet thick, are almost earthquake-proof and rarely catch fire, a heavy deluge would be likely to wash away the walls, reducing most of the town to a mud heap. It is fortunate that almost from one year's end to another the city is without rain. Earthquakes have been frequent and disastrous, and dense fogs which prevail in winter render the climate unpleasant and at times unhealthy.

Lima lies in a broad valley, six miles east of Callao, with which port it is connected by railway. There are several handsome boulevards in the city, and numerous public squares. On one stands the cathedral—the finest of the 70 churches in Lima and one of the most note-worthy in Spanish America—with two lofty towers. The national University of San Marcos was founded in 1551 and is the oldest in the Americas. The city possesses zoological and botanic gardens, and an immense bull-ring. Manufactures include pottery, silver-ware, textiles, paper, soap, furniture, cocoa, tobacco, and copper and iron articles.

Lima was founded in 1535 by Pizarro, the Spanish conqueror of Peru, and became the capital of the Peruvian Republic in 1824 at the termination of Spanish rule. The population is about 628,820.

Lime. Often, among the limestone hills, you may come across curious little brick-built kilns, without much in the way of a visible chimney, and with a smoke-blackened, tunnel-like entrance. Usually such kilns are quite deserted and are merely signs of a forgotten, or rather a transformed, industry. For these are lime-kilns, in which the lime used to be burned by the local people for agricultural or building purposes. But now the industry of lime-burning, intimately connected as it is with those of cement- and concrete-making, has been centralized, and where a district may have supported 20 or more little kilns, it now has one vast cement works. That is why you seldom see a small lime-kiln being used, although lime itself is still as necessary as ever.

The process called lime burning consists of heating pure limestone or chalk (calcium carbonate, $CaCO_3$), whereby the gas carbon dioxide is liberated and quicklime (calcium oxide, CaO) is formed, thus:

$$CaCO_3 \rightarrow CaO + CO_2$$

When we treat quicklime with water, the lime

crumbles away and gets very hot, and we obtain slaked lime, calcium hydroxide, $Ca(OH)_2$, thus:

$$CaO + H_2O \rightarrow Ca(OH)_2$$

Lime is used in many processes and plays a part in removing hairs from hides, correcting acidity in soils, softening hard water, preparing insecticides like lime-sulphur wash for fruit trees, steel-making, glassmaking, the chemical industries, and in making mortar and plaster.

To make lime mortar, lime is slaked by adding water; then sand, fine cinders or pulverised stone are mixed in. As the mixture dries it absorbs carbon dioxide from the air to form calcium carbonate, and also combines with the silica of the sand to form calcium silicate. These substances bind the bricks or stones together. Quicklime exposed to air is ruined for mortar-making by absorption of carbon dioxide (air-slaking). Lime mortar is now less used than formerly, having been to a considerable extent replaced by Portland cement mortar. Lime plaster is made by mixing hair with water-slaked lime.

When a lump or stick of quicklime is heated by means of an oxy-nydrogen blowpipe flame (see Hydrogen), the lime emits a very intense white light—the limelight which once was used for stage lighting, projection lanterns, and so on. The electric arc has now largely replaced the limelight as a source of intense illumination.

A solution of calcium hydroxide in water is called lime-water. This is used in medicine to correct acidity, to prevent milk from curdling in large lumps, and with certain oils, as the emollient carron oil for burns. Lime-water reveals the presence of carbon dioxide by becoming cloudy, and you can show that your breath contains carbon dioxide by blowing through a tube dipped into lime-water. (See Cement).

Lime (LINDEN). Beneath a tall tree you may chance to find in summer-time a collection of insects, chiefly humble-bees and hive-bees, all more or less dead or crawling feebly about. This is almost certain to be a lime tree, and the bees and other insects are suffering through their own greed. For the lime tree (*Tilia europaea*), sometimes called the linden, has flowers which have an unusual amount of nectar and a strong smell. These attract the insects, which are tempted to gorge. Honey which hive-bees make from the nectar has a delicious flavour.

The common lime is not a native of England but was introduced from the Caucasus hundreds of years ago. It is a favourite tree for avenues, lives to a considerable age, and may reach a height of 100 feet. The leaves are heart-shaped, large, and pale green. The flowers are small, greenish or yellow in colour, and are attached in clusters to a leaf-like scape (leafless stem), which later bears the fruits—hard little objects like nuts with a rather woolly covering. Of the other species of lime, the bass-wood (*T. glabra*) is an important timber tree, providing light and white wood for utensils of all sorts as well as pulp for paper; its fibrous inner bark (bast) is used in the making of mats, chair seats and baskets.

These trees are not to be confused with another lime, a native of south-eastern Asia, particularly of the sub-continent of India. This is *Citrus aurantifolia*, a member of the orange family, whose fruits, like small and green lemons, provide the lime juice so popular as a drink. It is largely grown in the United States, the West Indies and Mexico.

Limerick. In the province of Munster, Eire, adjoining Tipperary, Kerry, and Cork on the south and west, and having for its northern boundary the lower reaches of the River Shannon, lies Limerick, the county of the Golden Vale and the most fertile tract in all Ireland. This meadow land is given over to grazing, and on large farms along Shannon's shores many of the finest cattle in Ireland are reared. The Shannon, navigable up to Limerick city, is well stocked with sea trout. In the south rise the Galty Mountains.

Oats and potatoes are the staple crops, but more and more land is being given to pastures on which

H. Bastin

FLOWERING LIME THAT THE BEES LOVE
Few trees attract insects so much as the common lime, for its sweet-smelling blossoms exude sticky substances that bees especially delight to feed on. Here is a big spray of the common lime, with its broad, heart-shaped leaves and small yellowish flowers, each group of which is supported by a greenish bract. The tree is quite hardy in Britain.

great numbers of live-stock are fattened for market. Milling, lace-making—for which Limerick is celebrated—and bacon-curing are important, as also is the salmon fishery. The small town of Foynes on the Shannon estuary is part of Shannon airport, which is a stopping-place for the Trans-Atlantic air services. At Ardnacrusha is the power-station of the Shannon hydro-electric plant, which supplies electricity to most of the country.

Limerick (population, 42,522), the county town, is one of the oldest cities in Ireland; it existed in the first centuries of the Christian era. County Limerick covers over 1,030 square miles, and has a population of 142,000.

Keystone

FLYING-BOAT AT FOYNES, COUNTY LIMERICK
On the estuary of the Shannon in County Limerick is the town of Foynes, which was used as a temporary base by British and American flying-boats making the first experimental flights across the Atlantic to and from Newfoundland. Above is a British flying-boat preparing for its first flight in July 1937.

Limericks.

Most people know these verses, with jingling metre and rhymes between the first, second, and fifth, and the third and fourth lines. Here is a famous example:

> There was a young lady of Riga,
> Who smiled as she rode on a tiger.
> They returned from the ride
> With the lady inside,
> And the smile on the face of the tiger.

This is the generally accepted form of a limerick. There are examples in which the last line especially

UNDERGROUND LAKE IN LIMESTONE COUNTRY
Because streams can cut deep channels in limestone, underground water often makes great caves and lakes. This lake, beneath Ingleborough Mountain, Yorkshire, is 300 yards long and 20 feet wide, and so deep that no plumb-line has yet touched the bottom.

is halt and lame, and the verse loses its point and, so to speak, drags its tail; whereas a good limerick has the greatest possible sting in its tail. Even most of the famous ones created by Edward Lear (*q.v.*), who first popularized this form of verse, have that failing, for he was prone to have the last line terminating in the same word as the first—a fault, because it wastes a chance for further humour.

It is said that the limerick originated at parties in the part of Ireland that bears that name, when each guest would compose a line towards a verse in this metre, the whole ending with the chorus, " Will you come up to Limerick ? " Another and, perhaps, more plausible theory is that the form of verse was brought to Limerick from France by returned Irish mercenary soldiers about 1790; it had long existed on the Continent.

Limestone.

One of the commonest and most useful rocks is limestone, which serves for building, for road-making, as a flux in smelting iron and lead ores, as an ingredient in Portland cement and, when burnt to lime, for making mortar and chloride of lime, as well as in numerous industrial processes.

Limestone is a sedimentary rock formed under water (*see* Geology), and is composed chiefly of calcium carbonate ($CaCO_3$). Most limestones are made of shells of molluscs and foraminifera, coral skeletons, fragments of sea-lilies, etc. ; together with such other substances as clay, iron, silica and magnesia. Fossilized shells are plainly to be seen in some limestones. Oölitic limestone resembles in texture the mass of eggs seen in fish-roe (whence its name, from Greek ōon, " egg "), and is a good building stone. Well-known varieties found in Britain are Bath, Portland, Clipsham and Ketton stones; the egg-like particles are seen noticeably in Ketton stone. Other limestones are formed by the deposit of calcium carbonate from "hard" water.

Chalk is a white soft limestone composed chiefly of the shells of foraminifera (see Chalk). Dolomite is a limestone which contains carbonate of magnesium as well as calcium. Marble is a " metamorphic " limestone—i.e. one which has suffered a change of state during its formation. It has been crystallized under pressure. Limestone, calcined in kilns (the process being called " lime-burning "), produces " stone-lime." Chalk, calcined in the same way, yields " chalk-lime."

In England, the South Downs, the Chilterns, and the other chalk ranges; the Cotswolds and the coast scenery of Dorset; the greater part of the Pennine chain, including the Yorkshire Moors and much of the Derbyshire dale scenery—all are composed chiefly of limestone, and so is much of the Silurian series of Wales.

The Carboniferous limestones are best seen in Yorkshire, in the central part of the Pennines. The limestone is easily worn by water and weather, producing the most curious formations in the rocks. There are rounded, smooth surfaces, breaking off into a sudden, knife-like edge, which may lead to a crevasse in the rock many feet in depth and only a few inches across. Such crevasses often lead into great caves, and it is in these limestone districts especially that the finest caves and " pot-holes " occur, the exploration of which is a popular sport. The Jurassic limestones of the Cotswolds give a very different type of scenery. (See also Geology ; Lime; Marble; Pennine Chain.)

From LOG CABIN to WHITE HOUSE

The greatest of American presidents, save perhaps for George Washington, and inventor of the slogan 'Government of the people, by the people, for the people,' Lincoln was a prime founder of modern democracy.

Lincoln, ABRAHAM (1809–65). As a boy the future President of the United States had few advantages, and his achievements all came from his own efforts. Lincoln was born near Hodgenville, Kentucky, United States, on February 12, 1809, when the so-called pioneer era of American history was just emerging from the Indian fighting and hunting period. The conditions of life in southern Indiana, whither the family removed in 1816, were as primitive as in Kentucky. There, on the farm near the Ohio river, Lincoln's young mother died for lack of medical attendance, in 1818.

As President, Abraham Lincoln led the Northern States to victory in the American Civil War (1861–65).

The boy of nine helped his father, a cabinetmaker by trade, to make the rough coffin in which his mother was buried. Then he wrote his first letter, one to an itinerant preacher, asking him to stop on his next round and say a prayer over her grave. To his mother, who urged him to "learn all he could and be of some account in the world," and to his capable stepmother, with her sympathy and insight, he owed much in the shaping of his character.

In the autumn of 1830 he tied his extra shirts and home-knit socks in a big cotton handkerchief, and turned his face to the nearest settlement of New Salem—to begin life as a man. He made two voyages down the Mississippi to New Orleans; served as captain of a company of volunteers against the Indians in the Black Hawk War of 1832; was a clerk in a store; acted as village postmaster, carrying all the mail in his hat; and learned surveying.

Self-educated, he began to read law, starting his legal career in 1837. He had now entered political life, but much of his time was needed to attend to his growing practice. In 1846 he served one term in Congress (parliament), but had little chance to distinguish himself. From 1848 to 1854 he was out of politics, but he was making a reputation as a lawyer and as an orator. The slavery question now became prominent, threatening to split the country in halves, and in a speech in 1858 Lincoln made an observation that set the nation thinking. " A house divided against itself," said he, " cannot stand. I believe this Government cannot endure permanently, half slave and half free." In seven public debates between Lincoln and S. A. Douglas, who upheld slavery, Lincoln proved superior to his opponent, who had been looked upon as probably the next President; and in May 1860 Lincoln was elected President by a great majority. So the man who had been born in a log cabin went to live in the White House, the President's official residence in Washington.

Lincoln was not pledged to abolish slavery—only to preserve the Union by which the States were held together to form one country, and to prevent the spread of slavery. Even after the American Civil War between the slave-owning Southern States and the Northern States broke out in 1881 the government offered to purchase the freedom of slaves in the slave States that remained loyal—Kentucky, West Virginia and Missouri. But the movement on the part of the Southern States to form a separate Government had begun as soon as Lincoln's election in November 1860 was assured. When his inauguration as President took place, on March 4, 1861, seven States had left the Union and formed the Confederate Government.

In his inaugural address Lincoln declared that the Federal Government would not attack the rebellious States, but it would " defend, protect, and preserve if attacked." A month later the

President mobilized the regular army and issued a call for volunteers. Soon all the States had arrayed themselves on one side or the other, and the Civil War that was to last four years had begun.

Lincoln's part was to steer the ship of State through the troubled waters of civil war. For two years he kept consistently to the task of preserving the Union. On January 1, 1863, he issued the Slave Emancipation Proclamation, freeing all slaves in territory occupied by the Northern armies and allowing them to enlist in the armed forces, and from then on the prosecution of the war had the added purpose of freeing the slaves.

The battle of Gettysburg was fought in July 1863, and in the following November the battlefield was dedicated as a national cemetery. Lincoln's brief speech on that occasion will ever remain one of the greatest uttered, both for its lofty sentiment and for its literary style.

" Fourscore and seven years ago our fathers brought forth on this continent a new nation, conceived in liberty and dedicated to the proposition that all men are created equal. Now we are engaged in a great civil war, testing whether that nation or any nation so conceived and so dedicated can long endure. We are met on a great battlefield of that war. We have come to dedicate a portion of that field, as a final resting place of those who here gave their lives that that nation might live. It is altogether fitting and proper that we should do this.

" But, in a larger sense, we cannot dedicate—we cannot consecrate—we cannot hallow—this ground. The brave men, living and dead, who struggled here, have consecrated it, far above our poor power to add or detract. The world will little note, nor long remember, what we say here, but it can never forget what they did here. It is for us the living, rather, to be dedicated here to the unfinished work which they who fought there have thus far so nobly advanced. It is rather for us to be here dedicated to the great task remaining before us—that from these honoured dead we take increased devotion to that cause for which they gave the last full measure of devotion—that we here highly resolve that these dead shall not have died in vain—that this nation, under God, shall have a new birth of freedom—and that government of the people, by the people, for the people shall not perish from the earth."

Love, reverence and gratitude were in the votes by which Lincoln was re-elected President in 1864. In his second inaugural address, he set forth the moral significance of the conflict then drawing to a close, and declared that the task would be finished " with malice toward none, with charity for all." On April 14, 1865, five days after the end of the war, President Lincoln was shot in Ford's Theatre, Washington, by John Wilkes Booth, an actor, and died next morning. In 1920 a statue of Lincoln, a replica of one by A. St. Gaudens in Chicago, was placed opposite Westminster Abbey, London.

Lincolnshire. Lying between the Wash and the Humber this county of East Anglia (the second largest in England) contains, within an area of 2,665 square miles, what is perhaps the most extensive and richest tract of uniformly fertile farming land in the whole of England. The county is divided into three parts—Lindsey (in which are the Wolds), Kesteven and Holland. It is drained by three rivers—the Trent, Witham and Welland.

ABRAHAM LINCOLN AMONG HIS STATESMEN

Just after the battle of Antietam, Lincoln issued his famous Proclamation of Emancipation of the Negro slaves. He is here seen reading it to the members of his Cabinet. From left to right : Stanton, Chase, Lincoln, Welles, Smith (standing), Seward (seated), Blair and Bates. The proclamation called on the Southern States to return to their allegiance before the end of the year ; otherwise their slaves would be declared free men. The Confederates (or Southerners) ignored the injunction, and the proclamation came into force, though effective only in States under Federal control.

Portions of southern Lincolnshire, within the region of the fens, have been reclaimed either from the sea or from the marshes, and the fertility of this land is extraordinary. The sugar-beet industry has added greatly to the county's prosperity in recent years; the growing of potatoes and bulbs is also of importance. The flatness of the land has facilitated the construction of a number of aerodromes, the most notable of which is Cranwell, home of the R.A.F. College.

Lincolnshire is rich in historical interest. Lincoln, the county town (with a population of 22,600) was one of the great strongholds of the Romans and afterwards of the Danes; the city has great agricultural implement factories and a noble cathedral (see illus. page 722).

The largest town in the county is Grimsby (population 78,000), one of the great fishing ports of England. Another seaside town is Skegness. Grantham (q.v.), like Lincoln, stands on the River Witham, and is an important railway junction. It has an ancient church (St. Wulfram) and market cross. Boston gave its name to the greatest city of Massachusetts, United States, the name being a contraction of Botolph's-town. The western tower of St. Botolph's Church is popularly known as Boston Stump (see illus. page 529). The population of the county is 624,500.

HIGH BRIDGE, LINCOLN

One of the very few bridges in England on which houses still stand is High Bridge (above) in Lincoln, the county town of Lincolnshire. Situated on the River Witham, Lincoln is important for its manufacture of agricultural implements.

B. C. Clayton

Lindbergh, CHARLES AUGUSTUS (born 1902). On May 20 and 21, 1927, Charles Lindbergh, then 25 years old, flew alone in a single-engined monoplane from New York to Paris. He was the first airman to conquer the Atlantic Ocean alone.

Lindbergh was born on February 4, 1902, in Detroit, Michigan, and at 18 entered the University of Wisconsin to study mechanical engineering. In March 1924 he enlisted as a flying cadet in the United States Army. The following year, having left the Army, he tested aeroplanes for a firm of aircraft manufacturers. Seasoned by more than 1,500 hours of flying, he decided to try for a prize offered for the first non-stop flight between New York and Paris. Early in the morning of May 20, 1927, Lindbergh climbed into his aeroplane, the Spirit of St. Louis, at Roosevelt Field on Long Island, New York, taking off at 7.52 a.m. At 10 p.m., local time, on May 21, a crowd at Le Bourget Airport, Paris, heard the drone of an engine.

Twenty minutes later the little machine landed, having flown 3,600 miles in 33 hours and 29 minutes.

In 1931 Lindbergh and his wife blazed a northern air route from New York to China, Mrs. Lindbergh being radio operator, navigator and co-pilot. In 1933 they made a 30,000-mile air trip to study routes and bases for commercial transatlantic flying. Lindbergh also made contributions to archaeology and the technique of medical research. In 1929, flying over Yucatan, Mexico, he photographed hitherto unknown ruins of the Mayan civilization. Working with Dr. Alexis Carrel of the Rockefeller Institute for Medical Research, he developed a new method for separating red corpuscles from blood serum. In 1935 he perfected an "artificial heart and lungs." Following the kidnapping and death of their first child, the Lindberghs settled for a time in England in 1935. They returned to the United States in 1939.

Linen. "Purple and fine linen" was the raiment of princes in Biblical days, and fine linen, which is flax fibre in a manufactured form, is a luxury still. The glossy lustre of fine table damask rivals silk brocade. The whiteness of bleached linen and its smooth, dirt-repelling surface make it most suitable for shirts, collars and handkerchiefs. Because it is an excellent conductor of heat, linen sheets and garments are delightfully cool for summer. Linen towels are preferable to cotton because they absorb moisture more readily. Its great strength when stretched makes linen desirable for sail-cloth and for the most delicate hand-made laces.

Linen is woven from the fibres of flax (q.v.), and gets its name from the Latin *linum* (flax). The fibres are freed from other vegetable matter in the plant stems by "retting," or soaking in water. Certain kinds of bacteria, thus encouraged to grow, weaken the resinous substance which binds the fibre to the flax-straw. The stalks are then passed through fluted rollers to break them and facilitate the removal of the straw. Next the flax is combed and straightened, and the short fibres—known as tow—are removed from the longer ones. Following these preliminary processes, the fibre is spun, and then goes as yarn to the mills for weaving into linen.

The valley of the Nile was the original home of flax and linen and, being a symbol of purity, linen was the only material that Egyptian priests

Fox

IRISH LINEN LAID OUT TO BLEACH
World-famous for its quality is the linen made in Northern Ireland from home-grown and imported flax. In this field at Muckamore, Co. Antrim, wet linen is being laid out in strips on the grass to be whitened in the sun.

a generic and a specific name (*see*, particularly, pages 434–5 in our story of Biology). These names are given according to the "Linnean system" of nomenclature, and it was invented by Carl von Linné. Indeed, the title of "The Father of Modern Botany" may well go to the first and greatest of classifiers, so fundamental was the work of the great Linnaeus—to use the Latinized form of his name.

For it is to Linnaeus that we owe the system of nomenclature now used to designate every plant; he it was who first worked out, perhaps roughly and inaccurately in detail, the great system of natural classes, orders, families, sub-families, genera, species

were allowed to wear. Some of the chief centres of linen manufacture today are Belfast (Northern Ireland), Dundee and Dunfermline (Scotland), Leeds (Yorkshire), and certain towns in northern France, Belgium, and, in normal times, Germany.

Linné, CARL VON. (Pron. lin-nā). (1707-78). As you read the numerous articles in this book dealing with living things you will notice that they all have scientific names, consisting of two parts,

and varieties, upon which botanical study was built; and it was Linnaeus who invented the "binomial" naming of plants, *i.e.* the use of two Latin names, one for genus, one for species, by which every plant is labelled.

Carl Linné—he was later ennobled as Carl von Linné—was born at the little village of Reashult, in the province of Smaland, Sweden, on May 23, 1707. His father was the village pastor. At a very early

Reproduced from Linnaeus, by B. D. Jackson

LINNAEUS TIRED OUT AFTER A DAY IN THE FIELDS
Many were the delightful days young Carl Linné (or Linnaeus) would spend wandering in the fields and lanes round his home in Sweden in search of some new object for his beloved botanical collection. Even as a child plants and flowers interested him far more than toys, and what was first a youthful hobby became the study of a long lifetime of hard work.

age the boy knew the names of the plants in his father's garden and in the neighbourhood. It was intended that young Linné should become a pastor, eventually, like his father, and he took up theological studies at Lund. But his teachers found that he had so little aptitude for classical languages and for theology that it was deemed futile to go on. They advised the father to apprentice the lad to some handicraft. Happily a professor of medicine discerned Linné's gifts, and offered to help him in the study of medicine. So the youngster took up the new learning, first at Lund and then at Upsala university. He made friends with the botanical professor at Upsala, who lent him books, and all the while his passion for studying flowers increased.

After two years at Upsala, Linné was lucky enough to get an appointment as junior professor of botany, and the gardens of the botanical department were placed under his care. Then Rudberg, senior professor of botany, recommended that young Linné should be sent out to make a study of the flora of Lapland for the Swedish Academy of Sciences. Later he went to Holland to study further and to work for his degree as Doctor of Medicine, which he took at Leiden (Leyden).

His first great book, Flora Lapponica, was published in 1737. His work attracted the attention of a Dutch banker, who made him director of his extensive gardens and greenhouses. It was during his stay in Holland that Linné gave the world his most important works, Systema Naturae, Fundamenta Botanica, and Genera Plantarum. After a visit to England, another stay in the Netherlands, and a visit to France, Linné returned to Sweden. In 1742 he was appointed professor of botany at Upsala, having already held the professorship of medicine. At Upsala, Linné remained for the rest of his life, and it was there that he died, on January 10, 1778. In his various works Linné set out

CARL LINNÉ, FATHER OF BOTANY
Naturalist and physician, Linné—or Linnaeus, as he is more familiarly known—brought into use the system of naming plants and animals generally employed today. This statue of him was erected in 1948 at Reashult, his birthplace in Sweden.

his now universally accepted system; he made mistakes in details, as was to be expected of a pioneer in this field, but the fundamental principles he established remain as the basis of modern systematization, though some of his ideas have been modified and many of his names abandoned. His manuscripts, library, and collections of plants were obtained in perpetuity by the Linnean Society of London. His published works number more than 180.

In 1948 a new statue of Linné, by Gerda Sprinchorn, was erected on the spot where the house had stood in which the great botanist was born. It depicts him as a youth admiring a flower which he holds.

Linnet. One of the commonest birds of agricultural districts in Britain, living in hedgerows and on gorse-covered lands, the linnet is a member of the finch group. The cock linnet (*Linota cannabina*), notable for its twittering song, is marked in summer with bright red on head and breast; the upper parts of its body are rich brown in colour. The lead-blue of the conical beak is in sharp contrast. The nest is placed deep in a hedgerow, often in a thorn bush, or among thick brambles or gorse. It is made of twigs and fibres, lined with moss and hairs, and contains four or five bluish, red-spotted eggs. Usually there are two broods in a season.

Other birds sometimes called linnets are the twite, or mountain linnet (*L. flavirostris*), a brownish finch living in moorland districts; and the greenfinch, often called the green linnet. Closely related to the linnets, and resembling them in their habits, are the redpolls, of which one, the lesser redpoll (*Acanthis linaria*), is common in parts of England. This is a smaller bird than the linnet — indeed, the smallest British member of the finch family; it is a rich red-brown above, pink on the breast, and white below. It can be recognized by its continual twittering, and by the red crown which gives it its name.

C. W. Teager

SONGSTER LINNET
The twittering song of the common linnet is a familiar sound in the neighbourhood of British hedgerows and on gorse commons. Except during the breeding season these birds are seen in flocks. They feed upon the seeds of thistle and dandelion.

Linoleum AND OILCLOTH. Linoleum was introduced as a floor covering in England in 1860 by Frederick Walton, who coined the name from two Latin words meaning flax and oil, and patented the special process of manufacture. It is made by mixing ground cork, oxidized linseed oil, various gums, and colouring matter, then pressing the mass on a backing of jute burlap (coarse canvas). It is hung in drying rooms to season for a period of one to six weeks, depending on the thickness and quality of the material.

Plain linoleum has no pattern and is in solid colours, or in two tones of one colour. Printed linoleum is made by impressing a design of oil paints on a plain lino. Inlaid linoleums, the most expensive kind, have the colour and pattern extending through to the canvas backing. The pieces, of varying shape and colour, are cut from plain linoleum material of a superior kind, and in the course of manufacture are laid on the backing and bonded to it. Inlaid linoleum thus shows the pattern all through its wearing life.

An inexpensive felt-base floor-covering which resembles printed linoleum has a base of paper or felt saturated with asphalt and finished with paint and a printed design. Oilcloth is made by coating coarse cloth with white lead mixed with pigments, then printing a pattern on the surface.

The WONDER-MACHINES of PRINTING

The Linotype has made the speedy production of newspapers possible, by casting lines of type as an operator taps out the words on a keyboard. Moreover, the Teletypesetter enables an operator hundreds of miles away to work it!

Linotype. Of all the crafts that men practise, printing is one of the most intricate and complicated, and for that reason it was one of the latest to be mechanized. Perhaps the most important progress made in the development of letterpress printing is that associated with the actual type setting. For nearly 450 years all type was set from single type characters, which characters were picked up one at a time by the compositor, inserted in a special box, known as a composing stick, and when the line was approximately full, spaced out in a like manual way. This was an expensive as well as a slow process, and the average compositor setting type in that way could not compose more than about 1,000 letters per hour on an average.

Very many attempts were made by engineers and others to reduce this laborious method of type setting to a purely mechanical effort. At first the inventors endeavoured to use ordinary type characters, and by means of a keyboard mechanism to assemble them more quickly than they could be set by hand, and several kinds of this form of machine were made.

But, in a way, the inventors were on the wrong track. What really mattered was that the printer should be able to get a column of type, or a solid printing mass which corresponded to a column of type, without the labour of picking up all the thousands of pieces of type which go to make a column. To give you an idea of this task, one of our own full text columns contains about 3,000 separate letters, punctuation marks or spaces. By the old hand-setting method every one would have to be picked up separately from the type-case and arranged in lines. Then, after a stereo plate had been made from the column—or, of course, from two columns arranged in a page—every piece would have to be distributed, or put back into its proper box ready for setting up into the next job. Ottmar Mergenthaler (1854-99) invented the first model of the Linotype and by the year 1886 he had built a practical working machine. He was a German by birth and a watchmaker by trade, emigrating to the United States of America when 18 years of age. His machine did not set up type. Instead, it arranged in lines the moulds which formed the tops of type letters, bearing the characters, and from these moulds, placed on a box forming the shank or the rest of the cast "slug," a line of type was cast in type-metal. At one stroke Mergenthaler had abolished not only the labour of setting type by hand, but also the fiddling job of putting the type back into the boxes again after printing or stereotyping.

This book is printed from separate type cast and assembled by the 'Monotype' (*q.v.*), not from slugs made by the Linotype. Most books are set up by 'Monotype' or other typecasting and setting machines, because correction of errors is more easy. Individual letters or words can be picked out by the correcting compositor and altered. If an alteration has to be made in Linotype-set work, the entire line-slug must be taken out and be replaced by a new line in which the desired alteration has been made. For this reason Linotype is used for newspaper work generally, and the other type of machine for bookwork.

Although the Linotype of 1886 was commercially practicable, it did not meet all the demands of the printer or satisfy the inventors, despite the fact that they had already suffered 10 years of disheartening failure. But it contained many mechanisms which are still part of the modern Linotype.

The initial effort which in due course led up to the invention of the Linotype was the result of an inspiration which occurred to five shorthand writers in 1876, as a result of a conversation between them. At that time they had no idea of producing a type-composing machine, but had in mind the production of a machine operated by a keyboard to indent steel characters on papier-mâché, which papier-mâché in strip form was then crimped so as to re-adjust the words for line spacing. These strips in due course were pasted into column form and ultimately into page form, to make a mould from which stereotypes were cast. This ingenious method failed, as did many other developments which followed it. In due course a stage was reached where strip brass matrices, each bearing a different character, were arranged side by side to form a mould from which " slugs " were cast.

Linotype & Machinery, Ltd.

MACHINE WHICH ASSEMBLES MATRICES AND CASTS LINES OF TYPE

The Linotype assembles in lines, properly spaced out word by word, the matrices which constitute the top of the line-moulds and determine the 'characters' of the individual letters. The other three sides of the line-mould are formed by the mould-box against which the assembled line of matrices is brought. Molten lead is pumped into the mould-box, the resultant slug being pushed out and trimmed. After use, the matrices are distributed to the magazine again.

Ultimately the matrix characters were separated and stored in a magazine for use again, and there-after the Linotype machine gradually assumed the shape more or less as we now know it.

The Linotype, as we have seen, is not a type-setting machine ; it creates lines of metal which can be used for direct printing or, as in newspaper work, can be used for making papier-mâché moulds from which stereotype plates are produced. Each of these lines of metal, or slugs, is the length and width of a line of type, and has on its upper edge the necessary type characters to print an entire line. After use these slugs are melted down and used for recasting into other slugs. The practice of returning every single type character and space to its particular box, as with hand-set types, is thus done away with.

A matrix consists of a flat metal plate which has on its vertical edge a die or dies such as would be formed if we pressed a separate printing type into some soft substance such as wax. The matrix has in its upper portion a series of teeth in a V-shaped notch which are used for selecting and carrying it to its proper place in the magazine or container. This container has a series of grooves or channels along which the matrices slide on their edges, and from its lower end they drop, one by one, when released by the depression of a key button on the keyboard.

When the operator depresses a key it releases a matrix from the magazine above. The matrix falls down on to a constantly revolving belt into a box, which represents the stick of the hand compositor. The matrices come down in the order required for making words. After each word a " space-band " is inserted by depressing a key. When the matrices and space-bands have been assembled to fill a line, the operator raises the whole line by depressing a handle. Thereafter the entire operation of casting the line and returning the matrices to their original places is affected mechanically, and the operator can begin to assemble the next line.

The line just assembled is transferred to the front of the mould, which is slotted from the front to the rear and is of a size determined by the " body " (or depth) and the length of the slug to be cast. (The slot forms three sides of a mould corresponding to a line, and the row of matrices makes the fourth side.) While the line of matrices and space-bands is in front of the mould, the space-bands, which are like double wedges, are spread upwards until the words are spaced out to fill the line. At this moment the slot in the mould and the dies of the row of matrices are filled with molten metal to produce a slug.

The molten metal is contained in a pot behind the mould wheel, and is kept in a molten state within by a Bunsen gas flame or by electrically heated elements. The molten metal is forced into the mould and matrices by a plunger, which pumps the metal up the delivery mouth into the mould, where it solidifies and forms a slug. After casting, the mould wheel revolves and brings the slug into a vertical position, where it is pushed by an ejector

through two parallel trimming knives into a tray or " galley." At the back of the mould wheel is a knife which trims the bottom of the slug.

While the slug is being trimmed and ejected, the matrices and space-bands, having finished their work, are returned for use to their original places. The matrices are first lifted vertically to an intermediate channel, thence they move sideways to the right until their teeth engage in the ribs of a bar which has descended to receive them. This bar then rises and lifts the whole line of matrices to the distributor mechanism at the top of the magazine. In the meantime the space-bands, which have remained behind (because they have no teeth to engage in the bar), are transferred by a " grabber " to their original position in their own box again.

The method by which each matrix is returned to its proper channel in the magazine is very ingenious and is as follows : Each matrix, as we have said, has a number of teeth in a V-shaped notch formed by its top portion. These teeth are not the same in every matrix, but are arranged in a particular order or combination, according to the characters—letters or punctuation marks—the matrices bear. Every matrix differs in its combination from a matrix bearing any other different character, and the teeth play an important part in effecting the return of the matrices to their respective places. We may compare the toothed V-notch to a key; it will allow the matrix to drop only when opposite its proper place.

A rigid notched bar is fixed in position above the open ends of the magazine mouth, and is so made as to engage the teeth and hold them in suspension. The ribs of the bar vary in number and continuance along its length. The matrices are pushed on the bar at one end and carried along it over the mouths of the channels. Each matrix is engaged by its teeth on the bar *until it arrives over its proper channel*, where the correct combination of teeth allows the matrix to disengage itself, at gaps in the grooving of the bar, so that it falls into its own channel. The matrices are carried along the bar by means of longitudinal screws, which lie below the bar in such a position as to engage the edges of lugs on the matrices, and carry them along the bar.

So far, we have described the Linotype as a manually-operated machine; but it can also be remotely controlled— that is to say, the operator can be stationed many miles away from the Linotype which produces the type matter he is composing. The apparatus responsible for this wonderful development is known as the Teletypesetter; and, as its name denotes, the work of the operator is conveyed to the machine by telegraph.

In order better to understand how the apparatus functions let us give an actual example of what happens in the case of one of our big national daily newspapers, The Scotsman. It is printed and published in Edinburgh, but some of the typesetting (or shall we say the means of typesetting) is done on the first floor of a building in Fleet Street, London.

Linotype & Machinery, Ltd

KEYBOARD OF A LINOTYPE MACHINE
Pressure on a key releases a matrix from the magazine, and in this way matrices for a line of words are assembled. The long keys at either side (above) control the space-bands. On the keyboard the letters are arranged in the approximate order of frequency with which they occur in English.

Before the Teletypesetter was installed, such news matter as the stock market prices were telegraphed from London to Edinburgh every evening. That was a slow and laborious process. But nowadays the telegraphists in the London office operate keyboards which perforate continuous paper strips. The holes in the paper are arranged to form certain coded combinations representing the type characters they are to reproduce. These per-

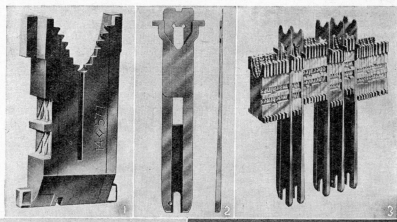

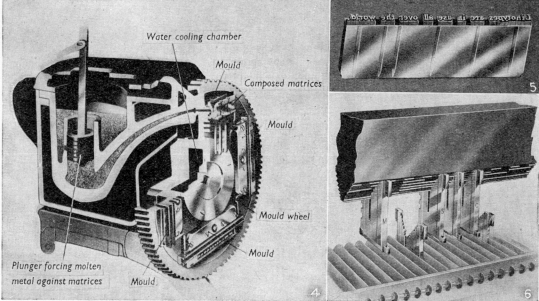

Linotype & Machinery, Ltd.

SOME OF THE MORE IMPORTANT DETAILS OF THE LINOTYPE

The matrix (1) can be used for two alternative letters ; note the toothed V-shaped notch at the top. Front and side views of a space-band are shown (2) ; these wedge-shaped pieces of metal are in two parts and are wider at the bottom than at the top, being pushed up if wider spacing is needed. The space-bands are the long members seen in (3) ; two of the words are at a higher level, to allow the alternative (italic) letters on the matrices to be used. An assembled line of matrices is seen against the mould on the mould wheel in (4), ready to be cast into a slug like that in (5). After use, the matrices slide along a grooved bar (6), dropping off into their respective magazines where the grooving corresponds with the arrangement of the teeth in the V-shaped notch and by which, until then, they had hung on the bar.

forated rolls of paper are fed into telegraph machines, which cause electrical impulses to travel over the wire to the office in Edinburgh, where the receiving apparatus reproduces a duplicate of the perforated roll made in London.

The rolls are then taken to the Teletypesetter-equipped Linotypes, and are inserted in the operating units attached to the keyboards. At each forward movement of the paper tape, six pins rise against the tape. According to the code in position at that instant some of the pins pass through the holes of the tape while others are blocked. This movement of the pins controls the setting of six code bars extending beneath the Linotype keyboard, which, in conjunction with a revolving cam, operate that keyboard.

But this apparatus does a good deal more, for it also determines whether the type characters are to be in a bold face, roman, or italic ; and it sends the matrix lines away for casting. In short, the Teletypesetter performs every function that would normally be done by a human operator.

Lion. Strange as it may seem, the lion and domestic cat belong to the same family of animals. In fact, they are much alike, except in size and colour. Of course, there are other differences of minor importance. Thus, the pupil of the cat's eye is elliptical; that of the lion is round. The cat is a good tree-climber, while the lion does not normally climb trees. The cat's fur is of nearly equal length all over its body, while the male lion possesses a mane which, when at its best, covers the fore-part of its body, including the head, and gives it a majestic appearance. The lion also has a tuft of black hair at the tip of the tail.

In ancient times the lion (*Felis leo*) inhabited the whole of Africa, all the southern part of Asia, and a large part of south-eastern Europe. It is still found in parts of Africa and in the north-west of the sub-continent of India, though in reduced numbers.

A large lion measures from nine to 10 feet in length, including the tail, and is four feet high at the shoulder. Its strength is prodigious. With a single blow of its massive forepaw it can crush the skull of an ox or break the back of a horse, and it is capable of carrying off a bullock in its jaws. It can cover 30 feet at a bound, and few animals other than antelopes can outrun it over short distances. Its tawny colour blends readily with its natural surroundings, making it almost invisible at a short distance.

Authorities disagree in regard to the hunting habits of lions. It seems probable that as a rule they live and hunt singly, except during the mating season and while the young are half-grown, when the whole family unites in the chase.

In common with most members of the cat family, the lion prefers to hunt at night, setting forth at sunset and lying in wait for its prey at a water hole, or stalking its quarry stealthily, taking advantage of every bit of cover.

Man-eating lions are not common. It is said that usually they are very old lions, too slow to catch the alert and speedy antelopes or zebras which formed their prey when young, and that, like the tiger, when once they taste human blood they persist in the habit as long as they live. Man-eating lions have been known to enter native villages and carry off a man or a woman in their jaws, in spite of fires and shouts and beating drums.

The young of the lion, generally only two in a litter, are born in a den in some secluded spot selected by the mother lion, who guards them and does not permit even the male lion to approach. Like the tom-cat, the lion is inclined to make a meal of his offspring. The mane begins to grow on the young male lion during its third year, but it does not attain its full growth until the seventh or eighth year. In captivity lions sometimes reach the age of 15 ; in the wild state they live for over 30 years.

ANDROCLES'S ADVENTURES WITH A LION

EARLY one morning in the 1st century of the Christian era a weary man came to a cave in an African desert, and flinging himself on the ground fell asleep. He was a Roman slave named Androcles (pron. an'-dro-klēz), or Androclus, who

Androcles removing the thorn from the lion's paw ; from the painting by Briton Riviere, R.A.

had been carried from Rome to northern Africa and for long had watched his chance to escape.

He was awakened by a terrific roar, and starting up he saw a lion standing at the entrance to the cave. He had been sleeping in the lion's den. There was no way of escape ; the beast barred the way. Terror-stricken, he waited for it to spring upon him and tear him to pieces. But the lion did not move. It stood there moaning and licking one of its paws. Then Androcles noticed that the paw was pierced by a big thorn and that blood was flowing from the wound. Seeing the animal in pain he forgot his fear, and taking the paw in his hand drew out the thorn and stopped the blood.

For three years Androcles and the lion lived together in the cave. They hunted together, ate together, and slept together. But Androcles longed to be once more among his fellow-men, and one day he left the cave—and was caught by some soldiers and sent to Rome. In those days the Romans ordered runaway slaves to be thrown into the arena to fight wild beasts for the public amusement.

Androcles was pushed into the arena, a lance was thrust into his hand, and he was told to defend himself against a lion which had been kept without food for several days in order to make it more ferocious. Androcles shook with fear as the cage was opened and the lion sprang out. But instead of rushing upon him, the animal began to lick his hands. Then he saw it was the lion that had been his companion in the cave. Androcles leaned against the lion's mane and wept.

Naturally the people who were watching the show marvelled at the sight. The emperor sent for Androcles, and when he

THE MAJESTIC LION ON THE ALERT AND AT PLAY

Daily Mail; Sport and General

Conditions in a modern zoo are so arranged as to be as nearly 'natural' as can be contrived, and most animals soon become 'at home.' Even the King of Beasts, the majestic lion, does not appear to be unhappy, as these photographs show. At the top, zoo lion cubs are trying to get father to wake up and play with them. The lower photograph was taken at the Zoological Society's open-air establishment at Whipsnade, in Bedfordshire, which was opened to the public in 1931. This head-on view of two fine males suggests something of the prodigious strength of the lion. A large specimen may measure 10 feet from muzzle to tail-tip and be four feet high at the shoulder.

2 IR 4

heard his story he set him free and presented him with a large sum of money. After that, whenever Androcles walked through the streets of Rome, and wherever else he wandered, the lion followed him about like a dog.

This story was told by the Roman author Aulus Gellius (*c.* A.D. 130–180).

Liquorice. Used as a flavouring for sweetmeats and for medicinal purposes, liquorice is made from the juices of a member of the pea family, *Glycyrrhiza glabra*. They are obtained from the long plant roots which extend down for more than a yard. The plant is cultivated in the warmer parts of the Old World, especially Turkey, Russia, Italy, Iraq, the sub-continent of India, and Spain, and has long been valued. The generic name *Glycyrrhiza* is a Greek word meaning sweet-root.

Stick liquorice is made by straining and concentrating the solution obtained by boiling the crushed roots. Mixed with sugar it is made into cough-drops, syrups and sweetmeats, and is used to disguise distasteful medicines.

Lisbon. Nine miles from the Atlantic, up the wide, swift channel of the River Tagus, lies Lisbon, the capital of Portugal and most western seaport of continental Europe. The approach from the sea is like a trip up the neck of a gigantic bottle, for immediately above the city the river broadens out into a tidal lake, four to eight miles wide and 11 miles long, forming one of the best harbours in the world. The wharves and quays stretch along the northern banks of the river and lake for five miles. Beyond them the city rises in terrace upon terrace of white houses and green parks, backed by the lofty granite mountains of the Cintra range.

Lisbon is almost entirely a modern city, for the earthquake of 1755, which killed more than 30,000 of its inhabitants, left only a small section of the town standing. That part contains interesting relics of ancient days. Here in the cathedral, first built in 1150, is the tomb of St. Vincent, patron saint of Lisbon. The modern part is not surpassed in beauty by any European capital. The streets are straight and broad, the finest being the Avenue of Liberty, a mile long and 300 feet wide, with a double row of trees down the middle ; its name commemorates the freeing of Portugal from Spain in 1640. Between the terraced levels of the city, lifts carry people up and down. Lisbon boasts one of the finest botanical gardens in Europe.

The industries include distilling, dyeing, the manufacture of silk, linen, wool, and cotton cloths, pottery, soap, paper, chemicals, cement and glass, and preserved foods. It is a busy railway centre, and its fisheries are very profitable.

Lisbon was probably founded by the Phoenicians, for it was a flourishing town before the Romans occupied it. It was held by the Moors from 711 to 1147. Vasco da Gama set sail from Lisbon on his voyage round Africa in 1497, and it was from here that the Spanish Armada started on its ill-fated voyage in 1588, while the city was in the hands of Spain. Lisbon was the chief scene of the Revolution of 1910, when the crews of revolting warships shelled the palace, and King Manuel (1889–1932) was driven from Portugal and the republic established. The population of the city is 709,180.

Dorien Leigh

SPLENDID BOULEVARD IN PORTUGAL'S CAPITAL

One of the finest streets of Lisbon is the broad Avenida da Liberdade, seen above, which runs through the heart of the city. It is a mile long and is lined by handsome stone houses, while ' islands ' planted with palms and Judas-trees divide it into three carriage-ways. The monument in the foreground commemorates Portugal's emancipation from Spanish rule in 1640; that at the farther end was erected to the Marquis of Pombal, a statesman of the 18th-century.

Lisle, CLAUDE JOSEPH ROUGET DE (1760–1836). The most stirring and famous national song in the world, the French Marseillaise was composed, both words and music, in an hour by Rouget de Lisle, while sitting alone in his lodgings with his violin beside him. The song proved to be the greatest inspiring force of the French Revolution, and became the national anthem of the Republic.

De Lisle was born at Lons-le-Saunier in the department of Jura on May 10, 1760. As a young man he was fond of music and the drama, and was in a humble way a poet and a novelist. While a captain of engineers in the army, he was in Strasbourg at a banquet given by the mayor on April 25, 1792, a few days after war had been declared by France against Prussia and Austria. Something was said about the need for a national patriotic song, and in a state of excitement de Lisle went home and composed the Marseillaise, or, as he first entitled it, Le Chant de Guerre de l'Armée du Rhin. Revolutionaries from Marseilles first made the song with its rousing air their own, and when they reached Paris it electrified the capital, becoming known as the Marseillaise. De Lisle was an old man before he received a State pension and the cross of the Legion of Honour as a reward for composing the song. He died at Choisy-le-Roi on June 26, 1836.

Lister, JOSEPH LISTER, 1ST BARON (1827–1912). Few men have been privileged to confer such great benefits on humanity as did Lord Lister by his discovery of antiseptic surgery. Before his day a serious operation meant almost certain death, because gangrene and blood-poisoning nearly always occurred in the wound made by the surgeon's knife.

When in 1862 Pasteur announced his theory of fermentation and putrefaction, Lister was quick enough to apply the new theory to surgery, realizing that the formation of pus was due to bacteria. In 1866 he made the discovery that the surgical evils of his time were the result of germs, and that by the use of carbolic acid the wound could be kept antiseptic and proof against the action of germs. He also carried out important researches on materials for absorbent ligatures, the drainage of wounds, and antiseptic dressings.

From the painting by Isidore Pils, in the Louvre; photo Mansell

FRENCH NATIONAL SONG SUNG FOR THE FIRST TIME
The Marseillaise, the stirring battle song of the Revolution, later adopted as the French national anthem, was written and composed by the young soldier Rouget de Lisle. In this picture we see him singing it for the first time in public—to a group of his friends who are listening with rapt attention to the moving words and thrilling tune.

Although much of Lister's technique, particularly the use of the carbolic spray for disinfecting the air surrounding patient and operator, has become obsolete, it is untrue to say that his work has in any way been superseded. While he did appear to lay great emphasis on antisepsis—that is, the killing of germs and the destruction of septic matter in and around the wound under treatment—both his constant striving after perfect cleanliness in surgery and his occasional use of the actual term asepsis—the preventing of septic conditions due to infection with germs—prove that his work was on right and permanent lines. If today carbolic acid is little used and asepsis is attained by heat sterilization without the use of antiseptics, these are but matters of evolution which could only have begun with Lister's work. The rigorous aseptic routine of the modern operating theatre is but a continuation of Lister's meticulous care in excluding germs from wounds, infections that slew more than 1 in 5 in surgical wards in the 60's of last century.

Joseph Lister was born at Upton, Essex, on April 5, 1827, and was most of his life engaged as a professor of surgery and lecturer at Edinburgh and Glasgow Universities, and at Kings College,

Elliott & Fry
LORD LISTER
By his work in perfecting the technique of antiseptic surgery Joseph Lister made one of the most valuable of all contributions to medical science.

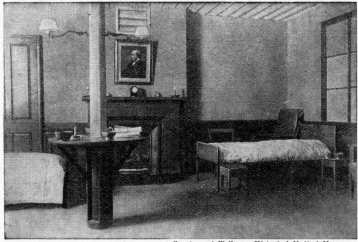

Courtesy of Wellcome Historical Medical Museum

WHERE LISTER WORKED

The great pioneer of antiseptic surgery, Lord Lister (portrait in page 1963) did much of his more important work in that connexion at the Glasgow Royal Infirmary, between the years 1861 and 1869. This photograph shows a section of a reconstruction of one of the Infirmary wards where he laboured to such good effect in the cause of suffering humanity.

customary reserve, he took the child in his arms and kissed him. At 14 years of age Liszt composed a successful operetta.

Liszt's life was a long series of artistic triumphs. As a concert pianist he has, perhaps, never been excelled. It is said that he showed the world how to perform feats in piano playing which before his time had been considered impossible. His compositions include works for the piano, organ, orchestra, and voice. He became a great teacher, counting among his pupils many of the foremost musicians of the 19th century. He became director of music to the Grand Duke at Weimar (Germany) and was decorated by every court of Europe. In 1861 he retired from public life to Rome, and later joined the Franciscan order of friars. He died on July 31, 1886, at Bayreuth, Bavaria, where he had superintended the productions of Wagner's operas.

London. He was made a baronet in 1863 and a baron in 1897. In 1902 he was created an original member of the new Order of Merit. He died on February 10, 1912.

Liszt, FRANZ (1811–86). The flickering lights of a gipsy camp-fire fell upon the gaudy garments and dark passionate faces of a group of singers gathered about it. Slightly apart in the shadow sat a pale, dreamy-faced stranger, listening. The fire burned low, and the song with its glad, mad gaiety and plaintive wistfulness died away; but still the stranger sat, transfixed and silent in the darkness.

It was the great musician Franz Liszt; and that night by the gipsy camp-fire there were born in his soul the strains that later were to leap forth at the touch of his fingers upon the piano keys in the melodies of the Hungarian Rhapsodies.

Born at Raiding in Hungary on October 22, 1811, this "Hungarian wonder child," as Liszt was called, began his public career at the age of nine. His father, an accomplished musician, taught him the theory of music and to play the piano. But the strange rhythms and weird sweet melodies of his compositions he owed to the wandering gipsy bands of his childhood home. At the age of 12 his playing so moved Beethoven that, dropping his

FRANZ LISZT

Perhaps never excelled as a concert pianist, the Hungarian composer Liszt began his public career as a musician at the age of nine.

Literature, CHILDREN'S. In any large bookshop today you will find a whole department devoted to "children's books," from picture-books for the very young to adventure stories and classics of all kinds. Yet even a century ago the number of books likely to appeal to children was comparatively limited.

Fairy stories, woven from folklore and recounted to numerous generations, are found in many medieval romances. In England until the 17th century, however, there were no printed versions. Tales and poems of animals, elves, goblins, stories of gods and heroes, were recounted throughout history; but the famous fairy stories such as Cinderella, Bluebeard, and Puss-in-Boots, were written by Charles Perrault, a member of the French Academy, and a friend of La Fontaine. His first book of fairy tales, the first to be written and published for children, appeared in France in 1697 under the title Contes de ma Mère l'Oye (Tales of My Mother Goose), and many of these stories were popular at the court of Louis XIV; they were translated into English some 30 years later.

The first story-books written for children's entertainment were published in England in the middle of the 18th century by John Newbery, a London bookseller and friend of Oliver Goldsmith—who is believed to have been the author of the most famous of them, The History of Goody Two-Shoes (1765). In The Vicar of Wakefield, Goldsmith describes the enterprising publisher of these little books, bound in "flowery and gilt" Dutch paper, as "the philanthropic bookseller of St. Paul's Churchyard." Later in the 18th century the French philosopher Jean-Jacques Rousseau, influenced by John Locke, advocated a return to the "natural state," as opposed to the highly artificial condition of society of his own day. His Emile (1762), designed primarily as an example of the philosopher's theories concerning the education of children, was a story of a boy who spends his life out-of-doors. He is allowed no books until he is 12, and then he is given Robinson Crusoe, and is supposed to relive Crusoe's experience.

To Rousseau, and to those who believed in his "noble savage," Emile represented "the natural boy." These romantic theories about children were developed by Maria Edgeworth (1767–1849) and her friend Thomas Day. Moral Tales, by Maria Edgeworth, and Thomas Day's Sandford and Merton deliberately put into nursery tales the doctrines of Rousseau. These books formed the basis of Mrs. Sherwood's The Fairchild Family (1818), just as Robinson Crusoe, by Defoe, inspired a Swiss pastor, J. D. Wyss, to write The Swiss Family Robinson (1813). Neither Robinson Crusoe nor Swift's Gulliver's Travels—both firm favourites—was intended to be read by children; the one was inspired by the adventures of the shipwrecked Alexander Selkirk; the other was a political satire.

The philosophic attitude of the 18th century suffered a reaction in Sir Walter Scott, whose romantic novels and poems introduced a new school of writers. As a boy, Scott was attracted to Percy's Reliques of Ancient English Poetry, delighting in its many fine ballads. His own Minstrelsy of the Scottish Border, The Lady of the Lake, and Marmion have a similar simplicity and directness. From Scott it is an easy transition to Macaulay's Lays of Ancient Rome—narrative poems which strongly appealed to the Victorian schoolroom and

Shock-headed Peter

Just look at him! there he stands,
With his nasty hair and hands.
See! his nails are never cut;
They are grimed as black as soot;
And the sloven, I declare,
Never once has combed his hair;
Anything to me is sweeter
Than to see Shock-headed Peter.

Courtesy of Blackie & Son, Ltd.

STRUWWELPETER

One of the most famous of children's books is Struwwelpeter or, as it is called in English, Shock-headed Peter. It was first published in Germany in 1847, and has been translated into nearly every European language. Above is a page from the book by Heinrich Hoffmann.

which have many adherents today. The Water-Babies, by Charles Kingsley, immensely popular with children of all ages, was written in part to draw attention to the hardships to which chimney-sweeps were exposed. To us it appears as a delightful fantasy, and though we have long grown familiar with such imaginative stories they were once rare in literature.

Catherine Sinclair's Holiday House, which E. V. Lucas called "the first children's book in which the modern spirit manifests itself," introduces a comic giant. This character was "so tall that he was obliged to climb up a ladder to comb his own hair." How far removed is this conception from the moral tales and model characters of an earlier age! This giant was the forerunner of a hilarious company of characters invented by writers who were masters of fantasy. Among famous examples are Heinrich Hoffmann's book Struwwelpeter (Shock-headed Peter), Edward Lear's Book of Nonsense (which, by odd twist of time, now appeals to adults rather than to children), and Lewis Carroll's Alice books.

The generation which delighted in Sir J. M. Barrie's whimsical play Peter Pan delighted also in the animal fantasies of Beatrix Potter in The Tale of Peter Rabbit (1902), Jemima Puddleduck, and Tom Kitten, just as an earlier generation sought out the works of Mrs. Molesworth (The Cuckoo Clock, 1877) and Frances Hodgson-Burnett (Little Lord Fauntleroy, 1886). Louisa M. Alcott's Little Women (1868) and its successors Good Wives and Little Men have never lost their first popularity.

The 19th century showed a remarkable development in the art and scope of literature for children. At the beginning of the century the Brothers Grimm published Kinder and Hausmärchen (Children's and Household Stories) in Germany in 1812. The two brothers collected and wrote down these stories in many different dialects. Jakob, the elder, was an authority on the derivation of words (etymology). The value of folk-tales as records of social life and of primitive beliefs is of the utmost importance, and the brothers spent 13 years in transcribing their fascinating collection.

Lighter in style, and more sentimental, are the fairy tales of Hans Christian Andersen. Even the traditional stories of Scandinavia are retold in his own manner, but the unique achievement of his invention is the "wonder story," which has had countless imitators. The Constant Tin Soldier, The Nightingale, and The Lamplighter remain supreme examples of their kind. The stories were published a few at a time between 1835 and 1872.

It is in William Blake's Songs of Innocence, published in 1789, and in Wordsworth's Lyrical Ballads, published in 1798, that the beginnings of poetry for children and the first clear recognition of childhood as a distinct element in human life are to be found. Having once discovered the "new continent of childhood in the spiritual world," poets and story-writers evolved a special literature, prose and poetry alike, created for sheer joy of companionship with children—with birds and animals, earth and sky, mountains and sea as they appear to children. To this special literature belong Wordsworth's Alice Fell, and We Are Seven, and Blake's The Lamb, and The Little Black Boy. In more recent times Walter de la Mare (born 1873) has reflected in the most imaginative poetry and prose the moods and images of childhood. His Peacock Pie, Songs of Childhood, and his anthologies Come Hither and Poems for Children have a unique place in English literature.

Anthologies designed to give children and young people the most memorable examples of poetry have been in process of making and remaking since the appearance of The Golden Treasury of Songs and Lyrics, by F. T. Palgrave (1861); The Children's Garland, compiled by Coventry Patmore (1862); and Andrew Lang's Blue Poetry Book. Poetry inspired by memories of childhood, which captured the imagination of a later generation, was R. L. Stevenson's A Child's Garden of Verse and the verses in Kipling's Jungle Book and Just-so Stories. In lighter vein during the 1920's came A. A. Milne's When We Were Very Young, and Now We Are Six, in which the hero Christopher Robin was the author's own son.

The first retelling of a classic to achieve a distinctive place in literature for children belongs to Tales from Shakespeare, by Charles and Mary Lamb. The stories of 20 plays are included in the collection published in 1807 in two small volumes. Charles wrote the tragedies, Mary the comedies. The Adventures of Ulysses, published in 1808, was the work of Charles Lamb alone. Since then there have been many translations from Homer. Hawthorne's Tanglewood Tales and Kingsley's The Heroes serve as excellent introductions to Greek mythology. Later retellings of stories from the classics include The Adventures of Odysseus, by Padraic Colum (the same author has retold also tales from the Celtic and Norse), and the fine renderings of William Morris, Sir Arthur Quiller-Couch, Andrew Lang, James Stephens, and Walter de la Mare.

School-stories and tales of adventure hold a high place in the affections of most boys and girls. The most famous school-story designed for boys is probably Tom Brown's Schooldays, by Thomas Hughes, a realistic tale of Victorian public-school life (1857); Kipling's Stalky and Co. belongs to a later age, but in the public-school tradition, and represents that educational system during one of its most properous periods. Stories of girls' schools came somewhat later. Pioneers in this field included L. T. Meade, and one of the most popular writers for girls was Angela Brazil (died 1947). The interest of the novel and short story widens as the reader grows older. Facts closely packed in school histories are apt to seem dull; for many children, indeed, they have to be related to human beings, preferably beings resembling themselves.

The historical novel, with its background of picturesque detail and its chief characters behaving in a picturesque and romantic manner, belongs to the 19th century. Scott's Kenilworth, Kingsley's Westward Ho!, and Bulwer Lytton's The Last Days of Pompeii, became standard works. The remote past can be conjured up by an imaginative and skilful writer. The Gallic Wars, for example, become of supreme interest in The Conquered, by Naomi Mitchison (1923). The same author's Boys and Girls and Gods (1931) brings before us the poetry and beliefs of the ancient world in vivid and readable form. Many historical novels combine adventurous episodes—chiefly fictitious episodes—with historical facts, and the majority of such works are characterized by a careful blending of the two for the purposes of plot. Later novelists have discarded much picturesque detail, and concern themselves with presenting historical characters in a less romantic but more accurate light.

Mark Twain, no less than Charles Dickens, turned to his own youth in The Adventures of Tom Sawyer (1876), which describes the lawless but lovable side of vagrant boyhood, and in Huckleberry Finn (1885), another reflection of youth set against the background of the Mississippi. To this period belong also R. L. Stevenson's exciting adventure stories, Treasure Island (1882) and Kidnapped (1886).

Edith Nesbit (1858–1924) introduced a refreshing naturalism of manner into children's literature. Her delightful stories The Would-be-Goods (1901) and Five Children and It (1902) are among the best examples of her art. This naturalism and simplicity marked all that was distinguished in children's books during the 20th century. Puck of Pook's Hill (1906) and its sequel, Rewards and Fairies

Illustration by Arthur Hughes to an edition of 1890, courtesy of Macmillan & Co.

TOM BROWN DEFEATS THE BULLY

After Tom (in the book Tom Brown's Schooldays) had been 'roasted' by the bully Flashman, he and his friend East decided to 'lick' him, and in hall one evening, while Diggs, an older boy, acted as referee, they set about Flashman. By means of an old wrestling throw, Tom brought him down with a crash, as shown here. The bully never attacked them again.

(1910), by Rudyard Kipling, were new and vivid interpretations of the history of England. In his Jungle Books Kipling introduced unforgettable animal characters: Bagheera the panther, Baloo the bear, and Shere Khan the tiger. The little creatures of the English countryside are the characters in Kenneth Grahame's The Wind in the Willows (1908); animals in more fantastic guise appear in The Story of Dr. Doolittle and other books by Hugh Lofting. Among the most popular writers of a later day is Arthur Ransome, the creator of stories in which fishing and sailing play a leading part. His Swallows and Amazons (1930) and Peter Duck (1932) were followed by a long series of similar books.

Lithography. This is a method of *plane* or *surface* printing from smooth stone slabs or zinc or aluminium plates. The original process as invented by the German, Alois Senefelder, in 1796, is as follows. The design is drawn on the specially prepared surface of a large, thick slab of close-texture stone, either in a greasy lithographic ink or by lithographic crayon, which is composed of soap, lamp-black, wax and oil. The essential is that the crayon or the ink shall be of a *water-repelling* character. The stone is then lightly etched with a solution of acid and gum arabic, the purpose being to set the ink of the design and to render the blank parts of the stone more retentive of water.

In printing the surface is wetted, but the water remains only upon the blank portions of the stone, being repelled by the greasy portion where is the design. When the printing rollers, carrying a special greasy lithographic ink, are run over the stone, the ink is taken only by the parts covered by the design. A sheet of damp paper is then pressed upon the slab in much the same manner as that adopted in the case of ordinary printing. If several colours are to be used, a different stone must be prepared for each colour, and the paper is printed in turn from each. If the stone is not kept wetted, it will take up ink upon other parts than those bearing the design.

The difficulty of obtaining large-size flawless slabs of the stone used (an especially porous form of limestone, called lithographic stone and found only at Solenhofen, Bavaria) led to the use of zinc sheets and, later, aluminium as substitutes. These sheets have an added merit over the heavy stones in that they can be shaped to a curved cylinder, enabling rotary printing machines to be used, with more rapid printing; but they have certain disadvantages, and real stone is still used for the finest work.

Some artists prefer not to draw direct on the stone but to transfer a drawing made on paper, also specially prepared for the purpose. The drawing is made in red pencil or charcoal and gone over with lithographic crayon. It is then damped and pressed on to the stone. The drawing is then transferred, and all marks not covered by the lithographic crayon are later etched off with the acid solution.

Apart altogether from its commerical uses, lithography is a favourite medium of expression, by artists who make original drawings on stone and then print them off or arrange for them to be printed by a firm specialising in such art work. It thus ranks with engraving in this respect, and comparatively few prints are produced of any subject, the artist amending or altering his drawing, perhaps, as he sees the result.

Among outstanding artists who have done lithography are the German, Adolph Menzel; the Frenchmen Honoré Daumier and Ignace Fantin-Latour; the Spaniard Francisco Goya; and, in Britain, Samuel Prout. Whistler did much to revive lithography in America. Poster artists of note who used this medium include Henry Bone, Louis Raemakers and George Pennell.

It should be borne in mind that lithography, as we said earlier, is a *plane* (surface) printing; the surface is neither raised, as in letterpress printing, nor sunk, as in intaglio printing (*see* Engraving), but is level. It is much used commercially for labels, posters and other such work besides the reproduction of pictures. Photographic designs can be readily produced by transferring the original to the metal printing plate; colour lithography by the three- or four-colour process can be carried out after the preparation of the colour originals and the transference of the designs to the set of plates.

Another method is called offset printing. If anyone by mischance lays his arm upon a printing block or a page of type, which has been inked, a fine impression comes off upon the skin. If now one lays his arm upon a sheet of paper and presses down, much of the inked impression will be " offset " on to the paper. This offset will be in reverse, but if we take an offset from a reversed block in the first place, the final result will be an impression the right way up.

In offset lithographic printing the design from the plate does not go directly on to the paper, but on to an intermediate rubber-covered cylinder. This cylinder, in turn, transfers the design to the paper. When first introduced, offset lithography was welcomed because it enabled printing to be done on fairly rough-surfaced paper, instead of on the smooth and well-finished paper needed for direct printing. The result was not so crisp and clear, but in time offset came to be used for all kinds of work, and the slightly less sharp outline of design or type form was appreciated for its pleasing effect.

Lithuania. One of the largest States of Europe at the beginning of the 15th century, its boundaries extending from the Black Sea to the Baltic, this Soviet Socialist Republic is bounded on the north by Latvia, on the east by White Russia, on the south by the Russian Soviet Federal Socialist

---

Extent.—22,959 square miles. Population, 2,879,000.

Physical Features.—A level forested area. Chief river, the Niemen.

Principal Products.—Cereals, flax, potatoes ; dairy produce ; timber.

Chief Cities.—Vilnius (Vilna), the capital, 207,750 ; Kaunas (Kovno) 152,365 ; Memel (Klaipeda) 50,000.

Republic and Poland, on the west by the Baltic. The country has an area of 22,959 square miles, forests, lakes and marshes covering much of the land. Of its many rivers the chief is the Niemen.

Lithuania is an agricultural country, more than three-quarters of the population being engaged in this industry. Rye, wheat, oats, barley, potatoes and flax are the principal crops. Poultry farming—particularly the rearing of geese—and bee-keeping are other important occupations. In normal times the main exports are grain, cattle, dairy produce, flax, timber, wool and hides. There are 1,200 miles of navigable waterways and as many of railway, connecting the chief towns of Vilnius (Vilna), Kaunas (Kovno), Memel (Klaipeda), and Shavli (Siaulai), with the Russian and Polish railway systems. The capital is Vilnius, with a population of 207,750.

In the 13th century Lithuania became a Grand Duchy, reaching the height of its power in the 15th century. United with Poland in 1569, the country passed to Russia in 1776, remaining a Baltic province of the Russian Empire until February 1918, when it declared its independence of the newly-created Bolshevik Republic. In August 1940 the Lithuanian Republic was admitted to the Soviet Union as a Soviet Republic. The country was occupied by German forces from June 1941 until its liberation by Russian troops in January 1945 (during the Second World War, 1939–45). The population of Lithuania is 2,879,000.

Liver. This is one of the most important organs in the body and is found in all animals that have a backbone, as well as in some that have not. The liver in Man is situated in the abdominal cavity, on the right side, slightly above and behind the stomach. It is the largest gland organ of the body, weighing from three to four pounds.

The liver has four main functions: (1) It produces bile, which aids in the digestion and absorption of fats, and acts as a disinfectant in the gut. Bile is stored in the gall bladder, a little pouch beneath the liver, until digestion challenges its discharge into the small intestine. (2) Glycogen (or animal starch) is formed from the sugar circulating in the blood after digestion, and is stored away in the liver cells, to be given out again to the blood as sugar when it is needed by the muscles of the body for energy. (3) The liver, during the digestive process, forms urea—one of the wastes of the human body resulting from protein metabolism—which must be excreted (see Kidneys). (4) The liver also prepares fats for oxidation in the body.

Among its numberless other tasks is the preparation of a chemical on which depends the clotting of the blood; the manufacture of another substance which antagonizes a substance made by the kidneys, and which keeps the blood pressure within normal limits. Yet another substance made by the liver affects the health of the red blood cells.

The liver differs from all other organs of the body in that nearly all the blood passing through it is venous blood. Blood flows into it from two sources; the small hepatic artery brings arterial blood to feed the liver cells, and the large portal vein brings all the venous blood from the stomach and intestines to the liver before it goes back to the heart. This forms what is called the portal circulation and may best be likened to a short circuit in the general systemic circulation. The liver makes important changes in this blood before it passes on to the general circulation, taking from it several nutritive elements and giving to it waste products which will later be excreted by the kidneys.

Jaundice occurs when the bile which should be secreted into the gut finds its way instead into the blood stream, because of some inflammation or blockage of its proper channels. The liver substance may harden and be put out of action by a condition known as cirrhosis (the name is derived from a Greek word meaning " tawny " and a suffix denoting a disease). This condition is common in persons addicted to alcohol, but is caused rather by the poisons dissolved out in the gut by the alcohol than by the alcohol itself. Persons also who do not take alcoholic drinks are found with cirrhosis, and the horse suffers from this disease.

Cancer frequently attacks the liver. Failure of this most important organ to keep " foreign " substances out of the blood stream is associated with the troublesome disturbance called allergy : certain foods which most people can eat with enjoyment upset those who are allergic to these foods.

Liverpool. If you pay a visit to this great English port by steamer you may not be impressed by the seven-mile stretch of grey granite-walled docks ; but look well at those docks, for they are among the busiest in the world. Fleets of ships arrive and leave by every tide, and the warehouses store goods from all quarters of the globe.

The Mersey estuary, on the Lancashire shore of which Liverpool is situated, suffers from shifting sand-bars across the channel, and from a tide with a vertical rise and fall of 30 feet. To remove the sand the Mersey Docks and Harbour Board keeps a fleet of powerful dredgers constantly at work. The advantages of a tideless harbour have been practically secured by a wonderful system of " wet docks," operated like the locks on a canal. When a ship enters one of these docks, a water-gate closes behind it and remains closed, holding the water at a constant level, until the ship is ready to sail. The docks have a water area of about 475 acres with 29 miles of quays. One dock, the Gladstone, can take vessels up to 70,000 tons. The floating landing-stage is really a half-mile long raft on floating pontoons.

The Docks and Harbour Board, occupying one of the largest buildings on the waterfront, also controls the dock system on the Birkenhead side of the Mersey, to which side runs an underwater tunnel nearly three miles in length known as Queensway. The Anglican cathedral, designed by Sir Giles Gilbert Scott, was begun in 1904. Sir Edwin Lutyens and Adrian Gilbert Scott designed the Roman Catholic cathedral.

Liverpool has many industries, including ship repairing, flour-milling, tobacco and rubber processing, sugar refining, and seed oil extraction ; but it does not owe its importance to them. Its fortune has always lain on the water, even in ancient days when a safe beaching ground for fishing boats, out of the swift currents of the Mersey, was afforded by a shallow little tributary, the Pool. The Pool was filled up long ago when the docks and quays of the port were being built. The gigantic seaport of Liverpool lives today by grace of the Mersey, as did the fishing hamlet eight or nine centuries ago.

Liverpool's commercial importance began late— with the Stuart Restoration in the 17th century— and it had to outstrip first Chester and then Bristol before its position became commanding. In the latter half of the 18th century the power loom began to make Lancashire the world's greatest cotton-manufacturing centre, and Liverpool its chief port. Raw cotton is still the chief import, and the cotton goods of Manchester and other Lancashire towns the chief export, though some trade is now diverted through the Manchester Ship Canal.

Fox

LIVERPOOL : BRITAIN'S VAST PORT IN LANCASHIRE

On the estuary of the Mersey, Liverpool is one of the leading ports in Great Britain. Here we see that part of the waterfront which is close to the huge floating landing-stage. In the foreground on the left is a block of offices, the Royal Liver building ; then come the Cunard-White Star Line's headquarters, and the domed structure housing the Mersey Docks and Harbour Board. The white tower in right background marks the entrance to the Mersey Tunnel.

During the Second World War (1939–45), 75 million tons of cargo were handled at Liverpool and over 4,700,000 Allied troops passed through the port. The Battle of the Atlantic, waged against German submarines, was directed from an underground control-room in an office block adjoining the town hall. German aircraft made repeated bombing raids on the city, especially in one week in May 1941 when more than 2,500 people were either killed or seriously injured. The population in 1947 was 756,230.

Liverworts. The next time you notice a flat, creeping, rather fleshy-looking plant, with rounded lobes to its leaf-like body, and no separate stem, leaves or flowers, examine it carefully. It is probably a liverwort—a simple flowerless plant, one of the first types of land plants in the earth's history. The liverworts got their name from the fact that they were once believed to be beneficial in diseases of the liver, or perhaps from their shape.

They are usually of a bright green hue, and they grow most luxuriantly on wet rocks, logs, or on the ground in ravines and other moist, shady places. Many are so small they are easily overlooked. Others are much like mosses and are often confused with them. Others, again, are large and conspicuous, with their upper surface green, and the lower surface covered with numerous fine white hairlike rootlets called rhizoids. Some of these liverworts have little

R. M. Adam

AN ATTRACTIVE LIVERWORT

Liverworts are flowerless, flat, greyish or greenish plants, fond of moist places and damp walls. This one (*Marchantia polymorpha*) is producing an enormous number of archegonia, the female organs of reproduction.

green cuplike organs, called cupules (Latin *cupula*, little tub), containing tiny greenish balls, known as brood buds, which grow into new plants.

The liverworts have also another mode of reproducing, by growing tall umbrella-like organs, some of which (called archegonia) bear little eggs, while others (antheridia) bear very tiny, actively swimming cells, called sperms. During wet weather the sperms swim to the archegonia and there fertilize the eggs, which grow into tiny plants, rooted in the archegonium, and containing many very small brownish spores. These spores fall upon the ground and there grow into liverwort plants, and so the cycle goes on.

The liverworts are in many ways related to the mosses, and with them compose a great division of the vegetable kingdom, the *Bryophyta*, the liverworts forming the group *Hepaticae*.

Livery Companies. The City Guilds or Livery Companies of the City of London are descended from the old medieval trade guilds.

It was compulsory for every craftsman or trader to join his particular company, and to wear its livery, but nowadays membership is not reserved for followers of any particular profession.

There are 79 guilds in existence, the twelve great London companies being the Mercers, Grocers, Drapers, Fishmongers, Goldsmiths, Skinners, Merchant Taylors, Haberdashers, Salters, Ironmongers, Vintners, and Clothworkers. Each Company is governed by a court, which includes the Master, or Prime Warden, and Wardens, and controls the Company's funds.

Formerly the courts regulated the trade of the Company and looked after the general welfare of the members. Most of the Companies have considerable funds at their disposal, and education in particular has benefited greatly by their generosity (*e.g.* City and Guilds of London Institute). Members of the Livery Companies are Freemen of the City of London, an honour which now carries with it few practical advantages. (*See* Guilds.)

The MISSIONARY-EXPLORER of AFRICA

This is the wonderful life-story of David Livingstone, who braved the many dangers of the African wilds during 30 years of exploration and missionary work—a man of the highest ideals and greatest courage.

Livingstone, DAVID (1813–73). How does it feel to be crunched in the jaws of a lion? Dr. Livingstone, the famous British missionary and African explorer, was one of the few men who knew and lived to tell the tale. Soon after he began his work in South Africa he was sent to establish an advanced station in the heart of the wilderness 800 miles north-east of Cape Town. The site was infested with lions.

At a distance of 30 yards Livingstone fired two bullets into one of the beasts, severely wounding it. The lion hurled itself upon him, crushing his left shoulder in its jaws and bearing him to the ground. "Growling horribly, close to my ear," wrote Livingstone, "he shook me as a terrier does a rat. The shock produced a stupor similar to that which seems to be felt by a mouse after the first shake of a cat. It caused a sort of dreaminess, in which there was no sense of pain nor feeling of terror, though I was quite conscious of all that was happening." Fortunately the lion soon let go of Livingstone, and fell dead of its wound.

No dangers, neither hunger, fever, attacks by hostile Boers or native cannibals, the treachery of Arab slave traders, nor any of the perils that beset him could damp his ardour or make him abandon his chosen field. His patient resourcefulness, courage, fair dealing and Christian character laid

Scottish missionary and explorer, David Livingstone died in Africa on May 1, 1873, and was buried in Westminster Abbey, London.

the basis for missionary work over a large part of South and Central Africa. In addition, no other explorer ever did so much for African geography.

He was born on March 19, 1813, at Low Blantyre, Scotland. As his parents were poor, he went to work in a cotton mill at the age of 10, and with his first earnings he bought a Latin book for beginners. Although work at the factory began at six in the morning and lasted 10 hours or more, he attended night school and studied at home. In his 20th year he was thrilled by reading an account of a missionary's labours in Asia, and, as he says, "resolved to devote my life to the alleviation of human misery." Then followed college classes in Glasgow, examination and acceptance by the London Missionary Society, the completion of his medical education in London, and studies of theology, botany, zoology, geology, chemistry, and astronomy—all with a view to his future life-work. At last came his arrival at Cape Town, in 1841.

For over 30 years Dr. Livingstone travelled up and down Africa, from the Cape nearly to the Equator, and from the Atlantic to the Indian Ocean. He discovered the Victoria Falls on the Zambezi, Lake Nyasa, Lake Bangweolo (where he was to die), and the upper course of the Congo, called the Lualaba and thought by Livingstone to be the upper Nile. He also explored much of Lake Tanganyika, which Burton (*q.v.*) had discovered in 1858.

Two purposes specially dear to Livingstone were the stopping of the Arab slave trade in Africa, which he called the "great open sore of the world," and the discovery of the sources of the Nile. The descriptions of the horror of the slave raids which he sent to England helped in time to stamp out this ghastly trade. He was never to find the sources of the Nile, however.

About six months before he died a relief expedition sent by the New York Herald under H. M.

LIVINGSTONE'S LAST SAD JOURNEY TO THE SEA

It was a fitting tribute to the epic grandeur of Livingstone's life of sacrifice and service in Central Africa that after his death at Illala, beside Lake Bangweolo, his body should be carried to the sea by his devoted African servants through 1,000 miles of savage waste. This picture shows some of the perils of that journey to Zanzibar, whence his remains were taken to England.

It is estimated that in 33 years, attended in the main by only a few native servants, Livingstone travelled more than 30,000 miles of country hitherto unknown to the white man. Through him the slave trade received its death-blow, owing to the horror his accounts aroused in the civilized world. A statue of him was unveiled at Victoria Falls, Southern Rhodesia, on August 5, 1934.

Stanley (*q.v.*) found him at Ujiji on Lake Tangan-yika, suffering great privations and weakened by fever following the desertion of some carriers with supplies and his medicine chest. Stanley tried in vain to persuade him to return to civilization.

After the relief party had left, Livingstone again started west, looking for the sources of the Nile. His old enemy, dysentery, attacked him, with complications brought on by excessive hard-ships, and he grew steadily worse. On the morning of May 1, 1873, his men found him kneeling beside his cot, dead. His faithful native attendants, who loved him, preserved the body as best they could and carried it halfway across Africa to Zanzibar. From there it was taken to England and buried with all honours in Westminster Abbey, London. A monument was erected where he died, and there is a statue of him at the Victoria Falls.

Livy (59 B.C.–A.D. 17). Among the literature called classical, the works of Titus Livius, commonly called Livy, the Roman historian, will always hold an honoured place. Livy was born at Patavium (Padua), in Northern Italy, and after settling in Rome he became one of its leading citizens. The great work of Livy's life was the writing of a history

of Rome from the traditional date of the founda-tion of the city, 753 B.C., to 8 B.C.

Originally it consisted of 142 books, but of these only 35 have survived in their entirety, although the existence of a sort of abridged edition of the whole history has enabled the blanks in the original work to be filled in to a certain extent. His object, as he says in his preface, was to recall to his con-temporaries Rome's mighty past, and to hold up former celebrated characters as examples to them. He excelled in his vivid descriptions of battles and sieges. It is wonderful how his works survived at all, considering the calamities which befell Rome in its fall, and some of Livy's writings were not dis-covered by scholars until medieval times.

He was held in high esteem by the scholars and writers of Rome who came after him. There are several English translations of Livy, but though they give us the substance of his work they give us no adequate idea of his literary style. Among scientific historians Livy has no place, as he was quite un-critical in his methods, being content to accept his facts from previous writers without any attempt at independent investigation. Yet for all his faults Livy remains among the immortals.

BASILISKS and DRAGONS of TODAY

We no longer believe that the glance of a lizard can turn the beholder into stone, or that there are real fire-breathing dragons. But the appearance and habits of the lizard family are strange enough.

Lizards. If you saw together a specimen of each of the 1,700 different kinds of lizards that have been found in the world you would hardly believe that animals of such widely different shapes, sizes, colours, and habits could possibly belong to the same big group of reptiles.

You would see tiny creatures two or three inches long lying beside giants measuring from 10 to 12 feet. Bright greens, blues and reds would stand out among dull greys, browns and blacks. Most of them would show four sturdy legs, with long toes and claws; but there would be some with only front legs, some with only back legs, and some with

no legs at all. Tree-lizards, ground-lizards and water-lizards would be included, some darting about, others sluggish and still.

Here and there you would find a sleek, slender, lively and even graceful creature, but many of them would probably impress you as misshapen, repulsive monsters. Yet, if you judged by looks alone, you would do the lizard tribe an injustice, for only two of the 1,700 species are poisonous—the helo-derm of western Mexico and the Gila monster of the south-western United States.

Present-day lizards are blood brothers of the snakes, and both orders together form the sub-class *Sauria* of the reptilian class of animals. The relationship can be traced through many details of internal anatomy.

While lizards are found in nearly all except the colder parts of the earth, they reach their greatest numbers in tropical lands. Most of them catch living prey, the smaller ones feeding usually on worms and insects, the larger ones devouring mice, frogs, other lizards, snakes, young turtles and crocodiles, fish, birds—in fact, almost any animals they can overpower.

There are some important varieties, however, that prefer a vegetable diet, notably most of the larger members of the iguana family of tropical America, some of which reach a length of six feet.

E. J. Hosking

BEAUTIFUL SAND LIZARD OF THE HEATHS

The handsomest of English lizards is the one seen here—the sand lizard (*Lacerta agilis*). The colour varies considerably, but brown predominates on the females and green in the males, rows of dark and light spots occurring in both sexes. It is not very common, but is found on sandy heaths in the south of England.

THE FRILLED LIZARD—A STRANGE REPTILE

W. S. Berridge

Found in Queensland and New South Wales, two States of Australia, the frilled lizard is one of the strangest of creatures, with a large collar or frill of loose skin around its neck. This is raised when the reptile is frightened or annoyed—perhaps it is a bit of bluff to make it seem a terrible monster! Then there is its queer habit when running of rising up on its hind legs and proceeding, more like a human being than a reptile, on two legs alone. In all. the frilled lizard is about three feet long.

To face page 1972

'DRAGONS' OF TODAY : A PAIR OF THE GIANT MONITOR LIZARDS OF KOMODO

The largest living lizards are the 'Komodo dragons,' inhabitants of one of the remote islands of the East Indies, after which they are named. Until this photograph was taken there was little reliable information concerning their habits and real appearance, for so large are they—their length is over 12 feet—that exaggerated reports made them seem unbelievable. They have a power and dignity not seen in any other lizards, except perhaps the great marine iguanas : but unlike those creatures the 'dragons' are carnivorous.

To face page 1975

Perhaps the most amazing peculiarity found in the lizard tribe is the faculty which many of its members possess of casting off their tails. When seized by a foe from behind, the tail breaks off between two of the joints of the backbone. The severed part continues to wriggle for some time, catching the attention and satisfying the hunger of the pursuing foe, while the more important part of the lizard escapes. Some species will abandon their tails even before they are seized. Such mutilation seems to cause them no inconvenience, for they at once set about growing a new tail. This is an example of what the scientist calls "r e g e n e r a t i o n"—the power of reproducing, by new growth, parts that have been lost. It is seen in the British lizard known as the slow-worm (*Anguis fragilis*), which is often mistaken for a snake because of its long, serpentile tail and the absence of legs.

Another strange p r a c t i c e among certain large lizards, notably the frilled lizards of Australia and the teguexin of the West Indies and South America, is that of running swiftly and for great distances on their hind legs. When doing this, their front legs swing to and fro like the arms of a human

supporting the lizard like a parachute as it glides through the air, often for remarkable distances.

The frilled lizard previously mentioned gets its name from the broad collar of loose skin it wears round its neck, which it spreads out like an umbrella when frightened or angered, at the same time opening its mouth wide and hissing—all of which is pure bluff. Such " scarecrow " tricks are common among lizards. The hooded basilisk, which is

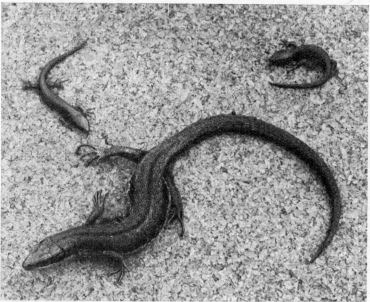

named after the fabled monster that was supposed to turn a beholder to stone with its glance or breath, is a conspicuous example of such tactics. Being about three feet long, and possessing jagged crests which it can raise at will on its head, back, and tail, this creature is regarded as an object of terror by the native children of Central America.

Some lizards are by no means placid. Though non-poisonous and inclined to mind their own business, some of them are fierce fighters and biters when annoyed. This is particularly true of the monitor family, whose members are scattered through Africa, Arabia, southern Asia and Australia. One water-loving species (*Varanus salvator*) sometimes attains a length of more than eight feet, while the largest of the whole lizard tribe is the Komodo dragon, *V. komodoensis*, which is very possibly the original of many oriental dragon legends.

In contrast with this vigorous and short-tempered creature are those most helpless of all lizards, the slow-worms mentioned earlier, sometimes called glass-snakes or blind-worms; and the strange amphisbaenas. Both are devoid of legs, although some possess useless external flaps in place of feet. The slow-worm is, of course, neither a snake nor a

A. B. Thompson; John Kearton

LIZARDS, WITH AND WITHOUT LEGS

Both these photographs show lizards, though the creatures in the lower one are not easily recognizable as such : they are slow-worms—British lizards that have no legs. The others (top) are the common lizard (*Lacerta vivipara*), a female with her newly-born young. This species also is found in Britain.

runner and their tails project stiffly backwards and upwards to balance them, making them look like strange birds. Indeed, the whole performance recalls sharply the fact that millions of years ago birds emerged from reptilian ancestors.

The nearest thing to flying found among the lizards, however, are the long sailing leaps from tree to tree performed by the small flying-dragons of the Malayan countries. The " wings " of these creatures are formed by the outward extension of the ribs, which are connected by thin membranes of skin. When at rest they lie close to the creature's sides, but when a leap is made they spread out like fans,

worm, nor is it blind. Its small bright eyes are equipped with eyelids, a thing unknown among true snakes. The " glass " part of its name arises from the fact that it becomes rigid when captured and breaks off at the tail if not handled very gently. This creature is common in many parts of England.

The amphisbaena has eyes and ears both concealed by growths of skin. This lizard lives in the ground, and it can move backwards or forwards with equal ease like an earthworm.

Although most of the lizards have no voice beyond an angry hissing, the night-loving gecko family is distinguished for its ability to emit a variety of cries, all resembling more or less the sound from which they derive their name. The geckos are small creatures, very useful for the number of insects they destroy. Some are sand-runners, others tree-dwellers, and a few varieties penetrate dwellings in search of food. These have feet equipped with tiny pads and hairs, which enable them to climb up a pane of glass or walk on a smooth ceiling.

While the geckos have been in many lands unjustly persecuted from the popular belief that they spread mysterious poisons, another group of small lizards, the skinks, have been regarded from the earliest times as possessed of equally mysterious medicinal properties. The head and feet of the common sand-burrowing skink were preserved in wine and imported in great quantities to ancient Rome. The Arabs of today still use them as medicine and food. Nor is this the only example of lizards being eaten by Man, for the iguanas of America and many Australian, Asiatic, and African species are highly relished by the natives.

Among the best-known of North American lizards are the poisonous Gila monster and the gentle, friendly " horned toad." The former, which sometimes reaches a length of two feet, was first found in the Gila river valley in Arizona. Its sluggish body is marked with big orange or pinkish blotches and rings on a black background. The poison-sacs lie near the root of its grooved teeth, and its bite quickly kills the small animals on which it preys. In rare cases it has been fatal to Man. Its near relative, the heloderm, has yellow instead of orange spots.

The horned toad, so called because of its flat, squat, toad-like body, is found throughout the dry plains and deserts of the western and south-western United States and in Mexico. It is covered with short sharp spines, particularly about the head, which protect it against being swallowed by snakes. Similar but not closely related forms occur in Australia.

Besides the slow-worm we have in Britain two other native lizards, the common lizard (*Lacerta vivipara*) and the sand lizard (*L. agilis*), while several others, such as the true green lizard (*L. viridis*) and the wall lizard (*L. muralis*) have been introduced. All are typical little lizards, quick-moving, amusing, and difficult to catch. (*See* illus. pages 1972 and 1973.)

Two close relatives of the lizard tribe, the

chameleon and the tuatara (*Sphenodon*) of New Zealand, are of immense interest to scientists. The story of the chameleon is told elsewhere (*see* Chameleon). The tuatara deserves mention here because this singular creature is the sole surviving member of a group of reptiles otherwise extinct millions of years ago. The bodily structure of this " living fossil " has given science a key to the evolution of the whole reptile group, for it retains traces of many of the primitive bodily forms once common to the group, but since evolved away —notably a well-developed pineal body or " third eye " buried beneath the skin of its forehead, which is a remnant of a third eye thought to be possessed and used by certain prehistoric reptile ancestors. A pineal body, much less well developed, is present in existing lizards and reptiles.

W. S. Berridge; G.P.A.

POISONOUS GILA MONSTER AND A SKINK

One of the few poisonous members of the lizard tribe, the Gila monster (lower) of North America was first found in the Gila river valley in Arizona ; it is marked with pinkish or orange on a black background. Its bite quickly kills the small animals on which it preys, but is rarely fatal to Man. Various parts of the skink (upper) have long been used in Oriental medicine, and the Arabs still eat these small lizards.

SURVIVORS FROM PREHISTORIC DAYS
The tuatara (Sphenodon), a relative of the lizards native to New Zealand, is a most remarkable creature, for it is a survival of lizard types that died out elsewhere millions of years ago. In it a pineal (shaped like a pine cone) body suggestive of a third eye is well developed. These specimens were photographed in the London Zoo.

Lizards are " cold-blooded," like all reptiles. Some lay from one to 20 eggs, but others produce living young (the slow-worm hatches its young within the body), and the specific name of our own *Lacerta vivipara* refers to this. Their skin, like that of snakes, is normally covered with scales, and at intervals they shed the thin, horny outside coating.

The family history of the lizards is particularly interesting because of its many relationships with the birds and mammals. You might think at first that the lizards are very small descendants of the prehistoric monsters that once roamed the earth. But the original reptiles were evolved from amphibians (*see* Reptiles), and from them developed the monsters, which, however, proved unable to survive. On the other hand, the primitive reptile stock was still in existence and Nature's second effort produced small, fleet animals, capable of surviving under the new conditions. These were the lizards and reptiles as we now know them.

At about the time when the lizards were appearing, Nature was also producing (perhaps from the same primitive reptile type) the first birds, and possibly even forerunners of early mammals.

Llama. Although related to the camel of the Old World, the llama, which is found only in South America, has no hump. It is a domesticated form of the wild guanaco, which is found in the Andes. Its wool is not so highly valued as is that of the alpaca and the vicuña, its relatives, which, like the llama, live in the Andes of Bolivia, Peru, and Chile; for llama wool is coarse and rough and is suitable only for twine and very coarse cloths. The male llama is chiefly valued as a beast of burden, and the females are useful for their milk and meat, which latter resembles mutton.

When the Spaniards conquered Peru in the 16th century they found the Incas using hundreds of thousands of llamas as riding animals and beasts of burden. In the whole New World these were the only domesticated animals except dogs, and the lack of such useful beasts as the horse, ass, ox, sheep, and pig was one of the reasons why the New World lagged behind the Old in civilization. The Spanish conquerors used the llamas, and long strings of these animals in the charge of a few native drivers were soon carrying silver by the narrow mountain trails from the mines to the coast. Until the middle of the 19th century llamas remained almost the only means of transportation employed in the Andes. Even today, in the more inaccessible parts, this beast is still essential for transport purposes.

The llama (*Lama huanacus glama*) is about three feet high at the shoulders and is capable of carrying 120 lb. at the leisurely rate of 12 miles a day. If treated well, llamas are willing and docile. They are hardy, and can travel over places too rough and steep for any other burden-bearing animal. If overloaded, they will lie down and refuse to move. When annoyed they are apt to spit a ball of food and saliva at their tormentor.

Sport & General

LLAMAS OF THE ANDES
Most very young animals have a peculiar charm, and this little llama with its mother is no exception. Though related to the camels of the Old World, these beasts have no hump and are only about three feet high at the shoulder. The male llama is chiefly valued as a beast of burden, the female for its milk and meat.

Lloyd George, DAVID LLOYD GEORGE, 1ST EARL (1863–1945).

At the age of 17 this Welshman, who for six epoch-making years was Prime Minister of Britain, visited the House of Commons for the first time. He wrote in his diary, " I will not say that I eyed the House of Commons in the spirit in which William the Conqueror eyed England on his visit to Edward the Confessor." But already he was dreaming of future political greatness.

Born on January 17, 1863, in Manchester, the family was left in poverty, when he was only 18 months old, by the death of his schoolmaster father, William George. Lloyd George was reared and educated by his mother's brother — R i c h a r d Lloyd, a village cobbler of North Wales—from whom he received his second name of Lloyd. Starting to study law at the age of 14, he was articled to a firm of solicitors in 1879, and became a qualified solicitor in 1884. In 1890 he was elected to Parliament as Liberal member for the Welsh constituency of Caernarvon, a seat which he held for nearly 55 years.

In Parliament he showed himself fearless, quick and biting in reply, and he speedily won at ten tio n. When the Liberals came into power at the end of 1905, Sir Henry Campbell-Bannerman, the Prime Minister, offered Lloyd George a place in the Cabinet as President of the Board of Trade. When, in 1908, Asquith succeeded Campbell-Bannerman as Prime Minister he asked Lloyd George to take the second place in the Cabinet, that of Chancellor of the Exchequer. The friend of the poor now had his chance. It was his first duty to bring in the Budget, the annual statement of the nation's finances. To provide funds for the Old Age Pension Act, Lloyd George proposed new taxes. But the House of Lords rejected the Budget, and then the Prime Minister gave notice that the government proposed to limit the power of the Lords. A general election showed that the mass of the people favoured Lloyd George's Budget, the Prime Minister and the Liberal Party being returned to Parliament in 1910 with a big majority, and the Parliament Act passed in 1911 ended the power of the Lords to reject a money bill, such as the Budget.

Immediately, Lloyd George produced a new programme of social reform. The chief measure passed provided working men with state-guaranteed insurance against sickness and unemployment, with free medical service, payment of partial wages during periods of disablement, hospitals for tuberculosis, and maternity benefits for their wives. This legislation entitles Lloyd George to rank as one of the greatest practical social reformers in the history of England or, indeed, of any country.

Howard Coster

DAVID LLOYD GEORGE
Prime Minister of Great Britain from 1916 to 1922, the leadership of this Welsh statesman inspired the people of the British Empire during the latter half of the First World War (1914–18). Made an Earl in January 1945, he died on March 26 of the same year.

When the First World War broke out in 1914 he was one of the first to realize that Britain was being outstripped by Germany in the quantity and quality of shells manufactured, and he was given the new post of Minister of Munitions. By his enthusiasm and dynamic energy he organized the manufacture of munitions in every corner of the kingdom, and soon the British Army was as well equipped with armaments as the German.

In December 1916 Lloyd George became Prime Minister, with the consent, and at the wish, of the leading politicians and soldiers. In his new capacity he gathered round him trained men and gave new impetus to the British war effort. He stood out firmly against the talk of a " peace by compromise," rallied the faint-hearted, pressed the supplies of munitions, and re-organized the Army staff in spite of opposition. The outcome of the war abundantly justified his policy, and in the general election of November 1918 his party held the majority of seats in the House of Commons, and Lloyd George continued in office as Prime Minister.

At the Peace Conference, held in Paris in 1919, Lloyd George steered no consistent course. At one time he seemed to be with France in her efforts to destroy Germany once and for all; at another to be with President Wilson of the United States in his efforts for a peace based upon reconciliation and the rights of nationalities. Here, however, as earlier in his career, he showed his genius for conciliating and bringing to agreement persons of widely opposing views. In the troubled times which followed the Peace, Lloyd George faced tremendous problems connected with Ireland, labour, and reconstruction. Towards the close of 1922 criticism of his Near-East policy foreshadowed the government's fall. At a meeting of the Conservative Party it was decided that the Party would not support the Liberal Prime Minister at the forthcoming election, and on the resignation of certain of his ministers Lloyd George relinquished the Premiership. In 1929 he made a last bid for political power, but failed to win the support of the people.

His War Memoirs, in six volumes, appeared during 1933–36. In his later years Lloyd George devoted much time to his farm at Churt, in Surrey. He had been awarded the Order of Merit on the signing of peace at Versailles in 1919; in January 1945 he was made Earl Lloyd George. He died on March 26, 1945.

Lloyd's.

There is no higher praise than to be classed as " A 1 at Lloyd's " (*see* A 1), whether or not the expression, which is derived from this oldest and greatest of marine insurance societies, refers to health condition or to financial stability.

Lloyd's had its origin in the coffee-house in Tower Street, London, of one Edward Lloyd, about 1690. Very little is known of Lloyd, other than that he had three wives and many children and had been a constable. His establishment was a resort for business men interested in shipping and foreign trade, some of whom were willing to act as insurers. Ship-owners and others looking for insurance underwriters soon found it easier to go to Lloyd's than to make the rounds of offices. Thus the first great insurance committee originated out of a mixture of social custom and convenience.

It differs from the usual insurance company in one fundamental respect : the corporation as such does not write insurance, but the risks are assumed by the underwriters (insurers) individually, each of whom is personally liable for the amount of insurance he guarantees. Risks of non-payment are fully safeguarded against, and large risks are distributed among many underwriters. The corporation makes audits of each member's accounts and, in other ways, provides a constant check to safeguard its members' interests. It takes all forms of insurance except life, accepting such insurances as those against weather, chances of public or private functions being cancelled, or fog spoiling a " first night " show at a theatre. In fact, Lloyd's insures against almost any contingency.

Lloyd's, which is in Leadenhall Street, London, close to the Royal Exchange and Bank of England, is noteworthy for the traditions still preserved there. When, for example, a ship is reported missing, the great Lutine bell which hangs in Lloyd's building (so called because it was recovered from the wreck of H.M.S. La Lutine, a captured French man-o'-war that sank off the Dutch coast with a large quantity of specie on board in 1790) is rung. Should an overdue vessel be reported safe the bell clangs twice. Lloyd's List, in which the movements of the world's shipping are reported daily, dates from 1696, and is probably the oldest daily newspaper in Europe.

Lloyd's Register, which is distinct from the marine insurance corporation, is a British society that exists to certify the seaworthiness of ships of all kinds. Its surveyors examine all ships built to its requirements and classify them in various

LLOYD'S FAMOUS BELL
One of the most celebrated bells in the world is the Lutine bell at Lloyd's in London, which is rung when a ship is missing or is later reported safe. It was recovered from the wreck of H.M.S. La Lutine, a captured French man-o'-war.

grades, the highest being 100 A1 at Lloyd's. It is controlled by a committee of shipowners and others and publishes every six months a register of ships of every class excepting those of the Royal Navy. The society dates from 1834. Its head office is in Fenchurch Street, London, and it has surveyors in most of the ports of Great Britain and throughout the world, for Lloyd's Register is the standard for ships of all nations.

Lobster. What a curious creature the lobster is, with its powerful claws and long antennae, the eyes mounted on the ends of movable eyestalks, and an armour-like shell of dark blue covering body and tail ! Blue ? Yes, for it is only when the lobster is boiled or otherwise cooked that it turns brilliant red, as we are accustomed to see it on the fishmonger's slab.

The lobster (*Homarus gammarus*) belongs to the group Crustacea and is a big relative of the crayfish, prawn, and shrimp. Its tail is made up of six jointed segments ; it breathes by means of gills enclosed on each side of the body under the shell

F. Martin Duncan
LOBSTER CRAWLING OVER THE SEA-BED
In summer lobsters are found amongst rocks in shallow water, but with the approach of cold weather they usually move out into deep water. This one is feeling its way by means of the long antennae that reach well beyond the two big claws.

Fox

LOBSTER POTS

The fishermen of Sennen Cove, Cornwall, depend mainly on lobster fishing for their livelihood. This man is preparing to embark with five lobster pots. They are of wicker, and when the lobster enters through the funnel-shaped aperture in the top it cannot get out again.

of the head and thorax. Of its two large claws one grows somewhat larger than the other and is used for crushing its prey; the smaller claw, set with sharp teeth, tears its food. Behind these claws are four pairs of legs, the first two pairs of which end in small claws. Each joint of the abdomen has a pair of swimmerets or paddles. The last joint ends in a fan-shaped tail-piece, which serves as a rudder and a means of propulsion.

The lobster lives sometimes in shallow water near the shore and sometimes in deep water, but at all times it prefers a rocky bottom and reaches its greatest size in such places. Lobsters eat living and dead animals, and vegetable matter to a less extent. They are well protected by their hard shells and powerful claws and by their habit of burrowing among the rocks; but when they are very small, or when they shed their shells (as the males do twice a year, the females once), great numbers are destroyed by fishes, for at those times they are soft-skinned and helpless.

The female lobster produces a great many eggs, from 3,000 to 70,000 according to her size and age. These eggs are attached to the swimmerets by a sort of glue, and after about 11 months they hatch into larvae. For six to eight weeks these remain as free-swimming larvae, moulting five or six times with various changes of colour. The adult form is attained after 15 to 18 days when the larva is about three-quarters of an inch long; at this stage it sinks to the bottom near the shore and begins its lobster life. As a general rule a lobster 10 to 12 inches long is about five years old. Great age and size are sometimes attained, individuals weighing more than 30 lb. having been caught.

The method of capture is simple. A slatted box or wicker basket called a " pot," with a funnel-shaped opening of coarse netting in the ends, is baited with stale fish, weighted with a flat stone and sunk to the bottom on a line. The lobster can enter easily but finds it very difficult to escape.

Locke, JOHN (1632–1704). Today the pursuit of knowledge implies that first we examine and classify facts, and then we build up a theory which explains them, or tries to do so. If the theory does not fit the known facts, we modify it or reject it. But early philosophers thought that Man had a natural " knowledge " of things by reason of " innate ideas." The Greeks sought to explain Nature by symbolism, and made great play with numbers. Thus there were the four elements— earth, water, air, fire; and the four " tempers "— blood (sanguine); black bile (melancholy) ; yellow bile (choleric); and phlegm (phlegmatic). Such fantastic notions persisted well into medieval times.

John Locke in 1687 wrote his famous Essay on Human Understanding. He had had a political career as secretary to the earl of Shaftesbury, and as secretary to the Board of Trade. When Shaftesbury had to flee the country, Locke went with him to Holland, and there he wrote his great book. Knowledge, he says, cannot derive from our own natures ; therefore it must come from experience. We reflect upon the impressions we receive from sensation, and so we get ideas of duration, substance, infinity, power, good and evil. Sensation and reflection make up the sum of our experience.

Locke ranks among the great English philosophers. He was born at Wrington, Somerset, on August 29, 1632, and was the son of a lawyer. He was educated at Westminster School, and at Christ Church, Oxford. He became a tutor at Christ Church, studying science for several years; he also practised as a physician. His political career began in 1666. After his exile with Shaftesbury he returned to England with William of Orange, and settled at Oates, near High Laver, in Essex. He died on October 28, 1704.

JOHN LOCKE

Ranking among the great English philosophers, Locke in his writings maintained the principles of liberty of thought and speech. His Essay on Human Understanding is famous.

Locks and Keys.

The essential fact about a lock is that it affords security against unauthorised opening of the door, box-lid, or other object to which it is fitted. This is done by making that lock *different* from other locks, so that only the proper key will operate it and allow its bolt to be shot or withdrawn. The invention of the first locks, like that of many other things, has been attributed to the Chinese. It is certain that the ancient Egyptians had locks with movable tumblers; the Greeks also had tumbler locks, one of which is illustrated. The key was something quite different from our modern key. We also show an ancient

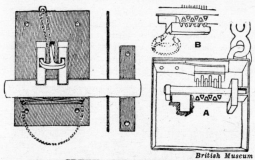

British Museum

GREEK AND ROMAN LOCKS

On the left is an ancient Greek lock, restored. The key, shown inserted, catches in the tumblers and lifts them free from the bolt. In the Roman lock (right) pins pressed into perforations in the bolt (A) are pushed up by the teeth of the key (B); the bolt is then moved forward by the key.

Roman lock, in which pins fit into perforations in a bolt, and are pressed up by teeth in the key. The key can move the bolt forward or backward.

The key in this Roman lock, as in modern ones, has to do two things; to lift pins, or raise levers or tumblers, in a certain manner to free the bolt; it has also to propel the bolt outwards to fasten the door, or to draw the bolt backwards to allow the door to be opened. A third requirement is that the bolt has to be "locked" against movement after it has been shot or withdrawn; this is often done by the key, just as it finishes its movement of the bolt, allowing a stud to fall into a notch in the bolt, or a notch in a separate sliding member called a follower. Other methods are to allow the tumbler to drop on to a fixed stud and lock the bolt in that manner. You can see these devices in our diagrams.

Ancient keys, like the locks to which they belonged, were large by modern standards. Some were beautiful pieces of metalwork, chiselled and chased on the bow and shank. Initials, monograms or designs representing heraldic emblems were often formed in the bow. The bitt—the part which enters the lock and moves the tumblers—was generally very complicated in appearance, with its many clefts and slits to allow it to

pass the ring-shaped wards or the standing wards (which were intended to baffle entrance and movement by any alien key). But some of these shapings were mere shams which, as in some factory-made keys of today, are intended to give an impression of greater security than is really afforded.

The first of the "modern" locks was that invented by Joseph Bramah (1749–1814) He was the son of a small farmer, and when a disabled ankle prevented him from following the plough he was apprenticed to a carpenter. Later, having served his time, he came to London and set up as a cabinet-maker, but turned his inventive faculties to improving water-cocks and pumps. He became famous by his hydraulic press and his new locks. As a boy he had made friends with the village blacksmith, who taught him much and made tools for him out of old files and odd pieces of steel.

Bramah's lock was patented in 1784; it had a sort of nozzle or cylinder projecting from the front, in which were the sliding tumblers which had to be moved in order that the key might shoot the bolt. The key was small, in comparison with earlier ones. Bramah made use of the permutation of numbers, by using several sliders. Thus, with three sliders, these might be arranged in six different ways— 3 x 2 x 1—6; four sliders enabled 24 different arrangements or permutations—4 x 3 x 2 x 1—to be used; five sliders increased the number of different arrangements in the same lock to 120— 5 x 4 x 3 x 2 x 1. This was an important advance, since Bramah, with the same basic type of lock, could guarantee to his customers secure and individual locks which only the appropriate key would open. Moreover, merely by altering the shape of his keys, and forming the keyhole of the lock to suit the new shape, he could turn out another series different from the first.

Bramah, like other locksmiths, aimed at preventing his locks being "picked"— that is, opened by shaped wires called picks, as used by thieves. He exhibited a notice in the window of his shop in Piccadilly, London, offering £200 to anyone who should succeed in picking his improved patent lock. After some years this reward was won by an American lockmaker, Hobbs. Bramah's locks were sold in large numbers for many years. Meanwhile, another famous English locksmith was giving his attention to the problem. This was Charles Chubb (1772–1845), who started in business at Winchester and later built up a concern of world-wide renown in London. He patented what he called his "detector" lock in 1818, using pivoted

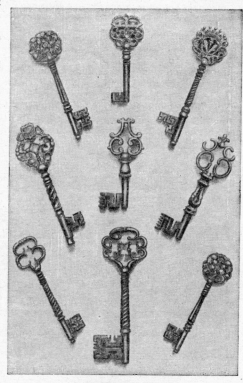

ARTISTRY IN KEYS
In the 16th and 17th centuries keys were often really beautiful pieces of metal-work, as shown by these chiselled steel examples.

tumblers. With his brother Jeremiah he patented various other locks, and designed burglar-proof safes. The firm which he founded was continued by his son John (1816–72), and exists today, though the complex and wonderful locks for safes and bank strongrooms which are now turned out bear small resemblance to those fashioned a century and more ago.

The pin-tumbler lock, produced by the American Linus Yale (1821–68), had two great advantages:

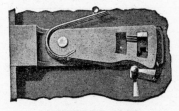

A TUMBLER LOCK
When the key is turned, the tumblers are raised just enough to release the small oblong bolt projection (upper right-hand corner).

desire, while giving your guests the security of an individual lock and key for their rooms, to be able yourself in emergency to open any door. This is the locksmith's problem, and he solves it in various ingenious ways of " mastering and differing." The pins of the pin-tumbler lock may be made in three pieces or " breaks " instead of two, so that while the individual key will turn the cylinder, the master-key will also do so—in this case using another " break " in the pin.

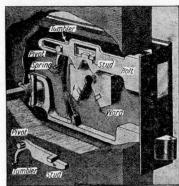
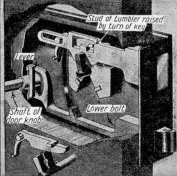
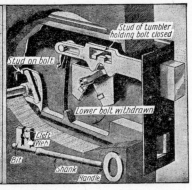

HOW AN ORDINARY DOOR-LOCK WORKS

As the key turns in the lock, it raises a tumbler (shown separately at the bottom of the left-hand picture), which is a pivoted lever held down by a spring. When the key raises the tumbler a stud on it is lifted, as shown in the centre picture, and the bolt can be moved by a further turn of the key, as in the third picture. The tumbler then falls into position, and the stud drops into the other notch of the tumbler, thus holding the bolt immovable until again unlocked by the key.

the key could be small and the lock small and compact. Its principle is well explained by the diagrams at the bottom of this page. Here again the important point is the use of permutations, these being represented by notches of different depth in the key, and by spring-loaded pins of different length in the lock cylinder. Unless the proper key is used, so that all the pins are pushed up clear of the top surface of the cylinder, the cylinder cannot be turned, and the bolt withdrawn. Keys with various groovings are used.

You may have heard of " master-keys." If you were the owner of an hotel you might reasonably

Combination locks will not open, or allow the key or bolts to be operated, unless a series of figures or letters on a number or rings or dials is brought to a number or word which represents the " combination " to which the lock has previously been set. Such locks range from a simple brass padlock, which can be bought for a few shillings, to an elaborate and complicated lock for a safe, which might cost several thousand pounds. In time-locks, a clock governs the time at which the lock can be operated, even if the proper combination is worked; not until the exact time comes round (pre-set beforehand) can the door guarded by a time-lock be opened.

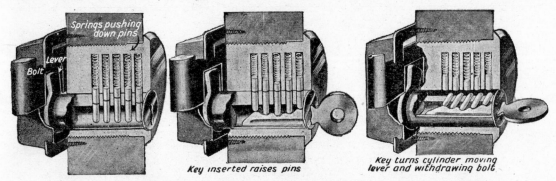

THE MECHANISM OF THE 'YALE' TYPE PIN-TUMBLER LOCK

The pin-tumbler lock for a street door has a narrow cylinder which moves inside another, fixed, cylinder (left). In the movable cylinder is a twisted keyhole, and when the key is inserted a number of notches in it raise up pins in the lock until their ends are in a straight line, as in the centre picture. As the key is then turned the small cylinder is moved round, and the bolt of the lock is drawn back (right). Each lock of this kind has its own individual key.

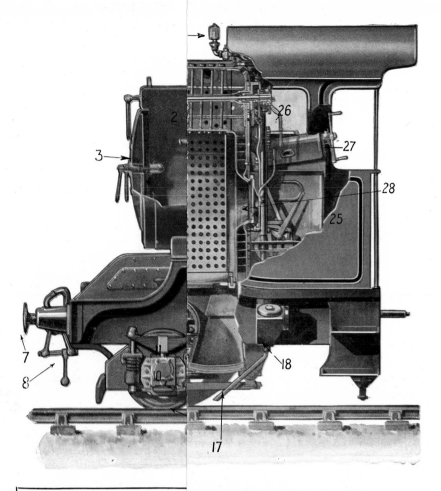

HOW A C
EXPRESS

THIS diagram shows the chief w
so called because these engi
this type haul many of the most i
such famous " fliers " as the Corn
cylinders, two inside the frame and
wheels and the outside cylinders t
and exhaust of the steam to the c

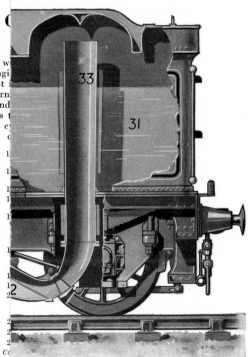

1. Chimney.
2. Smoke-box, which collects the smoke and ashes drawn through the tubes from the fire-box, the smoke being discharged through the chimney.
3. Smoke-box door.
4. Blast pipe, through which the discharge of steam from the cylinders is carried into the smoke-box.
5. Regulator valve, through which steam is admitted to the cylinders.
6. Steam chest, through which the steam enters the cylinders.
7. Buffer.
8. Screw coupling.
9. Bogie wheels.
10. Outside axle bearing for bogie.
11. Bogie spring.

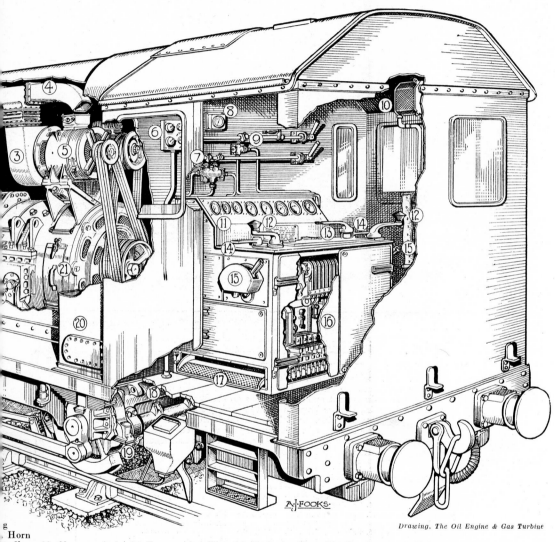

Drawing, *The Oil Engine & Gas Turbine*

g
Horn
andles ; 13. Master switch ; 14. Reverser handles ; 15. Brake handles ; 16. Control gear cubicle ; 17. ' Dead-man ' pedal ;
nk ; 21. Main dynamo ; 22. One point of three-point suspension ; 23. Battery isolating switch ; 24. Battery box.
ind the auxiliary dynamo (5) and the radiator for cooling the main engine is at the front of the loco.

To face page 1981

LOCOMOTIVE

WONDERS *of the Modern* RAILWAY ENGINE

Present-day Steam and Electric and Diesel-electric locomotives represent almost incredible advances on the old 'Rocket' and 'Puffing Billy,' astonishing as these forerunners were in their time.

Locomotive. Like all great inventions, the locomotive ("a machine that can move from place to place") developed through the slow accumulation of improvements made by different inventors. Men in England and France were working on the idea as early as the middle of the 18th century. Some "locos" were designed to run on the ordinary highways, and were forerunners of the motor-car. Richard Trevithick (1771–1833), in England, was the first to make a steam-driven engine which travelled on rails. It was used at the Penydarran ironworks, near Merthyr Tydvil, in 1804, and hauled a load of 20 tons at the rate of five miles an hour. In 1808 Trevithick demonstrated another locomotive in London; it travelled on a circular track at 12 miles an hour. William Hedley improved on this (1813) with his Puffing Billy, built for the Wylam colliery, near Newcastle.

The first really successful locomotive, however, was the work of George Stephenson (*q.v.*), and was used to haul coal for the Killingworth colliery, Northumberland, in 1814. In 1825, at the opening of the Stockton and Darlington railway—a line measuring 37 miles—a Stephenson engine weighing eight tons and capable of 16 miles per hour was used. Of the early locomotives, the Rocket, produced by George and Robert Stephenson, was perhaps the most notable. At the world-famous locomotive trials held at Rainhill, Lancashire, in 1829 this engine is credited with having attained a maximum speed of 29 miles per hour.

Britain's 125 m.p.h. Record

These early locomotives were pygmies compared with the heavy, fast, and powerful machines of today. Speeds exceeding 100 miles per hour have been achieved by express locomotives, the British record of 125 m.p.h. (Mallard) at present standing to the credit of the London & North Eastern Railway (North-Eastern Region, British Railways). Typical British locomotives of the larger types weigh about 160 tons, and can haul a load of 500 tons at 55 miles per hour in everyday service.

The modern steam locomotive has not a high thermal efficiency (*see* Heat), when comparison is made with the fuel used; but in a country like Great Britain, where water power is not generally available to produce cheap electricity, the steam locomotive is an economical means of providing motive power except on lines which carry heavy traffic. It is relatively inexpensive compared with electric traction, and continual attempts are being made to reduce the cost of construction and maintenance, and to add to its efficiency.

Considerable improvements have been attained without changing the general design, which remains much as it was left by Stephenson and other early constructors. Improvements in construction and in the materials used, together with the addition of the superheater (*see* page 489) are, taken together, the greatest advances made so far.

The principal parts of the steam locomotive are:
1. The boiler, including the boiler barrel and fire box, and also the smoke box, ash pan, and other portions connected with the generation of steam.
2. The engine, which includes the cylinders, pistons and piston rods, connecting rods and cranks, also the valves, valve gear, and reversing apparatus.
3. The frame on which the boiler is mounted and to which the cylinders and other working parts are attached; the wheels, four, six or eight in number, two or four of which are revolved by the cylinders; and the bogie, a four-wheeled truck which carries the front part of the engine.
4. The tender, or, in the case of tank engines, the tanks and coal bunkers which carry the supplies of fuel and water.

The boiler (*q.v.*) consists of four main portions—the inner fire box, the outer fire box or shell, the barrel containing the tubes, and the smoke box. In the inner fire box the fire is placed, and the heated gases from it are conducted through a large number of tubes—heating in their passage the water surrounding the tubes and superheating the steam supplied to the cylinders—to the smoke box at the other end, and thence to the chimney. The smoke box also contains the blast pipe, out of which the exhaust steam from the cylinders issues, and which causes the draught for the fire.

With the many tubes the heating surface in contact with water in the boiler is very large. The typical express locomotive already mentioned has a boiler 30 feet long, a total heating surface of 3,600 sq. feet, and a working pressure of 250 lb. per sq. in. Every stroke of the piston sends a discharge of steam through the blast pipe up the chimney, withdrawing a percentage of the contents of the smoke box with it and leaving a partial vacuum in that chamber. Then, to destroy this condition of lowered pressure, atmospheric air rushes through the fire from beneath, producing the rapid combustion desired.

Mechanism of the Steam Engine

We will take next the engine or mechanism by means of which the energy of the steam is transformed into useful work by propelling itself and its load. Primarily, the engine consists of the cylinders in which the steam acts on the pistons, whose reciprocating (to-and-fro) motion is transformed through the medium of the piston and connecting rods into a rotary one at the crank axle, propelling the engine either backwards or forwards as required.

If there are two cylinders there are, of course, two cranks. These are set at an angle of 90 degrees to each other, so that when one piston is at the end of its stroke, or on the "dead centre," the other is in its position of maximum effort. Three- or even four-cylinder locomotives are common.

Steam is admitted alternately on opposite sides of the piston through two steam ports, one at each end of the cylinder, leading from the steam chest. A third port—the exhaust port—allows the steam to escape to the blast pipe. These ports are opened and closed by a valve in which a piston moves backwards and forwards. The piston valve is enclosed in the steam chest into which steam passes from the boiler by means of the main steam pipe. The movement to the valves is imparted by eccentrics and link motion, which serves as a reversing gear.

There are several forms of valve gear, the principal being Stephenson's shifting link motion, Gooch's stationary link motion, Allan's straight link motion, Joy's radial valve gear, and Walschaerts's valve gear. The Stephenson, or shifting link, motion was introduced in 1843, and has been commonly used to this day for locomotives. It is being gradually supplanted, especially in outside-cylinder engines, by Walschaerts's gear.

In the Stephenson motion there are two eccentrics connected to a slotted link; this link is curved, the radius of curvature being that of the eccentric rod. It is capable of being raised or lowered by a lever operated by the driver, and accommodates in its slotted portion a block which slides in the slot, and this is connected directly with the valve by a rod. Therefore, in the mid-position, the valve is not moved by either eccentric. When the block occupies the top or bottom position of the link, it is brought under the influence of either eccentric, and the valve travels its full distance. The extreme positions serve to determine the direction in which the engine will run, backward or forward.

Walschaerts's valve gear has one eccentric and a slotted link, and takes its valve movements also from the crosshead. It produces a more uniform steam distribution than the Stephenson gear.

How Engine and Boiler are Carried

We will now describe the framing and running gear. The engine and boiler are arranged and carried on a framing supported by the wheels and axles. In Britain the frames are usually built up of plates, the two inner ones inside the wheels being the main frames, and the two outer ones supporting the footplates, splashers, etc.

The main frames are arranged vertically, and have to be connected to each other to give them sufficient lateral (sideways) stiffness and to maintain them at the proper distance apart. They are steel plates $1\frac{1}{4}$ to $1\frac{1}{2}$ inches thick, shaped to take the axles of the wheels, and drilled for attachment of the engine details. Firmly bolted to the frames and fitted into the horns are the cast steel horn blocks, having rectangular faces inside which the axle boxes can ride up and down freely.

The connexions of the springs to the frames are by brackets secured on each side of the axles, in which there are holes for the spring hangers to pass through. The hangers are pinned to the top ends of the springs, and are secured below the brackets by nuts, sometimes with rubber washers between. The springs lessen the shocks received by the wheels when running, and are of several forms. Spiral springs are often used for the driving wheels; and laminated, or plate, springs for the carrying wheels. The greater part of the engine is spring-borne; that is, the weight is first conveyed through the brackets to the nuts beneath them; the nuts transmit it to the spring hangers, so that there is a pull at the top-end pins on each side of the spring, which deflect according to the load.

There is an important part of the engine which is not spring-borne. This consists of the wheels and axles themselves, and the driving axle, with the eccentrics and cranks, which really form part of it. Consequently, these details are made as light as possible, consistent with strength. The wheel centres are now usually cast steel, with rolled steel tires shrunk on. Axles also are of steel, with portions at each end carefully turned to form the axle journal bearings and wheel seats. The wheels are pressed on to the axles by hydraulic pressure. Crank axles are solid forgings formed to take the ends of the two connecting rods; or are of the built-up pattern, now a very usual form of construction.

The leading end of express engines is often carried on a separate four-wheeled truck or bogie. Connexion between the main frame of the engine and this bogie is made by a centre pivot and pin, about which the bogies can swivel, as the frame of this is quite separate from the main frame. Besides serving to distribute the weight at the front end of the engine, the bogie gives lateral flexibility on curves. Radial trucks, however, are frequently used, having one pair of wheels only.

Buffer and draw gear next claim our attention. The side buffers, with which all standard gauge engines in Britain are provided, are attached to the buffer beam, arranged to meet those of the vehicles forming the train. A common form of buffer comprises a hollow plunger fitting easily in a casing. Within the plunger is a coiled steel spring; a central pin passes through a hole in the base plate, and after the whole has received an initial compression it is secured by a cotter behind the back plate. There are many other designs in use.

The draw-hook has a shank, which passes through the buffer beam at its centre and pulls on to steel or rubber springs. Through a hole in the hook a link of the shackle of the screw coupling is passed, a swivel being attached to the two ends of the shackle, securing them and the screw together. The screw is revolved by means of the hanging arm and turns in a nut fixed to the other link of the shackle; this second link is hooked on to the next vehicle, and, as the screw is turned, the necessary tension is secured, whilst the weight hanging down prevents the screw from slacking.

Locomotive's Miscellaneous Fittings

Here we can only briefly consider some of the miscellaneous fittings necessary for the running equipment of the locomotive. The adhesion, or resistance to slipping, of the wheels is dependent on the weight placed on the drivers, but qualified by the condition of the rails. In order to work under the most advantageous conditions on wet or greasy rails, and obtain as much adhesion as possible, it is necessary to fit sanding gear, operated by steam or compressed air, for allowing sand to run upon the rails in front of one or more pairs of the coupled wheels.

In reference to running gear, that very necessary item lubrication must be mentioned. When the part to be lubricated has no movement apart from the whole movement of the engine, such as slide bars, axle boxes, etc., the oil is siphoned by worsted trimmings fed from an oil reservoir by capillary attraction. Parts which are subject to violent movement, such as eccentric straps, have oil

Keystone

FULL SPEED AHEAD WHILE STANDING STILL

It is not necessary to run a locomotive on rails to test its efficiency, for this can now be done in the works with far greater accuracy. The engine is mounted on circular disks instead of rails, and on these the wheels can revolve freely while the engine is stationary. The resistance of the disks can be regulated to represent varying loads and gradients, while elaborate mechanism registers the horse-power developed, the fuel consumption, and other facts useful to the designer.

cavities fitted with plug trimmings, which are made by forming a loop of copper wire and wrapping strands of worsted round it, then pushing the whole into the oil hole. As the oil is thrown about by the movement of the part to which it is fixed, some of the oil in the reservoir above the plug passes through it to the bearing.

The brake gear may be arranged to work by hand or power, but in all passenger engines, and most goods engines, power is used (*see* Brakes). The power may be obtained from (1) compressed air, (2) atmospheric pressure, as in the vacuum brake, or (3) steam. The coupled wheels of the engine and the tender wheels are fitted with brake blocks. Engine bogie wheels are not as a rule fitted with brakes.

A brake cylinder and piston are fixed beneath the foot-plate, and the end of the piston rod is connected to a bent lever, which has an arm attached to a cross-shaft, the other end of the lever being connected to the end of one of the brake rods. When air or steam is admitted to the brake cylinder, the rods are pulled, and with them a series of cross-beam levers, forcing the blocks hard against the wheels. Brake gear is usually compensated so as to give equal block pressures on all wheels.

Engines intended for short runs are often provided with tanks for water and with coal bunkers upon their own frames. Wash plates are provided in these tanks to prevent the water from washing from one end to the other when the brakes are applied. Sometimes the tanks are made semi-circular in shape to fit on top of the boiler—these are called saddle tanks. Tank engines are so designed with respect to their wheel arrangement as to run equally well in either direction.

Tenders on standard British locomotives are constructed to carry up to 5,000 gallons of water and nine tons of coal, and usually run on six or eight wheels. The coal space is above the tank, and is made with a sloping bottom so that there is a tendency for the coal to shake forward towards the door, thus being convenient for the fireman. This is known as self-trimming. Water pick-up arrangements are fitted to tenders, when water troughs are available. This reduces the tank capacity necessary when water pick-up gear is not used.

Passing mention may be made of the application of compounding to locomotives. In a compound engine, the steam in passing through one (high-pressure) cylinder expands only partially, and is then exhausted into the larger low-pressure cylinder

AT THE BIRTH OF AN EXPRESS LOCOMOTIVE

Western Region, British Railways

The preliminary stages in the building of a locomotive are shown in these two photographs, both taken in the Swindon works of the Western Region, British Railways (formerly the Great Western Railway). In that at the top the framework of an express engine of the King George V type is being laid down. The lower photograph shows a later stage in the process of erection; facing the camera at the right is a pair of inside cylinders, mounted between the frames of a four-cylinder engine. The boiler will rest on the curved saddle seen above the cylinders. On the left the building of a similar locomotive has been taken a stage further, and we see the outside cylinders bolted on to the frame.

A RAILWAY GIANT RECEIVES ITS BOILER

When the framework is in position and the cylinders have been bolted into place, as shown in the facing page, the next stage is to put the boiler in position. Travelling cranes convey the huge structure from one point to another, and in the top left photograph it is seen held front downwards over a riveting machine. In the top right photograph the completed boiler has just been lowered into position on the frame for attachment. In the centre of the lower photograph is seen an array of pairs of wheels on to the proper complement of which the frame and boiler will be lowered.

or cylinders, in which expansion is completed, and finally exhausts into the air.

While most locomotives have two cylinders only, there are large numbers of three- and four-cylinder engines in service. They offer certain advantages compared with ordinary two-cylinder types, but are, of course, more complicated. Three-cylinder engines have three cranks, usually arranged to divide the crank circle into three equal parts, meaning that they are at 120 degrees to each other. This provides an even turning moment and tends to prevent undue slipping of the wheels, especially at starting. Four-cylinder engines are largely used for passenger trains, especially on the G.W.R. (Western Region, British Railways). Such engines have four cranks, so arranged that they divide the crank circle into four equal parts; this means that they make angles of 90 degrees to one another. With this arrangement the cranks for adjacent cylinders are placed opposite to each other, while each pair is at 90 degrees to the other pair.

Balancing Weights in Wheel Rims

This plan enables a certain amount of balance to be obtained for the parts like the pistons and their rods and the crossheads which move to and fro—reciprocate, as it is called. Both three- and four-cylinder engines move more steadily over the track than those with only two cylinders. Whatever the type of cylinder arrangement adopted, provision must be made to balance completely the revolving parts of the motion ; and at the same time some additional weight is added to the balance weights seen in the wheels to compensate the disturbances caused by the reciprocating parts of the motion.

When the balancing weights in the rims of the wheels are rising as the wheels revolve, they tend to lift the wheels from the rails ; and conversely, when they are moving downwards towards the rails, there is a tendency to press the wheels downwards on to the rails. This action is due to the fact that, as already stated, there is more mass in the balance weights than is required to counteract the revolving parts, so that there is a certain amount of free centrifugal force (q.v.), which acts to balance the reciprocating parts in the longitudinal direction. In the vertical direction, there is not only no reciprocating balance due to the balance weight, but actually there is a vertical disturbance tending to lift or force the wheels off or on to the rails.

With these considerations in mind, reciprocating parts are made as light in weight as possible, and only a small proportion of their weight is balanced. The large locomotives now required are so heavy in themselves that but a small part of the reciprocating parts needs balancing, because the mass of the locomotive resists longitudinal fore-and-aft disturbances which are the result of the unbalanced reciprocating masses.

Thus far we have considered only steam locomotives of normal types, and have not mentioned what are called articulated (jointed) designs. In many instances these special types are required especially to obtain high powers on lightly constructed tracks, and where sharp curves are to be negotiated. Different forms of articulated locomotives have been brought out from time to time. Such engines have used various methods for obtaining a flexible wheel base so that they can travel round curves while at the same time running on a number of wheels, and so can reduce the weight borne by any one pair.

The best known of the articulated designs are now the Beyer-Garratt, the Mallet and the Shay locomotives. The Beyer-Garratt is very extensively employed on many railways, amongst which is the great railway system of the Union of South Africa. The design is relatively simple : the fundamental principles involved include a boiler carried by a frame in the form of a cradle, which at each end rests on pivot centres attached to "power bogies." These bogies comprise the cylinders, driving gear and the wheels. The wheel arrangement of each of the two bogies is alike and is designed to suit the track and the tractive force required. Flexibly designed steam and exhaust piping are employed, and supplies of fuel and water are accommodated on the power units that, at the end of the boiler next the driver's cab, carry the fuel as well as part of the water.

The Mallet, largely used in America, especially in the United States, has been developed to very high powers. Such engines have a boiler of the normal type, carried by two separate groups of driving wheels. One group at the hind end is rigidly held in a framing supporting the fire box end of the boiler; and the leading group of wheels is held in a separate framing, hinged at its hind end with the front of the trailing set of frames. The weight of the front end of the boiler is borne by a sliding support fitted to the front engine frames. The front engine frame is the articulated feature, as it can swing about the hinged joint with the rigid rear frame, and can so accommodate itself to any curvatures in the track.

Each of the two sets of engines has identical cylinders, driving gear and wheels. As in the case of the Beyer-Garratt, the power units have wheel arrangements to suit the tractive force required and the wheel loadings allowed. Modern Mallet type engines have four equal sized cylinders, all receiving steam from the boiler; though, when first introduced, such engines were compounds having two small cylinders, taking boiler steam, fitted to the rear frames and exhausting into larger low pressure cylinders at the front end. Formerly these locomotives were principally used for helping heavy trains on steep gradients, but now they are found in general heavy use.

For Lightly Constructed Tracks

The Shay locomotive differs materially from those mentioned. In this case the driving engines, of the three-cylinder type, are arranged in an entirely different manner, being built as a unit attached on one side of the boiler, the drive being taken by a flexible line of shafting to the bogies carrying the locomotive. The main shaft drives the axles through gearing made up of bevel wheels, protected by casings.

Engines of this kind are used for relatively slow haulage over lightly constructed tracks, such as may be found at mines; and are also largely used by lumber companies (see Lumber) in their felling regions, where the tracks are often rather roughly laid. They can haul heavy loads at low speeds and, as their weight is distributed on several wheel pairs, they are suitable for tracks composed of lightweight rails.

The fuel most commonly used for steam locomotives is coal, and in the case of large and powerful engines mechanical stokers are fitted in order that sufficient coal can be fired to produce the high powers required. Mechanical stokers are fitted as standard for locomotives using coal in the U.S.A. and in Canada, and to some extent on the South African Railways.

Powdered coal has been tried, but so far without success. On some railways steam locomotives are fired with oil. This is, of course, more particularly the case where oil is more easily obtainable than coal. Some railways in Russia and Persia use oil, and some railways of the U.S.A. (especially those in the Western States which are far removed from coal fields but have access to oil supplies). Oil has a higher heat value than coal and therefore less is required; but it is more costly. It can be used quite readily with only relatively small alterations to the fire box as used for coal-burning engines.

For oil burning, a tank is fitted on the engine tender to carry the oil fuel. This is fitted with heating coils to maintain the oil sufficiently liquid to flow to the burners in the lower part of the fire box, which is lined with firebricks to protect the fire box plates from the great heat of the flame. The usual grate bars for a coal fire are not fitted.

Steam locomotives, though still moving not less than 90 per cent of the world's rail traffic, have to meet competition set up by both "straight" electric and Diesel-electric locomotives. Both of these rivals to the steam loco. offer certain advantages as compared with steam traction, but both are extremely costly per locomotive. Further, in the case of electric traction, to the high unit cost of each locomotive must be added the cost of the electric generating plant and the transmission system. Electric traction can, in general, only be justified where line occupation is exceptionally dense—as, for instance, where there are very frequent and extensive suburban passenger services. Main line traffic over heavy grades sometimes calls for electric traction, and is economically possible where hydro-electric generating plant can be made available.

Electric locomotives may be of great power on account of the practically limitless energy that can be made available by large generating stations. Therefore, heavy fast traffic may be readily operated.

STREAMLINED TO LESSEN AIR RESISTANCE
This Pacific type locomotive of the Southern Region, British Railways, is of the West Country class and shows a great advance in railway engine design. Air-smoothed, it is a 3-cylinder high pressure locomotive, similar to the Merchant Navy class, and built during the Second World War (1939–45).

The availability of electric motive power units is high because they require only minimum attention. This is a great advantage.

As an alternative to "straight" electric traction and to the steam locomotive, considerable progress has been made in the development of Diesel engines (q.v.) for locomotive purposes. To use effectively the Diesel motor, however, involves the employment of the electric transmission of power between the engine and the rails. This complicates the locomotive as well as adding considerably to the expense, already high by reason of costly Diesel multi-cylinder engines. Like a steam locomotive, the Diesel-electric is a self-contained unit, being independent of an outside source of power supply, unlike an electric locomotive.

Electric locomotives comprise electric motors, usually geared to several pairs of carrying wheels. The current is taken from overhead wire equipment, or from a third rail. The engine cab contains the switchgear, train heating equipment, and the driver's control. There must also be equipment for operating the continuous brake for the train, and the brake gear for the locomotive itself. "Regenerative" braking is also provided, consisting of apparatus permitting of changing over the traction motors to generators; these act as dynamos when the locomotive is running down grades, enabling the current thus generated to be supplied to the mains. The power so produced and absorbed acts as a brake for controlling the speed of the train. The line voltage is usually much higher than that which can conveniently be supplied to the traction motors; therefore, further equipment in the form of transformers is required. The traction motors have often to meet an overload, and to enable them to do so, and to run continuously on normal power for long periods, blowers are provided to ventilate each motor, thereby keeping them cool, which is a matter of considerable importance.

Diesel locomotives, as used for main line traffic, comprise a multi-cylinder vertical engine, directly connected to an electric generator. This generator provides electrical energy for traction motors, as used for "straight" electric locomotives. Power and speed are obtained by a controller of the same general type as for electric locomotives. Thus the Diesel-electric locomotive is really a mobile

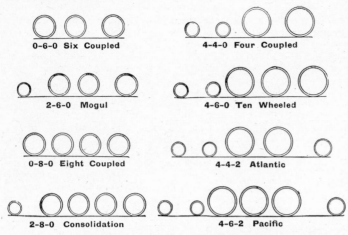

0-6-0 Six Coupled

4-4-0 Four Coupled

2-6-0 Mogul

4-6-0 Ten Wheeled

0-8-0 Eight Coupled

4-4-2 Atlantic

2-8-0 Consolidation

4-6-2 Pacific

LOCOMOTIVE WHEEL ARRANGEMENTS

Here are shown the wheel arrangements now most generally used on British railways. First (left to right) come the ' idle ' wheels, then the main driving wheels, and last the trailing wheels. The four types on the left apply to goods engines, those on the right to express locomotives.

electric generating station using its electric current for traction purposes.

As in the case of the " straight " electric locomotive, a large amount of auxiliary equipment is necessary. For the engine there must be lubricating apparatus; radiators and fans for the cylinder-jacket cooling water; and an auxiliary exciter for the generator ; also a fuel oil tank. Electrically-driven air blowers are needed to keep the traction motor cool; an electrical air compressor, or exhauster, is fitted for the continuous brake, according to whether this is the Westinghouse or automatic vacuum. A carriage warming steam boiler is also fitted; and electric storage batteries to furnish current to drive the main generator when starting the Diesel engine.

For high powers, Diesel-electric locomotives are made up of two, three or four units, each of, say, 2,000 h.p., providing therefore 4,000, 6,000 or 8,000 h.p. The first cost of each unit is very high compared with that of the steam locomotive of equivalent power; but, to offset this, high " availability " is claimed, due to the short time required to turn round after each trip. This can only be attained if proper facilities are available, and in the U.S.A., where great advances have been made in high capacity Diesel-electric locomotives, very elaborate terminal facilities have been provided. The high cost of these locomotives makes it necessary that they should be utilised to the greatest extent in revenue-earning traffic.

Locomotives are usually classified according to their wheel arrangement—giving, in order, the number of "idle" wheels in front, of main coupled driving wheels, and of idle trailing wheels. An outstanding class is the 4-6-2 or Pacific. This includes some of the finest locomotives in Britain, such as the stream-lined Coronation Scot and the Princess Elizabeth of the L.M.S. (Midland Region and Scottish Region), the Coronation and Silver Jubilee and long-famous Flying Scotsman of the L.N.E.R. (North-Eastern Region and Scottish Region). No. 6202 of the L.M.S.—Britain's only turbine locomotive—is also a Pacific.

The 4-6-0's—i.e., locomotives with a leading four-wheeled bogie and six coupled wheels—include the Royal Scots of the L.M.S., Castles and Kings of the G.W.R. (Western Region) and Lord Nelsons and King Arthurs of the S.R. (Southern Region). Other notable wheel arrangements are the 4-4-0 (e.g. the S.R. Schools class), 4-4-2 or Atlantic; and, for very heavy mixed or goods trains, the 2-6-0 (Mogul) and 2-8-2 (Mikado). The locomotive with the greatest number of wheels (if one excepts articulated types like the gigantic Beyer-Garratt) is probably a 4-14-4 built in Russia in 1935. (See Railways).

Lodge, SIR OLIVER JOSEPH (1851-1940).

When Lord Kelvin was invited to join the board of directors of the newly-formed Marconi Wireless & Telegraph Co. he stipulated that Oliver Lodge should also be asked, because he recognized that the name of Lodge must for ever be associated with those of Clerk-Maxwell and Hertz in the brilliant researches and mathematical deductions which made wireless telegraphy possible.

Born at Penkhull, Staffordshire, on June 12, 1851, Oliver Lodge was, at 24, a lecturer at Bedford College, London, and at 30 professor of physics at Liverpool University. Later, he was appointed first principal of Birmingham University, and at various times was President of the British Association, of the Physical Society of London, and of the Society for Psychical Research. He was knighted in 1902 and elected F.R.S. The Royal Society presented him with the Albert Gold Medal for his work in wireless telegraphy.

It is for his discoveries in wireless communication, and his tuning method, that Lodge is best

SIR OLIVER JOSEPH LODGE
Pioneer work of this British scientist was done in examining the nature of electro-magnetic waves and in wireless telegraphy. Knighted in 1902, Sir Oliver Lodge died on August 22, 1940.

known. In 1894, using a " coherer " invented by Edouard Branly,

MONARCHS OF THE STEEL HIGHWAY

The famous Golden Arrow express train. running over the Southern Region, British Railways, between London's Victoria Station and Dover, Kent, is here shown headed by an equally famous locomotive of the Merchant Navy class. These engines have several features novel in British practice, including an automatic power-operated fire-door. They are of the three cylinder pattern and have the Pacific or 4–6–2 wheel arrangement. Including the tender, running on six wheels, the total weight of the locomotive, when it is fully loaded and ready for the road, is 144 tons.

A HUNDRED YEARS OF LOCOMOTIVE PROGRESS

Photopress: Fox

The top photograph shows a modern reproduction of George Stephenson's pioneer locomotive the Rocket standing against one of its present-day successors. Below are three locomotives which span the history of railways for 100 years. Left is the Lion built in 1837 for the Liverpool and Manchester Railway and now preserved in Lime Street Station, Liverpool. Centre is the Coronation built in 1911 and named to commemorate the Coronation of King George V. Right is the Midland Region streamlined locomotive Coronation built in 1937 to mark the Coronation of King George VI. It was then a leading example of high-speed passenger locomotive design.

BROAD GAUGE AND NARROW GAUGE OF THE G.W.R.

Courtesy of the Western Region

The Great Western Railway, now the Western Region, British Railways, was originally built with a gauge of seven feet, whereas all other railways had a gauge of four feet eight and a half inches. In the early '90s, however, the Great Western decided to abandon the broad gauge and conform to that of other lines. The top photograph shows the last broad gauge train passing through the Sonning cutting on May 23, 1892. Below is a modern express train, the Cheltenham Flyer, on its run to London, travelling on the narrow gauge lines which are now universal in Great Britain and are in general use in most Continental countries and all the principal railways of the United States and Canada.

SIX 'KINGS' SPICK AND SPAN FOR A DAY'S RUN

Topical

When a train arrives at the end of its journey, or when locomotives are changed during the run of a long-distance express, the engine is taken to the sheds to prepare it for the next day's work. This photograph shows a row of engines of the King class on the Western Region just after leaving the sheds. The furnaces have been re-lit and steam is up, while the paint and brass have been polished till they shine again. The tenders have been filled with coal and water, and one by one these engines, which have the 4–6–0 wheel arrangement, will back on to the trains they are to haul.

STREAMLINED GIANTS IN THEIR SILVER ARMOUR

Fox

The three locomotives on the left of this photograph are streamlined; that is to say, the boiler and all external working parts are encased in a covering designed to offer the least possible resistance to the air. They were employed in drawing the fastest long-distance trains on the London and North-Eastern Railway, now part of the Eastern and North-Eastern Region, British Railways. The first one, named Silver Jubilee, began to run in 1935, the year of the Silver Jubilee of King George V. The names of the earliest engines of this class included the word 'silver.'

ENGINES OF POWER AND SPEED ON TWO CONTINENTS

Courtesy of Swiss Federal Railways and Canadian National Railways

In this page are shown two of the most powerful locomotives in the world. The top one is an electric locomotive of the Swiss Federal Railways used for hauling the heaviest trains over steep gradients. The Swiss Railways have been almost entirely electrified, for Switzerland has an abundance of water power and electricity can be generated cheaply. The lower photograph shows a semi-streamlined steam locomotive of the Canadian National Railways. Capable of a speed of 100 miles per hour, it hauls trains far heavier than those on British railways.

AMERICAN RAILWAY MAMMOTH THAT LIVES ON OIL

J. R. Hind

This photograph shows the front of an American stream-lined locomotive, suggesting in a remarkable degree its speed and strength. The motive power is a 2,400-h.p. Diesel motor, which works on heavy oil. This engine was designed to haul a train known as the City of San Francisco, making round trips between Chicago and San Francisco The train consisted of 11 carriages, including dining and sleeping cars, and provided all the comforts of a hotel for the passengers. This type of engine, capable of a speed of 100 m.p.h., was also put into service in Britain in 1948.

1995

WASH AND BRUSH-UP AT THE END OF A RUN

When a locomotive is taken to the engine shed at the end of a turn of duty it will be cleaned before returning to work. To save valuable time new devices are being employed, one of which is shown in operation above. Hot water under pressure and mixed with a small quantity of oil or a special compound quickly washes off accumulations of grease and dirt. This is an important job, because all moving parts have to be carefully examined by experienced workmen, to see that they are in perfect order ; and that cannot be properly done unless the parts are reasonably clean.

Thos. Walker & Son, Ltd.

HOW A SHIP'S LOG MEASURES A VESSEL'S SPEED

To ascertain the speed of a vessel a taffrail log (upper left) is fixed to the upper part of the ship's stern, the cable being allowed to stream in the water. At the end of the cable is a rotator (top right) which when dragged through the water revolves, thereby rotating the cable and operating gears in the log, the hands of which indicate the distance traversed. The electric log (lower left) is connected to a registering instrument (lower centre) on the ship's bridge (lower right).

Lodge succeeded in picking up wireless signals made by electro-magnetic oscillations sent out by Hertz's method. The distance was only about 150 yards, but in the words of the French proverb, " It is only the first step which matters," and Lodge had shown the way, with this and other early experiments.

Only Lodge's compeers in science are able to estimate the great value of all his labours in physics, especially in electro-magnetism. He discovered, almost simultaneously with Hertz, the evidence of electric waves ; his experiments illustrating the vibrations excited when a Leyden jar (q.v.) is discharged were the first practical demonstrations of electric waves. In his devising of a practical means of tuning a wireless circuit, so that it would respond only to a particular frequency of signal, Lodge anticipated Marconi.

Retiring from the principalship of Birmingham University in 1919, Sir Oliver devoted himself to the study of psychical problems, and eventually became a firm believer in the possibility of real communication with the dead. His son Raymond had been killed in the First World War, and, in his memory, he wrote Raymond, or Life and Death (1916), in which he expounds his views on spiritualism.

Among his scientific publications were Signalling without Wires, Electrons, Ether and Reality, Relativity, Man and the Universe, Life and Matter, and Science and Human Progress.

Log, SHIP'S. The speed of a ship is reckoned by a device called a log. The simplest is a wooden board with a line attached, thrown from the stern. The board, called the log-ship, is shaped like the sector of a circle, and is weighted on the curved edge so that the "ship" floats with its point upwards. The log-line is attached by two short lines to two holes, one in each lower corner; one such attachment is fixed, but the other is made by a bone peg fixed to the end of its line and pushed into the hole in the log-ship.

The idea is that when both short lines of this " harness " are attached to the board, the latter floats upright in the water and offers resistance; hence the line unwinds on its reel as the ship goes on. When it is desired to pull the log-ship and line back into the vessel, the line is checked, and the resistance causes the bone peg to pull out of its hole. Then the board, being attached to the log-line now by only one short rope of the harness, drops from its upright position and floats flat on the water, offering little resistance and being readily pulled in.

The log-line is marked off into divisions called knots, by coloured pieces of cloth. Commonly these " knots " are 47·33 inches apart. A sand-glass is used to measure the period of time during which the knots are counted, as the line runs off its reel after the log has been " heaved " by hurling the log-ship over the stern of the vessel. This glass is shaped like an egg-glass, and its sand runs out in 28 seconds. The length of a division on the log-line bears to the nautical mile of 6,080 feet the same ratio as 28 seconds does to one hour. The log is heaved and the sand-glass turned; then, when the sand has quite run out, the line is checked and the nearest knot noted. The number of knots of line run out gives the speed in " knots," or nautical-miles per hour.

The hand log is used only for slow speeds, and did very well in the days of sailing ships ; it is said that the name came from a primitive method of throwing out a piece of wood at the bows of a ship and counting the time taken by it to pass two marked points on the deck. But all such facile derivations are suspect, and it is possible that the name came instead from " clog," a wooden block used to check movement.

The mechanical log used today works somewhat on the same principle as a speedometer, and shows the distance in miles traversed directly on a dial. The log-line is attached to a spinner not unlike that which the angler uses when spinning for pike in a stream, with propeller-like vanes which cause it to rotate as it is dragged through the water by the motion of the ship. A line connects the spinner with the registering mechanism in a case fixed to the stern of the ship. The spinner twists the line, and the movement is communicated to the wheels in the recording apparatus, so that the distance is shown by the pointers of the dial. A stage further in development is the electric log, which is con-nected to a registering instrument on the navigating bridge, where the officer can see it at all times.

From the practice of entering the speed and distance in a book regularly this book came to be called the log-book, or log for short. In such a book all important events and details are entered, and it is the diary or journal of a ship's voyage. When a member of the crew commits an offence his name and the particulars are entered in the log, and he is said to be " logged." The practice of keeping a log was extended to aircraft, in whose log details of flights, etc., are recorded. Motorists also keep a log-book for their cars, in which registra-tion particulars are written. The book goes with the car in any change of ownership, and changes in registration are noted in it, together with a record of licences issued and other official particulars.

Logarithms.
If we want to use the simplest and surest method of multiplying or divid-ing complicated numbers (whole numbers or deci-mals of any magnitude), then we must learn logarithms, rightly described as one of the most valuable inventions ever made in practical mathe-matics. They make the hardest sums easy. With logarithms we multiply by adding, and divide by subtracting; and the numbers we add or subtract in order to do complicated multiplication and division sums are all set out in the logarithmic tables found in most mathematical text-books.

Logarithms were invented by the Scottish mathe-matician, John Napier (1550–1617), 8th laird of Merchiston, who in 1614 published a treatise in Latin of only 97 pages called Mirifici Logarith-morum Canonis Descriptio. He himself coined the word logarithm from two Greek words meaning " ratio " and " number."

The logarithms we use mainly today are com-puted to the base of 10, and are called " common " logs. " Natural " or Napieran logs. are computed to the base of 2·7183, for which the symbol is e. Napier's great contribution to mathematics was the compilation of numbers in a tabular system so that calculation could be simplified and made more rapid. Such tables of logs. may be calculated to few or to many places of decimals. Four-figure tables are accurate enough for most work with which the young student is concerned ; such tables are often given in elementary books of mathematics. (Seven-figure tables, of numbers up to 100,000, are published by W. & R. Chambers, Ltd., of Edin-burgh. A Ministry of Education pamphlet giving four-figure tables from 10 to 99, and corresponding tables of anti-logarithms, is published by His Majesty's Stationery Office.)

The idea of logarithms is based on another one which we meet in algebra. You probably know that to multiply a^2 by a^3 we merely add together the *indices*, or *powers*, as the small figures are called (the answer being a^5); while to divide a^6 by a^4 we sub-tract (the answer being a^2). Now, suppose that a represents 10. Then we can state the sum 100×1000 as $10^2 \times 10^3 = 10^5 = 100,000$; and the division sum $1,000,000 \div 10,000$ as $10^6 \div 10^4 = 10^2 = 100$.

In " common " logarithms every number is re-duced to a power of ten, which is called the *base;* thus, for instance, the number 2·643 can be expressed as $10^{0.4221}$ and the number 372·7 as $10^{2.5713}$. Or, to say it in the correct way, the logarithm of 2·643 to base 10 is 0·4221; the logarithm of 372·7 to base 10 is 2·5713. Therefore, if we want to multiply these numbers we can state the sum 2.643×372.7 as $10^{0.4221} \times 10^{2.5713}$. Adding the indices, or logarithms, the answer is 2·9934, which represents the number 985, as obtained by simple multiplication.

But it is obvious that we cannot spend our time in working out what powers of 10 the numbers 2·643 and 372·7 are, even if we knew how, or what number is represented by $10^{2.9934}$. And, indeed, there is no need for us to do that, for it has already been done for us in the logarithm tables. A short extract from four-figure tables is printed here to explain the method of use.

For clearness we will keep to the same sum: 2.643×372.7. Look in the left-hand column of the table for **26**; then look along the same line until, below the number 4 at the head of the column, you see **4216**. This is the log. corresponding to 264. Now look at the right-hand part of the table (which is called the table of " mean differences "). Here, on the same line as 26, and under the number 3 at the top of the column, we find the number **5**. This must be added to 4216, giving **4221** as the logarithm corresponding to the number 2643. As you will observe, no notice has yet been taken of the decimal point in our original number.

The number to the left of the decimal point in a log. is known as the *characteristic*, and is deter-mined by reference to how many digits there are (to the left of the decimal point) in the original number (2·643) whose log. we seek. There is *one* digit in the number whose log. we seek. There-fore there are *no* digits to the left of the decimal point in the log.; or we can express this by saying that the digit is " zero," 0. We write the log. as 0·4221. The decimal portion of the log. is called the *mantissa*. The rule for the characteristic is as follows: the characteristic is always one less than the number of digits to the left of the decimal point in the original number whose log. we are seeking. For example, it would be 2 for 739; 3 for 7396; 4 for 73981, and so on. Adding the characteristic and mantissa together gives the logarithm sought.

Now let us find the log. of the other number in our sum—372·7. The number obtained from the table (column 1) alongside 37 and under the main column headed 2 is **5705**; we add 8 for the fourth figure, got from the table of mean differences under the right-hand column headed 7: this makes a total of **5713**. Now the original number (372·7) has three digits to the left of the decimal point; this, by our rule, denotes that the characteristic of the logarithm must be 1 less—that is, 2. So the logarithm of the second original number is **2·5713**.

All this sounds complicated, and you will probably be wondering where the quickness of the logarithmic method comes in. But the task takes very much less time than its explanation. Now for the multiplication. It is done by *adding* the two logs.: 0·4221+2·5713=**2·9934**. We look this up in the log. table, where it can be found quite as easily as in a table of anti-logarithms. Look for the number **9934** in the body of the log. table; it corresponds, we find, with 985 (**98** in column 1, and the third figure, **5**, at the head of the column in which we find the log. 9934). So **985** is the number resulting from multiplying 2·643 by 372·7.

To use the table of anti-logarithms for finding the number corresponding to 2·9934, look first for the first two figures (**99**) in column 1; under the third figure (**3**) of the log. we find the number **9840**. There is still the fourth figure of the log. to evaluate, and we refer to the column headed 4 in the table of mean differences; here in the same line in which we found 9840, we now find the figure **9**, which is to be added to 9840, making a total of **9849**, actually **984·9**. The slight difference between this and the

number (985) obtained by the first method is due to our using four-figure tables. In seven figure tables we find the log. of 985 to be 9934362; that of 984·9 is 9933921.

The log. of a number less than 1 is a *minus* quantity; the log. of a number greater than 1 and less than 10 is a *fraction*. The logs. of numbers greater than 10 and less than 100 are between 1 and 2—*i.e.* 1 plus a decimal; those of numbers greater than 100 and less than 1,000 are 2 plus a decimal portion.

Now, suppose we want the answer to the division sum 6794÷86; we proceed exactly in the same manner, writing down for 6794 its characteristic 3 and its mantissa ·8321 (thus log.6794=3·8321); and for 86 we write its characteristic 1 and its mantissa ·9345 (thus log.86=1·9345). As it is a division sum, we must *subtract* to find our answer: 3·8321−1·9345=1·8976. We turn to the table of anti-logarithms to find the numerical value of 1·8976, knowing that it must consists of at least two whole numbers, since its characteristic is 1; we find that 1·8976 is the logarithm of 79, which is our answer.

It is often troublesome to find by arithmetical means the square, cube, or higher power of even comparatively small numbers, but never so by logarithms. And in finding the powers of large numbers the saving of time is remarkable. Suppose we want to find the cube of, say, 17, all we have to do is to look up our tables and find log.17=1·2304489, multiply this by 3 to get 3·6913467, and so get the logarithm of the required cube. Turning to the table of logarithms we find that 3·6913467 (actually 3·6913468 in seven-figure table) is the logarithm of 4913, which is our answer. Thus, instead of doing the laborious sum (17×17×17), we merely write down log.(17)³=3 log.17, and consult the tables.

Similarly, if asked to find the cube root of 2197, we merely look up its logarithm 3·3418301 and divide it by 3, giving us 1·1139433. Looking up 1·1139433 in the logarithms table (actually 1·1139434 in seven-figure table), we get the value

	0	1	2	3	4	5	6	7	8	9	1	2	3	4	5	6	7	8	9
26	4150	4166	4183	4200	**4216**	4232	4249	4265	4281	4298	2	3	5	7	8	10	11	13	15
27	4314	4330	4346	4362	4378	4393	4409	4425	4440	4456	2	3	5	6	8	9	11	13	14
28	4472	4487	4502	4518	4533	4548	4564	4579	4594	4609	2	3	5	6	8	9	11	12	14
29	4624	4639	4654	4669	4683	4698	4713	4728	4742	4757	1	3	4	6	7	9	10	12	13
30	4771	4786	4800	4814	4829	4843	4857	4871	4886	4900	1	3	4	6	7	9	10	11	13
36	5563	5575	5587	5599	5611	5623	5635	5647	5658	5670	1	2	4	5	6	7	8	10	11
37	5682	5694	**5705**	5717	5729	5740	5752	5763	5775	5786	1	2	3	5	6	7	8	9	10
38	5798	5809	5821	5832	5843	5855	5866	5877	5888	5899	1	2	3	5	6	7	8	9	10
39	5911	5922	5933	5944	5955	5966	5977	5988	5999	6010	1	2	3	4	5	7	8	9	10
40	6021	6031	6042	6053	6064	6075	6085	6096	6107	6117	1	2	3	4	5	6	8	9	10
96	9823	9827	9832	9836	9841	9845	9850	9854	9859	9863	0	1	1	2	2	3	3	4	4
97	9868	9872	9877	9881	9886	9890	9894	9899	9903	9908	0	1	1	2	2	3	3	4	4
98	9912	9917	9921	9926	9930	**9934**	9939	9943	9948	9952	0	1	1	2	2	3	3	4	4
99	9956	9961	9965	9969	9974	9978	9983	9987	9991	9996	0	1	1	2	2	3	3	3	4

ANTI-LOGARITHMS

	0	1	2	3	4	5	6	7	8	9	1	2	3	4	5	6	7	8	9
·96	9120	9141	9162	9183	9204	9226	9247	9268	9290	9311	2	4	6	8	11	13	15	17	19
·97	9333	9354	9376	9397	9419	9441	9462	9484	9506	9528	2	4	7	9	11	13	15	17	20
·98	9550	9572	9594	9616	9638	9661	9683	9705	9727	9750	2	4	7	9	11	13	16	18	20
·99	9772	9795	9817	**9840**	9863	9886	9908	9931	9954	9977	2	5	7	9	11	14	16	18	20

Portions of tables of logarithms and anti-logarithms to explain methods of calculation described in the text are shown. The figures in bold type are those used in the examples.

1300, and since there must be two whole numbers in the answer, we get 13 as the cube root of 2197. From these examples it is clear that the principal qualities of logarithms are represented by the equations:

$$\text{Log. }(xy) = \log.x + \log.y; \quad \text{Log. }(^x/_y) = \log.x - \log.y;$$

$$\text{Log.}x^y = y\log.x; \quad \text{Log.}(\sqrt[y]{x}) = {}^1/_y\log.x;$$

where x and y are any quantities, and the common base is 10. Of course, these equations may be expanded indefinitely, as, for example, log.(wxyz) = log.w + log.x + log.y + log.z.

This simple method of multiplication and division, or of obtaining powers or roots, which takes only a few seconds—not nearly as long as you require to read this explanation—is not confined to whole numbers only, but is also applied to decimals. The characteristic in the case of decimals is treated as *negative*, while the mantissa is *positive*; the rule holds that the characteristic is one less than the whole numbers of the expression. Thus while log.20 = 1·3010, and log.2 = 0·3010, log.0·20 = $\overline{1}$·30.0 (with a " bar " or minus sign written above the characteristic to show it is negative), the mantissa being the same in either case. All operations with negative characteristics are performed according to algebraic rules.

The reader interested in logarithms is recommended to purchase a book of seven-figure logs.; and to evaluate any logarithms by reference to these tables rather than to anti-logarithm tables. An important application of logarithms is in the slide-rule calculator used by engineers and others.

Lohengrin. (Pron. lō'-en-grin). According to a medieval German romance, Elsa, a fair young daughter of the Duke of Brabant, was in distress, having been falsely accused by Count Frederick of Telramund of the murder of her brother, and was waiting despairingly for someone to come to her aid, when there appeared a knight in a boat drawn by a silver swan. This was Lohengrin, the son of an English knight Sir Perceval (Parsifal), whom King Arthur had sent from the castle of the Holy Grail to fight as her champion. Having overcome her enemy, Lohengrin married Elsa but made her promise that she would never ask his name or whence he had come. They lived happily until Elsa, yielding to her curiosity, asked the forbidden question; thereupon Lohengrin bade her farewell. The swan-boat reappeared on the river and bore him away, never to return. Wagner (q.v.) made this legend the subject of one of his most popular operas.

Loire, RIVER (Pron. lwahr). The longest river in France, the Loire rises in the south-eastern part of the country, 85 miles north of the Mediterranean, flows northward for half its course, then sweeps in a great curve toward the south-west, discharging its waters into the northern part of the Bay of Biscay at St. Nazaire. Its whole course covers about 610 miles.

Rising in a spur of the Cévennes Mountains 4,500 feet above sea-level, its headwaters are fed by melting snows. From the mountains it emerges upon green fields where cattle graze. Farther on, where the country is again mountainous, the river flows through a valley planted with vineyards and orchards, with here and there a strip of forest. At the northernmost point reached by the river,

75 miles south-west of Paris, is Orléans, an old city of historic memories, delivered from the English in the 15th century by Joan of Arc (q.v.). Below Orléans the Loire enters the province of Touraine, where there are Roman ruins, and castles whose halls once echoed to the mailed tread of French chivalry. About 75 miles south-west of Orléans rise the towers of Tours. Thirty-five miles from the river's mouth is Nantes, where Henry IV of France signed the famous edict giving religious liberty to the Huguenots (1598). At this point the Loire widens into an estuary with several islands, over portions of which Nantes, now an important manufacturing city, has spread. The port of St. Nazaire, accessible to the largest ocean-going vessels, lies where the river mingles its waters with those of the Bay of Biscay.

The Loire is not a great commercial waterway, because in many places it is choked with rocks and gravel carried down from the mountains, or with sand and clay, rendering its channel uncertain. In the wet season its tributaries so increase the volume that it floods wide stretches of land along its banks; in the heat of summer it shrinks to a shallow stream. Canals, however, have been built as an aid to navigation, notably those connecting it with the Seine, the Saône, and (at Nantes) with the harbour of Brest.

Lombards. The most productive region of Italy, the fertile valley of the Po is still called by the name Lombardy, from the barbarian Lombard hordes who overran it in the 6th century. These people, the last of the Germanic invaders of Italy, pressed down from the north (568 A.D.) within 15 years of the time when the emperor Justinian the Great had expelled the East Goths. They soon gained the mastery of most of the Italian peninsula, though Rome, Ravenna and a few other fortified cities, successfully resisted their assaults. They failed, however, to establish a strong central government, the elected king having only nominal power. Small dukedoms grew up, thus splitting Italy into numerous divisions whose jealousies and rivalries led to disunion which lasted until the unification of Italy in 1861.

The Lombard kingdom in the valley of the Po lasted a little more than two centuries; it was finally overthrown, in 774, by Charlemagne (q.v.), who invaded Italy at the request of the Pope, dethroned the king, and was himself crowned with the " iron crown " of Lombardy—so called because beneath the gold was a circlet of iron, said to be made from one of the nails with which Christ was crucified. After the break-up of Charlemagne's empire the Lombards gradually merged with the other peoples of Italy.

The energetic race which grew up from this fusion of Latin and Teuton became conspicuous from the 13th to the 16th centuries for the success of its members as merchants and moneylenders. They found their way to London and other European cities in such numbers that north of the Alps all Italians came to be known as Lombards, and finally the name Lombard came to have the same meaning as moneylender. One of the streets in the City of London is called Lombard Street after members of this race who were said to have settled here as early as the 12th century.